Th...
the Tho...
and ...

D0370926

The Book of
the Thousand Nights
and One Night

RENDERED INTO ENGLISH FROM
THE LITERAL AND COMPLETE
FRENCH TRANSLATION OF
DR J. C. MARDRUS
BY POWYS MATHERS

Volume IV

ROUTLEDGE

LONDON AND NEW YORK

Reprinted ten times
Second edition 1964
Reprinted 1972
First published as a paperback in 1986
by Routledge & Kegan Paul plc

Reprinted 1989 by
Routledge
11 New Fetter Lane, London EC4P 4EE
29 West 35th Street, New York, NY 10001

Printed in Great Britain by
The Guernsey Press Co. Ltd.,
Guernsey, Channel Islands

No part of this book may be reproduced in
any form without permission from the
publisher except for the quotation of brief
passages in criticism

ISBN 0-415-04542-8 (vol. IV)
ISBN 0-415-04543-6 (set)

Contents of Volume IV

CONTENTS OF VOLUME IV

CONTENTS OF VOLUME IV

The Tale of Pearl-Harvest

IT is related in the writings of the wise past that the Commander of the Faithful, al-Mutasid Billāh, sixth Khalīfah in the line of Abbās, grandson of al-Mutawakkil, grandson of Hārūn al-Rashīd, was a prince of lofty soul and fearless heart. He was noble and beautiful, royal and intelligent, he had the courage and strength of lions, and a genius which made him the greatest poet of his time. He kept sixty zealous wazirs about him in Baghdād to watch day and night over the welfare of his people; so that no trifle escaped him in all his mighty empire, from the desert of Shām to the Moorish confines, from the mountains of Khurāsān and the western sea to the furthest bounds of India and Afghanistan.

One day, as the Khalīfah was walking with Ahmad ibn Hamdūn, his intimate friend and chosen cup-companion (to whom we owe the oral transmission of the fairest tales and verses of our ancestors), he came to a lordly dwelling folded pleasantly among gardens. Its harmonious architecture said more of its owner's fine taste than the tongue of an eager friend, and to a man of the Khalīfah's subtle and attentive soul seemed eloquence itself.

As the two men sat down on a marble bench which faced the gate, to rest from their walking and breathe an air laden with the souls of jasmine and lily, they saw two youths of moon-like beauty coming towards them out of the shades of the garden. One was saying to the other: 'Would that heaven might send some chance guests to our master on this delightful day. He is sad when he has to eat alone.' 'This is the first time that such a thing has happened,' answered the second youth. 'It is strange that no citizen has walked out to see our gardens on this fair Spring day.'

These words astonished al-Mutasid in two particulars: that there should be a lord of high rank so near at hand whose name he did not know, and that this lord should have so strange a taste as to dislike solitude. 'I am the Khalīfah,' he said to himself, 'and yet I often love to be alone. I would soon die if I had to feel some strange life for ever beating with mine. There is nothing so precious as occasional loneliness.' Then to his companion he said: 'O Hamdūn, O honey-tongued teller, surely you, who know the present as well as the past, have some knowledge of the man who owns this palace? Do you not think that we should make ourselves known to so strange a being?

Do you not find this an occasion for proving that we also can be generous to a chance acquaintance?' 'I do not think the Commander of the Faithful would ever regret a visit to this man,' answered Hamdūn. 'I will call those two delightful boys and tell them to announce our presence to their master.' He left al-Mutasid sitting, in his usual disguise as a merchant, and went up to the youths, saying: 'The blessing of Allāh be upon you! Tell your master that two strange merchants beg to be allowed to present their homage to him.' The two boys ran joyfully to the palace, and very soon the master of that place appeared upon the threshold.

At this point Shahrazād saw the approach of morning and discreetly fell silent.

But when the eight-hundred-and-fifteenth night had come

SHE SAID:

He was a man of kindly aspect and great elegance, with delicate features and a clear-cut face, dressed in a tunic of silk from Nīsābūr, having a mantle of gold-fringed velvet over his shoulders and a ruby ring upon his finger. He came forward with a smile of welcome and pressed his left hand to his heart, saying: 'Cordial greeting to the kind lords who honour us with the supreme favour of their coming!'

He then led them into his palace, and they supposed that they were straying among the chambers of Paradise, for the interior beauty of that place was greater than the exterior, and would have made a tortured lover forget love.

In the guest hall a little garden was mirrored by singing diamonds of water which fell into an alabaster basin; from its very smallness it was an enchantment and a cool delight. For if the great gardens belted that palace with all the flowers and green leaves of Allāh in a bright riot which was near to folly, the little garden was the very wisdom of flowering things. It held four blossoms only; but the like of those blossoms has not been seen since the first innocence of time.

The first was a rose lolling upon her stem; not a rose of rose trees, but the rose of the world, sister of the rose which flowered in Eden before the coming of the angry sword: a flame of red gold, a glowing fire of joy, a velvet virginal blood-tinted cloud. Its heart burned with the purple of a king's robe and its scent upon the breeze opened the fans of the heart, saying to the soul: 'Be drunk!' and to the body: 'Here are wings!'

The second was a tulip, tall and lonely; not the tulip of a Sultān's terrace, but the tulip of fable, fed on the blood of dragons in Many-Columned Irām. Its colour said to a cup filled with old wine: 'Their lips do not touch me and yet I madden them!' and to a flaming coal: 'Lo, I am not consumed!'

The third was a straight hyacinth; not of earth's gardens, but hyacinth, mother of lilies; a white fragility, saying to the swan: 'Return to the water, for I am queen!'

The fourth was a carnation leaning lonely; not such as young girls water at evening, but an incandescent bubble, a fragment torn from the western sun, a crystal holding the soul of peppers; brother to that carnation which the King of the Jinn gave to Sulaimān to lie in the hair of Bilkīs; from which our Lord made the Elixir of long life, the spiritual Balm, the royal al-Kilā, the Theriac.

Even when the diamond of the fountain was still, the water moved a little in emotion to reflect these flowers.

There was nothing to take the eye in that hall of white marble save these flowers; but the eye was satisfied.

The Khalīfah and his friend sat upon a couch covered with the carpets of Khurāsān, and fed exquisitely from heavy gold plate upon low bamboo tables. It was a feast of friends, made gay by the coming of four girls: a lutanist, a cymbal player, a singer and a dancer. While these concerted a harmonious entertainment, the host and his guests drank wine and ate fresh fruit.

Though Ibn Hamdūn, the teller of tales, was used to the sumptuous entertainments of his master, the generous wines and chosen beauty of that place inspired him to make a song about a certain youth who was a friend of his. In his fine voice, he sang:

> Idol carved by Chinese hands
> From a wild-rose, leave your lazy
> Lazy couching, eyes of jade,
> Pour me out the young undying
> Tulip-coloured wine from Chinese places.
>
> Pour it laughing to the cup,
> Laughing in the lips of folly,
> Yet as pure as your boy's heart;
> I will set my mouth to drinking,
> Sucking blood from the black throats of wineskins.

Tell a man who was born drunk
Wine's betraying? Never do so.
(As the curling of your hair
My desires are complicated.)
Bad for poets? While the sky's blue tunic

Hangs at the green door of earth?
I will drown myself in wine baths;
When they smell the scarlet rose
From my heart below the meadow,
Pretty weeping boys shall laugh home reeling.

When he had made an end, he looked to the Khalīfah for a smile of pleasure, but saw his face so filled with anger that he dropped his cup of wine. Fearing lest he had mortally offended in some way, he ventured a second glance, and was relieved to see that his master did not appear to have heard the song, but to have been occupied during the singing with some deep problem of the mind. 'As Allāh lives,' he said to himself, 'he was delighted a minute ago, yet now a blacker storm is brewing than I have ever seen before. Allāh preserve us all!'

While Hamdūn continued to speculate on the cause of this sudden anger, the Khalīfah cast an offended glance at his host and cried, in defiance of all the laws of hospitality: 'Who are you, O man?' The host turned pale, and answered: 'I am usually called Abū al-Hasan Alī ibn Ahmad of Khurāsān.' 'And do you know who I am?' asked the Khalīfah. 'I have not that honour, my master,' replied the man, turning paler still.

At this point Ibn Hamdūn rose, and said to the youth: 'O host, you are in the presence of the Commander of the Faithful, the Khalīfah al-Mutasid Billāh, grandson of al-Mutawakkil Alā Allāh.'

The master of the house fell trembling to the ground and kissed the earth between the Khalīfah's hands, saying: 'O Khalīfah, O Prince of Believers, I conjure you, by the virtue of your pious ancestors, to pardon in your slave any lack of politeness, submission, or generosity which you may have found in him.' 'It is not of these things that I will complain,' answered the Khalīfah. 'You have proved yourself a better host than many kings. I would have thanked you for your generous hospitality had I not suddenly discovered a most grave cause of anger.' 'Surely, my lord,' cried Abū al-Hasan, 'you will not let the heaviness of your wrath overwhelm your servant and at the same time not tell him his fault?' Then said the Khalífah: 'I have seen that all the furnishing of this house and all the garments which you wear carry the name of my grandfather, al-Mutawakkil Alā Allāh. Can you explain this thing? Have you dared to pillage the dwelling of my sacred ancestors? You have a choice between speech and death.'

At these words their host smiled again and seemed relieved. 'May the grace and protection of Allāh be upon you, my lord!' said he. 'Truth is your inner garment, your outer garment is sincerity; therefore I shall speak without reticence and with perfect truth.' 'Be seated, then, and speak!' cried the Khalifah.

At this point Shahrazād saw the approach of morning and discreetly fell silent.

But when the eight-hundred-and-sixteenth night had come

SHE SAID:

So Abū al-Hasan sat down again, and said: 'Know first, my lord, that I am not a king or a king's son, as one might suppose, nor in any way of royal blood; but the tale of my life is so strange that, if it were written with needles on the interior corner of an eye, yet would it serve as a lesson to the circumspect. Also, I make sure that, when you have heard all, the weight of your displeasure will be dispersed.' Abū al-Hasan paused for a moment to collect his thoughts and then began:

Though not of noble birth, my father was the richest and most respected merchant in Baghdād, and I was his only son. He was not a merchant in one market only, but had a shop in all, and ever the finest; he had a shop among the druggists, among the changers, among the silk-merchants. Each shop had a clever salesman in charge, and also a private apartment at the back in which my father could take his ease during the heat of the day. It was his custom to sleep, with a slave fanning him, and he gave special instruction to the youth to direct the air upon his testicles, which were very sensitive to the heat.

As I was his only and much loved son, my father denied me nothing and spared no expense in my education. His riches increased year by year and had become past counting when he died. May Allāh cover him with His mercy, and admit him into His peace! May He add the days which my father lost to the span of the Khalīfah.

When I inherited my wealth, I carried on my father's shops as he had done, eating and drinking of the best, amusing myself with chosen friends and making life as happy for others as for myself. That is why my gaiety was without bitterness and felt no need of change. That which some call ambition, and some call glory, and some call fame, and some call noise, was insupportable to me. To such a thing I preferred myself, and calm, and my sweet-faced friends.

But no life, however clear and simple, is free from a menace of complication; and complication entered my life under the most desirable of all forms: a girl of fourteen, borrowing the face and form of a fourteen-year-old boy. It was such an apparition which sealed my thoughts for ever.

One day, as I sat before one of my shops and talked of this, that and the other with my friends, a dancing, smiling little girl stopped before me and threw one glance at me from Babylonian eyes. My soul and body shivered as at the first coming of happiness. 'Does this shop belong to Abū Al-Hasan ibn Ahmad of Khurāsān?' asked the child in a voice like running water. She stood slim before me and I could see that her tiny mouth beneath the muslin veil was as a purple flower in which white hail has fallen. 'This is the shop of your slave,' I answered, rising in her honour; and my friends discreetly withdrew.

The girl came into the shop, dragging my soul at her heels; she sat like a queen on the couch, and asked: 'Where is he?' My tongue was forked with emotion, but I babbled: 'I am he.' 'Tell your lad to count me out three hundred dīnārs,' she said, smiling with the smile of her mouth. I turned instantly to my first cashier and ordered him to weigh out the money; when he had done so, the girl rose and left me without thanks or farewell. But more than ever she dragged my soul at her heels.

'Dear master, in whose name shall I write the money?' asked my lad respectfully. 'How should I know?' I answered. 'Do the names of the hūrīs appear in account books? If you like you can write: *Three hundred dīnārs advanced to the Queen of Hearts.*' 'I see that my master is testing me,' cried the cashier. 'I will run after her and ask her name.' He ran zealously from the shop, but presently returned, holding his hand over his left eye and weeping bitterly. 'What is the matter?' I asked, as he sat down in his place and wiped his cheeks. 'Far be the Evil One!' he replied. 'I ran after the young lady, meaning to ask her name; but, when she knew that she was followed, she turned round and hit me in the left eye with her fist. She nearly drove it into my head; she is stronger than a blacksmith!'

Glory be to Allāh Who has given such prompt strength to the little light hands of love!

All day my soul lay in chains of memory, both tortured and refreshed. Next morning the girl came smiling again. As I would have greeted her, she interrupted me, saying: 'Have you not been thinking of me as a little baggage who played a trick on you for what she could get out of it?' 'The name of Allāh be upon you and about you, O queen!' I answered. 'You but took your own property; this shop and all which it contains belongs to you. Among the least of your goods I count myself.' At this the girl raised her little face veil and, bending like a rose on a lily's stem, sat down laughing, with a tinkle of bracelets and sighing of silks. It was as if a breeze from all the gardens of Baghdād had come with her. 'If that is so, O Abū al-Hasan,' she said, 'let me have five hundred dīnārs.' I had the money paid over to her, and she departed without a word. For the rest of that day I lay, a doubting prisoner in a web of sorcery. On the next day, as I sat pale and inactive in my place, she came again, with long eyes of darkness and flame, and small infatuating smile. This time she said no word, but, pointing to a square of velvet on which hung certain inestimable jewels, a little broadened her smile. At once I took down the velvet square and, folding it up with its contents, handed it to the sorceress, who took it and departed.

At this point Shahrazād saw the approach of morning and discreetly fell silent.

But when the eight-hundred-and-seventeenth night had come

SHE SAID:

Seeing her thus depart a third time, I could no longer consent to inaction, so, overcoming a natural fear lest I might meet with the same rebuff as my cashier, I rose and followed her. When she reached Tigris bank, she embarked in a small skiff, which was rowed by rapid oarsmen to a marble palace: the palace of the Prince of Believers, al-Mutawakkil, your grandfather, my lord. This sight disquieted me, and I said to myself: 'At last, O Abū al-Hasan, you have found an adventure and are carried into the mill of complication.' In spite of myself I recalled the words of the poet:

> Her small white arms are softer for your brow
> Than a swan's feathers. Oh, be careful now!

I gazed pensively for a long time upon the water and seemed to
see the calm monotony of my past life reflected in the stream of boats
which were borne down by the current; but suddenly I noticed that
the purple skiff lay moored at the marble stairs, bereft of men. 'Are
you not ashamed of this sleepy life, O Abū al-Hasan?' I cried.
'How dare you hesitate before the burning hours of complication?
Surely, another poet has said:

> The rose of life is wearying by your bed,
> Half drowsy with your sleep:
> O lover, rise and touch the crimson hours.
> It will be time enough to sleep
> When she is dead,
> As die she must although you spare her flowers.'

Stirred by these lines, I determined to lose no chance of reaching
the girl, now that I knew the place of her dwelling. As a preliminary,
I hastened home and told my dear mother all my troubles. 'Allāh
protect you, my child!' said she. 'Will you endanger the calm passage
of our lives with the turbulence of complication? If this girl lives at
the palace, you will be lost if you attempt to follow her. I conjure
you, by the nine months in which I nourished your blind life, to forget this unknown creature.' 'Calm your dear soul and refresh your
eyes, my mother,' I answered. 'Nothing will happen which is not
fated to happen, and Allāh knows all!'

Next morning, at my shop in the jewellers' market, I received a
visit from the manager who guarded my interest among the druggists, an old man in whom my father had had unlimited confidence.
After we had greeted, he said: 'Why this sudden change of colour,
good sir? Why this woeful countenance? Allāh protect us all from
bad bargains! But I see that you are in good health; therefore I cannot suppose that your trouble is without remedy.' 'I have not been
making any bad bargains, dear uncle,' I answered. 'My life has
changed its aspect, that is all; complication has set in upon it with
the passing of a little girl.' Then I told the old man what had happened, describing the ravisher of my soul as if she stood before me.

'It is a complication indeed!' exclaimed the sheikh, after reflection. 'But it does not take this old slave out of his depth. I have a friend in the palace itself, a tailor who makes for the eunuchs and officers of the court; I will introduce you to him and, if you give him some work at handsome pay, I warrant he will be of use to you.' He led me straight to the palace and conducted me to the apartment of his friend the tailor, who received us affably. To begin my employment of him, I showed him one of my pockets, which I had been careful to tear out as we walked, and begged him to sew it in at once. When he had dexterously done so, I slipped ten gold dīnārs into his hand, promising that I would reward him more generously in the future. He looked at me stupidly, and then replied: 'You are dressed as a merchant, my master, but you do not behave like one. A merchant would not have given a dirham unless my work had been worth ten; and you have paid the price of an amīr's robe. Surely only lovers act so strangely. Are you in love, my lord?' 'How would I not be in love,' said I, lowering my eyes, 'when I have seen what I have seen?' 'Fawn or gazelle?' he asked. 'Gazelle,' I replied. 'This should be easy,' said he, 'you will find me a good guide to the gazelles in this palace. What is her name?' 'Allāh alone knows,' I answered, 'unless you do.' 'Describe her,' said he. So I began describing her as well as I might, until he cried: 'As Allāh lives, it is Pearl-Harvest, the Khalīfah's lute-player! . . . I see her little eunuch coming even now; make the most of the meeting, my lord.'

As he spoke, a small white slave, as beautiful as the crescent moon of Ramadān, came into the apartment and saluted us most sweetly. He pointed out a little brocaded vest, saying: 'How much is this, O sheikh Ali? I need it very much, because I must soon walk abroad with my mistress, Pearl-Harvest.' At once I took the vest down from its place and gave it to the child, saying: 'It is already paid for.' The boy looked at me with a sidelong smile, just like his mistress, and then led me apart by the hand, saying: 'You must be Abū al-Hasan ibn Ahmad of Khurāsān.' Being astonished to find so much sagacity in one so young, I took a costly ring from my finger and slipped it upon his thumb, as I answered: 'You are right in your guess, my charming lad, but who told you my name?' 'Why should I not know it?' he retorted. 'I hear my mistress saying it fifty times a day. She is in love with someone whom she calls Abū al-Hasan Ali, the noble lord. I swear by the virtues of the Prophet (upon whom be all grace and benediction!) that, if you are as much in love as she, I will help you with all my might to come into her presence.'

When I had sworn to this child that I loved his mistress to distraction and would die if I did not behold her at once, he comforted me, saying: 'Now that I am sure of you, I am your slave. Wait here for a moment until I come back.'

At this point Shahrazād saw the approach of morning and discreetly fell silent.

But when the eight-hundred-and-eighteenth night had come

SHE SAID:

After a few moments of absence, the little eunuch returned with a packet from which he took a linen tunic embroidered in fine gold, and a mantle among whose thread was worked, in letters of gold, the name of al-Mutawakkil Alā Allāh. 'These are the garments which the Khalīfah wears, when he goes at evening to his harīm,' said the child, as he helped me into them. 'As soon as you reach the long interior gallery, which contains the rooms of the favourites, you must take a grain of musk from this flask and place it before each door; for this is a custom of the Prince of Believers when he passes down that gallery. When you come to a threshold of blue marble, open the door above, without knocking, and you will find yourself in the arms of your mistress. As to your coming away afterwards, Allāh will provide.' Then he wished me well in my enterprise, and disappeared.

Though I was not used to such adventures and was taking my first step in complication, I saw to the fit of the Khalīfah's garments and began walking through the courts and colonnades of the palace as if I had spent all my life among them. When I came to the long gallery of the harīm, I drew the flask of musk from my pocket and placed a grain in the little porcelain plate which had been set, for that purpose, outside each door. I came at length to a threshold of blue marble and was about to open for my desire, when I heard a noise of persons coming behind me and saw the advancing glare of many torches. It was the Khalīfah himself! I had not time to retreat, and, as I sped along the gallery, I heard the voices of two favourites talking afar. 'As Allāh lives,' said one, 'the Prince of Believers is paying a second visit. He has just passed and left the usual grain of musk, and now he is coming again. Yet we recognised him the first time by the smell of his garments.'

I could not halt in my flight because the noise of the Sultān's escort still approached; I could not continue to run on in that way without risking an alarm; so, forgetting my disguise, I chose a door at random and fled through it. I found myself in the presence of a girl with long affrighted eyes, who jumped from the carpets on which she lay and quickly covered her face and hair with the hem of her robe.

I stood gazing at her like a fool, wishing that the floor would open and swallow me, and cursing that detestable little eunuch in my heart. I had resigned myself to death, either by drowning or impaling, and held my breath for the terrified cries which would bring my executioners upon me, when the young lips moved beneath their muslin shield, and a charming voice spoke low to me: 'Be welcome to my apartment, O Abū al-Hasan, for you love my sister Pearl-Harvest and she loves you.' I threw myself face downwards before the girl and covered my head with her protecting veil, kissing it the while. 'Welcome and long life to generous men!' she said. 'You have come out very well from the proofs which my sister set you. She talks of nothing but her love for you. You may thank a kind Destiny which led you to me, instead of leading you to death. Have no fear for yourself now, for I promise that your future shall bear the seal of happiness.' I continued to kiss her veil in silence, and she went on: 'But before I interfere on your behalf, O Abū al-Hasan, I wish to be quite sure of your intention with regard to my sister. There must be no misunderstanding in that matter.' I lifted my arms on high, and answered: 'May Allāh guard and guide you, O mistress of my help! I swear by your sweet life that my intention is both pure and disinterested. I have but one desire in the world: to see your blest sister again, that the sight of her eyes may still the beating of this heart. As Allāh is my witness, it is only this and nothing more.' 'In that case, O Abū al-Hasan,' she said, 'I will lead you to the lawful goal of your desires.'

She clapped her hands, and said to the little slave who appeared upon that signal: 'Find my sister Pearl-Harvest, and say to her: "My mistress, Sweet-Almond, sends greeting and begs you to come to her without delay as she is sad to-night, and also has a secret for your ear."' The little slave hastened away with this message.

And soon, my lord, Pearl-Harvest entered in her beauty, in her light grace, wearing for sole garment a blue silk veil, and walking upon naked feet.

At first she did not see me, and said to her sister: 'Here I am, dearest. I came straight from the hammām and did not take the time to dress. Tell me your secret quickly.' By way of answer, Sweet-Almond beckoned me from the shadows.

When she saw me, my dear love showed neither shame nor embarrassment, but came to me, white and breathing and warm, and threw herself into my arms, as a child flies to the embrace of its mother. I held all the girls of Paradise against my heart, together with the melting delight of fine butter and a paste of almond. My arm scarcely dared press upon that childish body; a hundred years of new life came to me with that kiss.

I know not how long we clasped each other; for I was in a trance of ecstasy, or close to it.

At this point Shahrazād saw the approach of morning and discreetly fell silent.

But when the eight-hundred-and-nineteenth night had come

SHE SAID:

Soon I came a little to myself and was about to tell the girl how I had suffered for love of her, when we heard the noise of voices approaching down the gallery. I had hardly time to hide myself in a large chest, which the two sisters fastened upon me, when the Khalīfah himself entered to visit Sweet-Almond.

When your grandfather saw Pearl-Harvest, he said to her: 'I am rejoiced to meet you in your sister's room like this. Where have you been these last days? Why have I not seen you in any part of the palace? Why have I not heard that voice in which I take delight? Take your lute now and sing me a song of passion.' Pearl-Harvest knew that the Khalīfah was deeply in love with a young slave named Banjah, but she was herself too moved to find an appropriate song, she could only give free course to her own heart, and sing:

> My joy, O night,
> Was washed, O starry eyes,
> In roses, joy, my joy.
> My fresh, O night,
> Had eyes, O starry eyes,
> To snare, joy, O my joy,
> The kings, O night,
> Of Babylon, O starry eyes.
> Such was my joy, my joy,
> Such was my joy.

When the Khalīfah al-Mutawakkil heard this song, his heart was gladdened and he said to Pearl-Harvest: 'O girl of benediction, mouth of nightingale, express a wish and it shall be granted, even were it for the half of my kingdom.' Pearl-Harvest lowered her eyes, as she answered: 'May Allāh preserve the life of our master! I have no wish save that the Commander of the Faithful may continue to look kindly upon me and upon my sister.' 'You must ask something more than that, O Pearl-Harvest,' said the Khalīfah kindly; so she spoke again: 'Since our master commands me, I ask to be set free, and given as a present all the furnishing and contents of this room.' 'It is yours!' cried the Khalīfah. 'Sweet-Almond shall have the finest pavilion in the palace instead of it. You are free now, and may go or stay according to your wish.' With that the Khalīfah left us and went forward towards the apartment of young Banjah.

When we were alone, my love sent a eunuch to fetch porters and dismantlers, and had all the contents of that room, with stuffs, coffers and carpets, carried to my house. The first article of furniture to go, you may be sure, was the chest in which I lay.

That same day I married Pearl-Harvest before Allāh, in the presence of the kādī and witnesses, and the rest is a mystery of our Faith.

Such, O my Lord, is the story of this furniture and these garments, marked with the glorious name of your grandfather. I have neither added nor taken away a syllable of the truth. The Commander of the Faithful is the fountain of all generosity and of all goodness!

Abū al-Hasan fell silent and the Khalīfah al-Mutasid Billāh cried in joy: 'Upon your tongue is the honey of eloquence and your tale is a tale of marvel. Bring me pen and paper, I pray, that I may reward you according to your merits.' When pen and paper were brought, the Khalīfah handed them to Ibn Hamdūn, the tale teller, and made him write: 'In the name of Allāh, the Merciful, the Compassionate! Be it known by this firmān, signed by our hand and sealed with our seal, that we exempt our faithful subject, Abū al-Hasan Ali ibn Ahmad of Khurāsān, from all taxes during the rest of his life. Also we make him our principal chamberlain.' When he had signed and sealed the firmān, he handed it to Abū al-Hasan, saying: 'I desire to see you often at my palace, as cup-companion and good friend.'

After that, Abū al-Hasan was never separated from the Khalīfah; the two lived in all delight until that inevitable separation, which hurries those who have dwelt in palaces to dwell in tombs. But glory be to Him Who lives in a palace which is above the winds of Destiny!

As the dawn had not yet appeared when Shahrazād made an end of this story, she at once began The Tale of the Two Lives of Sultān Mahmūd.

She said:

The Tale of the Two Lives of Sultān Mahmūd

IT is related, O auspicious King, that Sultān Mahmūd, who was one of the wisest and most glorious of the Egyptian rulers, used often to sit alone in his palace, weighed down by a causeless sadness and beholding the world black before his eyes. At these times life was tasteless to him and without significance; yes, even though Allāh had given him, without stint, health and youth, power and glory, and, for his capital, the most delicious city of the earth, where his eyes might ever be rejoiced by flowers, serene skies, and women gilded like the waters of the Nile. These gifts were forgotten during the hours of royal sadness, and Mahmūd envied the lot of drudges bent over the furrow, and travellers lost in the waterless desert.

One day, as he sat with his eyes drowned in the blackness of dreams, in a dejection greater than ordinary, refusing to eat or drink or govern, desiring only death, his grand-wazir came to him in the chamber where he despaired, saying: 'Lord of my life, a very old man has come to our door from the extreme West, and solicits an audience. If I may judge by his words, he is the greatest sage, the wisest doctor, and the most extraordinary magician who has ever lived among the sons of men. Knowing that my lord is prostrated with sadness, I have dared to beg leave to lead this old man into the presence, in the hope that he may drive away the gloom which lies upon the thought of our King.' Sultān Mahmūd nodded his head, and the grand-wazir hastened to introduce the stranger.

At this point Shahrazād saw the approach of morning and discreetly fell silent.

But when the eight-hundred-and-twentieth night had come

SHE SAID:

There entered rather the shadow of a man than a living creature of Allah; if there were a question of age with such a being, it would have to be given in hundreds of years. For sole clothing he wore a prodigious beard over his grave nakedness and a large leather belt barring the parchment of his withered loins. You would have taken him for one of those corpses which Egyptian labourers find in the granite tombs; save that under the terrible white penthouse of his brows burned two eyes of living intelligence.

This pure old man, instead of bowing before the Sultān, said in a hollow and inhuman voice: 'Peace be with you, Sultān Mahmūd! I am sent to you by my brothers, the saints of the extreme West, to make you conscious of the gifts which Allah has showered upon you.'

Then, without a gesture of obeisance, he took the King by the hand and dragged him towards one of the windows. There were four windows in that chamber, each facing an astronomic point. 'Open!' commanded the old man, and, when the Sultān had, like an obedient child, opened the first window: 'Look!'

Sultān Mahmūd put his head out of the window and beheld a vast army of riders pouring down upon him from the mountain citadel, and waving naked swords. The first lines had already come to the palace foot and were climbing the walls with a clamour of war and death. Mahmūd understood that his troops had mutinied, and came to kill him. He changed colour, and cried: 'There is no God save Allāh! This is the hour of my Destiny!'

Immediately the old man shut the window and opened it again in the same movement. The army had disappeared; the citadel stood at peace in the distance, breaking the noon sky with its minarets.

Without giving the Sultān time to recover from his agitation, the old man led him to the second window, which looked down over the great city, bidding him open and regard. Mahmūd opened the window, and recoiled in horror. The four hundred minarets of the mosques, the domes of the palace, the thousand fair terraces stretching as far as the eye could reach, were all one flaming fire, fanned by cries of terror, and belching up black smoke to hide the sun. A savage wind whooped on the flames towards the palace, until the fair building was only cut off from that red ocean by the fresh green of the gardens. In great grief the Sultān let drop his arms, and cried: 'Allah alone is great! There is a Destiny upon things, even as upon men! To-morrow the desert will meet the desert upon a nameless plain which was to-day the fairest city of the earth. Glory be to the sole Living!' He wept for his city and himself; but the old man shut the window and opened it again in the same movement. All appearance of fire had vanished. The city of Cairo stretched out in its maiden glory among orchards and palms, while the four hundred voices from the minarets called the Believers to prayer, and rose like incense to the Lord of all.

The old man dragged the King to the third window, which looked over the Nile, and made him open it. Mahmūd saw that the river had broken its bed and was heaving its waters against the city. Already they had surpassed the highest terraces and were biting angrily at the palace walls. A wave, greater than all, threw down the ramparts and cast itself against the lower storey of the palace. The building began to melt like a lump of sugar in a cup, and was already toppling to one side, when the old man banged to the window. He opened it again instantly and lo! there had been no flood. The great river walked on majestically in its sleep, between infinite green fields.

The old man relentlessly opened the fourth window, before the Sultān had time to collect himself after these three shocks. Now this fourth window looked over that admirable plain of green which stretches to the horizon from the city gates: it is filled with running waters and happy flocks, sung by all the poets since Umar; the fields are carpeted with roses and sweet basil; narcissus and jasmine alternate with thickets of orange, whose trees are the homes of doves and nightingales, fainting for love; Sultān Mahmūd beheld a red and white desert of terror burned by an inexorable sun; among its aching rocks laired starving jackals and hyenas; vile snakes sped swiftly to and fro upon it. But when the old man had shut and opened this window, as the others, the plain smiled to the sky with flowers and gardens as before.

Sultān Mahmūd did not know whether he slept or waked, whether he had gone mad or been bewitched; but the sheikh, instead of allowing him to resolve these questions in peace, led him swiftly to a little fountain basin which refreshed the chamber with the tinkle of its water. 'Look!' said he, and the Sultān leaned over the basin to look; with a rough movement the old man forced his head down into the water.

Sultān Mahmūd found that he had been shipwrecked at the foot of a mountain which overlooked the sea; though he still wore the crown and attributes of royalty. A group of rough men stood not far off, laughing at him and making rude signs concerning him. Mahmūd's rage knew no bounds, but it was directed more against the old saint than the laughing strangers. 'O vile magician,' he cried, 'you have shipwrecked me, but surely Allāh will send me back to my kingdom that I may chastise you!' Then, pulling himself together, he walked towards the group of gaping farm labourers, and said most solemnly: 'I am the Sultān Mahmūd! Depart!' But they went on laughing, until their mouths were open from ear to ear. What mouths! What caves! The Sultan was about to turn tail rather than be eaten up alive, when one, who appeared to be the chief of these people, snatched off his crown and royal robe, and cast them into the sea, crying: 'That hardware must have been very warm, poor man! Come, dress yourself sensibly, as we do!' He stripped the King naked and forced him to put on a robe of coarse blue cotton stuff, a pair of old yellow slippers soled with hippopotamus hide, and a little bonnet of sad coloured felt. 'Come and work with us, poor stranger,' said he, 'for, in our country, he who does not work must starve.' 'I do not know how to work,' Mahmūd objected. 'But you can be an ass,' retorted the man. 'Anyone can be an ass.'

At this point Shahrazād saw the approach of morning and discreetly fell silent.

But when the eight-hundred-and-twenty-first night had come

SHE SAID:

These good peasants had already finished their day's work, so they were glad enough to have someone to carry their tools; Sultān Mahmūd was obliged to stagger behind them to their village, broken under an enormous weight of spades, harrows, pickaxes and rakes. When he came breathless and foundered between the houses, he was at once the butt of a crowd of naked children, who pursued him with a thousand insults. He was shut into a disused stable for the night, and given an onion and some mouldy bread to eat; in the morning he had become a proper ass, with hoofs and tail and trailing ears. They harnessed him for ploughing and led him out into the fields. When he refused to work, they handed him over to the miller, who soon tamed his spirit by blindfolding him and making him turn the mill.

For five years he turned the mill, with no rest save to snatch his ration of beans and drink a bucket of water. For five years he suffered the goad and the stick, together with privations and curses, and had no relief or consolation except in the eternal series of farts which he let from dawn to dusk as he tramped round. One day the mill fell in upon his head and he found himself returned to the shape of man. He was wandering among the markets of an unknown city and felt very weary. Seeing that he was a stranger, a venerable merchant politely invited him into his shop. When he was seated, the old man said: 'You are young and I do not think that you will be unhappy in our city, for young men come in for a deal of petting here; especially when they are solid lads like you. Do you think of staying with us long?' 'As Allāh lives,' answer the Sultān, 'I would stay in any place where they did not feed me beans!' 'Beans!' cried the old man. 'It is not beans, but strong salt fortifying meats that you will be given here; and you will find them necessary. Now listen to me: go and stand outside the hammām at the corner of this street, and ask every woman as she comes out if she is married or single. When one tells you she is single, you will become her husband instantly, for that is the law of our land. But be very careful not to omit a single woman from your questioning, or you will find yourself in grave trouble; for that also is a law of our land.'

Sultān Mahmūd hastened to the door of the hammām and, as he took up his position, beheld a delightful girl of thirteen come down the steps. 'This shall console me for all my troubles,' he thought, as he went forward to address her. 'Dear mistress, are you married or single?' he said. 'I was married last year,' she answered, and went her way.

The next to come out of the hammām was an old woman of terrifying ugliness; Mahmūd shivered with horror as he beheld her, and said to himself: 'I would rather die of hunger or become an ass again than marry this venerable ruin; but the merchant warned me, and I suppose that I had better question the vile old thing.' So he turned away his head, and asked: 'Are you married or single?' 'I am married, heart of my heart,' answered the beldame, with a dribble. What a relief! 'I congratulate you, good aunt,' said Mahmūd; but to himself he breathed a prayer that Allāh might have compassion on the husband.

As the old woman went upon her way, there appeared through the door of the hammām and came down the steps an antiquity, a monument of eld, infinitely more disgusting than she. 'Are you married or single?' asked Sultān Mahmūd in a trembling voice. 'Single, O eye of my eye,' she answered, blowing her nose in her fingers. 'Gently, now, gently!' cried Mahmūd. 'I am an ass, good aunt, I am an ass! Look at my ears, look at my tail, look at my zabb! Nice old women do not marry asses!' But the hoary tomb came up to him and would have kissed him; so he began to cry out again in terrified disgust: 'Gently, now, gently! I am an ass, dear lady, I am an ass! For pity's sake, do not marry me! Gently, now, gently!' And, with a superhuman effort, he lifted his head from the fountain.

Sultān Mahmūd found himself standing in his palace, with his grand-wazīr on his right hand and the strange old saint on the left. Before him, one of his favourite girls held out, on a gold salver, a cup of sherbert which he had commanded a few moments before the introduction of the sheikh. Gently, now, gently! He was a king! He was a king! His terrible adventures had only lasted during the moment his face had been covered with the water. He looked about him and rubbed his eyes. Gently, now, gently! He was a Sultān, he was the Sultān Mahmūd; he was neither a shipwrecked mariner, nor an ass, nor the husband of a redoubtable mausoleum. As Allāh lives, it was a pleasant thing to be a Sultān! He was about to speak, when the hollow voice of the pure old man addressed him, saying:

'Peace be with you, Sultān Mahmūd! I am sent to you by my brothers, the saints of the extreme West, to make you conscious of the gifts which Allāh has showered upon you.'

Then the saint disappeared, and none might tell whether he had departed by the door or by one of the windows.

Sultān Mahmūd understood the lesson of his Lord, and shuddered to think that these visionary misfortunes might have been the real incidents of his life. He fell to his knees, weeping; he banished sorrow from his heart, and, being happy, spread happiness about him. These are the two lives of the Sultān Mahmūd, the one which was and the one which might have been. For with Allāh all things are possible!

When Shahrazād had made an end of this tale, she fell silent; and King Shahryār cried: 'That is a lesson for me, O Shahrazād!' The wazār's daughter smiled and answered: 'It is not to be compared with the lesson of the Unending Treasure.' 'I have never heard of that treasure, Shahrazād,' said King Shahryār.

The Tale of the Unending Treasure

IT is related, O auspicious and exquisitely mannered King, that the Khalīfah Hārūn al-Rashīd, the most generous and magnificent prince of his time, had one weakness (Allāh alone has none!); he would boast that no man alive equalled him in giving.

One day, as he gave full rein to this tendency and praised those gifts which Allāh had but given him that he might be generous, his wazīr Jafar, whose delicate soul condemned this lack of humility in his master, resolved to adventure on the liberty of opening his eyes. He kissed the earth three times between the Khalīfah's hands, saying: 'O Commander of the Faithful, O crown upon our heads, I pray you pardon your slave that he dares to lift his voice in your presence in testimony that the chief virtue of a Believer is humility before Allāh, and that such humility can be the only lawful pride. The riches of this world, the gifts of the spirit, and the qualities of the soul are lent to man by the Highest; it can be no source of pride to man that he has received them; a tree is not proud of her fruit, nor the sea that she receives the waters of the sky. Leave the praises of your munificence to your subjects, for they are always ready to thank Allāh that they were born in your land and in the days of your life. Do not think, my lord, that it is you alone whom Allāh has loaded with riches and rewards past counting. There is a young man, a simple private citizen, in the city of Basrah, who lives with greater magnificence than the most powerful King. His name is Abū al-Kāsim, and even the Commander of the Faithful himself has not a hand so large and so often open.'

At this point Shahrazād saw the approach of morning and discreetly fell silent.

But when the eight-hundred-and-twenty-second night had come

SHE SAID:

The Khalīfah became red in the face when he heard this speech; his eyes flamed and he looked at Jafar haughtily, saying: 'Woe upon you, O dog among wazīrs! Do you not know that such a lie means death?' 'I swear by the life of your head, my lord, that I have dared to speak the whole truth,' answered Jafar. 'If you have lost faith in my words, send someone to control the truth of what I say. I am ready to abide by his decision. When I was last in Basrah, I was the astonished guest of young Abū al-Kāsim and my eyes have not yet forgotten what I saw. Even at the risk of disgrace, I affirm again that he is the most generous being of our time.'

Speechless with indignation, the Khalīfah signed to his guards to place Jafar under close arrest. While this was being done, he left the hall and hurried to the apartments of his Queen Zubaidah, who paled to see the usual signs of dark weather in his face.

Al-Rashid threw himself upon the couch without a word, his eyes staring from his head and his brows deeply drawn together. Zubaidah, who knew him too well to importune him with questions, filled a cup with rose-scented water and offered it to him, saying: 'The name of Allāh be about you, O son of my uncle! May this drink both refresh and calm! Life is of two colours, black and white; may only the white appear upon your days!' 'By my glorious ancestors,' cried al-Rashid, 'that day, at least, was black when I first set eyes on Jafar, the cursed son of the Barmakids! He dares to criticise my words, to comment on my actions; he dares to exalt private individuals at my expense!' He told his wife what had happened, and she readily understood that Jafar's life was in greater danger than it had ever been. She was too subtle to take sides with him openly, but contrived to introduce into her condemnation of him a suggestion that nothing should be done by way of punishment until someone had been sent to Basrah. Hārūn was calmed, as ever, by her talking, and answered: 'Such a course is only just, since I am dealing with the son of an old servant. As I can trust no eyes but my own, I will go myself to Basrah and see this Abū al-Kāsim. If his generosity has been exaggerated, Jafar shall hang.'

Then, though Zubaidah tried to dissuade him from going alone, he disguised himself as a merchant and immediately left Baghdād.

Allāh brought him in safety to Basrah, and he alighted at the chief khān. Before he would sit down or eat, he questioned the doorkeeper of the khān, saying: 'Is it true, O sheikh, that there is a young man called Abū al-Kāsim in this city, whose generosity passes the magnificent generosity of kings?' The old doorkeeper wagged his head wisely, and replied: 'Allāh bless him! Is there a single man who has not been raised up by his arm? For my part, had I a hundred mouths, with a hundred tongues in each, and a treasure of eloquence upon every tongue, I could not tell you how admirably the gift for giving sits upon that youth.' Then, as other merchants came to the door, he was obliged to break off his praises of Abū al-Kāsim, and Hārūn had to be content to retire for the night.

But next morning he rose early and went to walk among the markets; as soon as the shops were open, he approached one of them and begged the owner to direct him to the dwelling of Abū al-Kāsim. 'You must have come from far,' replied the man. 'Abū al-Kāsim's palace is better known in this city than is a king in his own chambers.' When Hārūn confessed that he had indeed come from far and for the sole purpose of becoming acquainted with that noble lord, the merchant gave him one of his boys as a guide.

Abū al-Kāsim's palace was admirably built of sprinkled marble and had doors of green jade. Hārūn saw a troop of young slaves playing in the courtyard and bade one of them tell his master that a stranger had journeyed from Baghdād to Basrah in order to see him. The slave judged that he had to do with no common man, so he ran within and carried the message to his master. Abū al-Kāsim promptly came down into the courtyard to receive his guest. After wishing him polite welcome, he took him by the hand and led him into a hall of strange beauty.

When they were seated on a large couch of gold-embroidered silk, which ran round the four sides of the hall, twelve young white slaves came in, bearing cups of agate and rock crystal worked on the outside with rubies and filled inside with the deeper ruby of old wine. Then twelve girls like moons brought in porcelain basins of fruit and flowers and large golden goblets of sherbert prepared with snow. The slaves and the girls tried these refreshments, before presenting them to host and guest; when Hārūn tasted, he had to confess that he had never known the like, although the East was daily ransacked for his palate.

Also Hārūn al-Rāshīd was forced to admit equal excellence to the meats, which were served to him on gold dishes in a second chamber, and to the further wines, the preserves and light pastries which were given him in a third. When singers and musicians played before him, he was constrained to say: 'There are indeed voices in my palace; there is indeed Ishāk from whom no instinct of music has been hidden; but I find in the dwelling of a private citizen a concert which I could hardly have expected in Paradise.'

While the Khalīfah was paying particular attention to the sweet enchantment of one young singer, Abū al-Kāsim left the hall and returned, carrying an amber wand in one hand and, in the other, a little tree whose trunk was of silver, whose leaves were of emerald, and whose fruits were of rubies. When his host set this tree before him, the Khalīfah noticed that there was a gold peacock of rare workmanship perched upon the top of it. As soon as Abū al-Kāsim tapped this bird's head with the amber wand, it stretched its wings, flirted the splendour of its tail, and began to turn round and round very fast upon itself. With this movement, it jetted threads of aloe and nard scent from a multitude of pin-pricks in its sides, until all the air of the hall was freshened with the perfume.

But, as soon as Hārūn had settled down to marvel at this object, Abū al-Kāsim quickly removed it from before his eyes and carried it forth. 'As Allāh lives, this is a strange thing!' cried Hārūn to himself in rising temper. 'Is this the behaviour of a host? I do not think Abū al-Kāsim understands the business of generosity as well as Jafar would have me think! I suppose that he was afraid that I would ask for the bird; I am not sorry that I came to test this famous hospitality.'

As Hārūn thought thus bitterly, Abū al-Kāsim returned, leading a little boy slave as beautiful as sunlight. This amiable child was dressed in a robe of gold brocade sewn all over with pearls, and he carried in his hand a cup, carved from a single ruby, filled with purple wine. He kissed the earth between Hārūn's hands and presented the cup to him; but, when the Khalīfah drank and handed it back to the pretty slave, behold! it was still full to the brim. He took it from the child's hand again and emptied it for the second time, but, even as he returned it, he saw it fill.

At this point Shahrazād saw the approach of morning and discreetly fell silent.

But when the eight-hundred-and-twenty-third night had come

SHE SAID:

The Khalīfah marvelled even more at the cup than at the peacock and could not help asking how the miracle was performed. 'My lord, there is really nothing astonishing in it,' replied Abū. 'It is the work of an old philosopher who knew all the secrets of the earth.' So saying, he took the child by the hand and hurried him away. 'By the life of my head,' thought the indignant Hārūn, 'either this young man has gone mad or else he has never learnt manners, which is perhaps a worse misfortune. He brings me all these curiosities without my asking, he shows them to me and, as soon as he sees that I am taking pleasure in them, snatches them away. I call it both vulgar and dishonest. I think, good Jafar, that I will soon teach you to be a better judge of men, and to turn your tongue a little about your mouth before you speak!'

At this point Abū al-Kāsim returned again to the hall, followed by a little girl whose beauty would be sought in vain among the gardens of Eden. She was clothed in diamonds, but her slim body shone through more brightly. Hārūn forgot the tree and the peacock and the inexhaustible cup, and sat with thralled soul while the child played to him in twenty-four modes upon a lute of aloe-wood and ivory. So great was her art that al-Rashīd cried: 'O youth, your lot is enviable!' But, as soon as Abū al-Kāsim heard this, he took the girl by the hand and ran with her out of the hall.

This third affront made the Khalīfah so angry that he knew he must let his indignation burst forth if he remained in that place. Therefore, when his host returned for a fourth time, he rose, saying: 'O generous Abū al-Kāsim, I am indeed confounded by the treatment which you have accorded to an unknown stranger. Allow me now to retire and leave you to your repose; for I would not trespass further on your munificence.' Not wishing to constrain his guest, the young man bowed to him most graciously and conducted him to the palace gate. There, before allowing him to go upon his way, he begged to be excused for having offered entertainment unworthy of so delightful a chance visitor.

As Hārūn walked back towards his khān, he said bitterly to himself: 'What an ostentatious fool! He feeds his vanity by displaying his riches before strangers; but if that be generosity I am a blind man. No, he is only a miser, and a miser of the most detestable sort. Jafar shall soon learn the penalty for vulgar lying.'

As he came angrily to the gate of the khān, he saw in the entrance court a crescent-shaped assembly of young slaves; one horn of the crescent being black slaves and the other white. In its centre stood the lute girl from Abū al-Kāsim's palace; on her right was the delightful boy holding his ruby cup, and another lad, no less delightful, waited on her left with the emerald tree and the peacock.

When the Khalīfah came through the door, all these slaves prostrated themselves before him, and the girl came forward to present him with a roll of silk paper on a brocaded cushion. Al-Rashīd unfolded the roll and read these lines:

'*Peace and benediction be upon a charming guest whose coming has honoured and perfumed our house! And after! O father of witty cup-companions, you are requested to look upon these few valueless articles, which our feeble and stinting hand has made so bold as to bring before you, and to accept them as the poor homage of one whose roof-tree has been lighted by your presence. We noticed that the various slaves who form an escort for this, we noticed that the two boys, the girl, the tree, the cup and the peacock were, in their own poor fashion, not displeasing to our guest; this fact gives us the courage to request that he will con-sider them as if they had ever belonged to him. All things come from Allāh and return to Him at last! May His name be exalted!*'

As soon as al-Rashīd had taken in the full purport of this letter, he marvelled and cried: 'By the merits of my ancestors (whom may Allāh esteem!), I think I misunderstood this young man! Where is your liberality now, Hārūn? It does not exist. The blessing of Allāh be upon you, faithful old wazīr, for you have chastised my self-sufficiency and my false pride. Here is a private individual who, without the least appearance of regret, gives away riches which would embarrass the generosity of any king. Yes, but in saying that he is a private individual surely I have put my finger on the diffi-culty? How is it possible for a plain young man to be so rich and I know nothing of his means? Even at the risk of seeming importun-ate, I must set my mind at rest upon this point.'

So he left his gifts in the courtyard of the khān and returned to Abū al-Kāsim, saying: 'O generous master, may Allāh increase His favours upon you! But your gifts to me are so prodigious that I fear to accept them, lest I should seem to be abusing my position as your guest. If I may do so without risk of offence, I ask to be allowed to return them, before I depart to spread the tidings of your magni-ficence in Baghdad.' But Abū al-Kāsim answered sorrowfully: 'My lord, I fear that you have found cause of complaint in my reception of you, or that my gifts have displeased you by their paltry nature; otherwise you would hardly have returned from your khān to in-sult me.' Hārūn—and you must remember that all this time he was disguised as a merchant—made haste to say: 'O too generous Abū al-Kāsim, I pray that Allāh would ever prevent me from insulting a host. My return was only impelled by a scruple lest you should ruin yourself by these extravagant presents to strangers; for, however great your treasure may be, it cannot be endless.'

'If such a scruple has in truth caused me the pleasure of your return, my master, I beg that you will cease to entertain it,' answered Abū al-Kāsim with a smile. 'For every day I pay my debt to Allāh by giving to chance strangers presents at least as valuable as those you have received to-day. In truth He has given me a treasure which is unending. I see that I will have to tell you the episodes of my life in order to convince you. And indeed the tale is so astonishing that, were it written with needles on the interior corner of an eye, yet would it prove a lesson to the circumspect.'

So saying, the young man led his guest by the hand into a cool hall where small braziers were burning sweet perfumes. He begged the Khalīfah to be seated on a tall gold throne, with a soft foot carpet woven into the appearance of coloured flowers, and, taking his place beside him, began to speak as follows:

I must tell you first, my master (Allāh is the Master of us all), that I am the son of Abd al-Azīz, the great jeweller of Cairo. Though he belonged to that city and though his father and grandfather had lived there all their lives, his riches obliged him to flee from the cupidity of the Sultān of Egypt and come to establish himself in Basrah, under the sheltering wing of the Abbasids. May Allāh bless them! My father married the only daughter of the richest merchant in this place and I was the sole fruit of that marriage. Therefore, when my parents died, I found myself, while still very young, the master of enormous riches.

At this point Shahrazād saw the approach of morning and discreetly fell silent.

But when the eight-hundred-and-twenty-fourth night had come

SHE SAID:

But, as I loved expense and prodigality, I so conducted my life that in two years my inheritance was spent. All comes from Allāh and returns to Him! Seeing myself destitute, I determined to leave Basrah, where I had cut a striking figure, and bear my poverty among strangers. I sold my house, which was my last possession, and journeyed with a caravan of merchants, first to Mosul and then to Damascus. Then I crossed the desert on pilgrimage to Mecca, and finally made my way to the great city of Cairo, which was the cradle of my race.

When I found myself at last among the fair houses and numerous mosques of Cairo, I called to mind my father, Abd al-Azīz, and wept as I conceived his shame if he could behold me as a beggar where he had lorded it among the merchants. While, heavy with such thoughts, I wandered out along the banks of the Nile behind the Sultān's palace, I was called to myself by the face of a girl at one of the windows above me. Even as I looked, this apparition of beauty disappeared and, though I stayed in that place till nightfall, I could not get sight of it again. At last I returned unwillingly to the khān where I was lodging; but in the morning I came out again and watched the window. On this second day no face appeared at all, but I fed my sudden love on a little trembling of the curtain and a hint of dark Babylonian eyes behind the lattice. On the evening of the third day the lattice was thrust aside and the curtain parted, to show a face of starlight before which I eagerly prostrated myself. Having shown my humility, I rose saying: 'O queen of day, I am a stranger whose first hour in Cairo was made fortunate by the sight of beauty seen at unawares. May I pray that Destiny, who has led me so far, will complete this adventure according to your slave's desire?' I fell silent, but, instead of answering, the girl showed such a face of fear that it was only by an effort that I kept my place. Yet I was soon rewarded for my bravery; for the girl leaned over the window frame, and whispered in a trembling voice: 'Return at midnight, but now depart!' Then her face disappeared as if by enchantment, leaving me in so deep a joy that I forgot the misfortune of my life, and returned gaily to the khān. I sent for a barber to shave my head and groin and armpits, and then made my way to the poor man's hammām where, for a few copper pieces, I was bathed, perfumed and refreshed. I came forth with my body as light as a feather and well disposed for every dalliance.

I crept through the midnight darkness to the palace window and, finding a silk ladder hanging from it, climbed boldly up until I gained the shelter of the lattice. Then I made my way softly through two unlighted chambers to a third, where the girl lay smiling on a silver bed. Dear guest, no riches of mine could purchase eloquence to paint her eyes. As I stood speechless before her, she half rose and, in a voice sweeter than candied sugar, bade me lie beside her. I lay beside her and, as well as I could for passion, told my story. But nothing would be gained by repeating it in this place.

She listened with grave attention and, when I saw her eyes wet with tears, I cried: 'Dear mistress, one of those tears has washed away all memory of my grief.' We cast our arms about each other, and the girl said: 'O Abū al-Kāsim, I am the lady Labībah, the Sultan's favourite wife. I am surrounded by jealous rivals who have sworn my downfall, and also I grieve because Allāh, Who has given valiance to the meanest cock in the farmyard, has forgotten my husband in this matter. I looked from the window and seemed to see that you were strong; prove to me, my love, that I was not mistaken.'

It was for that very thing that I had come; therefore I wasted no time in the singing of verses, but cast myself upon the charge. Even as our bodies met, there came a violent knocking at the door, and Labībah cried in accents of terror: 'None but the Sultān has a right to knock! We are betrayed and lost!'

My retreat to the silk ladder was cut off; as I scrambled beneath the bed, I was seized by twenty terrible black hands and borne aloft. The eunuchs carried me to one of the windows and thrust me through it; as I was about to fall, I saw the body of my mistress cast through a neighbouring lattice. We fell together into the fast waters of the Nile.

It was written in my Destiny that I should not drown; though I lay for a moment on the bed of the river, I was able to fight my way to the surface of the water and swim through the darkness to the opposing bank. But, though I dived again and again for the body of the charming girl whom I had betrayed through my imprudence and ill luck, I could not find it. Bitterly repenting, I made all haste to leave the land of Egypt and came without accident to Baghdād, the City of Peace.

I changed the last dīnār which remained in my belt and bought a trifle of sweetmeats, scent apples, balms, and rose conserve. These I placed on a wicker dish and hawked among the shops of the market, singing their excellence, instead of crying it, as is the custom in Baghdād. As I had been dowered with a beautiful voice I soon began to gain sufficient livelihood. One day, when I was perhaps singing more musically than usual, a venerable old man, who owned the largest shop in the market, called to me and chose out one of my scent apples. I accepted his invitation to sit by him; but, when he asked me my name, I replied: 'Dear master, I do not wish to open a wound which time begins to assuage.' I spoke so sadly that he changed the conversation to the profits of my peddling and, when I left him, gave me ten gold dīnārs with such sweet speech that I could not possibly refuse and kissed me as a father kisses his son.

At this point Shahrazād saw the approach of morning and discreetly fell silent.

But when the eight-hundred-and-twenty-fifth night had come

SHE SAID:

Though I was not quite certain of my benefactor's intention, I returned to his shop next day. He chose some incense from my wicker dish and then, making me be seated as before, so pressed me for my name and story that, for very gratitude, I had to yield. When I had told him all, he said in a voice charged with emotion: 'My son, you have found a richer father than Abd al-Azīz (Allāh be good to him!) and one who will love you no less than he. As I have neither child nor hope of child, I adopt you, Abū al-Kāsim. Calm your dear spirit and refresh your eyes, my son; for, by Allāh's grace, the trials of your life are over.' The old man took me to his heart, and then constrained me to throw away my wicker dish. He shut his shop and led me by the hand to his own home, saying: 'To-morrow we will leave for the city of Basrah, which is also my city, and there live together in comfort until the end.'

As we journeyed towards Basrah, those who met and recognised me rejoiced that I had come under such an influence; and you may be sure that I used all my wit to please my guardian. While we dwelt together in this palace, he would often say: 'I bless the day of our meeting, Abū al-Kāsim. You are not only worthy of my confidence and affection, you are worthy of the provision which I mean to make for you after my death.'

When we had lived together for a year, during which I shunned the companionship of young men and devoted myself entirely to win the smiles of that good old man, the merchant was taken ill of a sickness for which the doctors could find no cure. He called me to his bedside, saying: 'My blessing upon you, dear son! You have given me a year's happiness, and most men may not hope for more than a day of it in all their lives. Therefore, before the Separator comes to stand where you stand now, I would quit myself of my great obligation. The treasure which I leave will make you richer than all the kings of the earth; it has belonged to the folk of my house since the beginning of time and came I know not whence. My grandfather told my father the secret place of it, and my father told me.'

The old man whispered certain directions in my ear, and then said:

'Give with an open hand, my son, for you will never exhaust the unending treasure of my line. Seek happiness before all things! May the blessing of Allāh be upon you!' Those were his last words—may Allāh have him in compassion and spread about him the blessing of His peace!

I paid the final duties of an heir to my dead friend, and then entered upon my inheritance. Those who had known me in the days of my first prosperity were not slow to prophesy that I would soon run through my second fortune; but months passed and I continued solvent, though I increased my expenses every day and entertained each stranger who came to Basrah as if he had been a king.

It was not long before the rumour of my prodigalities appealed to the greed of the city authorities. One day the chief of police came to visit me and, after chatting of this and that, said softly: 'Lord Abū al-Kāsim, my eyes see and my ears hear; but it is not for a humble policeman, who works for his living, to call a young man to account for his extravagance. I have come for the sole purpose of telling you that, if I am at all clever in my profession, I owe my proficiency to Allāh and am not proud. A strange thing has happened: just as the price of bread has gone up, our cow has ceased to give any milk.' 'O father of detectives,' I asked, 'how much do you think it would cost to buy bread for your family and replace the milk which your cow refuses to supply?' 'Not more than ten gold dīnārs a day, my lord,' he answered. 'That is not enough,' I cried. 'It will be a pleasure to give you a hundred. If you come here at the beginning of each month, my treasurer will count you over the trifling sum.' The man would have kissed my hand, but I prevented him; for I remembered that all riches are a gift from God.

Next morning the kādī called me into his presence, saying: 'O young man, Allāh is the Master of all treasures and there is a quaint old law which lays down that a fifth shall be given to His poor. We judges have to know about such things.' 'I am not very sure of our master's meaning,' I replied, 'but for a long time I have meant to beg a favour at his hands. Might I venture to hand over a daily thousand dīnārs for the well-known justice of the kādī to distribute among the afflicted of Allāh? I pray you not to refuse me, for I have considered that my life might pass without vexatious interruption if I were giving to the poor.' The kādī kindly consented to be my almoner.

Three days later, I was called into the presence of the walī of

Basrah. He greeted me very kindly, and said: 'Someone was telling me the other day that if a young man were to show me some vast treasure in confidence, I alone of all my noble calling would not reprove him for any youthful extravagance.' 'Would that I had a treasure which I could show the walī!' I cried. 'Recently I have been thinking that my life might pass with less vexation if I could find some very holy man to distribute for me, out of the pittance on which I live, a matter of some two thousand dīnārs every day to those who walk in religious poverty.' The walī was very good to me and, in the end, consented to distribute my alms among deserving persons.

Since that time I have punctually paid this extortionate blackmail, and the three functionaries have allowed me to live my life in my own way, giving as it pleased me, with both hands. Such is the story of my treasure, dear guest. I have told it to none before yourself.

The Khalīfah felt an overpowering desire to see Abū al-Kāsim's treasure, so he said to him: 'O generous host, is it really possible that there can exist a treasure upon earth which the pleasant expansion of your nature is not able to exhaust? By Allāh, I will not believe, unless I see it with my own eyes! I swear by the sacred rites of hospitality that I will not violate your confidence, if you do me this unique favour.' 'I am afraid,' answered Abū al-Kāsim sadly, 'that I could only grant your wish under a somewhat humiliating condition. Indeed, I should refuse altogether if it were not that to send away a guest unappeased is to me a grief more bitter than death itself. Are you ready to go with bandaged eyes and bare head, and for me to carry a naked sword with which to combat the least hostile movement?' 'I do not care for a thousand such conditions,' answered the Khalīfah.

Abū al-Kāsim blindfolded his guest and conducted him by a secret staircase to a vast garden which had no other entrance. After walking him about and about through interlacing alleys, he led him into a deep cave and thence, by a sloping corridor, to a mighty hall, far down below the level of the earth. Here the Khalīfah was allowed to take off his bandage and dazzle his eyes in the radiance of countless carbuncles, let into the walls and ceiling. By this fiery light he saw a pond of white alabaster, one hundred feet in circumference, which was filled entirely with gold pieces. Round the rim stood twelve statues, each cut from a different jewel and standing upon a gold column as if to guard the central sea of gold.

Abū al-Kāsim led the Khalīfah to the side of the basin, saying: 'There is no bottom to this pond; in all the years of my people the level of the gold has not sunk by half an inch.' Then he took him into a second hall, graced by a sea of cut and uncut gems, greater round than the pond of gold and shaded by two lines of trees like that which had borne the peacock. Round the dome of this second hall there blazed an inscription written in jewels: *He has the most who the most freely spends; for nothing is worth having except friends.*

When the Khalīfah was weary of beholding these and further rooms of treasure, his host led him back by the same way, blinded with the same kerchief.

At this point Shahrazād saw the approach of morning and discreetly fell silent.

But when the eight-hundred-and-twenty-sixth night had come

SHE SAID:

When they were seated again in the palace, the Khalīfah said: 'Dear master, if I may judge by the young slave and two delightful boys whom you have given me, you must be very happy, you must have girls from all the East and out of the islands of the sea.' 'I have many beautiful women in my home, my lord,' answered the young man sadly, 'but they weigh very little against the bitter memory of one who was cast into the waters of the Nile for love of me. I would give all the treasure which you have seen if it would buy back my lost Labībah.' Hārūn al-Rashīd, though he applauded such constancy, exhorted Abū al-Kāsim to forget his sorrow in the joys of the present.

Then he took leave and returned to Baghdād, with the slaves and precious gifts he had received. His first action was to release Jafar from his dungeon and present him with the two delightful boys, as a sign that he was returned to favour. Then he said: 'O Jafar, tell me what I can do to reward this Abū al-Kāsim; for any present which I could send would seem poor in his eyes.' 'You could make him King of Basrah,' suggested Jafar. 'I will do so,' answered al-Rashīd. 'Set forth immediately, my faithful wazir, and, after handing him his patent of royalty, bring him back with you, that his coronation may take place before our eyes.' Jafar departed and Hārūn al-Rashīd went to his wife's apartment. He gave Zubaidah the little girl, the tree, and the peacock; but kept the inexhaustible cup of purple wine. The

Queen found the young lute-player so charming that she smiled at her lord and assured him that such a pledge of self-sacrifice should not be wasted. Then she begged him to tell her the story of his journey.

When Jafar returned and led Abū al-Kāsim into the Khalīfah's presence, Hārūn rose in his honour and embraced him as a son. He himself led him to the hammām, an honour which he had not accorded to any since he had mounted the throne, and, while the two were being served with sherberts and fruits after the bath, commanded a young slave whom he had just bought to sing before them. When Abū al-Kāsim looked upon the slave's face, he uttered a great cry and fell swooning to the floor; but al-Rashīd, taking him in his arms, soon succeeded in bringing him to his senses.

This young singer was none other than Labībah, who had been queen of the Sultān of Cairo. A fisherman had saved her from the Nile and sold her into slavery; her purchaser had kept her for a long time hidden in his harīm and then taken her to Baghdād, where she had been purchased for the palace. Thus Abū al-Kāsim, King of Basrah, found his love again and lived with her in all delight until they were visited by the Destroyer, the inexorable Builder of tombs.

But do not think, O King, that this story is as astonishing or as moral as The Adventures of the Royal Bastard. 'What bastard is that, Shahrazād?' cried King Shahryār, knitting his brows. 'The tale will tell you,' answered Shahrazād, and began:

The Adventures of the Royal Bastard

IT is related—but Allah knows all—that there were once three friends in a certain city of Arabia, who were genealogists by profession. The meaning of this will be explained more fully later, if Allāh wills.

These good fellows were all dowered with such subtlety that they could, for pure amusement, take a miser's purse and get away with it unsuspected. They would meet every day in a chamber which they had hired for that purpose in a lonely khān, to plan some pleasant trick upon the city with which to divert their morrow. Yet it must be said at the outset that their diversions had ever more of wit and less of malice than is the custom of jesters, that their manners were excellent, and their faces pleasing. They kept common purse of their takings, great and small, and spent an equal sum each day on food for the body and hashish for the soul. When they sat at night before the lighted candles to take their drug, its course was to expand and elevate their humour; and they never fell to brawling or bad words. Their intelligence mounted as the hashish diminished and it was in those delightful moments that they hit upon the most inspired of their drolleries.

One day the herb, fermenting in their brains, suggested an audacity to them greater than any exploit which they had yet attempted. Having talked over the matter in all its details, they walked together to the wall of the King's garden and there began a loud quarrel in which, much against their usual custom, they cursed and derided each other, with many threats of slaughter or buggery at the least.

The King, who was walking in his garden, heard the tumult and bade the eunuchs hale the disturbers of his morning peace into the presence.

When the three genealogists stood before him, he cried angrily: 'Who are you, O rogues? And how do you dare conduct your shameless quarrels under our very walls?' 'O King of time, we are the masters of our art,' they answered. 'We each practise a different profession, and we came to words as to which of these professions is the noblest. Words led to anger, and the distance between anger and vulgarity is very short. To our shame, we forgot the possible presence of our master and began to lay our tongue to all the buggers and sons of bitches and zabb-swallowers which we had ever heard. Anger is a poison to good manners, O King of time! We have sinned, and stand before our lord without excuse.' 'What are your professions?' asked the King, and the first of the three kissed the earth between his hands, and answered: 'I am a genealogist of precious stones; I have heard it said that there is no one else so learned in the art.' 'You look more like a tramp; but perhaps the two things are not incompatible,' said the King. 'Explain the trade to me.' 'It is the knowledge of the origin and race of every precious stone,' replied the man. 'It is to distinguish the true from the false at a single glance or by a touch of the fingers.' 'I shall find a way of proving you,' said the King.

At this point Shahrazād saw the approach of morning and discreetly fell silent.

But when the eight-hundred-and-twenty-seventh night had come

SHE SAID:

Then the Sultān turned to the second hashīsh-eater, saying: 'And what is your profession?' The man kissed the earth between his hands, and answered: 'I have been called the most expert genealogist of horses in all Arabia. My art is to tell at a single glance and with never a mistake the race of a horse, the blood of a horse, the tribe which bred him, and the kind of country which pastured him. I can give instantly the distance any horse would travel in a given time at a gallop, at an amble, or at a quick trot. I can tell hidden disease or disease which is to come; I can describe the causes of death of the sires and dams back to the fifth generation. I can cure equine ills which had been written as incurable, and have a dying horse win races in an hour. I might say a great deal more if I were not so modest. But Allāh knows all!' So saying, the second hashīsh-eater demurely lowered his eyes and fell silent.

'You look more like a tramp,' exclaimed the Sultān, 'but I shall find a means of testing you.' Then he turned to the third brawler and asked his trade.

The third, who was the cleverest, kissed the earth and answered: 'O King of time, my profession is at once worthier and more difficult; for I am a genealogist of man. I can tell the true origin of my kind; not the supposed, but that which the mother can hardly know and the father never. By glancing once at a man or by once hearing the vibration of his voice, I can say whether he is true born or a bastard, and whether his father and mother were true born or bastards, and whether all the various members of his family, back to our father Ismāïl ibn Ibrāhīm (upon whom be the mercy and chosen blessing of Allāh!), were true born or bastards. Thanks to the art with which Allāh has seen fit to dower me I could disillusion a great many nobles concerning their birth, and prove to them beyond possibility of doubt exactly what their mothers had done with camel-boys cooks, false eunuchs, and slaves. Also, my lord, if I look at a woman veiled, I can tell her race, her origin, and the profession of her parents. I would say more, O King of time, but, were I to attempt to give you a full description of my art, you would have to tolerate my heavy presence for many hours. Therefore I will content myself with claiming that I am the one infallible genealogist of the world.' So saying, the third hashīsh-eater modestly lowered his eyes.

'This is an astonishing collection of talent!' cried the King. 'If what you say is true you are certainly the three wisest men of your time. I will keep you with me and, as occasion serves, make a test of the skill of each of you. If your boasts are without foundation I have an impaling stake which can reduce you to a like condition.' Then he turned to his grand-wazir and bade him give each of the three sages an apartment in the palace with a daily ration of meat and bread, and water at discretion. As the three companions were led away, they exchanged glances which signified: 'A wise and generous King! But we are not genealogists for nothing; our time will come.'

They were right. On the next day a neighbouring King sent rich presents to the Sultān, and among them was a clear white diamond of a water as pure as a bird's eye. The Sultān sent for the first hashīsh-eater and bade him examine the stone and give an opinion on it. 'By the life of the King's majesty,' answered the man. 'I do not need to examine it or take it in my hand. Let me touch it with my left little finger when my eyes are closed.'

'Now we shall test his pretension!' exclaimed the King, as he held out the diamond. The man shut his eyes and applied the tip of his left little finger to one of the facets of the stone. At once he recoiled and began to shake his hand as if it had been bitten or burned. 'My lord,' he said, 'the thing is of no value. Not only is its origin impure, but there is a worm in its heart.'

'Say you so, O son of a pimp?' cried the furious Sultān. 'This is the gift of one king to another, and the light shines through it as through water.' With no thought save for the insult, he called his executioner, saying: 'Pierce this liar's fundament!' The executioner, a man of gigantic stature, lifted the expert like a bird, and was about to spit him, when the grand-wazir, who was prudent and of a good intelligence, besought the Sultān, saying: 'O King of time, it is obvious that this man has exaggerated his powers; but it is possible that there is a grain of truth in what he says. Should that prove to be the case after he had been impaled, you would not be able to excuse his death in the sight of Allāh. Spare him, I pray you, until the stone has been tested, for the life of a man weighs more in the scales of Allāh than a hundred diamonds. Let the stone be broken; if there is a worm in its heart, spare this man. If it be sound all through, let the executioner continue.'

The Sultān recognised the justice of this suggestion, so he bade the executioner strike the diamond with his mace. The stone broke into fragments and a white worm wriggled out from the midst of them; as soon as it felt the touch of air, the creature burst into flame and was consumed.

'How did you know it?' gasped the astonished King, and the expert modestly replied: 'I have sensitive fingers, and the diamond was hot.' 'Free him!' commanded the Sultān. 'Let him be given a double ration of bread and meat, and water at discretion.' So much for the genealogist of jewels.

A few days later the Sultān received a beautiful brown bay horse as a sign of loyalty from an important chief in the heart of Arabia. In his delight he passed many hours in the stable, admiring the fine points of the beast; then he sent for the second hashīsh-eater, and said to him: 'Do you still pretend to know as much about horses?' 'Certainly, O King of time,' answered the man. Then cried the Sultān: 'I swear, by the truth of Him Who has set me as a King upon the necks of His servants, Who says to each thing: "Be!" and lo! it is, that you shall die the worst of deaths if you make a single error or confusion in the test which I propose for you.' 'Be it so, my lord,' replied the second hashīsh-eater, and the Sultān bade his grooms bring out the horse. After one glance at the fine animal the genealogist pursed his lips and turned to the King with a smile, saying: 'I have seen and known.' 'What have you seen and known?' demanded the Sultān.

At this point Shahrazād saw the approach of morning and discreetly fell silent.

But when the eight-hundred-and-twenty-eighth night had come

SHE SAID:

Then said the second genealogist: 'O King of time, this horse is of rare beauty and excellent breed; he is well-proportioned and has a proud carriage; he has great staying power and a perfect action. He is fine in the shoulder and the arch of his neck is excellent; he is high in the saddle, the curve of the tail is proud and correct. Also, his mane is heavy and sweeps the ground. His head is all that an Arab head should be, large, well-developed above, long from ear to ear and from eye to eye, but short from ear to ear; the brow stands out, the eyes are clear and flush with the head, the space about them is bare of hair and shows fine black skin. The bones of the cheeks are wide and spare, while those of the jaw are clearly outlined; the front narrows to the muzzle and turns sharp at the lip; the nostrils in repose are level with the front and seem like one pinched slit. The lower lip is larger than the upper; the ears are fine and large and long, their outline is clear cut. His colour is the queen of colours, and I should call him the king of horses were it not for one serious imperfection.'

The Sultān, who had listened in marvelling delight to this clear description, made after one fleeting glance, flamed into anger when he heard the end of it. 'What is that, vile cheat?' he cried with sparkling eyes. 'Do you dare to speak of an imperfection in the last marvel of the Arab race?' 'If the Sultān is moved by the slave's words,' answered the second hashīsh-eater calmly, 'the slave has nothing more to say.' 'Yet I command you to speak!' shouted the Sultān. 'I will not speak unless I am given security,' replied the man; but when the King had given him security, he said: 'He is a horse of pure race on his sire's side; but of his dam, I dare not speak.' 'Dare, and dare instantly!' cried the enraged King. 'My lord, his dam was a sea-buffalo cow,' answered the genealogist.

The Sultān swelled like a frog in his rage; then he breathed out, and then he swelled again. At last he panted to his executioner: 'Pierce this dog's fundament! Impale this genealogist!' The giant lifted the unfortunate man until his bottom was above the spike, and was about to let him drop, when the grand-wazīr begged the King for a few moments' grace, saying: 'O my lord, it is true that this genealogist has been both imprudent and foolish in suggesting that a wonderful horse like that could be dropped by a sea-buffalo cow; but would it not be better to prove to him that his punishment is just by sending for the groom who brought the horse? In this case, the matter is easy to control, for all steeds of noble blood have sworn pedigrees fastened about their necks.' 'Be it so,' answered the Sultān.

The groom was fetched and commanded to produce the pedigree. He drew from his breast a copper case, worked and encrusted with turquoises. From this the Sultān took a parchment, sealed with the seals of that tribe from which the horse came and attested by those who had witnessed the serving of the female. This pedigree proved beyond a shadow of doubt that the horse had been sired by a pure

Arab stallion on a sea-buffalo cow, whom he had met one day while being exercised along the shore and had covered three times with whinnies of delight. The grooms had captured this aquatic beast and, at the end of her term, she had dropped a bay-brown foal and given it milk for a whole year among the tribe.

When the Sultān had read this confounding document, he marvelled at the infallible art of the genealogist and bade his executioner lift the man down. 'How could you tell?' he asked, when the man stood again before him. 'You have proved to be exactly right and now I would know the signs by which you recognised that blemish.' 'The thing was easy enough,' answered the hashīsh-eater. 'The King has but to look at the creature's hoofs.' So the King looked, and behold the hoofs were forked and coarse and long like those of buffaloes, instead of being compact and light and round, like those of horses. 'Allāh is all powerful!' cried the Sultān. 'Let this learned man be given a double portion of meat and two loaves to-day, also water at discretion.' So much for the genealogist of horses.

Now that the Sultān had beheld these two tests, he was more than ever anxious to try the learning of the third hashīsh-eater. So he sent for him, and said: 'Do you still persist in your claim to tell the true origin of any man; not the supposed, but that which the mother can hardly know and the father never? That by looking at a woman veiled, you can know her race, her origin, and the profession of her parents? If so, I will give you a chance to make good your claim.' 'I said that I could do so, O King of time, and I can do so,' answered the third hashīsh-eater. 'But Allāh alone knows all!'

Then said the Sultān: 'Follow me!' and, after warning all the women to veil their faces, led him into his harīm. When he came to the apartment of his favourite of the moment, he turned to the genealogist, saying: 'Kiss the earth before your mistress, and look upon her that you may tell me afterwards what you have seen.' The hashīsh-eater kissed the earth between the girl's hands, and turned away, saying: 'I have seen, O King.' 'Follow me!' said the Sultān, and led the way back to the throne room. He dismissed all save his wazīr and then bade the hashīsh-eater make a report upon his favourite. 'My lord,' said the man, when he had collected his thoughts, 'I have seen the queen of charm and excellence, the empress of modesty and beauty. She has all gifts to enchant the heart and lift up the eyes; she is full of proportion and harmony; if I may judge by the intelligence of her regard she has every interior quality of subtle apprehension. There is nothing lacking in her. But Allah knows all.' 'I do not want to hear all that, O genealogist,' exclaimed the Sultān. 'I wish you to tell me what you have discovered of this honourable lady's origin.'

At this point Shahrazād saw the approach of morning and discreetly fell silent.

But when the eight-hundred-and-twenty-ninth night had come

SHE SAID:

The third hashīsh-eater took on an air of discreet reserve, and answered: 'The matter is a delicate one, O King of time. I do not think that I should speak of it.' 'In Allāh's name, O fool, for what did you think that I commanded your presence?' cried the Khalīfah. 'Say what you have to say, vile wretch, and weigh your words!' 'Then, by the life of our master,' replied the genealogist calmly, 'I should say that lady would be the most perfect of Allāh's creatures if she had not one fault of birth which overshadows her perfections, all her qualities.'

The Sultān drew his sword and rushed upon the man in a fury, crying: 'Dog and son of a dog, are you going to tell me that my favourite was born of a sea-buffalo cow, or that she has a worm, or something of that kind? Son of a thousand shameless horns, taste my sword!' He would infallibly have run the poor man through, had not his wise wazīr held his arm, saying: 'My lord, it would be better to spare this man until he has been proved wrong.' 'Speak, you!' said the Sultān to the man on whom he knelt. 'What is the fault?' The third hashīsh-eater sat up, and replied without emotion: 'O King of time, my mistress, your noble lady, is in herself all perfect beauty; but her mother was a dancing girl, a free woman of the wandering Ghāzīyas, a daughter of prostitution.'

The Sultān strangled for a moment with fury, then bade his wazīr fetch his favourite's father, who was intendant of the palace. When the old man came, he cried out on him: 'Do you see this stake? If you do not wish to feel it through your bum, tell me the true story of your daughter's birth.' The girl's father bowed, and answered:

'Dear master, I will tell you the truth, because in the truth lies salvation. In my youth I lived the free life of the desert, escorting the caravans across the land of my tribe for hire. One day, when we were in camp near the wells of Zubaidah (the mercy of Allāh be upon her!), there passed a troop of women of the wandering Ghāzīyas, whose daughters, from the moment they are ripe, prostitute themselves to the men of the desert, wandering from one tribe to another and from one camp to another, selling their charms and dexterity to the young riders. These women stayed with us for some days and then departed to traffic with our neighbours. When they had left, I saw a little girl of five years old crouching beneath a tree near the wells, where she had either been lost or forgotten by her mother. The child was as brown as a ripe date and so slight and pretty that I swore to adopt her. Though she was as wild as a hind among trees, I succeeded in taming her; and she grew up with my children. When she reached puberty, she was as desirable as any girl could be, and therefore, because I loved her and would not take her, I married her. For our great pride, Allāh gave us a daughter whom my King has deigned to regard as his favourite. I swear by the Prophet that that is the whole truth. But Allāh knows all!'

When the Sultān heard this simple tale, his breast was relieved of the torture of uncertainty, for he had at first imagined that his favourite was the daughter of a prostitute and now he knew that her mother, although belonging to the Ghāzīyas, had been a virgin until her marriage. He marvelled at the penetration of the genealogist and asked him how he had discovered this thing. 'The matter was easy,' answered the third hashīsh-eater. 'The women of the Ghāzīyas have thick eyebrows which just touch at the root of the nose; also their eyes are the darkest in all Arabia.'

The King felt that he could not dismiss this remarkable man without a reward, so he said to his slaves: 'Allow this sage a double ration of meat and two loaves to-day, also water at discretion.'

So much for the genealogist on that day; but his adventures are not yet finished.

The Sultān passed that night in reflecting on the strange powers of these three companions and, in the morning, said to himself: 'I think that the third must be the most learned man in all my kingdom, but perhaps his skill is all in bastardy; I wonder what he could tell me of my origin, who am the true son of true kings?' He sent for the man afresh, and said to him: 'Now that I know that you speak the truth, tell me something of my own origin.' 'I hear and I obey, O King of time,' answered the third hashīsh-eater. 'But first I must have security. The proverb says: *If the king's vexed, run hard and do not halt; the best way to be hanged is by default.* And I've so sensitive a breach, so tender to the least assault; if I must suffer for free speech, I'd rather suffer by default.' 'I absolve you in advance,' answered the King and presented him with the kerchief of safety. 'In that case, let us be alone, O King of time,' whispered the man. 'Why?' asked the King. 'Because, among the sacred names of Allāh, there is the name of the Veil.' So the Sultān ordered everyone to leave the hall, including his wazīr.

When they were alone, the genealogist whispered in the King's ear: 'My lord, you are not only a bastard, but a very low bastard.'

At this point Shahrazād saw the approach of morning and discreetly fell silent.

But when the eight-hundred-and-thirtieth night had come

SHE SAID:

When he heard these terrible and audacious words, the Sultān staggered as if he were drunken without wine; his face turned yellow and he foamed at the mouth; he made a strange noise in his throat and fell all along the ground, so that the hashīsh-eater did not know whether he was dead or half-dead or still alive. Very slowly he came to himself and, leaning up on his elbow, spoke calmly: 'Now I swear, O man, by the truth of Him Who has placed me as a King upon the necks of His servants, that, if I acquire proof positive of what you say, I will abdicate my throne in your favour, for I shall be no longer worthy of it. But if you have told me a lie, I will cut your throat with my own hand.' 'It is permitted,' answered the hashīsh-eater.

The Sultān then rose to his feet and ran, with a naked sword in his hand, to the apartment of the Queen Mother. When he saw her, he said: 'I swear, by Him Who divided the waters, that if you do not answer with the truth, I will mince you to pieces!' He brandished the blade above the old woman, who replied in fear and anger: 'The name of Allāh be about you, my child! If you will calm yourself and ask me plainly what you want, I will speak you truly enough.' Then said the Sultān: 'Tell me quickly and without preamble if I am the son of the King, my father!' 'Quickly and without preamble,' she replied haughtily, 'you are the son of a cook. It happened in this way:

'When the former Sultān married me he coupled with me according to custom; but Allāh did not favour us with offspring, and I was not able to give an heir to the throne. Because of this lack the King fell into a profound sadness which robbed him of appetite and sleep. His mother worked upon him to take another wife, and he did so. But Allāh decreed that that union also should be barren. His mother worked upon him to take a third wife; so I, seeing that I would soon be of no account at court, resolved, if an occasion should offer, to save my influence and also to preserve the throne that it might not go to strangers.

'One day the Sultān, with the caprice of a sick man, greatly desired to eat a stuffed chicken, and ordered his cook to take one of the birds from the special coops which stood below the palace windows. As the man was doing so, I looked upon him from above and saw that his strength and youth were what I needed. I signed to him to come up to me by the secret door, and received him in my apartment, where that which was necessary passed in a flash of time. As soon as he had fulfilled my need, I plunged a dagger into his heart and he fell dead. My girls took him up and buried him secretly in the garden. That day the Sultān did not have his stuffed chicken, but he lost a cook. Nine months later I bore a son, as fine and healthy as you are to-day. The Sultān recovered his health, showered presents upon all who came within sight of him, and held public rejoicing for forty days and nights. That is the truth of your birth. I swear by the Prophet I have spoken of certain knowledge.'

The Sultān said no word, but walked away weeping and, when he came into the throne room, sat down on the floor opposite the third hashīsh-eater in silence. For an hour the tears fell from his eyes and trickled through his long beard; at length he raised his head, saying: 'O mouth of truth, how in Allāh's name did you know?' 'Dear master,' answered the genealogist, 'when each of us proved our great talent before you and caused you much delight, you ordered us to be given a double ration of meat and bread, and water at discretion. From such mean recompense, and especially from the form of that recompense, I knew that you must be the son of a cook and of a long line of cooks. Kings, who are sons of kings, do not recognise intellectual merit by altering a sage's diet, they give him robes of honour and royal uncounted gold. The matter was easy: you were a king, supposed to be sprung from a line of kings, and yet you had the soul of a cook, therefore you were a bastard.'

When the genealogist had given his explanation, the Sultān rose and bade him remove his garments; he took off the robes and attributes of his own royalty and dressed the other in them. He set him upon the throne and kissed the earth before him; then he called the whole court together and made them swear fealty to their new sovereign. The hashīsh-eating King's first act was to send for his two companion genealogists and raise them to an equal honour only less than his own. As he was a just man, he retained the former grand-wazīr in his high office. Time showed that he was a great King. So much for the three hashīsh-eaters. But the royal bastard's story is just beginning.

At this point Shahrazād saw the approach of morning and discreetly fell silent.

Little Dunyazād who, day by day and night by night, had been becoming more beautiful, more mature, more understanding, more attentive, and more silent, half rose from her carpet, saying: 'Dear sister, your words are delectable and sweet, savoury and alluring.' Shahrazād kissed her, and answered with a smile: 'They are nothing to those which I would employ for our great King's entertainment to-morrow night, if he were to allow me to live.' 'Have no fear, Shahrazād,' cried King Shahryār, 'to-morrow you shall tell us the rest of this extraordinary story. You may even continue to-night if you are not too weary; for I burn to know the fate of that royal bastard. May Allāh curse all women! And yet I must confess that that man's mother, the old queen, had an excellent intention when she coupled with the cook. She did not merely seek to satisfy a bodily letch. May Allah have her in His mercy! But that vile wanton, that insatiate bitch, had no such noble purpose when she lay with the negro Masud. Allāh forget her for ever!' The King frowned terribly and showed the whites of his eyes; but he added: 'I begin to think, Shahrazād, that you are not altogether such an one as those whom I have beheaded.' Shahrazād bowed, and answered: 'At least, my lord, let me live until to-morrow night, so that I may tell you what happened to the royal bastard.' Then she fell silent.

But when the eight-hundred-and-thirty-first night had come

LITTLE DUNYAZĀD SAID TO SHAHRAZĀD: 'In Allāh's name, dear sister, if you are not sleepy, please tell us what happened to the Sultān who was the cook's bastard.' 'With all my heart and as in duty bound to this auspicious King!' answered Shahrazād, and she continued:

As soon as the old Sultān had given up his throne to the third genealogist, he dressed himself in the garments of a wandering darwīsh and, without waiting to make farewells which had ceased to be significant, set out for the land of Egypt, where he intended to pass the rest of his days forgotten, and in close consideration of his Destiny. Allāh had written him safety and he came, after a weary journey, to the splendid city of Cairo, that vast capital, which is so different from the towns of his own country and whose circumference is three days and a half of walking. He saw that she is the fourth marvel of the world, fit to take her place with the bridge of Sanjīyah, the Alexandrian pharos, and the Amawī mosque at Damascus. He found the words of the poet true, who said: 'O Egypt, whose dust is gold, whose river is a benediction; O Egypt of pleasant peoples, O prize for the strong hand!'

As he wandered about, looking and marvelling, he rejoiced in the liberty of the poor and forgot the cares of a king. 'I give praise to Allāh,' he murmured, 'for He has made care and power to be sisters, and a light heart to be the bride of poverty!' Rich in the memory of fair things seen, he came at last to the palace of Sultān Mahmūd.

He halted beneath the windows, leaning upon his darwīsh-stick, and began to speculate on the preoccupation and responsibility of him who dwelt within. He rejoiced exceedingly in the sudden disgrace which had made him free of the air and given him the sufficient revenue of his clothes. He felt a great serenity fall upon his heart and stood at gaze, so that he did not notice the Sultān return from hunting and go up the steps of the palace. Mahmūd looked upon the noble detachment of this figure, and said to himself: 'As Allāh lives, this is the first darwīsh I have seen without an outstretched hand. His story should be a strange one!' As soon as he had a little reposed from the fatigue of hunting, he sent one of his lords to bring the darwīsh into his presence. When this had been done, he received him affably, saying: 'Be very welcome, O venerable darwīsh of Allāh! To judge by your appearance, you are the son of some noble Arab.' 'Allah alone is noble, my lord,' answered the darwīsh, 'I am but a poor man, a beggar.' 'It is permitted,' answered the Sultān Mahmūd. 'But why have you come to our country and why did I see you standing below the walls of our palace? In Allāh's name, O darwīsh of benediction, tell me the story of your life without delay.' The darwīsh let fall a tear and felt the hand of the past grasping his heart. 'There is bitter as well as sweet in my memories,' he said at length, 'but I will hide nothing from you, O King. Yet I would not speak in public.' Sultān Mahmūd rose from his throne and, taking the darwīsh by the hand, led him into a retired chamber. 'Now you can speak without restraint,' he said.

The darwīsh told the whole story of his abdication and pilgrimage; but nothing would be gained by repeating it in this place.

Sultān Mahmūd heard him out with attention and then embraced him with great love, saying: 'Glory be to Him Who, by His power and according to His wisdom, humiliates and honours His people! Your tale is a noble tale, my brother, and the lesson which it teaches is a true lesson. Grief is a cleansing fire, the return of time opens the blind eyes of birth. Now that wisdom has made her abode in your heart and humility has raised you to a noble height unknown to true born princes, may I, O greater than myself, be allowed to make a request?' 'Be it upon my head and before my eyes, O magnanimous King!' answered the pilgrim Sultān, and Mahmūd murmured: 'I would wish to be your friend.'

Then he embraced his guest again, saying: 'What a delightful life ours is going to be henceforth, my brother! We will go out together, we will return together; at night we will disguise ourselves and wander through the city, learning the lessons of life. The half of all that may be found in my palace is yours; therefore do not refuse me. Remember that to repulse a seeming obligation is one of the forms of parsimony.'

The pilgrim Sultān accepted this offer of friendship with tears in his heart, and Mahmūd added: 'Now that we are brothers and friends, I would have you know that there is also a story hidden in my life, and it is so astonishing that, if it were written with needles on the interior corner of an eye, yet would it prove a lesson to the circumspect. I will tell it to you now, as I wish you to know what I am and what I have been, before we take up our pleasant life together.'

So Sultān Mahmūd, after collecting his thoughts, told his new friend:

The Tale of the Ape Youth

You must know, good brother, that my tale flows in an opposite course from yours. You began by being a Sultān and have ended as a darwīsh. I was a darwīsh in my youth and have ended as a Sultān upon the throne of Egypt.

My father was a very poor man and earned a sparse living as a waterer in the streets; each day he carried a heavy goatskin bag on his back and sprinkled his water before the shops and houses. As soon as I was old enough, I was given a waterbag just too heavy for my strength, and had to help him with his trade. When he died, he left me the larger skin as sole inheritance and I followed in his footsteps as far as possible; for he had been a favourite waterman, sought after by shopkeepers and the porters of rich houses.

But a son is never as strong as his father, and I found the great skin too heavy for the bones of my back; so, rather than grow for ever humped, I became a begging darwīsh, living on alms in public places and sleeping at the entrance of my mosque. At night, after I had eaten my meagre bread, I would close my eyes, saying, as is the custom with such folk: 'Allāh may send a better day to-morrow!' Yet I never forgot that every man has his hour upon this earth and that mine would come whether I wished it or no. Therefore, fearing to miss it by sleep or distraction, I watched for my hour as a dog for game.

In the meanwhile I was so poor that I could have no pleasure, and, when an unexpected alms of five silver dirhams was given me by a generous lord, from whom I begged on his birthday, I clenched the money in my hand and ran to the principal market, promising myself that I would dine delicately, and sniffing on all sides to give my nose the first choice.

At this point Shahrazād saw the approach of morning and discreetly fell silent.

But when the eight-hundred-and-thirty-second night had come

SHE SAID:

As I ran I heard in the market the laughter of a crowd and beheld a grinning rabble treading the heels of a man who led a chained ape, a young and well-built ape, with a rose-coloured behind. This animal made eyes and grimaces to the people as he went along, and held out his paw for nuts.

'O Mahmūd,' I said to myself, 'how do you know that your Destiny does not hang round this ape's neck? Would it not be better to buy him with your five dirhams than spend the money on a feast which will be soon forgotten?'

When the crowd thinned, I went up to the man, saying: 'Will you sell me that ape for three dirhams?' 'He cost me ten,' the owner replied, 'but you may have him for eight.' 'Four,' said I. 'Seven,' said he. 'Four and a half,' said I. 'Five, and that is my last word,' said he. 'Pray for the Prophet, my friend.' 'The prayer and peace and blessing of Allāh be upon him!' I answered. 'Here are the five.' I loosened my hand's iron grip on the money, and led away the ape by his chain.

Knowing that, if I appeared at my usual mosque with my new possession, we should both come in for hard words, I made my way to a ruined house which I knew, and prepared to pass the night there with my ape. Hunger began to torture me and I reflected wistfully on all the things which I might have bought at the market; also I began to doubt my power of furnishing victual for my future stock-in-trade. But I might have spared myself this anxiety, for the ape soon began to shake himself in a curious way, and changed in one moment from a hideous animal with a bright behind to a youth as fair as the full moon. He stood before me in an attitude of charming submission, and addressed me in a voice of sugar, saying: 'O Mahmūd, you have spent all your money upon me and now you can see no way to get us food.' 'As Allāh lives, that is true,' I answered, 'but why did I do it? And who are you, and where do you come from and what do you want?' 'Not so many questions, I beg,' he answered with a smile. 'Instead, take this gold dīnār and buy us good food. Also remember, Mahmūd, that your Destiny is fastened about my neck, as you supposed, and that I will surely bring you wealth and happiness. Only go quickly now, for we are famishing.'

I ran to the market and soon returned with a more liberal meal than I had ever eaten. When the last morsel had disappeared, it was already late and we lay down side by side. I covered the delicate body of my friend with my old mantle and, when he fell asleep all against me, did not dare to make the least movement, lest he should wake, doubt my intention, and turn again into a flay-bummed ape. As Allāh lives, I found the touch of that soft body pleasanter than the two old waterskins which had been the pillows of my poverty! I fell asleep with the pleased assurance that I lay beside my Destiny, and my last thought was a glorification of Allāh that it had come in so seductive a form.

Next morning the youth woke me, saying: 'After this night on the bare ground, I feel ready for you to hire us some palace in this city. Do not, I pray you, stint the furnishing of it.' He gave me gold, and I bargained so well with it that, in a few hours, we were both installed in the most splendid palace of Cairo. Then the youth said to me again: 'Now, Mahmūd, are you not a little ashamed to come so near me in those rags and with a body which serves as the Paradise for every known variety of flea and louse? Why do you not go to the hammām and improve yourself? You can have more money than all the kings of the earth put together; your only difficulty in acquiring suitable garments will be an embarrassment of choice.' I bowed low and hastened to the hammām, where I had an astonishing bath and left much of the accumulated discomfort of my youth.

When I returned to my friend, clad in all the sumptuous richness which had suggested itself to my starved fancy, he examined me closely and then said: 'That is how I would have you, Mahmud. Now sit down close to me.' So I sat down close to him, thinking: 'My time has come at last.' Soon he tapped me in friendly fashion on the shoulder, and exclaimed: 'What do you say to a king's daughter for your wife, a king's daughter fairer than the moon of Ramadān?' 'I would say that she was welcome, my master,' I answered. 'Then rise up, now,' said he, 'take this packet and present yourself before the Sultān of Cairo, to ask for his eldest daughter. She is written in your Destiny, and, when her father sees you, he will acknowledge you as her chosen lord. But offer him this packet before you speak.' As he had said that this thing was my Destiny, I set forth, accompanied by one of our slaves bearing the packet, and made my way to the palace.

The eunuchs and the guards were impressed by the magnificence of my new clothing, so they asked me my desire very respectfully and, when I said that I had a present for the throne, led me, after formality, into the Sultān's presence. Instead of losing countenance, I stepped forward as if I had been ever the companion of kings, and greeted the Sultān deferentially but without platitude. When he had answered my greeting kindly, I offered him the packet, saying: 'O King of time, deign to accept this trifle, whose value suits more with my poverty than with your great desert.' The Sultān caused his grand-wazīr to open the packet; when he saw that it contained incredible jewels and ornaments of every regal sort, he marvelled and exclaimed: 'It is accepted! Now tell me your desire; for kings are not backward in the giving of gifts.' 'O King of time,' I answered promptly, 'O Sultān of the age, I ask for wage that hidden pearl, that flower in calice curl, that lady in silk furl, your eldest girl!'

After the Sultān had looked at me for an hour of time, he

answered: 'It is permitted.' Then he turned to his wazīr, saying: 'And what do you think of this noble lord's demand? For my part, I approve it, for I have read his Destiny in his face.' 'He is surely not unworthy,' answered the wazīr, 'but perhaps it would be better to make a further proof of him,' 'In what way?' asked the Sultān. 'I would suggest, O King of time,' ventured the wazīr after some thought, 'that you show him the fairest and largest diamond in your treasury and ask from him one of equal value for your daughter's dowry.'

Though my heart beat in fear, I put a bold face on the matter and asked the Sultān if I might have the princess on that condition. For answer, he gave the fairest diamond out of his treasury into my hand, and said: 'If you bring me a stone identical with this one, she shall be yours.' I examined the jewel carefully and fixed its details in my mind; then I took leave of the court, begging permission to be allowed to return on the morrow.

'How went your wooing?' asked the ape youth, when I returned to him. I told him the demand which had been made of me and described the diamond as closely as I could. 'There will be no difficulty about that,' said he. 'It is too late to do anything to-night, but to-morrow, if Allāh wills, you shall have ten diamonds to take to the King.'

At this point Shahrazād saw the approach of morning and discreetly fell silent.

But when the eight-hundred-and-thirty-third night had come

SHE SAID:

Early next morning the ape youth went out into our palace garden and, after an hour, returned with ten diamonds as large as pigeon's eggs and with the same sunlight purity as that which the Sultān had shown me. I took them at once to the palace and stood before the throne, saying: 'Excuse the poverty of my offering. I found that I had not one diamond, so I have brought you ten. I beg you to choose out those which please you and throw away the rest.' Then I opened the little enamelled casket in which I had brought the stones, and the Sultān fell back upon his throne to find them all the exact brothers of his chief treasure.

He signed to his wazīr with his hand, as much as to say: 'What shall I do now?' and the wazīr signalled back: 'Let him have the girl.'

At once orders were given that the wedding should be prepared;

the kādī and witnesses were sent for and a marriage contract written in their presence. When it was handed to me, I gave it into the hands of the ape youth, whom I had brought to represent me. Knowing that I could neither read nor write, he proclaimed the contents in a loud voice. Then he drew me aside, saying: 'Now you are legally married to the princess, Mahmūd. But I wish you to promise me something.' 'My life is already yours,' I answered. 'If that be so,' he said with a smile, 'I desire you not to consummate your marriage until I give you leave to touch. I have a thing to do while she is yet a virgin.'

When the bridal night came, I sat far from the princess, in the room prepared, nursing my desire with my eyes but making no motion to approach her. On the second and the third night I did the same; so that, when the Queen came each morning to ask after her daughter's virginity, my wife was obliged to say: 'He has not done anything yet.' On the fourth morning the old woman wept, and cried: 'Alas, alas, why does he humble us? Why will he not go near you? What will our relations and our slaves think? Will they not begin to imagine tortuous reasons and blemishes hard to tell?' She carried her anxious grief to the Sultān, and he exclaimed: 'If he does not break the seal to-night I will cut his throat!' This threat came to the ears of my wife and she told me of it.

I hastened anxiously to put my difficult situation before the ape youth, but he reassured me, saying: 'The time has come, O Mahmūd! I have only one condition to set you: before you go in to the girl, beg her to give you a bracelet which she wears on her right arm. When you have received it and brought it to me, you may begin a husband's work and thus satisfy all who may be concerned.'

As soon as I was alone with the girl that night, I said to her: 'Tell me, dear heart, in Allāh's name, are you desirous of joy to-night?' 'I am desirous,' she answered. 'Then give me that bracelet from your right arm,' said I. 'You may have it,' she cried in astonishment. 'But it is only a holy bracelet which my nurse gave me when I was a child.' She unfastened the trifle from her arm and gave it to me. Then I made an excuse to leave her, promising that I would soon return, and swiftly carried the bracelet to the ape youth. When he received it, he sighed with satisfaction, and said: 'Now you may return to your bride.' So I returned, on feet winged with desire, anxious to make up for lost time and to satisfy all who were concerned in the matter of my wife's virginity.

She waited in readiness upon our bed, but, as I stepped towards her, the light, I know not how, grew dark about me and I found myself lying among the ruins of that house to which I had taken the ape. My royal robes had disappeared and I was half-naked under my old patched tunic. My darwīsh-stick lay by me and the turban of my wandering was upon my head, as full of holes as a sieve. 'Do I wake or sleep?' I cried. 'Am I Mahmūd the beggar, or Mahmūd the prince?' I rose and shook myself, as I had seen the ape, but nothing happened and I was in no way restored.

In my distress of soul, I wandered about the streets at haphazard until I came, by chance, on a certain Moor of Barbary sitting upon a mat in a byway, with a small carpet spread before him to hold written papers and objects of various divination.

I rejoiced at sight of him and, squatting before him, begged him to consult the Invisible on my account.

He looked at me with eyes like swords, and asked, 'O darwīsh, is it you who have been separated from your wife?' 'In Allāh's name, it is!' I cried, and he continued: 'O poor man, the ape which you bought for your five dirhams, the animal which changed into a de- lightful boy, is no human at all, but a very evil Jinnī. He has used you for his own ends: being passionately taken with the charms of the Sultān's eldest daughter and not being able to get near her, be- cause of the holy bracelet which she wore on her right arm, he em- ployed you to rob her of this protection that he might bear her off with impunity. But I have a hope of destroying this vile spirit, for he was one of those baseborn Afārīt who revolted against our Lord Sulaimān (upon whom be prayer and peace!).'

When he had thus spoken, the Moor traced certain complicated characters on a piece of paper and handed it to me, saying: 'I would bid you have all faith in the greatness of your Destiny; carry this paper to the spot which I shall describe to you and, when a troop of beings pass, give it to him who seems to be their chief. As for my reward, you can give me that when your Fate has been accom- plished.'

I thanked the learned man and made haste to follow his direction. I walked all night and all day, and came on the second night to a desert place filled with wild grass and the invisible presence of God. As I sat down to wait what might befall, I heard all about me a flying as of night birds; yet I could see nothing. Terror was already taking hold of my heart when I beheld a great number of torches, which seemed to be borne along in the distance; but the hands which carried them and the folk they lighted were invisible. Soon, where the torches were the thickest, I saw a King borne by on his throne. As he passed before me he looked closely at me; but I could not speak to him because my knees were knocking together. After a long regard, he addressed me, saying: 'Where is the writing from my friend, the Barbary Moor?' I plucked up my heart and, taking a step forward, handed him the paper. At once he stopped the procession of torches and read the writing. Then, to an invisible someone, he cried: 'O Atrash, go swiftly to Cairo and bring me the Jinnī such and such in chains!'

At the end of an hour my ape youth was hustled into the presence of this King by unseen hands, chained and terribly scowling. 'Why have you cheated this human of his mouthful?' asked the King. 'Why did you swallow that mouthful yourself?' 'No harm has come to the mouthful,' answered the youth, 'and I prepared it for myself.' Then said the King: 'Give back the holy bracelet to this man or we shall talk together.' But the Jinnī answered with piggish pride: 'I have got it now and no one shall take it from me.' So saying, he opened his mouth, until it yawned and glowed like a furnace, and threw the bracelet into the depths of his throat.

The night King slowly extended his arm and, seizing the ape youth by the neck, thrust him down and down until his length entered into his breadth. Then he commanded one of the invisible torch-bearing hands to bring the bracelet out of that broken mass and return it to me.

At this point Shahrazād saw the approach of morning and discreetly fell silent.

But when the eight-hundred-and-thirty-fourth night had come

SHE SAID:

Dear brother, as soon as my fingers closed round the holy thing, the King and his guard of hands disappeared and I found myself standing in my royal robe before the bed on which my wife lay sleeping. As soon as I had fastened the bracelet round her arm, she woke with a cry of joy. I lay down beside her, as if I had never been absent. . . . And the rest is a mystery of our Faith.

Next morning the King and Queen were so delighted by my return and by my exorcization of their daughter's virginity, that they quite forgot to ask me where I had been. After that night of fulfilment we all lived together in calm harmony.

When the Sultān, the father of my wife, died without leaving an heir, I found that he had bequeathed the throne to me. Thus I became what I am, my brother. Allāh alone is great! We come from Him and to Him we return at the last!

As he made an end of this tale, Sultān Mahmūd saw that his new friend, the pilgrim King, showed signs of great astonishment, so he said to him: 'Do not be surprised, my brother, for that which is written must run, and nothing is impossible to Allāh's will. I have told you the whole truth, without fearing to lessen myself in your eyes, because I trust that my example may be a consolation to you and a proof that you may accept my friendship with a quiet mind. For you can see that I am not likely on any day to twit you with your origin. . . . And now, O very brother in Destiny and rank, I will make your position regular by appointing you my grand-wazīr. You shall be ever upon my right hand to advise me in all my doings, and nothing shall pass in my kingdom save through you and improved by your experience.'

Sultān Mahmūd called together his amīrs and the principal nobles of his kingdom and, in their presence, clad the pilgrim King in a magnificent robe of honour and gave him the seal of the reign in token of his new rank. The grand-wazīr held dīwān that day and for many days to come, acquitting himself with such justice and impartiality that folk flocked from the length and the breadth of the land to bring their disputes before him; and even those against whom he gave judgment went away praising his wisdom and benevolence. He passed his moments of leisure in intimate friendship with the Sultān and soon became the companion of his every thought.

One day Sultān Mahmūd felt himself weighed down by heavy depression, so he hastened to his new friend, saying: 'Brother and wazīr, my heart is heavy.' 'O King of time,' answered the other, 'all joy and sorrow comes from within, but sometimes outside shows may have an influence upon those humours. Have you made trial of any outside shows to-day?' 'I have made trial of all the jewels of my treasury,' replied the Sultān. 'I have taken up in my fingers and let fall rubies, emeralds and sapphires, and every colour of precious stone; but not one of them lifted my soul to pleasure. I have been to my harīm and passed in review the white and the brown and the fair, the copper-coloured and the dark, the heavy and the slim; but none lifted up my soul to gladness. I went to my stables, but none of my countless beautiful horses could take my fancy, and the veil of the world has not lifted. So now I have come to you, O wisdom, that you may find a cure for me.'

'What do you say to a visit to the māristān, my lord? We have often spoken of exploring a house of fools together, but we have never done so yet. To my way of thinking the mad have a more subtle understanding than the sane. They behold differences and affinities which are hidden from common men, and are often visited by strange vision.' 'Allāh lives,' cried the Sultān, 'let us visit the māristān at once!'

The two left the palace without an escort and soon came to the māristān; but, as they wandered through its chambers and galleries, they found only the guards and the chief of keys. Of lunatics they could see no trace at all. The Sultān questioned the chief of keys concerning this strange dearth, and he answered: 'We have not had any fresh cases for a long time; I attribute the falling off in custom to a general deterioration of intellect in Allāh's creatures. But I am glad to say that I can show you three mad men, all of whom were left here by persons of the highest rank with strict orders that they should be shown to no one. Without doubt they are very learned men, for they read in great books all day.' So saying, he led the Sultān and his wazīr to a pavilion apart and, after opening the door for them, respectfully retired.

The two visitors saw three young men chained to the wall, one reading aloud and the other two listening with great attention. All were handsome and well-built, showing no sign of either raving or melancholy madness; so the Sultān turned to his companion, saying: 'Surely the stories of these three young men would be very astonishing, if only we could come to hear them.' Then he said to the prisoners: 'Have you been shut away for madness?' 'As Allāh lives,' they answered, 'we are neither raving mad nor melancholy mad, O King of time. We are neither idiots nor normally stupid persons. But our adventures have been so singular that, were they written with needles in the corners of our eyes, yet would they serve as a lesson to the circumspect.' The Sultān and his wazīr sat down on the ground opposite the three young men, saying: 'Our ears are open, and you have all our attention.'

So the first, he who had been reading aloud, said:

The First Madman's Tale

M Y lords and crowns upon my head, I used to be a silk merchant, as my father and grandfather had been before me, and I
sold only expensive Indian pieces of lively colouring. To this ex-
clusion I owed my great profits.

One day, as I sat in my shop, a venerable old woman entered and
gave me good day. When I had returned her salutation and prayed
her to be seated, she asked me whether I kept any choice silks of
India. I answered that I had nothing else, so she begged me to show
her a sample of my wares. I rose and, taking a most expensive square
of embroidered silk from a special cupboard, displayed it before her
delighted eyes. When I told her that she could have the piece for five
hundred dīnārs, she drew out her purse and paid over the money at
once; then she departed with her purchase. Allāh in that moment had
given me a profit of three hundred and fifty dīnārs.

Next morning she came again and paid me a further five hundred
dīnārs for another piece. The same happened on the third day, and
every morning until two weeks had passed since her first coming.
On the sixteenth day she chose a fair Indian silk at the same price,
and then felt for her purse. When she discovered that she had left it
at home, I hastened to reassure her, saying: 'Great lady, there is no
hurry, no hurry at all. Take the silk now. Then, if you return with
the money you will be very welcome, and if you return without the
money you will be very welcome.' But she cried out that she would
never consent to take anything away from my shop without paying
for it, and we were soon engaged in a battle of courtesy, she refusing
and refusing and I politely insisting. I played my part with all the
more readiness since I could have afforded to let her take away
several pieces without payment, after the great profit which she had
brought to me. At last the old woman said: 'O Kwājah, I see that we
will never agree; so I suggest that you accompany me now to my
house, and receive payment there.' As I did not wish to deny so good
a customer, I left my shop and followed her. We walked along in
single file until we came to the beginning of the road which held her
house. There she stopped and drew a silken kerchief from her
bosom, saying: 'Will you allow me to blind your eyes?' I could not
help asking for what reason, and she answered: 'There are many
houses with open doors in this street and the women sit in sight with
their faces unveiled. If you saw one of them you might fall in love

with her, and love is a great vexation. You may think that I exaggerate your danger, but I assure you that, in our quarter of the city, there are many wives and virgins who could lead the oldest of ascetics from his path. I should be grieved indeed if your heart came to any hurt through me.'

At this point Shahrazād saw the approach of morning and discreetly fell silent.

But when the eight-hundred-and-thirty-fifth night had come

SHE SAID:

'Here is a wise old woman!' I thought, and I allowed myself to be blindfolded and led to a door, on which my guide knocked with an iron ring. As soon as we were inside, the old woman took off the bandage from my eyes, and I found myself, not as I had expected in some ordinary dwelling, but in a true palace of kings. O our master the Sultān, I had never seen the like of that dwelling in my life. The old woman left me in a small chamber, through whose doorway I could see into a larger hall of smooth white marble. Having nothing better to do until her return, I fixed my eyes upon this hall and soon noticed all the precious silks which I had sold for those fifteen days piled negligently in a corner. Before I had recovered from my astonishment at this, two girls, as fair as moons, entered carrying vessels of rose-water. Setting their burdens upon the white marble floor, they took up one of my costly fabrics at haphazard and, after tearing it in two, began to use the pieces for all the world as if they had been kitchen cloths. They raised their sleeves to their armpits and, plung- the rare silks into the rose-water, began to wash the marble; then they dried the whole surface of the floor with more of my rare stock, polishing it until the hall seemed to be filled by a lake of silver. Lastly they spread out gaily worked tissues over the expanse, and I could see that the least of these could not have been purchased with my whole fortune. Over the tissues they laid a carpet woven of musk-scented kid's hair, and scattered cushions of ostrich down. Then they spread fifty squares of gold brocade round the central carpet, and retired. Hardly had they gone when my staring eyes beheld fifty young girls walk in two by two, hand in hand, and each recline on one of the squares of gold brocade, with her face turned towards the central carpet. After this settling down of doves, ten maidens of strange beauty bore a curtained chair into the hall. Because of their whiteness and the black fire of their eyes, I dropped my lids and, when I raised them again, behold! the chair had disappeared and a branch of wild rose, a light and laughing queen, lay among the central cushions and looked upon her girls. As I gazed, my old guide plucked me by the sleeve and drew me forward into the hall. 'Surely they wish my death,' I whispered to myself. 'There is no power or might save in Allāh!'

But the royal girl smiled upon me and, wishing me welcome, bade me sit down beside her on the carpet. I obeyed, but sat gingerly and in a confusion which was only deepened when she said: 'Young man, what have you to say of my beauty? Do you think that I might win you for my husband?' 'Mistress,' I answered, 'how could I dare to think myself worthy? My loftiest dreams might reach to be your slave, but nothing more.' 'Yet I am speaking seriously,' said she. 'Answer as seriously and have no fear; for my heart is filled to the brim with love of you.'

I understood that, by some miracle of chance, the girl meant in truth to marry me, though she might have had the choice of the thousand finest youths on earth. As the inconceivable is beyond the torture of surprise, I made bold to answer: 'If you are sure that you are not making me a laughing-stock before these honourable ladies, I beg you to remember the proverb: *When the blade is red it is ripe for the hammer*, by which I mean that my heart is hot enough for us to come together. Tell me, I pray, what dowry I must bring?' 'It is paid,' she answered with a smile, 'and, as you are so pressing, I will send for the kādī and witnesses that we may be wedded without delay.'

And indeed, my lord, the kādī and witnesses soon came and joined us with a lawful knot. 'Do I sleep or wake?' I asked myself, when my miraculous bride sent me to the hammām in charge of her fairest slave. The bath hall was scented with the smoke of aloes and filled with expert girls, who undressed me and gave me a bath which made me lighter than a bird. When they had scented me and attired me richly though slightly, they led me from the hammām and left me at the door of a private chamber where my naked bride awaited me.

She came to me and took me, she tumbled me beneath her and rubbed me with astonishing passion, until all my soul rushed into a part of me which you can divine, my lord. I set to the work required of me, the work under my hand; I reduced that which there was to reduce, I broke that which there was to break, and ravished that which there was to ravish. I took what I might, I gave what I ought; I rose, I stretched, I drove in, I broke up, I plunged, I forced, I stuffed, I primed, I sank, I teased, I ground, I fell, and I went on again. I swear, O King of time, that my rascal earned his names of ram, smith, stunner, sweet calamity, long one, iron, weeper, workman, horner, rubber, old irresistible, staff, prodigious tool, pathfinder, blind fighter, young sword, great swimmer, nightingale, thick-neck father, father of nerves, him of the large eggs, old man with a turban, bald head, father of thrusts, father of delights, father of terrors, cock of the silence, daddy's little one, the poor man's wealth, old muscle of caprice, and mighty sugar-stick. I gave a separate example for each name and only made an end in time for the morning prayer.

We lived together thus in a sweet drunkenness of folly for twenty nights, but at the end of that time I remembered my mother and turned to my wife, saying: 'It is many days since I have been home or to my shop; my mother must be very anxious about me and my business must be going to waste.' 'Have no anxiety for that,' she answered. 'I am willing for you to go every day to see your mother and to attend to your affairs; I only require that the old woman leads you out blindfold each time, and brings you back in the same way.'

So that day the old woman led me forth blindfold to the end of the street. When I returned to the same spot in the evening, after having consoled my mother and seen to the accumulated business of my shop, she was waiting for me with the silk kerchief ready. As she bound it about my eyes, she said: 'This is the only safe way, my son. There are wives and virgins in this street who sit at their doors all day, smelling out for love as a horse smells out for running water.'

My wife received me with transports of excited joy, and I answered as an anvil to the hammer. Cock of the silence did not run away from this most appetising bird; ram butted his courageous ewe fully thirty times until she cried for truce.

For three months more I lived an active life in that palace, with night expeditions, morning assaults, and pitched battles through the day. I grew to marvel at my Destiny, saying: 'Why should this ardent girl have fixed on me? It is astonishing that Fate should have added to this portion of delightful butter an excellent palace and more than royal wealth!' Though I had often wished for the chance, it was not until after many days that I found myself alone with one of my wife's black girls and was able to question her. 'Maiden of benediction, O doubtless white inside,' said I, 'tell me all you know of your mistress, and your words shall be hidden in the darkest corner of my memory.' The girl trembled, as she replied: 'Dear master, the story of my mistress is a fabulous story, and I should surely die if I revealed it. I may only tell you that she looked upon you one day by chance in the market and chose you for herself out of pure love.' Then, when I tried to cajole her into saying more, the creature threatened to tell her mistress, so that I was fain to return to my wife and engage in some minor skirmish.

Life thus passed with me as a violent love tourney until one noon, as I sat in my shop, taking advantage of my wife's daily permission, I saw a veiled girl cross the street and come directly towards me.

At this point Shahrazād saw the approach of morning and discreetly fell silent.

But when the eight-hundred-and-thirty-sixth night had come

SHE SAID:

When she was before my shop, she greeted me most graciously, saying: 'Good master, I have here a golden cock picked out with diamonds, which I have tried in vain to sell for its cost price to the merchants of this market; but they have neither taste nor delicacy and have refused, simply because there is not much demand for such things. I have come to you because you are a man of finer clay.' 'I have no need of the toy,' I answered, 'but to please you, I will give a hundred dīnārs for it.' 'Take it then, and may it be a good bargain to you,' said she. Reflecting that the golden cock would make a pleasant gift to my wife, one which would remind her of my valiance, I took a hundred dīnārs from the chest and offered them to the girl, but she refused, saying: 'These are no good to me; my price is one kiss upon your cheek, young man.' 'As Allāh lives,' I said to myself, 'the thing is worth more than a thousand dīnārs, and I am going to get it for a single kiss. I can see no objection.'

The girl lifted the little veil from her face and took a kiss upon my cheek; but, at the same time, as if her appetite had grown with the touch of her lips upon my skin, she closed her sharp young teeth in my flesh and gave me a bite whose mark I carry to this day. Then she danced off with a satisfied laugh, leaving me to wipe the blood which flowed in abundance down my cheek. 'As Allāh lives,' I cried, 'if all the women are coming for samples of me, a bit of my cheek, a bit of my chin, a bit of you know what, I might as well throw away my merchandise and deal only in myself!'

I was half laughing and half angry when the old woman bandaged my eyes that evening, at the corner of our street. Though, as we walked along, I heard her mumbling a confusion of words between her teeth, I only thought: 'Old women love to grumble; after a certain age they would curse their own shadows.'

But I found my wife frowning and clad from head to foot in scarlet red, such as kings wear upon their angry days. Her face was pale and her expression relentless. Yet I went up to her as usual and, although she turned her face away, offered her the golden cock, saying: 'Dear mistress, pray accept this curious trifle which I have bought for your pleasure.' Her brow grew dark and she gave me a buffet which sent me spinning like a top, and nearly broke my left jaw. 'Dog and son of a dog,' she cried, 'if you bought the thing, why is there a bite upon your cheek?'

My head was singing and I felt as if I should swoon; but I managed to control myself until I saw four slaves come from between the curtains of the room, carrying the body of the girl who had kissed me, with her head severed and lying upon her breast. Then indeed I sank into darkness and did not come to myself until I had been chained to this wall as a sworn madman.

Such is the story of my incarceration here, and I think that Allāh must have sent you, O King of time, and you, judicious wazīr, to save me from my death. Judge for yourself, from the coherence of my tale, with what kind of madness I have been inflicted.

The Sultān and his wazīr stayed for an hour in deep reflection, and then the Sultān said to his companion: 'I swear by the truth of Him Who set me to govern that I will neither eat nor drink nor sleep until I have discovered the wife of this young man! Tell me now, what must we do to that end?' 'O King of time,' answered the wazīr, 'we must leave these two other unfortunates for the moment, and take this silk merchant with us up and down the city. When he recognises the street corner where his eyes used to be bandaged by the old woman, we will blindfold him and trust his memory to calculate the number of steps that he was used to take. After he has led us to the required door, Allāh must be our guide in a very delicate affair.' 'It shall be as you say, O wisdom!' cried the Sultān, and at once freed the young man from his chains.

When they had left the māristān, all came to pass as the wazīr had predicted: after some time the young man recognised the street corner and, being blindfolded, led his two companions to the door by which he had been used to pass. 'Far be the Evil One!' cried the Sultān, as he looked up at the palace before which they stood. 'One of the wives of the old Sultān lives here with her daughter; surely it must be the last who has married this young man. In Allāh's name, O wazīr, do you think that all king's daughters are fated to wed common folks like you and me? Let us go in and see the end of this.' They knocked with the iron ring and the door was opened by eunuchs who stared in dumb surprise when they recognised the Sultān, the grand-wazīr, and the husband of their young mistress.

At this point Shahrazād saw the approach of morning and discreetly fell silent.

But when the eight-hundred-and-thirty-seventh night had come

SHE SAID:

One of them ran to give tidings of this visit, and his mistress came swiftly forth from the harīm to present her homage to the Sultān and kiss his hand. You will remember that the Sultān had married a step-sister of this girl. He greeted her kindly, saying: 'O cousin, the past is with Allāh, our concern is only with the present. I wish you to be reconciled to your husband, for he is a youth of excellent quality, and desires nothing better than to be restored to you. I swear, by the merits of your dead father, that his was the lightest of faults and that he has already been far too gravely punished.' 'Our master's wishes are commands,' replied the girl, and the Sultān joyfully cried: 'Then I name your husband my first chamberlain; he shall eat and drink with me for ever. To-night I will send to bring you to my palace, where the two of you shall be formally reconciled. In the meanwhile, we will take your husband with us to hear the tales of his two companions. If you promise that there shall be no more secrecy and blindfolding on your side, I will undertake for him that he shall never allow himself to be kissed by any other woman.'

Such, O auspicious King, continued Shahrazād, was the end of the tale of the first young man whom the Sultān and his wazīr found chained in the māristān. If you would hear the adventures of the second victim, I will continue:

When the Sultān had returned to the māristān with his wazīr and chamberlain, he sat down on the ground opposite the second young man, saying: 'Now it is your turn.' And the other said:

The Second Madman's Tale

'THE reason of my imprisonment in this place is more astonishing than the story which you have already heard, for my companion suffered from his over-carelessness with women, but I from over-care. You will realise this if you allow me to present my tale in its proper order.' 'Certainly do so,' said the wazīr, 'for the better you order your narrative, the more convinced shall we be that you are not mad.' So the second youth began:

I am a merchant and the son of a merchant. Before I was thrown into this place, I had a shop in the market where I sold bracelets and other costly ornaments for women. This story begins when I was only sixteen years old and already had a reputation for seriousness, honesty and sound judgment. I never tried to make conversation with my women customers and only spoke the necessary words of purchase and sale; I practised the precepts of the Book and never lifted my eyes to any daughter of the Faith. Other merchants held me up as an example to their sons, and more than one mother entered into negotiation with mine on the subject of an honourable marriage for me. But my mother always postponed the matter, saying that I was young and an only son.

One day, as I sat reading in my account book, an affable little negress entered the shop and greeted me respectfully, saying: 'Is this the shop of the noble so-and-so?' When I replied that it was, she drew a folded note from her bosom, with infinite precaution and many glances to right and left. As she gave it to me, she said: 'This comes from my mistress and she waits the favour of an answer.' Then she stood aside and let me read the letter.

I opened the paper and found that it contained an ode in my honour, couched in terms of flame and having the name of the girl who wrote it woven into the substance of the last stanza.

Considering this communication an attempt upon my virtue, I was extremely shocked; I tore it into little pieces and stamped it under my feet; then I took the little negress by one ear and smacked her cheek soundly, before sending her through the door with a well-directed kick. I made great parade of spitting in her face as she lay outside, so that none of my neighbours might fail to remark my wisdom and virtue. 'Daughter of a thousand shameless horns,' I cried, 'carry this back to that pimp's bastard, your foul mistress!' As I turned back into my shop, I heard my neighbours murmuring their admiration, and saw them point me out to their sons, saying: 'Allāh will surely bless this good young man! Learn, my son, to repulse all perverse offers in the same noble way.'

This happened, my lords, when I was sixteen years of age. It was only later that I saw clearly how gross and foolish my conduct had been, how vulgar and hypocritical, how full of stupid vanity and unfounded pride. Whatever my punishment was to be later, surely that one piece of conduct earned me this chain about my neck, though, as you will hear, I was chained for quite another reason.

But, not to mix Shaabān with Ramadān, I will only say that the months and years passed and I became a man, bachelor still, but now fully experienced in the delights of love. I began to think that it was time for me to marry a wife in the sight of Allāh. And I did marry a wife. As Allāh lives, I did so!

One afternoon I saw five or six white slaves conducting towards my shop a girl worthy of all love; her nails were tinted with henna, her hair fell about her shoulders, and she came to me with a conscious noble swaying of her hips.

At this point Shahrazād saw the approach of morning and discreetly fell silent.

But when the eight-hundred-and-thirty-eighth night had come

SHE SAID:

She entered like a queen and favoured me with gracious greeting. 'Young man, have you a choice of gold and silver ornaments?' she asked and, when I answered as was fitting, bade me show her gold ankle rings. I brought her the heaviest and most beautiful which I had in the shop, and she cast a negligent eye on them, saying: 'Try them for me.' One of her slaves stooped and, lifting the hem of her silk robe, showed me the slimmest, whitest ankle that ever came forth from between the fingers of God. I tried on the rings, but there were none small enough to fit the intoxicating slightness of those perfect legs. Seeing my embarrassment, she smiled and said: 'Do not trouble about them, young man. I will ask you to show me something else. But first, do they tell me the truth when they say at home that I have an elephant's legs?' 'The name of Allāh be about you and about the perfection of your ankles, dear mistress!' I cried. 'Gazelles would die of jealousy on beholding them!' 'I thought they were quite otherwise,' she answered. 'Now show me some bracelets.' The vision of those damning ankles still floated before my eyes as I chose out the narrowest gold and enamelled bracelets for her choice. 'I am very weary to-day,' she said. 'Try them for me.' One of the slaves darted forward and lifted her mistress's sleeves: alas, alas, a swan's neck, whiter and smoother than crystal, a little hand, a melting wrist, and fingers of desire! Sugar, date paste, soul's joy, and pure delight! I tried my bracelets about her arms, but even those which had been made for babes gaped outrageously above each slim transparency. As I hastened to draw them off, lest they should roughen such tenderness, she smiled again, saying: 'What have you seen, young man? I am maimed and web-fingered, am I not? I have arms like a hippopotamus, have I not?' 'The name of Allāh be upon you and upon those white curves,' I cried, 'and upon your child's wrist, and upon fingers of a small hūrī, my mistress!' 'Then they were not right?' she said. 'Now show me some gold necklets and breastplates.' I staggered, as if I had drunk wine, while I brought out my richest and lightest necklets and breastplates of gold for her inspection. One of the slaves uncovered her mistress's neck with a priest's care, exposing part of the bosom at the same time. Two breasts, two breasts at once, O King of time! Two little round mutinous breasts of rose ivory, twins nestling to their mother! I turned away my head, crying: 'Cover them, cover them! Allāh veil them, veil them!' 'What,' said she, 'will you not try on the necklets and breastplates? It does not matter, I will ask you for something else. I am black and hairy, am I not, with dugs like a buffalo cow? Or is the other rumour correct: that I am all bone, and dry like a salt fish, and as flat as a carpenter's bench?' 'The name of Allāh be upon you and upon the hidden beauty and upon the hidden fruit!' I cried. Then said she: 'You think that they were fooling me, then, when they told me that I had the ugliest hidden things in the world? And have you any belts?' I brought the lightest, supplest belts of filigree gold, and laid them discreetly at her feet, but she cried: 'No, no! Try them for me, in Allāh's name!' I chose the smallest of those belts and girt her with it over her robes and her veil; but, although it had been made for an infant princess, it was too large for a waist which cast no shadow, for a waist which would fill the heart of a scribe with despair when he was making the letter alif, for a waist which would wither the branch of a ban tree from sheer spite, for a waist which would have melted fine butter in jealousy, for a waist which would have shamed the pride of a young peacock, for a waist which would have burnt a bamboo stem. Knowing that I could in no way fit her, I was about to make excuses, when she said: 'They say I am deformed, with a double hump behind and a double hump in front, with an ignoble belly and a back like a dromedary. Is this so?' 'The name of Allāh be about you and about your waist,' I cried, 'about that which goes before and that which follows after, my mistress!' 'You surprise me, young man,' she said. 'They have never been very complimentary about my waist at home. Perhaps you could find me some earrings and a gold frontlet for my hair.' She lifted her veil and showed me a face like the moon riding up the sky on her fourteenth night. Seeing the Babylonian diamonds of her eyes, her cheeks of anemone, and her mouth which was a little coral case holding a double bracelet of pearls, I ceased to breathe and stood stockstill. So she smiled and said: 'It appears that you also are not proof against such ugliness, young man. I know from many repetitions that my face is a hideous thing, a parchment pitted with smallpox, a blind right eye and a bleared left, a nose terribly knobbed, a stinking mouth with broken teeth, and a pair of cropped ears. They say that my skin is scabby, that my hair is broken and frayed, and that the invisible horrors of my interior are not to be named.' 'The name of Allāh be upon you and upon your beauty, visible and invisible, O queen, O garmented in splendour!' I cried out. 'May His name be upon your purity, O daughter of lilies, and upon your scent, O rose, and upon your white bright skin, O jasmine!' Then I clutched at a support, feeling mortally drunk.

The girl of love looked at me with a smile of her long eyes, saying: 'Alas, alas, why does my father hate me so? For it is my father who attributes all these horrors to my appearance. I give thanks to Allāh that He has allowed you to assure me that I am not so! I do not think my father wishes to deceive me; I imagine that he has an hallucination which casts an ugliness upon all he sees. But, whatever the reason, he so hates the sight of me that he is ready to sell me to a merchant of cast slaves.' 'And who is your father, O queen of Beauty?' I asked. 'The Sheikh al-Islām in person,' she answered; but I cried in passion: 'Rather than sell you, would he not let me marry you?' 'He is a very scrupulous man,' she replied. 'As he thinks his daughter a repulsive monster, he would not willingly wed her to a worthy youth. But you might do worse than try to gain his consent, if I were to show you a way of overcoming his scruples.'

So saying, she reflected for a moment, and then continued: 'When you present yourself before my holy father and ask for my hand in marriage, he is certain to say: "My son, I must open your eyes on this matter: my daughter is a cripple, a hump-back, she is built awry, she has . . ." But you must interrupt, saying: "I am content, I am content!" He will go on: "She is blind of one eye, her ears are cropped, she is lame and stinking, a dribbler, a pisser . . ." But you must interrupt, saying: "I am content, I am content!" He will continue: "But, my poor boy, she is disgusting and vicious, she is snotty and for ever farting . . ." But you must interrupt, saying: "I am content, I am content!" He will continue: "But you do not know, my son. She is bearded and flab-bellied, she has the paps of a prize cow, she is short of an arm and has a club foot, her left eye is covered with a film, her nose is a mass of oily pimples, her face is one sieve of smallpox, her mouth a cesspit, her teeth a wreck, her interior organs are one mutilation, she is bald and incredibly scabby, she is a horror, an abomination of desolation." But you must interrupt, saying: "As Allāh lives, I am content!"'

At this point Shahrazād saw the approach of morning and discreetly fell silent.

But when the eight-hundred-and-thirty-ninth night had come

SHE SAID:

At the bare idea that any man could apply such terms to the figure of perfect love, I felt my blood boil within me, but as I knew that it would be necessary to stand this catalogue from the old man's own lips if I were to win the pattern of gazelles, I said: 'The proof is hard, dear mistress, but Allāh will give me strength. When shall I present myself to the venerable Sheikh al-Islām?' 'To-morrow in the middle of the morning, without fail,' she answered; then she rose and left me caught in the snare of her last smile and drowned in the fiery river of impatience.

Next morning, at the appointed hour, I hastened to the dwelling of the Sheikh al-Islām and demanded an audience on important business. He received me kindly and, as he bade me be seated, I was able to remark his noble appearance, his snow-white and immaculate beard, and above all the hopeless sadness of his eyes. 'That is the hallucination of ugliness,' I thought. 'May Allāh cure him!' Twice I rose and twice saluted him, in order to show my sense of his importance, then at last I sat and waited for him to question me.

When the servant had set ceremonial refreshment before us and the old man had said a few words on the heat and dryness of the time, he begged me to state my business. 'My lord,' I answered, 'I have come to solicit you humbly for one who is hidden behind the chaste curtain of your honour, for a pearl sealed with the seal of discretion, for a flower hidden among the leaves of modesty, for that unparalleled virgin of my desire, your daughter!'

I saw the old man's face darken and then turn yellow; he looked down in silencè for some time upon the floor, before he answered sadly: 'May Allāh preserve your youth, my son, and keep you for ever in the path of His grace! My daughter, who dwells behind the chaste curtain of my honour, is a creature altogether helpless; there is nothing to be done for her. She is. . . .' But I cried: 'I am content, I am content, my lord!' 'Allāh thank you for that, my son,' he went on, 'but my daughter is not for any strong and handsome youth like you; she is a poor invalid; her mother, being frightened by a fire, bore her before the term. She is as writhen and hideous as you are straight and fair. As it is right that you should understand why I refuse your suit, I will, in brief, describe her. . . .' 'But I wish her with all her faults,' I cried. 'I am content!' 'You force me to the pain of plain speech,' said he. 'If you were to marry my daughter, you would be wedding the most terrible monster of our time. One glance at the poor child . . .' But I felt that I could not stand a repetition of the catalogue, so I interrupted, saying: 'I am content, my lord, I am content! Spare yourself the task of description, for I would go on soliciting your daughter in marriage whatever you could find to say of her. I have a taste for horrors, my lord, when they are such as afflict your honourable daughter. I can only repeat, my lord, I am content, content, content!'

When the Sheikh al-Islām realised that I was in strict earnest, he clapped his hands together in astonishment, and cried: 'My conscience is free before Allāh and before you, my son. The madness of such a step will rest with you. Divine precept forbids me to raise objection to a legitimate desire. Therefore I give my slow consent.' I kissed the old man's hand in great content and begged that the marriage might take place that very day. 'It is permitted,' he answered with a sigh. The contract was drawn up immediately before witnesses: it expressly laid down that I accepted my bride with all faults, deformations, infirmities, deformities, malformations, ills, diseases, uglinesses, and blemishes; also it stipulated that I should pay a ransom and dowry of twenty thousand golden dīnārs if ever I divorced her. But I agreed to these conditions, and indeed would have accepted a thousand more of the same kind.

When the contract had been made legal, my father-in-law said to me: 'You must live and consummate the marriage here, for your wife is too infirm to be moved to another place.' I agreed to this condition and in my heart I said: 'How can an obscure merchant have won to such happiness and nobility? Is it really true that I am to rejoice and take my ease with all that beauty, to drink my fill of those hidden glories, and sweeten my soul with those obscure delights?'

Hardly could I wait till night. At the first civil moment I went with a bounding heart to my bride's bed and lifted the veil from her face and looked upon her with my eyes and soul.

Allāh confound the Devil, my dear lord! May he never cause you to look upon such a sight! I saw the most repulsive, the most deformed, the most disgusting, the most repugnant, the most nauseous creature of a nightmare. She was worse than the description which that lovely and wicked girl had given of her. She was a monster of malformation, a rag so full of horror that I should retch if I described her even now. Let it suffice to say that I had willingly, eagerly, madly, married a nauseous compendium of all lawful faults and illegal abominations, of all impurities, decays, aversions, atrocities, and disgusts which have ever entered into the imagination of the damned. I pinched my nose and let fall the veil. Then I hastened to a far corner of the room and sat down; for, even if I had been an eater of crocodiles from the Thebaid, I could not have had fleshly contact with that blot upon the face of Allāh's world.

I sat there and rocked with grief all night. What remedy was there for me? Like a fool, a heavy pig, a gulled ox, I had cried: 'Content, content!' when the old man warned me. I had bound myself a mile deep in that accursed contract. I bit my fingers and raged against myself; my blood would not flow normally; all the long hours until the dawn I felt that I was being tortured in some prison of the Medes.

At this point Shahrazād saw the approach of morning and discreetly fell silent.

But when the eight-hundred-and-fortieth night had come

SHE SAID:

With the first light I fled from that sorrowful place and, at the hammām, made ceremonial ablution for impurity; then I staggered to my shop and sat there with reeling head, drunk without wine.

Soon my friends and acquaintances among the merchants came to me by ones and twos and threes and fours to congratulate me and offer wishes. Some said: 'A benediction! A benediction! A benediction! May joy abide with you! May joy abide with you!' Others said: 'We did not know that you were so mean! Where are the pleasant sherberts, where are the pastries? Where, oh, where, is the halwā? Surely love has turned his brain and made him forget his friends, but nevertheless may joy abide with him, may joy abide with him!'

I answered mumblingly and at random, not knowing whether they mocked me or wished me well, and bore this torture with tears very near my eyes, until I was relieved by the time of the noon prayer. But, soon after my friends had departed to pray, I saw the maiden of love made perfect, the vision of desire who had cast me into hell, come smiling towards me in the middle of her slaves. She balanced voluptuously to right and left among her silks, as supple as the young branch of a ban in a garden of spices. She moved with such conscious seduction that the folk of the market left their prayers and crowded about her passage. She entered my shop innocently, like a child, and sat down with a gracious greeting. 'May this be a day of benediction, O bridegroom!' she said. 'May Allāh put a crown upon your happiness!' she said. 'May joy abide with you, joy abide with you!' she said.

Seeing her add such audacious insult to that bitter injury, I felt all the low claptrap of my virtuous youth come to my lips, and my mouth showered curses upon her. 'O cauldron of pitch! O bowl of tar! O well of perfidy!' I cried. 'May Allāh curse the hour of our meeting, may He damn the foul blackness of your soul, you wanton whore!' 'What is all this, sounding brass?' she asked with a calm smile. 'Have you forgotten my ode and my poor little negress, and your great virtue?'

When she had said this, she wrapped her veils about her and rose to depart; but I suddenly understood that I had never reaped what I had sown in that far-off day, and felt the full weight of my hateful and heavy virtue. Therefore I threw myself at the perfect feet of love and begged for pardon, saying: 'In very truth I repent!' I called together words as sweet and tender as rain upon burning sand; so that at last the girl deigned to excuse me, saying: 'I pardon you this once, but you must never do the like again.' I kissed the hem of her robe and covered my brow with it. 'O mistress,' I cried, 'I kneel in your protection and look for deliverance at your hands!' 'I have already thought of that,' she answered with a smile. 'I caught you and it is only right that I should set you free.' 'Make haste, make haste, in Allāh's name!' I cried.

'Listen carefully,' said the girl, 'and you shall soon be freed from that poor woman.' 'O dew! O refreshment!' I murmured, bowing low, and she continued: 'Go to the foot of the citadel and call together all the acrobats, mountebanks, quacks, buffoons, dancers, rope walkers, ballad singers, ape leaders, bear masters, tambourines, clarinets, flageolets, cymbals, and funny men, and say to them such and such.'

At this point Shahrazād saw the approach of morning and discreetly fell silent.

But when the eight-hundred-and-forty-first night had come

SHE SAID:

When the girl of love's perfection had sketched out a plan to me, which seemed to promise a door of salvation, I cried: 'O queen of fair intelligence, I am ready to obey you in all things!' I hastened to make the preparations which she had suggested, and then proceeded to the palace of the Sheikh al-Islām.

We sat together upon the platform of the courtyard, drinking sherberts and talking pleasantly together, until suddenly the great door opened to admit the strangest procession. First came four acrobats walking on their heads, next four rope walkers balancing on their big toes, then four mountebanks leaping along on their hands, and lastly the whole dancing, yelling, tinkling, shouting, clattering, grinning, mimicking crowd of the city's foolery. Ape leaders led their apes, bear masters showed their bears, buffoons twirled their tinsel, quacks cocked their high felt bonnets, singers of lewd songs sang their lewd songs, and players upon instruments played upon their instruments, altogether and all out of tune. They collected round us in some sort of order and, at a single bang upon the drum,

fell into a solemn silence. The chief of the tribe came to the foot of
the steps and, in the name of all my family there assembled, wished
me prosperity in a ringing voice, and swore that none of those noble
professions would ever desert me. 'What is this?' cried the outraged
Sheikh al-Islām, as he pointed a trembling finger in my face. 'Are
you the son of a mountebank? Are these vile gipsies kin to you?'
'Because I love your daughter and her honour,' I answered, 'I cannot deny my birth and family. Blood remembers blood, and the river
her cradle among the hills.' 'In that case, young man,' he stormed,
'your marriage contract is illegal. In it you falsified your parentage.
You cannot stay in the house of the Sheikh al-Islām; should the
people hear of your presence, they would spit in your face, as if
you were no more than a Christian dog or a hog of Israel!' 'As
Allāh lives,' I cried, 'I have won her and will not divorce her for all
the kingdom of Irāk! Each of her hairs is more precious to me than a
thousand lives.' Then the holy old man, who knew full well that a
divorce under compulsion is forbidden by the Book, took me apart
and wheedled me for a long time, saying: 'Protect my honour and
Allāh will surely protect yours.' At last I consented to do his will. I
proclaimed in the presence of witnesses: 'I put her away; once, twice,
thrice, I put her away!' Also, because the father himself had urged
on this renunciation, I was not called upon to pay the ransom and
dowry which had been set down in the contract.

Without even taking leave of that sad old man, I ran off as hard
as I could and came breathless to my shop, where perfect love still
waited me. She welcomed and congratulated me sweetly, and then
said: 'Shall we not come together, dear master?' 'In your house or at
my shop?' I asked. 'Poor lad,' she answered with a smile, 'do you
not know that a woman has many a preparation before such things
can be? We will go to my house.' 'O queen,' said I, 'since when have
lilies gone to the hammām and roses to the bath? My shop is large
enough to hold a lily and a rose, and, if it burn to the ground, there
is always the vast chamber of my heart.' 'Your compliments have
improved in quality with the years,' she admitted with a laugh; but
nevertheless she bade me follow her.

I locked the door of my shop and followed my sweet mistress and
her slaves, until we came to a certain palace, whose doors opened to
let us pass. The girl gave a command to two eunuchs, who led me
forth to the hammām where they bathed me, perfumed me with
Chinese amber, and clothed me in sumptuous garments of my love's

providing. They they led me through many corridors to a hidden apartment, where the lily of my desire and perfect love lay careless upon a deep brocaded bed.

When we were alone together, she said: 'Come here, come closer, O sounding brass! As Allāh lives, you must have been a little booby in the old days to refuse such a night as this! But I will not confuse you by recalling the past.' Seeing her before me naked, white and fine, my lord, seeing those coveted delicacies in front, and those broad dimpled desires which lay behind, I felt the wasted days clamour within me, and made as if to leap. But she stopped me with a gesture and a smile, saying: 'Before the fight, O soldier, let me hear if you know the name of your antagonist.' 'River of grace,' said I. 'No,' said she. 'White father,' said I. 'No,' said she. 'Sweet fleshy,' said I. 'No,' said she. 'Peeled sesame,' said I. 'No,' said she. 'Basil of the bridge,' said I. 'No,' said she. 'Wild mule,' said I. 'No,' said she. 'I only know one more name,' said I, 'Father Mansūr's khān.' 'You are wrong,' said she. 'Come, tell me, sounding brass, did all your masters teach you nothing?' 'Nothing,' said I. Then she said: 'Listen to the thing's rightful names. They are: dumb starling, fat sheep, silent tongue, wordless eloquence, adjustable vice, sliding rule, mad biter, great shaker, magnetic gulf, Jacob's well, little cradle, nest without eggs, bird without feathers, dove without stain, cat without whiskers, silent chicken, and rabbit without ears.'

As soon as she saw that I had gathered the theory of these things, she grasped me hard between her thighs and arms, saying: 'In Allāh's name, dear sounding brass, be swift in the assault, be heavy in your fall, throw light, swim deep, cork close, and jump and jump again. Hateful are the once risers, the twice risers, and those who rise to fall! Come, stiffly stand to it, dear friend!' 'But there should be seemly order in all things,' I objected. 'Where shall I begin?' 'Where you like, sounding brass,' she panted. 'Then first I will give seed to the dumb starling,' said I. 'He is ready, oh, he is ready,' cried my love.

Then, O King of time, I said to the child of my inheritance: 'Feed the starling!' So he bountifully fed the starling with great handfuls, until the dumb starling signified after its kind: 'Allāh increase you! Allāh increase you!'

And I said to the child: 'Bow to the sweet fat sheep!' He bowed so low and bowed so deep to the sweet fat sheep, that the sheep answered after its kind: 'Allāh increase you! Allāh increase you!'

And I said to the child: 'Now speak to the silent tongue!' He rubbed the silent tongue with a finger so strong and young, that the silent tongue found voice and by it was sung: 'Allāh increase you! Allāh increase you!'

And I said to the child: 'Now tame the savage biter's bite!' The child caressed the savage wight, gripping so tight that he came forth unscathed in the thing's despite, and the mouth cried: 'A right drink, a right, a drink of delight.'

And I said to the child: 'Now fill up Jacob's well, O strongest man in Israel!' He filled that well so well that none might tell that there had been a well.

And I said to the child: 'Now heat the bird without feathers!' And the child outran all the tethers till the bird cried: 'Now I am warm for all weathers.'

And I said to the child: 'Now give corn to the dumb chick!' And he spread the corn so thick and so quick that the chick cried: 'O benediction, O benedic, dic, dic!'

And I said to the child: 'Do not forget the rabbit without an ear. It has fallen fast asleep, I fear!' And the child drew near and woke the rabbit and calmed its fear, with counsels queer and dear. The rabbit cried: 'I hear!'

At this point Shahrazād saw the approach of morning and discreetly fell silent.

But when the eight-hundred-and-forty-second night had come

SHE SAID:

And in this way, O King of time, I urged the child to converse with every aspect of his adversary, to say the correct thing and to draw the full savour from each answer. His reply to the cat without a whisker could not have been brisker, and nothing could have been more plain than his discourse with the dove which had no stain. Calling a space a spade'll give you an idea of his chat with the cradle; and he was at his best with the eggless nest. He adapted himself and was not over virtuous or nice with the adaptable vice; he did not slip like a fool with the sliding rule; also he showed himself steel filings to the magnetic gulf's beguilings, till the sweet possessor of all these things cried out: 'I choke, I choke! It is no joke, this mighty artichoke!'

But as soon as morning light appeared we said our prayer and went together to the bath. When we came out of the hammām and sat down to eat together, my love said to me: 'Sounding brass, you have proved yourself a champion, and I am content that I chose you out and waited for you. Would you like to be married to me, or would you like to leave me?' 'Rather the red death than to leave your white face, my mistress,' I cried, and she exclaimed: 'If you think so, we need the kādī.'

The kādī and witnesses were sent for; and after they had written out our marriage contract, we ate and waited for digestion. As soon as our stomachs were calmed, we sprang again to the assault and made the night a fellow labourer with the day.

Life and love lived love and life together for thirty days and nights, my lord. I crushed and filed and stuffed the stuffable, the fileable, the crushable, until a giddiness came over me and I dared to say: 'I know not why, my saint, but I feel I cannot plant the twelfth great lance to-day.' 'But the twelfth is the most necessary,' love objected. 'The eleven do not count.' 'Yet it is impossible, impossible,' said I. Then she with a laugh: 'You must have rest, my poor, you must have rest!' And when I heard that word, I lay down and fainted clear away.

I came to myself in chains, fast to the wall of this māristan, and when I asked the guards why I was here, they answered: 'You must have rest, you must have rest.' But I have rested now, O King of time, I have rested and am quite full again of love. Can you not of clemency arrange that I go back to the girl of love's perfection? I cannot tell you her name and quality, but I have given you the true tale, with all the orders and gradations of its intercourse. Yet Allāh knows all!

Sultān Mahmūd marvelled at the lucidity of this tale, and said: 'Even if you had been chained here for madness, I would have freed you on the clear evidence of your story. Do you know the road to your wife's palace?' 'I would know it with my eyes shut,' answered the youth. The Sultān knocked off his chains with his own hand and was preparing to lead him forth, when the third young man cried out from the wall: 'In Allāh's name, dear masters, do not leave me until you have heard a third and more marvellous story!' But the Sultān promised to return in a short time, and led his companions from the māristan.

They followed the young man until they came to a palace; and at the sight of it the Sultān cried: 'May the Tempter be for ever confounded! This palace belongs to the old Sultān's third daughter. Our Destiny is a prodigious Destiny! Praise be to Him Who reunites the separated and joins the torn rents in the lives of His creatures!' He led his companions into the palace, and his cousin hastened to present herself between his hands.

Now this was none other than the girl of perfect love. She kissed the hand of the Sultān, who was her sister's husband, and declared herself in all things ready for his wishes. 'Child of my uncle,' he said, 'I bring you your husband, whom I have appointed my second chamberlain, my friend and cup-companion; I know the trouble which was between you in the past but I take it upon myself that such a thing shall not happen again. Also, the lad is well rested and ready for anything.' 'I hear and I obey!' answered the girl. 'Now that he lies under the mantle of your safety, O King of time, and now that you assure me he is ready for anything, I am quite prepared to live with him again.' 'I thank you, my child,' answered the Sultān, 'you have lifted a great weight from my heart ... But I must take him away now, for we have to listen together to a tale which promises to be altogether extraordinary.' He took leave of the princess and left her palace with his wazīr and two chamberlains.

When they came to the māristān, they all sat down upon the ground facing the third young man, who had languished in his chains for their return. At once he began:

The Third Madman's Tale

O SOVEREIGN master, he said, wise wazīr, and honourable chamberlains who lived with me even now beneath these fetters, my tale has nothing to do with those which went before, for women came to my companions and tempted them, but with me it was different. I leave the moral of my life to your good judgment.

My father and mother passed into the compassion of Allāh when I was still very young, and I was taken into the house of poor and kindly neighbours, who had no money for my education and were forced to let me grow up in the streets, dressed only in the half of a blue cotton shirt. I cannot have been altogether revolting to look upon, for people would stop in the streets at the sight of my little body cooking in the sun, and cry: 'Allāh preserve this child from the evil-eye! Surely he is a fragment of the moon.' Sometimes, if a man passed eating halwā and chick-peas or that yellow pliant toffee which can be pulled out into long strings, he would hand me the delicacy, tapping my cheek, or stroking my head, or pulling at the little top-knot which rose from the middle of my shaven skull. Then I would open an enormous mouth and swallow the sweetmeat in one gulp, to the admiration of the giver and the envy of my friends. Such was my life until the age of twelve.

One day, as I was hunting for the nests of sparrow-hawks and crows on the roof of a ruined house, I saw, lying beneath a scanty palm-thatched shed in the abandoned courtyard, the dim and motionless figure of a man. Supposing this to be some Jinnī or Marid who was haunting the ruin, I slithered down from the roof and was about to run away, when a voice of great beauty called me from the shed, saying: 'Why would you run away from me, my son? Come and taste wisdom with me. I am no Ifrīt, but a man of the sons of men who finds it better to live in solitude and contemplation. Come to me, my child, and I will teach you to be wise.'

At this point Shahrazād saw the approach of morning and discreetly fell silent.

But when the eight-hundred-and-forty-third night had come

SHE SAID:

Checked in my flight by some power of this voice, I approached the shed and, entering, found myself face to face with a man incalculably old but having a face as bright as the sun. 'Welcome to the orphan who shall inherit my wisdom!' he said, and again, 'I shall be your father and your mother,' and again, taking my hand, 'You are my disciple. Some day you will have disciples of your own.' He gave me the kiss of peace and, bidding me sit down beside him, began my instruction without delay. The beauty of his teaching conquered my wayward will; I gave up all thought of playing with my comrades. The old man became in truth my father and my mother; I showed him tender respect and boundless submission. Five years passed away in my instruction and my spirit thrived upon the lonely bread of wisdom.

Yet all wisdom is vain unless it be sown upon a soil excellent in itself. Otherwise the first scrape of folly's rake effaces the image and exposes the dry and barren earth beneath.

One day my venerable master sent me to beg food in the court-yard of a mosque. Having received a sufficiency of alms, I took the road back to our solitude; but, as I went, I was met by a group of eunuchs who made room with their long staves for the swanlike walking of a veiled girl. Her eyes, seen dimly through the silk, had all the sky in them for me. 'The Sultān's daughter, the Sultān's daughter!' I heard men cry, and, by the time I had reached my master, five years of hoarded wisdom had slipped from my mind and my head burnt with an unknown fever.

The sage looked sadly at me, and I wept; we passed the night side by side without speaking. In the morning, as I kissed his hand, I said: 'O my father and my mother, pardon your unworthy disciple! I must glance once more upon the Sultān's daughter.' 'My child, you shall see her again since you desire it, but I charge you to reflect on the distance which lies between solitary wisdom and the loud pomp of kingship. Babe of my tenderness, have you forgotten that where king's daughters are there can be no true balance of the mind? Would you lose peace for ever? Would you have me die in the bitter knowledge that I carry the precepts of solitude down with me into the tomb? The richest thing in the world, my son, is renunciation, and to go without is to possess the world.' 'O my father and mother,' I answered, 'if I cannot look once more upon the princess, I shall die.'

'Would one glance satisfy you, my child?' asked my master. 'As-suredly,' I answered. So he came up to me sighing, because he loved me, and circled my eyes with a certain balm. Immediately the upper part of my body became invisible, and I was, as it were, legs and a waist walking. 'Hurry back into the city,' said the old man, 'and there wait upon your desire.' In the twinkling of an eye I had run to the public square, where I found myself the centre of a surging mob who could make nothing of my appearance. The miracle was noised abroad, and rumour of it came to the palace, where the Sultān's daughter dwelt with her mother. As they burned with curiosity to behold me, they sent eunuchs who brought me into the harīm. While they took their fill of novelty, I took mine of beauty. But when I was dismissed and had returned to my master, my soul was in a greater torment than before.

I found the sage lying upon his mat, very yellow about the cheeks and with signs of agony imprinted on his face; but I had too much trouble of my own to be concerned for him. 'Have you seen, my child?' he asked in a feeble voice. 'Yes,' I answered, 'and it is worse than if I had never seen. Now my soul will know no rest until I can sit beside her and gaze my fill.' 'I tremble for your peace, O disciple whom I love,' he sighed. 'How can there be aught in common between the people of Solitude and the Fools of Power?' But I answered: 'To rest my head near hers, O father, to touch her neck with my hands! Surely I shall die!'

'O child, you are full of life and have forgotten,' sobbed the old man. 'I will give you means to satisfy all your desires, but, as a last favour, I beg you dig my grave in this place and bury me with no stone or sign above.'

I leaned down over my master and he rubbed my eyelids with a fine powder of black kohl, saying: 'O dead disciple, you are now invisible and can go upon your chosen path unseen of men. I pray that Allāh may guard you among the pitfalls which it has seemed good to Him to set for the feet of Solitude!'

When he had thus spoken, my old master was as if he had never been. I dug a grave for him beneath that shed (Allāh give him a chosen place among His mercy!) and then hurried towards the Sultān's palace.

As I was invisible, I was able to enter the palace and pass through the harīm into the very chamber of the princess. She lay sleeping upon her bed, clad only in a chemise of Mosul tissue; I had never seen the nakedness of a woman before, and cried at the top of my voice: 'Allāh, Allāh!' The girl half opened her eyes and uttered a sigh of waking; but that, happily, was all. She turned over and settled to sleep again, showing me the inexpressible. I was thunderstruck that so frail and fine a girl could have so large a bottom; knowing that I was invisible, I dared to go nearer and lay the point of my finger to one of those sleek, dry, elastic surfaces. As this contact did not explain the mystery of their great size, I hastened to come into closer touch with their delightful mistress. I took infinite precautions of gentle silence and, when I judged that the first danger was over, allowed the child to play a little by himself. Yet he behaved so well, eschewing all that might be considered gross and reprehensible, that the matter would have passed off without accident, and both of us retired with a judgment formed and nothing more, had not the Devil tempted me to pinch the very centre of one of those mysterious cushions. Alas, alas, the impression of my fingers overcame her sleep for good and all; she leapt from her bed with a frightened cry and called loudly upon her mother.

At this point Shahrazād saw the approach of morning and discreetly fell silent.

But when the eight-hundred-and-forty-fourth night had come

SHE SAID:

In answer to these cries, her mother ran in, tripping over her robe in her anxiety, followed by several eunuchs and an old nurse. The girl continued to point at the place of the pinch and call upon Allāh to protect her; in one breath her mother and the nurse questioned her, saying: 'What is it, what is it? Why is your hand on the honourable? What is the matter with the honourable? What has happened to the honourable? May we not look at the honourable?' The nurse turned like an adder upon the eunuchs, crying: 'Leave us for a while!' and the eunuchs departed, cursing the calamitous old woman beneath their breath.

All these things I saw without being seen, thanks to the magic kohl. As the two old women craned their necks to behold the injury, the girl cried in a blush of pain: 'I have been pinched just there!' And, sure enough, the two old women beheld the red and inflamed trace of my thumb and finger exactly in the middle of the honourable. They recoiled in offended shock, crying: 'Who did that, you naughty girl, who did that?' 'I do not know, I do not know!' she answered through her tears. 'It happened while I was dreaming that I was eating a large cucumber.' Alarmed by this symbol, the two old women looked behind the curtain and draperies of the room. When they found nothing, they asked the child if she was sure that she had not pinched herself in her sleep. 'I would rather die than do such a cruel thing!' she answered. Then the old nurse gave her opinion, saying: 'There is no might or power save in Allāh! One of the unnameable folk of the air has pinched our daughter. He came in through the window and, seeing her sleeping with her honourable exposed, could not resist the temptation of pinching it. Before we put on a cold compress of water and vinegar, we must banish the evil presence. The Jinn cannot abide the burning of camel dung.' She carefully shut the window, and cried to the eunuchs beyond the door: 'Bring me a basket of camel dung!'

While she was waiting, the mother approached her daughter and said in a low voice: 'Are you sure that the nameless one did nothing else? You did not feel anything of you know what?' 'I do not know,' replied the child bashfully; so mother and nurse bent together and made an examination. They found no trace of violence upon either side, and that all was in its place; but that wicked old nurse's nose was over-sensitive, and she cried: 'There is the smell of a male Jinnī upon her! Where are those vile eunuchs? Where is the camel dung?'

At that moment the eunuchs arrived with the camel dung in a basket, and handed it through the door. The old woman took up the carpets and shook out the dung in a pile upon the marble floor. Then she set it on fire, tracing magic signs in the air with her finger and muttering strange words.

The reeking smoke of the burned dung chafed my eyes so unsupportably that they filled with water and I was obliged to keep on rubbing them with the tail of my garment. The same stupidity which had prevented me from bringing a supply of that kohl from my master's tomb blinded me to the fact that I was rubbing off that which made me invisible, until I saw the three women point to me and cry together: 'There is the Ifrīt! There is the Ifrīt!' They called in their fright on the eunuchs, who threw themselves upon me and would have killed me; but I cried in a terrible voice: 'If you do me the least harm, I will call my brothers and they shall pull down this palace upon your heads!' This frightened them and, although they held me, they did me no hurt. 'My fingers in your eyes!' cried the nurse; but I shouted angrily in answer: 'Be quiet, you disgusting old woman, or my brothers shall grind you to powder.' This silenced her for a moment, but soon she exclaimed: 'If this be an Ifrīt, we cannot kill him; but we can chain him up for the rest of his years.' So she plucked up courage, and cried to the eunuchs: 'Take him to the māristān, chain him to the wall, and tell the guardians that they shall die if they let him escape.'

O King of time, the eunuchs brought me to this place and here I met your two most noble chamberlains. Such is my tale for the Sultān's regale. I have told it all, with details great and small, in hope that the King will unchain me from this wall and release me from thrall. But Allāh knows all!

When Sultān Mahmūd had listened to this tale, he turned to his wazīr, the pilgrim King, saying: 'See how Destiny deals with my race! The princess with the pinched honourable is the late Sultān's youngest daughter. Now it only remains for us to arrange these matters suitably.' He knocked off the young man's chains, and said to him: 'Your story is indeed astonishing, my son; because of my delight in it, I will give you the hand of the princess in marriage. You know something of her already, and will be the more anxious to wed her, I am sure. Also I make you my third chamberlain.'

All five men left the māristān together and went to the Sultān's palace, where a great feast of public rejoicing was prepared to celebrate the marriage of the third youth and the reconciliations of the other two. The festivities were kept up for forty days and forty nights, and all those people concerned in them lived together in the joys of love and friendship until the inevitable separation.

Such, O auspicious King, continued Shahrazād, were the adventures of the royal bastard, who became first a pilgrim upon the road of Allāh, then the wazīr of Sultān Mahmūd, and lastly auditor of the three remarkable tales told in the māristān. But Allāh knows all! And you must not think that this tale is in any way more admirable and instructive than the Wisdom below the Severed Heads. 'What wisdom is that, O Shahrazād,' cried King Shahryār, 'and what severed heads are those?' So Shahrazād said:

Wisdom Below the Severed Heads

IT is related—but Allāh alone can tell the true and false—that there was once, in the antiquity of time, a just and powerful King who ruled over one of the ancient cities of Rūm. The greatest of the treasures of his reign was one son, who was not only the handsomest youth of his time but the possessor of a wisdom which, as you will see, grew to be the marvel of the earth.

In order to put this quality to the proof it was necessary for Allāh to turn the tide of prosperity against the King and Queen, and allow them to wake one morning in an empty palace, poorer than any beggar upon the road of generosity. Nothing is easier to Him than to break down the thrones of kings and give to beasts of prey and birds of night a habitation in high palaces.

At this point Shahrazād saw the approach of morning and discreetly fell silent.

But when the eight-hundred-and-forty-fifth night had come

SHE SAID:

Before this misfortune the gallant prince felt his hot heart tempered like a sword's blade in ice, and he said to the King his father: 'If you will deign to hear me, my lord, I suggest that we rise up now and go to some land which does not know our name. However bitter the immediate past, we are still masters of the present and may hope for new joys in a new life.' 'O excellent son,' answered the old King, 'your counsel is an inspiration from the Master of wisdom. May He conduct the affair for us!'

The prince made all preparations for a journey, and took his father and mother across plains and deserts until they came in sight of a great and well-built city. Then he left them to repose in the shadow of the walls and entered the streets by himself; but, as soon as he found out from the people that the city was ruled over by a just and high-minded King, he returned to his parents, saying: 'I intend to sell you to the Sultān of this city. What do you say to that?' 'Allāh has given you tenderness of heart and great intelligence, dear child,' they answered. 'Do with us as you think best.' So the prince took the old people by the hand and, after demanding an audience, led them into the presence of the King of that city. 'What do you wish, O youth of bright beauty?' asked the Sultān, and the prince answered: 'O my master, I have with me two gracious and well-born captives. They have both seen better days, and would make excellent slaves if you would deign to buy them.' 'If they belong to you, they are certain to please me,' said the King. Then he looked for the first time on the two old strangers, and cried: 'How can a King and Queen be slaves? Are you in truth the property of this fair youth?' 'We are his property, O King of time,' they answered.

The Sultān turned to the prince, saying: 'It is for you to set the price. There have never been two such slaves before.' 'I wish neither gold nor silver,' answered the young man, 'but only the loan of a prince's equipment and the fairest horse in your stables. On the day that I return these things, I shall take back my two captives, trusting that they have been a cause of blessing to you in the meanwhile.' The Sultān at once agreed to this arrangement; he robed the prince in all the accoutrements of a warrior king, and gave him a noble chestnut horse to ride.

The prince took leave of his parents and passed over field and fountain, moor and mountain, until he came to a city greater and more beautiful than the first. But, as he rode in, a strange murmur of surprise and pity followed him, with cries of: 'Alas, alas, for his youth!' 'He will be the hundredth, the hundredth!' 'How may he hope to succeed when so much wisdom has failed!' These cries increased as he rode along and soon his way was entirely barred by the weeping people. 'Good folk,' he cried, 'is it your custom to prevent strangers from coming to rest among you?' For answer, an old man caught his horse's bridle and looked up into his face, saying: 'O beautiful youth, we beg you to turn back, not to rush madly upon a certain death.' 'I do not understand you,' replied the prince, and the old man continued: 'I thought at first that you had come to attempt the hand of our Sultān's daughter; therefore I begged you to retire while there was yet time. For you must know that our princess, the wisest and most beautiful damsel of all ages, has determined not to marry until she has found a youth who can answer all her questions. Ninety-nine kings' sons have already failed. She lives in a tower above the city and alas, alas, that tower is hung with the heads of those who could not answer her.' 'Surely my Destiny waits me there!' cried the prince. 'Lead on, I pray, good people.'

Seeing that he was determined to make the attempt, the people fell in behind him with cries of lamentation, and escorted him outside the city to the tower. There he saw a princess seated high upon a terrace, dressed in royal purple and surrounded by slave girls dressed in purple also. Because of its red veil he could distinguish nothing of her face except two dark jewels which were her eyes, two black lakes lighted by a fire burning below the water. And, about that terrace, set equal distances from one another, ninety-nine young severed heads swung a little in the breeze. The princess leaned over and looked down as the prince halted his horse below the terrace. The crowd fell suddenly silent, and she said: 'Are you ready to answer my questions, O hundredth, O rash youth?' 'I am ready, O princess,' answered the prince.

'Now that you have looked upon me and upon those about me,' said the princess, 'tell me, without hesitation, what we resemble as we sit here in our high tower?' The prince answered without hesitation: 'O princess, you resemble an idol in a temple surrounded by those who serve the idol; you resemble the sun surrounded by the sun's rays; you resemble the moon surrounded by her young stars;

you resemble the month of Nīsān surrounded by all the flowers of Nīsān, feeding them with her breath.'

A murmur of admiration rose from the crowd, and the princess spoke in satisfaction: 'You have excelled, O young man, and your first answer is not worthy of death. As you have so aptly compared me with all these pleasant things, I will not try you with as difficult complications as I might. Tell me now the exact significance of these words:

'Give the son of the East to the bride of the West, and their child shall be the Sultān of beauty.'

'O princess,' answered the youth without hesitation, 'those words contain the whole secret of the philosopher's stone, and the translation of their symbol is: corrupt the healthy male earth of the East with the moisture which comes from the West and you will engender mercury, the sovereign power of nature, which will bear you the sun, and gold which is the son of the sun, and the moon, and silver which is the son of the moon, and will change pebbles into diamonds of beauty.'

At this point Shahrazād saw the approach of morning and discreetly fell silent.

But when the eight-hundred-and-forty-sixth night had come

SHE SAID:

'You have escaped death a second time, young man,' said the princess. 'Now tell me to what talismans owe their virtue?'

The young man answered from his horse: 'O princess, they owe their sublime virtues and miraculous effects to the letters which compose them; for there is no letter in the language which is not governed by a spirit, a ray, or emanation of the virtue of Allāh. The spirits of the intellect communicate with those of the soul, and those of the soul with those of the senses. Letters form words and words form sentences; and the sentences written upon talismans are nothing but a collection of spirits which, though they may astonish the ordinary man, do not trouble the wise; for the wise know the power of words and are aware that words govern the whole world. Whether they are written or spoken, words can destroy kings and ruin empires.'

A shout of joyful acclamation rose from the crowd at this answer, and the princess said: 'O young man, so far you have excelled; but now can you tell me who are the two eternal enemies?'

The prince on his horse made answer: 'O princess, I will not say that the two eternal enemies are heaven and earth, for the distance and interval between them, though they appear to be gulf on gulf, are not real but imaginary. The distance between heaven and earth may be bridged in the twinkling of an eye, without armies of the Jinn or a thousand wings; the distance between heaven and earth may be bridged by prayer. And I will not say that the two eternal enemies are night and day, for morning joins them and twilight separates them, again and again for ever. And I will not say that the eternal enemies are the sun and moon, for each of them lights the earth and they are joined by a bond of similar duty. And I will not say that the eternal enemies are body and soul, for though we know the first, we are utterly ignorant of the second; and we cannot form an opinion about that of which we are ignorant. But I affirm, O princess, that the two eternal enemies are life and death, for they are fatal to each other. They quarrel over the body of man, the body of man is their plaything. They grow fat and prosper at its expense; but the body of man, the plaything, is infallibly destroyed in their engagement. They are the two eternal enemies, enemies of each other, and enemies of each created thing.'

At this answer the crowd cried with a single voice: 'Glory be to Him Who gives knowledge and wisdom to His creatures!' The princess, sitting high in her tower among her girls, dressed all in royal purple, said again: 'O young man, so far you have excelled; but now can you tell me what tree has twelve branches, each bearing two clusters: one cluster of thirty white fruit and one cluster of thirty black fruit?'

The youth answered without hesitation: 'A child could tell you that, O princess. The tree is a year, the branches are months, the white clusters are thirty days, and the black clusters are thirty nights.'

'O young man, so far you have excelled,' said the princess, 'but now can you tell me what earth has seen the sun but once?'

He answered: 'The bottom of the Red Sea saw the sun once when the children of Israel passed over it through the power of Moses (upon whom be prayer and peace!).'

She said: 'Can you tell me who invented the gong?'

He answered: 'Noah invented the gong when he was on board the ark.'

She said: 'Can you tell me a thing which is illegal whether it is done or left undone?'

He answered: 'The prayer of a drunken man.'

She asked: 'What spot upon the earth is nearest the sky? Is it a mountain?'

He answered: 'The holy Kaabah at Mecca.

She said: 'Can you tell me what bitter thing should be kept hidden?'

He answered: 'Poverty, O princess! Though I am young I have tasted it; though I am a king's son I have found it bitter. Indeed, I have found it more bitter than myrrh and absinthe. It should be strictly hidden from all eyes, for friends and neighbours are the first to laugh at it.'

She said: 'What is the most precious thing after health?'

He answered: 'A tender friendship. But it is necessary to use both proof and choice in finding a friend. A man's first friend should never be denied; for a second friend is not easily kept. If you are wise your friends must be wise, for a crow will turn white before the fool understands wisdom. Words with beatings from a sage are preferable to the praises and flowers of the ignorant. For the wise man utters no word until he has consulted his heart.'

She asked: 'What tree is the most difficult to straighten?'

The youth answered without hesitation: 'A bad character. There was once a tree planted by a river of waters in an auspicious soil, but it bore no fruit. Its owner, after lavishing all the cares of his art upon it, wished to cut it down; but the tree said: "Plant me in another place and I will bear fruit." "You are planted by a river of waters and have borne nothing," answered the owner, and he cut it down . . . A wolf was once sent to school to learn to read. The master said: "Repeat after me: a, b, c." But the wolf said: "Sheep, kid, lamb," because that was all his thought and all his nature . . . A certain man wished to accustom his ass to cleanliness. He had him taken to the hammām and given a luxurious bath with many perfumes; he had him installed in a magnificent chamber and gave him a rich carpet on which to sit. At once that ass ranged through all those habits which would not have called for attention in a field, from the most untimely noises to the most indelicate exhibitions. Then he upset the copper pot of ashes in the middle of the carpet with his head, and rolled in the ashes with his four legs in the air, scratching his back and dirtying himself in every possible way. Slaves ran forward to beat him, but his master checked them, saying: "First let him roll and then take him back to his stable, for you will not be able to change his temperament." One day a man said to his cat: "If you will stop thieving I will make you a collar of gold and feast you every day on the liver, lungs and kidneys of birds and mice." The honest cat replied: "My father's business was theft and my grandfather's business was theft, why should I be untrue to my kind just to please you?" O princess, I have nothing more to add.'

At this point Shahrazād saw the approach of morning and discreetly fell silent.

But when the eight-hundred-and-forty-seventh night had come

SHE SAID:

Cries of admiration rose to the sky from a thousand throats, and the princess said: 'O young man, you have excelled; but my questions are not yet exhausted and the condition is that I should ask them until the time of the evening prayer.' 'O princess,' answered the youth, 'it is certain that you have many more problems and it is equally certain that, with Allāh's help, I would resolve them all. Therefore, in order that you may not fatigue your glorious voice, it would be better for me to ask you one question. If you can answer, my head will join these others; if you cannot answer, our marriage will be celebrated without delay.' 'Ask what you will, for I accept your conditions,' she answered.

Then said the youth: 'Can you tell me how I, your slave, sitting upon this noble horse, may yet be said to be sitting upon my own father, and how I, your slave, visible to you all in knightly habiting, may yet be said to be hidden by my mother's garments?'

The princess reflected for an hour, and then said: 'Give me the answer yourself, for I cannot find it.'

Before that assembled multitude the prince told his story in all its details to the princess; but nothing would be gained by repeating it in this place. 'And that is how,' he concluded, 'having exchanged my father for a horse and my mother for this equipment, I may be said to ride upon my father and be hidden by my mother's garments.'

Thus it was that the son of the ruined King and Queen married the princess of the riddles. When he became King, on the death of his wife's father, he was able to return the horse and equipment to their owner and fetch his parents to live with him in all delight. That is the tale of the youth who showed such wisdom beneath the severed heads. But Allāh is wiser still!

When she had made an end of this story, Shahrazād fell silent, and King Shahryār cried: 'I have been greatly entertained by the wisdom of this youth; but it is a long time since you have told me any short and delightful anecdotes, and I am afraid that I have exhausted your store of them.' 'Short anecdotes are the tales which I know best, O auspicious King. I will prove that fact to you at once,' answered Shahrazād eagerly.

And she said:

The Perfidy of Wives

IT is related, O auspicious King, that a certain celebrated jester once lived at a King's court. One day his master said to him: 'You are a bachelor, O father of wisdom, and I have a keen desire to see you married.' 'O King of time,' answered the jester, 'I pray you spare me that felicity. I am a bachelor through fear of the sex; I have abstained lest I should chance on some debauched, adulterous, or whoring woman. Therefore I pray you to remember all the vices and ignoble qualities of my life and, as a punishment for them, to deny me the blessing of matrimony.' The King laughed so much at this answer that he fell over on his backside. Nevertheless he cried: 'I cannot help your feelings; to-day you must be wed.' The jester assumed an air of resignation; he lowered his head and crossed his hands over his bosom, sighing: 'All right! All right! All right!'

The King ordered his wazīr to find a modest and beautiful wife for the jester. The wazīr entered into communication with an old woman whose trade was in such things, and the old woman speedily found a girl whom she vouched to be both fair and pure. The marriage was celebrated at once and the King showered presents upon his oddity.

For half a year or perhaps seven months the jester lived at peace with his wife; but after that there happened that which had been fated to happen; for no man may escape his Destiny.

During those months of peace the woman had contrived to add four men of different talent to her pleasures, over and above her husband. The first was a pastrycook, the second a greengrocer, the third a mutton-butcher, and the fourth, who was more important altogether, none other than the first clarinet of the Sultān's orchestra and syndic of the corporation of clarinets. One day the jester, the one-time bachelor, the new father of horns, was called early to the palace; so he left his wife in bed and hastened into the presence of the King. As chance would have it, the pastrycook felt in a mood for coupling that morning; so, having seen the husband depart, he came and knocked upon the door. 'You are earlier than usual,' exclaimed the woman, when she had opened to him. 'I am,' he answered. 'When I had prepared my dough and rolled it and leaved it and stuffed it with pistachios and almonds, I noticed that it was still too near the dawn to expect purchasers. So I said to myself: "Shake the flour from your clothes, my friend, and go to rejoice a little with your sweet!"' 'As Allāh lives, that was well thought of,' said the girl, and she played paste to his pin, while he played almonds to her pastry. They were just finishing their set of tarts when there came a knocking on the door. 'Who can that be?' asked the cook. 'I do not know,' she answered. 'Go and hide yourself in the privy while I see.'

The pastrycook departed for that place and the girl went to the door, where she found the greengrocer with a box of early vegetables. 'This is a little too soon,' she said. 'You have anticipated your hour.' 'You are right,' he answered. 'But, as I was returning from my kitchen-garden this morning, I said to myself: "It is too early for the market; you had better take these fresh vegetables to your sweet, for they will rejoice her!"' 'You are very welcome,' said she. He gave her her favourite vegetables: an heroic cucumber and an exceptional pumpkin; but they had not quite finished potting when there came a knock at the door. 'Who is there?' cried the greengrocer. 'I do not know,' answered the woman. 'Go and hide in the privy while I see.' The man took his box of vegetables and carried them to the privy, where he found the pastrycook. 'Why are you here? What have you been doing?' he asked. 'I have been doing what you have been doing, and I am here for the same purpose as yourself,' replied the pastrycook. With that, they sat down peaceably side by side.

In the meanwhile the woman had gone to the door and admitted the butcher, who brought her a present of a handsome sheepskin with curly wool and two fine horns attached. 'You are a little too soon,' she said, and he replied: 'When I had killed to-day's sheep and cut them up on my shop, I noticed that the market was still quite empty, so I said to myself: "You had better take your sweet this sheepskin; it will make a soft carpet for her feet, and she will start your morning well for you."' The woman became more tender to him than the tail of a fat-tailed sheep, and he gave her what rams give; but their exercise was not yet over when there came a knocking at the door. 'Quick, take the skin and hide in the privy!' cried the woman. So the butcher went to the privy, but found the pastrycook and the greengrocer already in possession. He asked them why they were in that place, and they answered: 'For the same reason as yourself.' So the butcher took his place amicably among them. 'You are earlier than usual,' said the woman, when she opened the door and found the first clarinet waiting outside it. 'You are right,' he answered. 'I went forth from my apartment this morning to hold a rehearsal of the King's music for to-day; but, when I found that none of the players had yet come, I determined to wait in the dwelling of my sweet.' They played the clarinet together, but they had not finished the first tune, when there came a violent knocking upon the door. 'Who is that?' cried the clarinet. 'Allāh alone knows!' she answered. 'Perhaps it is my husband. Take your clarinet and hide yourself in the privy.' The man went to that place and found it already occupied by the pastrycook, the greengrocer, and the butcher. 'Peace be with you, my friends!' said he. 'What are you doing in this singular apartment?' 'The peace and mercy and blessing of Allāh be upon you!' they answered. 'We are here for the same reason as yourself.' So the four men ranged themselves in friendly fashion side by side.

As soon as the woman opened the door for the fifth time, the jester rushed in, holding his belly in two hands and crying: 'Give me an infusion of anise and fennel, good wife! Things are moving, things are moving! I could not stay at the palace. I had to come home to bed. Things are moving, things are moving!' Without noticing his wife's confusion, he ran straight to the privy and, flinging wide the door, saw four men squatting upon the tiles above the hole.

At this point Shahrazād saw the approach of morning and discreetly fell silent.

But when the eight-hundred-and-forty-eighth night had come

SHE SAID:

The jester realised at once the exact nature of his misfortune, but he was a wise man and, fearing that they would kill him if he threatened them, at once pretended to be mad. He cast himself on the privy floor and cried to those who sat there: 'O sacred messengers of Allāh, I know you, I recognise you well! You, who are stained with leprous whiteness and might be mistaken for a pastry-cook by the profane, are without doubt the holy patriarch, Job, the leprous, the ulcerous. And you, O saint with the box of excellent vegetables, must be great Khidr, who guards each orchard, who clothes each tree with a green diadem, who loosens the streams in Spring, who spreads the scented carpet of the meadows and covers the sky at evening with the light grass tint of his garment. And you, O warrior of the lion's skin, surely you are Alexander of the Double Horn. And you, you, O glorious angel with the heavenly trump, are certainly Isrāfil who shall summon us on the last day!'

The four rogues pinched each other's thighs, and whispered: 'We must fool him in this bent, for it is our only chance of safety.' They rose together, crying: 'You are not mistaken, O man. We are even as you have named us, and we came into this privy because we wished to enter your house and reward you for your great virtue. We could find no other chamber open to the sky.' Still bowing low, the jester answered: 'Since you have done me so great an honour, O illustrious saints, will you grant me one wish?' 'Speak, speak!' said they, and he went on: 'Come with me to the palace of the Sultān, for he is my master and will be greatly obliged when I introduce such famous visitors to him.' The four hesitated, but were forced to reply: 'We grant you that peculiar grace.'

The jester led them into the Sultān's presence, saying: 'O my lord the King, allow me to present you to these four sacred personages: the first, with the flour on his clothes, is our lord Job, the leper; this, with the box of vegetables, is our lord Khidr, father of all green things; this, with the horned skin, is Alexander the Great; and this, with the clarinet in his hand, is the angel Isrāfil, who shall announce the Last Judgment. I owe the great honour of their visit to the saintly qualities of the wife whom you so generously gave to me, my lord. I found them squatting, one behind the other, in the privy of my harīm.'

The Sultān looked closely at the four men and then burst into so great a convulsion of laughter that he fell over on his backside, kicking his legs in the air. 'Have you gone mad or do you want to kill me?' he cried. But the jester answered: 'I only tell what I have seen; I surely saw what I have told.' 'Yet,' objected the King, 'do you not see that the prophet Khidr is only a greengrocer, the prophet Job only a pastrycook, Alexander the Great only a butcher, and the angel Isrāfīl only my first clarinet, the master of my music?' Yet the jester would shake his head and say: 'I only tell what I have seen; I surely saw what I have told.'

At last the King saw through the jester's stratagem, and fixed his eyes wrathfully upon the four lechers, crying: 'Sons of a thousand shameless horns, tell me the truth or you shall lose your eggs!' Trembling and fearing for their inheritance, the four told the whole truth, and the astonished King exclaimed: 'May Allāh exterminate that traitorous sex!' Then he said kindly to the jester: 'O father of wisdom, I grant you a divorce here and now. You are a bachelor again.' He robed him in a magnificent robe of honour and then said to his executioner: 'Cut off the eggs of these four men, that they may be eunuchs and serve this honourable bachelor.'

Then the prophet Job, or rather the pastrycook, kissed the earth between the King's hands, saying: 'O most magnanimous of Sultāns, if I tell you the story of an intrigue more wonderful than our intrigue in the house of this honourable bachelor, will you let me keep my eggs?' The King questioned his jester with a look and when the man nodded his head, promised the cook mercy if his story turned out to be truly marvellous. So the first lecher said:

The Pastrycook's Tale

IT is related, O auspicious King, that the governor of a certain city had a wife who was altogether an astonishing tumbler and true companion of calamity. This honest man knew nothing of the perfidy of women, nothing at all; also he had grown to that age when he could do nothing with his wife, nothing at all. Thus the woman excused her wanton loves by saying: 'I must take bread where I find it.'

Her favourite lover was a young groom belonging to her husband, but as time went on and the governor took to being more and more at home, their difficulties became correspondingly greater. At last the wife said to her husband: 'O my master, I have learnt that my mother's dearest neighbour is dead. I feel it only right that I should spend the three days of the funeral at my father's house.' 'May Allāh add the lost days of the dead woman to your span, my dear,' answered the governor. 'You may certainly go for the three days to your mother.' 'But I am young and timid; I cannot go alone,' objected his wife. 'Why should you go alone?' asked the husband. 'Have we not an honest and zealous groom who can put the red saddle for you upon the ass, and lead you to and from your father's house? Tell him not to excite the animal with shouting or the goad; for I do not wish you to have a fall.' 'Will you not tell him these things yourself, O my master?' ventured the woman. 'I am too modest.' The governor called the muscular young rascal into his presence and, to his great delight, ordered him to saddle the ass for his mistress and go along with her.

The groom put his red saddle upon the ass and started off with the woman; but did they go to the funeral? Assuredly not. They took a bountiful provision of meat and old wine to a certain garden which they knew. There, in the cool shadow, the groom generously brought forth all the goods which his father had left him and displayed them before the ravished eyes of his mistress. She put them in her hands and rubbed them to test their quality and, when she found them of the finest, complimented their owner and set diligently to work at her sewing. Nor did she leave off until it was too dark to thread a needle.

When night fell, they made their way to the groom's house and, after giving his ration to the ass, made ready to give a ration to each other. They fed each other with such generous vigour that they were soon forced to sleep from repletion; but, after an hour, they woke again and did not cease from mortifying their desires until morning. Even when day came they could find no better employment than to go again to the garden and attempt the manipulations of the day before.

For three days they went at it without repose, showing the way the millrace flows, and how the industrious spindle goes. They gave the lamb suck, they startled the buck, they tried on the finger-ring for luck. They cradled the child, they kissed the twins, they polished the sword till it had not speck, they taught the sparrow how to peck, they made the camel show his neck, and fed the bird at the barley bins. They gave the little pigeon seed, and put the rabbit out to feed, with many another pretty deed, till they blew a hole in the shepherd's reed.

On the morning of the fourth day, the groom said: 'The three days of leave are over.' 'When I am allowed three days, I take six,' answered the woman. 'Therefore we have plenty of time in which to eat our fill. Let that absurd old pimp, my husband, rot alone at home; if he wants company he had better thrust his head between his legs like a dog.'

So she said, and so they did; joyfully coupling on the next three days and only returning on the morning of the seventh. The old governor received his wife without the least suspicion, saying kindly: 'I thank Allāh that you have returned safe and sound! Why have you been so long, O daughter of my uncle?' 'O my master,' she answered, 'they gave me the orphan child to console, and I have laboured with him for three days and then three days.' Then said the governor: 'I know you would always tell me the truth.'

And such is my tale, O King of truth.

The King laughed so much that he fell over on his backside, but the angry jester exclaimed: 'The governor's evil was not as great as mine.' So the King turned to the pastrycook, saying: 'As the judge has condemned you, I shall only be able to leave you one egg.' Content with this triumph, the jester said sententiously: 'And he deserves it, the human dreg, who throws a leg and shows a peg and broaches another person's keg, and yet, O mighty King, I beg, that you will spare his second egg!'

At this point the second lecher, the greengrocer, kissed the earth between the King's hands, saying: 'O great and generous sovereign, if I can astound you with my story, will you spare me also?' On a sign from the jester, the King agreed to the test, and Khidr the Prophet, or rather the greengrocer, said:

The Greengrocer's Tale

I T is related, O auspicious King, that there was once a great astronomer who was also deeply learned in the reading of faces and the divining of hidden thoughts. He had a very beautiful wife who was never tired of vaunting her virtue, and saying: 'O husband, I do not think I have my equal among the sex for chastity.' As she had a pleasant innocent face, the astute physiognomist believed her, and would be always boasting her decent purity among his friends. In speaking of his harīm thus, he was himself transgressing the bounds of decency; but the manners of learned men, and especially of astronomers, are not ordinary manners.

One day, as he gave great praise to his wife's virtue in the presence of certain strangers, one of them rose, saying: 'You are a liar, my friend.' 'How am I a liar?' asked the astronomer angrily, turning very yellow in the face. 'Either a liar or a fool,' continued the inter-rupter calmly, 'for, in point of fact, your wife is a common whore.' The old man leaped upon him to strangle him and suck his blood, but the crowd parted them, crying: 'Make him prove his words! If he cannot do so, then you have our leave to suck his blood.' 'But how?' asked the old man. 'Pretend to go upon a journey for three days,' suggested the offender, 'but, as soon as you have departed, return and watch the house from some place of concealment.'

The astronomer went home with trembling beard, and said to his wife: 'O woman, rise up and prepare me provisions for a journey; for I am compelled to leave you for four days or it may be six.' 'Do you want me to perish of loneliness or die of grief?' cried the woman. 'Why do you not take me with you, to serve you on the journey and care for you if you fall sick? You cannot find the heart to leave me pining?' 'Surely she is the woman of Allāh's choice,' thought the old man, and he answered aloud: 'Light of my eye, I will only be gone four days, or it may be six.' 'I am unhappy and abandoned, I am not loved!' wailed the virtuous wife; so the astronomer tried to comfort her with a promise of presents on his return. He left her fainting in the arms of her women, and went his way.

After two hours he returned and, slipping into the garden by a hidden door, found a hiding-place from which he could see into the house without betraying his presence.

At this point Shahrazād saw the approach of morning and discreetly fell silent.

But when the eight-hundred-and-fiftieth night had come

SHE SAID:

He had not lain in concealment for an hour before he saw a certain man, who sold sugarcane in a shop opposite the house, enter his wife's apartment. She came towards him swinging her hips and re-ceived a stick of sugarcane with laughing goodwill. 'Is that the only piece you have brought?' she asked, and the man answered: 'Dear mistress, the visible sugarcane is not to be compared with the invis-ible.' 'Give it to me, give it to me!' she cried, and, as he presented it for her inspection, he answered: 'Here it is!' 'And how is that pimp of my arse, the excellent astronomer?' he asked at length. 'Allah break

all his bones!' she cried. 'He has gone away for four days, or even
six; it is to be hoped that some minaret falls on top of him before he
comes back.' She began to peel the man's sugarcane and press it in
the approved fashion; then the two embraced and clipped each other,
and took their fill.

At length the merchant of sugarcane went upon his way, but the
unfortunate astronomer almost immediately saw his place taken
by the principal poultry-merchant of the neighbourhood. The girl
went forward to meet him, swaying her hips. 'Greeting, O father
of fowls!' she said. 'What have you brought me to-day?' The man
kissed her and answered: 'I have a chicken for you to thicken, a
chicken only you can quicken.' At once she cried: 'I undertake it!'
He thrust and panted: 'Thus I bake it!' So she played with that excellent fowl again, the trick she had played on the sugarcane; but
the honest poulterer, after the play, shook down his clothes and
went his way.

In a few moments the unhappy sage saw the chief donkey-boy of
the quarter enter his wife's chamber, and heard the girl cry: 'What
have you brought me to-day, O father of asses?' 'A banana, an excellent banana, dear mistress,' he replied. So the girl laughed, and
sighed: 'Dear ass, I do not understand, for I see nothing in your
hand, no ghost of a banana.' 'O lighter yourself than a branch of
ban, it belonged to my father, a worthy man, who used to conduct a
caravan; but he died of a fondness for the can, and left me his
banana.' 'Dear ass, I ask not whose it was, but where it is, dear ass,
because I want to see your banana.' 'O queen, it fears the evil-eye,
so I keep it hidden when folk are by and only produce it on the sly.
. . . But . . . here is my banana!'

Before the banana was quite eaten, the astronomer uttered a great
cry and fell down dead of a broken heart. Allāh have him in mercy!
Afterwards it was proved that the girl preferred bananas to sugarcane or chicken, for she married the donkey-boy.

And such is my story, O King of glory.

The King was convulsed with glad merriment, and said to his
jester: 'I swear that this piece of cuckoldry was more than yours; we
shall have to spare the greengrocer his eggs.'

The man retired and his place was taken by the third lecher, who
asked and obtained the same condition as the other two.

Alexander the Great, or rather the mutton-butcher, said :

The Butcher's Tale

THERE was once a man in Cairo whose wife was famous for beauty and piety; she had a pair of plump geese in the house, heavy with delicious fat, and, never far away from the house, a stalwart lover whom she loved to distraction. One day the lover saw the geese and felt his appetite tempted by them; so he asked if his mistress would not cook them for him. 'I will stuff them and cook them and you shall have them all,' she replied. 'Light of my eyes, I promise that my bastard of a husband shall not have a taste of them.'

When her husband returned at sunset, she began twitting him for his meanness, saying that he never asked a guest to dine with him. 'That is easily remedied,' answer the man. 'I will buy you a dish of lamb and rice to-morrow, and ask one of our intimate friends to eat it with us.' 'Rather buy me some good stuffing,' she said, 'and kill the two geese in the morning, before you go to work. I shall stuff and roast them to a turn, and your guest will be the more delighted.'

Next morning the good man killed the geese and bought the ingredients of a savoury stuffing. As he handed these things to his wife, he begged her to have all ready by noon, and then went upon his way.

The wife at once set to work: she plucked and drew the geese, she stuffed them with a marvel of minced meat, rice, pistachios, almonds, raisins, pine-seeds, and fine spices; and finally watched over them in the oven until they were cooked to a golden brown perfection. Then she sent the little negress for her lover, who speedily answered the summons. They clipped each other and went to it with mutual satisfaction until the morning grew late. At last the woman gave him the two delicious geese in their entirety, and sent him back to his own house. So much for him.

At this point Shahrazād saw the approach of morning and discreetly fell silent.

But when the eight-hundred-and-fifty-first night had come

SHE SAID:

At noon the woman's husband returned home with a guest; but she told him that the geese would be enough for three or four and bade him hasten to invite more of his friends. As soon as he had gone forth in all docility to do her bidding, she went up to the guest and said to him in a voice trembling with emotion: 'Alas, alas, why do you not escape while there is yet time?' 'What is the matter, O wife of my friend?' asked the man, and she answered: 'As Allāh lives, my husband is offended with you and has laid a snare for you to cut off your testicles and to reduce you to the sorry condition of a eunuch. He has even now gone out to collect friends to hold you down during the operation.'

Without waiting to hear more, the guest jumped to his feet and, leaping into the road, ran away as if he were pursued by a Jinnī. At that moment the husband returned with two more friends, and the girl met him with a bellow: 'Police, police! The geese, the geese!' Then he cried: 'Peace, good woman, peace!' But his wife went shouting without cease: 'The geese, the geese, the geese, the geese! Your guest has stolen them, bones and grease! He climbed out by the window piece! Run after him, all of you, quickly, please, for he has stolen the geese!'

The husband rushed into the street, and beheld his late guest speeding away, with his tunic held between his teeth. 'Come back, come back, in Allāh's name!' he cried, 'I will not take the two, you can keep one of them!' But as he ran, the fugitive shouted over his shoulder: 'Old fool, you will have to get young legs, before you catch me and take my eggs!'

Such is my story, O King of glory.

The King nearly swooned from laughing. When he had a little recovered himself, he forgave the butcher and commanded his jester to do the same.

The butcher retired and the fourth lecher sought and obtained the same trial as the other three. The Sultān lay back with folded hands and the angel Isrāfīl, or rather the first clarinet, said:

The First Clarinet's Tale

An old man of Egypt had a pubic son who occupied himself all day in the industrious development of the only inheritance which he had as yet received; for the rest, he would be sniffing about his father's fifteen-year-old wife, in the hope of finding an opportunity to show her the difference between iron and wax. To prevent his wife being seduced, the old man married a second, even younger and more beautiful, so that each might be a protection to the other.

'I shall have a double mouthful,' thought the son. And, when he heard the two wives assuring their husband that they would slipper the young rascal about the face if he said the least improper word to them, he smiled and murmured: 'We shall see.'

One day, the house ran out of corn and the old man bade his son follow him to the market to fetch a new supply. But when they had got to the end of the road, he discovered that he had left his slippers behind, which he used to carry slung across his shoulders; so he told his son to run back and fetch them. The sly child returned breathless to the two girls, who were watching the departure from the terrace. 'What have you been sent back for?' they asked, and he replied: 'To come up and embrace you as much as I like.' 'Vile little dog,' they cried, 'you know that you are lying!' 'I am telling the truth,' said he. 'I will prove it if you like.' With that he shouted at the top of his voice: 'Father, father! One, or both? One, or both?' 'Both, you wanton, both, and may Allāh curse you!' came the far away answer.

'He has told the truth after all!' cried the two girls. 'I suppose we must not hinder him.'

And that, O King, is the trick of the slippers by which that wantonest of nippers got the two women in his grippers. He ran to his father with the slippers, but the best of women, after a trip, errs, and both were eternally crying: 'Clip us!' to the lad who fetched his father's slippers.

And that is my story, O King of glory.

The delighted King excused the first clarinet the loss of his testicles and dismissed the four lechers, saying: 'First kiss the hand of this honourable bachelor and ask his pardon. 'So the five men became reconciled to each other and lived together on the best of terms.

But the tale of the Perfidy of Wives is so long, O auspicious King, that I would rather tell you at once the marvellous Tale of Alī Bābā and the Forty Thieves.

The Tale of Alī Bābā and the Forty Thieves

AND SHAHRAZĀD SAID TO KING SHAHRYĀR:

I T is related, O auspicious King, that there were once long ago, in a certain city of Persia, two brothers whose names were Kāsim and Alī Bābā. But praise be to Him Who takes no account of names, and beholds the soul of man in the mystery of its nakedness! Amen.

And after!

Their father was a poor man of the common people, and, when he died, the two brothers were left with so small a share of the world's goods that they soon found themselves with long faces and no bread and cheese. See what it is to be a fool in youth and to forget the counsels of the wise!

Soon Kāsim, who was the elder and more astute of the brothers, put himself into the hands of an old bawd (Allāh curse the same!) who tested his powers of mounting and coupling, and then married him to a girl with money and appetite. Thus he was saved from starvation and became the owner of a well-furnished shop in the market, for such was the Destiny written upon his brow at birth. So much for him. Alī Bābā, the younger brother, being devoid of ambition and having modest tastes, became a woodcutter; but though his takings were small he lived so wisely that, in the end, he was able to buy, first one ass, then two, and finally three. He would lead these beasts to the forest and load them with the faggots which he cut there. After he had bought the third, he became a person of importance among the woodcutters and one of them offered him the hand of a daughter in marriage. The three asses were written down in the marriage contract as dowry, though the girl, being poor, brought no portion at all. But poverty and riches endure for a breath. Allāh only is eternal!

To Alī Bābā and his wife were born children as fair as moons, and the family lived together in the honest enjoyment of the small money which the sale of firewood brought them.

One day, while Alī Bābā was cutting wood in a thicket of the forest, with his asses comfortably grazing and farting at no great distance, Destiny came to him. He heard a muffled noise as of galloping hoofs and, being of a peaceful and timid disposition, climbed up into a high tree, which stood on the top of a small hill and gave a view of the whole forest. He had done well to hide himself, for soon a troop of armed riders came towards the tree, and he could judge by their dark faces, eyes as of new copper, and beards parted terribly in the centre like the wings of a carrion crow, that he was in the presence of the worst kind of outlaw robbers. When they had come nearly to the tree, they dismounted at a signal from their gigantic chief and, after fastening their horses, slung forage sacks of barley for them to eat. Then they took off the saddle-bags and, bearing them up, came into file so slowly that Alī Bābā was able to count them at his ease and determine that there were forty robbers, neither more or less.

At this point Shahrazād saw the approach of morning and discreetly fell silent.

But when the eight-hundred-and-fifty-second night had come

SHE SAID:

The forty thieves carried their loads to the foot of a large rock which lay at the bottom of the little hill. Then they set down the bags, and the chief cried out in the direction of the rock: 'Open, Sesame!' At once the surface of the rock gaped. The captain waited until his followers had passed with their burdens through the opening, and then carried his bag in after them. 'Shut, Sesame!' he cried from within, and the face of the rock closed upon him. Alī Bābā was astonished at these things, and said: 'Allāh grant that their sorcery cannot find me in this tree!' He sat, without making a movement, and fixed anxious eyes upon his asses, who were feeding noisily in the thicket. After a long time, a sound like distant thunder made itself heard and the rock opened to give forth the forty thieves, carrying the bags empty in their hands. When the band of thirty-nine had mounted, their chief cried again: 'Shut, Sesame!' and, while the surfaces of the rock came close, rode off at the head of his pitch-faced and hog-bearded followers.

Fearing that they might come back and surprise him, Alī Bābā stayed in his tree until they had long been out of sight, and, when he ventured at last to climb down, he did so with a thousand precautions, ever turning his head to right and left as he let himself from a higher to a lower branch.

As soon as he came to the ground, he walked on tiptoe, holding his breath, towards the mysterious rock. At any other time he would have had no thought save for his asses, which were the wage-earners for all his family, but now a curiosity wholly foreign to his nature burnt in his mind, and his Destiny pushed him forward. He found the surface of the rock entirely smooth and without the smallest crack against which he might have pressed the point of a needle. 'Yet I saw the forty thieves go in,' he thought. 'Surely the place must be guarded by strange spells! Though I know nothing of spells, yet I certainly remember the words of opening and closing. Had I not better try them over, to see if they have the same power in my mouth as upon the lips of that terrifying man?'

Still pricked on by Destiny and quite forgetting his usual fear, Alī Bābā turned to the rock, saying: 'Open, Sesame!'

Though these two magic words were uttered weakly and without assurance, the rock gaped. Alī Bābā would have turned to flee, but Fate kept him in that place and forced his eyes to look within. Instead of seeing some cave of dark horror, he beheld a spacious gallery whose level floor led to a large hall, hollowed in the heart of the rock and well-lighted by slits contrived in the roof. Alī Bābā plucked up his courage and, murmuring: 'In the name of Allāh, the Merciful, the Compassionate!' walked along the gallery to the hall. As he went, the two halves of the rock came together soundlessly, but this did not dismay him, for he well remembered the formula of opening.

Arrived at the entrance of the hall, he beheld, all along the walls and piled from floor to ceiling, a profusion of rich merchandise, with bales of silk and brocade, bags of varied food, great chests filled to the brim with minted silver and silver bars, with golden dīnārs and bars of gold. And, as if these were not enough, the floor of the cave was heaped with loose gold and precious stones, so that the foot could hardly find a resting place, but tripped over some rich sample of the jeweller's art or sent a cascade of gleaming gold before it. Though Alī Bābā had never in his life seen the true colour of a dīnār or smelt the smell of it, he was able to judge that the cave, with its vast treasures heaped at haphazard and its innumerable costly ornaments, the least of which would have honoured a king's palace, had been, not only for years but for hundreds of years, the store house of generations of robbers, descendants, perhaps, of the mighty Babylonian thieves.

When he had recovered a little from his astonishment, he cried: 'As Allāh lives, O Alī Bābā, it is a Destiny of fair white face which has led you from your asses and firewood to a bath of gold, such as neither Sulaimān nor Alexander saw! O excellent woodcutter, you hear magic words of potency, and straight you have them off by heart! Surely He Who rewards all men has made you master of the fruit of countless crimes, that you may put it to the innocent uses of your family!'

Having thus eased his conscience, Alī Bābā emptied the food out of one of the bags and replaced it with close-packed golden coins. Taking no thought for the silver, he carried the great weight on his shoulders to the outer end of the gallery; then he repeated the task, until he had collected together as many sacks of treasure as he supposed his asses could carry. Standing by his spoils, he cried: 'Open, Sesame!' and, as soon as the two halves of the rocky door had moved asunder, went forth and led his asses to the entrance. He loaded the sacks of gold upon their backs and hid them carefully with brushwood; then he spoke the magic words of closing and waited until the surface of the rock was once more undisturbed.

Alī Bābā urged his asses forward with respectful shouts and not with those curses and sounding oaths which it is usually necessary to employ. Though, like all men of his profession, Alī Bābā would often address his cattle as zabb-worshippers, parts of your sister, sons of a bugger, and fruits of bawdry, he loved them as his own children and only flavoured his speech in order to make them listen to reason. On this occasion he felt it to be unjust to give them such names, when they were carrying more gold than there was in the Sultān's treasury; so he exhorted them inoffensively and let them take their own time back to the city.

At this point Shahrazād saw the approach of morning and discreetly fell silent.

But when the eight-hundred-and-fifty-third night had come

SHE SAID:

When he arrived before his house, Alī Bābā found that the door of the courtyard was fastened on the inside with a great wooden bolt, so, wishing to see whether his knowledge of magic would be available in any place besides the cave, he cried out: 'Open, Sesame!' At once the bolt was shot and the door stood open, so that he was able to drive the asses into the little courtyard without announcing his presence. 'Shut, Sesame!' he exclaimed, and at once the door closed of itself and the bolt moved into position.

When Alī Bābā's wife saw the donkeys in the courtyard and her husband beginning to discharge them, she ran out, beating her hands together, and crying: 'O my husband, how did you open the door after I had bolted it?' Instead of answering, Alī Bābā said: 'These sacks are from Allāh, good wife. Help me to carry them into the house instead of tormenting me with questions about bolts.' The woman came forward to help and, as she handled each sack, became convinced that they all contained money. Though she only supposed that the money was old copper coins, she at once grew very frightened and became certain that her husband had joined himself to a robber band or some such terrible institution. When all the sacks were in the house, she could contain herself no longer; so she began to beat her cheeks and tear her garments, crying: 'O woe upon us, woe upon us! The poor children! O gallows!'

'Gallows in your eye, vile wretch!' answered Alī Bābā in some indignation. 'What are you grumbling about?' 'Bad luck has entered the house with these sacks, O son of my uncle!' she wept. 'Load them again on the asses and take them to some far place, I pray you!' 'Allāh confound all women, for they are fools!' cried Alī Bābā. 'Do you think I stole the sacks? Let me assure you that Allāh showed me my Destiny in the forest this morning! First I will empty the things, and then tell you how I came by them.'

He poured out flashing streams of gold upon the mat, until all the sacks were empty; then he sat down proudly on top of the glittering mound and told the women his adventure. But nothing would be gained by repeating it in this place.

When his wife heard the story, her fear gave way to an extravagant joy, and she cried: 'O day of milk, O white, white day! Glory be to Allāh Who has made these ill-gotten riches well-gotten, by setting them in the path of His poor slaves!' She squatted down on her heels before the gold and began to count the incalculable dīnārs one by one. 'What would you do, poor woman?' asked Alī Bābā with a laugh. 'You could never count all that. Rise up now and help me to dig a ditch in the kitchen where we can hide all traces of the gold. If we leave it here it may stir the cupidity of our neighbours and the police.' But his wife, who loved order in all things and wished to know exactly how rich they were, cried: 'I must at least weigh it or measure it. Give me but time to go to one of the neighbours for a measure and you shall know how much we have. I will do the measuring while you dig the ditch, and thus, before putting the gold away, we can have a clear knowledge of our children's inheritance.'

Although Alī Bābā found this step superfluous, he would not argue with his wife on so fortunate a day. 'Go quickly, then,' he said, 'and take great care not to say a single word about my discovery.'

Alī Bābā's wife went straight to the house of Kāsim, which was near by, and sought out the presence of Kāsim's wife, a vulgar and pretentious woman (she had never visited Alī Bābā and his wife and had never given any sugared chick-peas to his children, such as the very poor give to the very poor). After greeting, she begged for the loan of a wooden measure for some minutes.

When Kāsim's wife heard the word 'measure,' she was astonished, for she knew that Alī Bābā was a very poor man and could only buy a day's or a week's supply of grain at a time. Under other circumstances she would have refused to lend the wooden vessel, but her curiosity was so excited that she cried: 'Allāh increase His blessings upon you, O mother of Ahmad! Do you want the large measure or the small one?' 'The small one, if you please, my mistress,' answered the poor woman, and Kāsim's wife went into the kitchen to fetch the thing.

But she was a bawd's client and had the mind of one—may Allāh refuse His blessing to all such!—therefore feeling curious to know what kind of grain her poor relation wished to measure, she conceived a true harlot's trick and rubbed some suet on the under side of the measure. Then she returned to the poor woman and handed her what she wished, with many excuses for keeping her waiting.

When Alī Bābā's wife reached home, she set down the wooden measure upon the great pile of gold and began to fill and empty it, marking a single stroke in black charcoal upon the wall for each measure. As she was finishing her work, Alī Bābā entered from digging a hole in the kitchen floor. His wife proudly showed him the marks on the wall and then left him to bury the treasure, while she herself returned in all haste to Kāsim's wife. She did not know, poor creature, that a golden dīnār had stuck to the suet on the underside of the measure.

She gave back the measure to her rich kinswoman, that whore's daughter, and thanked her, saying: 'I wished to bring it back at once, my mistress, so that you would not mind my borrowing it again at some other time.'

Her visitor's back was hardly turned when Kāsim's wife inverted the measure and saw, not beans, barley, or oats stuck to the place of her contriving, but a bright dīnār of gold. Her face became the colour of saffron and her eyes of pitch. In a devouring jealousy, she cried: 'Ruin seize their house! How have these rats got gold to measure?' So furious was she that she could not wait for her husband to return from his shop but sent her servant in all haste to fetch him.

When he crossed the threshold, quite out of breath, she showered him with a clatter of shrill abuse, as if she had caught him doing something to a little boy.

Without giving him time to recover from this storm, she thrust the dīnār under his nose, crying: 'You see it, you see it? It is a cast off from your wretched brother's house, a thing thrown away! Fool, fool, you go about rubbing your stomach and congratulating yourself that you have a shop, while your brother only has three asses! You deceive yourself! That hollow-bellied woodcutter, that nothing, has not time to count his gold; he measures it! By Allāh, he measures it as a grain-seller measures grain!'

In a tempest of vociferation she told her husband of her trick and its astonishing result. 'The thing cannot rest here,' she screamed. 'You must go immediately and force that vile hypocrite to reveal the source of his treasure. I tell you he measures it, he throws it about in cartloads!'

Kāsim was quite convinced by his wife's words that Alī Bābā had in some way found a fortune, but, instead of being happy to know that his brother would now be for ever beyond the reach of poverty, he was stricken by a bilious jealousy and felt his gall bladder swelling from spite. Therefore he rose, as soon as he recovered his breath, and ran to his brother's house to see what might be seen.

At this point Shahrazād saw the approach of morning and discreetly fell silent.

But when the eight-hundred-and-fifty-fourth night had come

SHE SAID:

He found Alī Bābā with the pickaxe still in his hand, and addressed him thus angrily, without civility or greeting: 'How is it, O father of asses, that you dare to be reserved and secretive with us? That you go on pretending to be poor and humble, when you measure gold by the bushel in your lousy dwelling?'

Alī Bābā was troubled by these words, not because he was avaricious but because he knew the evil greed of Kāsim and his wife. Therefore he answered: 'By Allāh, I do not know what you would say. If you will only explain, I will answer you frankly and in good faith, although for all these years you have forgotten the tie of blood which is between us and have turned your face away from me and mine.'

'All that is beside the point, Alī Bābā,' cried the imperious Kāsim. 'It is no use to play the ignorant with me, for I know what you are hiding.' He showed his brother the dīnār, still smeared with suet, and went on: 'How many bushels of this have you got in your store, O thief? O shame of our house, where did you steal it?' He told Alī Bābā in a few words of the trick which his wife had played, and the poor woodcutter, seeing that the harm was done, could only answer: 'Allāh is generous, my brother! He sends to His own what pleases Him, therefore let His name be exalted!' Then he told Kāsim the story of his adventure in the forest, without revealing the magic words, and added: 'Dear brother, we are sprung from the same mother and father; that which is mine is yours and, if you will be so good as to accept it, I freely offer half of the gold I have brought from the cave.'

But Kāsim, who was as greedy as he was black at soul, made answer: 'So you say, so you say. But I also wish to know how to enter the cave myself, in case I should care to do so. I advise you not to give me any false direction, for I feel inclined, as it is, to denounce you to the law as an accomplice of thieves.'

The excellent Alī Bābā pictured to himself the fate of his wife and children if he should fall into the hands of justice, and even more he remembered the days when he and Kāsim were boys together; so he confided to his brother the two magic words which would open and close all doors. Kāsim at once resolved to obtain all the treasure for himself, and left his brother hastily, without a word of thanks.

Before daylight on the following morning he set out for the forest, driving ten mules loaded with ten empty cases. He meant to spy out the extent of the hoard and afterwards to return, if necessary, with a whole train of camels. He had refused Alī Bābā's offer to act as guide, but followed the directions which he had given in all confidence.

Soon he came to the rock and recognised it by its smooth surface and the great tree which grew above it on the hill. He stretched forth his two arms towards it, crying: 'Open, Sesame!' and at once the face of the rock gaped to let him pass. Leaving his ten mules tied to trees, he entered the cave and closed the rock behind him with the necessary words. Surely he would not have done so if he had known the fate which lay before him!

He was stunned and dazzled by the sight of the bright gold and the colours of the winking jewels; his desire to be sole master of this fabulous treasure increased and fastened to his heart; also he calculated that he would need not one caravan of camels to empty the hoard but all the camels which ply ceaselessly between the frontiers of India and Irāk. In the meantime he contented himself with filling as many sacks as he thought his ten mules could carry in the chests upon their backs. When this work was completed, he returned to the gallery and cried: 'Open, Barley!'

The wretched Kāsim, unbalanced by the sight of so much gold, had forgotten the necessary word. He shouted again and again: 'Open, Barley! Open, Barley!' but the rock remained impenetrable. Then he cried: 'Open, Oats!'

But the rock remained impenetrable.

Then he cried: 'Open, Beans!'

But the rock remained impenetrable.

Kāsim lost patience and began to shout at the top of his voice: 'Open, Rye!—Open, Millet!—Open, Chick-pea!—Open, Maize!— Open, Buckwheat!—Open, Corn!—Open, Rice!—Open, Vetch!

But the rock remained impenetrable.

Kāsim stood shaking with terror before the cruel door, and muttered over the names of every cereal and seed which the hand of The Sower had cast upon the fields since the birth of time.

But the rock remained impenetrable.

Alī Bābā's unworthy brother forgot one name, one magic name, Sesame, that wonder-working word!

It is thus that, sooner or later, and often sooner than later, Fate blinds the memory of the wicked and, at Allāh's word, steals away the light from before their eyes. The Prophet (upon whom be prayer and peace!) has said: 'Allāh shall take back from them His gift of light and leave them groping among shadows. Blind and deaf and dumb, they shall not return upon their way.' And the Prophet (upon whom be prayer and peace!) has said: 'Their hearts and their ears are sealed for ever by the seal of Allāh. Their eyes are veiled with a bandage. A punishment is reserved for them.'

Kāsim racked his brains in vain and then in terror and rage ran up and down the cave, seeking for an outlet. Granite walls of desperate smoothness met him at every turn; his mouth ran foam and blood, as does the mouth of a rutting beast. But this was only the first part of his punishment. Death was the second.

At this point Shahrazād saw the approach of morning and discreetly fell silent.

But when the eight-hundred-and-fifty-fifth night had come

SHE SAID:

At noon the forty thieves returned to their cave; when they saw the ten mules fastened to trees, with empty chests upon their backs, they drew their swords with one single ferocious movement and galloped up to the face of the rock. As one man they leapt to the ground and then scattered to find the owner of the mules. When they could not do so, the robber chief pointed towards the invisible door with his naked sword, and cried the two words which made it open.

As soon as Kāsim heard the cries and hoof-beats, he hid himself in a corner near the door, ready to make a final dash for safety if a chance were given him. At the word 'sesame,' he lowered his head like a ram, and rushed forward, but with so little care that he directly butted the robber chief and brought him to the ground. As the giant fell he clutched Kāsim, one hand in his mouth and the other in his belly, and held him until the band could run up and chop at him with their swords. In the twinkling of an eye Alī Bābā's wretched brother sighed out his soul at unawares and lay at the entrance of the cave in six parts. Such was his Destiny. So much for him.

The thieves wiped their swords and, hastening into the cave, emptied out the sacks of gold which Kāsim had prepared, without noticing the absence of that which Alī Bābā had taken away. Then they sat in a circle and deliberated upon what had happened; but, being unaware that Alī Bābā had spied on them, they could come to no satisfactory conclusion. As they were active men not given to many words, they soon preferred to leave their speculation and go out afresh to harry the roads and cut off the caravans. But we shall find them again when the time is ripe.

Although Kāsim richly merited his death, it was certainly the fault of his wife, that vile creature. She had loosed an action upon the world when she invented her detective suet, and it culminated in the division of her husband into six parts. She prepared a special meal to celebrate Kāsim's return with the treasure and, when night fell without the shadow or smell of him, became very anxious. Not because she loved him extravangantly, but because he was necessary to her life. At last she pocketed her pride, the whore, and ran to Alī Bābā's house. 'Greeting, greeting, dear brother of my husband,' she said. 'Brothers owe a certain duty to brothers and friends to friends. My soul is in a torment of anxiety because Kāsim has not returned from the forest. In Allāh's name, O face of fair omen, go forth at once and see what has happened to him.'

Alī Bābā, who was notoriously soft-hearted, shared the woman's alarm, and answered: 'May Allāh protect him from all harm, my sister! If he had only let me be his guide . . . But you must not allow yourself to fret just yet awhile; for he may have determined to avoid notice by returning late at night.'

This was a sensible speculation, but it was groundless; for by this time Kāsim's two arms and trunk, two legs and head, had been piled together behind the invisible door in the rock, that the horrid sight of them might appal and their increasing stench drive back any other stranger who should be rash enough to cross the threshold.

Alī Bābā constrained his brother's wife to take his bed for that night, promising that, as nothing of advantage could be done in the dark, he would set forth at dawn.

True to his promise he drove his three asses from the courtyard just as the sun was rising, and came in due course to the rock which he knew so well. When he did not see his brother's mules, he had to admit to himself that the worst had probably happened; when he saw blood at the foot of the rock, he knew for certain, and it was in a trembling voice that he cried: 'Open, Sesame!' Also his legs trembled as he walked across the threshold of the cave.

His knees knocked together when he saw the six parts of Kāsim; but his brotherly feeling overcame his fear and, in order that the dead man should not lack the last rites of the Faith, he fetched two large sacks from the cave and distributed the six parts between them. He loaded the sacks on one of his asses, covering them carefully with leaves and branches, and then, that the other two animals might not make a useless trip, loaded each with a sufficiency of dīnārs, taking care to hide the bags as carefully as he had hidden the remains of his brother. After that he commanded the rocky door to shut, and set out upon his homeward journey with a sad heart.

When he had driven the asses into the courtyard of his house, he called the slave, Marjānah, to help him unload them. This Marjānah was a girl whom Alī Bābā and his wife had taken into their house as a baby and brought up with as much care and love as if she had been their own child. She had grown to womanhood in that house, helping her adopted mother and doing the work of ten persons. She was as adroit as she was sweet-tempered, and could quickly resolve any difficulty to which she applied her mind.

She descended and kissed her father's hand in welcome, as she did ever on his return. 'Marjānah, my girl,' said Alī Bābā, 'to-day needs a proof of your wit and discretion.' He told her of the dreadful fate which had overtaken his brother, and concluded: 'Now the six pieces of him are upon the third ass. While I go up and break the sad news to his widow, you must think of some way by which we can bury him with all the appearance of his having died a natural death.' 'I will try,' said Marjānah, and Alī Bābā hastened upstairs.

Kāsim's wife could see by the poor man's face that something terrible had happened, so she began to utter loud cries. She was getting ready to tear her hair and lay fingers to her cheeks, but Alī Bābā told the bad news very quickly and added, before she had time to make up her mind whether she should scream or not: 'Allāh has given me riches more than my need, dear sister, and if it would be any consolation to you in your great grief to accept your share of what I have and to remain in this house as my second wife, you are very welcome. You will find the mother of my children a loving and attentive sister to you, and we shall live together in all tranquillity, talking over the merits of the dead.' Having thus spoken, Alī Bābā fell silent and waited for an answer, and in that moment Allāh lighted the heart of the wicked woman, and purged it of its spite and pride. She understood Alī Bābā's goodness and generosity, and accepted his offer with a grateful heart; thanks to her marriage with this noble man, she became an excellent woman.

Alī Bābā, having thus prevented the woman from alarming the neighbourhood with her cries, left her to the care of his first wife and went down to find young Marjānah.

He met her as she was returning from a visit in the town; for she had lost no time in concocting a plan and putting it into execution. She had gone to a neighbouring druggist and asked for a special theriac which is used for the cure of mortal ailments. The druggist had sold her the draught and asked her who was ill. She sighed, and answered: 'Alas, alas, the red evil has stricken down my master's brother, and he has been carried to our house for better attention. But we can do nothing for him; his face is quite yellow, he is dumb and blind, he is deaf and motionless. Our only hope is in your theriac, O sheikh.' She carried the drug back and told Alī Bābā briefly of her scheme, which he applauded with genuine admiration.

At this point Shahrazād saw the approach of morning and discreetly fell silent.

But when the eight-hundred-and-fifty-sixth night had come

SHE SAID:

Next morning Marjânah returned weeping to the druggist and asked for a certain electuary which is only used upon patients whose cases seem to be hopeless. 'If this does not succeed,' she mourned, 'all is lost, all is lost!' Also, as she departed with the electuary, she took care to spread the evil tidings among the folk of that quarter. Therefore the people were not surprised to be woken on the following morning by piercing and lamentable cries, and to be informed of the death of Kâsim.

Now Marjânah had said to herself: 'It is not enough to make a violent death seem natural, my girl. You will have succeeded in nothing if you cannot hide the fact that the body has been cut into six parts.' As soon, therefore, as she had played her part in the mock mourning, she walked to the shop of an old cobbler in a quarter of the city where she was quite unknown. She slipped a dînâr into the cobbler's hand, saying: 'We have need of your great skill to-day, sheikh Mustafâ.' 'You bring me a fortunate morning, O face of the moon,' answered the gay and talkative old man. 'Speak, dear mistress, and all shall be as you require.' 'You have only to collect what you need for sewing leather, and to follow me,' said Marjânah, 'but first it is necessary that I blindfold you, for that is a strict condition of the work.' She bound a kerchief about his eyes, but he recoiled, saying: 'Would you make me commit a crime or deny the Faith of my fathers for one poor dînâr?' So Marjânah soothed him with a second dînâr, saying: 'Your conscience may be clear, O sheikh. We only want you to do a little sewing.'

This satisfied the cobbler and he allowed himself to be led along the streets and down into the cellar of Alî Bâbâ's house. There Marjânah removed the bandage and showed him the six pieces of the body which she had set in order. Then she gave him a third gold coin, saying: 'I wish you to sew the pieces of this body together; if you work quickly, you shall have a fourth dînâr.' This munificence decided the old man and, in a very short time, he had joined the unfortunate Kâsim into one body. Marjânah gave him the rest of his wage, and led him back blindfolded to the door of his shop. Then she returned home, taking care that the old man did not spy upon her direction.

When she reached the cellar again, she washed the reassembled body, perfumed it with incense, and smeared it with aromatic oil. Then she shrouded it, with Alī Bābā's help, and went forth to purchase a litter.

For this she paid well, and insisted on carrying it to the house herself, so that no porter might spy upon her master and herself. The body was covered with thick shawls bought for the purpose, and then the Imām and other dignitaries of the mosque were invited to attend. Four neighbours took up the litter, the Imām headed the procession, the readers of the Koran went next, followed by Marjānah uttering lamentable cries and beating her breast, and Alī Bābā with his friends brought up the rear. While the train went on and came to the cemetery, Alī Bābā's two wives mourned loudly in the house, and all the women of the quarter mourned with them. Thus Kāsim was buried, and no one outside that household had a suspicion of the way in which he had met his death.

When the forty thieves returned after a month to their cave, they found no sign at all of Kāsim's pieces or Kāsim's putrefaction. Their captain thought deeply over the matter, and then said: 'My men, our secret is known; unless we wish to lose all the riches which our fathers collected with such noble labour and to which we ourselves have added so notably, we must find out the accomplice of the man we killed, and kill him also. The best way to do that will be for one of us, who is both brave and circumspect, to disguise himself as a darwīsh and enquire about the city until he hears some whisper concerning a man cut into six parts. As it is absolutely necessary that no word of our doings should leak out, it will be as well to pass sentence of death upon our messenger in the case of his unsuccess.' But in spite of this threat one of the thieves volunteered for the duty, and was dismissed with praise and congratulation.

He came to the city in the early morning and found all the shops shut save that of Mustafā, who stood at his door, awl in hand, and was already engaged upon the confection of a saffron leather slipper. The craftsman lifted his eyes and beheld a darwīsh watching his work with obvious admiration; he gave him good morning, and the holy man at once expressed surprise to see such excellent eyesight and such nimble fingers in so venerable a cobbler. The old man preened himself and answered: 'Thanks to Allāh, O darwīsh, I can still thread a needle at the first attempt. I can still sew together the six parts of a dead body in a dark cellar without a light.' The robber nearly fainted for joy and sent up a silent prayer of thanks that he should have been led to his desire by so short a road. He feigned astonishment and cried: 'The six parts of a dead body, O face of fair omen! What do you mean by that? Is it a custom in this country to cut the dead into six parts, and then sew them up again? Do they do it to find out what is inside?' Mustafā laughed, as he replied: 'As Allāh lives we have no such custom! But I know what I know and no one else shall know it. I have reason enough for keeping silence, and my memory is always bad in the early morning.' The pretended darwīsh laughed heartily, in order to win the old man's favour; making as if to shake hands, he slipped a gold coin into the other's palm, saying: 'O uncle of eloquence, Allāh preserve me from poking my nose into other people's business! But if I felt that I had a stranger's right to express a wish to you, I think I would ask you to tell me the position of the house where you sewed the dead man together.' 'But how should I know the position of it, O head of all the darwīshes?' cried the cobbler. 'I was blindfolded and led to the place by a girl, who went so quickly from one thing to another that half the time I did not know what I was doing. Yet I think, my son, that if my eyes were bandaged afresh I could find the house again by certain indications which came to me through the sense of touch. You must know, O holy brother, that a man sees as well with his fingers as with his eyes, unless his skin is as hard and gross as a crocodile's back. I myself have many honourable customers who, though blind, see better with their finger tips than the vile barber who shaves my head each Friday and scarifies my poor old hide. May Allāh do so to him and more also!'

At this point Shahrazād saw the approach of morning and discreetly fell silent.

But when the eight-hundred-and-fifty-seventh night had come

SHE SAID:

'Praise to the breast which gave you suck!' exclaimed the robber. 'Long may you thread needles in this world, O sheikh of excellence! I would like nothing better than to see if you can find your way back to that cellar.' The man's admiration was so obvious that old Mustafā allowed his eyes to be bandaged and, with his hand on the other's sleeve, groped his way to Alī Bābā's house. 'This is most certainly the place!' he cried. 'I recognise it by the smell of asses' dung and by this post against which I stubbed my toes when I came before.' The delighted robber removed the old man's bandage and then hastened to mark the door of Alī Bābā's house with a small piece of chalk. He slipped a second dīnār into the cobbler's hand, promising that he would buy all his slippers from him for the rest of his life, and sent him back to his shop. Then he made all haste to the forest and told his chief of his success.

When the diligent Marjānah went out soon afterwards to buy provisions, she saw the white mark on the door and thought: 'This did not write itself. This is the work of an enemy and we must find some conjuration against it.' She fetched a piece of chalk and made exactly the same mark on the same part of every door in the street, and, as she made each mark, she addressed the unknown foe, saying below her breath: 'Five fingers in your left eye, five fingers in your right!' For she knew that this was a most powerful spell against threats from the unknown.

Next morning, when the thieves came two by two into town to lay aboard the house which their companion had marked for them, they were greatly embarrassed to find all the doors in that long street bearing the same sign. In order not to attract attention, their chief sent them back to the forest, where they condemned their unfortunate spy to death and cut off his head without delay.

Their rage against the unknown trespasser increased a hundredfold, and one of their number eagerly volunteered to run him to earth. He went disguised into the city, as his dead comrade had done, entered into conversation with the old cobbler, and was conducted to the door of Alī Bābā's house. He marked this with a small red mark in an inconspicuous place, and then returned to the cave. He did not know that when a head is destined to make that fatal leap from the shoulders, it will make that leap and no other.

When the thieves came two by two into the town, they found that the excellent Marjānah had made identical small red marks on all the doors of the quarter. Therefore they returned to their lair and cut off the head of the second spy. Thus the band was reduced by two without nearer approach to the solution of its difficulty.

'I will have to go myself,' said the robber captain, and he went down into the city in disguise. But when the cobbler Mustafā had shown him Alī Bābā's door, he did not mark it in white or red chalk, or even blue; instead, he gazed long till he had fixed its appearance in his memory, and then returned to the forest. He called together the thirty-seven surviving thieves and said to them: 'I know the house for certain now, and, as Allāh lives, the fate of it shall be terrible. The first thing for you to do, my hearties, is to bring me thirty-eight large earthenware jars, with wide necks and swelling bellies. One of them must be filled with olive oil, the rest must be empty.' The thieves, who always obeyed their chief without question, rode off at once to the potter's market and brought back thirty-eight jars, slung in twos upon their horses.

Without unloading these, they took off all their clothes, at the chief's order, and, keeping only their turbans and slippers, climbed into the empty jars, so that one was balanced by the olive oil, and the rest balanced each other. They slung their slippers on their backs and squatted down in the jars with their knees to their chins, like chickens of the twentieth day curled in their shells. The captain armed each with a scimitar and a club, and plentifully daubed the outside of the pots with some of the oil from the full jar. Finally, after stoppering the mouths of each vessel with palm fibre so that the men inside should be hidden and yet breathe freely, he drove the horses down towards the city.

At nightfall he came to Alī Bābā's house, and Allāh even saved him the trouble of knocking, for the honest woodcutter sat on his threshold, gratefully breathing the cool air of evening.

At this point Shahrazād saw the approach of morning and discreetly fell silent.

But when the eight-hundred-and-fifty-eighth night had come

SHE SAID:

The robber chief checked his horses and greeted Alī Bābā most politely, saying: 'O my master, your slave is an oil merchant; he is ignorant of this city and does not know where to pass the night. He hopes that you will give hospitality, for himself and his horses, in the generous courtyard of your house.'

Alī Bābā remembered his own poverty and at once rose in the stranger's honour, answering: 'O oil merchant, O my brother, be very welcome to my house and the repose of my house and the life of my house.' He took his guest by the hand and led him into the courtyard, calling Marjānah and another slave to help with the unloading of the jars and to feed the horses. When the jars had been ranged in good order at the back of the courtyard and the horses fastened along the wall, each with a feed of barley and oats, Alī

Bābā conducted his guest, whom he was very far from recognising, into the reception hall of his house. Bidding him take the place of honour, he sat down beside him and served him with food and drink; but, as soon as both were satisfied and had given thanks to Allāh, the courteous woodcutter retired, saying: 'Good master, the house belongs to you.'

As he was going away, the robber chief called after him: 'In Allāh's name, dear host, show me that part of your honourable house where it is lawful for me to give peace to the motion of my bowels and make my water.' Alī Bābā led his guest to the privy, which stood at the corner of the house nearest the old jars. 'In there,' he said, and hastened away, so as not to incommode the digestive functions of the stranger. The robber captain did what he had to do, and then went to each of the jars in turn, whispering into their mouths: 'When I throw a pebble against your jar from my bedroom window, come out speedily and run to me, for there will be killing.' Then he returned to the house, where Marjānah lighted him to his bedroom with an oil lamp and wished him good night. As he felt that he would need his full strength for the great vengeance which he had in mind, he lay down and was soon snoring like a washerwoman's copper.

While Marjānah was washing the dishes in the kitchen, her lamp went out for lack of oil. As she had forgotten to lay in a fresh provision that day, she called her fellow slave Abdallāh and explained the difficulty to him. But Abdallāh broke into a laugh, saying: 'In Allāh's name, my sister, how can you say that we are out of oil, when there are thirty-eight jars full of it in the courtyard? And good oil, too, if I can judge from the drippings! I do not seem to recognise the resourceful Marjānah to-night. . . . I must go back to sleep, my sister. I have to be up early in the morning to accompany our master to the hammām.' He returned to his chamber, which was near that of the oil merchant, and was soon snoring like a marsh buffalo.

Marjānah, who had been a little put out by Abdallāh's jesting, went to one of the jars in the courtyard, removed the palm fibre from it, and plunged the measure through the gaping mouth. But—O wide eyes, dry throat, and working bowels!—instead of reaching oil, the measure bumped against something hard, and a voice came forth from the interior of the jar, saying: 'Pebble did he say? I should call it a rock. But, be that as it may, now is the time!' And a bearded head appeared above the rim of the jar.

Any but Marjānah would have shrieked aloud; even she allowed herself to think: 'Now I am dead!' In a moment, however, she collected all her faculties, and said coolly: 'Not yet, not yet, my man. Your master is still asleep. Wait till he wakes.' She had already divined the whole plot; therefore she visited each of the jars in turn, to count the number of her foes, and bade each head, as it appeared, have patience. When she had counted thirty-seven thieves and one full jar of oil, she returned to the kitchen, lighted the lamp, and set about the execution of a project which she hoped might save the house.

She lit a great fire under the cauldron which was used for washing clothes and then, going backwards and forwards with the measure, filled the cauldron with oil from the thirty-eighth jar. As soon as it boiled, she brimmed a large stable bucket with the death-dealing stuff and, going softly up to the first jar, snatched away the palm fibre from its top. Relentlessly she poured the boiling oil through the mouth on to the thief's head, so that he swallowed death with the cry which rose to his lips.

With sure hand and unhurried pace Marjānah burned and stifled the rest of the thieves to death; for no man, though he be hidden in a sevenfold jar, can avoid the Destiny which hangs about his neck. When she had completed her work of destruction, she put out the fire, stoppered the jars, and returned to the kitchen to wait in the dark for what should come.

At midnight the robber chief woke and put his head out of the window. Seeing no light and hearing no noise, he supposed that all the house was plunged in sleep. Therefore he took a handful of pebbles which he had brought up with him and began to throw them dexterously at the jars. He could hear by the noise they made that they had reached their marks; but there was no answer, no rushing of armed men, no sign, no sound at all. 'The dogs have gone to sleep,' he muttered, as he ran down to the courtyard; but there the smell of burning oil and roasting flesh took him by the throat, and his heart misgave him. He set his hand to one of the jars and found its surface as hot as an oven; he ventured to kindle a handful of straw and, examining each jar by its light, found every man of his crouched down smoking and lifeless.

Realising that he had terribly lost his band, he reached the top of the courtyard wall with one prodigious bound, leapt down into the road, and took to his heels. He fled among the shadows of night till he reached his cave, where he sat to brood sullenly upon the next step he should take. For the moment, so much for him.

At this point Shahrazād saw the approach of morning and discreetly fell silent.

But when the eight-hundred-and-fifty-ninth night had come

SHE SAID:

Marjānah, knowing that the house was safe, waited calmly till the morning, and only woke her master at the time appointed. Alī Bābā dressed himself and came down to the courtyard; not till then did Marjānah hint to him of her adventure. She led him up to the first jar, saying: 'Good master, I pray you lift the cover and look inside.' Alī Bābā did so and recoiled in horror; but when he had heard Marjānah's story, he wept joyful tears and cried: 'Blessed be the womb which bore you, O daughter of benediction! Surely the bread which you have eaten is a little thing compared with this. Henceforward you shall be our eldest child and the head of our house.'

With Abdallāh's help, Alī Bābā buried the thirty-seven bodies in a great pit in his garden, and was rid of them for ever. Then all the household returned to their quiet life and continued to make much of the astute Marjānah.

One day, Alī Bābā's eldest son, who now looked after the shop which had been Kāsim's, said to his father: 'I do not know how I can make a return to my neighbour Husain for all the favours which he has shown me since he took a shop in our market. Five times I have shared a midday meal with him, without returning his hospitality. I think you will agree that we ought to give some fine feast in his honour.' 'That is but fitting, my son,' answered Alī Bābā. 'You should have spoken of the matter earlier. To-morrow is Friday, the day of rest, and we cannot do better than ask the excellent Husain to take bread and salt with us in the evening. If he is inclined to make excuses of politeness, press him strongly, my son, for I am sure that we can entertain him in a fashion not unworthy of his generosity.'

So next morning Alī Bābā's son invited Husain, the new merchant, to walk with him, and took him towards his father's house, where Alī Bābā waited smiling on the threshold. The young man led his long-bearded friend up to his father, who thanked him with great civility for his many kindnesses, and pressed him to feed with them that evening. 'The grace of Allāh be upon you, good master!'

answered the venerable Husain. 'Your hospitality is a great hospitality but I cannot accept it, for I made a vow before heaven many years ago never to eat meat flavoured with salt or to taste that substance in any form.' 'Surely that is no difficulty,' cried Alī Bābā. 'I have but to give orders in the kitchen and our repast will be cooked without salt or any savour of the kind.' Thus he wrung an acceptance from his son's friend, and hurried into the house to tell Marjānah that all salt must be left out of that evening's meal. This condition greatly surprised the slave, but she handed on the command to the black woman who did the cooking.

When night came and the guest sat with Alī Bābā and his son before the well-piled cloth, Marjānah and Abdallāh waited upon them, and the former, with the natural curiosity of a woman, took every chance she could get of examining the old man who did not like salt. Yet, when the meal was over, she went forth and left the three men to talk together at their ease.

At the end of an hour this delightful girl entered the hall again and Alī Bābā was astounded to see that she was dressed as a dancer, her brow starred with gold sequins, her neck hung with beads of yellow amber, her waist pressed in a supple belt of gold, and having sounding gold upon her wrists and ankles. From her belt hung a jade-hilted dagger, as is the custom with dancers, so that the long blade may swing out and mimic the figures of the dance. Her dark, deep, glittering eyes had been heavily lengthened with black kohl, and her brows met in a threatening passionate bow. Behind her walked young Abdallāh, holding a tambourine with metal castanets, upon which he beat a gentle rhythm to the paces of the girl. When she arrived before her master, Marjānah bowed gracefully and then, signing to Abdallāh that he should a little quicken and louden his measure, began dancing like a happy bird.

She danced tirelessly and with all perfection, as the shepherd David danced before the black sadness of Saul. She danced the kerchief dance and the dance of veils, she danced after the manner of the Jews and of the Greeks, Ethiopian and Persian figures she danced, and the figures of the desert, as light and beautiful as Bilkīs who loved Sulaimān.

When the hearts of the three men waited upon her feet and their eyes were fixed in dream upon her body, she danced the swaying dagger dance. Drawing the gilded blade from its silver sheath, she swayed and leapt with blazing eyes, on wings that might not be seen.

She balanced like an angry snake, darting her point in every quarter of the air and then turning it against her own sweet breasts. The three men uttered frightened cries when they saw the white roses of her bosom menaced by the dagger's silver; but in a moment Marjānah turned the blade again, and reeled about and about, stabbing her imagined foes ever more quickly. Suddenly she sank to her knee and signed to Abdallāh to throw her the tambourine; she caught it in her hand and, again after the fashion of dancers, presented it to her master for a wage. Alī Bābā was a little offended that she should carry the imitation so far, but he could not resist her appeal, and therefore dropped a gold dīnār upon the sounding parchment. His son did the same, and the venerable Husain was feeling in his purse for money when lo! the dancer cast herself upon him and stabbed him to the heart. He opened his mouth and shut it again, gave a half sigh, and fell dead among the carpets.

Alī Bābā and his son thought that their slave had gone mad; they threw themselves upon her to restrain her, as she stood there wiping the blood from the dagger on a silken shawl. But she spoke to them calmly, saying: 'O my masters, let us give thanks to Allāh that He has strengthened the hand of a weak woman to save this house. This offal is no more a venerable Husain than it is an oil merchant.' So saying, she snatched the long coarse beard from the face of the corpse and showed the astonished Alī Bābā the features of the robber chief.

When Alī Bābā recognised the oil-seller and the captain of the thieves in that one body, and realised that Marjānah had saved the house a second time, he kissed her between the eyes and took her to his breast crying: 'Marjānah, my child, my daughter, will you be my daughter in very truth, will you marry this handsome young man, my son?' 'Be it upon my head and before my eyes!' answered Marjānah, as she kissed her master's hand.

Marjānah was wedded to Alī Bābā's son on that same day; there was feasting and rejoicing in the house. Late that night the woodcutter buried the robber chief in the ditch which had served for his band. May Allāh have him never in compassion!

At this point Shahrazād saw the approach of morning and discreetly fell silent.

But when the eight-hundred-and-sixtieth night had come

SHE SAID:

After his son's marriage, Alī Bābā kept away for a long time from the secret cave, for Marjānah feared that he might meet the two thieves whom she supposed to be alive. But we know, O auspicious King, that they had been beheaded for failing to mark down Alī Bābā's house. At the end of a year, however, the woodcutter set out, with his son and Marjānah, to inspect the place. The girl, who had quick eyes for anything upon the way, noticed that shrubs and tall grasses had overgrown the little path which led up to the rock and that there were no traces before the rock of man or beast. Therefore she concluded that the place had been abandoned, and said to Alī Bābā: 'We may enter safely, O my uncle.'

Alī Bābā stetched out his hand towards the invisible door of rock, crying: 'Open, Sesame!' and again the door gaped, as if by the impulsion of an unseen hand. Alī Bābā soon saw that the treasure was untouched since his last visit, and it was with some pride that he pointed out this vast inheritance to the two young people.

After a delighted examination of all the marvels, they filled three large sacks with gold and precious stones, and departed for the city. All the people of that house lived together in happy peace thenceforward, prudently spending the fortune which the Great Giver had sent to them. Thus it was that Alī Bābā, from being the owner of three asses only, became the richest and most honoured man of his town. Glory be to Him Who gives to the humble without counting!

And that, O auspicious King, is all that I know of Alī Bābā and the Forty Thieves. But Allāh knows all!

'Indeed, Shahrazād, the tale is both excellent and astonishing!' cried King Shahryār. 'There are no girls like Marjānah in these days. I ought to know, who have had to cut off so many women's heads.'

Seeing that the King began to frown at his memories, Shahrazād hastened to begin . . .

Meetings of Al-Rashīd on the Bridge of Baghdād

IT is related, O auspicious King, O crown upon my head, that the Khalīfah Hārūn al-Rashīd—whom may Allāh bless!—left his palace in disguise one day, accompanied by his wazīr Jafar, and Masrūr his sword-bearer, to walk about the streets for his diversion. When he came to the stone bridge which spans the Tigris, he saw a very old blind man sitting cross-legged upon the ground and begging alms from the passers-by in the name of Allāh. The Khalīfah paused and placed a gold dīnār in the extended palm, but the beggar strongly seized the royal hand, saying: 'O generous giver, may Allāh repay your gift with the choicest of His blessings! But before you pass on I beg you to lift your arm and give me a buffet on the lobe of the ear.' So saying, he let go Hārūn's hand but took care to hold him by the skirts of his long robe until he should comply with this extraordinary request.

'Good uncle,' cried the astonished Khalīfah, 'may Allāh do so to me and more also if I obey you! Such an action against so old a man would be unworthy of a Believer, and he who has acquired merit by giving an alms should not destroy that merit by giving a blow.'

He made as if to break away, but found that he had calculated without the vigilance of the blind beggar, who held him by force, and answered: 'Forgive my importunity, O father of gifts, for I cannot, without perjuring myself in the sight of Allāh, receive the alms without the blow. And if you knew the reason of my oath, you would not hesitate to humour me.'

'There is no help save in Allāh against this old obstinate,' muttered al-Rashīd, and, rather than stay to attract the notice of the passers-by, he gave the beggar a buffet on the ear and made off, followed by the thanks and blessing of the blind old man.

As he passed on, al-Rashīd said to Jafar: 'By Allāh, this blind man's story must be a strange one; return to him now and tell him, from the Commander of the Faithful, to present himself at the palace at noon to-morrow.'

When Jafar had obeyed this order and returned, the three walked on across the bridge; but they had not gone far when they saw a second beggar, lame and with a split mouth, also stretching out his hand for alms. At a sign from his master, Masrūr handed to this second unfortunate that which was written in his Fate for the day. At once the man lifted his head and laughed, saying: 'As Allāh lives, when I was a schoolmaster, I never earned so much!' 'By the life of my head,' cried Hārūn to Jafar, 'if this man is really a schoolmaster and has been brought so low as to beg for his bread in the streets, the story of his life must be a strange one. Bid him present himself at my palace to-morrow at the same time as the blind man.'

Jafar obeyed this order and the three walked on; but, before they were out of earshot, they heard the second beggar overwhelming a certain sheikh with so great a babble of blessing and thanks that it appeared certain that he had given an alms of extravagant size. Al-Rashīd expressed astonishment that a private citizen should give more freely than himself, and sent Jafar back to bid the generous old man present himself at the palace at noon on the following day.

As the three continued their way across the bridge, they saw a magnificent procession coming towards them, such as might be supposed only to attend upon kings. Heralds on horseback rode before, crying: 'Room, make room, for the husband of the King of China's daughter! Room, make room, for the husband of the daughter of the King of Sind and Ind!' Behind the heralds pranced a charger of noble race, bearing upon its back a princely boy shining in all the nobility of youth. Behind him, again, two grooms led a richly-harnessed camel by a halter of blue silk. This camel carried a double palanquin in which were seated, upon a dais of red brocade, two queenly girls veiled with orange silk. The rear of the procession was formed by a troop of musicians, playing Indian and Chinese airs upon instruments of unfamiliar form.

'Surely this is a more notable stranger than usually comes to my capital,' said Hārūn to his companions. 'I have received kings and princes and the proudest amīrs of the earth, the chiefs of the infidels beyond the seas, the Franks and the people of the farthest West have sent me ambassadors and deputations; but I have never seen a stranger show more pomp and beauty in our streets. Follow the procession, Masrūr, and invite that excellent young man to present himself before me at noon to-morrow. Then return to the palace and tell me all that you have seen.'

While Masrūr departed on this errand, the Khalīfah and his wazīr walked to the other end of the bridge and found themselves on the outskirts of the great polo-ground. There they saw an eager concourse of people watching a young man who galloped up and down upon a white mare of astonishing beauty. As he went he thonged and spurred the poor beast mercilessly, till she was covered with blood and foam, and trembled like a leaf.

The Khalīfah, who loved horses and would not suffer them to be ill-treated, furiously asked the bystanders the meaning of this exhibition. They answered: 'Allāh alone knows why he does it! We can only tell you that this young man comes here every day at the same hour and subjects his mare to the same inhuman treatment. After all, he owns the animal and can do what he likes with her.' But Hārūn turned to Jafar, crying: 'I charge you to find out the reason of this young man's conduct. If he refuses to tell you, command him most strictly to present himself before me to-morrow at the same time as the blind man, the lame man, the generous sheikh, and the noble stranger.' With that Hārūn al-Rashīd left Jafar on the polo-ground to carry out his instructions, and returned alone to the palace.

At this point Shahrazād saw the approach of morning and discreetly fell silent.

But when the eight-hundred-and-sixty-first night had come

SHE SAID:

Next day the Khalīfah entered the dīwān after the noon prayer, and Jafar introduced into his presence the five men whom he had met upon the stone bridge: that is to say, the blind man who wished to be buffeted, the lame schoolmaster, the generous sheikh, the noble stranger behind whose horse Indian and Chinese airs were played and the young master of the white mare. When the five had prostrated themselves before the throne and kissed the earth between the Khalīfah's hands, al-Rashīd signed to them to rise and Jafar arranged them in a half circle upon the carpet.

The Khalīfah then turned to the master of the white mare, saying: 'Young man, you showed yourself so inhuman yesterday in your riding that I must look most searchingly into your reason for ill-treating a dumb beast who cannot answer blows with blows and curses with curses. It is useless to tell me that you used your whip and spur to tame or train the animal or that you rode as you did to amuse those who watched you; for I have trained a great many stallions and chargers in my time without even maltreating them, and I saw for myself that the crowd which stood to watch you yesterday was horrified by what you did. I very nearly betrayed my presence and punished you on the spot; if you wish to escape most severe chastisement, explain yourself now, fully and without lying. If I find that you have an excuse, I will pardon you and forget your offence.'

The master of the white mare turned yellow in the face and hung his head in embarrassed silence. Also tears streamed down his face and fell upon his breast. Seeing his evident grief, the Khalīfah changed his tone, and said much more gently: 'O young man, forget that you are in the presence of the Commander of the Faithful and speak freely, as if you were among friends; for I swear, by the virtues of my glorious ancestors, that I will do you no harm.' Jafar also signed with his head and eyes, as if to say: 'Have no fear.'

The young man calmed the agitated breathing of his breast, and then lifted his head, saying:

The Master of the White Mare

O COMMANDER of the Faithful, I am known in my quarter as Sīdī Numān, and the tale which you bid me tell is a mystery of our Faith. If it were written with needles on the interior corner of an eye, yet would it serve as a lesson to the circumspect.'

The young man collected his thoughts for a moment, and then continued:

When my father died, he left me the inheritance which Allāh had willed for me and, on accounting it, I found that the Giver had blessed me with more than my soul desired. In one day I became the richest and best considered man of my quarter; but my new life, instead of filling me with pride, only helped me to satisfy my natural taste for a calm solitude. I lived as a bachelor, congratulating myself every morning that I had none of the cares and responsibilities of a family, and saying to myself each evening: 'O Sīdī Numān, how quiet and modest are your days! How sweet is the lonely life of a bachelor!'

But one morning, my lord, I woke with a violent and incomprehensible desire to alter the course of my existence and become a married man. Urged by this change of heart, I rose, saying: 'Are you not ashamed to live alone like a jackal in its lair, with no sweet presence by your side, with no fair body of a woman to delight your eyes, with no intimate love through which to feel the breath of God?

Will you wait till years have made you impotent before trying the pleasant attraction of our girls?'

I had no thought of fighting against this sudden and natural inclination; yet, as I had no liking for the marriage custom of my equals by which the bride's face is not seen until after the wedding, I preferred to choose a bride for myself in the slave market, for her charm alone. Therefore I left my house that morning and walked towards the market, saying to myself as I went along: 'You are right to marry a slave girl rather than seek alliance with some damsel of birth, O Sīdī Numān. You will escape both trouble and weariness; you will avoid the weight of a whole new family upon your back; you will avoid the hostile glances of a calamitous mother-in-law upon your stomach; you will avoid, upon your shoulders, a weight of brothers great and small and a horde of other relations; above all you will avoid, for your ears, the continuous recrimination of the bride herself, the claims that she is better born, that you have no rights over her, and that all the owing in your house is owing from you to her.'

Thus I arrived at the slave market, O Commander of the Faithful, in the fixed determination to choose a girl who should be at once charming enough to bring me happiness and worthy enough to call forth the great reserve of tenderness which I knew to be in my heart. That day the market had been enriched by the arrival of a new batch of varied women, drawn from Circassia, Ionia, the Isles of the Far North, Ethiopia, Khurāsān, Arabia, the Lands of Rūm, the Anatolian Coasts, Sarandīb, India and China. The brokers and auctioneers had already assembled them in different groups, according to their race, to avoid confusion; and each girl was placed separately and to advantage, so that she might be sold at her full value after a close examination. No man may escape his Destiny; mine led my steps at once to the women from the Isles of the Far North. My eyes were dazzled by them, for the light gold of their heavy hair and the whiteness passing silver of their bodies shone forth the more splendidly because of their darker rivals. These Northern girls seemed all strangely alike, as if they had been sisters of one begetting; their blue eyes had the sparkle of Iranian turquoises still wet from the rocks of their birth.

At this point Shahrazād saw the approach of morning and discreetly fell silent.

But when the eight-hundred-and-sixty-second night had come

SHE SAID:

I had never seen girls of so strange a beauty, and now I felt my heart straining and yearning in my bosom towards all of them. Even at the end of an hour I could not make the choice between their various perfections; therefore I took the youngest by the hand and bought her speedily at the first price asked for her. The graces of all womankind girt her as varied garments; her body was silver in the mine and blanched almonds, excessively clear and pale; her hair was a heavy fleece of yellow silk; her eyes were large and magical, shining with the lilt and savour of the sea, beneath sombre brows curved like the blades of scimitars. Seeing her, I remembered the words of the poet:

> Her mouth a birth of purple camomile,
> Her colour touched with the amber of a Chinese rose,
> Her agate eyes deepened with hyacinth,
> Longer than minions' eyes
> Dead on the tombs of Egypt;
> It needed but her black mole rose-thigh-islanded
> To tipsy the world.

> What are reeds looking down into water?
> I have seen her knees look down to her bare feet.
> When her beauty plays the lute and her body answers,
> The willows are white and shiver and do not move.

> She is a pirate ship calm on the green sea,
> Proud with the heavy metal of blue eyes.

I took the pale-coloured girl by the hand and, covering her nakedness with my mantle, led her to my house. Her silence and modesty pleased me, and I felt my heart drawn by her strange beauty, by her hair that was as yellow as liquid gold and her blue frightened eyes which avoided mine. As she could not speak my language and I could not speak hers, I did not weary her with questions, but thanked the Giver that He had given me a woman for my home whose simple appearance was an enchantment.

On that first evening I could not fail to remark the singularity of my bride; for, when night fell, her blue eyes became darker and, losing their daytime sweetness, seemed to shine with an interior fire.

She was shaken by some exaltation which paled her pale cheeks and gave a light trembling to her lips; from time to time she glanced sideways at the door, as if she wished to go forth; but, as it was time for supper, I sat down and made her sit beside me.

While I waited for food to be served, I profited by our nearness to show the tenderness of my heart and to prove that her coming was a blessing to me; I caressed her gently, trying to tame her strange soul; I carried her hand to my lips and to my heart, as carefully as if I was touching some very old and costly fabric which might dissolve in dust under my fingers. I passed my hand over the silk of her hair and, as Allāh lives, I shall never forget that contact; instead of the warmth of living hair it was as if these yellow tresses had been spun from some frozen metal, or as if my fingers dabbled in a silk floss dipped among melting snow. For a moment I had a terrible thought that she might have been made entirely from a cold and exquisite metal; but then I considered in my soul the infinite power of Allāh Who gives our girls hair as black and warm as the wing of night, and crowns the maidens of the North with frozen flame. Feeling my bride so different from the women of my own blood, I thrilled with fear and delight at once, and, as I gazed stupidly upon her, found myself attributing unknown and unnatural powers to her chill beauty.

When the slaves set food before us, I noticed in my wife an accentuation of wildness, a coming and going of red and white in her cheeks, and a dilation of the tempest-blue eyes. Thinking that these things might be due to her ignorance of our customs in eating, I began to devour a sweet dish of rice swollen in butter, eating with my fingers in order to show her the way. But I saw that, far from being reassured, she was seized with a sentiment of repulsion, if not of nausea. Instead of following my example, she turned her head as if looking for something, and then, after a minute's hesitation, took from her bosom a slender tube carved from a child's bone and drew from it a fine quitch stalk, like one of our ear-picks. With this she began to pick up grains of rice one by one, and eat them; but between each she let so long a time elapse that she had taken no more than a dozen when I had finished my supper. As she then made a sign as if she were satisfied, I did not press her to take more; and that was all the nourishment she accepted during our first day together.

'Perhaps she has already eaten,' I said to myself, 'or perhaps she is unaccustomed to sit down with men. If it is natural for her to eat so little, it shows that her body's needs are very different from those of our girls. And if her body's needs, why not the needs of her soul? Henceforth I will concentrate all my thought upon the needs of her soul.'

Though I burned indeed to possess this graceful mystery of the North sky, I very gently led her into her own chamber and left her there for that night. My pleasure was too precious a thing to be compromised by a little haste, and I felt sure that it would be to my advantage to prepare the soil and leave the acid fruit of the girl's love to grow to willing ripeness before I plucked it. Yet I could not sleep that night for thinking of the blonde strange beauty which perfumed my dwelling, and that there lay near me a body savoury as an apricot plucked in the dew falling, as downed and as desirable.

At this point Shahrazād saw the approach of morning and discreetly fell silent.

But when the eight-hundred-and-sixty-third night had come

SHE SAID:

Next day, when we met for the morning meal, I smiled upon my wife and bowed before her as I had seen the amīrs of the West, when they had come to our city on an embassy from the Frankish King. Among the dishes set before us was again one of rice boiled in butter, so well cooked that each grain fell away from the other, and delicately perfumed with cinnamon. My wife ate as before, taking up single grains at long intervals with her ear-pick. 'Why in Allāh's name does she eat like this?' I asked myself. 'Is it a custom of her people, or her own custom because she needs so little? Or does she want to count the grains so as not to eat more at one time than another? Or does she wish to teach me economy? I thank Allāh that I have no need for that!'

Whether she understood my perplexity or not, my wife continued, day after day, to eat in exactly the same fashion, and I began to think, when I realised that no woman could be sufficiently nourished in this way, that there was some mystery deep in the life of the girl which I should have to fathom before she would live with me in the way I wished. But I was far from dreaming of the terrible fashion in which my doubts were to be resolved.

After two weeks of patience and discretion, I determined to adventure upon a first visit to the bridal chamber; so, when I thought that my wife had been long asleep, I walked on tiptoe to the door of her room. This precaution I took because I dreamed of watching her sleeping at my ease, with her heavy lids closed and her long lashes lying idle.

But, when I came close, I heard the girl walking about within; being curious to know the reason of this, I hid behind the door curtain. Almost immediately the door was opened and my wife appeared on the threshold, dressed for the street, and began gliding across the marble of the courtyard, without making the least sound. As she passed me in the blackness, the blood stood still about my heart; for her face in the shadow was lighted by two green torches, eyes of a tiger moving swiftly upon some path of murder and blood. She had the appearance of an evil spirit sent in sleep to announce catastrophe to the world, or a Jinnīyah whose sole business was with cruelty. Her face was as pale as paper and her yellow hair stood terribly away from her head.

My teeth came together as if they would have broken, the wet of my mouth dried, and my breath ceased. My terrors froze me motionless and prevented me from betraying my presence in that place. I waited until the girl had disappeared, before staggering to the window which gave upon the courtyard of my house and looking out through the lattice. My first glance showed me her white figure passing through the gate into the road, on silent naked feet.

I gave her a few moments' advantage and then, taking my sandals in my hand, followed her across the courtyard, out of the gate, and along the road. The night was lighted by a just waning moon; all the sky trembled with light and spread out proudly above the earth. In spite of my dread and anxiety, I lifted my soul to the Master of all, praying within my thought: 'O Lord of exaltation and truth, bear witness that I have acted in all things discreetly and honestly towards this daughter of strangers, though she is unknown to me and perhaps belongs to a race of Unbelievers. I know not what she would do this night beneath the benevolent clarity of Your sky; but I declare that I am no accomplice of her actions and condemn them in advance, if they be not in accordance with the teaching of the Prophet (upon whom be prayer and peace!).'

Having cleared my conscience in this way, I followed my wife without hesitation. She led me through the streets of the city with as sure a movement as if she had been born among our houses, and I was able to keep in touch with her by the baleful gleaming of her hair, which lay on the night behind her like a torch. She came at length to the last houses, passed through the gates, and made for those barren fields which for hundreds of years have served as a home for the dead. The first cemetery, whose tombs are very old, she left behind her, and hastened to the one used for daily burial. 'She must have some friend or sister who came with her from the North, and died and was buried in this place,' I said to myself. But, when I recalled the expression of her face and the green fire in her eyes, the blood froze again about my heart.

And then I saw a form of shadow rise from among the tombs and come to meet my wife, and, by the foul face upon his hyena's head, I knew him to be a ghoul. My limbs gave under me and I fell behind a tomb, whence I was able to see the ghoul take my wife by the hand and lead her to the edge of an open grave. The two sat down upon the rim of it, facing each other across the cavity, and the ghoul, stretching down his hand, lifted a human head, fresh twisted from its body, and handed it to my wife. With the cry of a beast of prey she sank her teeth into the dead flesh, and began to chew and mumble it with savage appetite.

At this sight, my lord, I felt the sky tumbling its weight upon my head and I gave a cry of horror. In a breath I saw my wife standing upon the tomb which hid me and gazing upon me with the eyes of a starving tiger. Before I could make the least movement to defend myself or say one prayer against the unclean thing, she lifted her arm and uttered a long thin howl such as is heard when lions are hunting at night. Yet there must have been some devil's language in the sound, for I was turned straightway into a dog.

At this point Shahrazād saw the approach of morning and discreetly fell silent.

But when the eight-hundred-and-sixty-fourth night had come

SHE SAID:

My wife and the ghoul threw themselves upon me and kicked me so violently that, had not the awful terror of death given me unnatural endurance, I could never have escaped them. As it was, I bounded away over the tombs with my tail tucked between my legs, straining against my belly, and at the confines of the cemetery they gave up the chase. I ran on and on, howling miserably and falling over at every ten steps, until I dashed through the gates of the city. After a night passed in limping about the streets and fleeing from the cruel teeth of the dogs of each quarter, who thought that I had no right among them, I began to look about for some shelter. When the first shop was opened for the morning, I hurried through the door and curled myself up in a corner where my foes could not see me. This shop belonged to a seller of sheep's heads and trotters, and, at first, the owner took my part. But, after he had laid about him with his stick and scattered my aggressors, he came back into the shop with the evident intention of turning me out. I could see at once that this tripemonger was one of those conventional and superstitious fools who consider that dogs are unclean, and cannot find soap enough to wash their garments from the taint of even a puppy's contact. When he threatened me with his stick, I whined lamentably and looked at him with humble eyes; so he laid aside that weapon and, taking an odorous morsel of cooked trotter, showed it to me and then cast it far into the street. I ran for it and gobbled it greedily; then I returned to the man wagging my tail and begging, as well as I could, for shelter. 'Begone, you pimp!' he cried, lashing out with his stick; so I fled across the market and was soon a convergent point for all the other dogs. In deadly fear, I darted to the threshold of a baker's shop, not far from the dwelling of the inhospitable tripe-seller.

Even at first glance I could see that the baker was a gay and auspicious man, very different from his custom-ridden neighbour. He sat eating breakfast upon a mat and, before I had time to show him that I was hungry, he threw me a large piece of bread dipped in tomato sauce. 'Eat with delight, poor friend,' he said; but, instead of throwing myself eagerly upon Allāh's gift as ordinary dogs would have done, I first wagged my head and tail to express my gratitude, and then ate slowly and daintily, to show that I had no need of the gift and took it only to oblige the giver. He understood and signed to me to sit down near the shop; I did so with little whines of pleasure, and turned my back to the street to indicate that I asked for nothing of the world save his protection. Again he understood and patted me to give me confidence. I crossed the threshold slowly, looking up to him for permission, but, instead of being in any way offended, he pointed out a corner which I could make my own. I took possession of that place and kept it for as long as I dwelt in the house.

Quite soon the baker became very fond of me, and could not eat without my sitting by him to share his food. And I, on my side, kept my eyes fixed on him and paid no attention to anything else, either in the house or in the street. If he wished to go out, he would give one whistle and I would leap from my corner into the street and jump about, running gaily backwards and forwards until he was ready to depart. But, when we were well started, I would leave these games and walk sedately at his side, looking up pleasantly into his face from time to time.

After I had lived some weeks with the baker, an old woman entered the shop to buy a fresh loaf straight from the oven. She paid my master and was going towards the door with her purchase, when the baker, who had rung her coin, called to her, saying: 'O aunt, may Allāh grant you a long life! If it would not be offensive to you, I would rather have another piece of money.' At the same time he held out the coin, but the hardened old baggage refused, with a great deal of cackling, to exchange it, and said: 'I did not make the coin. Money is money; it should not be examined like vegetables.' This argument failed to convince my master, and he answered with a touch of disdain: 'The coin is so obviously false that this poor silly dog, this dumb animal, would not be deceived by it.' Then, simply to humiliate the calamitous old woman and with no expectation of a result, he called me by name: 'Bakht! Bakht! Here, come here, sir!' As I ran to him, wagging my tail, he put the suspect coin into his till and threw all the contents of the till on the ground before me. 'Look at these coins carefully, good Bakht,' he said, 'and tell me if you can find a false one.' I examined the heap attentively, pushing each coin lightly with my paw until I came to the counterfeit; then I withdrew the false coin from its fellows and firmly stood upon it, while I looked up at my master with little barks and wriggles of excitement.

The baker marvelled at my cleverness, crying: 'Allāh alone is great! There is no power or might save in Allāh!' As for the old woman, she could not believe the witness of her eyes and, in terror, threw down a piece of good money upon the heap and scuttled out of the shop.

My master at once called together his neighbours and all the shopkeepers of the market, and told them what had just happened. He did not fail to exaggerate a little, which was a pity, as the feat itself was astonishing enough.

At this point Shahrazād saw the approach of morning and discreetly fell silent.

But when the eight-hundred-and-sixty-fifth night had come

SHE SAID:

The crowd wondered at my intelligence, swearing that they had never come across such a dog. All produced from different places countless false coins which they showed me mingled with true currency, not because they doubted my master's word, but because they wished to have the joy of seeing with their own eyes. 'It is strange,' thought I, 'that so many honest folk should have so much spurious coin in their possession.'

Nevertheless, as I did not wish to blacken my master's face in the sight of his friends, I set to and distinguished the false money with my paw, so that my fame spread through all the markets of the city and even, thanks to the loquacity of my master's wife, into the harīms of the women. From morning to night the bakery was besieged by a curious crowd who wished to see me show my skill. I took care never to fail in the experiments, and thus the baker soon came to be more patronised than any other of his trade in the city, and hourly blessed the day of my coming. His success was bitter to the tripe-seller, who gnawed his fingers for spite, and jealously plotted against me. Sometimes he tried to have me carried away and sometimes he excited the dogs of the quarter against me; but in either case I had nothing to fear, as I was well guarded by my master from theft and, when I was abroad, I was vigorously defended from the other dogs by the numerous admirers of my small accomplishment.

Thus I lived for a long time, happy in all things save the memory that I had once been a man. It was not that I objected to being a dog through any sense of shame, but I could not help grieving that I had lost the power of speech and had to make myself understood through looks and gestures, helped out by a variety of barks. Also, when I remembered the night in the cemetery, my hairs stood up along my back and I shivered.

One day an old woman of respectable appearance came, as so many had done, to buy bread in our shop because of the rumour of my ability. Like others, also, she tested me with a false coin, and I at once selected it from a heap of true ones and held it under my paw to show that I had detected it. 'You have excelled,' she said, as she took back the money, and regarded me searchingly before paying my master for the bread. As she departed she signed to me quite clearly to follow her.

I was already sure, O Commander of the Faithful, that this old woman had reason for some more than ordinary interest in me, but from prudence I looked at her a long time at first without moving. Seeing that I did not follow her, she took some paces back and signed to me again; my curiosity was aroused and, taking advantage of my master's occupation with a batch of bread in the oven, I ran out into the street and followed my new acquaintance. As I walked behind her, I stopped from time to time, hesitating and slowly wagging my tail, but her encouraging smiles soon had me trotting along at a good pace, and I was by her side when she arrived at her house.

She opened the door and, passing through, sweetly invited me to follow her, saying: 'Come in, come in, poor friend. You will never repent that you have followed me.' So I entered the house.

The old woman led me through corridors into a small chamber, where a girl of moonlike beauty sat on a couch with her embroidery. Seeing me, she veiled herself with a quick movement, and the woman said: 'Dear daughter, I have brought you the famous dog who tells false money from true; you remember that I had my doubts of him when we heard rumours of his tricks. I have seen to-day that he can indeed perform that miracle and have brought him to you, to find out if you agree with me that he is not altogether what he seems.' 'You are quite right, dear mother,' answered the girl. 'I will prove it to you at once.'

The girl rose and, taking a copper basin filled with water, murmured over it low words which I could not hear; then she sprinkled me with a few drops, saying: 'If you were born a dog, remain a dog; but if you were born a man, shake yourself and become a man again, by virtue of this water!' Instantly I shook myself and broke the enchantment. I rose up no longer a dog, but a man upright among men.

After staring about me, I threw myself at my saviour's feet, kissing the hem of her robe, and saying: 'O child of blessing, may Allāh, by His choicest gifts, reward you for the great benefit which you have conferred upon a stranger! How can I find words for thanks, or pour down blessings upon you! I can only say that I no more belong to myself and that you have bought me for a price which far exceeds my worth. That you may know something of your new possession, I will tell you the story of my life in a few words.'

Then I gave both women a brief account of the weeks since my father's death, concealing nothing of my change of heart, my marriage, my patience with my wife, and my bitter disillusionment; but nothing would be gained by repeating it in this place.

The two women fell into violent indignation against my wife, and the elder said: 'O my son, it was a strange sin of yours to leave the excellent girls of our city and follow an unbelieving stranger. You must have been already under her witchcraft when you trusted your Destiny to one having different tongue and blood and origin. Satan, the Stoned, the Evil One, had a hand in all this, as I clearly see; but we must give thanks to Allāh that He has allowed my daughter to deliver you from that woman's evil!' I kissed her hand in answer, saying: 'O mother of benediction, I repent my rash act before Allāh and before your venerable face. I have no other wish than to enter your family, as I have entered your compassion. If you will accept me as the true husband of your noble daughter, you have but to say so.' 'I have no fault to find with the plan,' she replied. 'What do you think of it, my daughter? Does he suit you, this excellent young man whom Allāh has placed upon our way?' 'Indeed he does,' answered my preserver, 'but that is not the matter which should occupy us first. It is not enough that we have broken the enchantment; we must at once safeguard him from any further attack by that vile woman.' So saying she left us and returned in a few moments with a phial of water in her fingers. 'Sīdī Numān,' she said, as she gave it to me, 'my ancient books, which I have been consulting, tell me that your evil enemy is not at home, but that she will return presently. Before your servants she has pretended great anxiety because of your absence. While she is still away, you must return to your house and station yourself in the courtyard, so that, when she returns, she may meet you suddenly face to face. In her astonishment, she will turn to flee; it is then that you must sprinkle her with the water from this phial, crying: "Leave your human form and become a mare!" She will throw into a mare straightway, and you must jump upon her back, seizing her mane and forcing a double bit of great strength into her mouth. Then you must beat her with your whip for punishment until your arms can rise no more; and must continue every day, in Allāh's name, to school her in the same way. If by evil chance she took the upper hand of you, because you spared her, you would most grievously suffer for it.'

I agreed to the young girl's suggestion, O Commander of the

Faithful. I stationed myself in the courtyard of my house, and, when my wife would have turned her beautiful face and fled before me, I sprinkled her with the water from the phial, so that she became a mare.

Since then I have been lawfully married to the girl who saved me, and have exorcized the devil in that wicked woman every day upon the polo-ground. Such is my story, O Prince of Believers.

When the Khalīfah had heard this tale, he cried out in astonishment: 'Indeed, young man, your story is a strange one, and I must confess that the white mare has earned her punishment. But I wish you to intercede with your wife and beg her to find some way by which the mare, though still keeping her shape and being placed beyond the possibility of mischief for ever, may yet be spared that terrible treatment. If the thing be not possible, Allāh's will be done!' So saying, al-Rashīd turned to the handsome rider who had ridden so nobly at the head of the procession upon the bridge: the boy like a king's son, the boy followed by the palanquin of princesses, the boy followed by Indian and Chinese airs: and said to him. . . .

At this point Shahrazād saw the approach of morning and discreetly fell silent.

But when the eight-hundred-and-sixty-sixth night had come

LITTLE DUNYAZĀD CRIED: 'Please, please, dear sister, tell us what happened when the Khalīfah addressed the young rider behind whom Indian and Chinese airs were played!' 'With all my heart,' answered Shahrazād. And she continued:

'O young man, I judged you to be noble by your appearance, and have requested you to come before me simply in order that I may rejoice my sight and hearing. If you have any request to make or admirable story to tell, I pray you not to delay.' The young man kissed the earth between the Khalīfah's hands and then answered: 'O Commander of the Faithful, I have not come as an ambassador or deputy to Baghdād, nor have I come on any great or curious matter, but only to see again the land where I was born. But, for all that, my tale is so astonishing that I will not keep you for a moment longer in ignorance of it.'

And he said:

The Youth Behind Whom Indian and Chinese Airs were Played

KNOW then, O my master and crown upon my head, that I used to be a woodcutter, like my father and grandfather before me, and that I was certainly the poorest woodcutter in all Baghdād. My miseries were great and they were increased daily by the presence of my wife, a peevish, greedy and quarrelsome woman, with an empty eye and devilish disposition. There was nothing to be said in her favour; our kitchen broom was tenderer and more beautiful than she, but she was more tenacious than a horsefly and made more noise than a frightened hen. After interminable wrangles and disputes, I decided that the only way by which I could secure a little rest after my hard days was to give way to each caprice of hers and say no word. Thus, whenever the Giver rewarded my work with a few silver dirhams, the vile wretch met me on the doorstep and took possession of them all. Such was my life, O Commander of the Faithful.

One day, as I had need to buy a new rope to tie my faggots, because the old one had all ravelled out, I decided to tell my wife of this necessity, though I greatly dreaded the thought of speaking to her. Hardly had the words 'buy' and 'rope' come trembling from my mouth, when I supposed that Allāh had emptied all the tempests of His sky upon my head. An hour passed in a storm of reproof and recrimination with which I shall not weary the royal ears. At the end of it, she said: 'I know you, you foul rascal! You want to spend the money among the Baghdād whores, but I have an eye on you, I will come out with you and you can buy your rope in my presence if you want it.' So saying, she dragged me to the market and bought the rope herself, but Allāh knows that it did not change hands without another good hour of haggling, grimacing and vituperation.

Yet that was only the beginning, my lord. When we had left the market, I would have taken leave of my wife and gone to my work, but she cried: 'So that is it, is it? Very well, I am with you now and I shall not leave you.' Without more ado she climbed upon my ass, and said again: 'I shall certainly come to this precious mountain where you pretend to work; it will do you good to have my eye on you.'

Hearing this, I saw the whole world darken before my face and understood that nothing but death was left for me. 'O poor man,' I said to myself, 'now she will snatch away the last minute of peace which Allāh gives to you. At least you used to have calm in the forest, but now all that is over. There is no power or might save in Allāh, the Compassionate! From Him we come and to Him we return at last! And it is high time for me to return.' With that I made up my mind to throw myself flat on my belly, when we came to the forest, and stay thus until black death should take me.

I made no answer but walked along behind the poor ass, who now bore that great weight which had for so long stifled my soul.

Yet a man's life is dear to him and, as I trudged behind the woman, I hit upon a plan to save myself from death and better my condition generally.

When we came to the foot of the mountain and my wife had descended from the ass's back, I said to her: 'O wife, I must confess, since there is no way of deceiving you, that I did not need that rope for my work, but for an enterprise which will make us rich for ever.' While she trembled in indignation and surprise, I led her to the mouth of an old well, which had been dry for many years, and said further to her: 'This well contains our Destiny and, by means of the rope, I intend to set my hand upon it. I have known for a long time that there is a hidden treasure down below there, written in my name, and that it is on this day and no other that I must descend to take possession of it. That, dear wife, is why I begged you to buy the rope.'

When I made use of the word 'treasure,' that which I had planned came speedily to pass, for my wife cried: 'As Allāh lives, not you but I will go down into the well. You would never know how to open the treasure and bring it forth; also, I do not altogether trust your honesty.' She threw aside her veil and cried again: 'Fasten me to the rope quickly and let me down at once.' I made certain difficulties for form's sake, my lord, and then, in answer to her shrill oaths, sighed out: 'Allāh's will and your will be done, O daughter of excellent parents!' I passed the rope under her arms and tied her securely, then I let her slip gently down the whole depth of the well. But, when I felt that she had reached the bottom, I threw the rope down after her. The sigh of satisfaction which I breathed at that moment was the purest and deepest since I had left my mother's breast. Leaning over the rim of the well, I cried: 'O daughter of excellent parents, be kind enough to stay where you are until I come to fetch you.' Then I turned to my labours singing, and all that day, as I cut and stacked wood, I moved about the mountain as if on wings.

Having left the cause of all my troubles in the well, I enjoyed thenceforward the savour of perfect peace. But at the end of two days I said within my soul: 'O Ahmad, the law of Allāh and His Prophet (upon whom be prayer and peace) forbids one of His creatures to take away the life of another, and there is a chance that, if you leave your wife any longer in the well, she may perish of starvation. It is true that such a creature merits the worst of punishments, but you would not like to have her death upon your conscience. Draw her up, therefore, from the well and trust that the experience may have made her a better woman.' I bought a second rope and, going to the well, lowered it over the side, crying: 'Fasten yourself quickly, and I will pull you up. I trust that this will have been a lesson to you!' I felt the rope seized and, after giving my wife time to fasten herself securely, hoisted up the great weight with much grunting and sweating. But judge of my extreme terror, O Commander of the Faithful, when I found at the end of the rope, not my wife, whom I would have almost welcomed, but a gigantic Jinnī of repulsive aspect!

At this point Shahrazād saw the approach of morning and discreetly fell silent.

But when the eight-hundred-and-sixty-seventh night had come

SHE SAID:

Yet, as soon as the giant leapt safely to earth, he bowed before me, saying: 'I have countless thanks to give you, O Sīdī Ahmad, for the great service which you have rendered me. I am one of those Jinn who cannot fly, though I can travel along the ground as quickly as my brothers who have wings. Being a Jinnī of earth, I have lived for many years in that old well. My existence there was in every way quiet and suitable until the most wicked woman in the world came down to me two days ago. Not only has she abused me and tormented me ever since, but she has obliged me to work in her with scarce a pause for breath, though I am a bachelor, an anchorite among the Jinn. Also, I had almost forgotten how to do it. As Allāh lives, I have much, very much for which to thank you, and I will not rest content until I have paid you.'

He paused for a moment to regain his breath, while I, quite re-assured by what he had said, murmured to myself: 'Surely this woman is something horrible if she can frighten a giant and a Jinnī! It is astonishing that I, a simple human, could have borne with her so long.' I looked with great commiseration at the enormous Ifrīt and listened carefully, as he continued: 'O Sīdī Ahmad, you are a woodcutter now, but I shall make you equal to the greatest kings. Listen carefully: the Sultān of India has a little daughter, a girl as fair as the moon upon her fourteenth night. She is fourteen years and three months old; she is just ripe, and as virgin as a pearl within its shell. My project is to force her father, who loves her more than life, to give you her hand in marriage. I intend to journey swiftly from this place to his palace in India, to enter the body of his daughter and, for the time being, to take possession of her soul! Thus she will seem mad to all who know her, and the Sultān will try to get her cured by the greatest doctors of his kingdom. But none of them will know the real cause of her trouble, and my breath shall blow away their efforts on her behalf. Then shall you come and cure the girl yourself. It will be easy.' So saying, the Jinnī drew some leaves of an unknown tree from his breast and gave them to me, as he continued: 'When you come into the child's presence, you must examine her as if her disease were quite unknown to you, you must mutter, you must put your finger to your brow, and at last, having dipped one of these leaves in water, you must rub your patient's face with it. By the potency of the leaf, I shall be obliged to leave her body, and immediately she will recover her reason. Seeing the cure complete, the Sultān will sanction your marriage as a reward, and all will be well. That, O Ahmad, is the return which I intend to make you for the marvellous deliverance which you brought to me. Alas, alas, I had thought to end my days in that good well; but now the place is utterly impossible. May Allāh curse all foul calamitous women!'

The Jinnī took leave of me, after begging me to set out for India at once, and disappeared from my sight, racing across the surface of the earth as if he had been a ship driven before a tempest.

Knowing that my Destiny waited for me in India, I set out at once for that far country and came, after long days of danger, weariness and privation, which it would be useless to detail to our master, to the capital city where dwelt the Sultān whose daughter was to be my wife.

I learned that the princess had already been mad for some little time, that her illness had thrown the court and all the kingdom into a great consternation, and that, after exhausting the science of his greatest doctors, the Sultān had offered his daughter in marriage to whomsoever should cure her.

Confident of the result and strong in the instructions which the Jinnī had given me, I told my business to the King and soon found myself in the princess's chamber. I put on learned airs and made a serious consideration of the case until all those who were present began to have faith in me; then I moistened one of the leaves and rubbed the face of my patient with it.

At once the child was taken by a convulsion and, with a piercing cry, fell fainting to the floor. This condition was caused by the impetuous going forth of the Jinnī, and did not frighten me at all. I sprinkled the girl's face with rose-water, and, when she came to herself, she recognised those who surrounded her, called them each by name, and spoke wisely and sanely with them. A wave of joy swept from the palace and went about the city. The Sultān kept his promise to me, and my marriage was celebrated with great pomp on the very day of the cure. That was how I won the daughter of the King of India for my bride. As for the daughter of the King of China, who was seated on the left side of the double palanquin, I will tell you of her wooing now, my lord.

When the giant Ifrīt had left the body of the Indian princess, he looked about for a new abode, as he could not return to the dry well because of my wife's calamitous presence there. During his recent incarnation he had found the body of a young girl much to his taste, so, after reflecting for a short time, he set out across the earth to China as swiftly as a great ship ridden by the storm.

The Sultān of China's daughter was as beautiful as the moon upon her fourteenth night; she was fourteen years and three months old, and as virgin as a pearl in its shell. When the Jinnī entered into possession of her, she gave herself up to a series of wild contortions and incoherent words, which made all who were about her think that she was mad. The unhappy Sultān called all the most learned Chinese doctors to her; but they could not succeed in curing her. Therefore he despaired, until news came to him of the miracle which I had performed on the princess of India. At once he sent an ambassador to my father-in-law, begging me to come to China to undertake the care of his daughter, and promising me her hand in marriage in case of success.

When I heard of this proposition, I talked it over with my wife, and at length persuaded her that she would enjoy having the Chinese princess as a sister and fellow-bride. Then I departed for China.

Now all which I have told you, O Commander of the Faithful, of the possession of the Chinese princess, I only learned later from the lips of the Jinnī himself. I came to her father's court without the least knowledge of her disease, and placing all my trust in such a leaf as I had used before. Picture, then, my astonishment on being addressed in the Ifrīt's deep voice, speaking through the mouth of the princess, as soon as I was left alone with her. 'Is it you, O Sīdī Ahmad?' asked the voice. 'Is it my friend, whom I have loaded with my benefits, who comes thus to banish me from the dwelling of my election, the home of my old age? Are you not ashamed so to return evil for good? If you cast me forth, are you not afraid that I will go straight to India and attempt several extreme copulations upon the person of your wife, so that she die?'

This threat threw me into a panic, and the Ifrīt took advantage of my state to tell me the story of his house hunting and beg me to leave him in peace.

Deeply sensible that the good fellow had been the cause of all my fortune, I was about to depart from the girl's presence and go to inform the King of China that I could not undertake her cure, when a breath of inspiration descended upon me, and I said: 'O Chief and crown of the Jinn, O excellent, you entirely misunderstand my presence here. I have not come with any intention of curing the princess of China, but have only made this long journey to ask you to help me in a certain matter. Doubtless you recall that woman with whom you passed two rather unpleasant days in the dry well? That woman was my wife, my uncle's daughter; I myself threw her into the well in order to have peace. But calamity ever pursues me, and some unknown fool has pulled the bitch up and set her at liberty. Now that she is free, she follows hard upon my trail; she follows me everywhere, and alas, alas! she is close to me at this moment, very close. Even now I hear the crying of her vile voice in the courtyard of this palace. For pity's sake, good friend, help me, protect me!'

At this point Shahrazād saw the approach of morning and discreetly fell silent.

But when the eight-hundred-and-sixty-eighth night had come

SHE SAID:

When the Jinnī heard this, he was shaken with terror, and cried: 'My help, my protection, is it? Allāh grant I never come within a mile of such a woman again! Poor Ahmad, you must get out of this trouble as best you can, for I am off!' He left the body of the princess with a great heave, and sped away from that palace, annihilating distance under his feet, as if he had been a great ship ridden by the tempest. The Chinese princess returned immediately to perfect sanity, and became my second wife. Since that time I have lived in all delight with those two royal girls. A time came, however, when I knew that I should soon become Sultān of either India or China, and would then be able to voyage no more; so I undertook this journey, to revisit the place of my birth, Baghdād, the City of Peace, where I had toiled as a woodcutter.

That, O Commander of the Faithful, is how you came to meet me on the stone bridge, with my two wives behind me, and followed by the playing of Indian and Chinese airs.

Such is my story. But Allāh knows all!

When the Khalīfah heard the noble rider's tale, he rose in his honour and made him sit beside him on the bed of the throne. He congratulated him on having been chosen by Allāh to become heir to the kingdoms of India and China, and added: 'May He seal our friendship and guard you in the enjoyment of your future royalty!'

Then al-Rashīd turned to the generous and venerable sheikh, and said: 'O sheikh, I passed you yesterday on the bridge of Baghdād, and the sight of your modest generosity gave me a desire to know you. I am sure that the ways in which it has pleased Allāh to enrich you must have been unusual ways, and I yearn to hear of them from your own lips. Speak, I pray you, with all sincerity, and rest assured that you are covered with the kerchief of my protection, whatever you may have to say.'

The generous sheikh kissed the earth between the Khalīfah's hands, and said: 'O Prince of Believers, I will give you a faithful account of all which merits telling in my life. If my tale is astonishing, the power and munificence of Allāh are more astonishing!'

And he told the following story:

The Generous Sheikh

LORD of all good, I have been a rope-maker all my life, specialising in hemp, as my father and my grandfather did before me. My takings were hardly enough to feed my wife and children, but, as I had no capacity for another profession, I was content and did not murmur against the gifts of Allāh; nor did I attribute my poverty to anything except my own ignorance and dullness. In this I was right. I confess it, in all humility, before the Master of Intelligence. Intelligence has never been one of the gifts of rope-makers, specialising in hemp, and she has never chosen her dwelling beneath the turbans of those who specialise in hemp and are rope-makers. I tell you this that you may understand how I continued to eat the bread of Allāh without bothering my head with wishes for wealth, which in my case would have been as unlikely of fulfilment as the wish to make one jump from here to the top of Kāf.

One day, as I sat in my shop shaping a hemp rope which was fastened to my heel, I saw two rich dwellers in our quarter coming towards me. This was no unusual thing, for it was their custom to sit down upon the low front of my shop and chat of this and that in the cool air of evening. They were great friends, and it delighted them to discuss all things in heaven and earth while they told their amber beads. Yet never in all their discussions did either of them utter a loud word or depart in any way from those rules of conversation which are binding between true friends. When one spoke the other listened, and when the other began to speak the first fell silent. Thus their discourse was always clear and methodical, so that even a dull-witted person like myself could take profit from listening to it.

That day, when the three of us had greeted each other, the two friends sat down in their usual place and continued an argument which had already arisen upon their walk. The one, whose name was Saad, spoke to the other, whose name was Saadī: 'My friend, I do not say this for the sake of contradiction, but I must still contend that a man cannot be happy in this world unless he has great enough riches to live in absolute independence. The poor are only poor because they are born to poverty from father to son, or because they have lost riches through prodigality, through a bad bargain, or through one of those fatalities against which no human may avail. In all cases, O Saadī, I hold that the poor only remain poor because they can never collect a first small sum of idle money with which to lay the foundations of a fortune. And I contend that, if a poor man were to be enriched by finding such a capital, it would be quite possible for him to become really wealthy with the years.'

'Good Saad,' answered Saadī, 'I have no wish to contradict you, and, by Allāh, it grieves me not to share your opinion. Also, I must admit that it is usually better to live at ease than in poverty. But riches by themselves hold no temptation for an unambitious soul; they have but one use, that we may be generous to our neighbours, and the inconveniences attaching to them are a thousand. Surely the cares of our daily lives have taught us both that? Is not the existence of our friend Hasan, the rope-maker here, on the whole preferable to ours? The way by which you propose that a poor man should become rich, O Saad, does not seem so sure to me as it does to you, for it must be itself uncertain when it depends upon a host of uncertain chances. For my part, I believe that a poor man who is entirely destitute has as much chance of becoming rich as a poor man who puts aside a little; he may become fabulously wealthy in the night, without taking a single thought to that end, if such is written in his Destiny. I find economy a useless thing; I consider it ignoble and showing little faith in Allāh to behave as though He will one day forsake us. The surplus of rich man and poor alike should be given away for the relief of suffering. I myself never wake in the morning without saying: "Rejoice, O Saadī, for to-day's provision is in the hands of God!" In all my life I have never worked or taken thought for the morrow, and my faith has never been disappointed. That is my opinion.'

'O Saadī,' answered the excellent Saad, 'I see very well that neither of us will convince the other without proof. Therefore, I propose to find out some really poor but honest man, and place a small capital in his hand. The fortune of his life in the months following shall prove which of us is right: you, who leave all to Destiny, or I, who think that a man should build his own house.'

'Let it be so, my friend,' replied Saadī, 'but where will you find a better poor and honest man than our friend Hasan? He fulfils all the conditions of your test, and your generosity could have no worthier object.'

'As Allāh lives, you are right!' cried Saad. 'If I had remembered Hasan, I should never have thought of searching further.'

At this point Shahrazād saw the approach of morning and discreetly fell silent.

But when the eight-hundred-and-sixty-ninth night had come

SHE SAID:

Then Saad, who believed in the power of a small capital, turned to me, saying: 'O Hasan, I know that you have a numerous family, with mouths and teeth of their own, and that none of the children whom Allāh has given you is yet of an age to help you in the least; also I know that even such cheap raw material as hemp cannot be bought when the profits of a business are less than the expenses. Therefore take these two hundred golden dīnārs and use them for the enlarging of your trade. . . . Tell me, do you think that with this money you will be able to quicken your resources and set your life upon a wide and profitable basis?'

And I, O Commander of the Faithful, answered in this wise: 'Allāh will prolong your life and reward your generosity a hundred-fold, my master! Since you have deigned to question me, I dare assert that seed falls upon fruitful ground in my domain, and that with even a less sum I could become, first as rich as any of the chief rope-makers in my guild, and then, with Allāh's favour, richer than all the rope-makers in Baghdād put together.'

Saad was satisfied with this answer, and handed me a purse from his bosom, saying: 'You inspire me with great confidence, O Hasan. I trust that this purse may be the germ of mighty riches! Rest assured that both my friend and I will rejoice to learn that you have found a happiness in prosperity.'

My joy was so great, when I felt the coins actually between my fingers, that words failed me and I could only bow low before my benefactor and kiss the border of his robe. He bade me a kind and hasty farewell, and drew Saadī modestly away from the shop, so that they might continue their interrupted walk.

When they had departed, I cudgelled my brains for some place where I could hide the money, for my poor little house had one room only, and that contained neither cupboard, drawer, nor chest. At first I thought of burying the purse in the waste land outside the city, until I could find a way of employing my fortune; but then I considered that the hiding-place might be found by chance or that I might be overlooked by some workman. At last I decided to hide the purse in the folds of my turban; I shut the shop door and, after unrolling my headgear and removing ten dīnārs from the purse for current expenses, secured my treasure by folding the inner end of the turban about it and winding the four folds carefully again over my bonnet.

Breathing more freely, I opened my shop once more and hastened to the market, where I bought a modest quantity of hemp to last me for the next few days. I carried this back to my shop and then, as meat had long been a stranger to my house, bought a shoulder of lamb from the butcher. Finally, I directed my steps towards home again, dreaming of the tomato sauce which my wife would make, and of my children's ecstasy.

But my presumption was too great to pass unpunished: as I walked along, lost in a dream of opulence, with the shoulder of lamb balanced on my head, a famished hawk dropped from the sky upon the meat and, before I even knew what was happening, flew off with the shoulder in its beak and my turban in its claws.

My cries were so sorrowful that men, women and children ran to help me, but their concerted shouting, instead of making the bird drop its prize, hastened its flight, and soon it had disappeared, with all my prosperity, into the deeps of the air.

Sorrowfully I bought another turban, which made a new hole in the ten dīnārs I had saved, and, even as I put it on, my heart was darkened at the thought of the disappointment of my benefactor. For the time being, thanks to the remains of the ten dīnārs, we had no reason of complaint in my poor house; but, when the last small change had gone, we fell back into the same state of hopeless misery as before. Yet I guarded myself from murmuring against the decrees of Allāh, and would often say: 'He has given in His time and He has taken away in His time. Be it as Allāh wills!' I had however two further griefs: I had foolishly told my wife of the affair and she mourned bitterly for the lost fortune, and I had yet more foolishly told the neighbours, who frankly did not believe me but taught their children to cry as I passed: 'There goes the man who lost his head with his turban!'

Ten months after the swooping of the hawk, the two friends, Saad and Saadī, came to me to ask news of the money. As they approached, Saad said: 'I have been thinking of our friend for some time and I am delighted to think that we shall soon be witnesses of his prosperity. I am bound that you will find a great change.' 'It seems to me, my friend,' answered Saadī with a smile, 'that you are eating your cucumber before it is ripe. I can see Hasan still sitting in his shop with the hemp fastened to his heel, but as for any great change, that I do not see. His clothes are the same, except that his turban is a little less filthy and disgusting than it was ten months ago. Look for yourself, O Saad.'

By this time Saad was in front of my shop; he took stock of my appearance, and then said: 'Well, Hasan, why are you looking so down in the mouth? Business worries, I suppose, and the cares of opulence?' 'O my masters,' I answered with lowered eyes, 'may Allāh prolong the lives of both of you! Destiny is my eternal foe and I am in worse trouble now than I was before. The confidence which you placed in me, O Saad, has been most vilely betrayed, rather by the hand of Fate than by your slave.' Then, O Commander of the Faithful, I told them of my adventure with the hawk in all its details, but it would be useless to repeat it in this place.

When I had finished my recital, I saw Saadī smile maliciously.at the disappointed Saad. There was a moment of silence, and then my benefactor said: 'Indeed the experiment has not succeeded as well as I hoped. But I am not going to reproach you, although there is something strange about the tale of the hawk, and I might well have the right to suspect you of spending my two hundred dīnārs in debauch. Be that as it may, I wish to make a second attempt with you; for it would not be right to let my friend Saadī think that he had established his case by the one trial.'

So saying, he counted over a further two hundred dīnārs to me, and continued: 'I trust that you will not hide this in your turban.' As I was already lifting his hands to my lips, he withdrew from me and hastened off with his friend.

At this point Shahrazād saw the approach of morning and discreetly fell silent.

But when the eight-hundred-and-seventieth night had come

SHE SAID:

Instead of going on with my work after they had gone, I shut the shop and withdrew with my money into the back of my house, knowing that at that hour my wife and children would be absent. I set aside ten dīnārs and knotted the rest in a cloth which, after long consideration, I hid in the bottom of a large jar filled with bran. Replacing the jar in its corner, I prepared to depart. On the threshold I met my wife who was returning to cook the evening meal, and told her that I was going out to buy a fresh supply of hemp.

While I was at the market, a man passed along our street, hawking parcels of that earth with which women wash their hair at the hammām. My wife had not washed her hair for a long time. She called the man to her and, finding that she had not money with which to pay him, arranged to exchange our jar of bran for a quantity of his earth. When I returned at supper time, I stacked my hemp in a small loft which I had made near the ceiling of our room, and then strolled carelessly towards the place where I had left the jar, in order to see that it was quite safe. When I could not find it, I cried to my wife to know if she had moved it, and she answered me calmly with an account of the exchange which she had made. Red death entered my soul and I dropped to the ground, crying: 'Far be the Stoned One, O wife! You have exchanged my Destiny and your Destiny and the Destinies of our children for a little earth with which to wash your hair. This time we are lost past remedy!' In a few words I told her of my hiding of the money, and at once she began to scream and beat her breast and tear her hair. 'Woe, woe, through fault of mine!' she cried. 'I have sold the children's Destiny to a hawker and I do not know him. It is the first time he has passed this way and I shall never be able to find him again.' Then she began to reproach me with my lack of confidence in her, saying that the misfortune could not have happened if I had let her share my secret. O Commander of the Faithful, you know how eloquent a woman can be in times of trouble; I need not repeat to you the whole book of words which grief lent to my poor wife. In an endeavour to calm her, I cried: 'Be a little quieter, for pity's sake! We do not want to attract the attention of the neighbours. They have had enough amusement out of the story of the hawk; if they hear the story of the bran jar also, we shall have to move from this quarter. Let us rather thank Allāh that He has allowed us to keep ten dīnārs out of each of the lost sums. We are poor, it is true; but what are the rich? They breathe the same air, they rejoice in the same sky and the light as we; they die at the appointed time, as we do.' Very gradually, my lord, I managed to convince not only my wife but myself and, in a few days, I was working as blithely as if I had never in my life heard of hawks or bran jars.

Only one thing caused me anxiety: the grave disappointment which my benefactor would feel when he came to ask the use to which I had put his capital. He left me longer than before, but the dread day came at last. The two friends approached my shop, and I could almost hear Saad saying: 'I have left the good Hasan for a long time, now we shall see the full flower of his riches.' I could almost hear Saadī answering, with his wicked smile: 'As Allāh lives, I fear that we shall have to leave him until after we are dead, to find him wealthy. . . . But here we are, and there is Hasan ready with his fable.'

I was so confused at their coming that I wished nothing better than for the earth to open and swallow me up; though they stood before my shop, I pretended not to see them and went on diligently with my work. But when they greeted me I was obliged to greet them in return. I made one mouthful of the distressing news and told Saad of the bran jar. Then, with lowered eyes, I resumed my place on the floor of the shop and went on with my twisting. 'I have got the business over,' I said to myself. 'The rest is with Allāh.'

Instead of being angry or cursing me, instead of showing his chagrin at the disproof of his theory, Saad contented himself with saying: 'After all, Hasan, your tale is just possibly true, though it is a little strange that the hawk and the hawker should both have been so aptly at hand, and that you should have been so conveniently absent first in mind and then in body. Be that as it may, I do not think that I will make any more experiments.' But he said earnestly to Saadī: 'I still think that nothing is possible to a poor man without an initial capital.'

'You are quite wrong, O generous Saad,' answered Saadī. 'You have thrown away four hundred dīnārs, half to a hawk and half to a hawker, to prove your contention. I am not so prodigal, yet I am ready to risk a little to prove that a poor man is the sport of Destiny and nothing more.' He picked up an old plummet of lead from the dust, and showed it to me, saying: 'O Hasan, though fortune has not favoured you so far, I wish to help you, as my generous friend has helped you; but Allāh has not made me as rich as he, and I can only give you this piece of lead which some fisherman seems to have lost as he dragged his nets along the road.'

Saad burst out laughing; but Saadī took no notice of him and gravely held out the lead to me, saying: 'Take it, and let Saad laugh. If such be the decree of Destiny, a day will come when this fragment of lead shall be more useful to you than all the silver of the mines.'

Knowing that Saadī was both wise and kind, I took care not to be offended; instead I accepted the lead and fastened it carefully in my empty money belt. Then I thanked both men for their great kindness and watched them depart upon their walk before returning to my labour.

When evening came, I went back to my house and, after supping, betook myself to bed. As I undressed, something fell heavily to the floor; when I picked it up and found that it was the lump of lead, I set it aside in the first place that came to hand, deeming it of no importance. Then I fell into a heavy sleep.

At this point Shahrazād saw the approach of morning and discreetly fell silent.

But when the eight-hundred-and-seventy-first night had come

SHE SAID:

An hour or so after midnight, a fisherman, who lived near us, rose up, as was his custom, and began to inspect his nets before going down to the river. At once he noticed that a leaden weight was missing from the one place where its absence would gravely interfere with his fishing. As he had nothing with which to replace it and as all the shops were shut, he was thrown into a state of great perplexity, for he imagined that, if he were not at the waterside by two hours before sun-up, he would not make his expenses for the day. After consideration, he decided to send his wife to wake up the nearest neighbours, in spite of the hour, and ask them if they had such a thing as a piece of lead in their houses.

As our house was nearest, the woman knocked first at our door, though doubtless she said to herself: 'Nothing is to be gained by asking even for lead from a man who has nothing at all.' Her knocking woke me, and I cried out: 'Who is there?' 'I am the wife of your neighbour, the fisherman,' she answered. 'O Hasan, my face is blackened to disturb you in this fashion, but my children's bread-winner is concerned in the matter and I have therefore to constrain myself to this incivility. Pardon me, I pray, and tell me speedily whether you have a piece of lead in the house which you can lend my husband for his net!'

At once I recalled the excellent Saadī's gift. 'What better use could I make of it than to help a neighbour,' I said to myself, 'especially one who is a father of children?' I told the woman that I had exactly what her husband needed and, after groping until I found the lead, woke my wife that she might take it down to the door.

The poor woman rejoiced, and said to my wife: 'Dear neighbour, the sheikh Hasan has rendered us a great service this night and, in return, my husband will make his first cast to-morrow in your husband's name and bring you any fish that he may take with that cast.' She ran with the lead to her husband, who mended his net and departed for the fishing two hours before sun-up.

His first cast brought to shore one fish only, but it was more than a cubit long and broad in proportion. Though all the fish which he caught during the rest of the day were much smaller, the good man set aside the great fish and, before selling his catch in the market next morning, was careful to bed it in sweet herbs and bring it to our house, saying: 'May Allāh make it delightful for you! Although this gift is not sufficient, I pray you to accept it with a good heart, for it came to your chance, O neighbour.' 'I am afraid you have much the worse of the bargain,' I answered. 'Never has so fine a fish been sold for a lump of lead not worth a copper coin! But we accept the present in the spirit in which it is given, and thank you kindly for it.' After a few more civilities of this sort, the good man departed.

I handed my wife the fish, saying: 'You see, Saadī was quite right: a lump of lead can be as useful as all the gold of the Sūdān if Allāh wills. I am sure no king has eaten such a fish.' My wife rejoiced also, but asked: 'How am I going to cook it? We have no grill and none of our pans are large enough to take it.' 'It will eat just as well in pieces,' I answered. 'Take no thought for its outside appearance, but cut it up straightway and give us a stew.' My wife at once split the fish down the belly and took out the guts, but lo! in the middle of that mess something burned with a strange light. She drew it forth, washed it in the bucket, and held it out, so that I could see a round of glass as large as a pigeon's egg and as clear as rock water. When we had looked at it some time, we gave it to our children to play with, so that they should not bother their mother during her cooking.

At supper time that night, my wife saw that the room was well illuminated, although she had not yet lit the oil lamp. Looking about for the source of the light, she saw that it proceeded from the glass ball which the children had left on the floor. She picked it up and set it on the corner of the shelf instead of the lamp, and I cried in amazement: 'As Allāh lives, dear wife, Saadī's lead has saved us expense, not only in victual, but in oil.'

By the mysterious light of the glass egg we ate the delectable fish, chatting together of the day's events and giving praise to Allāh. That night we lay down to sleep in eminent satisfaction.

Before noon on the next day, the story of our discovery had spread through the quarter, thanks to my wife's long tongue. Soon that indiscreet woman received a visit from a certain Jewess among our neighbours, whose husband had a shop in the jeweller's market. After she had greeted my wife and looked long at the glass object, the woman said: 'You should thank Allāh, dear neighbour, that He has led me to you to-day, for that fragment of glass pleases me and, as I have a similar one and wish to make a pair, I am ready to buy the trifle for the enormous sum of ten dīnārs in new gold.' But, when the children heard tell of selling their plaything, they began to cry; so their mother, to appease them, and because the thing served her in place of a lamp, refused the tempting offer and sent the Jewess away in a bad temper.

When I returned home and was told what had happened, I said: 'If the thing had no value, a daughter of the Jews would not offer good money for it. I am certain that she will return and promise even more. Yet, if you take my advice, you will not sell without consulting me.' This I said, because I remembered Saadī's assurance that the lead would make me rich if my Destiny so willed.

Sure enough, the Jewess returned the same evening and, after greeting, said to my wife: 'Dear neighbour, how can you so despise the gifts of Allāh? Surely you do despise them when you refuse to sell a worthless fragment of glass! I have spoken to my husband about the thing and, because I am with child and the wishes of a pregnant woman should not be thwarted, he has given me leave to offer you twenty gold dīnārs for an object not worth a copper piece.'

Remembering my instruction, my wife replied: 'You make me ashamed to seem to hesitate but I have not the word in this house; my husband is the master. You must wait until he returns and then make your offer to him.'

As soon as I entered the house, the Jewess made the same offer to me, adding: 'I bring you much bread for your children in return for the glass trifle; but a pregnant woman's wish must be satisfied, and my husband does not care to have the thwarting of one such on his conscience. That is why he allows me to give so much gold.'

As I had given the woman her full say, I took my own time in answering, and after a minute or so, simply shook my head with no word spoken.

This daughter of the Jews became very yellow in the face and look at me with bitter eyes, saying: 'Pray for the Prophet, O Mussulmān!' 'Prayer and peace and the blessing of the One God be upon him, O unbeliever!' I answered. 'Why then this shaking of the head,' she asked, 'when Allāh has sent me with a fortune to your house?' 'The ways of Allāh are incalculable, O daughter of darkness,' I replied. 'We of the Faith can glorify Him without asking infidels to help us.' 'You refuse then?' she cried; but I only shook my head again. 'Will you be satisfied with fifty?' she asked; but I looked into a far corner and went on shaking my head.

At this point Shahrazād saw the approach of morning and discreetly fell silent.

But when the eight-hundred-and-seventy-second night had come

SHE SAID:

The woman gathered her veils about her and moved towards the door. Upon the threshold she turned, saying: 'A hundred is my last word, and, even so, I do not know what my husband will say.'

Then I condescended to answer her, though with an air of profound detachment. 'I would not see you go away in an ill-humour,' I said. 'Therefore, knowing full well the value of this thing and simply to oblige a neighbour, I will name you the only price at which I will sell: a hundred thousand dīnārs. Other jewellers, who understand these things better than your husband, would give me more; but I have never been a greedy man, and I swear before Allāh that I will not raise my price.'

When she heard and understood my words, the Jewess could only say: 'Buying and selling is not my duty; it is the business of my husband. If your price suits him, he will come and tell you so. In the meantime, will you promise not to sell to anyone else, until he has had a chance to see this miserable thing?' 'That I promise faithfully,' I answered, and the woman hurried away.

After that interview, I became certain that the egg was some marvellous gem of the sea, fallen from the crown of a marine king. I had often heard that mighty treasures lay in the depth of ocean, a plaything for mermaids, and this discovery in the fish only strengthened my belief in what I had been told. I glorified Allāh for His goodness to me and, at the same time, a little repented that I had been so hasty in fixing a price. Yet, as I had passed my word, I determined to abide by it.

As I had foreseen, the Jewish jeweller soon presented himself in person at our door. He wore an air of sinister cunning which warned me that he would try every trick known to the swine of his people in order to filch my Destiny from me. Thoroughly on my guard, I greeted him with a pleasant smile and a feigned air of stupidity. When he had taken his place on the mat and returned my greeting, he said: 'I hope, good neighbour, that the price of hemp is keeping low these days, and that business is none so bad?' 'Thanks to Allāh,' I answered, 'I have little of which to complain. I trust that things go well among the jewellers?' 'By the life of Abraham and Jacob, the trade is ruined, absolutely ruined!' he moaned. 'I can hardly scrape together enough money to buy bread and cheese for my family.' We went on chatting in this way, without coming to the point, until I had worn out the Jew's patience, and he said suddenly: 'My wife has been talking to me about a glass egg, or some such thing, of no value, as I gather, which you have given your children as a toy. Now the poor girl is pregnant and has the usual strange desires of her condition. Though there is no logic in such things, we have unfortunately to accept them. If a woman with child is thwarted in her wish, it sometimes happens that the thing desired marks and mars the unborn child. I am afraid that, if my wife does not obtain this silly glass egg, its form may be reproduced life-size upon our child's nose, or even upon a more delicate part which decency forbids me to mention. Show me the egg then, good neighbour, and, if I find that I cannot duplicate it in the market, I will willingly pay you a nominal sum for its possession. I am sure that I can rely upon you not to make a profit out of my wife's delicate condition.'

I rose and went to my children who were playing with their glass toy in the courtyard; they wept and protested when I took it from them, but I paid no heed. When I returned to the room where the Jew was sitting, I shut the door and windows, by his leave, that the place should be plunged in darkness, and then set the egg before him on a stool.

At once the room was lighted as if forty torches had been fired in it, and the Jew could not help crying: 'It is one of the gems of Sulai-mān, one of the jewels of his crown!' Then he realised that he had said too much, and added: 'Many such have passed through my hands. I have always sold them at a loss, as there is no great demand for the things. It is most inconvenient that my wife's desire should be fixed upon a thing which has no market value. How much will you take for this sea pebble, my friend?' 'It is not for sale, good neighbour,' I answered. 'I am willing to give it you, so that your wife shall not be thwarted to her hurt, and I have already named the price to her. Allāh is my witness that I will not raise it.' 'Be reasonable, be reasonable, O son of excellent parents!' cried the Jew. 'Would you ruin me? If I sold my shop and my house and myself and my wife and my children, I could not raise a tenth of the sum which you jestingly mentioned to my wife. A hundred thousand dīnārs, a hundred thousand dīnārs! It is my death that you are asking, neither more nor less!' As I was opening the doors and the windows, I answered calmly: 'A hundred thousand dīnārs; take it or leave it. If I had known that this marvellous jewel had belonged to Sulaimān (upon whom be prayer and peace!) I would have asked ten times as much and have compelled you to throw in a quantity of jewellery for my clever wife, whose gossip has been responsible for the sale. You should think yourself lucky that I am ready to abide by the ridiculously small price which I fixed in the beginning. Go and get your gold, O man.'

The Jew gave me a bitter look, and then said with a vast sigh: 'The money is at the door, give me the jewel!' So saying, he put his head out of the window and cried to a black slave, who stood at the door beside a mule charged with a quantity of bursting sacks.

The slave climbed up into my house with the sacks, and the Jew, slitting them open, weighed me out an exact hundred thousand dīnārs. My wife tumbled all our possessions out of the one great chest in which we kept them and, with my help, packed away the gold. Not till then did I hand the jewel to the Jew, saying: 'May you sell it at ten times the price!' He grinned from ear to ear as he answered: 'There is no question of selling the thing, O sheikh! My wife desires the bauble, that is all.' With that he departed. So much for him.

At this point Shahrazād saw the approach of morning and discreetly fell silent.

But when the eight-hundred-and-seventy-third night had come

SHE SAID:

Finding myself thus grown fabulously rich in a single day, I did not forget that I had been a poor rope-maker and the son of a rope-maker. I thanked Allāh for His blessing and was at first minded to seek out the excellent Saadī and tell him of the fortune which his gift had brought me. Then, because I was shy and because I did not know where he lived, I thought it better to wait till the two friends should come to ask news of poor Hasan—Allāh have him in compassion for he is dead and his youth was not a happy one!

In the meantime, instead of buying rich clothes or the like, I called together all the poor rope-makers in Baghdād and addressed them, saying: 'Since Allāh has seen fit to shower fortune upon the least worthy of our number, O brothers, I think it but right that we should all benefit. From to-day I take you into my service, so that you can continue with your rope-making in the assurance of receiving good pay. Thus you need never take bitter thought for the morrow as I used to do. For this purpose I called you together. But Allāh is more generous!'

The rope-makers thanked me and agreed to my proposal; since then they have all worked for me under excellent conditions, and my organisation has brought me in a steady profit, as well as assuring my position in the market.

I had already for some weeks abandoned the old house of my misery and gone to live in another which I had raised at great expense among the gardens, when it occurred to Saad and Saadī to come and learn my news. They were bewildered when they found my shop shut up, as if I were dead, and utterly astonished when the neighbours told them that I was still alive, that I had become one of the richest merchants in Baghdād, that I lived in a palace among the gardens, and that I was now known as Hasan the Magnificent.

They asked the direction of my new home and soon came to the great gates which give access to the gardens. The porter led them through a forest of orange and lemon trees, whose roots were refreshed by living water seeping through little channels from the river, and, when they came at last to my reception hall, they had already fallen under a cool spell woven of shadows, bird song, and the trickle of water furrows.

As soon as my slaves announced their arrival, I ran eagerly to greet them, and would have kissed the borders of their robes, but they prevented me and embraced me as if I had been their brother. I seated them in a small pavilion which gave upon the garden, and took my place at some little distance, as was fitting.

When we had been served with sherberts, I told them the whole story of my rise to fortune without omitting a single detail, but nothing would be gained by repeating it in this place. Saadī rejoiced greatly at my news, but to his friend he only said: 'You see, O Saad!'

They were still marvelling, when two of my children who had been playing in the garden ran up to me, bearing a large bird's nest which the slave who was in charge of them had secured from the top of a date palm. To my great astonishment I saw that this nest, which contained a brood of young hawks, had been built with a turban for its foundation. A closer examination showed me that this turban was my own, the one which had been stolen by the hawk. 'Good masters,' I said to my guests, 'do you remember the turban which I was wearing when Saad gave me the first two hundred dīnārs?' 'We do not remember it exactly,' they answered, and Saad himself added: 'I would know it for certain were it to contain a hundred and ninety dīnārs.' 'Let us see,' I answered, as I handed over the young birds to my children and unrolled the turban. As you will have guessed, the inner end was still safely knotted round the purse which Saad had given me.

We were still talking excitedly of this miracle, when one of my grooms entered, carrying a bran jar which I at once recognised as the one my wife had exchanged with the hawker. 'My lord,' said the man, 'I obtained this jar yesterday at the market, when I bought a measure of bran for the horse on which I was riding. I found it to contain this knotted bundle, which I have thought fit to hand to you.' Thus was Saad's second purse recovered!

Since then, O Commander of the Faithful, we three have lived together in perfect friendship and have conducted our lives on the assumption that none may tell the marvels of Destiny beforehand. As the goods of Allāh should return to His poor, I have never been weary of alms-giving. That is why, O King, you saw me behaving on the bridge yesterday in a manner which you have been pleased to call generous.

Such is my story.

'Indeed, O sheikh Hasan, the ways of Destiny are wonderful!'

cried the Khalīfah. 'And, as I wish to prove Saadī's contention up to
the hilt, I will show you something.' He whispered a few words into
the ear of his treasurer, and that dignitary departed, to return in a
short time with a small ivory box. This Hārūn al-Rashīd opened,
displaying before the eyes of the old man that same gem of Sulaimān which he had sold to the Jew. 'It came into my possession,' said
the Khalīfah, 'on the very day you parted from it!'

Then he turned to the lame and split-mouth schoolmaster, saying: 'Now, my friend, say what you have to say.'

The man kissed the earth before the throne, and began:

The Split-Mouth Schoolmaster

O COMMANDER of the Faithful, I began life as a schoolmaster and had twenty-four boys under my charge. The tale
of my adventure with those boys is indeed prodigious.

I must begin by telling you, my lord, that I was so severe and
strict that I made my pupils work even in the recreation times, sent
them home only an hour after sundown, and followed them to their
dwellings to see that they did not get into mischief by the way. It
was this very rigour of mine which brought down all my misfortunes upon my head.

One day, as we were all assembled for a lesson, my whole class
rose as one boy, saying: 'Dear master, you are very yellow in the
face to-day!' This surprised me as I was not feeling at all ill, and I
took no notice of their behaviour. 'Begin, you little ruffians!' I cried;
but my eldest pupil came up to me with an expression of deep anxiety
upon his face, and said: 'As Allāh lives, O master, you are indeed
yellow in the face! May He banish all evil from you! If you are too
ill, I will take the class instead of you to-day.' At the same time, all
the other lads looked at me with as much commiseration as if I were
about to die on the spot; so I came under the influence of their suggestion and said to myself: 'You may be seriously indisposed without knowing it. The worst ills are those which enter the body sur-
reptitiously and do not at first make their presence felt.' I rose from
my place at once and, confiding the class to the eldest pupil, entered
my harīm, where I lay down at full length, saying to my wife:
'Prepare me some drink which is efficacious against a determination
of yellow to the face.' This I said with sighs and groans, as if I

were already gripped by the pest and all the red maladies of the world.

Soon my eldest pupil knocked at the door and entered with a sum of twenty-four dirhams in his hand. These he handed to me, saying: 'O our master, your excellent pupils have contributed this sum between them in order that our mistress may cure you with no thought for the expense.'

I was touched by this generosity and, as a mark of my appreciation, gave the boys a whole holiday, without suspecting that the whole matter had been combined to that end. For who can guess the satanic ingenuity of youth?

Though delighted with the money, I passed that day in a lowered state of mind, brooding upon my illness. In the morning the eldest pupil came again, and cried when he saw me: 'May Allāh guard our master from all evil! You are much more yellow in the face to-day. Rest, rest, and do not trouble about us.'

At this point Shahrazād saw the approach of morning and discreetly fell silent.

But when the eight-hundred-and-seventy-fourth night had come

SHE SAID:

Mightily impressed by his words, I said to myself: 'It is your duty to take a thorough cure at the expense of your pupils,' and aloud I answered: 'Take the class yourself, just as if I were there.' I groaned over my heavy misfortune, and the boy left me to tell his companions the good news.

This state of things continued for a week and, at the end of that time, the senior pupil brought me another twenty-four dirhams, saying: 'Your excellent pupils have contributed this sum in order that our mistress may cure you without regarding the expense.' I was even more touched than the first time, and thought: 'Surely this is a blessed illness which brings in more money than all your teaching! The longer it lasts the better.'

By this time I knew very well that I was not ill, so I determined to practise a deception on my side also. Each time the spokesman of my class came to me, I told him that I was dying of inanition, as my stomach refused all nourishment, though, as a matter of fact, I had never had such excellent food or eaten so much of it.

One day this same pupil entered my apartment just as I was about to eat an egg. When I saw him, I slipped it whole into my mouth, lest he should see that I was able to eat. The egg was excessively hot and burnt me terribly; but, instead of tactfully departing, the lad looked at me with compassion, saying: 'Your cheeks are all swollen; you must have some malignant abscess.' Then, as my eyes were popping from my head because of the pain and I did not answer, he cried: 'It must be pierced, it must be pierced!' and advanced towards me with a large needle extended between his fingers. I jumped to my feet and rushed into the kitchen, where I spat out the egg, but the inside of my mouth was already so badly burned that a veritable abscess declared itself and I had to call the barber in to empty it. My mouth is still split and deformed as a result of that operation.

When I had recovered from my burn and returned to my class, I became more severe than ever, as the lads had got a little out of hand during my absence. I used my stick freely and inspired so much respect in the hearts of my pupils that when I sneezed they would leave their books at once, stand up straight in a line with crossed arms, bow low to the earth before me, and cry together with one voice: 'Benediction! Benediction!' Then I would answer, as politeness demanded: 'You are pardoned! You are pardoned!' I taught them a thousand similarly useful things, as I did not wish their good parents to spend money in vain upon their education. I must confess that I had high hopes that they would all turn into respectable citizens and good business men.

One day, as I was taking them for a walk, I led them further than usual and we all became very thirsty because of the heat. When I saw a well at the side of the road, I resolved to descend into it to allay my thirst with the cool water and to bring up a bucket, if I could, for my pupils.

As there was no rope, I knotted all the boys' turbans together and fastened one end of this improvised cord round my waist; then I bade my class lower me into the well. I climbed over the edge and the boys began to let me down with infinite precaution, so that I should not strike my head against the stone sides. But the passage from warmth to cool and light to darkness gave me a desire to sneeze, and I could not check it. As soon as they heard the familiar noise, either from habit or malice, the whole class let go the cord, crossed their arms, and called out together: 'Benediction! Benediction!' I was unable to answer, since I was already falling heavily to the bottom of the well. As the water was not deep, I escaped drowning, but I broke both legs and one shoulder. Terrified by the accident, all the boys ran away, and it was only after I had shouted in pain for a long time that certain wayfarers drew me out of the well. They set me on an ass and led me back to my house, where I languished at death's door for many weeks. I have never recovered from that misadventure and am no more able to practise as a schoolmaster.

That is why I have to beg in the streets to keep my wife and children, O Commander of the Faithful, and that is why you were able to see me and succour me on the bridge of Baghdād.

Such is my story.

When the lame and split-mouth schoolmaster had made an end of this tale, Masrūr helped him back to his place, and the blind beggar, who had asked to be buffeted after receiving an alms, groped his way forward to the throne and told the following story. He said:

The Blind Man Who Would be Buffeted

FROM my youth up, O Commander of the Faithful, I was a camel-driver and, thanks to my perseverance, I early acquired eighty camels of my own. These I hired out to caravans for business or pilgrimage, and drew from them a yearly profit which greatly increased my capital. Day by day I kept only this dream before me, to become the richest of my trade in Irāk.

One day, as I was returning with my beasts from Basrah after delivering at that port certain goods which were destined for India, I halted at a water cistern to refresh the camels and let them graze. As I was sitting down to eat, a darwīsh approached and, after cordial greeting on both sides, sat down beside me. We shared provisions and ate together, as is the custom of the desert; then we began to talk of this and that, and question each other concerning our journeys and destination. He told me that he was going towards Basrah, and I said that I was making for Baghdād. Intimacy being thus established, I spoke to him of my profits and outlined my dreams of wealth.

The darwīsh heard me without interrupting, and then said with a smile: 'O Bābā-Abdallāh, you yearn with great pains towards a result which is of little account, when we consider that Destiny could make you, at the turning of a road, in the twinkling of an eye, not only richer than all the camel-drivers in Irāk, but more powerful than all the combined powers of the earth. O Bābā-Abdallāh, have you never heard of hidden treasure and subterranean wealth?' 'I have often heard of such things, O darwīsh,' I replied. 'We all know that each of us could be raised above kings by a caprice of Destiny. There is no hind labouring in the earth who does not dream that one day his spade shall strike against the sealed stone of some miraculous treasure; there is no fisherman casting his net who does not surmise an hour when he shall draw to shore a marine jewel, to place him beyond the need of work for ever. I am no more ignorant than my fellows, O darwīsh, and I am well aware that the men of your guild hold words and secrets of great potency.'

The darwīsh ceased turning over the sand with his stick and looked at me afresh, saying: 'O Bābā-Abdallāh, when you met me to-day, I do not think that it was an unlucky meeting; rather I think that, at this hour, you will find yourself face to face with your Destiny at the turning of the road.' 'If that is so, I am ready to grapple it with a will,' I answered, 'and whatever it brings me I shall accept with a grateful heart.' 'Then rise up, poor man, and follow me,' he said.

I rose and walked behind him, thinking to myself: 'After all these years fortune has come at last!' In an hour's walking we reached a wide valley, whose entrance was so narrow that my camels could not pass two abreast. But, once we were well in, we could move easily and soon came to the foot of a remarkably steep mountain. 'This is the place,' said the darwīsh. 'Now halt your camels and make them lie on their bellies, so that there will be no delay when we come to load them.' I thanked him for this advice and made the beasts lie in a flat open space at the foot of the mountain walls.

When I rejoined the darwīsh, I found him setting light to a pile of dry brushwood. As soon as the flame had well taken, he threw a handful of male incense upon it, murmuring words which I did not understand. A thick column of smoke sprang up into the air and, when he had divided the vapour with his stick, behold! a large rock facing us split in two, showing a yawning cave.

At this point Shahrazād saw the approach of morning and discreetly fell silent.

But when the eight-hundred-and-seventy-fifth night had come

SHE SAID:

Within were hummocks of coined gold and bright jewels, massed as one sees salt upon the sea shore. I threw myself upon the first gold like a falcon plunging upon a pigeon, and began to fill a sack which I had brought with me from the camels. But the darwīsh laughed in my face, saying: 'Such labour will hardly pay you, poor man. If you fill your sacks with coined gold your beasts will not be able to carry them. Fill them rather with those gems which you see a little further off, for they are a hundred times lighter and a thousand times more valuable than the money.'

'You are right, O darwīsh,' I answered, as I began to fill my sacks with jewels and load them upon the camels. My companion stood still, watching me all the time with a slight smile, and, when I had finished, said to me: 'Now only remains to close the treasure and depart.' He made his way into the rock and approached a large jar of carved gold which stood on a pedestal of sandal-wood. As I watched, and cursed my luck that I had only eighty camels and not eighty thousand, he dipped his hand into the jar and drew forth a small gold pot which he hid in his bosom. Seeing the question in my face, he said: 'That is nothing. A little pomade for the eyes.' He gave no further explanation and, when I would have possessed myself also of a little pot, prevented me. 'That is enough for to-day!' he exclaimed, as he pushed me back into the sunlight. When we were outside, he muttered words of power, and the two halves of the rock joined smoothly together, leaving only a wall of stone before our faces.

'O Bābā-Abdallāh,' said the darwīsh, 'we will now leave this valley, and, when we come to the place where we first met, there shall be an equal and friendly division of these riches.'

I led my camels in good order from that valley, and we walked along until we came to the place of our separation. But, as we went, I had been brooding on the division of the jewels and had come to the conclusion that the darwīsh was asking too much. It is true that he had opened the treasure, but he could have done nothing without my camels. Also it was likely that the treasure had been written in my name and could only have been opened in my presence. He had stood smiling, while I had the labour of loading the jewels upon the camels; what right, then, had he to expect half of the treasure and forty of my beasts as well?

Therefore, when the time came for division, I said: 'O holy man, what will you, who are sworn to take no care for the riches of this world, do with the loads of forty camels? That is to say, if you are unjust enough to take them as a price for your indication of the treasure?' Instead of becoming angry, as I had half expected, the darwīsh answered in a calm voice: 'You are right, O Bābā-Abdallāh, when you say that I must have no care for the riches of the world. I take my equal share, not for myself, but to distribute to the poor and disinherited as I go about the world. As for injustice, you do not seem to realise that a hundredth part of what I have given you would make you the richest citizen in all Baghdād. You must remember that I was under no necessity to speak to you of the treasure, and could easily have kept the secret to myself. Set aside this feeling of greed, my friend, and be content with the benefit which Allāh has brought to you.'

Though I was quite convinced that I was wrong and that there was no equity in my claim, I changed the face and form of my question, saying: 'O darwīsh, you have convinced me; but I must point out that though you, as a darwīsh, know all that there is to be known about serving God, you do not know the least thing about driving camels. What will you do with forty such, who have only learned to obey their master's voice? I advise you, in all friendship, to take as few camels as possible, and to return some other day for jewels, since you can always open the cavern at your will. It would grieve me to think of you hurrying hither and thither over the desert, trying to control so large a band of Allāh's most stubborn creatures.' Just as if he could refuse me nothing, the darwīsh answered: 'I had not thought of that point, my friend. I do not imagine that I should like to trust myself with so many of the animals. I beg you choose out the twenty which please you most from my forty, and then depart under the safeguard of Allāh.'

Hiding my astonishment that he was so easy to move, I chose out the twenty best of his forty camels and then, thanking him heartily for his good offices, took leave and began to lead my sixty beasts towards Baghdād.

But I had only gone a few steps when Satan breathed envy and ingratitude into my heart, so that I regretted the camels which were now going towards Basrah and especially the loads which they carried upon their backs. 'Why should the vile fellow cheat me of twenty camels when he is the sole master of an unending treasure?' I asked myself. I halted my animals and ran back, calling to the dar-wīsh at the top of my voice and signalling to him to stop. Soon he heard me and halted his twenty. When I came up to him, I said: 'O my brother, I have had great anxiety for you since we parted. I cannot leave you without begging you, for your own sake, to content yourself with of the camels, which are, I assure you, all that so holy a man can possibly control. I am quite willing to take on the responsibility of the rest, for, thanks to my training, I can as easily drive a hundred as one.' My words had the effect which I desired, the darwīsh handed over ten of his twenty to me and I beheld myself master of seventy camels, each carrying a king's ransom in precious stones.

You would think, O Commander of the Faithful, that I would have been satisfied; but I was not! My eye remained empty and my greed increased rather than diminished. I redoubled my solicitations, prayers and importunities, and worked upon the darwīsh's generosity to make him yield the whole treasure to me. I embraced him and kissed his hands with such fervour that, at last, he consented, saying: 'O my brother, make a wise use of the riches which Allāh has given you, and sometimes remember the darwīsh who met you at the turning of your Fate.'

At this point Shahrazād saw the approach of morning and discreetly fell silent.

But when the eight-hundred-and-sixty-sixth night had come

SHE SAID:

But instead of rejoicing that I was now master of the whole of this cargo of bright stones, I was pricked on by my avarice to ask for something else. And that was the beginning of my desolation. It occurred to me that the little gold pot should belong to me also. 'It may have strange virtues,' I said to myself. 'At any rate the darwīsh can get as many as he likes from the cave.' So, when I embraced him finally in farewell, I said: 'Tell me, in Allāh's name, my brother, what you intend to do with that little pot of pomade you have hidden in your bosom? Surely a darwīsh knows nothing of pomades, and has no use for them? Give me the little pot and I will carry it away in memory of you.'

I had rather expected the good man to refuse me in anger, and I was ready to take what I wished by force, stunning him if necessary and leaving him to die in that deserted place, but he smiled good-naturedly and gave me what I asked, saying: 'May it satisfy the last of your desires, O Bābā-Abdallāh! But if you think there is any more that I can do for you, you have but to say so.'

I opened the pot and, after considering its contents, said: 'In Allāh's name, my brother, put a crown upon your goodness by telling me the uses and virtues of this paste.' 'It was prepared by the fingers of the earth Jinn,' he replied. 'If a man smears a little on the outskirts and the lid of his left eye, he will see all the deposits of hidden treasure beneath the surface of the world. But if, by ill-fortune, it should be applied to the right eye, both eyes will immediately become blind. Such is the use and abuse of this pomade, my brother. And Allāh be with you upon your journey!'

He would have taken leave of me for the last time, but I held him by the sleeve, saying: 'By your life, do me a last service. Apply a little of the balm to my left eye, for I do not understand such matters and yet stand upon knife blades of impatience to see the things of which you speak.' Not wishing to gainsay me, the good man took a little of the pomade upon the end of his finger and smeared it upon my left lid and about my left eye, saying: 'Now open the left and shut the right!'

I opened the treated eye and shut the other; at once the visible and accustomed things of life disappeared from my sight and their place was taken by an innumerable series of flat maps, one above the other, showing subterranean caves and sea caves, hollows among the bases of gigantic trees, respositories hewn in the solid rock, and hiding-places of every kind. These were brimmed with precious stones, with wrought gold, with heavy silver, and all sorts and colours of precious things. I saw the metals in their mines, virgin silver and natural gold, jewels crusted in their vein-stones, and all the precious lodes with which the earth is pregnant. I gazed until my right eye became weary and I had to open it; at once the objects of that landscape came back about me and all the magic maps had disappeared.

Convinced now of the power of the pomade when applied to the left eye, I began to doubt whether the darwīsh had told me the truth with regard to its use in the right. 'He is wily and deceitful,' I thought. 'He has only been so obliging in order to fool me in the end. It is impossible that a single balm could have two such contrary effects.' I laughed, and cried aloud: 'O father of guile, I see well enough that you are having a joke with me! I have an idea that, if this balm were applied to my right eye, it would make me master of all the treasures which its use about my left could only make me see. Am I not right? Whether or not you admit that I have discovered the truth, I mean to experiment for myself; therefore I pray you, smear my right eye and keep me no longer on tenterhooks.' For the first time the darwīsh grew angry. 'O Bābā-Abdallāh, what you ask is both fatal and unreasonable,' he cried. 'I will never allow myself to do you harm after I have done you so much good. Let us leave each other now as brothers in Allāh, and each go upon his way.' But I would not let him depart, for I was sure that he wished to trick me out of my right in the world's treasures. 'As Allāh lives,' I answered, 'if you do not wish to spoil all your kindness by this one trivial refusal, you will treat my right eye at once. I am stronger than you are, and will not depart until you have done so.'

My companion's face turned pale and hard. 'It is yourself who blinds you!' he exclaimed, as he rubbed a little of the balm about my right eye. Then, with both eyes, I saw but the shadows of darkness; they have stayed with me ever since, O Commander of the Faithful.

I stretched out my arms, crying: 'Save my sight, save my sight, O brother!' but there was no answer. He was deaf to my prayers, and I heard him driving away the eighty camels which bore my Destiny upon their backs.

I fell to the ground with no strength to move for many hours. I would certainly have died of grief and the confusion of blindness in that place, if a caravan from Basrah had not picked me up on the following day and brought me to Baghdād.

Since then I, who once had all power and happiness within my grasp, have begged about the roads of generosity. Repentance for my great greed and my abuse of Allāh's kindness has entered deeply into my heart and I have sworn that, wherever I take an alms, I also take a buffet on the ear.

Such is my story, O Commander of the Faithful. I have told it in all the details of its low impiety, and I am very ready to receive a hard slap from each of the honourable men who are here assembled. But the mercy of Allāh is infinite!

'O Bābā-Abdallāh,' cried the Khalīfah, 'your crime was great, your greed unpardonable, but I think that they are forgiven now because of your repentance and humility. Therefore, rather than that you should be condemned any longer to such public ill-treatment, I decree that the wazīr of my treasure shall give you ten dirhams a day that you may have food and lodging until the time of your death. May Allāh have you in His compassion!' He ordered a like pension to be paid to the split-mouth schoolmaster, and kept with him for sumptuous entertainment, according to their rank, the master of the white mare, the sheikh Hasan, and the youth behind whom Indian and Chinese airs were played.

But do not think, O auspicious King, continued Shahrazād, that this tale is at all to be compared with that of Princess Zulaikah. And then, as King Shahryār did not know the story, she continued: . . .

The Tale of Princess Zulaikah

IT is related, O auspicious King, that there sat once upon the throne of the Umayyads in Damascus a Khalīfah who had for wazīr a man of great wisdom and eloquence, who, having read in the books of the poets and annalists, remembered his reading and was able to tell his master such stories as agreeably passed the time for him. One day, when he saw that the King had some grief, he resolved to distract him, and therefore said: 'My Lord, you have often questioned me concerning the details of my life and have asked for the story of my past, before I became your slave and the wazīr of your power. Until now I have excused myself, fearing to seem conceited, and have preferred to tell you those things which have befallen others. But to-day, though manners still give me a certain hesitation, I will tell you of the set of extraordinary circumstances which marked my life and led me at last to the threshold of your greatness.' Then, seeing that his master listened eagerly, the good wazīr told the following tale:

I was born in this fair city of Damascus, O my lord and crown upon my head, and my father was a certain Abdallāh, one of the richest and best considered merchants in all the lands of Shām. He spared no expense upon my education, and I received a training from the wisest masters in theology, jurisprudence, algebra, poetry, astronomy, calligraphy, arithmetic, and the traditions of our Faith. Also I was taught all the languages which are spoken within your dominion, far and wide, from sea to sea; so that, if I had chosen through love of travel to take my way right across the world, I could always have made myself understood. Beside the various dialects of our own tongue, I mastered Persian, Greek, Tatar, Kurdish, Indian and Chinese. My application to study was so great that my masters held me up as an example to the idle, and my father, seeing my progress, beheld without bitterness or consternation the approach of that death which visits all creatures at the last.

At this point Shahrazād saw the approach of morning and discreetly fell silent.

But when the eight-hundred-and-seventy-seventh night had come

LITTLE DUNYAZĀD rose from her carpet and embraced her sister, saying: 'O Shahrazād, pray be quick and tell us the rest of the tale of Princess Zulaikah.' 'With all my heart and as in duty bound to this courteous King,' answered Shahrazād, and she continued:

Before he passed into the peace of our Lord, my father called me to him, saying: 'My son, the Separator is about to cut through the thread of my life, and you will be left without a guiding hand. But I console myself with the thought that your excellent education has fitted you to grasp a favouring Destiny. Yet, my child, no man may know what Fate has in store for him, and no precautions may avail against the decrees of Allāh. If, then, a day should come when life turns against you and all the world seems black, I charge you to go out into the garden of this house and hang yourself from the main branch of the old tree which stands there. This shall be a deliverance to you!'

My father died with these strange words upon his lips, and, during all the time of the funeral and the mourning weeks which followed afterwards, I pondered over the singularity of such last advice from the mouth of a true Believer. 'Why should he have told me to commit suicide, against all the precepts of Allāh,' I would say, 'instead of bidding me trust in His tenderness towards His creatures? Surely this thing passes understanding.'

Little by little, however, the memory of my father's last words faded from my mind and I began to give free rein to all my natural instincts for pleasure and expense. I lived riotously for many months in the breast of folly, until I woke one morning as destitute as a babe snatched naked from its mother's arms. I bit my fingers, saying: 'O

Hasan, O Abdallāh's son, you are ruined through your own fault and not by the treachery of time. Nothing remains save to sell this house with its garden and, leaving the friends who will not look upon you in your poverty, beg your bread upon the roads of the world. Nor will many take pity on one who has pulled his dwelling upon him with his own hand.'

Then suddenly I remembered my father's last words and, for the first time, saw sense in them. 'Better die than beg!' I cried, as I rose in search of a rope.

When I had obtained a cord of sufficient thickness, I walked out into the garden and fastened the end of it to two large stones which I set up under the main branch of the old tree. Then I threw the other end of the rope over the limb and, after making a running noose about my neck, launched myself from the top of the stones, with a prayer to Allāh for pardon. I was already strangling and gasping, when the branch broke beneath my weight and fell away from the trunk. I came to the ground with it and lay for some time in a great bewilderment.

When at last I understood that I was not dead, I was deeply mortified to have made my effort so clumsily. I was about to repeat my criminal attempt, when I saw something like a pebble fall from the tree and lie blazing upon the ground, with all the fires of a burning coal. This was only the first of a shower, and, when I looked up to the place where the branch had been torn away from the trunk, I saw that it was hollow within. Climbing upon my two stones, I examined the opening and found that the tree also was hollow as far as my eye could reach. Even as I watched, more and more diamonds and emeralds escaped through the broken place and joined their fellows on the ground.

At last I understood the true meaning of my father's words and saw that he had arranged this unknown treasure for me, with the intention that I should be comforted in my last despair.

Singing for joy, I fetched an axe from the house and began to enlarge the opening in the tree. I speedily discovered that the whole interior of the wood, from the roots up, was one hollow store of rubies, diamonds, turquoises, pearls, emeralds, and every other jewel of the earth and sea.

As I stood there glorifying Allāh and blessing the memory of my father in my heart, I suddenly felt a revulsion of feeling against the debauched and prodigal life which I had been leading, and swore most solemnly that I would be thenceforth a worthy and abstemious citizen.

As a first step in reformation, I made up my mind to leave the city which had been witness of my extravagance and to yield to the attraction which Shīrāz in Persia had always had for me, since the day when I had heard my father say of it that all elegance of wit and suavity of life were there united. 'You must install yourself as a merchant of precious stones in Shīrāz, O Hasan,' I said to myself. 'Thus you will make acquaintance with the most polished citizens in all the world. As you can speak Persian, the change will not be difficult for you.'

I at once put this project into execution, and Allāh granted me a safe journey to the city of Shīrāz, over which the great King Sābūr-Shāh reigned at that time.

I descended at the most expensive khān and hired a lofty chamber. Then, instead of resting, I changed my travelling clothes for new and beautiful garments, and went to walk among the streets and markets.

As I was leaving the great porcelain mosque, whose beauty had thrown me into an ecstasy of prayer, I saw one of the King's wazīrs passing by. He halted when his eyes fell upon me, and stood at gaze as if I had been an angel. Then he said: 'O fairest of all boys, I see by your habit that you are a stranger. From what land do you come?' 'I am a citizen of Damascus, good master,' I replied with a bow, 'and I have come to Shīrāz to be educated by contact with her inhabitants.' The wazīr rejoiced at my words and clasped me in his arms, saying: 'O sweet words of your mouth, my son! How old are you?' 'Your slave is in his sixteenth year,' I answered. At this he rejoiced still more, for he was directly descended from Lot. He said: 'It is a fine age, my child, a fine age. If you have nothing better to do, I will take you to the palace to present you to our King, for he loves handsome faces and will make you one of his chamberlains. Surely you will be the crown and glory of them all!' 'Be it upon my head and before my eyes!' I answered.

He took me by the hand and we walked on together, talking of this and that, and my companion marvelled not only at my charm and elegance, but also to hear me speak Persian with purity and assurance. 'As Allāh lives,' he cried, 'if all the youth of Damascus are like you, the city must be an outskirt of Paradise and the stretch of sky above it Paradise itself!'

When I was introduced into the presence of King Sābūr-Shāh, he smiled at me, saying: 'Damascus is welcome to my palace! What is your name, delightful boy?' 'The slave Hasan, O King of time,' I answered. 'Never was name more fitting!' he exclaimed in high delight. 'I appoint you, forthwith, one of my chamberlains, that I may rejoice my eyes with the sight of you each morning.' When I had kissed his hand and humbly thanked the King, my friend the wazīr led me away and himself clad me in the robes of a page. Then he gave me my first lesson in my duties and formally took me under his protection. I became his friend, and all the other chamberlains, a young and handsome band, became my friends also. My life promised to be one river of happiness among the delicacies of that palace.

Up to that time, my lord, no woman had entered my life; but she was soon to appear and, with her, complication.

At this point Shahrazād saw the approach of morning and discreetly fell silent.

But when the eight-hundred-and-seventy-eighth night had come

SHE SAID:

I must tell you first of all, my lord, that my protector had said to me on the day of our meeting: 'You must bear in mind, my dear, that it is forbidden to all chamberlains of the twelve chambers, as well as to the dignitaries of the palace, the officers and the guards, to walk in the gardens after a certain hour; for in the late evening they are reserved for the sole use of the women in the harīm. Should any man, by ill fortune, be found there during the time of reservation, his head would answer for it.'

One evening, however, the cool sweet air wooed me to sleep on a bench in the gardens and, after a time, I heard women's voices, saying in my dream: 'It is an angel, an angel, an angel! How beautiful, beautiful, beautiful!' I woke with a start and, seeing no one in the shadows about me, supposed that I had imagined these exclamations in my sleep; also I saw that my slumbers had betrayed me into staying long beyond the permitted hour. I rose briskly, intending to run for the palace, but suddenly a girl's voice called to me from out the shadow and silence, saying with a trill of laughter: 'Whither away, O handsome waker?' More startled than if I had been pursued by the harīm guards, I fled along an alley. But, as I turned a corner of it, the moon came out from behind a cloud and showed me a woman of white beauty standing before me, smiling into my face with wide dark loving eyes. Her attitude was queenly and the moon in Allāh's sky less bright than her face.

I could do nothing but halt before this apparition. I stood in confusion, with lowered eyes, while she said gently: 'Where are you going so quickly, O light of my eye? Why should you run so?' 'If you belong to the palace, lady,' I answered, 'you know already why I run. The gardens are forbidden to men after a certain hour, and I shall have my head cut off if the guards see me. Allow me, of your kindness, to pass.' 'Breeze of my heart, you are a little late in remembering the edict,' she laughed. 'The hour is long past and you would do better to stay for the rest of this white and blessed night in the garden than risk an entrance into the palace.' But I trembled and lamented: 'Alas, alas, my death is certain! O daughter of excellence, O my mistress, you would not have my destruction as a load upon your beauty?' I made as if to move forward, but she checked me with her left arm, while with her right hand she unveiled completely. 'Look at me, young madman,' she said without a laugh, 'and say if you can find such youth and such beauty every evening. I am only just eighteen and no man has ever touched me. My face is not altogether ugly, but, such as it is, no man has ever looked upon it before. You will offend me greatly if you attempt to flee after you have seen it.' 'O Queen,' I stammered, ' you are the full moon of beauty and, although the jealousy of night hides much of you from me, that which I have seen is sufficient for my enchantment. Yet surely you see that these facts do not make my situation any less delicate.' 'Your situation is delicate indeed,' she replied, 'but not in the way you think. You know nothing of my rank, but I will tell you this: the only danger you run, now that I have taken you under my protection, is the danger of offending me. . . . Tell me who you are and what you do in the palace.' 'I am Hasan of Damascus,' I answered. 'I am the King's new chamberlain and the favourite of his wazīr.' 'So you are the handsome Hasan who has crazed Lot's grandson!' she cried. 'Joy, oh, joy, oh, joy, that I have you alone for myself this night, my love! Come, my heart, come, let us not poison these sweet minutes with the bitterness of thought!'

She drew me to her with all her strength and rubbed her face against mine and passionately set her lips against my lips. Though it was the first time that such a thing had happened to me, my lord, I felt the child of his father come furiously to life under this contact. So, after I had returned the girl's embrace to the point of swoon, I drew him forth and showed him the way to the nest. But, instead of favouring me and lighting the path, the damsel pushed me roughly aside with a cry of alarm. I had hardly time to send the child home before ten girls ran out from a thicket of roses, laughing as if their hearts would break.

I understood at once that the woman had only been making game of me to amuse her companions. In a moment I was surrounded by them all, as they laughed and jumped up and down in the ecstasy of their joke. While their mirth rippled on, they looked at me with bright malicious curious eyes, and said to the one who had tricked me: 'Sweet Kāiriah, you have never done anything better! What a handsome, lively child that was!' 'And how quick!' said one. 'How irritable!' said another. 'How gallant!' said a third. 'How charming!' said a fourth. 'How big!' said a fifth. 'How sturdy!' said a sixth. 'How vehement!' said a seventh. 'How surprising!' said an eighth. 'Quite a little king!' said a ninth.

You must remember, my lord, that I had never looked upon the faces of women before; I stood there, more angry and confused than I can say. Surely these girls had more audacity than has ever been described in the impudic annals! I must have looked an imbecile as I stood amid their jeering.

But suddenly a twelfth girl slipped out like the rising moon from the thicket of roses, and at once the rest fell silent. Her beauty was sovereign and the flowers bowed upon their stems as she came towards us. The girls fell back and she looked me long in the face. 'Indeed, O Hasan of Damascus,' she said at length, 'I have never heard of such audacity as yours. It grieves me for your youth and beauty that your attempt at violation must be punished by death.'

Then the girl Kāiriah, who had been the cause of this trouble, came forward and kissed the hand of the last speaker, saying: 'O our mistress Zulaikah, I conjure you by your precious life to pardon him that impetuous movement. His fate is in your hands and it would be a pity if so charming an assailant were to lose his life.' Zulaikah reflected for a moment, and then answered: 'We will pardon him this time, since his victim intercedes in his favour. And now that his head is safe, we must try to make this adventure a little more agreeable for him, that he may remember his saviours with true gratitude.

Come, let us take him with us into the private rooms, where no man has set foot before.' She signed to one of her companions, who moved away lightly under the cypresses and returned soon after with a wave of silks beneath her arm. This she separated at my feet into the parts of a woman's charming robe, and then all the girls helped me to disguise myself as one of them. When Zulaikah approved me, I mingled with their pleasant band and made my way with them through the trees to the harīm.

As we came into the private reception hall of white marble crusted with pearl and turquoise, the girls whispered to me that this belonged to the King's only daughter, and that Zulaikah, who had spared my life, was the princess herself.

In this fair naked place were twenty squares of gold brocade, arranged in a circle on a large carpet. The handmaidens, who had not ceased till then from surreptitious touching of me and glancing, placed themselves on the squares, and then seated me in their midst close to the princess, who kept on looking at me with assassinating eyes.

Zulaikah commanded refreshments to be brought, and six new slaves, as fair and as richly dressed as my garden friends, served us with silk napkins on gold plates, while ten more followed them about with large porcelain bowls, the sight of which was a cool refection in itself.

At this point Shahrazād saw the approach of morning and discreetly fell silent.

But when the eight-hundred-and-seventy-ninth night had come

SHE SAID:

These porcelain bowls contained sherbert of snow, curdled milk, citron preserve, and sliced cucumber flavoured with lemon. Princess Zulaikah served herself first and fed to me, in the same gold spoon, a slice of preserved citron, a spoonful of milk, a touch of sherbert. The same spoon went round from hand to hand until all the bowls were empty, and then the slaves provided us with fair water in crystal cups.

The party became as lively as if we had all been drinking wine, and I was astonished to hear such bold words from the girls' lips; they laughed consumedly at each strong jest which was made concerning the child of its father, which seemed to be a mental preoccupation with them all. The delightful Kāirīah, my victim, if victim there had been, bore me no grudge and told me plainly with her eyes that my vivacity had been forgiven. I lifted my eyes to her from time to time, and then dropped them quickly when I found her gaze upon me; for, in spite of all my efforts to be assured, I still sat in great embarrassment among these strange maidens. Seeing that the conversation of her attendants could not make me bold, the princess said to me at length: 'When are you going to become easy and free with us, O Hasan of Damascus? Are you afraid that we will eat you? You run no risk at all in the apartments of a King's daughter, for no eunuch dare enter here without permission. Have you forgotten who I am? Do you think that you are talking with the daughters of petty shopkeepers? Lift up your head, boy, and look about you; then tell us frankly which of us pleases you most.'

Instead of being reassured by this command, I could only blush and stammer incoherent words, devoutly wishing at the same time that the earth would open and swallow me up. 'I see that my request has embarrassed you, O Hasan,' said Zulaikah. 'But, if you think that you will offend the others by showing a preference for one, let me tell you that my girls and I are such close friends that we could not be affected in our relations with one another by any man. Put aside all fear, therefore, and examine us closely; we will strip ourselves naked if you cannot make a decision without that.'

At this I plucked up what little courage was left to me and, after looking round, determined that, though Zulaikah's attendants were all of perfect beauty and that the princess herself was no less marvellous, all my heart beat for the quick delicious Kāirīah, friend of the child of his father. But, in spite of Zulaikah's reassurance, I was not such a fool as to express my preference aloud. Instead, I bowed and said as sweetly as I could: 'O my mistress, I would not know how to make a choice: the moon is perfect and remains the moon even among perfect stars.' At the same time, I sent a covert glance in the direction of my choice, so that the sweet child might understand that all this was only politic flattery of the princess.

Zulaikah smiled at this answer. 'Though the compliment is somewhat obvious, Hasan,' she said, 'you have acquitted yourself well in a difficult position. But now leave me out of account, and make your choice among my girls.' All the young women encouraged me to obey, and Kāirīah was the most ardent in bidding me speak my secret thoughts.

Throwing aside my bashfulness suddenly, I pointed to young

Kāirīah and cried to the princess: 'O Queen, this is the one I wish! As Allāh lives, this is my great desire!'

As I spoke, all the girls broke into silver cascades of laughter, without showing the least spite, and, as I saw them all nudging each other with the greatest good humour, I thought: 'A prodigy! Are these really women? Are these really girls? Since when has the sex had so much of virtue and detachment in its composition? Even sisters could not show so much forbearance to each other; they would be scratching each other's eyes out by now. This passes understanding!'

Zulaikah did not leave me long in perplexity. 'I congratulate you, Hasan of Damascus!' she cried. 'The young men of your land have a fine taste, a quick eye, and abundant wisdom. I am delighted that your preference lies with mine; Kāirīah is the chosen of my heart and my dear love. You are not likely to repent your choice, O ruffian! And as yet you do not know a tithe of the child's excellence; in wit and beauty she surpasses us all, and, though in appearance it does not seem so, she is a queen among slaves when she sits with us.'

Then the other girls, one after another, began to praise Kāirīah's charm and jest with her on her success; nor was she backward in her replies, but found the fitting arrow to return to each.

When they had all had their say, Zulaikah picked up a lute and gave it into the hands of her favourite. 'Soul of my soul,' she whispered, 'you must give your lover a taste of your quality or he will think that we have exaggerated.' So the delectable girl tuned the lute and, after a ravishing prelude, sang in a half voice, to her own accompaniment:

> Love has filled my soul with wine and gold
> But I keep them for him
> Who has pastured the black scorpions of his hair
> Upon my heart.
>
> He is a sword,
> A bow with black arrows,
> He is a white song written in tears of roses.
>
> Come with me to the bath, beloved,
> Nard shall burn his faint blue kisses about us
> And I will lie singing upon your heart.

When she had finished, she turned her eyes so tenderly upon me that I forgot all else and threw myself in a loving passion at her feet. To smell the smell of her garments and feel the warmth of her body made me mad drunk. I took her all in my arms and kissed her where I could, while she lay quivering and passive, as a dove in the hand. I was only recalled to myself by the hearty laughter of that strange assembly, who delighted extravagantly to see me unchained at last like a ram who has fasted since the time of his ripeness.

At this point Shahrazād saw the approach of morning and discreetly fell silent.

But when the eight-hundred-and-eightieth night had come

SHE SAID:

After this we ate and drank, with folly and caressing, until an old woman entered to announce the approach of dawn to that company. When she had thanked her nurse, Zulaikah rose, saying: 'It is time that we went to rest, O Hasan. You may count upon my help and protection in your love, for I will spare no trouble in aiding you. But the most important thing for the moment is to let you out secretly from the harīm.'

She whispered a few words into the ear of the old nurse, who looked me in the face for a moment and then took me by the hand, bidding me follow her. With a bow to this troop of doves and a passionate glance towards the delectable Kāiriah, I allowed myself to be led from the chamber and thence by a thousand turnings to a small door. This my companion opened with a key, and I slipped forth to find myself outside the precincts of the palace.

As the sun was already up, I hastened in by the chief door and took care to be noticed by the guards. When I reached my own chamber, I found the wazīr, my protector, the child of Lot, waiting for me in a manifest state of anxiety. He clasped me in his arms and embraced me tenderly, saying: 'O Hasan, my heart went grieving after you. I have not shut my eyes all night for fear that you, as a stranger, had fallen into the hands of the night rovers. Where have you been so far away from me, my dear?' Instead of telling him of my adventure, I answered that I had met a Damascene merchant who was about to leave Shīrāz for Basrah and that he had constrained me to spend the night with him. My protector believed this tale and, though he chid me, it was with laughing sighs and as a friend.

All that day and the next night I lay in the sweet bonds of my love, and I was still occupied with my memories on the following morning when a eunuch knocked at my door, gave me a folded paper, and disappeared.

I unfolded the note and read these lines, traced with intricate calligraphy: 'If the fawn from the lands of Shām will come with the moon to-night to sport among the branches, he will meet a lovesick hind already half faint at his approach. She will tell him in her own language how she rejoices to have been preferred among all the hinds of the forest.'

The reading of this made me drunk without wine, for, though I understood that I had found favour with Kāirīah on that first night, I had not dared to hope for so strong a proof of her attachment. When I had recovered from my emotion, I presented myself before the wazīr and kissed his hands many times until I had put him into a favourable humour. Then I asked permission to go that night to visit a darwīsh of my acquaintance who had recently come from Mecca. The old man gave me leave, and I returned to my own place, where I hastened to choose out, from my hoard of precious stones, the fairest emeralds, the purest rubies, the whitest diamonds, the largest pearls, the most delicate turquoises and the most perfect sapphires. Of these I made a chaplet upon a gold thread. Then I perfumed myself with musk and, after leaving the palace, crept through the small door, which had been left open for me, and entered the garden.

I soon came below the cypress, at whose foot I had slept on that first evening, and set myself to wait with panting heart for the coming of my love. . . . At first I thought that time had ceased to walk, but suddenly a white shadow moved among the trees and my own heart stood before me. I threw myself at her feet and stayed thus silent, with my face pressed to the earth, until Kāirīah said in a voice like running water: 'O Hasan of my love, rise up now and, instead of this tender passionate silence, give me some proof of your love! Is it really possible that you found me sweeter than my companions and the princess herself? I must hear it again from your dear lips before I can believe it.' She leaned over me and helped me to rise. I took her hand and carried it to my lips, crying: 'O queen of queens, see here is first a worthless chaplet of toys from my land, on which you may tell the hours of happy life. And with the chaplet take the love of all my life.' 'I am ravished that I have run the risk of to-night for so true a love, O Hasan,' she replied. 'But I know not, alas, whether my heart should rejoice at conquest or grieve at calamity. So saying, she leaned against my shoulder and I could feel the sighs of some grief lifting her breast. 'Why should the world seem black to you on this white night?' I asked. 'Why these false presentiments of doom?' 'Allāh grant them false, Hasan,' she murmured, 'but sorrow, sorrow! my fears are not groundless, O lover of lovers. Princess Zulaikah loves you in secret and goes about for an opportunity to tell you so. How will you answer her pleading? Will your love for me stand out against the temptation of glory?' 'It will, my sweet,' I interrupted. 'Your image is stronger in my heart than a thousand princesses. Would that Allāh might send a more dangerous rival, that I could give you proof of my constancy. Even should Sābūr-Shāh die and leave his throne in charge for his daughter's husband, my choice would be unalterable.' 'You are blind, blind, Hasan!' my mistress cried. 'Have you forgotten that I am only one of Zulaikah's slaves? If you were to spurn her love making, both you and I would never see another dawn. Our only way of safety is to give way to the greater power and trust that Allāh will assuage the bitterness of our disappointment.' Instead of agreeing to this, I grew wroth against the princess and pressed the slave in my arms, crying: 'O choicest of the gifts of God, do not torture me with such terrible sayings! If a breath of danger threatened your dear head, we could flee together to my country and hide in some deserted valley where all the power of Persia could not find us. Thanks to Allāh, I am rich enough to keep you in comfort at the other end of the world.'

Then, at length, my sweet friend gave herself up with a sigh of content into my arms, saying: 'O Hasan, I no longer doubt your love, and therefore no longer need to practise my deception. I am not Kāiriah, the favourite, but Zulaikah, the princess, for she whom you have taken for Zulaikah is Kāiriah. I only wished to be quite, quite certain of my lover. Lo, here is proof!'

She gave a low call and the erstwhile Zulaikah glided from the shade of the cypresses. She kissed her mistress's hand and bowed low before me. 'Will you love me so much, now that I am not a slave?' asked the true Zulaikah, and I answered simply: 'Because you have humbled yourself, I am exalted above all the kings of earth.'

At this point Shahrazād saw the approach of morning and discreetly fell silent.

But when the eight-hundred-and-eighty-first night had come

SHE SAID:

But she interrupted me, saying: 'O Hasan, you should not be astonished at anything that I have done for you; for I saw you sleeping in the moonlight beneath the tree and my heart gave itself to you as I looked.'

That night, while Kāiriah watched for us, we gave free course to the river of our love, though the bounds we kept were lawful. We kissed and talked tenderly together until the girl came, saying that the time for separation was at hand. But before she left me, Zulaikah said: 'My memory goes with you, O Hasan. Soon I will show you how I love you.'

I threw myself at her feet in gratitude, and we parted with tears of passion, she to the harīm and I to the small door.

Next day my soul stayed on the knife edge of hope, but when the hours passed with no message I could not eat or sleep. In spite of the many kindnesses with which my friend the wazīr sought to distract me, the sunshine grew hateful to me and I could not answer him. On the evening of the second day, I went down into the garden during the permitted time and saw to my consternation that all the thickets were occupied by armed men. I returned hastily to my own apartment and there found the princess's eunuch waiting for me in terror. He darted his eyes into every corner and, after slipping a folded paper into my hand, ran out as if the Sultān's army were behind him.

I opened the note, and read: 'O kernel of my heart's tenderness, when the hind quitted the gracious fawn she was surprised by the hunters. Now they range through all the forest and she dare not move. She may not again come to find her fawn in the moonlight. Be on your guard for pitfalls and, above all, do not give way to despair whatever you should hear these days, even though news of my death should come to you. Do not be so mad as to forget your prudence. And Allāh guard you!'

At this reading, O King of time, my foreboding grew into a giant too great to combat. When on the following morning news flew through the palace, like the beating of an owl's wings, that the Princess Zulaikah had died suddenly in the night, I hardly felt a greater pang. Without astonishment I slipped into darkness and fell swooning between the wazīr's arms.

I lay as one dead for seven days and seven nights; only my old friend's constant watching saved me for life and sanity. I crawled back to an existence which had no savour for me, and found that a disgust of living had me by the throat. I could stay no longer in the shadows of that palace, and watched for an occasion to flee forth to some place where I should be companioned only by the wild grass and the presence of God.

As soon as the shadows of that night fell thick, I collected the most precious of my jewels, cursing the branch of that old tree the while that it had not sustained me in my suicide, and stole away from the city of Shīrāz to wander in the desert.

I walked straight before me all that night and the following day. When I halted at evening near a little eyelet of living water beside the way, I heard the thunder of hoofs behind me and saw a young rider coming up against the setting sun, which flamed on his face and gave him the appearance of the angel Ridwān. He was dressed as a king's son, but surely he was no Mussulmān, for he greeted me with his hand only and not with words. I answered his salute in silence, grieving that so marvellous a youth should be an infidel. Then I invited him to rest and water his horse, saying: 'My lord, may the cool of the evening be propitious to you, and this water delightful to the weariness of your noble steed.'

The youth smiled and leapt to the ground. He fastened his horse by the bridle near the pool and then, suddenly throwing his arms round my neck, kissed me with singular ardour. My first feeling of surprise gave way to a cry and madness of joy, when I found that I was clasping Zulaikah.

And how, my lord, can I tell you of our delight? My tongue would become hairy before I could picture to you a shadow of those minutes. Suffice it to say that we stayed long in each other's arms, and that then my princess explained to me how she had escaped her father's vigilance by feigning death with the connivance of her favourite. She told me that she had escaped from the palace in time to watch over the effects of my grief, to follow me far off, and to come up with me, bearing a heart ready to renounce all grandeur and consecrate itself to my happiness. We passed that night in joys given and taken under the eye of heaven, and next day, we both set out upon Zulaikah's horse along the road to Damascus.

Allāh decreed, O King of time, that we should arrive in all safety, that I should be led into your presence, and become at length the wazīr of your power. Such is my story. But Allāh knows all!

But do not suppose, O auspicious King, continued Shahrazād, that this story of the Princess Zulaikah is to be compared with those contained in the Sweet Tales of Careless Youth.

Then, without giving King Shahryār time to express an opinion concerning the conduct of Zulaikah, she said:

SWEET TALES OF CARELESS YOUTH

Hard-Head and His Sister Little-Foot

IT is related—but Allāh knows all!—that there were once in a certain village a man and wife who believed in God and had two children, a boy and a girl. The boy was born with a hard head and a wilful temperament, the girl with a tender soul and delicious little feet. When the man was about to die, he called his wife to him, saying: 'I recommend you with my last breath to look after our son, the light of our eye. Whatever he does, do not scold him; whatever he says, do not contradict him; and, above all, let him have his own way in a life which I trust will be long and prosperous.' His weeping wife promised obedience, and the good man died happy.

After certain further years the wife also took to her bed—Allāh alone lives for ever! When she knew that she was about to die, she called her daughter to her, saying: 'My child, your father, before his death, made me swear never to go counter to your brother's will. And now I require the same oath from you.' The girl swore obedience to this last wish, and the mother passed smiling into the peace of her Lord.

After the funeral, the boy said to his sister: 'Listen, O daughter of my father and mother. I am going to put every single thing which has been left us for inheritance, furniture, cows, buffaloes, goats, money, everything, into the house, and then set fire to it.' The girl opened wide eyes and, forgetful of her oath, cried out: 'But if you do that, my dear, what will become of us?' 'I want to,' answered Hard-Head, and he did. But, as their inheritance was going up in flames, the boy discovered that his sister had managed to hide some of their possessions with the neighbours. So he found the various houses by following the tiny footprints of his sister, and set fire to them, one after the other, with all their contents. The wild-eyed owners armed themselves with pitchforks and ran after the two children to kill them. Half dead with fright, Little-Foot cried to her brother: 'Save me, save me!' and the two fled off together across the country.

After they had given their legs to the wind for a day and a night, they succeeded in throwing off their pursuers, and came breathless but safe to a large farm, where the harvest was being gathered in. They offered themselves for the work and were accepted because of their charming appearance.

A few days later, the boy was alone in the farm house with the three children of the owner. He tamed them with a thousand caresses, and then said: 'Let us go out to the threshing-floor and play at flails.' The four went out hand in hand to the barn, and Hard-Head in-augurated the game by lying down and letting the others beat him as if he were grain. They did not, of course, beat him severely, but only enough to make the play. Yet when it was their turn to be grain, Hard-Head beat them and beat them until they were not grain but a paste over the threshing-floor, so that they died. So much for them.

When the girl perceived her brother's absence from the house, she was convinced that he would be destroying something some-where. She set out to look for him and found him just as he was giv-his last blow to that which had been the three children. 'We must fly, we must fly, my brother!' she cried. 'And oh, we were doing so well on this farm!' She succeeded in dragging him with her in her fright, but he would certainly not have gone if he had not wanted to. . . . When the poor farmer found his children impasted upon the thresh-ing-floor and saw that the two strangers had fled, he collected all the farm hands and armed them terribly with bows and cudgels; then he led them forward along the paths which the children had taken and camped them for the night at the foot of a very tall tree.

Now the brother and sister were hiding in the top branches of this tree. When they woke at dawn and saw all their pursuers sleep-ing below, Hard-Head pointed down at the bereaved father, and said to his sister: 'You see that big one? Well, I am going to do things on his head!' The sister beat herself across the mouth for terror, and cried: 'O our loss! Do not do it, my dear! They do not know that we are up here and if you keep quiet they will go away.' 'No! I am going to do things on the head of that big one,' insisted Hard-Head and, squatting down on the topmost branch, he pissed and dropped dung on the head and face of the farmer until it was entirely covered.

The man woke with a jump on feeling these things, and saw the boy calmly wiping himself with leaves at the top of the tree; he furiously seized his bow and loosed a flight of arrows at the brother and sister, but they fell short and were deflected by the branches, because the tree was very tall. 'Cut down this tree!' he cried in a voice of thunder which woke his band. 'I told you so, we are lost!' sobbed Little-Foot. 'Who told you so?' demanded Hard-Head. 'We are lost! We are lost!' she repeated, but he replied: 'They have not caught us yet.'

Even as he spoke, a giant Rūkh, spying the two children as he sailed above the tree, pounced down upon them and bore them off in his talons. They were already in the air when the tree fell under the violent axe strokes of those below. The bereaved farmer saw them escape and his heart broke from bitter rage.

The Rūkh flew on with the children in his claws and made across an arm of the sea, intending to set them down when he should have reached the mountains. But, as he was borne along, Hard-Head cried to Little-Foot: 'Sister, I am going to tickle this bird's arse!'

At this point Shahrazād saw the approach of morning and discreetly fell silent.

But when the eight-hundred-and-eighty-second night had come

SHE SAID:

'For pity's sake, my dear, do not do so!' cried the girl. 'He will let go of us and we shall fall.' 'But I want to tickle his arse,' objected her brother. 'Then we shall die,' moaned Little-Foot. 'This is how it is done,' he answered, and put his plan into execution. The sensitive bird turned a somersault in the air and instinctively loosed his grip upon the captives.

The two children fell into the sea and were carried to the bottom, but, as they were both able to swim, they succeeded in rising to the surface and reaching the shore. As they set foot on land, they could see no more than if it had been the middle of the night, for they had chanced upon the country of shadows.

The boy at once groped until he found two pebbles, which he rubbed together until sparks came; by their light he made a large pile of driftwood and set fire to it. The bright flames comforted them, but before their clothes were well dried they heard a bellowing as of a thousand wild buffaloes and saw a black gigantic ghoul speeding across the sand towards them. As he came into the light of the fire, he cried from the furnace of his throat: 'What rash fool has dared to make light in the land which I have vowed to darkness?'

Little-Foot was terrified, and gasped: 'O son of my father and mother, here is death at last! I am so frightened!' She hid herself half fainting against her brother; but he, without a moment's loss of composure, seized the burning brands of his fire, one by one, and hurled them into the bellowing throat before him. As the last coal descended, the ghoul burst asunder in the midst and sunlight sprang down again upon the land of shadows; for the darkness had been caused by that ghoul ever keeping his gigantic bottom between the sun and the earth. So much for the ghoul's bottom.

While Hard-Head lay resting behind a rock and Little-Foot watched beside him, the King of that country saw the sun shine again after many years and knew that the terrible ghoul was dead. He therefore left his palace, followed by his guards, and set out in search of the valiant hero who had destroyed the scourge of his kingdom. He came down to the seashore and soon found the smoking remains of the children's fire. When she saw the oncoming of the armed men, with the King shining at their head, Little-Foot was again thrown into terror and begged her brother to escape while there was yet time; but he refused and still lay comfortably behind the rock.

Near the ashes of the fire the King found the body of the ghoul, blown into a thousand fragments, also a tiny sandal which Little-Foot had dropped when she retired with her brother behind the rock. 'Surely she who wore this sandal destroyed our foe,' cried the King to his guards. 'Scatter and find her!' But Little-Foot did not wait to be found. She plucked up her courage and came out from behind the rock. As the King walked to meet her, she threw herself at his feet imploring his safeguard, and, when he saw that she wore the fellow to the little sandal which he held in his hand, he raised and embraced her, saying: 'Little daughter of benediction, did you kill the ghoul?' 'My brother did, O King,' she answered. 'And where is the fine fellow?' he demanded. 'You will not hurt him?' she insisted. 'Most certainly not!' exclaimed the King. So Little-Foot retired behind the rock and led forth Hard-Head. When the two stood before him, the King said to the boy: 'O chief and crown of bravery, I give you the hand of my only daughter in marriage, and, because of her delicious little feet, I take your sister to be my Queen.' 'It is permitted,' answered Hard-Head.

And they all prospered in great delight.

And Shahrazād said again:

The Anklet

AMONG other sayings, it is said that there were once in a city three sisters, daughters of the same father but not of the same mother, who lived together and earned their bread by spinning flax. All three were as beautiful as the moon, but the youngest was also the fairest and the most charming; she could spin more than the other two together, and her spinning was faultless. This superiority roused the jealousy of the two elder sisters, for they were born of a different mother.

One day, the youngest went to the market and, with the money of her spinning, bought a little alabaster pot to set before her with flowers in it as she worked; but, when she returned with her purchase, her two sisters mocked her for foolish extravagance. In her shame and grief she answered nothing, but set a rose in the pot and, placing it before her, went on spinning.

Now this little alabaster pot was a thing of magic; when its mistress wished to eat, it brought her delicate food, and when she wished to dress, it gave her robes of marvel. But the child was careful to keep the secret of its virtue from her jealous sisters; while she was with them, she feigned to go on living as before and dressed even more modestly than they dressed. As soon as they went forth, however, she would shut herself up alone in her bedroom and caress the little alabaster pot, saying: 'Little pot, little pot, I want such and such today.' Then the little pot would bring her fair robes or sweetmeats, and, in her loneliness, she would put on garments of gold-embroidered silk, and deck herself with jewels, with rings on all her fingers, with bracelets and anklets, and would eat delicious sweetmeats by herself. When the sisters were due to return, the little pot would make the gifts of its magic providing disappear, and they ever found their youngest spinning flax, with the little pot in front of her holding a rose.

She lived in this way for many weeks, poor in the presence of her jealous sisters and rich when she was alone, until a day came when the King of that city gave a great feast in his palace and invited all his people to present themselves. The three sisters received an invitation and the two elder, bidding the youngest stay at home to mind the house, dressed themselves in their poor best and departed for the feast. As soon as they had gone, the youngest went to her own room, and said to the alabaster pot: 'Little pot, I want a green silk robe, a red silk vest, and a white silk mantle, all of the most lovely quality. I want rings for my fingers, turquoise bracelets for my wrists, and little diamond anklets. O little pot, I want to be the fairest of all at the palace to-night.' The alabaster pot provided these things, and the girl, dressing herself hastily, made her way to the palace and entered the harīm, where the women's side of the entertainment was taking place. Not even her sisters recognised her, so greatly had her magic apparelling enhanced her natural beauty. All the other women looked at her with moist eyes and went into an ecstasy before her. She received their homage like a sweet and gentle queen, and they fell in love with her.

When the feast was near its end, the girl took advantage of the chaining of the general attention by certain singers, to glide from the harīm and leave the palace. But in the haste of her flight she dropped one of her diamond anklets into the sunken trough where the King's horses were used to drink. She was not conscious of her loss, and her only care was to be waiting in the house when her sisters returned.

At this point Shahrazād saw the approach of morning and discreetly fell silent.

But when the eight-hundred-and-eighty-third night had come

SHE SAID:

Next morning the King's grooms took the horses out to drink, but they would not go near the water; their nostrils dilated in terror at the sight of something shining like a round of stars at the bottom of the trough and they backed away, panting and blowing. The grooms whistled them on and tugged at their halters in vain; then they let the beasts be and, looking down into the water, discovered the diamond anklet.

When the King's son, who always superintended the care of his own horses, had looked at the anklet and determined the wonderful slimness of the ankle which it must fit, he marvelled and cried: 'By my life, surely no woman born could wear it!' He turned it about and, seeing that each of the stones was singly worth all the jewels in his father's crown, he thought: 'By Allah, I shall marry the girl whom this anklet fits and no other woman!' He went and woke the King, his father, and, showing him the anklet, said: 'I wish to marry the owner of so slim an ankle.' 'I see no harm in that,' answered the King, 'but such things are in your mother's province, for she knows and I do not.

So the prince went to his mother and told her the story of the anklet. 'I trust you to marry me to the owner of so slim an ankle,' he said, 'for my father says that you know about such things.' 'I hear and I obey!' answered the Queen, and she called her women together and went out with them from the palace to search for the owner of the anklet.

They entered all the harīms of the city and tried the ornament upon the ankles of every woman, young and old, but none were found slim enough to wear it. After two weeks of vain pilgrimage, they came to the house of the three sisters and, when the Queen tried the anklet upon the youngest, behold! it fitted to a marvel.

The Queen embraced the girl, and the women of the court embraced her; they took her by the hand and led her to the palace, where her marriage with the prince was at once arranged. Feasts and entertainments of great magnificence were given, and lasted for forty days and forty nights.

On the last day, after the bride had been conducted to the hammām, her sisters, whom she had brought with her to share the enjoyments of her royal state, began to dress her and arrange her hair. But she had trusted in their affection and told them the secret of the alabaster pot, in order that they might not be astonished at the magnificent robes and ornaments which she had been able to obtain for her marriage night. When they had coifed her hair, they fastened it with a series of diamond pins.

As soon as the last pin had gone into place, the sweet bride was changed into a dove with a large crest upon her head, and flew away in fright through the window.

For the pins were magic pins which could transform all girls to doves, and the two sisters had required them from the pot to ease their jealousy.

The wicked women had been alone with their sister at the time and, when question was made, they told the King's son that his bride had gone out only for a moment. When she did not return, the young man sent search parties throughout the city and about all his father's kingdom, but these came back with no news at all. His loss plunged him into a wasting bitterness.

The dove came every morning and every evening to her husband's window and crooned there long and sadly. Soon the prince began to find an answer to his misery in this crooning, and came to love the bird. One day, noticing that she did not fly away when he approached the window, he stretched forth his hand and caught her. She shook in his fingers and went on crooning; so he began to caress her gently and smooth her feathers and scratch her head. While he did this last, he felt several little hard objects beneath his finger-tips, as if they had been the heads of pins. He pulled them from the crest one by one, and, when the last pin had come forth, the dove shook herself and became his bride again.

The two lived together in great delight and Allāh granted them numberless children as beautiful as themselves; but the two wicked sisters died of jealousy and a flowing back of their poisoned blood upon their hearts.

And that night Shahrazād said again:

The He-Goat and the King's Daughter

IT is related, among other relations, that there was once, in a city of India, a Sultān to whom Allāh had granted three daughters who were perfect in every part and a great delight to all beholders. As he loved them dearly, he wished, when they were ripe, to find them husbands who should esteem them at their proper value. To this end, he approached the Queen his wife, saying: 'Our three dear daughters are now ripe, and, when the tree is at her Spring, she must bear flowers, harbingers of future fruit, or she will wither. We must certainly find husbands for their happiness.' 'The plan is good,' answered the Queen, and she concerted with her husband as to the best way. On that day they sent out heralds to announce through the kingdom that the three princesses were of marriageable age, and that every unmarried man of their subjects should appear beneath the windows of the palace at a given hour. For the Queen had said to her husband: 'Wedded happiness does not depend on birth or riches, but upon Allāh. We must leave the choice of husbands for our daughters to the Destiny of each. When the time comes, they shall throw their handkerchiefs from the window among the suitors, and the handkerchiefs shall choose.'

The day and the hour came, and the polo-ground which stretched beneath the walls of the palace was tightly packed with suitors. A window opened and the King's eldest daughter looked forth with her handkerchief in her hand. She threw it into the air, and the wind took it and carried it gently, so that it fell upon the head of a young amīr, handsome and of noble birth.

Then the second princess appeared and threw her handkerchief, which lighted on the head of a young prince, as fair and delightful as could be wished.

The third daughter of the Sultān of India threw her handkerchief out over the crowd; the wind turned it and then stilled it, and it came to rest upon the horns of a he-goat who had pressed in among the suitors. Although the Sultān had devised this test, he considered that here was no fair use of it, so he bade the third daughter throw again; but again and yet again the wind lightly picked up the handkerchief and with it draped the horns of the he-goat.

At this point Shahrazād saw the approach of morning and discreetly fell silent.

But when the eight-hundred-and-eighty-fourth night had come

SHE SAID:

The Sultān's rage knew no bounds, and he cried: 'As Allāh lives, I would rather see her die an old maid in my palace than marry this filthy he-goat!' But the third princess wept and said, between two sobs: 'O father, if such be my Destiny, how can you prevent it? Each creature of Allāh carries his Fate about his neck, and if mine lies round the neck of this he-goat, is there any power can stay me from becoming his bride?' Her two sisters, who hated her in secret because she was younger and more beautiful, united their protestations with her own, hoping that marriage with a he-goat would avenge them for all. And the three of them so worked upon the King their father that at last he gave his consent to this monstrous bridal.

The three weddings were celebrated with all desirable pomp; the city was lighted with coloured fires and strewn with flowers, and for forty days and nights the people rejoiced with feasting, dancing and singing. One shadow only marred the minds of the guests, a fear for the result of a union between a virgin princess and a he-goat large even of his kind. During the days before the bridal night, the Sultān and his wife and the wives of the wazīrs and dignitaries of the court wearied their tongues in an effort to persuade the child not to consummate her marriage with an animal of naturally repulsive odour, fiery eye, and terrifying tool. But, to each and all, she answered: 'We carry our Fate about our neck and if it be mine to marry a he-goat, nothing shall stay me.'

When the night came, the three sisters were taken to the hammām, where they were bathed and ornamented and coifed. Then each was led to a chamber reserved for her, and to the two elder there happened what there happened.

As soon as the he-goat was led into the youngest princess's chamber, and the door had been shut upon them, he kissed the earth between his wife's hand and with a sudden shake threw aside his skin, to appear as a youth more handsome than the angel Hārūt. He kissed the girl between the eyes, upon the chin, about the neck, and a little everywhere, saying: 'O life of souls, do not try to find out who I am! Let it suffice that I am richer and more powerful than your father and the two young men who have married your sisters. I have loved you for weary months, but could not attain to you before. If you like me and wish to keep me, you will have to give me a promise.' 'What is the promise?' asked the princess, who found him very much to her taste. 'For love of your eyes I will execute it, however difficult it may be.' 'It is easy, lady,' he replied. 'I only require your oath that you will not reveal to a single person that I have the power of change; for if it were even suspected that I am sometimes a he-goat and sometimes a prince, I should be obliged to disappear at once, and you would find it very difficult to come upon a trace of me again.' At once the girl solemnly promised, adding: 'I would rather die than lose my sweet lord.'

Then, as there was no excuse for further delay, they gave rein to their feelings and loved with a great love, lip to lip and thigh to thigh, in pure delight until the dawn. With the first light the youth rose from between the whiteness of his bride and became a bearded goat again, with horns, split hoofs, and enormous merchandise. There remained no sign of that which had taken place, except a few blood-stains on the napkin of honour.

When the Queen came, as is customary, to ask news of the night and saw the proof of the napkin and beheld her daughter smiling and happy and the goat seated on a carpet at her feet, ruminating wisely, she ran and fetched her husband, who regarded these things with no less stupefaction. 'Is it true, my daughter?' he asked at length, and she answered: 'It is true.' 'You are not dead from pain and shame?' he demanded, and she replied: 'Why, in Allāh's name, should I be dead, with such a skilful and charming bridegroom?' 'You do not complain of him, then?' said the King. 'Not in the least,' answered the princess. 'As you do not complain, you must be happy,' admitted the Sultān, 'and happiness is all that we could wish for our dearest daughter.' So they left her to live in peace with the he-goat.

Some months later the King gave a great tourney in the polo-ground on the occasion of a certain feast and, among the other dignitaries who attended it, came the husbands of the two elder princesses. But the Sultān did not invite the he-goat, as he did not wish to be made a laughing-stock before his people.

The tourney began, and the riders, on their space-devouring steeds, jousted with loud cries and thrust strongly with their lances. Most successful of all were the King's two sons-in-law, and the people were cheering them to the echo, when an unknown knight cantered onto the ground, with such bright bearing that the brows of all the rest were lowered before him. He challenged the two royal bridegrooms to combat, one after the other, and, with a single blow of his lance, unseated each.

Amid the delighted cries of the assembly proclaiming him conqueror, he rode beneath the palace windows to salute the King with his lance, as is the custom. The two elder princesses looked down upon him with eyes of hatred, but the youngest, who recognised her lord in him, took a rose from her hair and threw it towards him, to the disgust and consternation of the King and of the Queen and of her two sisters.

On the second day, also, the young stranger bore off every event, and, when he passed beneath the royal window, his bride threw him a spray of jasmine. The King and Queen and sisters were more shocked than ever, and the King said to himself: 'Not content with darkening our lives by marrying that damned he-goat, she must publicly declare her passion for a stranger!' The Queen gave bitter sidelong glances and the two sisters shook out their dresses for horror as they looked upon their youngest.

Though she saw these signs of shame and animosity, the young princess could not help throwing down a tamarind flower, when her knight was acclaimed victorious on the third day.

The Sultān's rage burst forth, his eyes reddened, his ears trembled, and his nostrils shook. He caught his daughter by the hair to kill her, as he cried: 'Vile whore, was it not enough to bring a he-goat into my line? Must you go wantoning after strangers and catching for their desire? Die now and free us from this taint!' He was about to dash out her brains on the marble floor, when the princess bought her dear life by sobbing out: 'I will tell you the truth! Spare me, and I will tell you the truth!' Without taking breath, she told her father, her mother and her sisters that the he-goat was sometimes a man, and that it was her own husband who had been victorious in the jousting.

The Sultān and his wife and the two princesses marvelled to the limits of marvel, and forgave the bride; but neither the he-goat nor smell of him, nor the fair youth nor the shadow of him, was seen again about the palace. After many days and nights of fruitless waiting, the princess understood that he would never come, and fell straightway into a decline of tears.

At this point Shahrazād saw the approach of morning and discreetly fell silent.

But when the eight-hundred-and-eighty-fifth night had come

SHE SAID:

She lived for many days in wasting and continual tears, refusing consolation and answering all comfort with these words: 'It is all worthless. I am the most unfortunate of women and shall surely die.'

But, before dying, she wished to know if there were any woman upon Allāh's earth as hopeless and unhappy as herself. At first she decided to travel and make enquiry among the women of the cities through which she passed, but she abandoned this first idea for a second: to construct a splendid hammām at her own great expense, one which should not have its equal in all India. When the building was completed, she sent forth heralds to announce that entrance to the bath was free to all women, on condition that each told, for the distraction of the King's daughter, the greatest grief which had troubled her life. Those who had had no griefs could have no bathing.

All the afflicted females of the kingdom, all those who had been abandoned by Fate, those attacked by every colour of grief, widows and the divorced, together with all who had been wounded by the vicissitudes of time or the treachery of life, thronged to the new hammām, and each of them told the greatest grief of her life to the King's daughter, before she went down into the bath. Some detailed the ration of blows which their husbands allowed them, some shed tears over their widowhood, and yet others painted the bitterness of seeing their husbands prefer some hideous rival, some old woman or camel-lipped negress. And there were many mothers who found moving words to picture their sorrow at the death of an only son. But the princess could not find one, among all those thousands, who had a grief to be compared with hers, and she sank ever deeper in the dark waters of despair.

One day a poor old woman, already shivering beneath the breeze of death, entered the hammām, leaning on a stick. She approached the princess and kissed her hand, saying: 'O lady, my sorrows are more in number than my years, and my tongue would dry up before I had finished the tale of them. I will only tell you of my last sorrow, which was also my sorest because I can find no sense in it. It happened only yesterday and, if I tremble before you now, it is because I have seen what I have seen.

'You must know, O lady, that I possess no other chemise than this blue cotton which I am wearing now. As it needed washing before I could present myself fittingly at the hammām of your generosity, I went down to a lonely part of the river bank yesterday, where I might strip myself without being seen and wash my garment in the water.

'I had already cleansed the chemise and spread it on the pebbles to dry, when I saw a mule coming towards me, bearing two waterskins upon her back. As I expected the man who was driving her to appear at any moment, I jumped into my chemise, wet as it was, and let the mule pass me; but, when I saw that there was no shadow of a man following and that the animal walked along, wagging her head from side to side, as if sure of her direction, curiosity urged me to follow. I walked behind until the mule came to a hummock of earth near the river and, halting before it, struck the earth three times with her right hoof. At the third knocking the hummock opened in the middle and the mule went forward down a gentle slope. Plucking up courage, I went down after her and followed her into a cave below the earth.

'I found myself in a great kitchen as of an underground palace, where I saw fair red cookpots simmering on their stoves and sending up a savoury steam which dilated the fans of my heart and made the membranes of my nose to live again.

'I felt a great hunger grow in me and, seeing no one from whom I could ask for food in Allāh's name, lifted the lid of one of the cookpots. An odorous vapour enveloped me, but, with the vapour, a voice cried from the bottom of the pot: "Hands off, this is for our mistress! Touch not, or you die!" I dropped the lid in fright and ran from the kitchen into a second and smaller hall, where loaves and pastries of a delicious lightness were ranged on plates. I stretched out my hand to one of the loaves, which was still moist with heat, and received a slap on the fingers, while a voice cried from the plate: "Hands off, this is for our mistress! Touch not, or you die!" I fled again and passed through many galleries on the trembling of my old legs, until I came to a marble hall, such as your father perhaps has in his palace. In the middle of it was a basin of living water and about the basin there were forty thrones, one higher and more splendid than the rest.

'I was refreshing my soul with the cool and harmony of this place, when the silence was broken by a sound as of a flock of goats walking upon stones. I had just time to hide myself beneath a couch beside the wall, when I saw forty long-bearded he-goats enter in line, the last being borne by the last but one. This honoured one came down from the back of his porter and stood in front of the principal throne, while the others bowed before him with their heads to the marble pavement. Then, at a signal from their chief, they rose, and all forty shook themselves three times, to come forth from their skins as forty naked moon-white boys. They went down into the basin and bathed; they came up out of it, with their bodies glowing like jasmine, and sat upon the thrones, clothed only in their beauty.

'Then I saw that the handsomest of them all, who sat upon the principal throne, was weeping great and bitter tears, and that his companions were weeping lesser tears. They all sighed, saying: "Our mistress! O our mistress!" and their leader murmured: "O queen of grace and beauty!" Then I heard from the earth and from the dome, from the walls and doors and all the furniture, the same sorrowful murmuring: "O our mistress! O queen of grace and beauty!"

'When the band of boys had wept and cried for an hour, the prince of them rose, saying: "When will you come? I cannot go to you! I

cannot go to you, O queen, when will you come to me?" He stepped
down from the throne and got again into his goatskin, and the others
stepped from their thrones and got again into their goatskins, and
followed him away from that place.

'As soon as I had heard the last pattering of their feet, I crawled
out of my hiding place, and did not take a full breath until I had left
that underground palace behind me.

'That is my story, O princess, and the greatest sorrow of my life.
It was a double sorrow, because I did not eat and could not understand.'

The princess's heart had beaten ever more loudly as the old
woman's tale progressed, for she could not doubt that the chief of
the he-goats was her husband. 'O my mother,' she cried, 'Allāh in
His infinite compassion has led you hither that I may make your old
age a thing of happiness. From henceforth all that I have is yours,
and if you are grateful you can repay me in one moment by leading
me to the hummock into which you followed the mule.' The old
woman readily undertook to do this, and, when the moon rose upon
the terrace of that hammām, the two women went out together and
sought the riverside.

Presently the mule passed them, carrying two waterskins, and
they followed her until she came to the hummock and rapped thrice
with her right foot. When the slope appeared, leading down into the
earth, the princess bade her companion wait for her outside; but the
old woman refused to let her go alone.

They went down into the cave together and found in the kitchen
all the fair red cookpots singing upon their stoves and giving forth
a savour which expanded the fans of the heart, made the membranes
of the nose to live again, and put to rout all sorrow which infests the
spirit. The lids rose of their own accord as the princess passed, and
joyous voices from the steam cried: 'Welcome, welcome to our mistress!' In the second hall, where the pastries and puffed loaves were
ranged, happy voices cried from all the plates and pans: 'Welcome,
welcome!' and the air itself seemed to vibrate with an audible
joy.

Seeing and hearing these things, the old woman pointed out to the
princess the galleries which led to the hall of thrones. Then she said:
'Dear mistress, it is lawful for you to go forward; but a servant's
place is in the kitchen, and I shall stay here.' So the girl went on
alone, still companioned by auspicious music, and, coming to the

hall of thrones, sat down in the place of honour and waited, with her little veil over her face.

At this point Shahrazād saw the approach of morning and discreetly fell silent.

But when the eight-hundred-and-eighty-sixth night had come

SHE SAID:

She had hardly taken her place, when a soft noise was heard, not as of goats, but as of a boy lightly running, and her bridegroom entered to her in the diamond shine of his youth.

The two lovers came together joyfully in that hall, and all the palace sang music of itself to celebrate their rapture. After certain days spent below the earth in savouring their reunion, the two young people returned to the Sultān's palace, where they were greeted with acclamation by a whole people. And, after that time, the King and Queen befriended them, so that they lived together in great content. But Allāh knows all!

As Shahrazād did not yet feel weary, she said again:

The Prince and the Tortoise

IT is related, O auspicious King, that there was once, in the antiquity of time and the passage of the age and of the moment, a powerful Sultān whom Allāh had blessed with three sons: Ali, the eldest, Husain, the second, and Muhammad, the youngest. They were all indomitable males and heroic warriors; but the youngest was the most handsome, the bravest and the most generous. Their father loved them equally and, in the justice of his heart, had resolved to leave to each an equal part of his riches and his kingdom.

Also, when they came to marriageable age, the King called his wise and prudent wazīr to him, saying: 'O wazīr, I wish to find wives for my three sons, and have called you to me that you may give me your advice.' The wazīr reflected for an hour, and then answered, lifting his head: 'O King of time, the matter is delicate, for good and evil chance are not to be told beforehand, and against the decree of Destiny there is no provision. I suggest that you take the three princes, armed with their bows and arrows, up on to the terrace of the palace, and there, after bandaging their eyes, make them each turn round several times. After that, let them fire their arrows straight ahead of them, and let the houses upon which the arrows fall be visited. Have the owners of the houses brought before you and ask of each his daughter in marriage for the marksman of the arrow which fell upon his house. Thus each of your sons will have a bride chosen by Destiny.'

'Your advice is excellent and I shall act upon it!' cried the Sultān. As soon as his sons returned from hunting, he told them of the trial which was to be made and led them up, with their bows and quivers, to the terrace of his palace.

The dignitaries of the court followed and watched with breathless interest while the eyes of the young men were bandaged.

The eldest prince was turned about, and then discharged his arrow straight in front of him. It flew through the air with great swiftness and fell upon the dwelling of a most noble lord.

In like manner the second prince's arrow fell upon the terrace of the commander-in-chief of the King's army. But, when Muhammad drew his bow, the arrow fell upon a house whose owner was not known.

The King, with his retinue, set forth to visit the three houses, and found that the great lord's daughter and the commander-in-chief's daughter were girls as fair as moons, and that their parents were delighted to marry them to the two princes. But when the King visited the third house, on which Muhammad's shaft had fallen, he found in it no inhabitant except a large and lonely tortoise. Therefore, deeming that there could be no thought for a moment of marrying a prince to such an animal, the Sultān decided that the test should be made again. The youngest prince mounted again to the terrace and again shot an arrow blindfold, but it fell true upon the house of the large and lonely tortoise.

The King grew angry at this, and cried: 'By Allāh, your shooting is not fortunate to-day, my son! Pray for the Prophet!' 'Blessing and peace be upon him and upon his Companions and those who are faithful to him!' answered Muhammad. 'Now invoke the name of Allāh,' exclaimed the King, 'and shoot a third arrow.' 'In the name of the Merciful, the Compassionate!' exclaimed Muhammad, as he strongly drew his bow and sent a third shaft on to the roof of the house inhabited by the large and lonely tortoise.

When the Sultān saw, beyond any manner of doubt, that Destiny favoured the tortoise, he decided that his youngest son should remain a bachelor, and said to him: 'My son, as this tortoise is not of our race, or our kind, or our religion, it would be better for you not to marry at all until Allāh takes us again into His compassion.' But young Muhammad cried in dissent from this: 'I swear by the virtues of the Prophet (upon whom be prayer and peace!) that the time of my celibacy is over! If the large tortoise is written in my Destiny I shall assuredly marry her.' 'She is certainly written in your Destiny!' cried the astonished Sultān. 'But it would be a monstrous thing for a human being to wed with a tortoise!' 'I have no predilection for tortoises in general,' cried the prince. 'It is this particular one whom I wish to marry.'

The Sultān, who loved his son, made no more objections but, though the weddings of Alī and Husain were celebrated with great splendour for forty days and forty nights and then felicitously consummated, no one at court, neither his two brothers, nor their wives, nor the wives of the amīrs and dignitaries, would accept an invitation to Muhammad's bridal feast, and, instead, they did all in their power to spoil and make it sad. Poor Muhammad was bitterly humiliated by the mocking smiles and turned backs which everywhere greeted him; but of his marriage night he would say nothing, and only Allāh, from Whom no secrets are hid, can tell what passed between the two. It is certain, at least, that no one in that kingdom could imagine how a human youth might couple with a tortoise, even though she were as big as a stock-jar.

In the time which came after the three weddings, the years and preoccupations of his reign, added to the emotion of his disappointment in Muhammad, bowed the King's back and thinned his bones. He pined away and became yellow; he lost his appetite and, with his appetite, his vision, so that he became almost completely blind.

The three princes, who loved their father dearly, resolved to leave his health no longer in the ignorant and superstitious care of the harīm. When they had concerted together, they approached the Sultān and kissed his hand, saying: 'Dear father, your face is becoming yellow, your appetite is weakening, and your sight is failing you. If these things go on, we shall soon be tearing our garments for grief that we have lost the prop of all our life; therefore you must listen to our counsel and obey it. We have determined that our wives and not the women of the harīm shall henceforth prepare your food, for these last are great experts in the kitchen and by their cookery can give you back appetite which shall furnish strength, strength which will furnish health, and health which will restore your vision.' The Sultān was deeply touched by this care on his sons' part. 'May Allāh shower His blessings upon you!' he said. 'But I am afraid that this will be a great nuisance for your wives.'

At this point Shahrazād saw the approach of morning and discreetly fell silent.

But when the eight-hundred-and-eighty-seventh night had come

SHE SAID:

'A nuisance to our wives?' they cried. 'They are your slaves and have no more urgent object in life than to prepare the food which will restore you to health. We have agreed that each of them shall prepare a separate dish, and that you shall choose your favourite in appearance, odour and taste. Thus appetite will come back to you and your eyes be cured.' 'You know better than I do what is for the best,' answered the Sultān, as he embraced them.

The three princes went joyfully to their wives and bade them prepare the most admirable dish they could, and each said further, to excite a spirit of emulation: 'It is essential that our father should prefer the cooking of our house.'

After they had given their orders, the two elder brothers were for ever mocking Muhammad and asking him how a tortoise cooked, but he met all their jests with a calm smile. His wife, the large and lonely tortoise, had only been waiting for such an opportunity to show what she could do. At once she set to work, and her first care was to send a confidential servant to her elder sister-in-law, begging her to send back all the rat and mouse dung which she could collect in her house, that the tortoise, who never employed any other condiment, might use these matters for seasoning the rice dishes which she was preparing for the Sultān. 'As Allāh lives, I will do no such thing!' said Ali's wife to herself. 'If these things make really good seasoning let the wretched tortoise find her own; I can make all the use of them that is necessary.' Then aloud to the servant she said: 'I regret that I have to refuse your mistress's request, but I have hardly enough rat and mouse dung for my own requirements.'

When the servant returned with this answer, the tortoise laughed happily, and sent her to Husain's wife with a request for all the hens' and pigeons' droppings which she had by her. The servant returned from this mission empty-handed, with a bitter and disobliging message from the second princess; but when the tortoise had caused the words to be repeated to her, she fell into an ecstasy of contentment and laughed so heartily that she fell over on her backside.

As soon as she was a little recovered, she prepared those meats which she could cook best, covered the dish which held them with a wicker cover, and wrapped the whole in a rose-scented napkin. Then she despatched her servant with the dish to the Sultān, at the same moment as his other two daughters-in-law were sending theirs by slaves.

The time of the meal arrived, and the Sultān sat down before the three dishes; but, when he had lifted the lid of that sent by the eldest son's wife, there rose so foul a steam and odour of rat turds that it might well have asphyxiated an elephant.

The Sultān was so disagreeably affected by this stench that he fell head over heels in a swoon, and, when his sons succeeded in bringing him to with rose-water and the use of fans, he sat up and cursed his daughter-in-law heartily.

In a little while he became calmer and consented to try the second dish; but, as soon as it was uncovered, a fetid stink of burnt birds' droppings took him by the throat and eyes so that he thought that the hour of blindness and death was upon him. It was not until the windows had been thrown open and the dish removed and benzoin burnt with incense to purify the air, that the disgusted old man felt himself strong enough to say: 'What harm have I done to your wives, my sons, that they should try to dig me a grave before my time?' The two elder princes could only answer that the thing passed their understanding; but young Muhammad kissed his father's hand and begged him to forget his previous disappointments in the delight of the third dish. 'What is that, Muhammad?' cried the King in an indignant rage. 'Do you mock your old father? When women can prepare such frightful foods, do you expect me to touch the cooking of a tortoise? I can see that you have all sworn to destroy me.' Muhammad went on his knees and swore, by his life and by the verity of the Faith, that the third dish would make up for all, and that he himself would eat anything of it which was not to his father's taste. He urged with such fervour and humility that the Sultān at last signed to the slave to lift the third cover, and waited with a set jaw, murmuring: 'I seek refuge in the protection of Allāh!'

But it was the soul of all fine cooking which rose from the dish that the tortoise had prepared; it exquisitely dilated the fans of the old man's heart, it nourished the fans of his lungs, it shook the fans of his nostrils, it brought back lost appetite, it opened his eyes and clarified his vision. He ate for an hour without stopping, then drank an excellent sherbert of musk and pounded snow, and finally gurked several times from the very bottom of his satisfied stomach.

In great delight he gave thanks to Allāh and praised the cooking of the tortoise; Muhammad accepted his congratulations modestly, in order not to excite the jealousy of his brothers. 'That is only one of my wife's talents, dear father,' he said. 'Allāh grant that she may some day find a chance really to earn your praises.' Then he begged the King to allow his future nourishment to be entirely in the hands of the tortoise, and his delighted father readily agreed to the arrangement, which in a few weeks entirely re-established his health and eyesight.

To celebrate his cure the Sultān gave a great feast, and bade his three sons attend it with their wives. At once the two elder princesses began to make preparation that they might appear with honour and success before their father-in-law.

The large tortoise also schemed how to whiten her husband's visage before the people by the beauty of her escorting and the elegance of her clothes. Her first step was to send her confidential servant to Ali's wife with a request for the loan of the big goose which she had in her courtyard, that the tortoise might use it as a fitting steed on which to ride to the festivities. The Princess gave so peremptory a refusal that the good tortoise fell over on her backside in the convulsions of laughter which it occasioned her. Then she sent to the second sister to borrow her large he-goat for the same purpose, and never has tortoise been so convulsed and dilated with pure joy as was this one when she received a second and much ruder refusal.

The hour of the feast came, and all the old Queen's women were drawn up in good order at the outside door of the harīm to receive the three royal brides. As they waited, a cloud of dust rolled towards them and, when it dissipated, they saw a gigantic goose waddling forward with the speed of the wind, throwing her legs to left and right, beating her wings, and carrying the first princess of the kingdom clinging to her neck in disordered fright. Almost immediately afterwards, a he-goat, rearing and savagely bleating, came up to the entrance also, bearing upon his back the second princess, all stained with dust and dung.

The Sultān and his wife were deeply offended by this double exhibition, and the former cried: 'See, they are not content with strangling and poisoning me; they wish to mock me before the people!' The Queen received the two women coldly, and an uncomfortable pause was only broken by the arrival of the third princess. The King and his wife were full of apprehension, saying to each other: 'If two humans could show so absurdly, what can we expect from a tortoise? There is no power or might save in Allāh!' So saying, they waited with caught breath for what might appear.

At this point Shahrazād saw the approach of morning and discreetly fell silent.

But when the eight-hundred-and-eighty-eighth night had come

SHE SAID:

The first rank of couriers appeared, announcing the arrival of prince Muhammad's wife, and presently four handsome grooms, dressed in brocade and rich tunics with trailing sleeves, led up the palanquin. It was covered with bright-coloured silks, and the black men who carried it set it down by the stairs. An unknown princess of bright splendour stepped from it and the women, supposing her to be a maid of honour, waited for the alighting of the tortoise. Yet, when the palanquin was borne away and this delightful vision mounted the steps alone, they recognised her as Muhammad's bride and received her with honour and effusion. The Sultān's heart rejoiced to see her grace and nobility, her charming manners and musical movements.

At once the Sultān bade his sons and their wives be seated by him and by the Queen, and, when they had taken their places, the feast was served.

The first dish was, as usual, a profusion of rice swollen in butter. Before anyone could take a mouthful the beautiful princess lifted the dish and poured all its contents over her hair: immediately each grain of rice turned to a pearl and the pearls ran down the long strands of hair and tinkled to the floor in a bright cascade.

Before the company could recover its wits after so admirable a prodigy, she also lifted a large tureen, filled with thick green soup, and poured its contents over her head in the same way. The green soup changed to an infinity of emeralds among her hair, and these fell about her like green rain, to mingle their sea-tints with the pearls upon the floor.

During the delighted confusion which followed, the servants brought other supplies of rice and green soup for the guests to eat, and the two elder princesses, now yellow with jealousy, could not leave well alone. The eldest seized on the dish of rice and the second on the tureen of green soup; both poured the contents of these things upon their heads. But the rice remained rice in the hair of the first, horribly daubing her with butter, and the soup, remaining soup, ran down in a sticky course over the hair and face and garments of the second, for all the world like cow slop.

The Sultān was disgusted at these accidents and commanded his two elder daughters-in-law to withdraw from the feast, also he proclaimed that he wished never to see them again, or smell them, or hear of them. Their husbands, therefore, led them away in a great rage, and you may suppose that all four noses trailed very near the ground. So much for them.

When prince Muhammad and his magic princess were left alone with the Sultān, he embraced them and took them to his heart, saying: 'You alone are my children!' He wrote a will leaving his throne to his youngest son and, calling together his amīrs and wazīrs, made his intention known to them. Then to the two young people, he said: 'I wish you both to stay with me in my palace until the end.' 'To hear is to obey,' they answered. 'Our father's desire is upon our heads and before our eyes.'

That she might never again be tempted to resume the appearance of a tortoise and so shock the old Sultān, the princess ordered her servant to bring the large and lonely shell which she had left at home that day and, when it was fetched, burnt it without compunction. Ever afterwards she remained in her own delightful form. And glory be to Allāh Who gave her a faultless body, a marvel to the eyes of men!

The Giver showered His blessings upon these two and delighted them with numerous children.

Seeing that the King still listened without displeasure, Shahrazād also told that night the tale of:

The Chick-Pea Seller's Daughter

It is related that there was once, in the city of Cairo, an honest and respectable chick-pea seller, to whom Allāh had given three daughters. Though such could not usually be counted a blessing, the hawker received them with resignation and loved them dearly. This was the more easy as they were all as beautiful as moons, and as the youngest, who was called Zainah, was also an epitome of intelligence and charm.

The good man, wishing to fit them by education for a marriage above his own peripatetic class, spared every penny that he could afford for their teaching, and they would go every morning to learn embroidery upon silk and velvet from a mistress in that art.

Their way lay beneath the window of the Sultān's only son and, as they passed it each morning, a royal allurement with six Babylonian eyes snaring behind the little face veils, the youth would cry provocatively from his window: 'Greeting to the chick-pea seller's daughters! Greeting to the three straight letters!' The eldest and the next would answer with a light smile of their eyes, but the youngest would pass on without even lifting her head. Yet if the Sultān's son went further, asking, it may be, news of chick-peas and the current price of chick-peas and details of the sale of chick-peas and whether chick-peas in the abstract were good or bad, it was always Zainah who answered, without looking up: 'And what have you to do with chick-peas, old pick-cheese?' and the three would hurry laughing upon their way.

The prince, who had grown to love little Zainah, grieved bitterly at her coldness and irony. One day, when she had mocked him more than usual, he realised that he would obtain nothing by his gallantry, and determined to punish the child through her father, whom he knew she greatly loved. 'She shall feel my power at last,' he said.

As he was the Sultān's heir and had power over the people, he called the chick-pea seller to him, saying: 'You are the father of those three girls?' 'I am, my lord,' answered the trembling hawker, and the prince continued: 'To-morrow morning at the hour of prayer, I require you to return here, at the same time dressed and naked, laughing and weeping at the same time, and at the same time riding and walking. If you come as you are, or fail in only one of the conditions, your head shall answer for it!' The poor chick-pea seller kissed the

earth and departed, complaining bitterly to himself that his fate was
sealed.

He came back into the presence of his daughters with the sack of
his stomach turned upon him and his nose trailing to the ground.
The girls noticed his perplexity and little Zainah asked the reason of
it. 'My child,' he answered, 'a calamity has come upon me and my
breast is straitened with sorrow.' Then he told her of his interview
with the prince in all its details; but nothing would be gained by repeating them in this place.

At this point Shahrazād saw the approach of morning and
discreetly fell silent.

But when the eight-hundred-and-eighty-ninth night had come

SHE SAID:

Zainah heard her father through to the end and then exclaimed,
with a laugh: 'Is that all, dear father? If you follow my advice in this
matter, you need have no fear at all. Also we shall make that silly
prince burst from disappointment. To fulfil the first condition, you
have only to borrow a net from our neighbour, the fisherman, and
I will make you a garment of it to wear without anything else. Thus
you will be clothed and naked at the same time.

'For the second condition, you must take an onion with you to the
palace and rub your eyes with it on the threshold; then you will be
able to laugh and weep at the same time.

'The third condition is just as easy to satisfy, dear father. You
have only to go to our neighbour, the donkey-boy, and borrow his
little ass's foal. Then you can enter the presence of that young
ruffian with the foal between your legs and your feet touching the
ground; that is to say, both riding and walking. Such is my advice;
but Allāh knows all!'

The chick-pea seller kissed Zainah between the eyes, saying: 'O
daughter of your father and mother, who has such children does not
die! Glory be to Him Who has planted so much intelligence behind
your brow and such sagacity within your soul!' The world grew
white before his eyes, care fled from his heart, and the fans of his
bosom ceased from contracting. He ate and drank, and then went
forth to make the preparations which his daughter had suggested.

Next morning the chick-pea seller entered the palace, clothed and
naked, laughing and weeping, riding and walking, while the

frightened ass's colt brayed and farted among all the royal company. The prince felt his gall bladder like to burst against his liver, but he was obliged to send the hawker away in safety. At the same time he swore to be revenged, this time upon the girl herself. We will leave him cudgelling his brains for a plan, and return to young Zainah.

As she had a far-seeing eye and a nose for the future, she foresaw that the prince's next move would be against herself. 'Better attack than wait to be attacked,' she said, and straightway went forth to the shop of a clever armourer. After greeting, she said: 'O father of skilful hands, I wish you to make me a complete suit of armour all in steel, with thigh pieces, armlets, and helmet of the same. And you must so construct it that, at the least movement or touch, each piece will make a deafening noise and terrifying clatter.' The armourer set to work at once and, in a short time, delivered exactly the suit which the young girl required.

When night fell, Zainah terribly disguised herself in her iron garment, provided herself with a pair of scissors and a razor, and, taking up a large pitchfork, made her way towards the palace.

As she came along the road, the doorkeepers and guards fled in all directions; as she passed into the palace, the slaves and eunuchs, terrified by her appearance, scurried into dark holes and corners, and remained. Thus she was able to pass through corridors and come to that chamber to which the prince had retired for the night.

The young man, hearing the frightful noise of the armour and seeing the wearer of it in the half-light, supposed that some Ifrīt had come for his soul. His face became yellow, his teeth chattered, and he fell to the floor, crying: 'Spare me, spare me, O powerful Ifrīt, and Allāh shall spare you!' 'Keep your lips and jaws very, very still, O pimp!' answered the chick-pea seller's daughter in a voice of thunder. 'Otherwise I will thrust this fork into your eye!' The prince breathed no more words and lay without movement or resistance, while the girl shaved the half of his young moustaches, the left side of his beard, the right side of his head, and both his eyebrows. Then she rubbed his face with ass's dung and slipped a portion into his mouth. Finally she left as she had come, for no man dared to bar her way. As soon as she reached home, she hid away her armour and, lying down beside her sisters, fell into a deep sleep.

Next day, as usual, the three sisters, well washed, coifed, and dressed, left for the house of their embroidery mistress and passed under the prince's window. He sat there, in his daily position, but his face and head were muffled up in silk, so that only his eyes were visible. Contrary to their custom, the three looked at him with insistent coquetry, so that he said to himself: 'I think that I am taming them at last. It must be that my eyes are more attractive when the rest is hidden.' 'O three straight letters,' he called down to them, 'O daughters of my heart, how are the chick-peas this morning?' The youngest lifted her head and answered for her sisters: 'Greeting, O muffle-face! How are the beard and moustaches this morning? How are the lovely eyebrows? And did you like the taste of ass's dung, my dear? May it have been delicious in digestion!'

Then the three girls broke into laughter and ran on, with mocking and exciting gestures.

The prince understood that the Ifrīt of the night before had been little Zainah; he felt his gall bladder rising to his nose, and swore that he would be even with the girl or die. He waited until his beard, moustaches, brows and hair had grown again and then sent for the chick-pea seller, to whom he said: 'O man, I wish you to give me the hand of your third daughter in marriage, for my heart is lost to her. If you dare to refuse your head shall answer for it.' 'It is permitted,' answered the hawker, 'but I pray that our master, the prince, will allow me time to consult the child before I finally consent.' 'Certainly, ask her permission,' cried the prince, 'but remember that her refusal will mean a black death for both of you.'

The unfortunate man hurried home and told his daughter of the prince's command; but she laughed, saying: 'As Allāh lives, there is no calamity in that! This marriage will be a godsend to us all. I consent most readily.'

The chick-pea seller returned to the palace with this answer, and the Sultān's son rejoiced. Again we will leave him, this time making preparations for the marriage, and return to Zainah.

As soon as her father left the house, she hastened to the shop of an expert confectioner, whose chief skill was in the manufacture of sugar dolls. 'O father of light fingers,' she said, 'I wish a sugar doll which shall be a life-sized portrait of myself, with hair of spun candy, deep black eyes, a little mouth, a small pretty nose, long lashes, and all that is fitting in other places.' Straightway the confectioner collected his material and made so wonderful a resemblance of Zainah, that it only lacked speech for its humanity.

When the night of penetration came, Zainah dressed the doll in her own chemise, laid it with the help of her sisters in the bed, and lowered the light curtain about it. Then she gave final instruction to the others, and hid herself behind the bed.

As soon as it was time, the two sisters went for the bridegroom and introduced him into the marriage chamber. They gave him the usual wishes and recommendations: 'She is delicate! We trust her to you! She is gentle and sweet, you will have no fault to find!' and then retired.

The Sultān's son, as he stood by the bed, remembered all the slights which his bride had put upon him and all the angers which he had felt against her. With a quick movement he unsheathed his great sword and struck at the body through the curtain, so strongly that the head flew into pieces. One morsel entered his mouth, open for cursing, and the sweetness of its taste astonished him. 'By my life,' he cried, 'though she gave me ass's dung to eat, she is passing sweet in death!'

Racked with remorse, he would have passed the sword through his own belly, but little Zainah slipped from her hiding-place and held his arms from behind, embracing him and saying: 'If we forgive each other, Allāh will forgive us both!'

The prince forgot his rancour when he saw the exquisite smiling of the child. He pardoned her and loved her, and they lived in all delight, leaving a numberless posterity behind them.

As she was not yet weary, Shahrazād also told King Shahryār that night the tale of:

The Looser

IT is related that there was once in the city of Damascus, in the land of Shām, a young merchant so handsome, so like the moon upon her fourteenth night, and so irresistible, that all the women who came to buy in the market were instantly the victims of his charm. He was a joy to the eye and a damnation to the soul. Of him the poet sang:

> There is no corner of his body negligible,
> Surely his eyes have fired the houses of this city;
> He has black scorpion curls
> And tender limbs of silver silk,
> He's wild and witty;

> The steel light of his smile is not to tell,
> And his backside will shake like curdled milk,
> Poor girls.

One day, as he sat in the front of his shop, sowing destruction with his great dark eyes and with his roses, a woman entered to make a purchase. He received her with dignity, and a conversation began concerning the goods which she required; but very soon, quite subjugated by his charms, she said: 'O face of the moon, I will return to-morrow, and you shall be contented with me.' She threw down money and, snatching up some trifle, hastened upon her way.

Next morning she returned at the same hour, leading by the hand a girl much younger and more desirable than herself. The young merchant had no eyes save for the second beauty and paid no more attention to his customer of the day before than if she had not been there. At length she whispered in his ear: 'O face of blessing, your choice is a good one, and, if you wish it, I will be an intermediary between you and this girl, who is my own daughter.' 'Benediction is in your hand, O lady of Allāh!' replied the youth. 'I greatly desire your daughter, but, alas! to desire is not to have, and, if I may judge by appearances, she is too rich for me.' 'Let not that trouble you, my son,' replied the woman. 'We will forgive you all dowry and ourselves pay the expenses of the marriage. You have but to let yourself be and you shall find clean nest, warm bread, firm flesh, and wellbeing. When we find a man as handsome as yourself, we must take him as he is and only require an excellence in you know what, hard, dry and long.' 'It is permitted,' answered the youth.

At this point Shahrazād saw the approach of morning and discreetly fell silent.

But when the eight-hundred-and-ninetieth night had come

SHE SAID:

The three had a discussion on the spot and agreed that the marriage should take place as soon as possible, without ceremonies or guests, without dancers or singers, without processions or a showing of the bride.

On the appointed day, the kādī wrote out, in the presence of witnesses, a lawful marriage contract, and the mother led the young man into the bridal chamber. 'Rejoice in your Destiny, my children!'

she said, and left them to their game. There was not in all the city of Damascus that night a fairer couple than these two who lay in each other's arms, fitting as two halves of the same white almond.

Next morning, the youth rose and, after a visit to the hammām, went down to his shop, where he stayed until the closing of the market. Then he hastened back to the new house which had been purchased for him.

As he came into the bridal chamber, he saw his wife behind the light curtain of the bed clasped in love by a beardless boy.

The world darkened before his eyes and he fled from the chamber, but only to meet his mother-in-law upon the threshold. 'What is the matter, my son? Pray for the Prophet!' cried the woman, seeing his wild looks. 'Prayer and peace be upon him!' he answered. 'What, oh what, have I seen in the bed? I take refuge in Allāh from the acts of the Stoned One!' and he spat violently on the ground as if there were someone at his feet. So the mother reasoned with him, saying: 'Are you angry because your wife lies with someone else? Do you think that we can live on air? Do you think that you were spared all the expense of dowry and marriage in order that you might object to my daughter's caprices? How do you imagine two women can exist if they do not keep their freedom? You are very presumptuous indeed!' 'I take refuge in Allāh, the Merciful, the Compassionate!' cried the astonished husband, and the woman retorted: 'What, are you still complaining? If our way of life does not suit you, let us see the broad of your back!'

The youth flew into a mighty rage, and cried so that both mother and daughter might hear him: 'I divorce her! By Allāh and the Prophet, I divorce her!'

The girl, who had come out from below the curtain of the bed, veiled herself quickly before the man who had been her husband, for he had now become a stranger to her. At the same time the lover appeared from the bed, and lo! instead of being a beardless boy, her hair fell down to kiss her heels and she was a girl!

While the poor young merchant stood there stupid with surprise, two witnesses came out from behind hangings, and proclaimed: 'We have heard the words of the divorce and we bear witness that you have put away your wife.' 'Now you can go, my son,' said the elder woman with a laugh. 'Yet, as I do not wish you to have a bad impression of us, I will tell you that this lover, who has so excited your jealousy, is my younger daughter. The sin was born in

your imagination and lies upon your conscience. The explanation of
the mystery is this: your wife was married some time ago to a young
man who loved her and whom she loved; but, at the end of a trifling
quarrel, the husband cried to my child: "I divorce you the three
times!" That is the most serious and solemn formula which can be
used, and he who has said it cannot remarry his wife until she has
been married a second time and then divorced. We were in great
need of a looser, and at last we found one. As soon as I saw your
great dark eyes, your complacency, and your roses, I knew that you
were the perfect looser.'

So saying, she pushed him from the house and shut the door after
him, while the original husband came out of concealment and was
straightway married again to the woman of his heart.

Such, O auspicious King, is the tale of the Looser. But it is not so
delicious as the tale of:

The Captain of Police

THERE was once a Kurd in Cairo who had come into Egypt during the reign of the victorious Salāh al-Dīn (whom may Allāh
keep in His compassion!). This Kurd was a man terribly square and
thick, with great moustaches and a forked beard, all rising to the
level of his eyes, brows which fell down over his lids, and tufts of
hair jetting from nose and ears. So stern was his air that he had soon
become captain of police, and at the sight of him little boys would
run like the wind, as if a ghoul were chasing them. Mothers used to
still their babes when they were naughty by threatening to call in the
Kurdish captain. In a word, the hero of this tale was the bugbear of
the city.

One day he felt his solitary existence weigh upon him and
thought how good it would be to find young flesh waiting for his
tooth at home in the evening. Therefore he sought out a woman
expert in marriage, saying: 'I wish to take a wife; but I have had a
great deal of experience and know that the general run of wives is a
curse. To save complication, I wish a young virgin who has never
quitted her mother's robe and who will be ready to live with me in a
house of one room. Also, I make it a condition that she never leaves
that house and that room. Can you or can you not find me such a
bride?' 'I can,' answered the old woman, 'and I should like a little

something on account.' The captain gave her a dīnār, and left her to prosecute her search.

After several days of hurrying hither and thither, of asking and answering, the old woman found a girl who was ready to live with the Kurd and never to leave the single chamber of his house. She hastened to the captain of police with the news, saying: 'I have found you a young virgin who has never left her mother and who said, in answer to my demand, that she would just as soon stay prisoner in one room with a valiant captain as with a mother.' The Kurd was delighted, and asked: 'What is she like?' 'Fat, dimpled, and white,' answered the old woman. 'That is how I like them!' exclaimed the Kurd.

As the father and mother consented, and as the girl consented, and as the Kurd consented, the wedding took place without delay, and the father of great moustaches took his fat, dimpled, and white bride to the single room of his house and shut himself in with her and his Destiny. But Allāh alone knows what passed there on that first night.

Next morning, as the Kurd went forth upon the duties of his office, he muttered to himself: 'My Destiny is safe with the sweet child,' and, when he came back in the evening, a glance was sufficient to show him that all was well with his house. Every day he said in his soul: 'The man is not yet born who shall poke his nose into my dinner!' and every day his feeling of security was absolute. All his experience had not taught him that women have the Devil's own subtlety, even from the cradle, and that if they fix their mind upon a thing, nothing can stay them.

Facing their house on the opposite side of the street lived a mutton butcher, who had a son, a thoroughly delightful rascal. His nature was one of careless gaiety, and he sang from morning to night in an excellent voice. The captain's young wife was soon subjugated by the face and singing of this lad, and there came to pass what came to pass.

At this point Shahrazād saw the approach of morning and discreetly fell silent.

But when the eight-hundred-and-ninety-first night had come

SHE SAID:

One day the Kurd returned home earlier than usual and put his key in the lock. His wife, who was at that very moment under the

sway of copulation, heard the grating of the key, and let go of all in
order to spring to her feet. She hid her lover in a corner of the single
room, behind a cord hung with her own and her husband's garments.
Then she took up her great veil and ran down the little stair to meet
her husband, who was already half-way up and already suspicious.
'What is the matter?' he asked. 'Why are you holding your veil?' 'Dear
master,' she answered, 'the story of this veil is of such a nature that,
were it written on the interior corner of an eye, yet would it serve as
a lesson to the circumspect. Come and sit down on the couch, and
I will tell you about it.' She dragged him to the couch and, sitting
down beside him, thus continued: 'There was once in Cairo a terrible
and jealous captain of police, who kept unending watch on his poor
little wife. To make certain of her faith, he kept her shut up in a
house like this one, with only a single room; but, in spite of all his
precautions, she cuckolded him to her heart's content and coupled on
his very horns with the son of a neighbouring butcher. This she did
so often that she became careless and, one day, when her husband returned home earlier than usual, he began to suspect something.
When she heard him come in, she hastened to hide her lover and then
dragged her husband to a couch, just as I have done with you, my
dear. Finally she took a great veil which she carried in her hand and
wrapped it hard round her husband's head, like that!' So saying, the
young woman threw the veil over the Kurd's head and held it round
his neck, laughing as she continued her tale: 'When the son of a dog
had his head and neck well muffled in the veil, she called out to her
lover, who was hiding behind the husband's clothes on the line:
"Save yourself quickly, quickly, my delight!" At once the young
butcher ran from his hiding-place and leapt down the staircase into the
street. Such is the story of this veil, my lord!' As soon as her lover
was in safety, the young woman unwound the veil from the Kurd's
neck and laughed and laughed until she fell over on her backside.

The captain did not know whether to laugh or rage at the story
and the game with which his wife had entertained his home-coming.
But, after all, he was a Kurd, and perhaps that is why he never understood the signification of what had occurred. His moustaches and
hairs never drooped for shame, and he died a happy and prosperous
man, leaving many children behind him.

That night Shahrazād also told the following story, which poses
the question: who showed the greatest generosity, a husband, a
lover, or a thief?

A Contest in Generosity

IT is related that there were once in Baghdād a girl and boy who were cousins and had greatly loved each other from infancy. Their fathers and mothers had destined them for each other and would often say: 'When Habīb is big he shall marry Habībah.' The two had grown up together and their love had grown with them, but when they came to marriageable age, they were not destined to wed each other; for the girl's parents had suffered the reverse of time and were now so poor that they were obliged to accept the suit of a certain respectable sheikh, one of the richest merchants in Baghdād, when he asked for their daughter's hand.

After the marriage had been arranged, young Habībah sought out her cousin Habīb for the last time, and said to him through her tears: 'O my beloved, you have heard that my father and mother have given me to a sheikh whom I have never seen, and our love is frustrate for ever. Would not death be preferable?' 'Our Destiny is bitter; there is no meaning in our life henceforward,' answered Habīb sobbing. 'How shall we ever again savour the taste of life or delight in the beauties of the world? Alas, alas, sweet cousin, how shall we bear the weight of Destiny?' They wept together and were wellnigh swooning from unhappiness, when one appeared to separate them and tell the girl the time had come for her to be taken to her husband's house.

The desolate Habībah was carried in procession to the sheikh's house and there, after the usual blessings and wishings, left alone with him.

When the moment of consummation came, the old man entered the bridal chamber and found his wife weeping among the cushions, her bosom shaken with sobs. 'Surely she weeps after the manner of young girls, because she has left her mother,' thought the sheikh: 'Happily that does not last long. The stiffest bolt will yield to oil, and a kind word will tame a lion's cub.' So he went up to her, saying: 'O Habībah, O light of my soul, why do you destroy the beauty of your eyes? What grief is this which makes you forget that I am near you?' The girl redoubled her tears and sighs when she heard his voice, and thrust her head further among the cushions. 'Dear Habībah,' said the old man gently, 'if you are weeping for your mother, say so, and I will fetch her to you instantly.' The girl shook her head among the cushions, and the old bridegroom went on: 'If you are weeping for your father, or one of your sisters, or your nurse, or some pet animal, such as a cock, a cat, or a gazelle, tell me, and you shall be no longer separated from your desire.' A shake of the head was the bride's only answer. The sheikh pondered for a moment, and then said again: 'Is it the house itself for which you weep, Habībah, the house where you were young? If that is so, I will take you back there at once.' A little won over by her husband's kindness, Habībah lifted her tear-wet eyes and her cheeks with their fevered roses. In a small and trembling voice she answered: 'My lord, I do not weep for my mother, my father, my sisters, my nurse, or my pets; and I beg you not to insist that I shall tell you the reason of my tears.' The excellent sheikh, seeing her face for the first time, was softened indeed by her beauty, her childish charm, and the music of her voice. 'O fairest girl on earth, dearest Habībah, since the cause of your weeping is none of these things,' said he, 'I beg you all the more to tell me of it.' 'I cannot tell you of it,' she answered, and he went on: 'Then I know what it is; you weep because I am repugnant to you. If you had only told me through your mother that you did not wish to marry me, I should never have forced you into my house.' 'No, by Allāh,' cried the girl, 'I have no aversion from you. How could one whom I have never seen be repugnant to me? It is something else, for which I can find no words.' But the old man pressed her so kindly that at last she confessed with lowered eyes: 'My grief and tears are for a dear one of my house, a cousin with whom I grew up, a cousin who loves me and whom I love. O my master, love's roots are in the heart and, if love is plucked forth, the heart is plucked forth also.'

The sheikh lowered his head without speaking and reflected for an hour, then he raised his head, saying: 'Dear mistress, the law of Allāh and His Prophet (upon whom be prayer and peace!) forbids one Believer to snatch even a mouthful of bread from another Believer by force. How then could I, a Believer, snatch away your heart? Calm your dear soul and refresh your eyes, for nothing shall happen to you that is not written in your Destiny. Rise up now, O my bride of a minute, and go, with my full and free consent, to him whose right in you is more than mine. Give yourself to him freely and return here in the morning before the servants are awake. From henceforth you are my daughter, of my own flesh and blood, and a father does not touch his daughter carnally. When I am dead, you shall be my heir. Rise up now, my girl, and hasten to console your cousin, for he must be weeping as the dead weep.'

He raised her, dressed her himself in the fair robes and jewels of her marriage, and accompanied her to the door. As she walked into the street and started upon her way, she glowed like an extravagantly ornamented idol, such as the unbelievers carry on their feast days.

At this point Shahrazād saw the approach of morning and discreetly fell silent.

But when the eight-hundred-and-ninety-second night had come

SHE SAID:

She had hardly gone twenty paces down the deserted street when a black form fell upon her from the shadows, and a night-haunting thief, who had been attracted by the sparkle of her gems, began to snatch them from her, growling: 'If you open your mouth, I will smash you to the earth.' His hand was already fumbling with the collars about her neck when his eyes fell upon her face. 'As Allāh lives,' he cried, 'she is the richest jewel of them all, I must take her whole! . . . Dear mistress, I will do you no harm if you are complaisant, and I can promise you a blessed night if you will come with me. . . . She must be the wedding guest of some great lord to wear such things at night!'

When the girl wept, the robber cried: 'Why do you weep, my dear? I swear that I will neither hurt you nor rob you, if you give yourself to me freely.' At the same time he took her by the hand and would have led her off; but she found the courage to tell him who she was, how generous the sheikh had been, and the full details of her marriage. 'Now, when all was going well, I have fallen into your hands. Do with me as you will,' she said.

The robber, who was by far the most skilful craftsman in all the corporation of the city thieves, had sense enough to appreciate the husband's generosity. He reflected for a moment, and then said: 'Where does he live, this cousin whom you love?' 'In a room on the garden in such a house in such a street,' she answered. Then said the robber: 'Dear mistress, no one shall ever accuse a man of my profession of interfering with true love. May Allāh grant the choicest of His blessings to the two of you this night! I will now lead you to your cousin's house, as you might fall in with some vile thief if you were to go alone. The wind is for all, the flute for one, and that one is not I.'

So saying, he took the girl by the hand and escorted her, as if she had been a queen, right up to the house of her beloved. Then he took leave of her, kissing the hem of her garment, and went his way.

The girl walked across the garden and, listening at the window of her cousin's chamber, heard him sobbing alone. She knocked at the door, and a voice filled with tears asked who was there. 'Habībah!' she answered. 'O voice of Habībah!' said her cousin. 'But Habībah is dead! Who are you that speak to me in her voice?' 'I am Habībah,' she answered.

The door opened and Habīb fell swooning into his cousin's arms. She brought him to consciousness and, holding his head upon her lap, told him of the conduct of her husband and of the thief. At first Habīb could say no word, then he rose and murmured gently: 'Come with me, sweet love.' He took her by the hand, touching no more of her, and led her through the streets to the home of her husband.

When the sheikh saw his wife return with young Habīb and understood the reason which had brought them, he led them into his chamber and kissed them as a father kisses his own children. 'When a Believer has proclaimed his wife to be the daughter of his flesh and blood, no power can give the lie to his words,' he said in a grave voice. 'You owe me nothing, my children, for I am in bondage to my oath.'

So saying, he made over his house and goods to the two of them, and went to live in another city.

Shahrazād left King Shahryār to answer the propounded question himself, without requiring comment from him. That night she also said:

The Gelded Barber

IT is related that there was once in Cairo a youth of great merit and beauty, whose dearly loved mistress was the wife of a certain Guzbāshi, commander of a hundred police. This excellent husband was a man filled with courage and fire; one of his fingers could have crushed the girl and he was endowed to satisfy a large harīm. But the woman was one of those who prefer lamb for eating and beardless youth for coupling.

One day the Guzbāshi entered his house and said to his wife: 'I have been invited to go out to the gardens this afternoon to take the good air with my friends. If I am wanted for anything you will know where to send.' 'No one will want you to do aught save enjoy yourself,' answered his wife. 'If you take delight in the gardens, dear master, it will be an equal delight to me.' So the Guzbāshi went on his way, congratulating himself that he had such a loving, attentive and obedient wife.

As soon as he had turned his back, the woman cried: 'I thank Allāh that we have got rid of the wild pig for one afternoon! Now I will send for my heart's delight.' She called her little eunuch, saying: 'Run quickly to the house of such an one, my boy, and, if he be not at home, search for him until you find him.' The little eunuch ran off and, failïng to find the youth at his house, searched through all the shops of the market which it was his custom to frequent, until he found him having his head shaved in the booth of a certain barber. He entered just as the barber was winding a clean napkin round his customer's neck, with the words: 'Allāh grant that the refreshment of it be delicious!' The little eunuch tiptoed up to his mistress's lover, and whispered in his ear: 'My lady sends her choicest greetings, and bids me tell you that the Guzbāshi has gone to the gardens and that the coast is clear. If you would be master of the house for a little, come swiftly.' The youth immediately cried to the barber: 'I wish to go at once. Dry my head quickly and I will return another time.' So saying he slipped a silver dirham into the barber's hand, just as if the shaving had been completed, and the man, rejoicing at such generosity, said to himself: 'If he gives a dirham for nothing, how much will he not give for a shave! As Allāh lives, here is a client to be followed up. If I can once get him under my hands again, he will probably give me a handful of such dirhams.'

He followed the youth to the threshold, crying: 'Allāh be with you, my master! I trust that when you have completed your business you will return to my shop, to go forth fairer than you came in. Allāh be with you, Allāh be with you!' 'Certainly, certainly!' called the lover over his shoulder, as he vanished round a corner of the street.

He came at last to the house of his mistress and was about to knock when he was astonished to see the barber turn into that street from a byway and stand facing him. He paused with his hand lifted and heard the barber say: 'Allāh be with you, dear master! I pray you not to forget my shop, for it is perfumed and lighted by your coming. A wise man has said: "When a place has delighted you do not search for another place." The father of Arabic medicine, Abū Alī ibn Sīnā—may Allāh have him in keeping!—has also said: "There is no milk for a child like mother's milk, and nothing more delicious to the head than the fingers of a clever barber." I trust that you will be able to distinguish my shop from the many others in the market, O my customer?' 'Certainly, certainly, I shall be able to find the place,' answered the lover, as he slipped through the door, which had been quietly opened for him, and shut it behind him. He climbed up to his mistress, and did his usual with her.

Instead of returning to his shop, the barber stayed rooted in the street, opposite the door. 'If I do not wait for this excellent customer and lead him back myself,' he thought, 'he is certain to go to one of my rivals by mistake.' Thus he definitely took up his stand, never for an instant allowing his eyes to leave the door.

When the Guzbāshi came to the place of meeting, the friend who had invited him said: 'My dear sir, I trust you will pardon my rudeness, but my mother has just died and I must see about her burial. I will not be able, therefore, to enjoy your company to-day; but I trust in Allāh that it is only a pleasure deferred.' He took his leave, and the disappointed Guzbāshi said to himself: 'May Allāh curse all calamitous old women! They do nothing but interfere with our pleasure and spoil our holidays by dying! May Satan hurl them into the deepest holes of the fifth hell!' So saying, he spat furiously into the air and grumbled in his beard: 'Thus, O mother of spoilsports, I spit upon you and upon the earth which covers you!'

At this point Shahrazād saw the approach of morning and discreetly fell silent.

But when the eight-hundred-and-ninety-third night had come

SHE SAID:

He returned towards his house and his eyes were still rolling with wrath when he came to the street in which it stood. When he saw the barber standing still, with his face turned up towards the windows, like a dog waiting for a bone to be thrown to him, he touched him on the arm, saying: 'What is the matter? What have you to do with this house?' The barber bowed to the earth, as he answered: 'O our lord the Guzbāshi, I am waiting for my best customer. The bread of my life is in his hands.' 'What is that you say, O limb of the Afārīt?' demanded the astonished Guzbāshi. 'Is my house a meeting place for barbers' customers? Begone, you pimp, unless you want to feel the weight of my arm!' 'The name of Allāh be upon you, O our master the Guzbāshi, and upon your house, and upon those who dwell in your honourable house, which is the chosen home of all the virtues!' cried the barber. 'But I swear, by your precious life, that my best customer has been inside for a long time. As I can wait no longer, I beg you, when you go in, to reason with him and urge him to be quick!' 'What like is your customer, O son of a thousand bawds?' asked the Guzbāshi. 'A handsome youth with eyes like this, and a waist like this, and the rest to match,' replied the barber, with a double gesture. 'He is quite a dandy, and as generous as a prince! Sugar, my lord! Honeycomb, my lord!' The captain of a hundred police seized the barber by the neck and shook him, crying: 'O whelp of pimps, O bastard of a thousand whores!' 'It is permitted!' answered the barber courteously between the shakings. 'Do you still dare to defame my house?' panted the Guzbāshi, and the barber answered: 'You will see for yourself, my lord, when you tell the delightful young gentleman that I am waiting.' 'Stay here!' cried the Guzbāshi, and leapt foaming into the house.

While this discussion went on in the street, the wife, who had heard the beginning of it, had leisure to hide her lover in the cistern; therefore, when the Guzbāshi raged through the chambers, there was no sign or smell of any handsome youth. 'Yet he said there was a man here, my dear,' explained the Guzbāshi, and the woman cried indignantly: 'O shame upon our house and me! How could a man be here, dear master?' 'But there was a barber in the street who told me that his best customer was here, a most handsome young man,' insisted the Guzbāshi. 'And did you not smash him against the wall?' she asked. 'I will do so now!' he cried and, running down into the street, seized the barber by the neck again and spun him round. 'O pander to your own mother, O pimp to your own wife!' he yelled. 'How have you dared to say such things about the harīm of a Believer?' He would certainly have destroyed the man then and there, had not the barber protested: 'By the truth of the Prophet, O Guzbāshi, I saw him go in and I have not seen him go out!' The captain stopped his spinning, in astonishment that a man should uphold a lie in the face of death. 'I will not kill you until I have proved you wrong, you dog!' he said. 'Come now with me.' He dragged the barber into the house and hunted with him high and low. When all the rooms had been examined, they came down into the courtyard and ferreted vainly in odd corners. 'There is no one here,' said the Guzbāshi. 'But we have not tried the cistern,' said the barber.

The wife, who had listened to all their goings and comings, and had heard the barber's last words, ran down, cursing him beneath her breath, and cried to her husband: 'How long is this man, this bastard of a thousand shameless horns, to sniff through your house and harīm? Are you not ashamed to bring so vile a stranger into contact with your wife? Why do you not punish him!' 'You are right, he should be punished,' answered the Guzbāshi. 'But you are the offended party and it is for you to give the chastisement. Spare him not!'

The girl took a knife from the kitchen and heated it white-hot; then she approached the barber, whom the Guzbāshi had stricken to the earth with a single blow, and cauterised his knots and points, while her husband held him prostrate. When the operation was over, they threw the poor wretch into the street, where he lay until certain compassionate folk lifted him and carried him to his shop. So much for him.

The lover in the cistern waited until all the noises were stilled in the house and then, slipping from the courtyard, ran away. For Allāh veils as He pleases!

And Shahrazād would not let that night go by without telling King Shahryār the tale of:

Fīrūz and His Wife

IT is related that a certain King sat one day upon the terrace of his palace, taking the air and delighting his eyes with the sky above him and the gardens at his feet. Suddenly he caught sight of a woman on the terrace of the house opposite, and her beauty was such as he had never seen before. 'Whose house is that?' he asked of those who attended him, and they answered: 'It belongs to your servant Fīrūz, and that woman is his wife.' The King came down from the terrace, drunken with the wine of passion, and called Fīrūz to him, saying: 'Take this letter to such and such a city, and come back with an answer.' Fīrūz took the letter and, going to his house, slept with it beneath his pillow all that night. In the morning he rose, said farewell to his wife, and departed for the city in question, with no suspicion of the King's intent.

As soon as the husband had departed, the King went in disguise to the house opposite and knocked upon the door. 'Who is there?' asked the wife of Fīrūz, and he answered: 'The King, your husband's master.' She opened to him, and he entered and sat down, saying: 'We have come upon a visit.' 'I take refuge in Allāh from such a visit,' she replied with a smile, 'for I can suspect no good in it at all.' 'O desire of hearts, I am your husband's master,' said the King, 'and I think that you do not know me.' But she answered boldly: 'O our lord and master, I know you well, I know that you are my husband's master, and I know why you have come and what you wish of me. As a proof, I exhort you to remember your high estate and call to mind these words of the poet:

> I will not tread the path to the fountain
> If others may put their lips to the moist rock,
> I will push aside my pleasant meats
> When the black tempest of flies would share with me.

'O King, will you drink of the fountain where another before you has set his lips?' The King looked at her with stupefaction, turned his back upon her with no word to say, and fled from that house with such haste that he left one of his sandals behind him on the floor.

Fīrūz had not gone far when he felt for his letter and, not finding it, remembered that he had left it beneath his pillow. He returned to his house and, entering immediately after the King's departure, saw the royal sandal upon the floor, recognised it and understood why he had been sent upon that mission. Yet he kept silence and, after noiselessly retrieving the letter, departed without announcing his presence to his wife. He diligently carried the letter to its destination and returned with an answer to the King, who rewarded him with a present of a hundred dīnārs.

Fīrūz took the hundred dīnārs to the market of the goldsmiths and with the whole sum purchased magnificent ornaments, which he carried to his wife, saying:'These are to celebrate my return. Take them and all else that is yours, and return to your father's house.' 'Why?' she asked, and he replied: 'Because the King, my master, has loaded me with his favour and I wish all the world to know it. I wish your father to see what brave ornament the King's favour can bring to a woman.' 'I will go gladly,' said his wife.

She decked herself with all that her husband had brought her and all that she had before, and went to her father's house, where the old man rejoiced to see the richness of her habiting. For a whole month she stayed in her old home, and Fīrūz did not send once, either for news of her or to fetch her back.

At the end of the month the woman's brother sought out Fīrūz, saying: 'O Fīrūz, if you will not reveal the cause of your anger against your wife and the reason why you have abandoned her, you shall come and argue the case before the King, our master.' 'You may argue the case if you will,' answered Fīrūz, 'but I shall not answer.' 'You must come all the same,' cried the young man, 'for, if you will not argue the case yourself, at least you can answer my accusations.' So they went together into the presence of the King.

The King sat in the audience hall, with the kādī beside him, and, when the woman's brother had kissed the earth between his hands and announced that he had a case to argue, said to him: 'You must address yourself to the kādī.' So the young man turned to the kādī, saying: 'Allāh assist our lord the kādī! This is our complaint: we had a fair garden, shadowed and protected by high walls, wonderfully cared for, well-planted with flowers and fruit trees, and we hired it out to this man. But after he had plucked all the flowers and eaten all the fruit, he destroyed the walls and left our garden to the four winds. Now he wishes to break his lease, and give us back our garden as it is.'

'And what have you to say, young man?' asked the kādī of Fīrūz, and Fīrūz answered: 'I contend that I give them back the garden in a better state than it was before.' 'Do you admit the truth of that?' asked the kādī of the brother, and the brother answered: 'I do not, and I require him to tell us why he wishes us to take back the garden.' 'What do you say to that, young man?' asked the kādī, and Fīrūz answered: 'I give it back both willingly and much against my will. If they must know why: I entered the garden one day and found the footsteps of a lion among its beds, and I fear that if I ventured there again the lion would devour me. I have acted both out of respect for the lion and from fear for myself.'

At this point Shahrazād saw the approach of morning and discreetly fell silent.

But when the eight-hundred-and-ninety-fourth night had come

SHE SAID:

The King had been listening without appearing to do so. When he heard and understood the reason which Fīrūz gave, he sat up straight upon his throne, saying: 'O Fīrūz, calm your dear soul, lay aside your fear, and return to your garden; for, by the truth and holiness of Islām, it is the best defended garden in my kingdom. Its walls are unvanquishable by assault, its trees, its fruits, and its flowers are the most wholesome and the fairest which I have seen!'

Fīrūz understood, and returned to his wife, and loved her.

But neither the kādī nor any of the numerous courtiers and officials who were present understood the true meaning of that suit; it remained a secret between the King and Fīrūz and the bride's brother. But Allāh knows all!

And Shahrazād said again:

The Mind and the Soil

THERE was a Syrian to whom Allāh had given, as He has given to all Syrians, sluggish blood and a most heavy wit. For it is a notorious truth that, when the Giver distributed His gifts to men, He planted qualities and defects in the soil which bred them. Thus the people of Cairo have wit and polish, the men of Upper Egypt great copulative force, the Arabs a love of poetry, the riders of the middle kingdom a steadfast courage, the dwellers in Irāk civic genius, the wandering tribes a generous hospitality, the Syrians a low and greedy cunning together with a plentiful lack of any charm. This power of the soil is proved by the fact that to whatever part, from the salt sea to the Damascene desert, you transplant a Syrian, he will always be a muddy minded man, with a gross eye to the main chance instead of intelligence.

This man's evil Destiny, though his self-sufficiency would not have admitted that it was so, caused him to journey to Cairo, with its delightful and spiritual inhabitants, and to bring with him a precious collection of silks, brocades, wrought arms, and the like, with which to dazzle them.

He hired storage for his merchandise and a room for himself in a khān near the markets; then he began a series of daily visits among the merchants in order to make connection with possible purchasers. One day, as he went along a street, looking to left and right, he met three girls walking delicately and laughing at this and that. Their appearance was so delightful that his moustaches pricked to a swagger and, as they provoked him with their eyes, he was bold to say: 'Could you not come and keep pleasant company with me at my khān to-night?' 'Certainly,' they answered smiling, 'and we shall endeavour in all things to please you.' 'At my place or yours, dear ladies?' he asked, and they replied: 'At yours, in Allāh's name! Do you think that our husbands would like us to welcome strangers? Where do you lodge?' When he had told them, they recommended him to prepare a hot supper and expect them after the time of prayer. As soon as they had passed smiling down the street, he bought fish, cucumbers, oysters, wine and perfumes, and, with his own hands, prepared five different dishes on a meat ground, to say nothing of rice and vegetables.

At the time appointed the three girls arrived, muffled for safety in blue silk veils; but, as soon as they were in the Syrian's chamber, they threw these aside and sat down like three moons. Their host squatted opposite to them, with the grace of a water-jar, and served them with meat and wine according to their capacity. The cup went round and the Syrian missed no turn of it, until his head was nodding to all the points of the compass. The wine gave him courage to admire the beauty opposite to him, but it also caused him to wander between perplexity and stupefaction, to balance between extravagance and fear, and to confuse male with female. A memorable state was his, but a deplorable Destiny; he regarded without seeing, he helped himself with his feet, and would have walked with his head. He turned his eyes and shook his nose, then he blew his nose before he sneezed. He laughed and cried, and turned to one of the three, saying: 'What is your name, lady?' 'I am called Have-You-Ever-Seen-Anything-Like-Me,' she answered. 'Never!' he cried and, stretching himself on the ground supported by his elbows, asked the second girl: 'And what is your name, blood of the life of my heart?' 'You-Have-Never-Seen-Anyone-Like-Me,' she answered. 'Be it as Allāh wills, dear You-Have-Never-Seen-Anyone-Like-Me,' he cried, and then turned to the third, demanding: 'And what is your name, O scorch upon my heart?' 'Look-At-Me-And-You-Will-Know-Me,' she replied, and the Syrian rolled upon the ground, bellowing: 'It is permitted, dear Look-At-Me-And-You-Will-Know-Me!'

They sent round the cup again, pouring it down his throat when it came to his turn, until his blood stopped and he fell head over heels. Then they took off his turban and put a fool's cap upon his head, possessed themselves of all the money and precious things which lay to their hands, and left their host snoring like a buffalo in the midst of his pillaged chamber.

Next morning, when the Syrian came up out of his foul depths, he saw that his three charmers had swept the place for him, and the sight restored his senses. 'There is no majesty or power save in Allāh!' he cried and, leaping from the inn into the road, with the fool's cap still upon his head, began to question the passers-by concerning his three visitors. To one he cried: 'Have you seen Have-You-Ever-Seen-Anything-Like-Me?' and the man replied: 'Certainly not.' To a second he cried: 'I suppose you have not seen You-Have-Never-Seen-Anyone-Like-Me?' and the man replied: 'Certainly not.' To a third he cried: 'Have you seen Look-At-Me-And-You-Will-Know-Me?' and the man replied: 'I have seen, I have looked, but I do not know you and do not want to know you!'

At last a wise and charitable wayfarer said to him: 'O Syrian, your best course in this circumstance is to return at once to Syria, for the people of Cairo can turn light heads and heavy heads with the same ease, and juggle with stones as well as with eggs.'

With a long nose trailing to his feet, the Syrian returned to his own country, which he should never have left.

It is because such adventures happen so frequently that the natives of Syria cannot find a good word to say for the children of Egypt.

When she had made an end of this story, Shahrazād fell silent and King Shahryār said: 'O Shahrazād, these anecdotes have pleased me greatly and taught me not a little.' Shahrazād smiled as she replied: 'Allāh is the Sole Teacher! But what are these anecdotes compared with The Tale of the Magic Book?' 'What magic book is that?' cried King Shahryār, and Shahrazād answered: 'You shall hear tomorrow night, if Allāh wills and the King wills.'

When the eight-hundred-and-ninety-fifth night had come

LITTLE DUNYAZĀD rose from her carpet, saying: 'Dear sister, when are you going to begin The Tale of the Magic Book?' 'At once, since it is the King's will,' answered Shahrazād. And she said:

The Tale of the Magic Book

IT is related in the annals of the people and the books of old time— but Allāh alone knows the past and the future!—that the Khalīfah Hārūn al-Rashīd, of the orthodox line of the sons of Abbās, rose in his bed one night with a heavy heart and sent for Masrūr the sword-bearer. When Masrūr came, he said to him: 'This night is a heavy weight upon my heart which I require you to lift, O Masrūr.' 'Then rise up, O Commander of the Faithful,' answered the eunuch, 'and let us go out on to the terrace to see the tent of the sky pierced with stars, to watch the bright walking of the moon, to hear the music of the rippling water and the plaint of the water-wheels, of which the poet has said:

> The water-wheels, which weep from either eye
> Yet make a merry chanting as they spin,
> Are like young lovers who will groan and cry
> When all their heart is ecstasy within.

The same poet, O Prince of Believers, sang this on the subject of running water:

> My love is a young thing, she gives me wine
> With bread of gaiety, and she is mine;
> She is a garden with fountains, the twin still
> Waters her eyes, her voice the silver rill.'

But Hārūn shook his head, saying: 'I have no desire for that to-night.' 'O Commander of the Faithful,' ventured Masrūr, 'there are three hundred and sixty girls in your palace, robed by your generosity as if they were flowers of every colour, and all as beautiful as moons. Rise up and make a tour of their apartments, seeing without being seen. You will hear their songs and see the games they play, and perhaps one of them may attract you and you will join in her

game.' But Hārūn said: 'Send Jafar to me at once!' So Masrūr went
in search of Jafar, and said to him: 'Come to the Khalīfah,' and Jafar
dressed and followed him to the palace. He presented himself before
the Khalīfah's bed and kissed the earth, saying: 'Allāh grant that
there be nothing wrong!' 'Nothing is wrong, O Jafar,' answered
Hārūn, 'save that I am weary and oppressed this night. I wish you
to distract me.' Jafar reflected for a moment, and then replied: 'O
Commander of the Faithful, when neither love nor gardens are of
any avail, there remain only books. A library of books is the fairest
garden in the world, and to walk there is an ecstasy. Rise up now and
let us hunt at haphazard for some book among the shelves.' 'You
are right, O Jafar, though I had not thought of it,' answered Hārūn,
as he rose from the bed and made his way towards the hall of books,
followed by his two faithful servants.

Jafar and Masrūr held torches and the Khalīfah took books from
the cupboards and chests of scented wood, and passed his eyes over
their pages. After he had examined many shelves in this way, he
opened a very old book which came to his hand and, instead of casting it aside after a moment, began intently to turn page after page.
Suddenly he broke into so great a gust of laughter that he fell over
on his backside, but he still held the book and continued to read.
Almost immediately tears fell from his eyes and he wept so copiously
that the water trickled down through his beard onto the pages. Soon
he shut the book, slipped it into his sleeve, and rose to return to bed.

When Jafar saw the Khalīfah laugh and weep, he could not help
asking: 'O Commander of the Faithful and lord of the two worlds,
why did you laugh and weep at the same time?' But the Khalīfah
flew into a rage, crying: 'You are impertinent, O dog of the dogs of
Barmak! What business is it of yours? Really, your self-sufficiency
passes belief, and you forget yourself strangely. Now that you have
interfered in this matter, I bid you find me a man who can tell me
why I both laughed and wept, and who can divine the whole contents of this book from the first page to the last. If you do not find
such an one, I will have your head cut off, to teach you not to hold
yourself so high.'

'O Commander of the Faithful, I have been guilty of a fault,' confessed Jafar, 'but a fault is natural to such men as I, and to pardon is
natural only to the great of soul.' 'No, I have sworn, and therefore
cannot pardon,' answered Hārūn. 'You must bring me the man I require, or lose your head!' Then said Jafar: 'If Allāh created earth and

sky in six days, when He could have created them in an hour, it was to prove that haste, even in well-doing, is dangerous. How much more dangerous is it then in ill-doing! If you require me to find such a man for you, at least give me a delay of three days.' 'Three days you shall have,' answered al-Rashīd. 'Then I shall depart at once,' said Jafar, and straightway left the presence.

His heart was bitter with tears when he went to say farewell to his father Yahya, and his brother Al-Fadl. He told them of his trouble, adding: 'He who plays with a sharp blade shall cut his hand, and he who sports with a lion shall be destroyed. There is no place left for me at the side of the Khalīfah, for his presence is the greatest of dangers for me and for you, my father, and for you, my brother. It is better that I flee away from him, for life is the most precious of our possessions and distance is life's best preserver. The poet has said:

> If the crazed building makes to fall in thunder,
>> Friend, seek not to dissuade it,
>> But leap incontinently from under
> And leave the house to cry to him who made it.'

'Do not leave the city, O Jafar,' answered his father and brother, 'for the Khalīfah is certain to forgive you.' But Jafar insisted, saying: 'He has sworn my death if I cannot find a man who can explain the reason of his laughter and tears, and divine the contents of that cala-mitous book from beginning to end. You can see for yourselves that the condition is impossible.' 'You are right,' answered his father. 'I suggest that you journey to Damascus and stay there until your affairs are in better shape.' 'But what will become of my wife and my harīm?' asked Jafar. 'Think not of them,' replied Yahya. 'It is writ-ten in your Destiny that you should depart at once, and what happens afterwards is the care of Allāh.'

At this point Shahrazād saw the approach of morning and discreetly fell silent.

But when the eight-hundred-and-ninety-sixth night had come

SHE SAID:

Jafar listened to his father's advice; he filled a purse with a thousand dīnārs, girt on his sword and belt and, after saying fare-well, set forth, unattended, upon a mule. He journeyed in a straight line across the desert until he came, on the tenth day, to the Marj, the green mead, which lies before the delightful city of Damascus.

He saw the fair minaret of the Bride, dressed from base to summit in gilded tiles, rising from the green; he saw the gardens watered by rivulets and gay with flowers; he saw the fields of myrtle and rose laurel, and the hills of violet; and he listened to the birds singing to one another in the trees. He went up to a man who walked near by, and said to him: 'My brother, what is the name of this city?' 'My lord,' answered the man, 'this is that city which was called Jillik of old. The poet said of it:

> I am Damascus, the heart of bright waters,
> They flow silver under my walls
> And silver from my walls they flow again.
> I am His garden upon earth
> And splendour's golden bed;
> There is a blessing upon my terraces,
> The souls of those who have known my waters
> Sighing upon my terraces.

And her third name is Shām, for she is God's beauty-spot upon the body of the earth.'

Jafar took a lively pleasure in these explanations; he thanked the man and, dismounting from his mule, led her between the houses and mosques, going slowly and examining the fair buildings one by one. At length he saw, at the end of a well swept and watered street, a magnificent house rising in the centre of a great garden. There was a tent of worked silk in the garden, furnished with Khurāsān carpets, silk cushions, and beds of deep repose. A young man, as fair as the moon rising upon her fourteenth night, sat in the midst of the tent, lightly clad in a rose-coloured tunic. Before him were a troop of attentive guests and drinks of every worthy kind. Jafar paused for a moment to contemplate this scene, because the appearance of the young man delighted him, and, looking more closely, he saw that a young woman sat by the youth's side, like the sun in a clear sky. She had a lute at her breast, and sang this song:

> I gave my heart to love's hand yesterday,
>   His idle hand broke it in idleness.
> It was an unborn child he tore away
>   And now throws back breathless and beautiless.
>   Sing, bird: 'He tore it away.'

> I grew a little old in love study
>   And, when my heart stayed young, they buried it.
> Though I am blithe now to love carelessly,
>   They buried it, brother; and I bid you yet
>   Sing, bird: 'They buried it.'

Jafar gloried in this singing and stayed still, as the girl touched her lute afresh, and sang again:

> Knowing that you had love,
> My heart leaped lightly:
> I lifted my hand, sighing: 'Compassion, Compassion.'
> But ever you answered: 'Passion, passion, passion,'
> And the eyes of your slave are salt therefore.

For pleasure in this song, Jafar came nearer and nearer, and suddenly the young man saw him. He half rose, and said to one of his slaves: 'That man yonder is a stranger to our city, for I can see the stains of travel upon him. Run and fetch him to me, and take care to treat him with all civility.' The boy ran joyfully to Jafar, and said to him: 'In Allāh's name, my lord, have the great goodness to approach and greet my master.' Jafar gave over his mule to the boy and, crossing the threshold, came to the entrance of the tent. The young man, who had already risen in his honour, came forward with his arms stretched out in welcome; he saluted Jafar as if he had always known him and, after giving thanks to Allāh for such a sending, sang:

> O visitor, O wine upon our hearts
>   Making them dance, we laugh and live to-day,
>   We blossom in the warm benignant ray
> Which is our guest; we die if he departs.

'Will you be pleased to be seated, my lord?' he said. 'I give thanks to Allāh for your happy arrival!' Then, after reciting the guest prayer, he sang again:

> If we had known, prince of urbanities,
>   We would have made our welcoming more sweet
>   And spread our heart's red carpet for your feet
> And spread the soft black velvet of our eyes.

Then the youth kissed Jafar on the breast, and said: 'If to-day were not already a feast day, I should make it one.' He commanded

the slaves to bring what was ready, and Jafar was soon served with
excellent meats. To make his guest eat, the young man said sweetly:
'The wise have bidden us be content with little; but if we had known
of your coming we would have cooked the flesh of our hearts and
sacrificed our little children to the kitchen!' He helped Jafar with his
own hands and himself brought the basin and ewer for his ablution;
then he led him into the hall of drinks and there bade the girl sing
again. She took the lute to her breast, gentled its cords a little, and
then sang:

> Sweeter than wit and hope is our bright guest,
>> The dawn is shy to break, seeing his hair.
>> When I lie dying, if your guest be there,
>> Whether I live or die, it will be best.

Jafar rejoiced at his reception, and yet the memory of his quarrel
with the Khalifah weighed on him, and his host could see that his
heart was burdened with some unquiet secret. Though, from discretion and politeness, he would not question him, the young man
said at length: 'Listen, my lord, to these pleasant words of the wise:

> There's death in wine,
> White hands woo out from the green sleeves,
> There's death in wine, there's death to care,
> White hands win out from the green leaves,
> A web of drows'd forgetting the violet waves,
> And the narcissus has a Lethe'd hair,
> And there are girls.

Do not be sad, my master.' He made the girl sing again, and Jafar
was carried to marvel by the singing, so that he said: 'We shall go on
rejoicing, sometimes in songs and sometimes in words, until the
night comes.'

At this point Shahrazād saw the approach of morning and
discreetly fell silent.

*But when the eight-hundred-and-ninety-seventh night had
come*

SHE SAID:

The young man called for horses and gave his guest a mare fit to
carry a king. The two rode out together among the living spectacle

of the streets and markets of Damascus, until they came to a dwelling front brightly lighted with coloured lanterns. A great lamp of chiselled copper hung before it by a gold chain, and within were pavilions of wonderful statuary, containing also birds of every kind, and every garden flower. A domed hall with silver windows stood in the midst of the pavilions, and, when the young man opened the door of it, Jafar saw a paradisal garden, heard the lapping of streams between marble floors, and was welcomed by a cool scent of flowers. The whole hall was musical with bird song, carpeted with silk, and profuse in brocade cushions stuffed with ostrich down. The place was a treasure house of silver ware, far brought cups, gold perfume braziers, grey amber, powdered aloes, and dried fruit. A poet has said:

> So slight and gold the stone that the house seems
> Gilded with flame upon a base of dreams.

When Jafar was seated, the young man said: 'O my lord and guest, a thousand benedictions came upon us with your coming. With all my heart I tell you that your home and family are here; so may I ask why you have honoured our city with your journey?' 'I am a soldier, my master, the captain of a company,' answered Jafar. 'I fled from Basrah for my life as I could not pay my tribute to the Khalīfah.' 'Your misfortune was our fortune!' exclaimed the youth. 'And what is your name?' 'The same as yours, my master,' replied the wazīr, and his host retorted with a laugh: 'Then is your name Abū al-Hasan. I beg that you will not let any past trouble weigh upon you while you are here.' The two feasted together again and then went into an inner chamber, given over all to drinks, flanked by flowers and fruit. There the singer joined them, and sang so wonderfully that Jafar tore his garments and flung them from him. 'If you tore your garments from pleasure and not from sorrow, I am indeed satisfied!' cried his host, and he signed to his slaves, who brought Jafar new clothes, worth at least a hundred dīnārs, and clad him in them. 'Change the mode of your lute and sing again,' commanded the youth, and the girl sang:

> Once when I looked, his glance unto my glance
>   Was parallel always,
> But now I look upon an angle of his gaze,
>   Oh, lance, oh, lance!

Jafar again tore his garments, and the slaves brought him more costly ones. For an hour the two men talked together without interruption from the singing girl, and then the young man said: 'Listen, my lord, to a song which a poet made about the land to which a happy Destiny has led your feet. . . . Sing, my dear, the verses made in celebration of our valley, which in the old time was called the valley of Rabwah.' So the girl sang:

> Generous is the night in Rabwah valley
> Where the flowers give and the breezes carry.
> She has a collar of trees and she has rings
> Of flowers, and for her the moon brings
> Silver to work in the carpet of her fields,
> And her birds have silver wings.
> One dusk lemon tree her fruit yields
> To us drinking at night in Rabwah valley
> Where the flowers give and the breezes carry,
> Carry. . . .

Jafar cast aside his garments for a third time, and the young man kissed him upon the head as he clothed him in others. This youth was the most generous and magnificent of his time, his wide hand and lofty soul were a memory of Hātim of the tribe of Taiy. He talked with his guest concerning the news of the time and the heights of poetry, bidding him forget his cares. And Jafar said: 'I left my native city suddenly, meaning to enjoy myself and see the world; but, if Allāh ever sends me home and my friends ask me of the wonders which I have seen, I will tell them only of the conversation and hospitality which I met with in Damascus.' 'I take refuge in Allāh from all pride, for He alone is generous!' answered his host. 'You shall stay with me as long as you like, ten years or more; the house is yours and the master of it is yours.'

As the night drew on, slaves came in and spread a delicate bed for Jafar in the place of honour at the top of the hall, and set a second bed beside it. 'My host must be a bachelor. I will venture to ask him,' said the wazīr to himself, and then aloud: 'Dear master, are you married or single?' 'I am married,' answered the young man. 'Then why do you sleep at my side, instead of entering your harīm?' objected Jafar. 'My harīm will not fly away, dear guest,' replied the youth. 'It would be disgraceful and inelegant to allow a guest of Allāh to sleep alone. As long as you deign to honour my house with your presence, until you desolate me with farewell and return in peace to your own city, I shall lie each night at your side.' 'This is a prodigy, a marvel,' thought Jafar as he fell asleep.

Early next morning they rose and went to the hammām, whither the young man (whose true name was Attaf the Generous) had already sent a parcel of magnificent clothing for his guest's use. When they had taken the most delightful of baths, they mounted their horses, which stood saddled outside the hammām, and rode out towards the cemetery to visit the Lady's Tomb, at which they spent the day recalling the lives and deaths of worthy men. With daily visits of interest, and sleeping side by side at night, the two men spent four months together.

At this point Shahrazād saw the approach of morning and discreetly fell silent.

But when the eight-hundred-and-ninety-eighth night had come

SHE SAID:

At the end of that time Jafar became sad, and Attaf, finding him in tears one day, asked him the reason of them. 'My breast is straitened, dear brother,' answered Jafar. 'I should like to wander at haphazard through the streets of Damascus and calm my soul by viewing the mosque of the Umayyads.' 'You are free to walk where you wish and calm your soul in any way you like,' cried Attaf. 'I trust that you will soon be happy and smile again.' Jafar was about to go forth, when his host stopped him, saying: 'Have patience for a moment, my lord, and my people shall saddle a riding horse for you.' But Jafar replied: 'My friend, I would rather go on foot, for a man on horseback cannot freely observe the people; rather is he observed of the people.' 'As you will,' said Attaf, 'but at least let me hand you a purse of dīnārs, that you may give rein to your liberality as you walk abroad.'

So Jafar accepted a bag of three hundred dīnārs from his host, and departed from the house.

He went along slowly with his thoughts, brooding on his disgrace with the Khalīfah and grieving that no chance had brought him a solution of the problem which al-Rashīd had set him, until he came at last to the magnificent mosque, and mounted the thirty marble steps which led up to the principal door. He contemplated with delight the fair fittings of glazed earthenware, the gildings, the jewel work, the mighty marbles, and the fountains, where the water was so pure that the eye of man could not distinguish it from air. He gathered his soul together within him, made his prayer, and listened to the words of God, until a cool and a calm fell upon his spirit. Then he went out from the mosque and gave alms to the beggars at the door, murmuring these lines:

> I've seen the beauties grouped in Jillik's shrine,
>   I've seen their meaning written on the wall.
> Alone the calm, the ecstasy were mine;
>   But there is ecstasy and calm for all.

He wandered on again, dreaming and observing, until he found himself standing before a lordly house, with windows of silver in frames of gold, and silk curtains hanging before each window. A marble bench, covered with a carpet, opposite the door, wooed him to rest from the fatigue of walking; he sat down and began to speculate on the state of his fortunes and the possible happenings in Baghdād during his absence. Suddenly the silk curtain in front of one of the windows was drawn aside and a white hand appeared, carrying a little gold watering pot. The girl who owned the hand had a face to destroy the reason of a people; she stood for a moment and watered the flowers in their window cases, basil, double jasmine, carnation and gillyflower, and, as she did so, balanced like one of them. Jafar felt his heart wounded by love; he rose and bowed to the earth, and the girl, who had finished her watering, looked out into the street and saw him. At first she would have withdrawn but then thought better of it, and asked: 'Is this house your house?' 'As Allāh lives, my mistress,' answered Jafar, 'this house is not my house, but this slave is yours.' 'Since it is not your house,' she said, 'why do you not pass on?' 'Because I have paused, O lady,' he replied, 'to string together a few verses in your honour.' 'And what have you found to say of me, O man?' she demanded. So Jafar said:

> White is the diamond flame of your brown eyes,
>   White is your hand tending the tinted flowers.
> Lacking these two, O King of Paradise,
>   What white at all is ours?

Then, as she would have retired in spite of these lines, he cried: 'Wait a moment, my mistress, for there is another song.' 'What does it say this time?' she asked, and he recited:

Amazement, amazement,
A moon has risen in a little dusk,
A Mars of lips
In one small casement,
A rose in an eclipse
Of musk!

'You have excelled,' called down the girl, 'but your words are greater than you.' She sped a last glance to rankle in his heart, and then shut the window, leaving Jafar to wait through long hours in the vain hope of seeing her again. Each time he would have risen from the bench on which he had reseated himself, his passion bade him remain; and it was not until evening that he returned, with a chained heart, to the house of Attaf the Generous. His host was waiting for him on the threshold, and cried on seeing him: 'My lord, your absence has saddened all our day! My thoughts have been with you and would not stay at home.' He threw himself upon Jafar's breast and kissed him between the eyes; but the wazīr said nothing and seemed to be walking in his sleep. Attaf looked closely upon his face and there read many things. 'Your spirit is broken, my lord!' he cried, and Jafar replied: 'I have had a nervous headache all day because I slept on my ear last night. I could follow nothing of the prayers in the mosque; I fear that I am ill.'

Attaf led him to the hall where they were used to talk, and slaves set the evening meal before them; but Jafar would eat nothing and signed the food away with his hand. When his host questioned him, he said: 'This morning's repast is still heavy upon my stomach, but an hour of sleep will set me right and to-morrow I shall eat as usual.'

Attaf had his guest's bed prepared at once, and Jafar, after pulling the clothes over his head, filled his mind with thoughts of the magnificent beauty which Allāh had given to the girl at the window. He forgot his past, his quarrel with the Khalīfah, his friends and his native land. Desire buzzed in his head until he was sick, and he tossed from side to side in fever until the morning. It was as if he were borne up and down on the waves of love's sea.

Attaf rose first in the morning and bent over Jafar, saying: 'How are you? My thoughts were with you in the night and I know that you did not taste sleep.' 'I am not well, dear brother,' answered the wazīr. 'I have lost my kaif, my pleasure in living.'

At this point Shahrazād saw the approach of morning and discreetly fell silent.

But when the eight-hundred and ninety-ninth night had come

SHE SAID:

Attaf grieved at this answer and sent a white slave to fetch the best doctor in Damascus, the most skilful leach of all his time.

The great hakīm soon arrived and leaned over Jafar in his bed, studying his face and saying: 'Do not be excited by my coming. We will soon make you quite well. Give me your hand.' He felt his patient's pulse, and found that it was beating strongly and regularly; at once he correctly diagnosed the malady and, rather than speak of it in front of Attaf, wrote his prescription on a piece of paper, which he tactfully slipped beneath Jafar's pillow. 'The cure is under your head,' he said. 'I have prescribed a purge of sorts.' As he went forth to visit his numberless patients, Attaf accompanied him, and asked: 'O hakīm, what is the matter?' 'The prescription will tell you, if you insist on reading it,' replied the learned man, as he took his leave.

Attaf returned to Jafar, just as the latter had made an end of saying:

> 'Syrup of roses, ice, and stay in bed,'
>> Said the doctor who came
>> To physic my flame.
> 'Bring me her cheeks, her heart, herself,' I said.

Attaf sat by the bedside and asked to see the prescription; Jafar handed him the paper, and he read:

In the name of Allāh, the supreme Doctor—take three measures of her pure presence into which has been stirred a grain of prudence, three measures of union clarified with a pinch of absence, two weights of clear affection studiously free from wormwood, a heaped measure of incense of kisses high and low, a hundred kisses of the pomegranates, of which fifty shall be lip-sweetened, thirty pigeon-fashion, and twenty after the manner of little birds, two measures of Aleppo subtlety and sighs of Irāk, two ounces of tongue-ends worked diligently both in and out, three drachms of right Egyptian and pure white fat, boiled in love water and syrup of desire over the fire of pleasure: pour the mixture into a soft couch and quickly add two ounces of the water of her mouth. Take fasting for three days; on the fourth at noon eat a slice of the melon of

*desire, flavoured with lemon and white almond milk to taste, and wash
down with three measures of good thigh work. Then enter the bath
swiftly and deeply, for the health's sake. And may it be a cure to you!*

When he read this, Attaf could not help laughing; he clapped his
hands together, and said to Jafar: 'He is an excellent doctor, my
brother, for he has diagnosed your case aright. Tell me from whom
you caught the disease.' But he had to persuade and cajole for a long
time, blaming the wazīr for his lack of trust and affection, and ex-
pressing many fears that a stranger could not bring such an affair
to a successful conclusion, before Jafar raised his head and found it
in his heart to say: 'I will hide my trouble from my brother no longer, and no longer will I blame the impatience of lovers. A thing has
happened to me which I supposed would never happen, and I am
wounded unto death. The doctor has never had a more serious case.'
He told Attaf of the girl watering her flowers at the casement, and
added: 'My heart is sick for love of her. She shut the window very
quickly, and now I can neither eat nor drink nor sleep. That is the
history of my case, O Attaf, and you may rest assured that I have
hidden nothing from you.'

Attaf lowered his head and reflected for an hour, for he had recognised, from Jafar's description of the house, the window and the
street, that the girl was his own dearly loved wife, who lived with her
servants in a dwelling of her own. 'O Attaf, there is no power or
might save in Allāh! From Him we come and to Him we return at
last!' he said sadly to himself. 'I would not be in my friendship as
one who builds on the water and the sand; therefore I swear by the
generosity of God that I will feed my guest with all my soul and
substance!'

He turned a serene and smiling face to Jafar, and said to him:
'Calm your heart and refresh your eyes, dear brother, for I take your
affair upon myself. I know the family to which the girl belongs, and
I know that she was divorced from her husband a few days ago. I
will go and arrange matters at once, and you may await my return
in all tranquillity.' Then, after other words of encouragement to his
guest, he left the house.

He made his way to his wife's dwelling and penetrated to the
men's hall, without changing his garments or saying a word to any.
He called one of his young eunuchs to him and bade him fetch his
father-in-law. When the old man came, Attaf rose in his honour and

embraced him and caused him to be seated, saying: 'I announce nothing but good, my uncle. When Allāh is kind to His servants He shows them the way, and He has shown me mine. My heart inclines towards Mecca, I will visit the house of God and kiss the black stone of the Kaabah, then I will journey to Madinah to visit the tomb of the Prophet (upon whom be prayer and peace, benediction and mercy!). I have determined to make the pilgrimage this year and to return completed. Therefore I must leave no ties or obligations behind me, nothing to distract me in my going, for no man knows his Destiny. I have sent for you, dear uncle, to give you my bill of divorce from your daughter.'

When Attaf's father-in-law heard this, he was moved to the soul and cried: 'My son, why is it necessary for you to go to such an extreme? Though you leave your wife and are absent for a long time, she will remain your wife, just as your house will remain your house. There is no need to divorce her, my son.' But Attaf answered, with tears streaming from his eyes: 'I have made an oath, and that which is written in my Fate must have its course.' The old man was stricken down, and the young wife became as one dead, swimming in the bitter night of desolation. For she had loved her cousin Attaf since they were children together, and he was the light of her soul upon its way.

At this point Shahrazād saw the approach of morning and discreetly fell silent.

But when the nine-hundredth night had come

SHE SAID:

Attaf returned to his guest, saying: 'My brother, I have occupied myself in the affair. The girl is, as I said, divorced, and my suit for you has been successful. You will soon be wed. Rise up, now, and rejoice and put aside your grief!' Jafar rose and put aside his grief; he ate and drank with appetite and gave thanks to his Creator. When he had feasted, Attaf said to him: 'For complete success, I do not wish the girl's father to accuse me of trying to marry his daughter to a stranger, a man who is utterly unknown. To brush aside this difficulty, I intend to pitch tents outside the city, and provide sumptuous appointments and many horses. You will go out secretly, live for a time as if in your own caravan, and then make a public and magnificent entry into Damascus. I will take care to spread the report that you are a very great person in Baghdād, no less one, to wit, than Jafar al-Barmakī, coming on a visit as the Khalīfah's representative. When I tell the kādī, walī and nāib of our city that the wazīr Jafar is at hand, they will come forth to meet you, and you will entertain them according to their rank. While they are with you I will pay you a visit, and you must say to all of us: "I have come to your city for change of air and to find a pleasant wife. I have heard tell of the beauty of the amīr Amr's daughter. I think that I should like to wed with her." In that way, my brother, you will come to your desire.'

Thus spake Attaf to his guest, not because he had the least idea that he was in very truth Jafar al-Barmakī, but simply because they had eaten bread and salt together; for Attaf's soul was sublime, there has never been a man comparable upon this earth.

Jafar rose and would have kissed Attaf's hand, but Attaf withdrew it. That night the two slept together in the same bed, and, next morning, after their prayers and ablutions, Attaf led Jafar forth beyond the city. Then he returned and caused a secret provision of horses, camels, mules, slaves, mamlūks, chests of presents, and large coffers of gold and silver, to be taken to him. He clad him in a sumptuous robe, such as is worn by grand-wazīrs, and set him upon a grand-wazīr's throne under the principal tent. When all his preparations had been made, he sent slaves to inform the nāib of Damascus that an envoy of Hārūn-al-Rashīd was approaching the city.

The nāib of Damascus set forth, accompanied by the notables of the city, and came to the tents, where he kissed the earth between Jafar's hands, saying: 'Why did you not let us know earlier of your coming, my lord, that we might prepare a reception worthy of your greatness?' 'Such a thing is quite unnecessary,' answered Jafar. 'Allāh augment your health and favour you in everything! But I have only come for a change of air, and will remain only for the few days sufficient for my marriage. I have heard that the amīr has a noble daughter, and I wish you to speak to him concerning our wedding.' 'I hear and I obey,' answered the nāib. 'Her husband has just divorced her because he is going on pilgrimage. When the lawful period of separation has passed, nothing need interfere with your bridal, my good lord.'

He took his leave at once and, seeking out the amīr Amr, told him of the wazīr's wishes. Nor could the poor father answer save by hearing and obedience.

Jafar distributed robes of honour and gold from the store which

Attaf had provided; he called the kādi and witnesses, and had the marriage contract written, allowing the girl for dowry ten chests of costly ornaments and ten bags of dīnārs. He gave presents to great and small with the generosity of a Barmakid and, when the contract had been written out upon satin, had sugar water and choice meats set before his guests. These were followed by fruits, sweets, and refreshing drinks. As soon as the feasting was finished, the nāib of Damascus said to him: 'I go to prepare a house for your residence.' But Jafar answered: 'That may not be, for I am on an official mission from the Commander of the Faithful and must return with my bride to Baghdād, before the ceremony of our marriage.' 'Take the girl, then,' said her father, 'and depart in peace.' 'That also may not be,' replied Jafar, 'for I will not depart until I have prepared your daughter's plenishing.'

When the plenishing was ready, the amīr set his daughter in her palanquin, and the caravan set out, escorted by a crowd of the guests. At its head rode Jafar, with his face turned towards Baghdād.

They voyaged on until they came to Tiniat al-Iqab, which is half a day's journey from Damascus, and there Jafar, happening to look back, saw a rider hurrying after them from the direction of the city. He halted his caravan and dismounted from his horse to greet the rider, whom he soon recognised as Attaf. The young man embraced him, saying: 'My lord, I can find no rest away from you. My brother, my Abū al-Hasan, better that I should never have seen you than that I should lose you now.' Jafar thanked him, and answered: 'I can find no way to acknowledge all your gifts which lie heavy upon me, save to pray to Allāh that He shall soon unite us, and for ever.' He had a silk carpet spread and there feasted with Attaf on a roast cock, chickens, and sweetmeats, and drank with him for an hour. When they had remounted their horses, the wazīr cried: 'Travellers must journey on, my brother!' Attaf pressed him to his bosom and kissed him between the eyes, saying: 'O Abū al-Hasan, let there be no break in your sending of letters, but inform me of all which happens to you, as if I were by your side.' Then they said a last farewell and departed in opposite directions.

At this point Shahrazād saw the approach of morning and discreetly fell silent.

But when the nine-hundred-and-first night had come

SHE SAID:

But Jafar's bride had put her head outside the litter when the camels stopped and had seen Attaf and Jafar eating and drinking together. Within her soul she cried: 'There is my cousin, my dear love, and there is the man I saw from my window, the impertinent upon whom, Allāh forgive me, I think I sprinkled water from my little watering-pot. I see now what has happened: they are friends and, when this new husband of mine fell in love with me, my noble Attaf ceded me to him in the greatness of his soul.' She wept alone in the litter and lamented for what had happened. She recalled her past happiness and, while burning tears fell down her face, murmured these lines:

> Grief would be nothing were it not for places,
> Lovers go mad for places. God above,
> Let me go mad, or let me see the places,
> Just the places, just the places of my love.

And again she wept, and murmured:

> The past so prized,
> The present so despised . . .
> Oh, every time my heart beats I'm surprised.

And a third time she wept, and murmured:

> Once and for all we thought our hearts were riven,
> And clean departing was to make them whole;
> We gave each other back what we had given . . .
> But I forgot the pain, and you my soul.

When the caravan was again in motion, Jafar went up to the palanquin, saying: 'O mistress of the palanquin, you have surely slain us!' But his bride looked at him with modest sweetness, and answered: 'You should not speak to me, for I am the cousin and wife of your dear friend Attaf, the prince of generous friends. If you have a true feeling in your heart, you will give back the gift which he has made you.'

Jafar's soul was troubled, and he cried: 'Oh, is this true?' 'It is true,' she answered. 'After you had seen me at the window, you carried your love complaint to Attaf and he divorced me rather than

deny you anything you wished.' Then Jafar wept aloud, and exclaimed: 'We come from Allāh and return to Him at the last! Now,
O woman, you are forbidden to me and have become a sacred trust.'
He gave his wife into the care of the servants, and rode on day and
night at the head of the caravan.

Now you must know that the Khalīfah Hārūn al-Rashīd had
grieved at Jafar's absence and had regretted the hopeless task which
he had set him; he imagined him wandering as an outcast across the
deserts, and sent search parties into all wild places to look for him.
When these returned without news, he set himself impatiently to
await the fulfilment of time.

Therefore, when the coming of Jafar's caravan was reported, the
Khalīfah rejoiced and, going forth to meet it, took him to his heart.
They returned together to the palace, and the Commander of the
Faithful made his wazīr sit beside him, saying: 'Now tell me the whole
story of your wanderings since you left me.' So Jafar told him the
whole story; but nothing would be gained by repeating it in this
place. 'As Allāh lives, I desire to know your friend!' cried the astonished Khalīfah. 'You must certainly divorce this new wife of yours
and send her home under a faithful escort, for if your companion finds
a foe in you, he will become your foe, and if he finds a friend in you,
he will remain your friend. We will summon him to come to
Baghdād, for he is not a man to be neglected and his generosity will
teach us all a lesson.'

Acting on Hārūn's advice, Jafar installed the girl in a fair house
surrounded by a delicious garden, providing her with slaves, carpets, porcelains, and other necessaries. He never set foot in the place
himself, but daily sent greetings and promises that his bride should
speedily be reunited with her cousin. Also he allowed her a thousand
dīnārs a month for her upkeep.

When Attaf had said farewell to Jafar and returned to Damascus,
those who were jealous of him took advantage of the fact that his
name was on every tongue to say to the nāib of that city: 'Why do
you not guard yourself against that man? Do you not know that the
wazīr Jafar is his friend? Do you not know that he accompanied him
further than we did, even to Katīfah; that, on the way, he asked
Jafar for an edict from the Khalīfah to depose the nāib, and that Jafar
promised it? It is better to invite him to breakfast than to wait until
he invites you to supper, for success is only seizing the main chance
when it offers.' 'You have spoken wisely,' answered the nāib of

Damascus. 'Send for the man at once.' A mob ran to Attaf's house, where he rested in ignorance of the plot which had been spun against him, and threw themselves upon him with swords and sticks, beating him until he was covered with blood. They dragged him before the nāib, who ordered the immediate pillage of his house. His slaves, riches and kinsfolk were reft away from him, and, when he asked what was his crime, his enemies answered: 'O pitch face, are you so ignorant of Allāh's justice that you think you can attack a nāib of Damascus and sleep afterwards in peace?'

The nāib ordered his executioner to behead Attaf. The man tore away a strip of his victim's robe and bandaged the youth's eyes with it; but, even as the blade was about to fall, one of the amīrs rose, saying: 'O nāib, do not be in too great a hurry to cut off this man's head, for haste is a gift from Satan. Possibly those who have accused him are liars, for there is no man of eminence who has not jealous foes. Also, if the wazīr Jafar, who is Attaf's friend, hears how you have treated him, how long do you think your own head will remain upon your shoulders?'

At this point Shahrazād saw the approach of morning and discreetly fell silent.

But when the nine-hundred-and-second night had come

SHE SAID:

The nāib of Damascus came, as it were, out of his sleep and, staying the execution, ordered Attaf to be cast into prison. In spite of his cries and prayers, the poor young man was thrown into the city hold and chained there by the neck, to pass his days and nights weeping and calling upon Allāh to be his witness.

One night he woke and, after humbling himself before his Maker, walked up and down his cell, as far as his neck chain would permit. In doing so, he noticed that the gaoler, who had brought him his bread and water in the evening, had forgotten to shut his door. A feeble light showing through the crack acted upon him as a spur; he lifted his eyes to Allāh and, with a sudden miraculous effort, broke his chain. He felt his way, with a thousand precautions, among the complications of the sleeping prison, and discovered the key of the outer door hung in a corner near the lock. In a moment he was free and fleeing among the protecting shadows, which kept him safe until the morning. As soon as the city gates were opened, he mingled with the people and left Damascus for Aleppo, where he arrived after leagues of hardship. He made his way to the principal mosque and there fell into conversation with certain wayfarers who were journeying to Baghdād. These allowed him to join with them; in twenty days he reached Kūfah and, not long afterwards, came in safety to the City of Peace. He found it rich in towering palaces and delectable gardens, he found it full of wise men and fools, of rich men and poor, of good men and evil. He passed through the streets, exciting pity by his torn and dirty turban, unkempt beard and tangled elf-locks, and turned into the first mosque which met his gaze. While he sat in painful reflection, a vagabonding beggar squatted down opposite to him and drew, from an old sack, a loaf, a chicken, another loaf, some conserve, an orange, some olives, some date cakes, and a cucumber. The man began to eat, and Attaf, who had not tasted food for two days, watched the meal with famished eyes, as if it came from the very cloth of Jesus, son of Mary (the Blessing and Peace of Allāh be upon them both!). His hunger for these good things blazed so brightly from his eyes that at last the beggar noticed it. Meeting the other's glance, Attaf burst into tears, and the vagabond, after finishing his mouthful with a shake of the head, spoke as follows: 'O father of the dirty beard, why do you behave like a stranger or a dog, and only beg with the eyes? I swear, by the protection of Allāh, that you may shed a Jaxartes of tears, a Bactrus, a Dijlah, an Euphrates, a Basrah river, an Antioch river, an Orontes, a Nile, a salt sea, a very deep ocean of tears, and I will not give you a scrap of my food; but I do not mind giving you a bit of advice. If you want to eat white chicken, tender lamb, and all the jams and pastries of Allāh, you have only to knock at the door of the grand-wazīr Jafar, son of Yahya the Barmakid, for he received hospitality from a man called Attaf in Damascus, and it is in memory of this that he is feeding all and sundry. They say he neither rises nor lies down without mentioning that Attaf's name.'

Attaf lifted his eyes to sky, murmuring: 'O Allāh of impenetrable designs, again You have performed a miracle for Your servant!' And he recited these lines:

> When things fall odd,
> Sit down in peace and send your cares to Satan.
> If life's a tangle much too big to straighten,
> Give it to God.

Then he went to the shop of a paper merchant and begged from him the gift of a morsel of paper and the loan of a reed pen. The good merchant provided him with these things, and he wrote:

From Attaf your brother, whom may Allāh remember! Let him who possesses the world not be proud, for a day can cast him into the bitter dust. If you saw me, you would not recognise me, for poverty, misery, hunger, thirst, and a great journeying have reduced my body and soul to their starvation. I have come to you. Peace be with you!

He inquired his way to Jafar's house and stood at some distance from the door; the guards looked at him in silence, and he returned their glances without a word. As he was thinking to depart for very shame, a magnificent gold-belted eunuch passed by him, and he plucked up courage to kiss the man's hand, and say: 'My lord, the Prophet of Allāh (upon whom be prayer and peace!) has said that he who is go-between to a fair action has equal merit with the performer, and shall meet with reward in Paradise.' 'What do you want?' asked the eunuch, and Attaf replied: 'I wish you, of your great goodness, to carry this letter to the master of the house and tell him that his brother Attaf is at the door.'

The eunuch flew into a great rage, his eyes started from his head, and he cried: 'O shameless liar, do you pretend to be the wazīr's brother?' He beat Attaf in the face with his gold-shod stick, so that the blood ran out and the poor enfeebled youth fell all along the earth. But the Book says: 'Allāh has made good and evil even among slaves.' A second eunuch, who had watched from a little distance, came running up to the first, with his heart divided between angry indignation and a pity for the poor man who lay in the street. 'Did you not hear him say that he was the wazīr's brother?' asked the first eunuch, but the second cried: 'Man of evil, son of evil, slave of evil, pig and disgust, is Jafar one of our prophets? Is he not a dog of earth like the rest of us? All men are brothers, sprung from Adam and Eve, and the poet has said:

> Adam was my father, Eve your mother,
> You can't deny relationship, my brother.

There is only one difference between men, and that lies in goodness of heart, as you should know.'

He bent over Attaf and raised him up, he wiped the blood from his face, and shook the dust from his garments, saying: 'My brother, what is your desire?' 'I only desire that this paper be carried to Jafar,' answered Attaf. The compassionate eunuch at once took the letter and carried it into the hall where Jafar the Barmakid sat with his officers and friends, drinking, reciting verses, and listening to the music of lutes. The wazīr was standing on his feet, lifting his wine cup, and saying: 'Bodily absence, my friends, does not prevent a very real presence in the heart. Nothing can stay me from thinking and speaking of my brother Attaf, for he is the noblest man of our time. My friends, he gave me horses, black and white slaves, girls, fair fabrics, and coffer after coffer of magnificence. With these things he saved my life and had no thought of repayment, for he did not know that I had any power at all in the land.'

When the excellent eunuch heard these propitious words, he rejoiced in his heart and, bending low, handed the paper to Jafar. The wazīr took it and read it; but the charge of joy to his heart affected him as if there had been poison in the wine. He fell forward from his full height upon his face, still holding the letter and the crystal cup. The cup was broken into a thousand pieces and one of them entered deeply into Jafar's forehead, so that the blood gushed forth and the paper slipped from his fingers.

The eunuch saw this and fled, but Jafar's friends lifted him up and stanched the bleeding of his forehead. 'There is no power or might save in Allah!' they cried. 'These vile servants are all alike: they trouble the pleasure of kings. As Allāh lives, the man who wrote this paper shall be given five hundred strokes before the walī and then thrown into prison.'

The slaves ran out to hunt for the author of the letter, but they had not to look far, for Attaf said: 'I am the man, my masters.' They dragged him at once into the presence of the walī, who gave him five hundred strokes and cast him into prison, causing the words: 'For life,' to be written upon his chains.

At the end of two months a child was born to the Commander of the Faithful, who, to celebrate its coming, caused alms to be distributed among the people, and all the prisons to be emptied. As soon as Attaf came forth, tottering and hungry, he lifted his eyes to heaven, and cried: 'Our thanks are due to You, O Lord, in every circumstance. Doubtless I have suffered all these things in payment for some past fault. Allāh showered His blessings upon me, and I met them with disobedience and revolt. I have gone far enough in debauch and abomination, and now cry to Him that He may pardon me.' Then he recited these lines:

> It is our nature to forget in gladness,
>   And to remember only when we're glad,
>   Oh, may He too forget us when we're glad
> And yet be not unmindful of our sadness!

'But what shall I do now?' he asked himself weeping. 'If I departed for my own land, in my present state of weakness, I would surely die on the journey; and, if by chance I did arrive, I would lose my life at the hands of the nāib. If, on the other hand, I stay here to beg my bread, none of the beggars will allow me into their corporation, because I am a stranger. I shall leave my Destiny in the hands of its Master, for all else have turned against me and betrayed me. The poet has said:

> I wearied of my friend and of the East,
>   At morn I journeyed to the novel West;
> I found an unknown savour in the feast
>   And in the casual wine an unknown zest
>   (That day's first dusk had led me back to East
>   And I had lain all night upon his breast).'

At this point Shahrazād saw the approach of morning and discreetly fell silent.

But when the nine-hundred-and-third night had come

SHE SAID:

'O God, give me patience,' he murmured, as he made his way to a mosque and sat down inside it to wait upon his Destiny. At noon, when his hunger was sore, he prayed to Allāh, but would not stretch out his hand to any human. When night fell, he left the holy place, because he remembered the words of the Prophet: 'Though Allāh would let you sleep in His sanctuary, leave it for those who worship Him, since it was built for prayer and not for slumber.' He wandered up and down the streets and at last crept into a ruined house to sleep. In the darkness he stumbled over something and fell upon his face. When he felt for the thing which had tripped him, he found that it was the freshly slain body of a man, with a bloody knife lying beside it.

Attaf's rags were covered with blood; as he stood still in great perplexity, asking himself whether he should flee or stay, the walī passed that place with his police guard. Attaf hailed the men and they ran in with their torches; but when they saw the body of the murdered man and the knife lying beside him and the blood-smeared youth standing over it, they cried: 'O wretch, why did you kill him?' Then, as Attaf made no answer, the walī commanded: 'Bind him and throw him into a dungeon, until I have made my report of the case to the wazīr Jafar. If Jafar orders his death, we will execute him.' And the guards did as they were bidden.

Next morning Jafar was presented with a written report, conceived in these words: 'Yesterday we entered a ruined building and arrested a man who had killed another man. We questioned him and his silence confessed him the author of the crime. What are your orders?' The wazīr ordered the supposed criminal to be put to death, and Attaf was led from prison to the place of execution. The headsman blinded his victim's eyes with a strip torn from his rags, then he turned to the walī, saying: 'Shall I strike, my lord?' 'Strike!' answered the walī, and the executioner made a circle of sparks in the air with his sword. The blade was in the act to descend, when a voice cried: 'Stay your hand!' and Jafar, who was returning from a walk, laid his finger upon the man's arm.

The walī kissed the earth between Jafar's hands, and the wazīr asked him why a crowd had assembled. 'To see the execution of this man,' answered the walī. 'He comes from Damascus, and yesterday slew a youth of noble blood. He was caught well-nigh in the act and by his silence confessed the crime.' 'Alas, that a man should have come here from Damascus of all places and got himself into so unfortunate a scrape!' exclaimed the wazīr, and he bade the prisoner be led into his presence. When the condemned stood before him, Jafar did not recognise him, so changed was he by want and hardship. 'What is your country, young man?' asked the wazīr. 'Damascus,' answered Attaf. 'The city itself, or the neighbouring villages?' asked Jafar. 'The city itself,' answered Attaf. Then said the wazīr: 'Did you by chance know a man named Attaf, one justly famous for his generosity?' And Attaf replied: 'I knew him when you were his friend and dwelt with him in such a house in such a street; I knew him when the two of you used to walk together among the gardens; I knew him when you married his cousin; I knew him when you said farewell on the road to Baghdād, when you drank of one cup.'

'These things certainly happened,' exclaimed Jafar, 'but can you tell me what came to him after he left me?' 'Dear master,' answered Attaf, 'he was pursued by Destiny and such and such things happened to him.' He told the story of his adventures from the day of their separation to the moment when the executioner had brandished the sword above him. Then he recited these lines:

> Protector of the hunted from their foes,
>> Protector of the stranger near his end,
>> Gold lion of the hill, who called me friend,
> Behold, the valley wolves are very close!

Finally, he cried: 'O my lord Jafar, I know you, I am Attaf!' Jafar uttered a loud cry and threw himself into the poor man's arms. So great was their emotion that for many moments they did not know what went on about them; when they came to themselves, they embraced again and again, and could not be done with questions. Their confidences were in full tide when a shout was heard, and they looked round to find an old man coming towards them, crying: 'This execution must not be!' The stranger wore a beard dyed with henna and a blue handkerchief about his head. He bowed before Jafar, saying: 'Spare this innocent man, for he has killed no one. I am the murderer!' 'Had you no fear of Allāh, then,' asked Jafar, 'that you should take blood, and noble blood, upon your soul? Why did you kill him?' 'He belonged to me, I brought him up,' the old man answered. 'He took my money for his expenses every day, but he was not faithful to me. He would do it with Shumūshag, with Nagish, with Gasis, with Ghubar, with Gushir, with anybody. Even Odis, the scavenger, and Abū Butran, the cobbler, boasted of his favours before my face. Yesterday I caught him in that ruin with Shumūshag the tripe seller. The world darkened before my eyes, and I slew him. I kept silence about the matter until I heard that another was unjustly accused of my crime. Now I have come to give my life in exchange for the life of this youth. He must have been good looking in his time.'

Jafar reflected for a moment and then dismissed the old man, saying: 'The case is doubtful, and where there is doubt, it is best to leave well alone. Depart in the peace of Allāh, O sheikh, and may He pardon you!'

When the old man had gone, Jafar took Attaf by the hand and led him to the hammām. After he was refreshed and rested, he introduced him into the presence of the Khalīfah, kissing the earth before the throne, and saying: 'This is Attaf the Generous, O Commander of the Faithful. He was my host in Damascus and treated me as if I had been more precious to him than his own soul.' Al-Rashīd sighed when he saw the youth standing before him, meagre and exhausted, and heard him deliver his homage with great eloquence. 'And are you so reduced, poor man?' he asked; but Attaf wept. Yet, when Attaf told his story, it was Jafar and the Khalīfah who wept, though Hārūn could not help laughing heartily at the story of the old man with the dyed beard.

When the tale was finished, the Khalīfah looked at Jafar and asked him for a list of his indebtedness to Attaf. 'In the first place my blood belongs to him and I am his slave,' answered the wazīr. 'Then I owe him three million dīnārs in gold money, and countless other millions for the presents he made me. Until I can pay, he must stay with us for our delight; as for his cousin, who is his wife, that is a matter on which we must have further speech.'

The Khalīfah understood that the moment had come for leaving the two friends together, so he allowed them to depart from the presence. Jafar led Attaf towards his house and, as they went along, said with a smile: 'Dear brother, your wife, your cousin who loves you, remains untouched. I have never seen her face uncovered since the day when you and I separated from each other. I have divorced her, and now give back that precious trust.' Thus Attaf and his cousin found each other again, and the love of each merged together in one perfection.

At this point Shahrazād saw the approach of morning and discreetly fell silent.

But when the nine-hundred-and-fourth night had come

SHE SAID:

The Khalīfah sent orders to Damascus, and, in obedience to them, the nāib of that city was smothered with chains and cast into a dungeon until further notice.

Attaf spent many months of perfect happiness in Baghdād in the love of his wife and friend, and in the intimacy of al-Rashīd. He would have lived there for the rest of his life had not numerous letters come from his friends and relations in Damascus, begging him to return to them. The Khalīfah was loath to let him depart, and only allowed him to do so after appointing him walī of Damascus and providing an escort of noble riders, and a train of mules and camels loaded with magnificent presents.

His native city was decked and illuminated to celebrate the return of her most generous son; for Attaf was loved and respected by every grade of the citizens, and especially by the poor, who had wept for his long absence.

A second decree from the Khalīfah condemned the nāib to death, but Attaf interceded for him and caused the sentence to be commuted to one of life-long banishment.

No more was heard of the magic book which had made al-Rashīd laugh and weep, for the Khalīfah forgot all about it in the joy of his wazīr's return, and Jafar himself was careful never to allude to it. We need not ask of it, since we know that all those concerned in this tale lived in pleasure and untroubled friendship until they were visited by the Destroyer of joys, the Builder of tombs, the Servant of the Master of Destiny Who alone lives, Who alone is merciful.

Such, O auspicious King, continued Shahrazād, is the tale of Attaf the Generous as I heard it told. It is not to be compared with another which I hold in reserve for you, if my words have not begun to weary. 'The tale has instructed me and made me think,' answered King Shahryār. 'I am as ready to hear you now as I was upon the first day.'

So Shahrazād said . . .

The Splendid Tale of Prince Diamond

IT is related in the books of the sublime folk, the scholars and poets who opened the palaces of their mind to those who groped in poverty,—therefore chosen and multiple thanks be unto Him Who has given an excellence to certain men on earth even as He has placed the sun in the firmament, a lamp for the house of His glory, and has set the dawn upon the borders of the sky to be a torch for the nightly halls of His beauty; Who has mantled the sky with cool silk and put a bright green garment upon the earth; Who has decked the gardens with their trees, and the trees with verdant vests; Who has given streams of bright water to those that thirst; Who has given the shade of the vine to drunken men, to women beauty, and to Spring the rose; Who has created a smile to grace the rose and a nightingale to sing of her; Who has set woman before the eyes of man and has planted desire in his heart, a jewel within a stone!—that there was once a superb King in a great kingdom. His every step was a felicity, he kept fortune and happiness to wait upon him, his justice passed the justice of Khusrau-Ānūshīrwān and his generosity exceeded the generosity of Hātim of the tribe of Taiy.

This King with the serene brow was called Shams-Shāh, and he had an exquisitely-mannered son whose beauty exceeded that of the star Canopus shining upon the sea.

One day young Diamond, for such was the prince's name, sought his father, saying: 'Father, to-day my heart sickens of the city and I wish to go upon a hunting expedition. If I cannot do so I shall tear my garments to the very hem.'

As he loved his son, Shams-Shāh gave the necessary orders for this diversion. The officers of the hunt and the fowlers prepared the falcons, the grooms saddled the mountain horses, and Prince Diamond rode out joyfully at the head of a troop of ruddy-complexioned youth. Spurring forward in the heroic tumult, he came at last to the foot of a mountain whose summit wedded the sky. A great tree faced him and, at a stream, running by the roots of the tree, a deer drank with bended head. Diamond signed to his companions to halt and went forward, at the full fiery speed of his horse, to take the handsome prey alone. But the deer, realising his danger, escaped with a mighty bound and swift circling, and fled with the speed of an arrow across the plain. Diamond went headlong in pursuit, by sand and stone, until his horse came to a standstill, foaming and breathless, and lolled a parched tongue in the midst of a desert where there was no sign of human presence or hint that other than the invisible had ever harboured there.

At this point Shahrazād saw the approach of morning and discreetly fell silent.

But when the nine-hundred-and-fifth night had come

SHE SAID:

As the deer had disappeared behind a sandy hill, Diamond, in his despair, climbed to the top of this and walked to the farther side. From that new vantage point he beheld, not the pitiless drought of the desert, but a cool oasis of living green, cut with silver brooks, and so meadowed with white and red flowers that it seemed to hold the half light of evening and the half light of morning. The prince rejoiced and was at ease, as if he had entered that garden which the winged Ridwān guards.

After contemplating the admirable work of his Creator, the prince watered his horse and drank from a bubbling pool. Then he stood upright and looked about him. For the first time he noticed a lonely throne shaded by a very old tree whose roots must have reached to the innermost doors of earth. Upon this throne sat an aged King with a crown upon his head, and naked feet, who looked before him, wrapped in contemplation. Diamond respectfully greeted him, and the monarch answered his salutation, saying: 'O son of kings, what has led you to cross this savage desert where no bird may fly and where even the blood of beasts of prey is turned to gall?' The prince told the story of his hunting and then asked in his turn: 'O venerable King, why do you sit here surrounded by desolation? Surely your story is a strange story?' 'It is strange,' answered the King. 'It is so strange that you had better not ask to hear it, lest it be the cause to you of most unfortunate tears.' 'You may speak freely, O venerable monarch,' said the prince, 'for I drank my mother's milk and am the son of my father.'

He cajoled the old King, until he said from his throne beneath the tree: 'Listen, then, to the words which come from the very shell of my heart. Let none escape, but gather all into the robe-folds of your understanding.' He lowered his head for a moment and then, raising it, spoke again:

'Before I came to this isle in the desert, I reigned with riches and glory, with armies and a brilliant court, over the lands of Babylon, and Allāh had given me seven royal sons to be my joy. All was prosperous peace with me until my eldest son chanced to learn, from the lips of a traveller, of a certain princess called Muhrah, who dwelt in the far off countries of Sīn and Masīn. She was the daughter of King Kāmūs, son of Tammūz, and had not her equal in the world; the perfection of her beauty blackened the face of the new moon; Joseph and Zulaikah would have worn chains before her. In a word, she followed the verses of the poet:

> A thief of hearts equipped with all bright implements,
> With nard of gardens in her curls of hair,
> With lips of ruby-sugared condiments
> And in her cheek musk rose of gardens too,

And teeth like crystal when the sun is bare,
A thief of hearts equipped with all bright implements
    For breaking through.

'The traveller told my eldest son that King Kāmūs had no other
children and that, now that this charming bud from beauty's garden
had come to the Spring and the bees began to haunt about her flowering body, invitation had been sent into all lands that suitable princes
should come to woo her. Claimants for her hand had to answer the
princess's question: *What is the relation between Fircone and Cypress?*
and the correct reply was the only dowry asked of any suitor. It was,
however, made a condition that he who could not answer should
have his head cut off and spiked upon a pinnacle of the palace.

'When my eldest son learned these details, his heart burnt like
roasting flesh and he came to me in a tempest of tears, asking my
permission to depart for the countries of Sīn and Masīn. Frightened
by the rashness of his enterprise, I tried him with drugs and doctors
and, when none could cure him, said: "Light of my eyes, if your only
hope of life is to go to the countries of Sīn and Masīn, and interview
King Kamūs, son of Tammūz, the father of Princess Muhrah, I will
accompany you at the head of my armies. If the King consents to the
marriage, all will be well; if not, I swear by Allāh to shake the ruins
of his palace down about his head, to cast his kingdom to the wind,
and take his daughter for you by the strong hand.' But my son
would have none of this, and answered: "It would be against our
dignity, my father, to take what we cannot win. I must set out alone,
give the required answer, and woo the girl myself."

'Then I saw better than at any other time that no man can efface
one character which the winged scribe has written in the book of
Destiny. Conceiving certainly that this thing was written in my
son's Fate, I gave him leave with many sighs, and he departed to
follow his star.

'He came at last to the far kingdom of Kāmūs, presented himself
at the palace where the Princess Muhrah dwelt, and—could not
answer the question. His head was ruthlessly struck off and impaled
upon a pinnacle of the palace. I wept all the tears of despair and
shut myself in with my grief for forty days; my friends covered their
heads with dust, we tore the garments of patience, and all the halls of
my court sent up a noise of mourning and a confusion as of Resurrection Day.

'Then my second son wounded my heart, drinking the wine of death as his brother had done. He perished in the same enterprise, and the five others also died, martyrs to this disastrous love.

'Bitten to the heart by black fate and beaten down by grief, I wandered away from my country and my royalty. I passed like a man in sleep over these plains and deserts, and now, with naked feet and a crown upon my head, I wait for death to visit my lonely throne.'

When Prince Diamond heard the old King's tale, he was wounded by the murderous arrow of an unknown love, and sighed hot sighs. The poet says:

> I saw not love, my eyes were closed, a dart
> In by my ear made he.
> I do not know what has passed between some lady
> And my heart.

So much for the old King of Babylon upon his throne in the oasis, and for the sorrows of his life.

Though Prince Diamond had ordered his companions not to follow him, when they grew anxious at his long absence, they disobeyed and searched across the desert for him. They came upon him as he was leaving the oasis and, after clustering about him like butterflies about a rose, gave him a change horse whose action was lighter than the breeze and swifter than the imagination of man. He leapt into the gilded saddle and took the pearl-studded bridle in his hand; late in the day he came back to his father's palace with his troop.

Instead of finding his son healthily rejoiced by his hunting, Shams-Shāh saw that his colour was changed and that he was plunged in some dark sea of grief. For love had eaten to Diamond's bones and fed upon the strength of his heart and liver.

At this point Shahrazād saw the approach of morning and discreetly fell silent.

But when the nine-hundred-and-sixth night had come

SHE SAID:

At last the King's prayers prevailed upon Diamond to confess the reason of his grief; when the veil was torn aside, Shams-Shāh embraced his son and clasped him to his breast, saying: 'Refresh your eyes and calm your dear soul, for I will at once send my ambassadors to King Kāmūs, son of Tammūz, in the lands of Sīn and Masīn, with a letter in my own hand demanding marriage, and many camels loaded with robes of price, jewels, and coloured gifts such as are worthy of kings. If Muhrah's father is so ill-advised as to humble us by his refusal, I will despatch the armies of my devastation against him to roll his throne in blood and cast his diadem down the wind. Thus, in either case, the exquisitely-mannered Muhrah shall become yours in all honour.'

Thus spake Shams-Shāh from his gold throne, before his approving wazīrs, amīrs and ulamā; but Prince Diamond answered: 'O shelter of the world, this cannot be! I will go by myself, and answer the riddle myself. I will bring home the miraculous princess by my personal merit.'

The King groaned, as he replied: 'Son of my soul, so far my eyes have been bright and my body strong, because you are the consolation of my old royal heart and the sole prop of my brow. How can you now leave me, to run upon death?' But, though he spoke this and much like it, his pleading was in vain and, rather than see his son die before his eyes of frustration, he was obliged to give him leave to depart.

Prince Diamond mounted upon a horse as handsome as if it had been of fairy stock, and galloped out upon the road leading to the kingdom of Kāmūs, while his father and mother rubbed hands of despair and sank into the bottomless pit of desolation.

The prince journeyed from stage to stage, and came in safety to the city which he sought. He found himself facing a palace taller than a mountain and beheld, spiked by thousands upon its pinnacles, crowned heads and uncrowned heads with waving hair. Tents of gold tissues and Chinese satin, with curtains of gilded muslin, were pitched in the open square, and a jewelled drum, with an engraved stick, hung at the principal door of the palace. Upon the drum was written in letters of gold: 'Let any of royal blood who desires to see Princess Muhrah beat upon me.' So Diamond dismounted without hesitation, and beat so loudly with the jewelled stick upon the drum that all the city trembled.

Men came from the palace and conducted the stranger into the presence of King Kāmūs, who was so smitten by his beauty that he wished to save him from death. 'Alas upon your youth, my son!' he said. 'Why do you wish to throw away your life like all these others? Have pity upon yourself, renounce your wooing, and become my chamberlain. None but Allāh knows and can explain the fantastic mysteries which hive in a girl's head.' And, as Prince Diamond persisted in his demand, King Kāmūs said again: 'Listen, my son: it would be a great grief for me to see a handsome youth from the cultivated eastern lands die thus ingloriously in my kingdom. I beg you, therefore, to take three days of consideration before you again seek an audience which will infallibly lead to the separation of your delightful head from the citadel of your body.' So saying, he signed to the young man to retire.

Thus Prince Diamond was obliged to leave the palace on that day and to pass his time in an inspection of the shops and markets. Though he found the folk of Sīn and Masīn intelligent and polite, he could feel no peace till he had approached the dwelling of that lodestone which had drawn him, a needle, from his own land. He loitered before the garden of the palace and considered how he might enter to gain a sight of the princess; fear of being stopped by the guards prevented him from making the attempt, until he noticed a canal which passed under the wall and into the garden. 'Surely I can enter with the water,' said he, and immediately, plunging into the stream, he swam under the wall and climbed out upon the lawns of the garden.

He sat in a secluded place until the sun had dried his garments, and then began to walk slowly up and down among the thickets of flowers. The green garden bathed in her streams and was as richly dressed as a woman of rank upon a day of festival. The white rose smiled to her red sister, and the nightingales wooed both, as if they had been tender poets making love to the sound of lutes. Among the multiple beauty of the terraces, dew lay upon the purple of the roses, like tears upon the blushes of a startled girl. The birds were drunken with their own songs; in the cypresses by the water the obedient doves so crooned that the gardens of Irān seemed to be a thorn bush in comparison with that place.

As Prince Diamond slowly and cautiously made his way down an alley, a sudden turn brought him face to face with a white marble fountain beside which a silken carpet was spread out. Lying at ease upon this carpet, like a resting panther, lay a girl so fair that the whole garden shone because of her beauty. The smell of the curls of her hair rose up to Paradise, filling the dreams of the hūrīs with amber.

The prince, who could no more help looking than a man with the dropsy could help drinking the water of the Euphrates, understood that such beauty could only belong to Muhrah, for whom a thousand souls had perished like butterflies in the fire.

While he contemplated the princess in ecstasy, one of her girls approached the place where he was hidden, and leaned down to fill a gold cup at the stream. Suddenly she uttered a frightened cry and let the cup fall in the water. Trembling and with her hand to her heart, she ran and hid among her companions, and they led her up to their mistress that she might explain her clumsiness.

When the child, whose name was Coral-Branch, had a little recovered from her agitation, she said to the princess: 'O my mistress, O crown upon my head, while I leaned over the stream, I saw reflected in it so handsome a youth's face that I did not know whether it belonged to a mortal or an immortal. I was so moved by the appearance that I dropped the gold cup in the water.'

But when the nine-hundred-and-seventh night had come

SHE SAID:

Princess Muhrah at once sent another of her girls to look in the water, and the second damsel ran back, with a burnt heart and moaning for love, to say to her mistress: 'There is the face of an angel in the water, or the moon has fallen into the stream. I know not which.'

Muhrah felt kindle in her heart a spark of curiosity and a desire to see for herself; she rose to her charming feet and walked towards the stream with the pride of a young peacock. Upon its surface she saw Diamond's face reflected, and became pale and fell a prey to love.

Borne up in the arms of her girls, she called her old nurse to her, saying: 'O nurse, if you would not have me die, fetch me that boy whose face is mirrored in the water.' 'I hear and I obey,' answered the nurse, as she began to search among the thickets.

At length she discovered the delightful body of the prince in an angle of two trees, and saw a face of the sun of which the stars were jealous. The prince beheld her at the same moment and decided to pretend madness in order to save his life.

So, when the nurse, as if she were touching the wings of a butterfly, led him by the fingers into the presence of her peerless mistress, he laughed wildly and cried: 'I am famished, but I am not hungry. The fly has turned into a buffalo; but the water has changed the

cotton mountain into clay; I knew it would. The snow has melted all
the wax and the camel has eaten the coal. I will devour the world, no
one else shall do it.' He showed the whites of his eyes and poured out
a stream of the like insensate stuff, until the princess was convinced
of his madness.

Muhrah's heart was smitten with despair, she trembled like a half-
killed fowl, and cried to her girls: 'Alas, the pity of it!' for love had
entered her bosom for the first time.

It was only after a long look that she could tear her eyes away
from the young man, and say sadly to her following: 'This young
man is mad from possession, and I would have you remember that
the afflicted of Allāh are great saints, whom it is as impious to offend
as to doubt the existence of the Lord or the divine origin of the
Koran. He must be left here, to do as he wills in all liberty; none
must say him nay or refuse the least of his demands.' Then she turned
to the youth, and kissed his hand with religious diffidence, murmuring: 'O venerated saint, grace us by choosing this garden and that
pavilion as your home, for you shall lack nothing in the way of entertainment.' To this Diamond cried, with bulging eyes: 'Necessary
and nothing! Necessary and nothing! Necessary and nothing!'

Princess Muhrah left him after a final bow, and departed from him
with a heart half edified and half most desolate.

After this the young saint found himself surrounded by every sort
of reverence and little care. His pavilion was served by the most devoted of Muhrah's slaves, and was thickly piled, morning and evening, with dishes of varied meat and fruit conserves of every colour.
His holiness was the edification of the palace, the garden paths were
sedulously swept after him, and the rest of his meals, his nail parings,
and the like, were eagerly collected for amulets.

One day Coral-Branch, who was Princess Muhrah's favourite,
entered pale and trembling into the young man's presence, and laid
her head humbly against his feet. After sighs and groans, she said:
'O crown upon my head, O master of perfection, Allāh, Who made
your beauty, will, if you wish it, do more for you through my good
offices. My sad heart trembles and melts like wax because of you;
therefore have pity and tell me who you are and how you came to
this garden, in order that I may serve you better for the knowledge.'
Fearing some trick of the princess, Diamond would not allow himself to be influenced by the supplications and burning glances of the
girl. He babbled as if he had been really possessed and, though

Coral-Branch beat about him as a night moth beats about a flame, he would not yield. At last she said: 'The name of Allāh and His Prophet be upon you and about you! If you have any pity, open the fans of your heart and waft the sweetness of your soul in my direction. It is as certain that you have a secret as that my heart is a coffer whose key is thrown away. Speak, for the coffer is filled full with love of you.'

Convinced that the true perfume of love was in these words, the prince smiled quite sanely at the girl and then opened the fans of his heart, saying: 'Delightful child, my reason for coming through a thousand pains and perils to this place was to answer the Princess Muhrah's question concerning the Fircone and the Cypress. If, of your compassion, you could tell me the true solution, my heart would be greatly moved towards you. Surely you must believe me?'

At this point Shahrazād saw the approach of morning and discreetly fell silent.

But when the nine-hundred-and-eighth night had come

SHE SAID:

'Worthy young man,' answered Coral-Branch, 'I fully believe that the deer of your heart is compassionate, but, if you wish me to help you, you must first promise to marry me and set me at the head of all the palace women in your father's kingdom.' At once the prince kissed the girl's hand and carried it to his heart, with a solemn promise that he would obey her in this matter.

Coral-Branch rejoiced, and said: 'O capital of my life, there is a black man beneath Princess Muhrah's ivory bed. He took up his abode there, unknown to all save my mistress, after he had fled from his native city of Wakak. It is he who pricked on the princess to ask that difficult question of all her royal suitors. If you wish to find the solution, you must journey to Wakak, for there alone it is to be found. That is all I know of the Fircone and Cypress, but Allāh knows all!'

'O my heart,' cried Diamond silently, 'we must be patient until some light shines from behind the curtain of mystery. But, O my heart, surely many grievous things await you on the road to Wakak!' Then, aloud and to the girl, he said: 'O help of mine, until I have gone to the city of that black man and pierced the shadow of the riddle, dalliance is forbidden me, but, if Allāh allows me to return in success and safety, I will either accomplish your desire or never lift my head until the Resurrection.' He left the sighing, sobbing and moaning Coral-Branch and, making his way unperceived out of the garden, fetched his belongings from the khān where he had left them. Then, mounting upon his horse, as handsome as if it had been of fairy breed, he set out upon the road of Allāh.

As he did not know the situation of the city of Wakak or the road by which he might reach to it, he was looking about for some direction when he saw a darwīsh coming towards him wearing a green robe and citron yellow slippers. The man carried a stick in his hand and his face so shone with holiness and knowledge that he seemed like Khidr, guardian of all green things. Prince Diamond lighted off his horse and, after saluting the darwīsh, asked him the way to Wakak. The holy man regarded his questioner attentively for a whole hour and then answered: 'O son of kings, seek not a road endless and filled with terror, renounce your rash pursuit; for you might spend your life fruitlessly in searching for the way to Wakak and, if you stumbled upon it, you would lose your soul.' 'O respectable and venerated sheikh,' answered Diamond, 'my business and object in Wakak are so important to me that I would sacrifice a thousand lives as worthless as my own upon the journey. Therefore, if you know anything of the way, I pray you, who resemble Khidr in appearance, to be like him also in kindness and guiding quality.'

When the darwīsh saw that the prince would not be moved from his purpose, he was constrained to say: 'O youth of benediction, the city of Wakak lies in the centre of Kāf, and in and about Kāf dwell all the Jinn. There are three roads to it, but only the right-hand road is practicable. If you journey on from here for a day and a night you will behold, at the rising of the true dawn, a minaret bearing a plate of marble written upon in Kūfic character. Read that inscription and act upon it!'

Prince Diamond kissed the old man's hand in thanks and then continued his journey upon the right-hand road. After a day and a night he came to the minaret and found it as tall as the blue sky. Graven upon a plate of marble let into its surface were these words in Kūfic character: 'The three roads which lie before you lead to Wakak; if you take the left-hand road you will experience many trials and vexations; if you take the right-hand road you will bitterly repent of it; if you take the middle road you will find it terrible.'

After he had read, Prince Diamond lifted a handful of earth and cast it inside the bosom of his garment, crying: 'May I be dust before I fail!' He remounted and, choosing the middle and most dangerous road, galloped forward for a day and a night. In the morning he came within sight of an open space, covered with trees so tall that their branches brushed the sills of Paradise. These trees were disposed in straight lines to enclose a garden of living green and shield it from the savage wind. The entrance to this garden was blocked by a tall square of granite, and was guarded by so black a negro that his very presence shadowed all the flowers. This child of pitch was a giant, his upper lip rose above his nostrils in the shape of an artichoke, and his lower lip fell about his neck. He had the millstone of a mill slung for a shield across his breast, and wore a sword of Chinese steel, hanging from a belt formed of iron rings so great that a war elephant could easily have passed through each. At the time of the prince's arrival, this dark guardian, lying flat upon the skins of wild beasts, sent forth a thunderous snoring from his open mouth.

Diamond dismounted fearlessly, fastened his horse near the negro's head, and, climbing over the granite block, entered the garden.

The air of the place was such that the trees wavered and balanced as if they had drunken wine; in and out among them walked great deer with ornaments of jewelled gold hung about their horns, with brocade handkerchiefs fastened from their necks, and embroidered cloaks upon their backs. All these animals, with feet and eyes and brows, signed violently to the prince that he should not enter, but Diamond, construing these movements as abundant welcome, began to walk calmly up and down the alleys of the garden. He came at length to an immortal palace, and found the door as invitingly open as a lover's eye. In the entrance he could see a charming fairy head, smiling and glancing from left to right, white enough to have twisted the full moon with jealousy, and having eyes to shame the eyes of the jonquil.

When this vision of beauty beheld Prince Diamond, she was stupefied by his daring and captivated by his beauty. After a few moments' pause, she answered his greeting, and asked: 'Who are you, O daring youth, that you should allow yourself to profane a garden where even the birds of the air fear to move their wings?' Thus spake the girl Latīfah to Prince Diamond, and her beauty was the sedition of that time.

At this point Shahrazād saw the approach of morning and discreetly fell silent.

But when the nine-hundred-and-ninth night had come

SHE SAID:

Diamond bowed to the earth and then straightened himself, as he answered: 'O cast from the garden of perfection for too much perfection, O my mistress, I am Prince Diamond, son of . . .' and he told her his whole story from beginning to end; but nothing would be gained by repeating it in this place.

When she had heard all, Latīfah took him by the hand and drew him down beside her upon a carpet stretched in the shade of a vine. 'O walking cypress from the terraces of beauty,' she said, 'alas for your youth! O fretful plan! O difficulty! O great danger! If you love your dear life you must renounce your goal. You must stay here with me and touch the neck of my desire with the benediction of your hand; for it is better to lie with fair beauty than to chase the shadow of the unknown.' But Diamond answered: 'Until I have been to the city of Wakak and solved the riddle of the Fircone and the Cypress, all pleasure is a forbidden thing to me; but I swear, O very beautiful, that I will return, when I have succeeded, and place the collar of love about the neck of your desire.' 'Abandoned heart,' cried Latīfah, as she signed to certain rose-cheeked wine boys who stood far off. She summoned girls of astonishing loveliness, and cups of welcome were passed round, amid singing, to celebrate the coming of that charming stranger; yet the presence of the women mingled with the music until it overcame the wine.

When the cups were empty, the prince rose to take leave; after courteous thanks, he said: 'O princess of all the world, I seek your immediate permission to depart, for, if I stay a moment longer, the fire of love for you will spread among the harvest of my soul. But, if Allāh wills, I shall return to pluck the roses of desire and drink of another cup.'

Burning for the boy, Latīfah rose up also and, seizing a serpent-circled staff, breathed strange words above it. Then, with a sudden movement, she struck the prince on the shoulder, so violently that he spun round three times and fell to the earth; even as he touched the grass, he lost his human form and became another of the deer of that garden.

Latīfah fastened to his horns such an ornament as the other deer carried, tied a brocaded silk handkerchief about his neck, and loosed him into the garden, crying: 'Go to your kind, since you would have none of fairy beauty!' Diamond the deer went off on all fours, an animal in appearance but still a man within.

He wandered with his magicked fellows, meditating a way of escape, and thus came to a corner of the garden where the wall was sensibly lower than at any other part. Lifting his soul to the Master of Destiny, he leaped into the air and cleared the obstacle, but he came down in the same garden, as if he had never crossed the wall. Seven times he leaped forwards, and ever, because of enchantment, he found himself in the same place. The sweat of impatience poured from his hoofs and he paced up and down beside the wall like a caged lion, until, facing him, he saw a window-like opening, which had not been visible when he had passed that way before. Dragging himself painfully through, he found himself, this time, beyond the magic garden and in a second, the perfume of whose flowers lifted his brain like wine.

At the end of an alley he perceived a palace and, at a window of the palace, a young girl's face which had the tender colour of tulips and eyes which would have been the envy of a Chinese gazelle. Her amber-coloured hair held all the sun, the white of her cheeks was of Persian jasmine. Her head was outside the window, and she smiled in the direction of Prince Diamond.

As soon as the prince came near the window, the girl rose and ran down into the garden. She plucked a tuft of grass and held it out gently, with a soft clicking of her tongue, as if to tame this new animal and prevent him running away at her approach. Diamond the deer, who asked nothing more than to plumb this second mystery, ran up to the child as if he were hungry. When he was within reach, Jamīlah—for such was her name and she was the sister of Latīfah by the same father but not by the same mother—seized the silk cord about his neck and led him into the palace, where she fed him with fruits and other refreshments until he could eat no more.

When his meal was finished, Diamond dropped his head on the girl's shoulder and began to weep. She caressed him delicately and pitifully with her soft hands, so that he lowered his head to her feet and wept again. 'Why do you weep, my dear, my deer?' she said. 'I love you better than I love myself!' But he redoubled his tears and rubbed his head so sorrowfully against Jamīlah's feet that she understood at last that he was praying for his human form.

Though she held her sister in great fear, she rose and took a little jewelled box from a hollow in the wall. Then she made ritual ablution, dressed herself in seven robes of freshly whitened linen, and took a morsel of electuary from the box.

At this point Shahrazād saw the approach of morning and discreetly fell silent.

But when the nine-hundred-and-tenth night had come

SHE SAID:

She placed the fragment in the deer's mouth and at the same time pulled strongly on the cord about his neck, so that he shook himself and came out, a man, from the leathern skin.

He kissed the earth between young Jamīlah's hands, saying: 'O princess, you have saved me from the claws of destruction, and given back my life with my humanity. Though each hair on my head is filled with a separate praise of your goodness and great beauty, my tongue stumbles in its thanks, O glory!' But Jamīlah raised him and, after dressing him in royal garments, said: 'O prince with the white body, whose beauty has lighted our garden and our dwelling, what is your name? Why have you honoured us by your coming, and how did you fall into my sister's nets?'

Prince Diamond told his preserver the story of his adventure, and, when he had finished, she said: 'O Diamond, O eye of my heart, I beg you to give up this dangerous and barren undertaking, and not to expose your delightful youth and precious life to unknown powers. It is foolish to die for no profit. Stay here and fill the cup of your life with the wine of my desire. I am ready to serve you in all things, to put your interest before my own, and obey you as a child obeys its mother.' 'O princess,' answered Diamond, 'my debts to you weigh so heavily upon the wings of my soul that I feel I should flay away my skin and make sandals of it for those little feet. You clothed me again in the garment of humanity and my life belongs to you. But I dare to beg you to allow me absence for a few days; when, thanks to the security which Allāh will vouchsafe, I return from the city of Wakak and behold again the magic of your feet, my way shall be yours for ever.'

When Jamīlah saw that none of her entreaties would turn the prince from his purpose, she said with a deep sigh: 'Fruit of my heart, since no man may escape the Destiny which hangs about his neck, and since you are determined to leave me at this same moment of our meeting, I will give you the three objects of my inheritance to guard you upon your way and bring you back to me.' She opened another chest in the hollow of the wall and drew from it a gold bow with arrows, a sword of Chinese steel, and a jade-hilted dagger. These things she gave to Diamond, saying: 'This bow and these arrows belonged to the prophet Sālih (upon whom be prayer and peace!). This sword, which is known as the Scorpion of Sulaimān, is so keen that it could split a mountain as if the substance of it were soap. And this dagger, forged in the old days by Tammūz the Wise, preserves the wearer from all attack by a secret virtue in its blade. . . . But you will never reach the city of Wakak, which is beyond seven oceans, without the help of my uncle, the Simurg. Therefore place your ear to my lips and listen carefully to my instruction: dear friend, a day's march from this place is a fountain, and by the fountain is the palace of a negro King named Tak-Tak. It is guarded by forty bloody Ethiopians, each commanding an army of five thousand savage negroes; but King Tak-Tak will be your friend when he sees the arms which I have given you. He will be even gracious, though it is his custom to grill all strangers and eat them without salt or sauce. You must stay with him for two days and, after that time, allow him to send you with a guide to the palace of my uncle, the Simurg, by whose help it may be that you shall reach Wakak and resolve the problem of the Fircone and the Cypress. Above all, dear Diamond, take care not to depart by one hair's breadth from my advice.' She kissed him, and added: 'Because of your absence my life will be an evil upon my heart. Until you come back to me I shall not smile, I shall not speak, I shall not shut the door of sadness against my soul. Sighs shall rise like a fountain from my heart, and I shall have no more news of my body. Without the strength and prop which your love has given me, my body will be but a mirage of my soul.' Then she sighed out these lines:

> Far from the eyes which the narcissus loves
> Cast not my heart;
> Mock not the crying of the drunkards,
> Lead them back to the tavern.

The armies of his boy's beard
Compass my heart,
And, as a wounded rose,
The rent in my robe shall not be sewn.

O brown tyrannous beauty,
My heart lies at your feet of jasmine,
My heart of a little girl at your thief's feet.

Afterwards the girl took leave of Diamond with many prayers to
Allāh for his safety, and hastened back into her palace to hide her
tears.

The prince mounted his horse and rode on, in the immortal fairness of his youth, until he came to the fountain and the strong castle
of Tak-Tak, the terrible King of the negroes.

At this point Shahrazād saw the approach of morning and discreetly fell silent.

But when the nine-hundred-and-eleventh night had come

SHE SAID:

Though he found the approaches to the castle guarded by foul-
faced Ethiopians, each ten cubits tall, he dismounted fearlessly and,
after fastening his horse, sat down beneath the tree of the fountain to
rest himself. 'Fresh meat at last,' he heard one of the Ethiopians say,
and another answer: 'Let us carry the windfall in to Tak-Tak.' With
that, ten or twelve of the fiercest guards surrounded the prince and
would have dragged him into their master's presence.

But, when Diamond realised that the turning point in his life had
come, he drew Sulaimān's Scorpion from his belt and, rushing upon
his aggressors, sent many of them hurrying down the slope of death.
Even as their hellish spirits fled, news of the affair was brought to
Tak-Tak who, in a red rage, sent the pitch-faced Mak-Mak, his war-
chief, to bring in the audacious stranger. This Mak-Mak, who was
the well-known calamity of that time, came on at the head of his tar-
coloured army, as if leading an eruption of hornets, and black death
looked forth terribly from his eyes.

The prince rose up on his two feet and waited with stretched
thews. The calamitous Mak-Mak, hissing like a horned viper and
bellowing through his nostrils, came all against him and brandished
a smashing club above his head; but Diamond stretched forth his

hand, clasping the dagger of Tammūz, and thrust it between the giant's ribs. This son of a thousand horns drank death in a single draught, and the Angel of Allāh came near to him.

Seeing their chief fall, the rest fled, as sparrows flee before the Father of Beaks; but Diamond pursued them and slaughtered as many as he chose.

When King Tak-Tak learnt of Mak-Mak's discomfiture, rage rose in his nostrils until he could not distinguish his right hand from his left. Stupidity sent him forth to attack the crown of valley riders, Diamond, the peerless knight; but, when he saw the hero stand shouting before him, this black son of fat-nosed shame felt his muscles relax, the sack of his stomach turn upon him, and the wind of death pass over his brow. Diamond took him for target, and sent against him one of the arrows of the prophet Sālih (upon whom be prayer and peace!) so that he swallowed the dust of his own heels and hastened to those lost places where the Nurse of Vultures is accustomed to set down her load.

As soon as the prince had heavily crusted the meat of the dead king with his dead servants, he went up to the palace and knocked upon the door with the air of a conqueror. A girl opened to him, whom this same Tak-Tak had cheated of the throne of her inheritance; she stood like a frightened deer, and her face was salt upon a lover's wound. Truthfully, if she had not gone further to meet Diamond it was because the heavy haunches slung to so slight a waist prevented her, and because her backside, dimpled with valleys, was so remarkable a benediction that she could not move easily without it trembling like curdled milk in a Badawī's porringer or quince jelly heaped on a plate perfumed with benzoin.

She received her liberator with effusion and would have had him mount her dead father's throne, which had been reft away by Tak-Tak, but he refused any reward. Quite won over by his generosity, she asked: 'O handsome youth, what religion is it which makes you do good with no thought of recompense?' 'The Faith of Islām is my Faith, O princess,' answered Diamond, 'and her Belief is my Belief.' 'In what does that Faith and that Belief consist, my master?' she asked again, and he replied: 'Simply in attesting the Unity, through the profession revealed by our Prophet (upon whom be prayer and peace!).' 'And what profession can make men so perfect?' she demanded. 'These simple words: *There is no God but Allāh and Muhammad is the Prophet of Allāh!*' replied Prince Diamond. 'He who pronounces them with conviction is, at the moment, ennobled in Islām. Were he the last of unbelievers, yet he would become the equal of the most noble Mussulmān.' Princess Azīzah felt her heart moved towards the true Faith. Of her own accord she raised her hand and, lifting her index finger to the height of her eyes, pronounced the Shihādah. Thus was she ennobled in Islām.

At this point Shahrazād saw the approach of morning and discreetly fell silent.

But when the nine-hundred-and-twelfth night had come

SHE SAID:

Then she said to Prince Diamond: 'O my master, now that you have made me Queen and I have been lighted into the way of truth, I stand between your hands ready to serve you with my eyes and to be a slave among the slaves of your harīm. Will you, as a favour, accept the Queen of this land for your bride and live with her in whatever place is pleasing to you, whirling her delighted in the auriole of your beauty?' 'My mistress, you appear to me as life itself,' answered Diamond, 'but at the moment I am engaged upon a very important business, for which I left my father and my mother and my native land. It may be that, even now, King Shams-Shāh, the author of my days, weeps me as dead. My Destiny waits for me in the city of Wakak, but, if Allāh favours me and I return, I will marry you, take you to my native land, and rejoice eternally in your beauty. . . . Can you tell me where I may find the Simurg, the uncle of Princess Jamīlah? Only he can guide me to Wakak, but at present I am ignorant of his dwelling and his kind. If you know anything of him, hasten to tell me, for the sooner I am gone the sooner I will return.'

Queen Azīzah mourned bitterly in her heart, but, seeing that her tears and sighs could not turn the prince from his purpose, she rose from her throne and, taking him by the hand, led him in silence through the galleries of the palace and out into the garden.

It was such a garden as Ridwān watches: its avenues were unending lines of roses and, as the light wind wandered sifting out their musk, the heart was lifted into Paradise. The tulip opened, drunk with her own blood, and the cypress murmured throughout all her leaves praise of the measured singing of the nightingale. The streams ran like laughing children at the feet of rose trees, rhyming with their roses.

For all the heavy splendours below her slight waist, Princess Azīzah managed to lead Diamond to the foot of a great tree, whose generous foliage was shading the sleep of a giant. She brought her lips close to the prince's ear, and whispered: 'This is he whom you seek, the Flying Simurg, Jamīlah's uncle. If, on waking, he opens his right eye first he will be pleased to see you and, recognising the arms which his niece has sent, will do all that you may ask. But if, by evil fortune, he opens his left eye first, you will be lost, for your great valiance cannot prevent him lifting you in the air, as a falcon lifts a sparrow, and breaking your dear bones, my love, against the ground. And now, my sweet, may Allāh guard you and send you back to her who is already weeping for your absence.'

Then she quitted him hastily, her eyes filled with tears and her cheeks turned suddenly pomegranate flowers.

Diamond waited an hour for the Flying Simurg to wake, and meanwhile said to himself: 'Why do they give him that name? How could so great a giant rise in the air without wings, even on the ground how could he move except clumsily?' At last he lost patience at the monster's snoring, which was like that of a herd of young elephants, and, bending down, began to tickle the soles of his feet. Immediately the giant twitched and, kicking the air with his leg, let a terrifying fart. At the same moment he opened both eyes at once. When he saw the prince and recognised him as the author of his waking, he lifted one leg and thundered forth a procession of farts which lasted for an hour of time, and surely should have poisoned every living thing within a radius of four parasangs. Indeed Diamond only escaped the infernal tempest by the virtue of the weapons which he carried.

At this point Shahrazād saw the approach of morning and discreetly fell silent.

But when the nine-hundred-and-thirteenth night had come

SHE SAID

When the Simurg had exhausted his provision, he sat up and looked at the prince with stupefaction. 'What is this, O human?' he cried. 'How did you escape the blastments of my bum?' He looked more closely at the youth and, seeing the weapons, rose hastily to his feet. 'Pardon my behaviour, master,' he said with a low bow. 'If you had warned me of your coming by some slave, I would have strewn your path with all the hairs of my body. I trust that you will forget my quite involuntary greeting. Also I hope that you will tell me at once what pressing business has brought you into this place, which neither man nor animal can reach unaided, that I may assist you the more quickly in it.'

After assuring the Simurg of his goodwill, Prince Diamond told him every detail of his story and his desire. When he had finished, the giant lifted the young man's hand to his heart, his lips, and his brow, saying: 'Be it upon my head and before my eyes! We will set out for the city of Wakak as soon as I have prepared my provisions. For that it will be necessary for me to hunt down some of the wild asses which infest our forest here, that I may make kabābs with their flesh and waterbags out of their skins. When that is done, you shall mount on my shoulder and I will fly across the seven oceans with you, sustaining myself with the kabābs and the water, until we reach the city of your desire.'

Without further delay he strode into the forest and caught seven wild asses, one for the transit of each ocean. As soon as the kabābs and the waterskins had been prepared, he filled the latter and swung them about his neck; then he loaded the former into a foodbag, which he wore about his waist, and helped the prince to sit astride his shoulder.

Finding himself in this position, Diamond said to himself: 'Here is a giant larger than an elephant and yet he pretends that he will fly with me in the air without the use of wings! As Allāh lives, it is a prodigy, an unheard-of thing!' But, even as he thus reflected, he heard a noise as of wind passing through the chink of a door, and saw the giant's belly swell and swell, until it became as large as a dome. The noise of wind grew into the noise of bellows, as the giant extended.

Suddenly the Simurg beat the earth with his foot and a moment later was planing above the garden. He moved his legs in the air, as a frog swims in water, until he came to a height which pleased him; then he went forward in a straight line towards the west. Whenever he found that the wind lifted him too high, he would let one or two or three or four farts, of varied length and strength; when, by this perdition, his belly sagged, he took in air through mouth and nose and ears.

The two journeyed thus, as swift as birds, across one ocean after another, and, when the transit of each sea had been safely made, they would come to earth for a short time, in order to eat their kabābs of wild ass and drink the water from the skins. Also, the giant would lie down for a few hours to reinforce his strength.

At this point Shahrazād saw the approach of morning and discreetly fell silent.

But when the nine-hundred-and-fourteenth night had come

SHE SAID:

After seven days of this aerial flight, they found themselves one morning above a shining white city which slept among its gardens. 'You are now as a son to me,' said the Simurg to the prince, 'and I regret none of the fatigues which I have endured in bringing you to this place. I will set you down on the highest terrace of the city, for we have reached Wakak, the place of the black man who lives under Princess Muhrah's ivory bed. Here, if anywhere, you will find out about the Fircone and the Cypress.'

The Simurg let out air and floated down until he could gently set Prince Diamond on the terrace. In taking leave he gave him a tuft of his beard hairs, saying: 'Guard these carefully and, when trouble comes to you or you have need of me to carry you back, burn one of them to summon me.' Then he took in air again and, swimming easily up into the sky, set off rapidly towards his home.

Diamond sat down on the terrace and was reflecting how he might descend to the street without attracting attention when the master of the house, a youth of unparalleled beauty, came up on to the terrace and greeted him with a smile, saying: 'O most handsome of men, you have brought bright morning to my terrace. Are you an angel or a Jinnī?' 'Dear youth, I am a human being who has begun his day delightfully through seeing you,' answered Prince Diamond. 'It is my Destiny which has led me to your most fortunate dwelling; that is all I can tell you.' He clasped the young man to his breast, and the two swore eternal friendship. They went down together into the guest room and feasted in company. Glory be to Allāh for uniting two such fair creatures, and freeing their path from complication!

When they had sealed their friendship by eating and drinking together, Prince Diamond turned to his host, who was none other than Farah, the favourite of the Sultān of Wakak, and said to him: 'O Farah, as you are loved of the Sultān and must know all the secret affairs of the kingdom, will you do me a favour which can cost you nothing?' 'Be it upon my head and before my eyes!' replied young Farah. 'Speak, and, if it be sandals made out of my skin that you require, I will give them willingly.' Then said Diamond: 'I only wish you to tell me what is the relation between Fircone and Cypress, and to explain the business of the negro who lies beneath the ivory bed of Prince Muhrah, daughter of King Kāmūs, master of Sīn and Masīn.'

Young Farah changed colour and his eyes grew troubled: he trembled as if he had seen the angel of death and, when Diamond tried to calm him with gentle words, said in a voice from which he strove to keep his anguish: 'O Diamond, the King has ordered the death of any citizen or traveller who utters those two words, for he himself is Cypress and the name of his Queen is Fircone. That is all I can tell you in answer to your question. Of their relations I know nothing, and of the negro below the bed I know nothing. The King alone holds the answer to your riddle. If you like I will take you to the palace and make you known to him, for you are certain to please him mightily.'

Diamond thanked his new friend, and the two set out hand in hand, as it had been two angels walking, to the palace. King Cypress rejoiced at the sight of Diamond and gazed at him a full hour before bidding him approach. The prince kissed the earth between this monarch's hands and, after greeting, offered him a red pearl threaded on a chaplet of yellow amber, so precious that the whole kingdom of Wakak could not have bought its like. Cypress accepted the present with great content, and then said: 'O youth girt with all grace, ask me any favour in return and it shall be granted.' 'O King of time,' answered Diamond, who had eagerly expected these words, 'Allāh prevent me from asking aught save the favour of becoming your servant! Yet, if you insist that I ask more, grant me a promise of safety and I will speak from my heart.'

At this point Shahrazād saw the approach of morning and discreetly fell silent.

But when the nine-hundred-and-fifteenth night had come

SHE SAID

When King Cypress had given him leave to speak and promised him safety, Prince Diamond reflected for a moment and then answered boldly: 'My lord, the deaf and the blind are happy, for they are immune from those evils which enter by our ears and eyes. O shield of the world, since the evil day when I heard tell that which I shall now relate, I have known neither happiness nor sleep.' When he had told his whole story from beginning to end, he added: 'Now that my Destiny has led me rejoicing into your bright presence, and now that you have deigned to promise a gratification of my wish, I ask simply: what is the exact relation between our master, King Cypress, and our mistress, Fircone, and what is the negro doing under the ivory bed of Princess Muhrah, daughter of King Kāmūs, son of Tammūz, master of Sīn and Masīn?'

The King's colour and manner changed together; he became like a flame, his breast bubbled like a cauldron upon coals. 'Woe, woe upon you, O stranger!' he cried. 'I swear by the life of my throne that, if I had not promised you security, your head would be already severed from your body!' 'Pardon my indiscretion, O King of time! But I have only acted as you gave me leave,' ventured the prince. 'Whatever you feel in the matter, you are bound by your oath to tell me what I wish to know, for you have granted me the fulfilment of my desire, and my sole desire is to be told.'

King Cypress was thrown into perplexity and despair, his soul wavered between a wish to keep his oath and a wish to kill his questioner; the second instinct was the stronger, but for the time being he schooled it, saying: 'O son of Shams-Shāh, why will you force me to give your life to the wind, with no profit to yourself? Abandon this rash idea and ask me for something else, even for half of my kingdom.' 'My soul desires nothing but an answer, King Cypress,' insisted the prince. 'It is permitted,' sighed the King, 'but, when I have told you the secret, you must surely die.' 'Be it upon my head and before my eyes, O King of time!' answered Prince Diamond. 'When I have learnt the relation between Cypress and Fircone, and the business of the negro, I will make my ablution and deliver my head to the sword.'

Cypress grieved doubly, for his secret and for the handsome prince's life. For an hour he reflected with bent head and then, after whispering certain instructions to his guard, caused them to clear the hall. Soon a troop of soldiers entered leading a handsome greyhound by a jewelled red leather trace; when they had ceremoniously spread a square brocaded carpet, the greyhound sat down upon one of its corners. Immediately twelve bloody Ethiopians led in a slim and tender girl, of marvellous beauty, with her hands tied behind her

back, and set her down on the opposite corner of the carpet, facing
the greyhound. Then they placed before her a dish containing a
negro's head, so subtly preserved with aromatic salts that it seemed
to have been freshly severed. At a sign from the King, the master
cook of the palace supervised the placing of a whole service of delightful meats before the dog; the animal ate till it was satisfied and
then the broken food was piled on to a dirty common plate, and set
in front of the bound damsel. At first she wept and then she smiled;
the tears that fell from her changed into pearls, and the smiles that
escaped her into roses. With great care an Ethiopian picked up the
pearls and roses, and gave them to the King.

'Now either the sword or the rope remains for you,' said King
Cypress, but the prince answered: 'I will die when I have heard the
explanation of what I have seen, but not before.'

So King Cypress folded the hem of his royal robe over his left
foot and, cupping his chin in the palm of his right hand, spoke as
follows:

'O son of King Shams-Shāh, the girl, whose tears were pearls and
whose smiles were roses, is Fircone and my Queen. I am King
Cypress, master of the land and city of Wakak.'

At this point Shahrazād saw the approach of morning and discreetly fell silent.

But when the nine-hundred-and-sixteenth night had come

SHE SAID:

'One day I left my city to go hunting and was overcome by
burning thirst in the desert; I hunted on all sides for water but I was
well-nigh exhausted before I found a shadowy cistern, which had
been digged by some ancient people. Thanking Allāh, I made my
painful way across obstacles of ruin, and let my bonnet down into
the cistern at the end of a rope fashioned from my turban and my
belt. My heart was refreshed even by the sound of this improvised
bucket striking the water, but alas, wrestle as I might, I could not
pull it up again. The bonnet had become as heavy as if it were filled
with all the calamities of the world. "There is no power or might
save in Allah!" I cried down from my parched throat. "O dwellers
in this cistern, whether Jinn or human, have compassion upon a poor
man dying of thirst, and let go of my bucket! O illustrious inhabitants, my breath is almost spent, my mouth burns!"

'I cried and groaned in my torment until an answer came up to me: "Life is better than death, O servant of Allāh! If you pull us up out of the well, we will reward you! Life is better than death!"

'Forgetting my thirst for a moment, I assembled my waning forces. With one great effort I drew up the bonnet and beheld, clinging to it by their fingers, two very old blind women, each bent like bows and so thin that she could have been passed through the eye of a bodkin. Their eyelids lay deep in their heads, their jaws had no teeth, their heads wagged lamentably, their limbs trembled, and their hair was as white as carded cotton. Quite unmindful now of my thirst, I asked them pitifully the reason for their prisoning in the cistern, and they said: "O young man of our help, we once incurred the anger of our master, King of the Jinn of the First Bed, so that he blinded us and threw us into this place. We will now show you a way to bring back our sight and, when we are cured, will satisfy the least or greatest of your desires. Not far from here you will find a river upon whose banks a cow comes frequently to graze. If you collect some of her dung and smear it on our eyes, our seeing will return to us. . . . But you must be careful not to let the cow see you, for, if she does, she will not ease herself."

'I made my way to the river, which I had not seen in my searchings, and hid myself behind the reeds there. Soon a cow as white as silver came up out of the water, eased herself largely, cropped some grass, and then disappeared again into the stream. I hastened with a considerable supply of the fresh dung back to the cistern and there anointed the eyes of the two old women, until they saw clearly and looked round eagerly.

' "O master," they cried, kissing my hands, "do you wish wealth, health, or a sample of beauty?" "Good aunts," I answered without hesitation, "Allāh, of His generosity, has given me both health and wealth; but with beauty no man can fill his heart enough. Let me have the sample of which you speak." "Be it upon our heads and before our eyes!" said they. "This sample is the daughter of our King. She is a laughing rose leaf, nay, she is the rose itself, wild rose and garden rose at once. Her eyes languish as with wine, and one of her kisses would calm a thousand griefs. The sun is beaten back from the sky by her beauty, the moon burns for her. Her father and mother love her so that she lies ever upon their breasts; her beauty is the beginning of their day. She shall belong to you, with all that there is hidden of her, and you shall rejoice together in your youth." '

At this point Shahrazād saw the approach of morning and discreetly fell silent.

But when the nine-hundred-and-seventeenth night had come

SHE SAID:

' "We will lead you to her now, and all that there is to do you can do together. But take care that her father does not see you, or he will cast you alive into the furnace. Yet, even if that worst befall, we shall be there to save you; we shall smear your body with the oil of Pharaoh's serpents, so that you can lie for a thousand years in the bosom of the flame and come up out of it refreshed as by a bath in the streams of Irān."

'After thus temping and warning me, the two old women transported me into an inner chamber of the palace which belonged to the King of the Jinn of the First Bed, and there I saw the girl of my Destiny, a smiling body compact of light, lying upon a bed. To look at her long would have washed your mind of reason and life itself. The arrow of desire passed through my heart; I stood with my mouth open, while the child of my inheritance struggled awake and asked no better than to take the weather.

'Seeing the effect which she had upon me, the damsel of delight pursed up her rose leaf lips as if offended, but her mischievous eyes said very plainly: "Yes!" In a voice which she strove vainly to make harsh, she said: "O human, what gave you the audacity to come here? Are you not afraid that you will wash your hands of life?" But I, reading her true thoughts, made bold to answer: "O delicious mistress, would not I buy this sight of you with life itself? As Allāh lives, you are written in my Destiny and I but come in obedience to my Fate. By those dark diamonds which are your eyes, I conjure you not to waste this useful time in idle words!"

'Suddenly the girl quitted her careless pose; she ran to me and took me in her arms, she pressed herself hotly to me, she relaxed in a pale yielding. Soon she moved and wriggled and panted with so much energy that the child slipped into its cradle without cry or pain, as a fish slips back into the water. There were none present save ourselves and God, so that I gave my body to a pure and faultless joy. We passed all the day and all the night together without speaking, eating or drinking in an ecstatic movement and counter-movement of our thighs. The horning ram had no mercy on the battling ewe, he was the true thick-necked father, and the jam he served was the jam of the great muscle; white father was equal to the prodigious tool, and sweet-flesh fell a prey to the blind fighter; the mule was tamed with the holy man's stick, and the dumb starling rhymed with the tuneful nightingale; the earless rabbit and the voiceless cock made up a pair, the muscle of caprice well moved the silent tongue; the ravishable was ravished, the reducible reduced, and we did not cease from our labour until dawn called us to prayer and bathing.

'A month slipped by without anyone suspecting my presence in the palace, or dreaming that two led a life of silent coupling in that chamber. My joy would have been complete had not the fear of discovery a little daunted me, and torn the heart from the heart of my dear mistress.

'At last the dreaded day fell upon us. One morning the girl's father came early to his daughter's room and saw that the moonbeam freshness of her beauty had declined, as it were from some deep fatigue. He called his Queen to him, saying: "Why has our daughter's colour changed? Do you not see that the deadly wind of Autumn has withered her roses?" Her mother looked long, in a suspicious silence, at the sleeping child and then, quickly snatching up her chemise, divided the two charming halves of her daughter's being with her fingers. At once she had peremptory proof that the virginity of the jasmine-tinted rabbit had faded into the invisible.'

At this point Shahrazād saw the approach of morning and discreetly fell silent.

But when the nine-hundred-and-eighteenth night had come

SHE SAID:

'The Queen staggered in her emotion, and cried: "Her shame, her honour have been pillaged! O vile and calmly-sleeping girl! O stains upon the garment of her chastity!" Then she shook her daughter furiously, screaming: "If you do not tell the truth, you bitch, I have a red death for you!"

'The girl woke with a start and, seeing her mother's nose filled with black hatred, confusedly realised that the worst had happened. Instead of confession or denial, she lowered her lids and remained silent. From time to time she would lift timid and astonished eyes to her mother's wrath, but as for answering one way or another, that she refused to do. When the Queen felt her voice grow hoarse and her throat refuse its office, she went out in a tumult and instituted a search throughout the palace for the author of this harm. Very soon the slaves ran me to earth, for they traced me by my human smell, which was different from theirs.

'They seized me and dragged me outside the palace; they piled together a great quantity of wood and threw me naked upon it; but, at that moment, the two old women of the cistern appeared, and said to the soldiers: "We are going to pour this jar of inflammable oil on his vile body, so that he may burn the better and the more quickly." The soldiers gave ready permission, and my two deliverers rubbed every part of my body with the miraculous oil of Pharaoh's serpents. Then the soldiers lifted me back on to the pyre and set fire to it. In a moment I was surrounded by furious flames, but their red tongues were sweeter and cooler in licking me than streams in the gardens of Irān. From morning to night I lay in the belly of the furnace, as safe as if it had been my mother's womb.

'The Jinn of the First Bed, who had piled fuel on the fire all day, went at sunset to ask their master what they should do with my charred bones, and he bade them collect them and burn them again. "But all of you piss on them first," added the Queen. So the servants extinguished the fire in order to piss on my bones, and found me laughing and intact within.

'The King and the Queen were forced to pay astonished tribute to my power; after reflection, they became eager to marry their daughter to so eminent a person. They took me by the hand and excused their treatment of me; when they heard that I was the son of the King of Wakak, they rejoiced exceedingly that Allāh permitted a union between a princess of their line and the noblest of the sons of men. Thus it was that I married this body of a rose in all magnificence.

'When I expressed a desire to return to my kingdom, my father-in-law gave unwilling permission and, after loading me with presents of jewels, prepared for my journey a gold car drawn by six pair of flying Jinn. After sorrowful leave-taking, my bride and I were transported in the twinkling of an eye to my city of Wakak.

'The girl whom you have seen, O youth, with her hands tied behind her back, is none other than my Queen, Fircone, daughter of the King of the Jinn of the First Bed. About her lies the explanation which you demand.

'One night, soon after my return, I lay sleeping beside my wife and, contrary to my usual custom, woke because of the heat. Yet I noticed that, in spite of the stifling weather, Fircone's feet and hands were colder than snow. In a panic lest she were seriously ill, I roused her gently, saying: "My charming, your body is frozen! Are you sure that you do not suffer?" "It is nothing," she answered indifferently, "I went out to satisfy a need just now, and my consequent ablution has left me cold." On that occasion I thought that she was speaking the truth, and lay down again.

'A few nights afterwards, the same thing happened and Fircone gave the same explanation. But this time I was not satisfied, and felt vague suspicions penetrate my soul. But though, thereafter, I was troubled, I took care to close the coffer of my heart upon my doubts and place the lock of silence upon the door of speech.'

At this point Shahrazād saw the approach of morning and discreetly fell silent.

But when the nine-hundred-and-nineteenth night had come

SHE SAID:

'As a cure for my foreboding, I went one morning to look at the handsome horses in my stable and, to my consternation, saw that my own private chargers, erewhile swifter than the wind, had become thin and worn, with bones piercing their hides, and their backs galled in many places. I called the grooms into my presence, and said: "O sons of dogs, what is the meaning of this?" They threw themselves on their faces before my wrath, and one of them a little lifted his trembling head to say: "O our master, if you will spare my life, I can tell you something in secret." I threw him the kerchief of security, bidding him at the same time hide nothing if he wished to escape the impaling stake. Then he said: "Every night without fail the Queen our mistress comes to the stable, dressed in royal garments, with jewels and tires upon her, like Bilkīs who loved Sulaimān. She chooses one of our master's own coursers, and rides him away. When she returns before dawn, the horse is good for nothing and can only fall upon his straw. We have not dared to tell our King of this!"

'My heart was troubled at this news; suddenly all my floating suspicions had taken firm root. The day passed, and not for one hour did I find the calm necessary to sit in judgment upon the affairs of my kingdom. My legs and arms stretched with impatience towards the night, until at last it came. I went to my wife at my usual hour and found her already undressed and yawning. "See how heavy are my eyes with sleep," she said. "I wish nothing but rest to-night. Ah let us sleep!" I pretended to be even more weary than she and, fighting down the trouble of my mind, lay out beside her and snored like men in a tavern, to make her think I slept.

'The ill-omened girl rose up as quietly as a kitten, and spilled the contents of a cup between my open lips. It was with difficulty that I did not betray myself. I turned a little to the wall, as if still in my sleep, and spat the liquid banj noiselessly into the pillow. But Fircone was so certain of the drug's effect that she came and went openly in the room; she washed and cared for herself, she was prodigal of kohl upon her eyes, nard in her hair, Indian sumar upon her brows, Indian misī for her teeth, jewels and volatile essence of roses over all her body. When she had gone forth, drunken with the wine of some expectation, I rose and, throwing a hooded cloak about my shoulders, followed her softly upon my naked feet. I saw her go to the stable and ride off upon a horse as handsome and light as the courser of Shīrīn. Fearing that the noise of pursuing hoofs would give her warning, I was constrained to gird up my garment in my belt, in the manner of grooms and messengers, and run with all the speed of my body after the fugitive. When I tripped and fell, I fearlessly rose again, and, when the pebbles of the road cut my feet, I took no heed.

'Now I must tell you that the greyhound, which you have already seen, followed me unbidden and ran faithfully beside me without once giving tongue.

'After many hours of this cruel travel, my wife came to a naked plain, holding only a low mud-walled house such as negroes use. She dismounted and entered; but when I would have followed her, the door was shut, and I had to content myself with looking through a window. Inside were seven great black men, looking like buffaloes. They greeted my Queen with terrible oaths and, throwing her upon the ground, beat her so soundly that I thought her tender bones would have broken. But, though she bears the marks of those blows upon her back and belly to this day, she seemed not to care for them, and said presently to the negroes: "O my dears, I swear, by the ardour of my love for you, that I am only late to-night because my King, that scab, that evil arse, stayed awake longer than usual. Do you think, otherwise, I would have wasted a minute before running to the wine of our coming together?"

'I thought that I was a prey to some horrible dream; I heard myself saying: "By Allāh, I have never beaten her even with a rose!" Meanwhile the black men stripped my wife naked, tearing her royal clothes and snatching away her jewels. Then they fell upon her as one man and defiled her in all directions, while she answered their violence with panting, ecstatic eyes, and sobs of deep content.

'Not being able to control myself any longer, I burst through the window into that room and snatched up one of the vile dogs' own bludgeons. I threw myself upon the swarm of lechers, while they still thought that I was some avenging Jinnī, and sent five of them straight to a deep hell even upon the body of my wife. The two others pulled themselves loose and would have fled, but I was able to reach one and stretch him unconscious at my feet. When, however, I leaned over him to bind his wrists and feet because he was not dead, my wife pushed me so violently from behind that I fell to the floor. The negro took advantage of this intervention to rise and perch upon my chest. He had already lifted his cudgel to make an end of me, when my faithful greyhound seized him by the throat and rolled him over and over upon the dry mud. I fell upon him and bound his arms and legs; then, and still in raging silence, I fastened Fircone in the same way.

'Leaving the bodies in the house, I dragged the negro outside and lashed him to the tail of my horse; then I mounted and, slinging my Queen in front of me like a bundle, rode off with the faithful dog running at my stirrup.

'When I reached my palace, I cut off the negro's head with my own hand and fed his body, which was already a quivering rag because of his journey, to the good greyhound. I had the head salted, and it is my wife's punishment every day to look at it and to eat, if she must eat, the rest of the dog's food.

'The seventh negro, who had succeeded in escaping, ceased not his flight until he came to the lands of Sīn and Masīn, to the court of Kāmūs ibn Tammūz, and, by a series of typical machinations, found asylum beneath the Princess Muhrah's ivory bed. He is now her intimate counsellor, and no one knows of his presence in the palace.

'Such, O youth, is the whole story of Fircone, and of the presence of a black man beneath that young assassin's ivory bed.'

At this point Shahrazād saw the approach of morning and discreetly fell silent.

But when the nine-hundred-and-twentieth night had come

SHE SAID:

Thus spake King Cypress, master of the city of Wakak, to young
Prince Diamond. Then he added: 'And now that you have heard
that which no other living person knows beside myself, stretch forth
your head, for it is no longer yours, and wash your hands of life.'

But Diamond answered: 'O King of time, I know that my head
is between your hands, and I am ready to lose it without too great
regret. But at present the most important point of your story seems
to have been left out, and I do not know why the seventh negro hid
himself under Princess Muhrah's bed when he had all the world from
which to choose, and especially I do not know why the princess lets
him stay there. Explain these mysteries and then I shall be willing to
make my ablution and to die.'

King Cypress was prodigiously astonished by this request, for he
had not expected such a question and had never had the curiosity
to go into these details. Rather than appear ignorant upon so vital a
matter, he said: 'O traveller, those things which you wish to know
are a state secret and their revelation would be fatal to myself and my
kingdom. Rather than answer you, I prefer to grant you your life
and pardon your indiscretion. Now be gone from my palace before I
change my mind!'

Prince Diamond, who had never thought to get off so easily,
kissed the earth between the King's hands and left the palace, hug-
ging the answer to his riddle and giving thanks to Allāh for his
safety. He took leave of his friend Farah, who wept to let him go,
and, mounting upon the terrace of the fair boy's house, burnt one of
the Simurg's hairs. Immediately a tempest blew and the Father of
Flight appeared before him. When he had expressed the desire, his
good friend took him up and, after carrying him safely across the
seven oceans, cordially received him in his own palace.

He made him rest for a few days and then transported him to the
dwelling of the delicious Azīzah, among the rose trees rhyming with
their roses. He found her weeping for his absence and sighing for his
return, her cheeks changed to pomegranate flowers. When they
entered, she rose trembling, a calling hind; and the Flying Simurg
had the thought to leave the hall. When he returned in an hour's
time, he found them still laced, splendour upon splendour.

'O our benefactor, O father and crown of giants,' said Prince

Diamond, 'I wish you to carry us to your charming niece, Jamilah, for she waits me on the red coals of desire.' The excellent Simurg took them both up and, in the twinkling of an eye, set them down where they could find the gentle Jamilah, lost in sadness, having no news of her body, and still saying over these lines:

> Far from the eyes which the narcissus loves,
> Cast not my heart;
> Mock not the crying of the drunkards,
> Lead them back to the tavern.

> The armies of his boy's beard
> Compass my heart,
> And, as a wounded rose,
> The rent in my robe shall not be sewn.

> O brown tyrannous beauty,
> My heart lies at your feet of jasmine,
> My heart of a little girl at your thief's feet.

Diamond had not forgotten that he owed to this child deliverance from her sister Latifah and the magic arms which had served him so well. After the first rapture of greeting, he prayed Azizah to leave him alone with his preserver for an hour, and Azizah, considering that the request was just, went out with the Simurg. When they returned in an hour, Jamilah still lay in her lover's arms.

Then Diamond, who loved method in all things, turned to his two wives and the Simurg, saying: 'I think that the time has come to cry quits with Latifah.' 'It is permitted!' they answered with one voice. The Simurg hastened through the air and speedily returned, bearing his iniquitous niece, with her arms tied behind her back. The four sat round her in a circle to judge her, and the giant gave his opinion first. 'The human race should certainly be rid of this foul creature,' he said. 'I suggest that we hang her upside down, impale her, and finally feed her to the vultures.' But Queen Azizah, when Diamond asked her, said: 'I think that it would be best to forget the harm which she did to our husband and, in the joy of our marriages, pardon her.' Jamilah also counselled that her sister should be forgiven, on condition that she restored to their human shapes all the youths whom she had changed into deer. So Diamond threw her the kerchief of his safety, saying: 'I pardon her, and must now request to be left alone with her for an hour.' The other three withdrew and, when they returned, found Latīfah both pardoned and content in Diamond's arms.

When the sorceress had given back humanity to the princes and other noble young men whom she had changed into deer, and had dismissed them with suitable food and raiment, the Simurg took Diamond and his three wives on his back and brought them to the city of Kāmūs ibn Tammūz, father of Princess Muhrah. He pitched tents for them outside the city and left them there to rest, while he himself visited the harīm of the palace, at Diamond's suggestion, and sought out Coral-Branch. As soon as she heard of the return of the youth for whom she had sorrowfully waited, she allowed the Simurg to carry her to the prince's tent and, leading forth the three other brides, to leave her alone with him. After the first ardours of greeting, Diamond proved to Coral-Branch that he had not forgotten, and spoke to her in so fitting a language that she shone beautiful indeed in her contentment, and quite won the hearts of the three other girls when they returned.

As soon as Diamond had regulated the private affairs of his four wives, he set himself to the principal object of his quest. Leaving the tents, he made his way alone to the square before the palace, above which the crowned and the uncrowned heads moved in the wind, and beat loudly upon the jewelled drum, to signify that he was ready to answer Princess Muhrah's question.

At this point Shahrazād saw the approach of morning and discreetly fell silent.

But when the nine-hundred-and-twenty-first night had come

SHE SAID:

Guards came and led him into the presence of King Kāmūs, who at once recognised the charming youth to whom he had counselled a reflection of three days. 'Allāh protect you, my son!' he said. 'Do you still persist in your wish to sound the fantastic mysteries of a girl's brain?' 'Knowledge and divination come to us from Allāh,' answered Diamond. 'Not ours the pride! Your daughter has a secret in the coffer of her heart, but the key is with me alone.' 'Alas for your youth!' cried the King. 'The day has come for you to wash your hands of life.'

As he had no hope of turning the young prince from his deadly purpose, he ordered his slaves to announce to Princess Muhrah that a royal stranger was ready to unravel the weavings of her fantasy.

Soon she came into the hall, Muhrah the happy, the fatality of young lives; the eye could no more help regarding her than a man with the dropsy may refrain from drinking of the Euphrates; a thousand souls had died for her, like butterflies in the fire; and her coming was heralded by the odour of her curls. At the first glance she recognised the glorious saint of her garden, whose coming had so disturbed her heart; her astonishment gave place to rage when she remembered how he had secretly stolen away. 'This time he shall not escape me,' she muttered, as she sat down on the bed of the throne and regarded Prince Diamond with stormy eyes. 'All know the question!' she cried. 'What is the relation between Fircone and Cypress?' 'All know the answer!' retorted Diamond. 'The relation is bad; for Fircone, the wife of Cypress, King of the city of Wakak, is even now punished for a great wrong, and there are negroes in the matter.'

Princess Muhrah felt afraid, and her cheeks turned yellow; yet she fought down her disquiet, and said: 'There is nothing definite in your words. When you have explained, I shall know that you are lying.'

Seeing that the princess would not take his hint, Diamond said plainly: 'If you wish me to enter into details and lift the curtain from a thing rightly hidden, tell me first how you have learnt such things, for a young virgin should know nothing of them. It seems evident that you have someone here whose coming was a calamity to all those other princes.' Without giving her time to reply, he turned to the King, and continued: 'O King of time, it is not right that you should be kept any longer in ignorance of the mystery which surrounds your honourable daughter. I conjure you to press my question for me.' So the King signed with his eyes that the beautiful child should speak, but she would not.

Then Prince Diamond took King Kāmūs by the hand and silently led him to Muhrah's chamber. With a quick movement he stooped and pulled away the ivory bed. The flask of the princess's secret was shattered upon the stone of discovery, and the crisped head of the negro showed to the eyes of all. Kāmūs and those who were with him lowered their heads for shame and felt the sweat start out on their bodies. The old King would probe no further, lest the stain upon his honour should grow with explanation. Therefore he handed Muhrah to the prince to dispose of as he thought fit, saying: 'I only require that you take her away as quickly as possible, my son, so that my ears may not hear her speak, and my eyes not suffer the torment of her presence.' But the negro was impaled.

Prince Diamond had the confused princess bound hand and foot, and taken out to his tent. Then he begged the Simurg to carry them all as quickly as possible to the city of Shams-Shāh. The excellent giant obeyed in the twinkling of an eye and, when he had set down his young friend and the five women outside the gate, swelled up and floated on his way without waiting for thanks. So much for him.

When King Shams-Shāh learned of the approach of his dear son, the night of grief turned for him to the morning of joy, and the fountains of his eyes were stanched. While the good news ran about the city and happiness flamed up in all the houses, he went forth to meet the prince and took him to his breast, kissing him upon the mouth and eyes, and weeping and giving little cries of satisfaction. With his joined hands, Diamond strove to check his father's sighs and tears; when the first emotion of the two men was a little calmed, and the old King could speak, he said to his son: 'O eye and lamp of your father's house, tell me quickly each detail of your journey, that the recital of every day may bring a balm to the grief which I felt upon that day.'

At this point Shahrazād saw the approach of morning and discreetly fell silent.

But when the nine-hundred-and-twenty-second night had come

SHE SAID:

Prince Diamond told the old King the story of his adventures, but nothing would be gained by repeating it in this place. Then he presented his four wives, one by one, and finally pointed to the bound princess, saying: 'It is for you, O my father, to fix the fate of this woman.'

The wise Shams-Shāh divined that his son had a hidden love for the girl, since he had undertaken toil and danger to win her, though she had destroyed countless youths before him. Therefore, considering he would grieve the prince if his judgment were too harsh, he said: 'He who, by great trouble and difficulty, has become possessed of an inestimable pearl, should be in no hurry to cast it aside. A blind fantasy has led this princess into reprehensible actions, but it will be charitable to suppose that Allāh willed it so. Many young men have died for her, but they could not have died had not such a fate been written in their Destinies. Remember too, my son, that this girl treated you with kindness and reverence when you entered her garden. Finally, and most important, it is known that no hand of desire, either black or of any other colour, has touched the youthful fruit of her being; no man has savoured the apple of her chin or the pomegranate of her lips.'

As his four joyful and exquisite wives lent weight to his father's counsel, Prince Diamond chose an auspicious day and hour, and joined the bright sun of his body to this wild moon. His five wives bore him marvellous children who were as favoured as their father, Diamond the Splendid, and their grandfather, Shams-Shāh the Magnificent; like these they held fortune and happiness as slaves.

Such is the extraordinary tale of Prince Diamond. Glory and praise to those who have preserved the stories of old to be an edification to such modern ears as have the wit to seek for wisdom!

King Shahryār, who had listened with very great attention, for the first time thanked Shahrazād, saying: 'Praise, praise, O honey mouth! You have made me forget my bitter preoccupation.' But soon his face grew dark again, and Shahrazād hastened to answer: 'O King of time, this tale is nothing to certain things which I could tell you of the Master of Shifts and Laughter.' 'What master of what shifts, O Shahrazād?' cried King Shahryār, and Shahrazād said:

Some Jests and Suggestions of the Master of Shifts and Laughter

IT is related, O auspicious King, in the old annals of the wise, and it is also handed down to us by tradition, that there was once in the city of Cairo, that home of witty chatter, a silly-looking fellow who hid, beneath an extravagant buffoonery, an endless fund of intelligence and true learning. He was the most amusing, the best instructed, and the most ironical man of his time. His name was Goha and his trade was just nothing at all, though he would on occasion take the place of a teacher in the mosques.

One day his friends said to him: 'O Goha, are you not ashamed to pass your life in idleness, and work your ten fingers only in raising food to your mouth? Do you not think it high time that you left this vagabonding existence and conformed to the customs of other men?' Goha answered nothing. But one day, when he had caught a large and handsome stork, with magnificent wings to fly beyond the sunset, a beak which was the terror of the birds, and legs like lily stems, he took it up upon the terrace of his house and, in the presence of those who had reproached him, cut off its wings and beak and legs with a sharp knife. Then he kicked it into space, bidding it fly. 'Allāh curse you!' cried his scandalised friends. 'What is the meaning of this cruel folly?' 'The stork wearied me,' answered Goha. 'He weighed upon my sight, because he was different. Now I have made him conform to the customs of other men.'

On another occasion Goha said to a certain company: 'O Mussulmāns, do you know why Allāh gave no wings to the camel and the elephant?' 'We do not, O Goha,' answered his hearers, 'but you, from whom no secrets of science are hidden, can surely tell us.' 'If the camel and the elephant had wings,' explained Goha, 'they would perch on the flowers in your garden and, being very heavy, crush them to the earth.'

Once a friend knocked at Goha's door, saying: 'O Goha, for friendship's sake lend me your ass, for I have to go upon a sudden journey.' 'I would willingly have done so, but alas, I have sold him,' answered Goha, who had no great confidence in the man's integrity. At that moment the ass set up an interminable braying from the stable, and the friend cried: 'But your ass is here!' In a voice of deep offence, Goha replied: 'If you would take the word of an ass before that of a wise man, you are a fool and I do not wish to see you again.'

One evening Goha went by invitation to eat at a neighbour's house. A fowl was set before them, but after a few attempts at mastication Goha was obliged to leave his portion, for the bird was one of the oldest of its kind and its flesh was leather. He supped a little of the broth in which it had been cooked and then, arranging the fowl with its head towards Mecca, began to say his prayer above it. 'O blasphemy!' cried his host. 'To say your prayer over a fowl!' But Goha answered: 'O uncle, you are mistaken. Though this thing has the appearance of a fowl, it is, in reality, a very old and saintly woman, one who went down into the fire and the fire respected her.'

Again Goha made one with a caravan which was travelling on short rations. His belly was ever as large and desirous as that of a camel, but, when they all sat down to eat at the first stopping place, he hung back with great discretion and reserve. Knowing his usual appetite, his wondering companions pressed him to take the roll and hard boiled egg which was his share, but he replied: 'No, no, in Allāh's name, eat and be content! But, if you really insist upon my picking something, let each give me half his roll and half his egg, for my stomach could never compass the whole of either.'

Goha went one day to the butcher, and said: 'There is to be a festival in our house, so give me some of the best end of fat mutton.' The butcher gave him a fillet of considerable weight, which he carried to his wife with a request that she should make kabābs, seasoned to his taste with onions. Then he went out for a walk in the market.

As soon as his back was turned, his wife hastened to cook the mutton and to eat every scrap of it with the help of her brother. When Gola returned, his stomach watered at the good smell of cooking, but his wife only set before him some mouldy bread and a morsel of Greek cheese. When he asked after the kabābs, she said: 'The mercy of Allāh be upon you and upon the kabābs! The cat ate them all while I was in the privy.' Goha rose without a word and, seizing the cat, weighed it in the kitchen scales. Finding that it was not near as heavy as the meat which he had brought, he turned to his wife, crying: 'Foul daughter of a thousand dogs, if this is the weight of the meat, where is the cat? If this is the weight of the cat, where is the meat?'

On one occasion, when his wife needed to do some cooking, she handed their little three months' son to Goha, saying: 'O father of Abdallāh, nurse the child, and, when I have finished with the cook pots, I will take him again.' Goha, though he hated this kind of business, lifted the little boy; but, even at that moment, the child pissed all over his father's new kaftān. At once Goha set him on the ground and, in his fury, began to piss all over him. 'What are you doing on the child, O pitch-face?' screamed his wife. 'Are you blind?' he answered. 'Do you not see that he is our own dear little son and that I am pissing on him? As Allāh lives, if he had been anyone else's son, I might have turned my back.'

One evening Goha's friends said to him: 'O Goha, as you know all about astronomy, will you tell us what happens to the moon when it has passed its last quarter?' 'Were you taught nothing at school?' cried Goha. 'When the moon has passed its last quarter, Allāh breaks it up to make stars.'

Goha called one day on a neighbour and begged him for the loan of a stewpot in which to cook a sheep's head.

At this point Shahrazād saw the approach of morning and discreetly fell silent.

But when the nine-hundred-and-twenty-third night had come

SHE SAID:

The neighbour lent the stewpot and Goha returned it on the following morning with a second and smaller stewpot inside. When the owner expressed astonishment, Goha told him that his stewpot must have borne a child during the night. So the neighbour thanked him, and arranged the stewpot and her daughter on the same shelf.

Later in the day Goha returned and asked if he might borrow the two stewpots. 'With all my heart,' answered the other, as he handed the vessel to Goha with the little one.

When many days passed without a return of the stewpots, the neighbour went to ask for them, saying: 'I have no lack of confidence in you, O Goha, but to-day I need the vessel for myself.' 'What vessel, dear neighbour?' asked Goha. 'The stewpot which I lent you and which had a child,' replied the other. Then cried Goha: 'Allāh have her in His compassion! She is dead!' And, when the neighbour asked him how, in Allāh's name, a stewpot could die, Goha explained: 'All which is born and all which bears must die. We come from Allāh and to Him we return at the last!'

A fallāh gave Goha a fat fowl, and Goha asked the man to share it with him. They ate the bird and were content; but soon another peasant knocked at the door and demanded entertainment. 'You are welcome, but who are you?' was Goha's greeting, and the man replied: 'I am the neighbour of him who gave you the fowl.' 'Be it upon my head and before my eyes!' cried Goha, and so cordially fed the stranger that he departed in great good humour. A few days afterwards another peasant knocked at the door and, when Goha asked who was there, explained that he was the friend of the friend of the giver of the fowl. 'It is permitted,' said Goha as he led the man in and set him down before the cloth. He retired to the kitchen and returned with a bowl containing warm water, on whose surface floated a few little drops of grease. Seeing that there was no more to follow, the peasant asked: 'What is this, my host?' and Goha answered:

'This? The sister of the sister of the water in which the fowl was boiled.'

Certain of Goha's friends wished to play a trick on him, so they secretly provided themselves with eggs and invited him to go to the hammām with them. When they were all undressed and had entered the sweat hall, their spokesman cried: 'Now let each of us lay an egg, and he who cannot lay shall pay for the baths of all the rest.' At once the whole troop, except Goha, squatted down, cackling as well as they could, and, after a certain time, each produced an egg from underneath him. Immediately Goha brandished the child of his father on high and, crowing like a cock, threw himself upon his friends and began to assault them. 'What are you doing, vile libertine?' they cried, and Goha answered: 'As I seem to be the only cock among so many hens, surely I must do my kind!'

It is related that Goha used to stand every morning at the door of his house and make this prayer to Allāh: 'O Lord, send me a hundred dīnārs, for I need exactly a hundred. If the gift passes or falls short even by one dīnār, I cannot accept it.'

A certain neighbour, a Jew who had become evilly rich,—may he roast in the fires of the fifth Hell!—heard this loud daily prayer and thought to himself: 'By the life of Abraham and Jacob, I will try this fellow!' He made up a purse of ninety-nine gold dīnārs and threw it from the window at the feet of Goha as he prayed. Goha picked up the purse and, after counting its contents, lifted his hands on high, crying: 'O generous Giver, I render praise and thanks and glory! But the sum is not complete and I cannot accept it. I will give it to my poor neighbour the Jew, for he is a model of honesty and has many children.' So saying, he cast the purse through the Jew's door and went on his way.

'By the luminous horns of Moses,' cried the astonished Jew, 'this is a good man! But I have not tested him on the second point of his prayer.' Next morning he put a hundred and one dīnārs into a purse and threw them at Goha's feet as he prayed. Feigning to believe that this gift also came from Allāh, Goha counted the money and then cried, with his eyes lifted to heaven: 'O Father of a limitless generosity, I accept Your Gift.'

He slipped the purse into his breast and walked away, but the Jew, in a white heat of passion, soon overtook him. 'Give me the purse, give me the purse!' he cried, but Goha answered: 'Do you think that I should give you every purse which Allāh sends me? Your share this morning is one dīnār, dog of a Jew.' He gave the unbeliever one of the new coins and turned on his heel, exclaiming: 'Now I know what they mean when they speak of the uncounted blessings of Allāh.'

One day Goha listened to a preacher in the mosque and the preacher said, in explanation of a point of canon law: 'O Believers, if a husband does his duty at nightfall, it is equal to the sacrifice of a sheep. Lawful copulation during the day is equal in Allāh's sight to the freeing of a slave. And if the thing be done in the middle of the night the grace obtained is equal to the sacrifice of a camel.'

When he returned home, Goha reported this saying to his wife and then lay down by her side to sleep. But the woman, experiencing a violent desire, nudged him, saying: 'Rise up now, O man, and sacrifice a sheep!' 'Very well,' answered Goha, and he rose up, did the thing, and lay down again. Towards the middle of the night that dog's daughter again felt her inside attuned to coupling: so she roused Goha, and whispered to him: 'Let us sacrifice a camel.'

At this point Shahrazād saw the approach of morning and discreetly fell silent.

But when the nine-hundred-and-twenty-fourth night had come

SHE SAID:

Goha rose yawning and, with half-shut eyes, did what was required of him; then he fell into a deep sleep. But as soon as the sun rose his wife plucked him by the arm, saying: 'See, see, it is day! Let us free a slave!' 'Certainly,' answered Goha as he shut his eyes again, 'but let charity begin at home.'

Another day, at another mosque, Goha heard the Imām say: 'O Believers, O you who forsake your wives and run after the buttocks of boys, let it be known to you that each time one of the Faithful accomplishes the act of husbandry with his wife Allāh builds for him a shelter in Paradise.' Goha returned home and told his wife what had been said, and, though her husband thought no more of the matter, the woman remembered. When the children had been put to bed she said eagerly: 'Let us so work that a shelter may be prepared for our children in Paradise.' 'It is permitted,' answered Goha and he dug his trowel into the mortar box. Then he went to sleep.

An hour afterwards his wife woke him, saying: 'I forgot that one of our daughters is to be married and must therefore live alone. Let us prepare for her a shelter in Paradise.' 'If you insist on sacrificing the son for the daughter . . .' answered Goha, and he slipped the child into the cradle which gaped for it. Then he lay down again, breathing rather fast, and fell into deep slumber. In the middle of the night his wife pulled him by the foot, demanding that a shelter should be prepared for her mother in Paradise; but Goha cried: 'My good woman, we will none of us ever get to Paradise, if we keep the Almighty so busy building shelters.'

A certain woman who lived near Goha's house was praying one day when she accidentally let a fart. She was so new to this exercise that she could not be sure whether she had actually done the thing or whether she had scraped her foot along the tiles, or made some fervent noise in praying; so she went to consult Goha, who was famous for his knowledge of the law. His answer, when she had explained her difficulty, was to let a rather large fart and ask: 'Was it like that, good aunt?' 'It was louder than that,' insisted the pious old woman. Goha let a much louder fart, and asked: 'Was it like that?' 'It was louder,' she replied. Then cried Goha: 'As Allāh lives, the law takes cognisance of breaking wind but not of breaking tempests. Go in peace, O Mother of Airs, for if I try to rival you I may make some cakes.'

One day the conquering awe-inspiring Tīmūr lang, the lame man of iron, passed near the city where Goha lived, and the frightened inhabitants, after a thousand confabulations concerning the safety of the city, agreed to beg Goha to deliver them. He sent at once for all the muslin in all the shops of that place and rolled a turban as great as a chariot wheel about his head. Then he mounted his ass and went forth to meet the terrible invader. 'What is this turban?' asked the Tatar chief, and Goha replied: 'Turban, O sovereign of the world? This is my nightcap. I beg a humble pardon for coming out to meet you in my nightcap, but the cart and the oxen which carry my turban were not ready.' Judging the people by their turbans, Tīmūr lang left that city in peace, but for friendship's sake he kept Goha by him, and asked him who he was. 'I am the earth god,' answered Goha. So the Tīmūr, who like all men of his race was surrounded by many little boys with small and slanting eyes, showed them to Goha, saying: 'Well, earth god, what do you think of these delightful children? Have you ever seen their equal in beauty?' 'O sovereign of the world, I find their eyes too small and their faces rather plain,' replied Goha. 'I say it, not to displease you, but because you asked.' 'The matter is of little importance,' laughed Tīmūr, 'for, if you are the earth god, you can enlarge their eyes to please me.' Then said Goha: 'My lord, the eyes in the head belong to Allāh and only He can change them; being the earth god, I can do nothing but enlarge the eye which each has below his waist.' Tīmūr lang rejoiced at this reply and retained Goha in his service, to be his jester.

One day Tīmūr, who not only limped upon an iron foot, but was also one-eyed and extremely ugly, was talking with Goha and having his head shaved by the royal barber at the same time. When the man handed him a mirror, Tīmūr looked in it and wept. Goha also burst into tears. When the two had groaned and sobbed for three hours, Tīmūr made an end, but Goha went on with his lamentation. 'What is the matter?' said the astonished chief. 'I wept because I saw my surprising ugliness in the glass; but I have stopped now, while you, who had no cause for tears, are still continuing.' 'If I may say so with all respect, O sovereign of the world,' answered Goha, 'if you weep for three hours after one glance at your ugliness in the mirror, is it surprising that your slave, who has to look upon the same thing all day, should weep for even longer?' Instead of flying into a rage, Tīmūr laughed so heartily that he fell over on his backside.

When they sat at meat on another occasion, Tīmūr gurked near Goha's face, and the jester cried: 'My lord, you are not very polite.' 'We have no feeling against it in our country,' answered the astonished Tīmūr. Goha said nothing, but, when the meal was finished, let a sounding fart. Tīmūr was scandalised, and cried: 'Are you not ashamed, O son of a dog?' Then said Goha: 'Pardon, dear master, but I thought you did not understand our language.'

One day Goha consented to take the place of the Imām in the mosque of a neighbouring village. When he had finished preaching, he scratched his head and remarked to his congregation: 'O Mussulmāns, it is astonishing that the climate of your village and mine should be identical.' 'How so?' they asked, and he replied: 'I have been feeling my zabb, and I find it all slack and hanging on my testicles, just as it does at home. The name of Allāh be upon you all!'

Preaching at another mosque, Goha raised his hand to the sky and thus concluded: 'We thank You and glorify You, O living and all powerful God, that You did not see fit to situate our arses in our hands!' 'Surely this is strange praise!' ventured some of the congregation, but Goha answered: 'And yet praiseworthy, for if He had placed our arses in our hands, think how dirty our noses would have been.'

As he was preaching on another occasion, Goha said: 'O Mussulmāns, let us give thanks to Allāh that he did not put the front behind!' When they asked him to explain, he answered: 'If He had placed our sticks behind, think how easily we might have fallen into the sin of Lot!'

At this point Shahrazād saw the approach of morning and discreetly fell silent.

But when the nine-hundred-and-twenty-fifth night had come

SHE SAID:

One day, when Goha's wife was alone and naked in her room, she began to pat her affair with great love, and apostrophise it, saying: 'Dear treasure, why are there not two or three or four of you, O cause of all my joys?' Goha, who entered at this moment and heard these words, brought out his inheritance and, with tears in his eyes, began to curse it, saying: 'O dog, O pimp, O cause of all my woes, why are there any of you?'

Goha once went into his neighbour's vineyard and began to eat grapes like a fox, pulling down the clusters, crushing them in his mouth, and then letting the bare stems spring upwards. While he was thus engaged, the owner of the vineyard ran up, brandishing a stick, and cried: 'What are you doing here, O thief?' 'I had a colic,' answered Goha, 'and came here to relieve my belly.' 'If that is so,' retorted the other, 'where is what you have done?' Goha was at first nonplussed, but, when his roving eye caught sight of some ass's dung, he pointed to it, and cried: 'There!' 'You lie!' exclaimed the man. 'How long have you been an ass?' Goha pulled out his enormous zabb, and answered: 'Ever since Allāh gave me this calamitous tool!'

Goha was walking beside the river one day when a crowd of washerwomen swarmed about him like bees, and one of them, lifting her garment, showed her prime cut. Goha turned away his head, saying: 'O Protector of modesty, I take refuge in Your grace!' 'What is wrong with you, O sounding brass?' asked the offended washerwoman. 'Do you not know the name of this fortunate thing?' 'I know the name well,' he answered. 'It is called the Cistern of Calamity.' 'Not at all, not at all,' they cried. 'It is the Poor Man's

Paradise.' Goha walked a little apart and, after enveloping the child of his being in the stuff of his turban as if in a winding-sheet, returned to the washerwomen, who at once asked him what the thing might be. 'This is a poor man who died,' answered Goha. 'He wishes to enter the Poor Man's Paradise.' As they laughed loudly at this reply, they noticed a thing, which was no other than Goha's enormous purse, hanging outside the winding sheet. 'What are these two ostrich eggs depending by the body?' they cried. 'Those,' said Goha, 'are the man's two sons, who have come to visit his tomb.'

One day, when Goha was on a visit to his sister-in-law, the woman asked him to mind her baby while she went to the hammām. As soon as she had gone, the little one began to mule and pule with all his strength. So Goha pulled out his Turkish Delight and let the child suck it until he went to sleep. When the mother returned and found her bantling in a calm slumber, she thanked Goha for his care, but he replied: 'That is nothing at all, nothing at all. If you had but seen my sleeping draught you would have fallen head over heels at once.'

One morning, while Goha was covering his ass at the door of a lonely mosque, a worshipper came forth and, seeing his action, spat disgustedly upon the ground. Goha looked at him out of the corner of his eye, and cried: 'If I had not important business in hand, I would teach you to stop your dirty tricks!'

On another occasion, as Goha lay in the road in the heat of the sun holding his gallant stick naked in his hand, a passenger cried to him: 'What are you doing, O shameful?' 'I see nothing shameful,' answered Goha, 'in a father taking his son out for a little fresh air.'

During a legal consultation, Goha was asked what the congregation should do if an Imām let a fart in the mosque. 'Give him the usual responses,' answered Goha.

One day, as Goha and his wife walked along the banks of the rising river, the woman slipped and fell in. As she was being borne down by the current, Goha bravely threw himself into the river and began to swim with all his might upstream. People on the bank called to him to know what he was looking for, and he answered: 'By Allāh, I am looking for my wife. She has fallen in.' 'But the current is bearing her fast downstream, O Goha,' they cried. 'That shows all you know about my wife,' he spluttered. 'A contrary creature like that will be at the source by this time.'

During the time when Goha acted as kādī, a man was brought

before him who had been caught lining a cat in the open street. 'How did you do it?' asked Goha. 'Perhaps if you tell the whole truth, I will acquit you.' 'O our master the kādī,' answered the man, 'I put you know what to the door of grace; then, gripping the cat's paws in my hands and holding his head between my knees, I forced the door. Things went so well the first time that I was sinful enough to begin again. I confess my fault, O kādī.' 'Take this lying pimp and give him a good beating,' thundered Goha. 'I have tried thirty times and never succeeded once.'

During a visit which Goha paid to the kādī of a certain city, two litigants presented themselves before his host, saying: 'O our lord the kādī, we are neighbours and our houses actually touch. Last night a dog came and dropped a turd exactly half way between our two doors. We wish to know whose business it is to clean it up.' The kādī turned to Goha and said ironically: 'I leave you to give judgment in this suit; it seems worthy of you.' 'Is the turd not at all nearer to your door, O man?' asked Goha of the first. 'It is exactly between the two,' answered the man. 'Are you sure the turd is not a little nearer your door?' asked Goha of the second. 'I cannot lie, it stays in the road exactly half way between our doors,' answered the man. 'I have heard and now I give judgment!' proclaimed Goha. 'The onus ot cleaning away does not lie with either of you but with him whose duty is order in the public streets. Let the kādī see to it!'

Goha's son, a little lad of four years old, was once given a fine artichoke at a feast. 'What is that pretty thing?' asked the giver, and the child answered: 'A tiny calf which has not opened his eyes yet.' All laughed, but Goha said: 'As Allāh lives, I never taught him to say that!'

Once, when Goha felt like coupling and had uncovered his inheritance, a honey-bee came and perched on the tip of the thing.

At this point Shahrazād saw the approach of morning and discreetly fell silent.

But when the nine-hundred-and-twenty-sixth night had come

SHE SAID:

Goha swelled with pride, and exclaimed: 'As Allāh lives, you know what is good, O bee! You have found the best honey maker in all the garden.'

'These, O auspicious King,' continued Shahrazād, 'are only a few of the jests and suggestions of that master of shifts and laughter, the delightful, the unforgettable Goha. May Allāh have him in His mercy! May his memory live until the Day of Judgment!'

'Goha has made me forget my heaviest cares, O Shahrazād,' replied King Shahryār, and little Dunyazād cried: 'O my sister, surely your words are a sweet and savoury refreshment!' 'Yet what I have told you is not to be compared with The Tale of the Girl Heart's-Miracle, Lieutenant of the Birds,' said Shahrazād, and King Shahryār cried: 'As Allāh lives, I have known many girls, and seen even more; but I do not recall that name. Who was Heart's-Miracle, and how came she to be Lieutenant of the Birds?'
So Shahrazād said:

The Tale of the Girl Heart's-Miracle, Lieutenant of the Birds

IT is related, O auspicious King, that in Baghdād, the city of peace, the home of joy, pleasure's dwelling, and the garden of wit, the Khalīfah Hārūn al-Rashīd, Vicar of the Lord of the Three Worlds and Commander of the Faithful, had, as his cup-companion and perfect friend, a man whose fingers were wrought of harmony, whose hands were loved of lutes, whose voice was a lesson for the nightingale, the marvel of music, the king of singers, Ishāk al-Nadīm of Mosul. Hārūn had given him, in pure love, the fairest of his palaces, and Ishāk's duty there was to instruct the ablest of those girls sought in the markets of the world for his master's harīm in the arts of music and singing. When one of them excelled her companions in mastery of song and of the lute, Ishāk would take her to the Khalīfah, and she would sing and play before the throne. If she gave pleasure, she was raised straightway to the harīm; if her accomplishments were not sufficient, she returned to her place among the pupils in Ishāk's palace.

One day the Prince of Believers, feeling weary and oppressed, sent for his wazīr Jafar the Barmakid, Ishāk his cup-companion, Masrūr the sword-bearer of his vengeance, al-Fadl brother of Jafar, and Yūnus the scribe. They found him disguised as a plain citizen and were bidden to put on the same kind of clothes themselves. As soon as the whole band had the appearance of simple friends, they went forth secretly from the palace and, taking boat on the Tigris were rowed through the cool of the evening to Al-Tāf. There they disembarked and set off at hazard along the road of unexpected adventure.

As they walked, talking and laughing together, a venerable old man with a white beard bowed before Ishāk and kissed his hand. The singer at once recognised him as one of the chief furnishers of boys and girls to the palace, a sheikh with great aptitude for finding new pupils for the school of music.

Though he had no idea that he was in the presence of Hārūn, the old man excused himself for interrupting Ishāk's walk, and added: 'Dear Master, I have long been wishing to see you, and had almost made up my mind to seek you at the palace. But, now that Allah has set me upon your way, I beg to be allowed a moment's conversation. I have at my slave house a girl already quite proficient with the lute, who, I am certain, would in a short time be an honour to your school. She is as beautiful as she is talented, and I should be deeply obliged if you could spare a moment to see her and hear her voice. If she pleases you, I will send her to the palace at once; if not, I will sell her to some merchant.'

Ishāk consulted the Khalīfah with a quick glance and then replied: 'O uncle, precede us to your slave house and make ready the girl to appear before us, for I will follow you with my friends.'

The old man hurried off, and the Khalīfah and his companions proceeded more leisurely in the same direction.

This was no great adventure or out of the ordinary, but they accepted it as a good fisherman accepts the first fish which Allāh sends. Soon they reached the slave house and found it easily large enough to contain all the tribes of the desert. They crossed the threshold and entered a large hall supplied with benches for the convenience of purchasers. There they sat down and waited, while the old man went to fetch the girl.

Soon she entered with the grace of a balancing reed, and took her place on a throne of precious woods, covered with Ionian embroidery, which had been prepared for her in the middle of the hall. When she saluted the company it was as if the sun looked forth out of heaven, but her hands trembled as she raised a Damascus lute with strings of gold and silver. She took it to her breast, as a sister might caress her little brother, and, after preluding upon the docile cords, sang this song:

Sigh, O morning, I will send your sighs
As flower-scented salutes to the loved land,
To the far, shining band
With whom for a small change of love
I pawned my destinies.

My desire is stronger and climbs above
The difficult mountains, but, until I cross,
My feet are wounded on the diamond steep.
Also, my soul couched in its jewelled loss
Has taught my eyelids to forget their sleep.

As he heard, the Khalīfah could not help crying: 'Your voice and
your art are a glory of Allāh, O benediction! In very truth you have
excelled!' Then, remembering his disguise and fearing to be recognised, he fell silent, and Ishāk began in his turn to compliment the
girl. But no sooner had he opened his mouth than the harmonious
child ran from her seat to him and kissed his hands, saying: 'O
master, arms grow dull in your presence and tongues fall silent!
Eloquence, meeting you, is stricken dumb! Only you of all men,
master, can lift the veil of my need!' And as she spoke she burst into
tears.

At this point Shahrazād saw the approach of morning and
discreetly fell silent.

But when the nine-hundred-and-twenty-seventh night had come

SHE SAID:
Ishāk was both surprised and moved by her grief. 'Treasure
among women,' he said, 'why are you sad? And who are you, sweet
and unknown?' The girl lowered her eyes without replying and
Ishāk, understanding that she would not speak in the presence of
others, sought leave from the Khalīfah with a glance, and led the
slave into a curtained space apart.

When she saw that she was alone with Ishāk, the young singer
gracefully lifted her face veil and showed brows of starlight with
black curls on either temple, a straight nose which seemed to have
been carved by a master from transparent pearl, a mouth shaped
from the flesh of ripe pomegranates, a laughing chin, and darker eyes
under the darkest brows.

'Speak in all confidence, my child,' said Ishāk, and the girl, in a voice like the falling of fountain water, spoke: 'Long waiting and the torment of my soul have changed me, master; the tears have washed all the roses from my cheeks.' 'There are no roses in the moon,' objected Ishāk with a smile. 'But why should you belittle your great beauty?' 'How can one who has lived only for herself lay claim to beauty?' replied the girl. 'My lord, the days have passed into months here and, at each new auction, I have devised some way to escape being sold. I have waited your coming that I might enter your music school, for the fame of it has spread even to the far plains of my country.'

As she was speaking, the old man entered, and Ishāk turned to him, saying: 'What is her price? And, first of all, what is her name?' 'Her name is Heart's-Miracle, Tufhah al-kulūb,' answered the slave master. 'And her price is at least ten thousand dīnārs. I have had great argument about the sum with certain rich lovers who would have purchased her, but I must confess that it was not the price but the girl herself that prevented the sale on each occasion. Knowing that I would never sell her without her consent, she made such pointed objections to the appearance of each of my clients that, eventually, for fear of her tongue, no one would bid for her. Therefore, in honesty, I cannot ask you more than ten thousand dīnārs, although that sum will hardly pay my out-of-pocket expenses.' Ishāk smiled as he replied: 'O sheikh, add twice ten thousand dīnārs more, and we will feign that we have reached her value. Send her to my palace to-day and the money shall be yours.' He left the astonished old man and the delighted girl, and, returning to the impatient Khalīfah, told him all that had passed. Then the disguised band went forth from the slave house to seek for new adventures.

In the meanwhile, the old man led Heart's-Miracle to Ishāk's palace and, after receiving thirty thousand dīnārs, went his way. The little slaves crowded round Tufhah; they gave her a delicious bath in the hammām, dressed her, arranged her hair, and covered her with ornaments of taste and cost, such as collars, rings, bracelets, anklets: gold-embroidered veils and silver breastplates. When they had had their will of her, her face was tender with the light of a moon looking down upon a king's garden.

When Ishāk came in and saw the girl standing in this greater beauty, as a new bride, he congratulated himself and said within his heart: 'As Allāh lives, when she has had a few months in my school, and has improved a little in playing and singing, and has, through happiness, won back her roses, she will be the conquering star of Hārūn's harīm. I do not think that she is altogether mortal.'

He gave orders that the best which the palace had to offer in instruction and entertainment should be placed at her disposal, and for some weeks the path to art and beauty was made delicious for her.

One day, when her fellow girls were all dispersed about the garden and the palace was empty, Heart's-Miracle rose from the couch on which she was resting and wandered into the teaching hall. She sat down in her usual place and pressed her lute against her breast with the gesture of a swan folding its head below its wing. Her beauty had come back to her, her pale languor had gone. The narcissus, dun-cheeked for the death of Winter, had fled from the plot and the anemone had come back in a second Spring. She was a balm and an enchantment, a light song going up to the God Who made her.

She sang alone to the lute, and the hollow wood grew drunken until it trilled like a forest of birds. There was a miracle in each of her fingers.

If there had been any to hear her, they would have set down Ishāk as the pupil and Tufhah as his master. You must remember that, since the day her hands and voice had trembled in the slave house, she had not played or sung except to herself, for Ishāk's pupils at their lessons played and sang in chorus.

When, with the lute, she had called back all the voices of the birds which had housed in its native tree, she lifted her head and sang:

At this point Shahrazād saw the approach of morning and discreetly fell silent.

But when the nine-hundred-and-twenty-eighth night had come

SHE SAID:

> Laughing you said: 'Doctors are unavailing,
> My eyes' black flasks hold the sole cure of worth.'
> I have become a little weary of your railing,
> Are there not other targets over the earth?
>
> Yet when the soul leans to the one companion
> Not even Destiny can stem that yearning;
> Fair hand on the rack screw, cease not turning,
> For I shall die when the torturing is done.

In the meanwhile Ishāk, who had entered after a morning with the Khalīfah, heard her voice singing, miraculous and sweet like the breeze of early morning kissing the palm trees, lifting the heart's strength as almond oil fortifies the body of a wrestler.

He could not believe that this was mortal song; it was so like an escaped music from Eden that he uttered a cry of fear and admiration. Tufhah ran to him, with the lute still in her arms, and found him leaning against the wall of the vestibule with his hand to his heart, looking so pale and troubled that she cast aside the instrument, and cried: 'Grace and deliverance from evil be upon you, my lord! I trust that you are not ill?' 'Was it you who played and sang in the empty hall?' asked Ishāk in a low voice. The young girl blushed and would not answer, fearing that he was angry, but, when he pressed her again and again, she said: 'Alas, my lord, it was I.' Ishāk lowered his head, and murmured: 'Behold the day of confusion! O proud Ishāk, you thought that yours was the supreme voice and the supreme art of the century, and now you are proved a beginner, a bungling slave!'

He took the child's hand and carried it respectfully to his lips and brow; but Tufhah, though well-nigh fainting from emotion, had strength to pull away her hand, crying: 'The name of Allāh be upon you, master! Since when has the artist kissed the hand of the slave?' 'Say not so, Heart's-Miracle, say not so,' he replied humbly. 'Ishāk has found his master; beside your music, his music is as a dirham to a dīnār. You are excellence itself and I shall take you straightway to the Commander of the Faithful. When his glance burns upon you, you will become a princess among women, who are already a queen among God's creatures. Your art and your beauty will be crowned together. Praise and praise to you, Heart's-Miracle! Do not quite forget Ishāk when you come to the palace.' 'My lord,' cried Tufhah in tears, 'how could I forget the well-spring of my life and the strength of my heart?' Ishāk laid her hand upon the Koran and, when she had sworn never to forget him, said: 'Your Destiny is a marvellous Destiny, for I see the Khalīfah's desire written upon your brow. I pray you sing the same song to him as you sang just now, when I heard you and thought that I had entered Paradise before my time . . . And now, as a last favour, will you tell me by what mystery a queen came to be among those slaves, and all Allāh's treasure of earth and sea put up for sale?'

Tufhah smiled as she answered: 'Dear my lord, Tufhah's story is so strange that were it written with needles on the interior corner of an eye yet would it serve as a lesson to the circumspect. One day soon, perhaps, I will tell you that story. Suffice it, for to-day, that I was a piece of Moorish loot and dwelt among the Moors . . . Now I am ready to follow you to the palace.'

Ishāk, who had a reserved delicacy, questioned her no further. Instead, he clapped his hands and, when slaves appeared, ordered them to prepare their mistress's walking dress. They opened the great chests of clothing and dressed Heart's-Miracle in fair robes of striped Nīsābūr silk, perfumed with volatile essences and as soft to the touch as to the eye. They covered her with agreeable jewels and placed seven robes of seven colours upon her, so that she shone with the glory of a Chinese idol.

They sustained her on either hand, they carried the fringed train of her robes, and led her forth from the music school, while Ishāk walked ahead, accompanied by a little black boy carrying the lute.

Ishāk left the girl in the waiting hall and went in alone to the Khalīfah. 'O Commander of the Faithful,' he said, after making obeisance, 'I have brought you a stray from Paradise, the chosen miracle of our God, Tufhah the singer, my teacher and not my pupil.' Al-Rashīd smiled, and asked: 'Is this masterpiece the same girl whom we saw at the slave house?' 'The same, my lord,' answered Ishāk. 'She is fresher than the first morning and more musical to hear than the song of water over pebbles.' 'Let the morning come in!' cried al-Rashīd. 'Let us hear the song of water over pebbles, for these things should not be hidden.'

At this point Shahrazād saw the approach of morning and discreetly fell silent.

But when the nine-hundred-and-twenty-ninth night had come

SHE SAID:

When Ishāk went forth for Tufhah, the Khalīfah turned to Jafar, saying: 'O wazīr, is it not a prodigy to hear Ishāk praising someone beside himself? I must confess that I am stupefied by this miracle. But we shall see.'

Ishāk soon returned, leading the girl delicately by the hand. The eye of the Khalīfah burned, his soul rejoiced, for her moving was the floating of silk scarves upon the West wind. As he gazed she kissed the earth between his hands and, uncovering her face, looked forth, white, serene, and pure as the full moon. Though she was troubled by the presence, she did not forget her natural and acquired politeness. 'Greeting, O child of high nobility!' she said. 'Greeting, O auspicious blood of our lord Muhammad (on whom be prayer and peace!). Greeting, O fold and shelter of the righteous, O upright judge of the Three Worlds! Greeting from the most submissive and forgotten of your slaves!'

Al-Rashīd rejoiced, saying: 'The blessing of Allāh be upon you, O mould of perfection!' Then he looked at her more closely and well-nigh swooned for joy, and Jafar and Masrūr well-nigh swooned for joy.

The Khalīfah rose from his throne and, going down to the girl, very gently returned the little silk veil to her face, as a sign that she belonged to his harīm, and that the fairness of her had already retreated into the mystery of our Faith.

Then he invited her to be seated, saying: 'O Heart's-Miracle, your coming has lighted our dwelling, but our ears wait upon you, even as our eyes have waited. May we not hear that music entered with you also?' Tufhah took the lute from the little black boy and, sitting down at the foot of the throne, made prelude as of birds waking and crying upon the strings. Then, as the men held their breath, she sang:

> When on the plains of air the young moon rises
> And meets the king of purple going to his bed,
>   In sudden white she kerchiefs her surprises,
> But she's a queen. Girls such as I are stricken dead.

Al-Rashīd looked at the singer with love pleasure, and came down to sit beside her on the carpet, saying: 'O Tufhah, as Allāh lives, you are the gift of gifts!' Then he turned to Ishāk, crying: 'O Ishāk, in all you said you did not grant her praise enough! I do not hesitate to affirm that she easily surpasses even you. Surely it was written that only the Khalīfah could appreciate her.' 'By the life of my head, you are right, my lord!' cried Jafar. 'She is a thief of souls.' Then said Ishāk: 'O Commander of the Faithful, I am the more ready to admit the truth of what you say, since, when I heard her singing alone, I knew that henceforth all the talent which Allāh has given me would be as nothing in my eyes.' 'Good, good!' replied the Khalīfah.

When Tufhah had sung again, al-Rashīd's emotion was so great that he did not care to let it be seen by his companions, so he turned to Masrūr the eunuch, saying: 'O Masrūr, conduct your mistress to the chamber of honour in the harīm, and see that she lacks for nothing.' The gelded executioner led Tufhah away, and the Khalīfah watched her graceful going with moist eyes. 'She is dressed with taste,' he said to Ishāk. 'Whence come they, those robes which have not their equal in my palace?' 'They come from your slave,' answered Ishāk, 'but they were only his because of the Khalīfah's generosity. They are a present to the girl from the Prince of Believers, a most unworthy present.' So al-Rashīd, who was never backward in munificence, bade Jafar give a hundred thousand dīnārs immediately to the faithful Ishāk, and send ten robes of honour from the particular wardrobe to his palace.

Then with his cares forgotten and his face shining like a flower, he went to Tufhah's new apartment and took her in his arms behind the veil of mystery. He found her as virgin as a pearl still wet from the sea, and rejoiced in her.

From that day Tufhah held the highest throne in his heart, and he could not abide to be separated from her for a moment. He put the keys of all government in her hands, for she was a woman of great intelligence, and the gifts which he gave her, beyond the settled allowance of two hundred thousand dīnārs a month and fifty young girl slaves, would have bought all the lands of Irāk and the Nile.

Love took so strong a hold upon him that he would trust none but himself to guard Tufhah, and carried away the key of her chamber whenever he left her. One day, as she sang before him, he was so exalted that he even made as if to kiss her hand, but she withdrew it with a movement of such briskness that she broke her lute and wept. Al-Rashīd wiped away her tears and asked in a trembling voice the cause of them. 'O Tufhah,' he cried, 'I pray to Allāh that you shall never weep again!' 'What am I that you should kiss my hand, my lord?' said Tufhah. 'There is no creature upon earth worthy of that honour, and, if I allowed you to do it, Allāh would surely punish my arrogance by taking away my happiness.' Al-Rashīd was content with this saying, and replied: 'I will not offend again, now that you know the true place which you hold in my soul. Refresh your dear eyes, and remember that I love none in the world but you, that I would die in loving.' Tufhah fell at his feet and clasped his knees, but the Khalīfah raised her and kissed her, saying: 'You are my sole queen; you are more to me than Zubaidah, my cousin and my wife.'

One day, when the Khalīfah had ridden forth to hunt, Tufhah sat alone, reading a book by the light of perfumed candles set in gold. Suddenly a scent-apple fell in her lap and, looking up, she beheld the Lady Zubaidah standing before her. She sprang to her feet, and after respectful salutation, said: 'I pray you grant me your excuses, O my mistress! As Allāh lives, if I had been free in my movement, I would have come every day to offer you my service as a slave. May Allāh never deprive us of your presence!' Zubaidah sat down beside her, and said sadly: 'I knew that you had a great heart, O Tufhah, and therefore your words do not surprise me. Generosity is your native garment. Now I swear, by the life of my Sultān, that it is not my habit to pay visits to all my husband's favourites. Yet I have come to you, because I think that you should hear of the humiliation which has been put upon me ever since your entry into the palace. I am cast aside, I am relegated to the importance of a barren concubine; the Commander of the Faithful neither comes to see me nor asks news of me.' Here Zubaidah wept and Tufhah wept also; but soon the Queen went on: 'I have come to request you to bring it about that al-Rashīd allows me one night a month, only one night, so that I may not seem altogether a slave.' Tufhah kissed her hand, and murmured: 'O crown upon my head, O mistress of us all, I wish with my soul that he would spend all of each month beside you, not one night only, if that might comfort you and win my pardon from my gracious lady. I pray that one day I may be nothing but your slave.'

At this point Zubaidah saw al-Rashīd approaching, for he had returned from his hunting and made a very straight line to Tufhah's pavilion. Therefore she slipped away, comforted by the girl's promise.

Al-Rashīd entered with a smile and sat down, taking Heart's-Miracle upon his knees. They ate and drank together and then undressed. Not till they were both naked did Tufhah beg her lord to be merciful to Zubaidah and to go to her that night. 'Sweet Tufhah,' answered Hārūn with a smile, 'if it is so very important that I should visit the Lady Zubaidah, why did you wait to ask me until we had undressed?' 'Because,' she replied, 'I remembered the words of the poet:

> If you would beg, plain nakedness is best,
>   A leg's a better beggar than all wailing,
> For there is no investment in a vest,
>   And only to be veiled is unavailing.'

Hearing this, al-Rashīd took Tufhah to his breast, and there passed what passed. Afterwards he left her to go to Zubaidah, locking the door behind him. So much for him.

But what happened to Tufhah after this is so prodigious, so quite extraordinary that it must be told slowly.

At this point Shahrazād saw the approach of morning and discreetly fell silent.

But when the nine-hundred-and-thirtieth night had come

SHE SAID:

When Tufhah wearied of her book, she took up her lute and played so exquisitely that the walls came closer to listen.

Suddenly she felt that some unusual thing was taking place in the candlelight beside her. She turned and beheld an old man dancing silently in the middle of the room; his eyes were lowered, his look was venerable, and his carriage was majestic; he danced a dance of ecstasy such as no human could have compassed.

Tufhah grew cold with fear, for the windows and doors were shut, eunuchs were guarding all entrance to her, and she could not remember ever having seen the old man in any part of the palace. 'I take refuge in Allāh against the Stoned One!' she murmured to herself. 'I will go on playing as if nothing had happened.' And she forced her fingers to the notes.

After an hour, the old man stopped dancing and came up close to the girl, kissing the earth between her hands. 'You have excelled, O marvel of the East and West!' he said. 'O Tufhah, O Heart's-Miracle, do you not know me?' 'As Allāh lives, I do not know you,' she answered, 'but I fear that you are some Jinnī from the lands of Jinnistān. Far be the Evil One!' 'You are right, Tufhah,' said the old man with a smile. 'I come from Jinnistān and am even its lord paramount. I am Iblīs.' 'The name of Allāh be upon me and about me! I take refuge in Allāh!' cried poor Tufhah; but Iblīs kissed her hand and carried it to his brow, comforting her and saying: 'Fear nothing, O Heart's-Miracle. You have long been under my protection, you

317

have long been the loved desire of young Kamarīyah, queen of the Jinn, who surpasses all other immortals as you all human kind. For many weeks I have come with her every night to gaze upon you. She loves you madly, your name and your eyes are the only oaths upon her lips these days. When she sees you sleeping, she dies for your beauty, and, when she has to leave you, she languishes until another night be come. I have consented to act as her messenger, her advocate. If you let me lead you to Jinnistān, you shall be raised to the place of government among us. To-day is auspicious; my daughter is to be married and my son circumcised; you will be the chief illumination of our double feast. You shall stay as long as you like, queening it over the hearts of the Jinn, and then, upon my sacred oath, return at the first moment of your desire to do so.'

When Iblīs (may he be confounded!) spoke in this sort, the terrified Tufhah did not dare to refuse him. She bowed her head, and at this sign Iblīs took up her lute and led her by the hand, through the locked doors, until they came to the privy.

You must know that privies, wells and cisterns are the only means by which the subterranean Jinn can reach humanity. That is why no one enters the privy without invoking the name of Allāh. Also, the Jinn go back by the same unsavoury way as they have come; that is a hard and fast rule, a rule to which there is no exception.

Finding herself among the privies with Iblīs, the terrified Tufhah felt that she was going mad, but the Father of Evil obfuscated her with pleasantries, so that she did not struggle when he went down with her into the stinking hole. Nothing untoward happened during this difficult passage, and Tufhah soon found herself walking along a vaulted corridor which led to the open air. A horse, saddled and bridled, was waiting at the end of the corridor. Iblīs lifted the girl on to the high-backed saddle, and she felt the beast rise up like a wave beneath her and heard the beating of great wings in the night. When she knew that she was flying through the air and that Iblīs was keeping pace beside her, she fell back and swooned.

But the whistling of the air past her face soon brought her to herself, and she saw that they were traversing a vast meadowland, so filled with flowers that it appeared like a garment of painted silk below them. In the middle of this meadowland rose a palace with monstrous towers and a hundred and eighty copper doors. Upon the principal threshold the chiefs of the Jinn, habited in their best, were waiting for her.

When they saw Iblīs, they cried: 'Tufhah has come, Tufhah has come!' and, crowding round, lifted her from the horse and carried her into the palace, struggling to kiss her hands the while. She was set down with great pomp on a red gold throne, heavy with sea pearls, in the midst of so large a gold-walled and silver-columned hall that the tongue of a man would grow hair before he could tell of it.

The chief of the Jinn ranged themselves about the steps of the throne. All showed the appearance of humanity save two, who had single eyes set askew in the midst of their foreheads and the projecting tusks of a wild pig. As soon as each had taken his place according to his rank, a gracious young Queen advanced through the hall, lighting the air about her with her smile; she was followed by three fairy girls, swinging their hips delightfully as they walked. They all saluted Tufhah, and the young Queen began to ascend the steps of the throne, while Heart's-Miracle came down to meet her. When they had met, the royal lady kissed her guest long upon the cheeks and mouth.

This was no other than Kamarīyah, who had fallen in love with Tufhah; and the three attendants were her sisters, Gamra, Sharara, and Wakhīmah.

Kamarīyah sat down on a gold seat, and then instantly sprang up again to embrace Tufhah for a second time, to press her against her breast and stroke her cheek.

When he saw this, Iblīs laughed heartily and cried: 'O the fair accolade! Be kind, my pretties, and take me between you.'

At this point Shahrazād saw the approach of morning and discreetly fell silent.

But when the nine-hundred-and-thirty-first night had come

SHE SAID:

A great laugh, in which Tufhah joined, ran through the hall, and the fair Kamarīyah cried: 'I love you, dear sister, and the depths of my heart can have no witness but my soul. I loved you even before I saw you!' To this Tufhah replied politely: 'By Allāh, you are very dear to me, Lady Kamarīyah. I have been your slave ever since my glance first rested on you.' The Queen kissed her, thanked her, and presented her to the three princesses, saying: 'These are the wives of our chiefs.' So Tufhah saluted each appropriately, as they bowed before her.

Slaves entered with a vast tray of meats, and the five young women sat about this tray, in the midst of which was engraved:

Hot
Meats,
Cheese,
Fish,
And
Sweets;
Bake,
Roast,
And
Stew;
Please
Take
What
Most
You
Wish

In spite of this invitation, Tufhah was so preoccupied with the sight of the two repulsive Jinn that she was unable to eat much, and could not help asking Kamarīyah who they were and why they were so horrible. 'That one, sweetheart,' answered Kamarīyah with a laugh, 'is al-Shisbān, and the other is the great Māimūn, the sword-bearer. You find them uglier than the rest because they have refused, through pride, to put on a human appearance in order not to frighten you.' 'I cannot look at them!' whispered Tufhah. 'Māimūn is especially terrifying. I am very frightened of Māimūn.' At this Kamarīyah burst out laughing, and Shisbān asked what was amusing her. She explained fully in the language of the Jinn, but Shisbān, instead of being angry, filled the hall with a tempest of answering laughter.

When the gay feast came to an end, great flagons of wine were brought, and Iblīs came up to Tufhah, saying: 'The sight of you has already exalted us more than wine, my mistress; but we all, Kings and Queens alike, languish for the greater drunkenness of your singing. The night is already far spent, will you not oblige us with a song?' Tufhah took up her lute and played so ravishingly that one might have supposed that the palace was dancing with her like an anchored ship. Then she sang:

Peace be upon all who have sworn faith with me!
Have I not said that I will meet you, O you who meet me?
I will reproach you in a voice softer than morning,
Cooler than crystal water.
My lids are faithful to tears
Because the essence of my soul is that wine
By which my friends can live.

This song threw the chiefs of the Jinn into an ecstasy of pleasure; the monstrous Māimūn began to dance with a finger thrust up his anus, and Iblīs cried: 'The joy is too much. It stops my blood, it hurts my breathing!' Queen Kamarīyah rose and kissed the singer between the eyes. 'Heart of my heart, cool of my soul,' she said, and begged Heart's-Miracle to sing again. The delightful child consented, and this was her second song:

> I feed my soul with crumbled hopes
>   Until the rocks die down like snow,
>   For patience has more power, I know,
> Than fifty gilded horoscopes.

After this, all the Jinn began dancing, and Iblīs kissed Tufhah's fingers, demanding another song. 'Why does not Kamarīyah ask me?' retorted Tufhah; but the young Queen ran up to her and kissed both her hands, begging most ardently for more. Then said Tufhah: 'As Allāh lives, my voice is tired from singing; but I will, if you wish, recite for you the songs of the light wind, of the flowers, and of the birds.'

She set aside her lute, and said, in the pleased silence:

THE SONG OF THE LIGHT WIND

> I am the messenger of lovers, the sigh carrier,
> Faithfully bearing secrets, remembering every word,
> The indefatigable laughing flatterer,
> Tender for love's adventure, softening my breath
> For true love, but by false love harshly heard.
> And if girls sigh to guess in leaves my death,
> Yet I hearten their lads with my presence
> To make their prayer
> To slenderness.

I am a lute in white air,
And my essence
Is tenderness.

If I am variable, it is a reasoned gadding
To follow my sisters, the seasons, in their way,
(Who call me useful, but I am only fair . . .)
In Spring I flow from the north, making night day,
Fanning the fruit seed here and there.
To favour the clusters of my trees
In the hot season I run from the east
And sigh on the burnish of the leaves, adding
My beauty to the least
Of these.

I come up out of the south in autumn time
To fill my fruits, my coloured loves
For prime.
My winter fingers from the west are doves
Whose grey wings free the branches, whose fans give
Dry healing that the tree may live.

At morn
I carry the scent,
I make flowers speak with flowers, I balance the corn,
I give streams their silver chain,
I quick the palm, and lead lost youth again
Back to a woman's tent.

At this point Shahrazād saw the approach of morning and
discreetly fell silent.

But when the nine-hundred-and-thirty-second night had come

SHE SAID:

And Tufhah said again:

THE SONG OF THE ROSE

My visit is shorter than a ghost's,
Between Winter, it is, and Summer.
Hasten to play with me, play with me;
Time is a sword.

I balm my breath,
I am the colour of love,
I tingle in the hand of the girl who takes me.
I am your guest,
Hope not to keep me long,
The nightingale loves me.

I am the glory,
But the glory is hardest pressed of all the flowers.
I am the ever wounded,
Thorns spring out on my youth,
Steel arrows splashing my silks with my blood,
Staining my silks vermilion.

Yet I remain the elegant of passing things,
The pride of morning.
I wear my beauty in a crystal shift of dew.

Men hurry me from my green to another crystal,
My body turns to water, my heart is burned,
My tears are collected
And my flesh is torn.
I feel the passion of fire,
My soul is fumed off,
My spirit goes in vapour;
My sweet sweat is a record of my pain.
The passionate
Breathe the musk of my cast garments with delight;
My body goes from you, but my soul remains;
The wise do not regret my little time in the garden,
But lovers would have me,
Silly pretty lovers,
Have me there for ever.

And Tufhah said again:

THE SONG OF THE JASMINE

Come to me and mourn not, I am the jasmine.
My stars are whiter than silver
On the blue noon of air.

I come from the breast of God
To the breasts of women,
And am an ornament for black hair.

Use wine with me
And your friend's laughter
Shall shine more white.

My tint attests the camphor;
I am here when I am not here
So sweet am I.

My name detects the error of despair,
I am white joy, my lords.

And Tufhah said again:

THE SONG OF THE NARCISSUS

My beauty is not wine to me,
For I have eyes of languor,
And balance like music
And am nobly born.

I consider the flowers,
I talk with the flowers in moonlight.
My beauty gives me a throne among them
Yet I am a slave.

I am a slave,
The cincture of obedience,
The good servant
Who stands with a straight body
And bowed head.

I bare my neck,
I abide in my pure tent
Pitched on an emerald column;
My robe is gold and silver.

My modesty will excuse the wantoning of my eyes
As I hang my head above the waters.

And Tufhah said again:

THE SONG OF THE VIOLET

I wear a green cymar,
A sea-purple robe of honour,
Being quite little
And delightful.

My sister the rose is the pride of morning,
And I am the mystery of morning,
I am the dark child
Who wears an early grief.

You would have thought the modesty of my short hours . . .

I ravish my darlings for half a day,
And they pull me and use me and sell me cheap,
Make songs about me
And then despise me.

But in the morning the wise lift me
From my pale drought of death,
And balm disease with me.

The scent of my small life delighted the lad,
And my body dies for him.

But, but,
A little army with purple shields,
With emerald helmets,
Riding to victory . . .

And Tufhah said again:

THE SONG OF THE NENUPHAR

My shame could not live naked in the air,
I chose the passion of the water,
Immaculate petals
Guessed at rather than seen.
(Lovers, remember this!)
The river places are the bed of my rest
For ever.

That I should thirst
When he has given me to drink
Is love.
I thrust my gold cup to the sun
But night on the waters
Draws me as the moon draws
The waters.

I take my dreams to the green nest of water.

You lose me?
I am carried with open eyes;
We die together, water and I,
And you say you lose me.

He gave me what I am,
My shame could not live naked in the air,
I chose the passion of the water;
Immaculate petals
Guessed at rather than seen.

At this point Shahrazād saw the approach of morning and
discreetly fell silent.

But when the nine-hundred-and-thirty-third night had come

SHE SAID:

And Tufhah said again:

THE SONG OF THE GILLYFLOWER

The yellow garment of love sickness,
The white and yearning robe,
The blue frustrated veil . . .

I am a wise white, He knows,
For they will not touch my unscented nakedness.

And I am a wise yellow, Allāh knows,
For I blab the scent of my secret,
But not your secret.

Also I am a grief-bound blue,
For light offends my mystery.

I break at night, He knows!

And Tufhah said again:

THE SONG OF THE BASIL

Coloured flowers
Now that you have decked my garden
Take me,
The stream's bride,
The wise listener in moonlight,
Take me, coloured flowers!

As a dance cannot be jocund without instruments,
So wit cannot rejoice without me.
If the Prophet has promised me in Paradise
Why remember the mint flowers,

The chattering mint flowers?

The stream's bride,
The wise listener in moonlight,
Now that you have decked my garden
Take me, coloured flowers!

And Tufhah said again:

THE SONG OF THE CAMOMILE

Symbolists, symbolists . . .
And, if not, sleep . . .

Have you seen my flowers spreading on the fields,
The far-noticed white,
And the yellow disk giving languor?
The verses of the Book,
The clear verses,
And the difficult verses?

You have come to me and delighted,
You have come to me again and lo! I was not.
And you have not understood.

My bruised soul
Mounts into the singing of the doves
And you have thought it pleasure;
Though my white is recognisable far off,
You lie in the fields of my painting
And have not understood.

And Tufhah said again:

THE SONG OF THE LAVENDER

I am no terrace flower,
Vile hands and foolish talk
Escape me,
I grow in the hot brown dust,
Loving not men, but man.

No slave, no city thing
Can touch me.
Come to me in the waste heart of Arabia
Far from the dwelling of pale men,
For my delight is there.

I am the mistress of hermits,
Wild bees, deer, and the bitter absinthe
Are my sisters,
I am a free girl knowing no market.
Lust seeks me not, but the wild rider
Seeks me.

I would wish you to come to the valleys
Where the breeze kisses me at morning,
I would wish you
To lie near the wine of me.

Allāh, Allāh,
Even the camel-boy, telling of me,
Forgets his oaths!

And Tufhah said again:

THE SONG OF THE ANEMONE

If my heart were my body,
I should be above
The crying of the coloured flowers.

For his girl's cheek
A lover carries my blood as a flask of praise.

Yet the vases of the feast do not invite me
Because my heart is black.

I will fight no more.

I am the bright still of unhappiness.

'And now that I have finished the songs of the flowers and the light wind,' said Tufhah, 'I will say over for you, if you wish, some of the songs of the birds.'

At this point Shahrazād saw the approach of morning and discreetly fell silent.

But when the nine-hundred-and-thirty-fourth night had come

SHE SAID:

And Tufhah said:

THE SONG OF THE SWALLOW

If I choose farmers and their terraces
It is to escape my brothers of the trees.
The part of stranger is my chief delight;
The average of the world is not polite
Except to strangers. I will do no harm
To the provision of my chosen farm,
Neither my building nor my food is theirs;
These things I gather all from Allāh's cares.
It is their wit and not their meat I wish,
Their conversation, not their supper dish,
Their altruistic phrases, not their seed;
And, as I cost them nothing for my feed,
They learn to love me as a friend indeed.

And Tufhah said again:

THE SONG OF THE OWL

They call me wisdom's fowl, I hear,
But is there wisdom anywhere?
Wisdom and peace and happiness,
These might be found in loneliness.

Have you a friend, do you see men,
One man? You will not find them then.
Even as a drop forecasts the sea
Two souls forecast calamity;
There are no friends, I thank my God,
In the old wall of my abode.
I doom all sumptuous palaces
To the ill-starred who dwell in these;
I wish all delicate meats to those
Most poor, whose money golden grows.
Leave me my soul, I've known my soul
In ditch, in wall, in hollow bole,
Potential good, potential ill,
And both still-born and frustrate still.
Nought's to be feared and nought enjoyed
In a void spun upon a void:
Dark speech, and answer dark again;
Some things are fatal to explain.
Those obligations? Very fine,
They forget theirs! and I with mine? . . .
They call me wisdom's fowl, I hear,
But is there wisdom anywhere?

And Tufhah said again:

THE SONG OF THE FALCON

That I am sombre and most spare of words
Is a notorious fact among the birds.
My one perfection and my single beauty
Is taciturn devotion to my duty.
I am not as that fatuous nightingale
Whose ceaseless singing wearies all the vale
And whose intemperate speech, when heard on high,
Brings down misfortune and calamity.
The rule of silence is my one profession,
And my sole virtue lies in my discretion.
When I am caught, I still remain discreet,
I give no sign that I have felt defeat;
You will not see my head turned and down cast
To weep above the footsteps of the past,

Rather I look far forward and still chase
The dove of wisdom on from space to space.
So in the end my master yearns to me
And, fearing lest my cold reserve should be
My loss of love, he blinds me with a hood,
(The Koran says: To veil the eyes is good.)
He binds my tongue down to my under beak,
(The Koran says: 'Tis wisdom not to speak.)
He checks my freedom with a silken chain,
(Walk not in pride—the Koran says again.)
Silent and uncomplaining, I abide
These holy bands by which each sense is tied.
My wisdom ripens in the hooded night
Till kings become the servants of my flight;
Their royal hands bear up my pinions' beat,
I spurn their wrists beneath ascending feet.

And Tufhah said again:

THE SONG OF THE SWAN

Mistress of each desire, I use the sky,
The water, and the meadow equally;
With the same calm of confidence I show
My lily-bended neck, my carven snow,
My pouncet box of amber golden-sprent,
My feet of bogwood in each element.
My royalty is whiteness, loneliness,
And dignity compact; I am mistress
Of water's mystery and of the green
Dim glinting drifts of treasure submarine.
While I, self-sailed and with myself for guide,
Grow rich with each adventure of the tide,
The timorous shore-building stay-at-home
Desiring pearls, still nets the bitter foam.

And Tufhah said again:

THE SONG OF THE BEE

I build my house within the hill,
And, in my feeding, do no ill

Upon the flowers I fasten to
For forage lighter than the dew.
When, with my harmless theft content,
And mind on meditation bent,
I go to my abiding place
And brood on bees' predestined grace,
My turn is met at every turn
By works where Euclid deigned to learn.
Of all my musings this is chief:
That toil can be both joy and grief;
For, if my wax is fruit of pain,
Honey is learning's golden gain.
And next I ponder how my sting
Teaches the whole of love making:
I give all sweet, she gives all sweet
To him who'll take a wound for it.
Love makes all heaviness seem light.
O fools, good-day! O wise, good-night!

And Tufhah said again:

THE SONG OF THE MOTH

I am the lover whose love endlessly
Burns up his heart. Life's and love's law for me
Is to be swift to perish of desire,
Is to count consummation worth the fire.
Her kisses tear the tissue of my wings,
But listen to the song the candle sings:
'Do not condemn me, for I suffer too;
The flame loves me, even as I love you;
The sigh of his approach must burn me up,
As he draws near to drink, he melts the cup.
It was by fire that I was driven away
Where I and honey loitered yesterday.
To shed my life, to waste, to weep hot tears,
To jet my little hour to light the years,
Dear moth, dear moth, that is my Destiny.'
But fire blazed out to candle and to me:
'You drank my death, eternity was in it.
Have you not lived all living in a minute?'

At this point Shahrazād saw the approach of morning and discreetly fell silent.

But when the nine-hundred-and-thirty-fifth night had come

SHE SAID:

And Tufhah said again:

THE SONG OF THE CROW

That, dressed in black, with harsh importunate cry,
I trouble all delight as I go by;
That, circling shadow-wise the camps of Spring,
I prophesy their bitter leave-taking;
That, when I see a love, I croak its doom,
Or, flecking some bright palace with my gloom,
Foretell the speedy ruining of it—
These and more sombre habits I admit.
If you, who blame me for such things, could guess
Wherein lay your abiding happiness,
You would wear midnight garments, even as I,
And curb your conversation to a sigh.
But no! Vain pleasure is your only goad
And vanity decoys you from the road;
You cannot realise that friendship is
To blame, not praise, to teach and not to please.
I, only I, of all religious folk,
Retain the symbol of a sable cloak,
And weep for passing time and groan to see
The caravans set out high-heartedly.
All men are deaf. Although I cry aloud,
They turn their backs upon the morning cloud:
Alive they will not heed me, though they could,
And dead they cannot hear me, if they would.

And Tufhah said again:

THE SONG OF THE HOOPOE

When I came up out of Saba
With a love writing for the gilded king,
A letter from the queen of long blue eyes,

333

Sulaimān said to me:
'O hoopoe, you have brought from Saba
News which has set my heart to dancing.'

He covered me with his blessing
And put a crown of pride upon my head;
I wear it still.

He taught me wisdom,
And even now,
When ages of dust are sifted above him,
I go sometimes apart
To say over the lessons of Sulaimān.

He said:
'O hoopoe,
If conscience were of good understanding
She would hear glad tidings.

If the soul were sleepless
She would receive a light not of the stars.

If the body were pure,
The eyes would see love.

If a man threw off the garment of pride
He would walk naked with God,
And there would be no more frozen thoughts.

If you were to shed that cloak
You would learn how the health of the soul
Poises upon a balance,
You would refresh yourself with the fan of hope,
You would plant the cherry tree of refuge
And the plum tree of correction,
You would mould a mortar for your soul out of patience,
You would fashion humility to a sieve,
And, after a night of waking,
Walk with the Friend alone at dawn.

Who sees no portent
In the crying of the door,
In the buzz of flies,
The murmur of insects in the dust,

He also will disregard
The walking of the mists,
The light of mirage,
And the colours of the sea fog;
For there is no wisdom in that man.'

When she had said over these songs of the flowers and birds, Tufhah fell silent, and exclamations of delighted reverence came to her from all the Jinn. Iblīs kissed her feet, and the Queens embraced her, weeping. All that host signified clearly with their eyes and hands: 'Our tongues are bound by admiration, and we are so exalted that we cannot speak.' They jumped up and down rhythmically in their seats, waving their legs in the air, an action which says among the Jinn: 'You have excelled and we thank you!' The Ifrīt Māimūn danced round and round, with a finger thrust up his anus, by which he sought to exclaim, 'I marvel! I marvel!'

'As Allāh lives, good masters and mistresses,' cried Tufhah, greatly affected by this praise, 'if I were not weary I would say many more songs for you. You should hear the songs of the nightingale, the quail, the starling, the canary, the dove, the woodpigeon, the goldfinch, the peacock, the pheasant, the partridge, the kite, the vulture, the eagle, and the ostrich; you should hear the songs of the dog, the camel, the horse, the onager, the ass, the giraffe, the gazelle, the ant, the sheep, the fox, the goat, the wolf, the lion, and many, many others. But, if Allāh wills, we shall meet again for another bout of poetry. For the moment, I beg the sheikh Iblīs to take me back to the palace of my master, the Commander of the Faithful, for he must be distraught because of me. I would willingly wait for the circumcision and the marriage, but I have not the strength.'

'O Heart's-Miracle,' answered the sheikh Iblīs, 'our souls are tortured by your wish to leave us. Is there no way by which I could persuade you to stay a little longer? We have but tasted the wine, and now you pluck the cup from our lips. Can you not have a few moments more, O Tufhah?' 'It is beyond my power to grant,' replied Heart's-Miracle. 'I must return at once to the Prince of Believers, for a child of earth can find no happiness away from earth, and my heart is sad to be so far from other hearts. Surely you would not keep me against my will?'

'Be it upon my head and before my eyes,' said Iblīs kindly. 'But first I must tell you, Tufhah, that I know your music master, the admirable Ishāk ibn Ibrāhīm of Mosul.' He smiled to himself a little, and then continued: 'And he knows me, too. Certain things happened between us on a winter evening, which I shall tell you some day, if Allāh wills. It is a long story; but he has not yet forgotten the new modes of the lute which I taught him, or, for that matter, the spirit girl with whom I made him glad. If you were not in such a hurry, I would let you hear all about it . . . At least I insist that you shall not depart empty-handed. I am myself going to teach you an expedient upon the lute which will win you renown throughout the world and increase the Khalīfah's love for you.' 'Do as you think best,' said Tufhah.

Iblīs picked up the girl's lute and played upon it in a quite new mode, with such unheard-of artifice and repetition, such perfection of tremolo, that Tufhah felt she was hearing music for the first time, and that all the teaching of Ishāk had been but error. She took the lute from Iblīs (may Allāh confound him!) and repeated the lesson note by note, so that all the Jinn cried: 'Excellent! Excellent!' and the Evil One himself said: 'You have reached the topmost pinnacle of this art, and I am going to give you a diploma, countersigned by all the chiefs of the Jinn, to the effect that you are the queen of earthly lute players. I shall also nominate you Lieutenant of the Birds, for your poems have proved you peerlessly entitled to that rank.'

At this point Shahrazād saw the approach of morning and discreetly fell silent.

But when the nine-hundred-and-thirty-sixth night had come

SHE SAID:

Iblīs had his chief scribe prepare a cock-skin and write on it, under his dictation, in flowing Kūfic character and with perfect alignment, a notice to the effect that the girl Tufhah had been appointed Lieutenant of the Birds and queen of all earthly lute players. This document was sealed with the seal of Iblīs, and countersealed by all the chiefs and Queens of the Jinn. Then it was shut in a little gold box and given, with high ceremony, to Tufhah, who carried it to her brow in sign of thanks.

Then, at a signal from Iblīs, twelve slaves entered the hall carrying twelve cupboards of identical size and ornament. Iblīs opened them, one by one, and, as he showed the contents of each to Tufhah, cried:

'These are yours!' The first cupboard was filled to the top with jewels, the second with coined gold, the third with gold in bars, the fourth with wrought gold, the fifth with gold candlesticks of great elaboration, the sixth with myrobalan and dried conserves, the seventh with silk underclothing, the eighth with cosmetics and perfumes, the ninth with lutes, the tenth with gold plate, the eleventh with brocaded garments, and the twelfth with robes of many-coloured silks.

When Tufhah had rejoiced over these gifts, Iblīs made a sign to the porters, who took up the cupboards upon their backs and ranged themselves in order behind the girl. The Queens came weeping to say farewell, and Queen Kamarīyah sighed out: 'Though you are leaving us, dear sister, I am sure that you will let us come to see you in your pavilion sometimes, to rejoice our eyes with the beauty which leaves us desolate. If you wish, I shall not be invisible next time. I shall assume the form of a little human girl, and wake you with my breath.' 'Please do so, O my sister Kamarīyah,' answered Tufhah. 'I shall rejoice to wake under your breath and feel you lying against me.' And they kissed for the last time.

Iblīs bent his back and took Tufhah astride on his neck. He rose into the air and left that tempest of sighs behind, and the porters followed him close. In less time than it takes to tell, Tufhah had been set down gently on her own bed and the cupboards had been ranged silently along the wall of her apartment. Then the thirteen spirits kissed the earth before the bed and retired, as they had come, like shadows.

It seemed to Tufhah that she had never left that place; to assure herself that her experience had not been a dream, she took up her lute and played upon it after the manner that Iblīs had taught her, singing at the same time verses of return. The eunuch on guard outside the door heard the playing and singing. 'As Allāh lives, it is my mistress Tufhah!' he cried, and began to run through the palace, though he was a heavy man, as if all the arms of the desert pursued him. After a deal of tumbling and scrambling to his feet again, he prostrated himself before Masrūr, who stood as usual on guard outside the Khalīfah's bedchamber. 'My lord, my lord,' he panted, 'wake the Commander of the Faithful, for I bring good news!' Masrūr cursed him, saying: 'O vile Sawwāb, you must be mad if you think I dare wake the Khalīfah at such an hour.' But Sawwāb kept on insisting so loudly that Hārūn al-Rashīd woke, and cried from within:

'What is the meaning of this tumult, Masrūr?' 'Sawwāb has come, my lord, bidding me wake you,' replied the trembling executioner. 'What has Sawwāb to say to me?' asked the Khalīfah in a threatening voice; but Sawwāb could only stammer out: 'My lord, my lord!' 'Go and see what is the matter,' said Hārūn to one of the girls who watched about his bed.

The slave came out and led Sawwāb into the presence, but the poor negro was so moved by the news he brought that he forgot to kiss the earth between the Khalīfah's hands and cried, as if he were talking to an equal: 'Get up, get up at once! My mistress Tufhah is singing and playing in her apartment! Just you come and hear her, my boy!' Then, as the Khalīfah looked at him without a word, he went on: 'Can you not hear what I am saying? I tell you Tufhah is playing and singing in her bedroom! Come on, lazybones!' Al-Rashīd leaped from his bed and struggled into the first garment which came to hand, crying the while: 'What are you saying, wretch? How dare you speak of your mistress? You know that she has disappeared, you know that the wazīr Jafar has assured me that it was a matter of enchantment, you know that folks who are stolen away by the Jinn never return! What maggot of a dream has entered your black head that you should disturb me in this way?' Then cried the eunuch in an ecstasy of impatience: 'I've had no dream in my black head, I have not even been to bed; I tell you Tufhah is not dead, so come along, my bean-face!'

The Khalīfah fell into a fit of laughter, and cried: 'If you are telling the truth, I will make your fortune; I will free you and give you a thousand dīnārs. But if you have been dreaming, I will have you crucified.' 'O Allāh, O Protector, O Master of salvation, grant that it was no maggot!' murmured Sawwāb, as he led the marvelling Khalīfah to Tufhah's door.

Al-Rashīd heard the singing and playing of his mistress; for a full minute he fumbled with the key in the lock, and then hurled himself into the room, calling to Allāh against the wiles of the Devil.

Tufhah ran up to him and caught him to her breast, but the Khalīfah uttered a cry and slipped down from her arms in a death-seeming swoon. She bathed his temples with musked rose-water; but, even when he came to, he was as one drunk, and the tears fell through his beard on to the marble. When at last amazement left him and he could sigh with delight in the girl's arms, he cried: 'O Tufhah, your absence was a marvel, but your return is a greater marvel.'

'Wait till you have heard all,' answered Heart's-Miracle between their kisses, and she told him of the silent dancing of the old man, of the descent into the privy, of the winged horse, of the palace of the Jinn, of the beauty of Kamarīyah, of the songs of the flowers and birds, of the Devil's music lesson, and of her brevet written upon cock-skin. When she had shown the document to the astonished Khalīfah, she opened each of the cupboards in turn, but a thousand human tongues could give no picture of the riches he beheld. Suffice it to say that those things were the foundation of the great wealth of the Abbāsids.

At this point Shahrazād saw the approach of morning and discreetly fell silent.

But when the nine-hundred-and-thirty-seventh night had come

SHE SAID:

Al-Rashīd's joy was so great, in his recovery of his dear Heart's-Miracle, that he had the city of Baghdād lighted with coloured fires and gave great feasts to the poor. And during these feasts Ishāk al-Nadīm, who was now held in greater honour than ever by his master, sang publicly a song which he had written to the air of Iblīs (may Allāh for ever confound him!).

Hārūn al-Rashīd and Tufhah lived together in love delight, until they were visited by the Inexorable, the Tomb Filler.

Such, O auspicious King, continued Shahrazād, is the tale of Heart's-Miracle, Lieutenant of the Birds.

And King Shahryār, who had marvelled at this story and, above all, at the songs of the flowers and birds, and, of these, especially at the songs of the hoopoe and the crow, said within his soul: 'As Allāh lives, this wazīr's daughter is my blessing! A woman of her quality does not deserve death. At least, as it is likely that she may have more stories to tell me, I will reflect for a little longer before deciding her fate.' In an unusual exaltation of spirit, he suddenly drew Shahrazād to his heart, crying: 'Blessed are your like, O Shahrazād! Your tale has delighted me, and your songs of the flowers and birds have edified me. If, O virtuous and talented, you have one or two or three or four more stories of the same kind to tell me, begin at once, for to-night my ears are open to your eloquence.' 'I am the King's slave,' answered Shahrazād, 'and his praises are far above my worth. If he wishes it, I would rejoice to tell him certain truths concerning women, police captains, and the like; but I must warn my King that the stories which I have in mind are a little daring.' 'You may certainly tell me of these things,' answered King Shahryār, 'for, if the matter of your discourse be woman, nothing can surprise me. I know that woman is like a twisted rib; if she is to be cured, she must be twisted further; and if she is twisted too far, she breaks. Speak as freely as you like, for we have been wise enough since the day our Queen betrayed us.' The King's face grew dark again and his brows came together at the memory of that old misfortune; so little Dunyazād made haste to cry: 'Dear sister, please, please begin your tales about women and policemen, and be as free as you like, for our King knows well the difference between gems and pebbles, women and women.' 'You are right, little one,' answered Shahrazād. 'I will now tell our master The Tale of al-Malik al-Zāhir Rukn al-Dīn Baibars al-Bundūkdarī and his Captains of Police.'

And Shahrazād said:

The Tale of Al-Malik Baibars and His Captains of Police

IT is related—but the Invisible knows all!—that there was once in Cairo, in the land of Egypt, a Sultān of the illustrious Turkish Bahris, whose name was al-Malik al-Zāhir Rukn al-Dīn Baibars al-Bundūkdari. During his reign Islām shone with unprecedented lustre, and the empire rolled gloriously between the extremes of east and west. Under the blue heaven of Allāh the strongholds of the Franks and the Nazarenes were not to be found, for their kings had become a carpet for al-Malik's feet. No voice was heard in the deserts and green meadowland save the voice of the Believer, no footprint seen that had not been made by one walking in the way of righteousness. Therefore be manifold blessing given to the Fortunate One, to our lord Ahmad Muhammad, son of Abdallāh, the Prophet of Allāh, because he showed the way of righteousness! Amen.

Sultān Baibars so loved and was so loved of his people that the least important custom, tradition, or local usage which concerned them interested him very deeply. Greater even than his passion for seeing with his own eyes was his eagerness to hear these matters treated of in stories, and thus it happened that the best tale tellers among his court were sure of the highest honours.

One night, when he was more hungry for instruction than usual, he called together his captains of police and bade them tell him of any matters which they considered worth recording. 'Be it upon our head and before our eyes!' they answered. 'Does our master wish us to tell him of things which we have experienced ourselves or of happenings which we have by hearsay?' 'That would be a delicate decision,' said Baibars. 'I think that I will leave you free to choose for yourselves, provided that your tales are sufficiently surprising.' 'Our tongues and souls belong to the King!' they cried.

The first to speak was a captain named Muīn al-Dīn, whose liver was rotten with the love of women. 'O King of time,' he said, 'I will tell you of an extraordinary adventure which happened to myself in the early days of my career.'

And he told:

The First Captain's Tale

O MY Lord and crown upon my head, when I first entered the police service at Cairo, under our chief Alām al-Dīn Sanjar, I already had a great reputation. Every son of a pimp, every son of a dog, every son of a gallowsbird, and, I think I may even say, every son of a whore, feared me and fled from me as if I had been the yellow pest. When I rode my horse through the city, people pointed at me and winked fearfully to each other and bowed to the very dust; but I took no more notice than if a fly's wing had brushed my zabb, and would ride on, swelling with pride.

One day, as I was busy in the walī's courtyard, lying down with my back to the wall and thinking of my greatness, something as heavy as the Day of Judgment fell from the sky into my lap. Picking it up, I found it to be a sealed purse containing a hundred dirhams. As I slipped the sweet child into her father's breast, I looked to every direction of earth and sky, but could see no one; therefore I gave thanks to Allāh and went my way.

Next morning my duty took me to the same place, but I had hardly lain down before something of painful weight hit me on the side of the head. I snatched it up in a fury and discovered that it was another purse, own sister to the child of my bosom. As I sent it to join her, I raised my head and twisted my neck and spun round and stood still, without being able to catch the least glimpse of any who might have sent this charming stranger. 'Are you asleep or are you not asleep?' I asked, and I replied: 'You are not asleep, you are not even sleepy.' Having satisfied myself on this point, I lifted the skirts of my garment and walked from the courtyard, casually and as if nothing had happened, spitting copiously at every few steps.

But on the third morning I took my precautions. As soon as I went on duty, I shut my eyes and began to snore like a troop of wild camels. Suddenly, as I lay there, my lord, I felt a hand hunting for something about my navel. As I had nothing near there which the right sort of person was not at liberty to steal, I let the hand continue its exploration; but when I felt that it had found the road, I gripped it suddenly with my own, crying: 'Whither away, my sister?' At the same moment I opened my eyes wide and sat up abruptly. The owner of the gentle little jewelled hand, a girl of fairy-like beauty, stood regarding me with a smile. O my lord the Sultān, she was like jasmine! 'Greeting, dear mistress,' I cried, as I took a firmer grip of the slender wrist. 'The goods are yours and the shopkeeper as well; but tell me, sweet, of what terrace are you the rose? Of what cluster are you the jacinth? Of what garden are you the nightingale, O most desirable of damsels?'

Without the least shame of gesture or voice, the child signed to me to rise, saying: 'O Muīn, follow me if you would know me.' Without an instant's hesitation I rose and walked along behind the girl, as if I had been her milk brother or had known her all my life.

When we came in this order to the bottom of a blind alley, the girl turned and signed to me to approach. I came up smiling and brought out the child of his father to take the air with her. 'Here is the little rascal, my mistress!' I exclaimed, but the girl replied most disdainfully: 'Put him away, Captain Muīn, or he will catch cold.' 'Certainly,' I answered, as I obeyed her. 'You are the mistress here and I have already been loaded with your favours. But tell me, O daughter of honesty, since the big muscle of conserve, my excellently furnished zabb, does not tempt you, why have you given me two purses, why have you tickled my navel, and why have you led me to the bottom of a blind alley, which is the very place for assaulting and giving in assault?' 'O Captain Muīn,' she replied, 'I have more confidence in you than in any other man of this city, but, though I have sought you out, it is for a very different reason from the one which you suppose.' 'Whatever your object, dear mistress,' I hastened to assure her, 'I am your debtor and your slave.' 'Very well,' she smiled. 'Now listen carefully, O captain: I am a woman who is madly in love with a girl; a scorching fire burns me day and night. If I had a thousand tongues and a thousand hearts I could not love her more dearly. She is the daughter of the kādī, and certain things have come to pass between us; but that is a mystery of love. There is a pact of passion, a promise and an oath between us that neither shall ever marry or be touched by man. Our relations had continued for a long time (we were inseparable, we ate together, we drank of the same cup, and slept in the same bed) when that foul old beard, her father, cut short our delights, locked up his daughter, and threatened to break my hands and feet if I ventured again into his dwelling. I have not seen my loved one since, but I have learnt that she is well-nigh mad because of our separation. It is to ease my heart and bring a little joy to her that I have called on you, O captain.'

As I looked at this incomparable child and heard what she said, my brain became clouded, and I exclaimed in my soul: 'O Allāh, Allāh, girls will be boys! But what sort of love can there be between two women? Can the cucumber spring up in the night from a place devoted to quite other planting?' I beat my hands together in surprise, and cried aloud: 'Dear mistress, I understand nothing of what you have said. Therefore please explain the whole thing to me from the beginning, in all its details. Do does sigh after does, hens after hens?' 'Be quiet,' answered the girl, 'for this is a mystery of love and very few may understand it.'

At this point Shahrazād saw the approach of morning and discreetly fell silent.

But when the nine-hundred-and-thirty-seventh night had come

SHE SAID:

'It is enough for you to know that I need your help to reach the kādī's house and that, when you have aided me, I will never forget my obligation.' 'Well, well, good Muīn,' said I to myself, 'so you have been chosen for the go-between of two women! There was never such a tale in all the history of pimping! At least there is no law against it; you may go forward!' So I cleared my throat, and said to the gilded woman: 'This seems a delicate matter, my pigeon; but the less I understand of it the more ready I am to help you. Yet I confess I do not see how I can be of any use.' 'I wish you to help me into the presence of my loved one,' she explained. 'That is all very well, my dove,' I replied, 'but here am I, as it might be here, and there is the daughter of the kādī, as it might be there.' At this she cried fretfully: 'Poor fool, do you think I would be so rash as to let you come near the sweet one in your own person? I only need you as a stick upon the road to ruse and stratagem.' 'Behold a stick both blind and deaf, my lamb,' I murmured, and she went on: 'Listen, then! To-night I will go, dressed up like a peacock in all my best and so veiled that none at all may recognise me, and seat myself near the Kādī's house. When you come along with your guards, the perfume which I shall be wearing will attract you and you will come up to me respectfully to ask what so noble a lady does alone in the street at that hour. To this I shall reply: "O valiant captain, I am a girl from the citadel; my father is one of the Sultān's amīrs. To-day I came down into the city to do some shopping, but before I had finished the gates of the citadel had been shut against me. I walked down again, hoping to find some friend with whom I could spend the night; but by ill-luck not one of them is at home. As a last resort I came to sit near the threshold of the kādī's house that his shadow might in some sort protect me. To-morrow I shall return to my parents." Then you, O Captain Muīn, as an intelligent and observant man, will say to yourself: "It is not lawful to leave a woman in the street when she is young and beautiful and covered with jewels, for she may be outraged and robbed. If such a thing were to happen in my quarter, I would be responsible to the Sultān. No, I must protect her in some way; I must set one of my men to guard her, or, better still (for you know what policemen are!) find her a lodging with respectable folk until the morning. By Allāh, I have it! Where could she be safer than in the kādī's house? She sought it out instinctively, poor lamb. Lodge her with the kādī, my fine fellow, and, in one of two ways, you are sure to be rewarded." Then you must knock at the kādī's door and, in a minute or so, I shall be beside my loved one in the harīm. Such is my plan, O captain.'

'Allāh increase His favours upon your head, O mistress!' I answered. 'The scheme is clever, and the more so because it is easy. Intelligence is a gift from God.' Then, when I had agreed with her upon our time of meeting, I kissed her hand and went my way.

Evening came and then night; soon after the hour of prayer I set out on my round, followed by my policemen bearing naked swords. After passing through many districts, we visited, at about midnight, the road where I expected to meet my lady of strange loves. Even as I turned the corner, a rich and astonishing perfume was wafted out to me, and presently I heard the tinkling of bracelets and anklets. 'I see a shadow there, my sons!' I shouted. 'And what a smell!' We all peered into the gloom and soon saw a veiled figure, heavy with brocade and bright with silk. At once I went forward and addressed the shape respectfully, saying: 'O my mistress, what does a fair and high-born lady alone at such an hour? Are you not afraid of the night and the violence of thieves?' She answered me according to our plan, and I turned towards my men, as if to ask their advice. 'O chief,' said they, 'if such be your wish, we will conduct this lady to your house, for she will be better there than anywhere. We do not think that you will lose by giving her hospitality, as she is both rich and beautiful. When you join her there, you can act as seems good to you, and, in the morning, restore her to her loving mother.' But I cried out: 'Be quiet! I take refuge in Allāh against such a suggestion! For one thing, I live far from here, and, for another, my poor abode is quite unworthy of an amīr's daughter. No, my best plan will be to ask hospitality for her from the kādī, whose house is both handy and suitable.' At once my ruffians began to knock upon the kādī's door, and, in a moment or so, the judge appeared in person, leaning upon the shoulders of two black slaves. After greeting, I explained the affair to the old man, while the girl stood meekly to one side, with her veils drawn close about her. 'She is welcome!' answered the kādī. 'My daughter will entertain her and see that she lacks for nothing.' At once I handed over my incendiary package and, as she was being led to the harīm, went forth again upon my round.

Next morning, as I walked towards the kādī's house to take possession of the goods, I said to myself: 'By Allāh, it must have been a white night for those two girls! Yet, in very truth, my brain would crack before I could imagine what two gazelles like that could do between them. I have never heard tell of such a thing.' Busy with these thoughts, I turned into the entrance of the house and fell among an extraordinary tumult and buzzing of frightened slaves and clamorous women. As I halted in amazement, the white-bearded kādī hurled himself towards me, crying: 'O shame of good-for-nothings! You planted a thief in my house last night and she has made off with all my fortune! Unless you find her, I will bring you up before the Sultān to taste of his red death.' I asked for further details, and he explained, in an outpour of menaces and curses, that the girl had disappeared from his harīm early in the morning and that a belt containing six thousand dīnārs had vanished with her. 'I hold you responsible!' he cried, and again: 'I hold you responsible!'

At first, my lord, I was too thunderstruck to speak. I bit the palm of my hand, thinking: 'O pimp, this lands you in the pitch for good and all! Where the devil is that girl?' Then I plucked up my courage, and said to the kādī: 'Good master, if this thing has happened, it is because it was fated. I only ask you to allow me three days in which to lay hands upon that prodigious female; if I do not succeed, you may have my head for all I care.' The kādī looked at me searchingly and then answered: 'I give you three days, but not a minute longer.'

I left his presence with my brain in a whirl, saying to myself: 'You have done it this time, you clumsy fool! How are you going to recognise one out of all the veiled women in Cairo? How can you examine the harīms when you are not allowed to enter them? You might just as well go to bed for your three days of grace, since there is no way of evading your responsibilities.' When I had made this decision, I went home and lay down on my mat, where I stayed sleepless for three days, mourning over my fate. At the time appointed, I rose and took my way with bended head towards the kādī's house; but, as I was passing through a street not far from it, I happened to look up, and saw the maiden of my troubles behind a half-opened lattice. She looked at me with laughing eyes and signed with her brows, as much as to say: 'Come up to me!' I did not need a second invitation, as I knew that my life depended upon this meeting; in the twinkling of an eye I stood beside her, and, quite unmindful of any salutation, cried briskly: 'My sister, I have hunted every corner of the city for you. Do you realise that you have played me a mean trick? Do you realise that you have made me descend the red stairs of very death?' She came to me and pressed me to her bosom, saying: 'Can Captain Muīn be afraid? Do not waste time in telling me what has happened, for I know all. It is true that I have waited till the last moment, but I can easily save you. I called you up to me for nothing else.' I thanked her cordially and could not refrain, because she was beautiful, from kissing the hand which had done me so much harm. 'Be at ease,' she said, when I had done this, 'for no ill shall come to you. Rise up now and look!' She led me by the hand into an adjoining chamber which contained two chests; one was filled with rubies and every other colour of rare jewel, the other was stuffed to the brim with gold pieces. 'If you like, Captain Muïn, you can take back the six thousand dīnārs which disappeared with the belt of that black-souled kādī, my sweet one's father,' said this mysterious lady, 'but I think they can be put to a better use. I only took them away because I knew that the old man was a miser, and I hoped that he would die of grieving. When one is as rich as I am, one does not steal. His daughter knows very well that I was only aiming at his life. Listen carefully and I will show you a way by which you can clear yourself and, at the same time, help on my plans for that vile old creature's death.' She paused for a moment, and then continued: 'The kādī will be waiting for you on the hot grill of impatience. You must go to him at once, and say: "Simply as a matter of duty I have searched for three days through the city, to see if I could find the woman to whom you gave hospitality at my suggestion and whom you accuse of having stolen six thousand dīnārs. But I know for a fact that the poor creature never left this house. None of the police can find one trace of her since that evening, and none of the female spies have been able to get news of her in any harīm. You accuse her, my lord, of having robbed you; yet I think that such an accusation should be proved, for it seems very much more likely to me that the girl was the object of some vile plot, or the victim of some foul assault while under your care. Allāh knows all, but I consider it my duty to make a perquisition in your house, in case this thief of yours did not quite escape!"

'Thus, Captain Muïn, from being the accused you will have become the accuser. The kādī will see the world grow black before his eyes, he will fly into a great rage, his face will grow like a red pepper, and he will cry: "You dare to accuse me, you dog! But it shall avail you nothing! Begin your perquisition at once. After you have proved yourself in the wrong, your punishment will be the greater." Then you must take your men as witnesses and make a thorough search of the house, though, needless to say, you will find nothing. When you have scrutinised every inch of the terrace, when you have rummaged every room and chest in the place, you must lower your head in cruel embarrassment and, as soon as you have reached the kitchen, begin to confound yourself in excuses. As you are stammering out your contrition, you must lift the cover from the great oil jar, which you will see there, and cast a careless glance inside.

Suddenly you will cry: "Oh, oh, one moment, one moment! What have we here?" You will thrust your arm into the jar, and feel a packet thrust well down below the oil. You must bring this forth, and there, for all the world to see, will be my veil, my chemise, my drawers, and all the rest of my garments, reeking with coagulated blood! You will be triumphant and the kādī confounded. He will become yellow, and his joints will turn to water; he will certainly fall to the floor and, if Allāh be good to us, he may die. If he does not die on the spot he will be ready to do anything to keep his name out of this disreputable business, and will gladly bribe you heavily to suppress your finding. That is my plan, good Captain Muīn.'

For a moment I was dazzled and dumbfounded by the brilliance of this scheme and the charm of its inventor; when at last I had sufficiently recovered myself to take my leave, the girl slipped a purse of a hundred dīnārs between my fingers, as I was kissing her hand, and said: 'These are for the expenses of to-day. But, if Allāh wills, you shall have better proof of my generosity in the future.' I thanked her warmly and added, before I could prevent myself: 'Dear mistress, when this business is finished to your satisfaction, will it please you to marry me?' 'You have forgotten that I am already betrothed to her who holds my heart, good captain,' she answered with a laugh. 'But Allāh alone knows the future! Depart now, my friend, in His name!'

At this point Shahrazād saw the approach of morning and discreetly fell silent.

But when the nine-hundred-and-thirty-ninth night had come

SHE SAID:

I went forth, blessing her, and led my men to the kādī's house. As soon as the old man saw me, he cried: 'Here is my debtor, but where is the amount of the debt?' 'O our lord the kādī,' I answered, 'my head is as nothing when weighed against your head, and I have no one to sustain me in any high position; but, if the right is on my side, Allāh will show it forth!' 'What is this talk of right?' shouted the kādī furiously. 'Do you think that anything can save you from your fate, if you have not found the woman and my belt? By Allāh, there is a great gulf fixed between you and any question of right!' On this I looked the old man very bravely in the eyes and brought forth the astonishing rigmarole which turned me from accused into accuser. The effect of my words was exactly as the girl had fore-seen: the kādī saw the world darken before his eyes, his breast be-came stuffed to bursting with anger, his face took on the appearance of a pimento, and he cried: 'What are these lies, O most insolent of all the police? Such disgusting insinuations will serve you nothing! Make your perquisition, in Allāh's name, for when it leads to noth-ing, your punishment will be the greater!' So saying, he went into an irruption, as if he had been a red-hot cook pot suddenly filled with water.

We laid aboard his house and rummaged high and low, not letting the least corner, chest, hole, or cupboard escape us. As we carried on this business, I saw that sweet gazelle, who was loved of her own kind, flit from chamber to chamber to escape us. 'The name of Allāh·be upon her and about her!' I murmured to myself. 'A reed, a wavering reed! All elegance and all beauty! Blessed be the womb which bore her, and thrice glorified the Creator Who moulded her in the mould of perfection!' I understood for the first time how such a girl might subjugate another of her like, and I murmured: 'Some-times the rose will lean towards the rose, the jonquil to the jonquil.' I was so delighted by this discovery that I wished to run with it at once to the prodigious damsel whose business I was now about, so that she might approve me and no longer think me lacking in delicacy and discernment.

We came at length to the kitchen, without finding a trace of the missing woman or any suspicious thing at all, and, by this time, the kādī's fury had no bounds.

Here I acted upon my instruction and, feigning great shame for my boldness, humbled myself in excuses before the kādī, who re-joiced in my embarrassment. A silly fly who could not see the web, he triumphed over me, saying: 'Insolent liar, son of a liar, and breeder of liars! Where are your threats now? Where is this body of which we have heard so much? Perhaps we will find her before the Sultān's throne!' During this speech I stood against the large un-stoppered oil-jar, with my head bent over it in an attitude of con-trition. Suddenly I threw up my chin, and cried: 'As Allāh lives, I may be wrong, but I seem to smell blood in this jar!' I plunged my hand into the oil and drew it forth, exclaiming: 'Allāh akbar! Allāh akbar! Behold!' and I displayed before the eyes of the kādī and my men the packet which my ingenious friend had left in the jar before she went away. It contained her veil, her head kerchief, her breast kerchief, her drawers, her chemise, her slippers, with other linens which I do not recall, and all were covered with blood.

As the girl had foreseen, the kādī was stricken down by the sight of these things; his face became yellow, his joints turned to water, and he fell head over heels to the floor in a swoon. When I had brought him round, I thought it was my turn to triumph, and so said: 'O our lord the kādī, which of us is the liar now? I can at least thank Allāh that I am cleared from all suspicion of theft, from connivance with the poor young dead. But I do not see how all his wisdom and all his jurisprudence is going to help the kādī! Oh, how could you, a rich man nourished in the laws, reconcile your conscience to such a hideous crime? How could a judge rob and murder a young girl, after, I make no doubt, violating her in the most shameful manners? The Sultān must hear of this at once, for, if I failed in my duty and kept silence, the thing would be sure to come out, and I should lose my office and my head.'

The unfortunate kādī stood before me, with round starting eyes, as if he heard and understood nothing of all this. His agony had stricken him as motionless as a dead tree. Night was upon his spirit, and it was long before he could distinguish his right hand from his left and say to me: 'Good Captain Muīn, this is a most obscure affair, and Allāh alone can understand it. But if you can find it in your duty not to noise the thing abroad, you shall in no sort lose by that.' He fawned upon me and thrust into my arms a sack holding as many dīnārs as he had lost. Thus he bought my silence and extinguished a fire, which might have been fatal to him, while it was still small.

I left him more dead than alive and ran with my news to the girl, who received me with a ripple of laughter, and said to me: 'Now it is certain that he cannot live much longer.' And, in fact, my lord, three days had not passed before I learned that the kādī had died by rupturing his gall bladder. When I went to carry these joyful tidings to the strange lady, I heard from the servants that their mistress had already departed for a property which she owned on the Nile near Tantah, and had taken the kādī's daughter with her. On looking back, I marvelled at that which had passed and, as I still could not understand what two gazelles could do together without one clarinet between them, I made many unsuccessful attempts to get upon their track. I have not yet quite lost hope of hearing news from them, a few words which will instruct me further in this curious love making.

Such is my story, O my lord the Sultān, the strangest adventure which ever came to me in the exercise of those duties with which your royal confidence invested me.

When Captain Muīn al-Dīn had made an end of his tale, a second policeman advanced between the hands of Sultān Bairbars, and, after greeting, said: 'O our lord the Sultān, I also will tell you of an adventure which happened to me personally, and, if Allāh wishes, it will delight you.' Then he said:

The Second Captain's Tale

BEFORE accepting me as a husband, O Sultān, my cousin (Allāh have her in His mercy!) said: 'Let us marry by all means, if such is God's will, but remember that I can only accept you if you agree in advance to the three conditions which I am about to make.' 'I see no objection to that,' I answered. 'But what are the conditions?' Then said she: 'You must never take hashīsh, you must never eat water-melon, and you must never sit on a chair.' 'Your conditions are very hard, my cousin,' I replied, 'but, though I do not understand them, I accept them.' 'That is well,' she exclaimed, 'for they are hard and fast.'

We were married, and all passed as it should. For many years we lived together in tranquil unity. But a day came when my spirit began to be tortured to know the reason of my wife's three conditions, and I said to myself: 'What possible object can she have in forbidding three things which are quite usual and harmless? There is a mystery in the matter which I would give my eyes to penetrate.' As my desire was as great as my curiosity, I entered straightway into the shop of one of my friends and, as a beginning, sat down in a straw-stuffed chair. Then I called for a fine cool water-melon and ate it greedily, and, finally, I absorbed a grain of hashīsh in the last of the fruit and sent my soul in search of fortunate dreams. Because of the hashīsh my soul knew perfect happiness, because of the water-melon my stomach found felicity, and my poor bottom, after all these hard years, discovered ecstasy because of the stuffed chair. But, O Sultān, when I returned home, the band began to play. As soon as she saw me, my wife jumped up and drew her veil across her face, as if I had been a perfect stranger; she looked blackly upon me, and cried: 'O dog, and son of a dog, is this the way you keep your promises? Come with me at once to the kādī, for I insist upon divorce!' As my brain was still exalted by the hashīsh, my belly still pleasantly heavy with the water-melon, and my haunches delightfully rested by the stuffed chair, I boldly denied my three transgressions; but, at my first 'No!' the woman exclaimed: 'Hold your tongue, O pimp! Do you expect me not to believe the evidence of my own senses? You stink of hashīsh, your clothes are covered with droppings of water-melon, and you have pressed your dark and dirty bum so hard upon a chair that the straws have left visible lines about your skirts. Henceforth we are nothing to each other!'

At this point Shahrazād saw the approach of morning and discreetly fell silent.

But when the nine-hundred-and-fortieth night had come

SHE SAID:

She drew her veils about her and dragged me to the kādī's court. When we were in the presence, she cried out: 'O our lord the kādī, your servant was legally married to this abject here, and, before the ceremony, he swore to observe certain conditions. For some time he kept his oath, but now he has broken it, and I demand divorce, together with the return of my dowry and my clothes.' The kādī asked to be told the three conditions, and my wife enumerated them. 'Now this gallows-child has sat on a chair,' she added, 'has eaten a water-melon, and taken hashīsh.' Then she brought forward her proofs, and they were so peremptory that I had not the heart to deny them.

But the kādī had a kind soul and pitied me; therefore, before giving his decree, he said to my wife: 'O daughter of excellent parents, you are within your rights, but it would well become you to be merciful.' Then, as the woman declared in a tempest of words that she would not listen to this plea, the kādī, and all who were by him, tried to persuade her to postpone action until she had had time to reflect. They spoke so feelingly that at last my wife, though ready to argue all day, consented to reconciliation with me, on condition that the kādī would find the answer to a question which she had in mind to put to him. 'I am agreeable,' answered the kādī. 'Ask your question, my good woman.' Then said my wife: 'First I am a bone, then I am a muscle, and finally I am flesh. What am I?' The kādī stroked his beard and reflected for a long time, then he looked at his questioner again, saying: 'To-day I am so wearied by my long session that I cannot answer even the simplest question; but this evening I will consult my books of jurisprudence and, if you care to return to-morrow morning, will have the answer ready for you.'

Soon he dismissed all his pleaders and returned to his house, where he became so immersed in the problem that he forgot the meal which his daughter, a girl of fourteen and a half, had set before him. 'First I am a bone,' he kept on saying half aloud to himself, 'first I am a bone, then I am a muscle, and finally I am flesh. What am I? Yes, by Allāh, what am I? Yes, yes, what is he? Yes, yes, yes, what is it, in Allāh's name?' He searched through his books of jurisprudence, his grammars, and his library of medical works, but could find no hint of an answer and no shadow of a hint of an answer. At last he cried: 'I give it up! There seems to have been no book written on the subject!'

His daughter, who had noticed his preoccupation and heard these last words, questioned him, saying: 'What is the matter, dear father? Why do you groan and rumple your hair?' 'Because I see no issue to a certain problem, my child,' answered the kādī. 'Tell me about it,' urged the little girl, 'for nothing is impossible to the wisdom of Allāh.' So the kādī told her the whole story and repeated my wife's question. 'O father, do you call that difficult?' cried his daughter with a laugh. 'It is as easy as running water. The answer boils down to this: in respect of vigour and consistency a man's zabb is a bone when he is between the ages of fifteen and thirty-five, a muscle when he is between thirty-five and sixty, and, when he has passed sixty, it is nothing but a useless bit of hanging flesh.'

The kādī rejoiced, saying: 'Glory be to Allāh Who gives intelligence to the meanest of His people! You have not only saved my honour, O daughter of benediction, but you have prevented the disruption of a loving family.' He rose impatiently at dawn and ran to the courthouse, where he had to wait for a long time before my wife appeared, dragging me with her. 'O our Lord the kādī,' said my wife, 'do you remember my question and have you found the answer?' 'Glory be to Allāh, Who gave me light!' exclaimed the kādī. 'O daughter of excellent parents, your question was too easy; everybody knows that the zabb of a man from fifteen to thirty-five is like a bone, from thirty-five to sixty like a muscle, and, after sixty, only an inconsequential piece of flesh.'

My wife, who recognised the subtlety of the daughter in this, easily guessed what had happened, and answered slyly: 'As Allāh lives, many who have grown old in the trade could not have done so well! I congratulate you most heartily upon your daughter, my lord! She is only fourteen and a half, but her head is twice as old. I think we may say that her future is assured.'

She signed to me to follow her and quitted the court, leaving the kādī in a vast confusion from which he did not recover for the rest of his days.

When he had thus spoken, the second policeman returned to his place, and Sultān Baibars said to him: 'The tale is strange! The mysteries of Allāh are unfathomable!' Then the third captain, whose name was Izz al-Dīn, came forward and kissed the earth before the throne, saying: 'O King of time, in all my life nothing has happened to me that I consider worthy to be brought to the ears of my lord. But I can tell him a tale which is no less pleasing and prodigious than a personal adventure.' And he said:

The Third Captain's Tale

M Y mother knew a great many stories of the past, and this was one of them:

There dwelt in a country near to the salt sea a fisherman, who was happily married to a very beautiful wife. Every day he would cast his net and, by selling his catch, earn just enough to feed them both. Once, when he fell ill, there was no food in the house for the whole day; so, on the following morning, his wife said to him: 'If you cannot fish, how are we going to live? If you care to rise up now, I will carry your net and your basket, and you shall direct me how to fish. If we only take two little ones, we shall be able to buy supper.' The fisherman agreed to this suggestion and, rising from his bed, made his slow way to a part of the shore at the foot of the Sultān's palace, which he knew to be fertile in fishes. His wife followed him, carrying the basket and the net.

As they walked, the Sultān was watching the sea from his window. When he saw the fisherman's beautiful wife and had feasted his eyes upon her, he felt himself moved with desire. So he called his grand-wazīr to him, saying: 'O wazīr, I have fallen violently in love with that fisherman's wife. There is not her equal for beauty in all my palace.' 'The business is a delicate one, O King of time,' answered the wazīr. 'What shall we do?' 'At least we shall not hesitate,' replied the Sultan. 'Bid the guards seize the man and kill him, and then I shall be able to marry his widow.' But the wazīr, who was a judicious man, objected, saying: 'It is not lawful for you to put him to death, unless you can bring some fault against him. People will accuse you of injustice, and say that you valued a woman more than the life of her husband.' 'That is true,' agreed the Sultan, 'but how else shall I reach to my desire?' 'There is a lawful way,' answered the wazīr after reflection. 'You know that the audience hall of the palace is a full acre in extent. Well, I shall summon the fisherman thither and command him, on pain of death, to cover the whole floor with a single-piece carpet. He will not be able to do this, and we can kill him without any of the people suspecting another motive.' 'Good, good,' replied the Sultan.

The wazīr sent at once for the fisherman and led him into the hall, where the Sultan waited. 'O fisherman,' he said, 'our master the King requires you to cover the floor of this hall with one carpet, woven in a single piece. He allows you three days, and, if in that time you do not bring the carpet, you shall be burnt in the fire. Write an agreement to this effect and seal it with your seal.' 'That is all very well,' replied the fisherman, 'but do you think that I am a man of carpets? I am a man of fish. Ask for every colour and variety of fish and I will bring them to you, but as for carpets, as Allāh lives, they do not know me and I do not know them, not even the smell of them! If it were a question of fish, I would gladly write an undertaking and seal it.' 'Enough of idle words!' cried the wazīr. 'The King has commanded this thing.' 'Then seal it yourself, in Allāh's name!' exclaimed the fisherman. 'Seal it a hundred times if you like!' With that he beat his hands together and ran from the palace in a great rage.

'What has annoyed you?' asked his wife, when he rejoined her. 'Be quiet,' he answered. 'Instead of vexing me with your babble, make our clothes into a bundle, for we must flee from this land.' 'Why?' she asked, and he replied: 'Because the King wishes to kill me in three days.' 'How is that?' she asked again, and, for answer, he told her of the carpet. 'Is that all?' she demanded. 'For if it is you may sleep in peace. I myself will bring you the carpet to-morrow, and you will have nothing to do but spread it out in the King's hall.' 'It needed but this!' cried the exasperated fisherman. 'Have you gone mad, like the wazīr?' But his wife answered: 'Since you seem anxious, you can have the carpet to-day. Listen carefully: go out towards the gardens and you will find a crooked tree which overhangs a well. Put your head over the side, and call: "O So-and-So, your dear friend Such-and-Such gives you greeting and begs you to send her the spindle which she forgot yesterday. We wish to carpet a room with it."' 'Oh, very well,' replied the fisherman.

He walked to the well beneath the twisted tree, and cried down into it: 'O So-and-So, your dear friend Such-and-Such gives you greeting and begs you to send her the spindle which she forgot yesterday. We wish to carpet a room with it.' Then that which was in the well (Allāh alone could describe her more fully!) called up in answer: 'How could I refuse anything to my dear friend? Here is the spindle! When you have finished with it, bring it back to me.' The fisherman caught the spindle, as it was thrown up out of the well, and, placing it in his pocket, returned home. 'The woman has made me as mad as she is!' he muttered as he went along; but, when he came into the presence of his wife, he said: 'Here is the spindle.' 'Good,' she answered. 'Now go to this calamitous wazīr and ask him for a large nail. When he gives it to you, you must drive it into the floor at one end of the hall and fasten the thread of the spindle to it. Then, as you move away, the carpet will unfold itself.' At these words the fisherman lost confidence, and cried: 'Do you want people to laugh at me and take me for a fool before I die?' But his wife grew angry, and retorted: 'Be quiet and do as I say!' So the fisherman carried the spindle to the palace and, as he went, murmured to himself: 'There is no power or might save in Allāh! This is the last day of your life, O most unfortunate man!'

At this point Shahrazād saw the approach of morning and discreetly fell silent.

But when the nine-hundred-and-forty-first night had come

SHE SAID:

When he came into the presence, the wazīr asked him where the carpet might be, and he answered that it was in his pocket. Both the wazīr and the Sultān burst out laughing at this, and said to each other: 'Here is a man who jests before his death!' Also the wazīr mocked, and asked: 'Is an acre of carpet to be carried in the pocket like a child's ball?' 'What is that to you?' replied the fisherman. 'You asked for a carpet and I have brought you a carpet. There the matter ends. If, instead of laughing at me, you would stir your stumps and get me a large nail, I could spread the carpet at once and go my way.'

As the wazīr rose with a smile and fetched the nail, he whispered to the Sultān's executioner: 'Stay here near the door and, when the fisherman fails to lay the carpet, strike off his head without waiting for further orders.' The sword-bearer bowed, and the wazīr handed the nail to the fisherman, saying: 'Now let us see the carpet!'

The fisherman hammered in the nail at the end of the hall and fastened the beginning of the thread to it; then he started to turn the spindle, saying: 'Spin my death, vile thing!' But lo! a magnificent carpet began to stretch out from the nail and had soon covered the whole space of the floor with a fabric of unequalled beauty. The King and the wazīr looked at each other in stupefaction for a whole hour, while the fisherman stood before them calmly and in silence. At length the wazīr winked at the King in knowing fashion, and said to the fisherman: 'The King is content with this, but he has another thing to ask. He requires you to bring him a little boy not more than eight days old, and he insists that the little boy shall tell him a story which is a tissue of lies from beginning to end.'

'Is that all?' cried the fisherman. 'That will be quite easy, if you will be so good as to place the new-born children of all the Jinn at my disposition!' 'Be quiet!' answered the wazīr. 'The word and the desire of the King must have their course. We give you eight days in which to find the child, but, if you fail, you shall most certainly taste red death before our eyes. Write out an agreement to this effect and set your seal to it.' 'Here is my seal, but I do not know how to use it,' objected the fisherman. 'I know something of fish and something of carpets, but of seals and lying babies I know nothing. Put a hundred seals to the thing if you like! As for me, I put my trust in Allāh.' The wazīr took the seal and set it to the agreement, while the fisherman ran out of the palace in a royal rage.

When he came into his wife's presence, he cried: 'Rise up now, for we must flee from this land. I told you once and you would not listen to me. Rise up now, for I am off.' 'But why?' she asked. 'Did no carpet come from the spindle?' 'The carpet came,' he answered, 'but that pimp, that wazīr of my arse, that son of a bitch, now insists that I shall provide him with a little boy, less than eight days old, and that the boy shall tell the Sultān a tale filled with lies from beginning to end. Out of his great generosity he has given me eight days in which to do the thing.' 'Good,' said his wife, 'we at least have time in which to concoct a plan.'

On the ninth morning the fisherman said to his wife: 'Have you forgotten about the little boy? This is the final day!' 'Then I will tell you what to do,' she answered. 'Go to the well beneath the twisted tree. Then, after you have given back the spindle with a few words of polite thanks, you must say: "O So-and-So, your dear friend Such-and-Such sends you greeting and begs you to lend her the boy who was born yesterday, for we have need of him in a certain matter."'

'As Allāh lives,' cried the fisherman, 'unless it be that pitch-faced wazīr, I know no more perfect fool than you! He at least permits the child to be eight days old, but you insist on lowering my chances by seven days.' 'That is no concern of yours,' she answered tartly. 'Go, and do as I say!' 'Very well,' he grumbled, as he left the house, 'since you want me out of the way, this is as good a plan as any.'

When he came to the well, he threw the spindle into it, calling down: 'Here is the spindle!' Then he added: 'O So-and-So, your dear friend Such-and-Such sends you greeting and begs you to lend her the boy who was born yesterday, for we have need of him in a certain matter. And for Allāh's sake be quick, for my head is not steady upon my shoulders!' Then that which was in the well (Allāh alone can describe her more fully!) called up in answer: 'Take the child, and say over him the words against the evil eye.' So the fisherman took the child which was handed up to him and said: 'In the name of Allāh, the Merciful, the Compassionate!'

As he went his way with the infant, he thought: 'Surely the children of the most powerful Jinn, even when they have reached their thirtieth day, could not talk and tell such tales as are required from this little one.' To set his doubts at rest he spoke to the swathed bundle in his arms, saying: 'Come, my child, talk to me a little, for I wish to know whether or not this is the day of my death.' Hearing his loud voice, the boy became frightened and, contracting both his face and belly, did after the manner of all bantlings; that is to say, he wept with terrible grimaces and pissed to the full extent of his power. The fisherman was both soaked and angry when he came into his wife's presence. 'Here is the child,' he said, 'but Allāh protect me from such children! The little devil knows how to cry and piss, but that is the extent of his wisdom. My garment is spoilt for ever.' 'That is no concern of yours,' answered his wife. 'Pray for the Prophet, O man, and do exactly as I tell you. Carry this infant to the

Sultān, and you will soon see whether he can talk or not. Only be sure to demand three cushions for him, and, when you have set him on the middle of a couch, put one on each side of him and one at his back. Also pray for the Prophet.' So the fisherman answered: 'On him be prayer and peace!' and went his way, with the child in his arms.

When the wazīr saw the fisherman arrive with his swaddled burden, he broke into a laugh, and addressed the infant in such tones as are used when speaking to a baby. 'There's a pretty!' he said; but, instead of speaking, the child screwed up his nose and mouth, and made a noise like: 'Mees! mees!' The wazīr ran in delight to the King, and whispered to him: 'I have spoken to the child but he has not answered; instead he has wept and made a noise like: "Mees! mees!" The fisherman is nearing his end. Now only remains for us to put him to confusion before all the amīrs and notables, and then cut off his head.'

The Sultān immediately summoned all his amīrs and notables, and accompanied his wazīr into the hall of justice. When all were in their places, the fisherman was introduced, and the wazīr, after reading aloud the sealed agreement, bade him bring forward the child. 'First I must have three cushions,' said the fisherman, 'then you shall hear what you shall hear.' Three cushions were brought, and the unfortunate man, after setting the baby in the middle of a couch, consolidated him with them. 'Is this the child who is going to tell us our tissue of lies?' asked the King.

Before the fisherman had time to answer, the one-day-old child remarked: 'Before all, greeting, O King!' Amid an astonished silence the no less astonished King returned this salutation, and said: 'Now, O Learned, I beg you to tell me some story which shall be one jam of lies.' 'Once, when I was in the prime of my young manhood,' began the child forthwith, 'I walked in the fields outside the city during the heat of the day, and, because I was thirsty, bought a water-melon from a man for one gold dīnār. When I had cut a slice and swallowed it with great delight, I looked inside the melon and saw there a city complete with its citadel. Without hesitating, I stepped over the rim, one leg at a time, and found myself inside the fruit. For a long time I wandered, looking at the shops and houses, until I came at length to the suburban fields. There I saw a date tree bearing a multitude of dates, each an ell long, and, as I hungered for dates, I climbed up into the tree to eat a few. But I found a quantity of peasants sowing seed among the dates, and cutting the ears, and flailing and husking the corn. I passed by these and met a man who was beating eggs upon a threshing-floor; as I watched him, I noticed chickens coming out of the eggs as they were beaten flat. The little cocks walked off to one side and the little hens to the other. At once I married the little cocks and the little hens, and, leaving them content, walked off along another branch. Soon I met a donkey, carrying a load of sesame cakes, and, being extremely partial to such things, helped myself to one of them. But as soon as I had swallowed it down, I found myself outside the water-melon and beheld the fruit close and become complete as it had been before. Such is my story, O Sultān.'

Hearing such words from one swaddled and newly born, the King cried out: 'Oh, ho, ho! O sheikh and crown of liars! Oh, ho, ho, my Learned, I swear there is not one word of truth in what you have said! Do you really think that we believe a single syllable of that devilish tale? Allāh, Allāh! Since when have there been cities inside water-melons, since when have chickens come out of eggs which have been beaten flat on a threshing-floor? Confess, O Learned, that you made the whole thing up.' 'I confess nothing and I deny nothing,' answered the child. 'Neither should you, O King, deny the real reason for your persecution of this fisherman. You wish to kill him because you saw his beautiful wife on the strand and lusted after her. Was this worthy of one rich in kingship? I swear, by Allāh and the virtues of the Prophet (upon whom be prayer and peace!). that, if you do not leave this man and his wife in quiet from now on, I shall so cleanse the world of men from you and your wazīr that not even the flies shall find a trace of you.'

When he had spoken these things in a terrifying voice, the child turned to the fisherman, saying: 'Now, uncle, take me up and carry me back to your house.' The fisherman took up little Learned and left the palace, no man staying him. As soon as he arrived home and told his wife of what had happened, she bade him take back the baby to the well, with many thanks; and this he did. When the infant had been received by that which dwelt in the well beneath the crooked tree, the fisherman returned to his house and, after ablution and prayer, did his usual with his delightful wife. From that time they lived together in prosperity and peace. So much for them.

When he had made an end of this tale, the third captain of police returned to his place, and Sultān Baibars said: 'An excellent story! But it was a pity, O Izz al-Dīn, that you had no further complication to tell us, no later strife between the Sultān and the fisherman.' Then the fourth captain, whose name was Muhyī al-Dīn, came forward, saying: 'O King, if you will give me leave, I will tell you the rest of that tale; for the end is more astonishing than the beginning.' 'With all my heart!' cried Sultān Baibars and Muhyī said:

The Fourth Captain's Tale

O KING of time, a man-child was born to that fisherman and his fair wife, and they called him Muhammad Learned, in memory of the miraculous infant who had saved them upon a certain day. And the son was as beautiful as his mother.

The Sultān also had a son of the same age; but he was ugly, and as dark in the face as any hind.

The two children went to the same school to learn to read and write, and, when the King's son, who was lazy and in a low class, saw the fisherman's son, who was studious and in a high class, he would say to him: 'Good morning, O fisherman's son!' Knowing that this was intended as an affront, little Muhammad Learned would answer: 'Good morning, O King's son! May your face be whitened, for it is as black as the strap of an old clog.' For a year the two children saluted each other in this way every morning, and at last, in a fit of rage, the King's son told his father that the fisherman's son ever drew attention to the fact that his face was as black as the strap of an old clog. The Sultān was angry but he dared not himself punish Muhammad, because of what had gone before. Instead, he called the schoolmaster before him, saying: 'O Sheikh, if you were by chance to kill little Muhammad, the fisherman's son, I would give you a fine present and send you many concubines together with fair white slaves.' 'My life is yours, O King of time,' answered the delighted old man. 'I will beat the little scoundrel every day until he dies.'

So, when little Learned went to school on the next day, the master bade the rest of his pupils fetch the stick and hold the poor child down. The boys seized Muhammad and, placing his feet in a wooden vice, stretched him out on the ground. Then the master beat him upon the soles, until the blood gushed out and his legs were all inflamed. 'You shall have another dose to-morrow, you little blockhead!' he cried. But Muhammad, as soon as he was loosed, fled through the door and ran all the way home. He sought his mother and father, and said to them: 'Look, look! The schoolmaster has beaten me almost to death because of the Sultān's son! I shall not go to school any more. I want to become a fisherman like my father.' The man at once gave him a net and basket, saying: 'Very well, my son. Here are the tools of our trade. To-morrow you may go out and see whether you can earn your keep.'

At dawn next morning Muhammad went down and cast his net into the sea; but, when he withdrew it, he found that he had caught only one little red mullet. 'I shall roast it in its scales,' he said, 'and eat it for my breakfast.' He collected a handful of dry grass and twigs, and, after lighting them, picked up the fish; but the red mullet opened her mouth, and said: 'Do not roast me, Muhammad! I am one of the Queens of the sea and, if you will throw me back into the water, I promise to come to your help in any time of trouble.' 'Very well,' replied Muhammad, and he cast the red mullet back into the sea. So much for her.

At this point Shahrazād saw the approach of morning and discreetly fell silent.

But when the nine-hundred-and-forty-second night had come

SHE SAID:

At the end of two days the Sultān called the schoolmaster into his presence, saying: 'Have you killed the boy Muhammad?' 'I gave him the stick on that first day until he swooned,' answered the old man. 'Then he fled, and I have not seen him since. I hear that he has turned fisherman like his father.' 'Begone, you son of a dog!' cried the Sultān. 'May your father be cursed, may your daughter mate with a pig!'

Then he called his wazīr, and said to him: 'The boy is not dead. What shall we do?' 'I have found a way,' answered the wazīr. 'I have heard tell of a very beautiful girl, who is the daughter of the Sultān of Green Country. Her kingdom is seven years' journey from this place. We will summon the fisherman's son, and I shall say to him: "Our master the Sultān has you in his favour and lays great store by your valour. He requires you to go to Green Country and bring back the daughter of its King, for he wishes to marry her and knows that no one can succeed in the quest except yourself."' 'An excellent plan!' exclaimed the Sultān. 'Let the boy be sent for at once!'

The wazīr hailed the protesting Muhammad into the presence, and said to him: 'Our master the Sultān has you in his favour and sets great store by your valour. He requires you to go to Green Country and bring back the daughter of its King, for he wishes to marry her and knows that no one can succeed in the quest except yourself.' 'And since when have I known the way to that place?' objected the boy; but the wazīr answered: 'It is the King's will!' So Muhammad went forth in a rage and told to his mother what had happened. 'Walk with your trouble by the riverside, near to where it joins the sea, my son,' she said, 'and your trouble will stand off from you.' At once her son walked with his trouble by the riverside near to where it joined the sea.

As he wandered here and there, the red mullet came up out of the water, and asked: 'Why are you angry, Muhammad Learned?' 'Do not ask me,' he replied, 'for the thing is hopeless.' 'Hope is in the hand of Allāh,' said the fish, 'therefore tell me of your trouble.' 'O red mullet,' answered Muhammad, 'that pitch-faced wazīr has bidden me set forth in search of the King's daughter of Green Country.' Then said the mullet: 'There is no difficulty in that. Go at once to the King and tell him that you will undertake the expedition if he builds you a river boat of pure gold at his wazīr's expense.'

Muhammad went straightway and made this demand of the King, who at once built him a river boat of pure gold at the wazīr's expense, and greatly against that person's will. When all was ready, the boy boarded his gold boat and set forth up the river.

His friend, the red mullet, swam before him, showing his course and leading him by a network of inland waterways, until he came to Green Country. On his arrival he sent the public crier through the streets to cry: 'Men, women and children, all are welcome to come down to the riverside to see the gold boat of Muhammad Learned, the fisherman's son!'

So all the people of that city, great and small, men and women, came down and regarded the gold boat for eight whole days. And the King's daughter, hearing a rumour of this, sought leave of her father, saying: 'I wish to go and see the gold boat, like everyone else.' The King consented and made proclamation that neither man, woman, nor child should leave the house that day, because the princess wished to go and see the gold boat.

When the King's daughter had taken her fill from the bank of that delightful sight, she signed to Muhammad to ask if she might come on board and see the interior of his boat; as soon as the boy had given permission with his eyes, she stepped on to the gold deck and began to look about her. But when Learned saw that her attention was well occupied with the bright fittings, he silently lifted the rope and stake, and dropped down stream.

Soon the princess of Green Country wished to go ashore and lifted up her eyes. When she saw that the boat was in motion and had already passed far beyond her father's city, she sought out the mullet's friend, and asked him: 'O Learned, whither are you taking me?' 'To a King who will be your bridegroom,' replied Muhammad. 'And is this King handsomer than you, O Learned?' said the girl. 'I do not know,' he answered. 'Soon you will be able to see for yourself.' At this she drew a ring from her finger and threw it into the stream (but the red mullet took it in her mouth and swam on to show the way) and said with a smile: 'I will never marry anyone but you. I give myself to you freely now.' So Muhammad took her pleasant virginity and rejoiced with her upon the water.

When they came to their destination, the fisherman's son sought out the King, and said to him: 'I have brought you the daughter of the Sultān of Green Country; but she says that she will not come out of the boat until you stretch a green carpet for her to walk on from the river to the palace. She will walk upon it in great beauty and grace.' 'Be it so,' answered the Sultān, and he bought, at the expense of his wazīr and much against that person's will, all the green silk carpets in all the markets, and spread them from the palace to the boat.

Then the princess of Green Country came down, clothed all in green, out of the gold boat, and walked, with gentle balancing, over the green silk carpets, so that the King saw her and desired her. As soon as she reached the palace, he said: 'I will have our marriage contract written out this evening.' 'If you wish to marry me,' answered the princess, 'you must first bring me the ring which fell from my hand into the river, while I was being carried to you.'

But the red mullet had already given this ring to Muhammad Learned, the fisherman's son.

The King called his wazīr to him, saying: 'Listen: this lady's ring has fallen into the river and she requires it to be brought to her. What shall we do now? Who shall find it for us?' 'Who but Muhammad?' answered the wazīr. 'For surely he is an Ifrīt and given over to evil.' This he said in order that the boy might be lost beyond recall.

At once the King sent for Muhammad and bade him find the ring;
but Muhammad held it out, saying: 'That is easy.'

As he returned the ring to the princess, the Sultān bade her prepare
for the marriage. 'I am ready,' she answered. 'But in our country
there is a certain custom.' 'And what custom is that?' asked the King.
'They dig a ditch from the bridegroom's house down to the sea,'
she replied. 'The ditch is filled with faggots and branches, and these
are set on fire. The suitor then casts himself into the trench and walks
through it down to the sea, where he bathes before seeking his
bride. Thus is he purified both by fire and water. Such is the marriage ceremony of Green Country.'

At this point Shahrazād saw the approach of morning and
discreetly fell silent.

But when the nine-hundred-and-forty-third night had come

SHE SAID:

Because he greatly loved the girl, the King ordered a trench to be
dug down to the sea, and filled with faggots and branches; then he
called his wazīr to him, saying: 'To-morrow you must be ready to
walk through the fire with me.'

On the following morning, when the time came to set light to this
strange river, the wazīr said to his master: 'It would be better for
Muhammad, the fisherman's son, to make trial of the flames first. If
he comes out unscathed, we can follow him in all confidence.'
'Good,' said the King.

Meanwhile the red mullet had climbed up on board the gold boat
and had said to her friend Muhammad: 'If the King bids you throw
yourself into the fire, O Learned, you need not be afraid. You have
only to plug your ears and breathe the saving words: "In the name of
Allāh, the Merciful, the Compassionate!"'

So, when the King set light to the wood in the trench and bade
Muhammad walk through the flames down to the sea, the youth replied: 'Be it upon my head and before my eyes!' He plugged his ears
and, murmuring the saving words, went down resolutely into the
fire. He came out into the sea looking more beautiful than ever, and
all the people marvelled at his appearance.

Then said the wazīr to the King: 'My lord, the flames will make us
as handsome as that devil's brat. Therefore let your son go with us,
that he may become as fair as we.' The King called his son, the ugly

child whose face was coloured like the strap of an old clog, and the three took hands upon the trench's brink. They leapt together into the fire and were immediately shrivelled up to ashes.

Then Muhammad Learned, the fisherman's son, sought out the princess of Green Country and married her. He sat upon the throne of the empire, and became both King and Sultān. He called his father and mother to him, to share his glory, and all four lived together in harmony and gladness, in prosperity and peace. Glory be to Allāh Who is the Master of peace and prosperity, the Giver of harmony and gladness!

When Muhyī al-Din had finished this story and been thanked by Sultān Baibars, his place was taken by another policeman, whose name was Nūr-al-Dīn. This man kissed the earth between the Sultān's hands, saying: 'O our lord and crown upon our head, I will tell you a tale which has not its equal among tales!' And he told:

The Fifth Captain's Tale

THERE was once a Sultān who called his wazīr to him, saying: 'O wazīr, I require you to have a seal drawn out and engraved which shall have this power over me when I wear it, that, if I am glad, I cannot become angry, and, if I am angry, I cannot rejoice. He who makes the seal must guarantee that it will have this power. And I allow you three days.'

The wazīr went to the seal makers of that city and required from them a seal according to the specification of the King; but none of them would undertake so difficult a task. So he rose up in a rage, saying to himself: 'I will not find it in this city. I must seek elsewhere.'

He went out through the gates and walked across the countryside, until he came upon an Arab sheikh thrashing corn in his field. 'Peace be with you, O sheikh of the Arabs!' he said, and the man returned his salute, asking: 'Where do you go, good sir, in this great heat?' 'I go upon the Sultān's business,' answered the wazīr. 'What business is that?' demanded the old man; and the wazīr said: 'I seek a seal which shall have this power, that, when the Sultān wears it, if he be glad, he cannot become angry, and, if he be angry, he cannot rejoice.' 'Since that is all your trouble,' replied the sheikh, 'sit down and I will bring you food.'

The Arab went to his daughter Yásamín, and said to her: 'O Yásamín, make ready a meal for our guest.' 'Whence comes he?' she asked and, when her father told her that the wazír came from the Sultán, demanded to know the object of his journey. Therefore the sheikh gave her the story of the seal, but nothing would be gained by repeating it in this place.

Yásamín of the Arabs made a dish with thirty eggs and much sweet butter, which she gave to her father with eight rolls of bread, saying: 'Carry this to the stranger and tell him that Yásamín of the Arabs will write his seal for him. Tell him that the month has thirty days, that the sea is full at this hour, and that there are eight days in a week.' 'Very well,' replied the sheikh, and he set forth, with the dish held carefully before him.

As he walked, the melted butter slopped over on to his hand, so he set down the dish and, after wiping his hand with one of the rolls, ate that and also an egg which took his fancy. Then he bore the dish to the wazír, saying: 'My daughter, Yásamín of the Arabs, greets you and says that she will write your seal. She also says that the month has thirty days, the sea is full at this hour, and there are eight days in a week.' 'Let us eat first,' answered the wazír. 'Afterwards we can consider the meaning of her words.'

But, when he had examined the dish and eaten his fill, the wazír said to the Arab: 'Tell her that she may write my seal, but that there is one day missing from the month, the sea is dry, and there are only seven days in this week.' The sheikh carried this message to his daughter and, as soon as she had heard it, she cried: 'Are you not ashamed of yourself, my father? You not only set down the dish on the way and ate one of the eggs and one of the rolls, but you took the dish to our guest without butter.' 'By Allah, that is true!' exclaimed her father. 'But the whole thing was an accident.' Then said Yásamín of the Arabs: 'Let us prepare the seal.'

She prepared the seal, with a weaving of these words: 'All feeling, whether it be joy or pain, must come from Allah.' When it was completed, she sent it to the wazír, who departed with a multitude of thanks.

The King read the inscription upon the seal and asked his messenger who had drawn it out. 'A young girl called Yásamín of the Arabs,' answered the wazír; and immediately the King rose to his feet, saying: 'Lead me to her father's house that I may marry her.'

The two set out hand in hand and, when they found the sheikh of

the Arabs, thus addressed him: 'O honourable, we seek alliance with
your line.' 'You are welcome!' he answered. 'But through whom do
you seek it?' 'Through your daughter, Yāsamīn of the Arabs,'
answered the wazīr. 'This is our master, the King, and he wishes to
marry her.' 'That is well!' said the sheikh. 'But, though we are your
slaves, my daughter must be set in the scales and balanced with gold;
for she is very dear to her father's heart.' 'It is permitted,' replied the
wazīr.

As soon as gold had been fetched from the palace, Yāsamīn sat in
one of the trays of the balance and dīnārs were poured into the other,
until the weights were equal. Then a marriage contract was drawn
out; the King gave a great feast to the Arab village and that night,
lying at her father's house, rejoiced in the virginity of Yāsamīn. In
the morning he departed with her and installed her in his palace.

But, when she had stayed in the palace for a few weeks, Yāsamīn
of the Arabs began to pine and dwindle; so the King called the
doctor and said to him: 'Go up quickly and examine Yāsamīn of the
Arabs, for I cannot tell why she pines and dwindles.' The doctor
went up to the Queen's apartment and soon came down to the King.
'She is not used to cities,' he said. 'She is a daughter of the fields, and
here her breast is straitened for lack of air.' 'What is to be done?'
asked the King, and the hakīm replied after consideration: 'Build her
a palace by the sea and she will soon become more beautiful even
than before.' The King gave immediate orders for his masons to
build a palace by the sea and, when their work was finished, caused
the languishing Yāsamīm to be carried thither.

At this point Shahrazād saw the approach of morning and
discreetly fell silent.

But when the nine-hundred-and-forty-fourth night had come

SHE SAID:

But, after Yāsamīn of the Arabs had dwelt some time in that
palace, she became plump again and lost her languor. One day, as
she leaned out of her window and regarded the sea, a fisherman came
to the shore below her and cast his net. When he drew it up filled
with shards and shells, Yāsamīn called down to him: 'Cast this time
in my name and I will give you a golden dīnār for your catch!' So
the fisherman cast in Yāsamīn's name and drew a copper flask to land.
The Queen muffled herself in her bed sheet, in place of a veil, and

ran down to the fisherman, crying: 'Here is a dīnār, give me the flask!' But the fisherman answered: 'By Allāh, I will only let you have it for a kiss upon your cheek!

As they spoke together, the King came upon them and, after passing his sword through the fisherman's heart, threw the body into the sea. Then he turned to Yāsamīn of the Arabs, saying: 'Go where you will, for I shall not look upon you again!'

Yāsamīn went from that place and walked, fasting and without water, for two days, until she came to a certain city. From morning till noon she sat at the door of a shop in the market, and at last the owner spoke to her, saying: 'Lady, though you are welcome to sit before my shop from morning till noon, I would fain know your reason for doing so.' 'I am a stranger,' she answered, 'I know no one in this city, and I have neither eaten nor drunken for two days.' At once the merchant called his negro slave. 'Lead this lady to my house,' he said, 'and tell them to give her food and drink.' So the negro led Yāsamīn to the house, and said to the merchant's wife: 'My master bids you give food and drink to this honourable stranger.' The woman looked at Yāsamīn and became jealous of her beauty; therefore she bade the slave conduct her guest to the hen-house, which was upon the terrace; and the negro did so.

Yāsamīn remained in the hen-house until evening, then, since no refreshment had been brought to her, she remembered the copper flask. 'Perhaps there is a little water in it,' she said, as she turned the stopper with her fingers. Immediately a basin and ewer came up out of the flask, and, when Yāsamīn had used them for washing her hands, they were followed by a tray of excellent meats and wines, so that she was able to eat and drink and sit content. When she turned the stopper again, ten young white slaves came up out of the flask, with crotals in their hands, and began to dance upon the floor of the hen-house. With the last movement of their dancing, each threw ten purses filled with gold into Yāsamīn's lap and returned into the flask.

For three days the girl remained unnoticed in the hen-house, eating and drinking of the best and beguiling her weariness with the skill of the white dancers. And, as she received ten times ten purses of dīnārs for each dance, the hen-house was soon filled to the top with gold.

On the fourth morning the negro slave, coming on to the terrace to satisfy a need, saw Yāsamīn in the hen-house and was astonished, for his mistress had told him that the guest had departed long ago. 'Has your master sent you with food and drink for me,' asked Yāsamīn, 'or does he wish my state to be more wretched than it was before his invitation?' 'O lady,' answered the slave, 'my master thought that they had immediately given you bread and that you had departed.' He ran to the shop and sought out the merchant, saying: 'That unfortunate woman, whom you bade me lead home, has been three days in the hen-house on the terrace without food or drink.' The kind-hearted merchant flew into a rage; he shut up his shop and ran home to his wife. 'Vile wretch,' he cried, 'you have kept our guest without food or drink!' and, so saying, he beat the woman with a stick until his arm could rise no more. Then he took bread, with other necessaries, and, climbing up to the terrace, said to Yāsamīn: 'Eat heartily, poor soul, and do not blame me too greatly for my forgetfulness.' 'Allāh increase you,' she replied, 'for I am as grateful as if your charities had reached their goal! If you would set a crown upon your kindness, do me this final favour: build me a palace outside the city which shall be twice as beautiful as the King's.' 'Certainly, certainly,' answered the merchant, and Yāsamīn continued: 'Here is gold. Take as much as you need, and pay the masons four dirhams instead of one for each day's work, if that will hasten them.'

The merchant took the money with a bow. He called together the architects and masons of that city, and these had soon built a palace twice as beautiful as the King's. When he had returned to the hen-house and informed his mistress that the work was finished, she gave him more gold and begged him to furnish the palace all in satin, and to collect negro servants who should know no word of Arabic. The merchant furnished the palace gloriously, collected Berber servants who knew no Arabic, and then returned to the terrace, saying: 'O my mistress, your home is now complete. Have the goodness to come and take possession.' But, before leaving her strange abiding place, Yāsamīn turned to the merchant with a smile, saying: 'The hen-house is full to the ceiling with new gold. Take it as a gift from me, for you have been very kind.' So much for the merchant.

Yāsamīn entered her palace and dressed herself in a royal robe of great magnificence, so that when she sat upon the throne there, she had the appearance of a handsome king. So much for her.

A few days after he had killed the fisherman and sent his queen away, the Sultān became calm; and for the whole of one night his thoughts were busy with Yāsamīn. In the morning he called his wazīr to him, saying: 'Let us disguise ourselves and set forth in quest of my lost lady.' So the two disguised themselves and wandered far, asking and listening, until they came to the city where Yāsamīn dwelt and beheld her palace rising to the sky. 'This building is new,' said the King, 'I have never seen it before in my journeys. To whom can it belong?' 'I do not know,' answered the wazīr, 'but perhaps it was built by some invading King, who has conquered the city without our knowledge.' 'By Allāh, you may be right!' exclaimed the Sultān. 'We can find out for certain by having proclamation made through the city that no light must be shown from any dwelling to-night. That will determine whether the folk in the palace are obedient subjects or invading kings.'

The proclamation was made, and, when night came, the Sultān and his wazīr walked through the city and beheld no light in any building save the new palace, which was splendidly illuminated and filled with singing and the sound of lutes. 'I was right!' exclaimed the wazīr; yet the Sultān would not be satisfied until he had questioned the doorkeeper. But the negro who stood upon the marble steps had come from Barbary and knew no Arabic; therefore he answered each inquiry with: 'Shanu!' which signifies in the Berber tongue: 'I do not know.' So the King and his wazīr were forced to depart unsatisfied, and could not sleep that night because of fear.

On the next day the Sultān had the same proclamation made, but, when he and his wazīr went their round that night, the palace was more than twice as brightly lighted as before. 'I was right!' exclaimed the wazīr. 'You were right,' answered the Sultān, 'but what shall we do now?' 'Sleep,' replied the wazīr, 'for the evil of to-morrow will come to-morrow.'

And the next day the wazīr said: 'Let us walk up and down in front of the palace like all the rest; then, if Allāh favours me, I shall creep into the building and find out something of this King.'

The Sultān readily agreed to the plan. While he held the door-keeper in uncomprehended conversation, the wazīr crept unseen into the palace and made his stealthy way to the throne hall. He saluted Yāsamīn, taking her to be a young King, and she cordially bade him be seated. She knew him instantly, in spite of his disguise, and was not ignorant of her husband's presence in the city; but she turned the stopper of her copper flask and, after giving refreshment to the wazīr, bade him keep the consequent gold. 'It is a gift, for I can see that you are poor,' she said; and the wazīr kissed her hand, as he answered: 'May Allāh grant you victory over all your foes, O King of time, and indefinitely prolong your days for our delight!' Then he took leave and descended to rejoin the King.

'What did you learn?' asked the King, and the wazīr answered: 'By Allāh, I was right when I told you that the city had been invaded! He gave me a hundred purses of gold to ease my poverty! Can you doubt that I was right?' 'Perhaps there is something in what you say,' replied the Sultān. 'But I think that I also will elude the vigilance of these Berbers and see for myself.'

Yāsamīn of the Arabs pretended not to know her lord. She rose in his honour and bade him be seated. Such submissive conduct reassured the Sultān, and he said to himself: 'This is a subject and not a King.' When he had eaten and drunken, he steeled himself to ask what might be the quality of those who dwelt in the palace, and Yāsamīn smiled, as she answered: 'We are rich, very rich.' As she spoke she turned the stopper of the flask, and ten white dazzling slaves came forth to dance to the crotals. When they had finished, each cast, as ever, ten purses into Yāsamīn's lap.

At this point Shahrazād saw the approach of morning and discreetly fell silent.

But when the nine-hundred-and-forty-fifth night had come

SHE SAID:

The King marvelled exceedingly at the flask, and cried: 'Will you tell me where you bought that prodigy, my brother?' 'I did not buy it,' she answered. 'I begged it from the owner in exchange for anything he wished. He would not sell it, but agreed to give it to me if I would once do cock and hen with him. I consented, and thus obtained the flask.'

Now Yāsamin only told this lie because she had an idea.

'You took an excellent and easy way!' exclaimed the Sultān. 'If you would care to give me the flask, I will readily consent to play that game twice instead of once.' 'Twice is not enough,' answered Yāsamīn. 'Then you may do it to me four times for the flask,' agreed the Sultān eagerly. So Yāsamīn bade him come into another room, and he rose and followed her.

But, as soon as the Queen saw the King kneel down and adopt

that posture which was necessary for the completion of the bargain, she laughed so heartily that she fell over on her backside. 'The name of Allāh be upon you and about you, O King of time!' she cried. 'You are a Sultān, and yet you would be buggered for a flask! How can you reconcile that with your rash slaying of the fisherman who only asked me a kiss upon the cheek for it?'

At first the Sultān was speechless with surprise. Then he began to laugh, saying: 'Is it you? Is all this coil from you?' He gave her the kiss of reconciliation, and the two lived thenceforth together in prosperous harmony. Glory be to Allāh from Whom all harmony and all prosperity must come!

When Nūr al-Dīn had made an end of this tale, the delighted Baibars praised him for it, in Allāh's name. Then a sixth policeman, whose name was Jamāl al-Din, advanced to the foot of the throne, saying: 'O King of time, by your leave I will tell you a most pleasing story.' 'You have our leave,' said Baibars, and Jamāl al-Dīn began:

The Sixth Captain's Tale

THERE was once a Sultān who had a very beautiful daughter, well-loved and petted and most elegant. Therefore she was called Dalāl.

One day, as she sat scratching her head, she caught a little louse; she looked at it for a long time and then carried it in her fingers to the provision cellar, which was filled with large jars of oil, butter and honey. Opening a big oil jar, she set the louse down gently upon the surface of its contents and then, replacing the lid, went her way.

Days and years passed by, and Princess Dalāl reached her fifteenth year, with no memory at all of the louse and its imprisonment.

But one day the louse broke the jar by its great bulk and came forth with the appearance of a Nile buffalo. The cellar guard fled in terror, calling loudly to the servants for help; and at length the louse was caught by the horns and led into the presence of the King.

'What is this?' cried the astonished monarch; and Dalāl, who was standing near, exclaimed: 'Yeh, yeh! It is my louse! When I was little, I found it in my head and fastened it in an oil jar. Now it has become so big that it has broken its prison.'

'My daughter,' answered the King, 'it is high time that you were married. The louse has broken his jar, and to-morrow we shall have you breaking your wall and going to men. Allāh protect us from such breakages!'

Then he turned to his wazīr, and said: 'Cut the thing's throat, flay it, and hang its skin to the palace gate. Then go forth, with my executioner and chief scribe, for I intend to marry my daughter to the man who can recognise the skin for what it is. Those suitors who fail shall have their heads cut off and their hides hung beside the louse.'

The wazīr cut the throat of the louse in that same hour and, after flaying it, hung its skin to the palace gate. Then he sent a herald about the city to proclaim: 'He who can recognise the skin upon the palace door for what it is shall marry the Lady Dalāl, daughter of our King; but he who fails to recognise it shall have his head cut off.' Many of the young men of the city defiled before the dubious hide; some said that it had belonged to a buffalo, some that it had been taken from a wild goat; and thus forty lost their heads and had their skins hung up beside the louse.

At this point Shahrazād saw the approach of morning and discreetly fell silent.

But when the nine-hundred-and-forty-sixth night had come

SHE SAID:

Then there passed a youth who was as fair as the star Canopus shining upon the sea. When he was informed that the suitor who recognised the skin for what it was might marry the King's daughter, he went up to the wazīr, the executioner and the chief scribe, saying: 'It is the skin of a louse which has grown great in oil.'

'True, true, O excellent young man!' they cried, and led him into the presence of the King. When he stood before the throne, he said: 'It is the skin of a louse grown great in oil.' And the King exclaimed: 'True, true! Let the marriage contract be written out at once.'

The wedding took place on the same day, and that night the star-like youth rejoiced in the virgin Dalāl, who learned all the beauty of love in his arms, for he was like the star Canopus shining upon the sea.

They stayed together for forty days in the palace, and then the youth sought out his father-in-law, saying: 'I am a King's son, and would take my princess to abide in my father's kingdom.' After trying to dissuade him from this course, the Sultān gave his consent, and said: 'To-morrow, my son, we will collect gifts for you, together with slaves and eunuchs.' But the youth replied: 'We have a sufficiency of such things, and I desire naught save Dalāl.' 'Take her, then, and depart in Allāh's name!' said the King. 'But take her mother also, that she may learn the way to your father's palace and afterwards visit our daughter from time to time.' But the youth replied: 'Why should we uselessly fatigue your queen, who is far on in years? I undertake to send my wife back once a month, to rejoice your eyes and tell you of her doings.' 'So be it,' answered the King, and forthwith the youth departed with Dalāl for his own country.

Now this handsome youth was none other than a ghoul of the most dangerous kind. He installed Dalāl in his house on the top of a lonely mountain and then went forth to beat the country, to lie in wait about the roads, to make pregnant women miscarry, to frighten old dames, to terrify children, to howl in the wind, to whine at doors, to bark in the night, to haunt ruins, to cast spells, to grin in the shadows, to visit tombs, to sniff at the dead, to commit a thousand assaults and provoke a thousand calamities. Worn out at length, however, he became a youth again and carried back a man's head to his wife, saying: 'O Dalāl, cook this in the oven and carve it so that we may eat.' But Dalāl answered: 'It is a man's head and I eat nothing except mutton.' So the ghoul brought her a sheep, and she was fed.

They lived together alone in this solitude, and Dalāl was defenceless against her horrible husband, who would come back to her with traces of murder and rape upon his body.

After eight days of such existence, the ghoul went out and changed himself into the appearance of his mother-in-law. He dressed in woman's clothes, knocked at his own door, and, when Dalāl asked from her window who was there, answered in the old woman's voice. Dalāl ran down and opened the doors, and behold! in those eight days she had become pale and thin and languishing. The false mother kissed her daughter, and said: 'My dear, I have come to see you in spite of all opposition, for we have learnt that your husband is a ghoul and makes you eat human flesh. Oh, how is it with you, my daughter? Alas, I fear that a time may come when he will be tempted to eat you also; so flee with me now, my dear!' But the loyal Dalāl answered: 'Be quiet, mother! There is no ghoul here, no trace or smell of a ghoul. Oh, my calamity, you must not say such things! My husband is a King's son and as beautiful as the star Canopus shining upon the sea. He gives me a fat sheep every day.'

The ghoul departed, rejoicing at his wife's discretion, and, when he returned in his male form, carrying a sheep, Dalāl said to him: 'My mother came to visit me; it was not my fault. She bade me salute you.' 'I am sorry that I did not hurry home,' answered the ghoul, 'for I should have rejoiced to greet so solicitous a lady. Would you like to see your aunt, your mother's sister?' 'O yes,' she cried, and he promised to send the old woman to her on the morrow.

Next morning, at dawn, he took on the appearance of Dalāl's aunt, and, and, when he came into her presence, kissed her upon the cheeks, weeping and sobbing as if his heart would break. Dalāl asked what was the matter, and the false aunt replied: 'Ay! ay! ay! Alas, alas! It is not for myself but for you that I lament! We have found out that you have married a ghoul.' But Dalāl cried: 'Be quiet! I will not listen to such wicked words! My husband is a King's son, even as I am a King's daughter; his treasures are greater than my father's treasures, and he is as handsome as the little star Canopus shining upon the sea.'

At this point Shahrazād saw the approach of morning and discreetly fell silent.

But when the nine-hundred-and-forty-seventh night had come

SHE SAID:

Then Dalāl fed the false aunt on sheep's head, to show her that mutton and not man was eaten there; and the ghoul departed in high good humour.

When he returned with a sheep for Dalāl and a freshly-severed head for himself, his wife said to him: 'My aunt has been to visit me, and sends you greeting.' 'Praise be to Allāh!' he answered. 'I take it kindly that your family do not forget you. Would you like to see your other aunt, your father's sister?' 'O yes,' she cried; and he continued: 'I will send her to-morrow and, after that, you shall see no more of your relations, for I fear their blabbing tongues.'

Next morning he presented himself before Dalāl in the form of her other aunt, and wept long upon her neck. 'Alas, what desolation upon our heads and upon you, O daughter of my brother!' she sobbed at length. 'We have found out that you have married a ghoul. Tell me the truth, my daughter, I conjure you by the virtues of our lord Muhammad (upon whom be prayer and peace!).' Then Dalāl, who could hold her terrible secret no longer, answered in a low voice: 'Be quiet, good aunt, be quiet, or he will destroy us both. He brings me human heads, think of it! When I refuse, he eats them all himself. I fear that soon he will make a meal of me.'

As she said these last words, the ghoul took on his own terrible shape and ground his teeth at her in fury. As she fell back, trembling for yellow terror, he spoke gently to her, saying: 'So you have already told my secret, Dalāl?' She threw herself at his feet, crying: 'Pardon me this time, spare me this time!' 'And did you spare my character before your aunt?' he asked. 'Where shall I begin to eat you?' 'If it is in my Destiny, then you must eat me,' she answered, 'but to-day I am dirty and would not taste at all pleasant. It will be well for you to take me to the hammām where I can wash myself for your table. After the bath, I shall be white and sweet, and my flesh a delicious savour in your mouth. Also I give you leave to start with any part you please.'

At once the ghoul collected suitable linens and a large gold basin. Then he changed one of his evil friends into a white ass and, after transforming himself into a donkey-boy, led the ass, with Dalāl upon its back, towards the hammām of the nearest village.

When he came to the hammām, carrying the gold basin upon his head, he said to the female guard: 'Here are three dīnārs for you. Give this King's daughter a good bath and return her safely to me.' Then he sat down outside the door to wait.

Dalāl entered the vestibule and seated herself sadly upon a marble bench, with the basin and the rare linens beside her. The young girls went into the bath and bathed, and were rubbed, and came out jesting happily with each other; but Dalāl wept silently in her corner. At length a troop of maidens came to her, saying: 'Why do you weep? Rather undress and take a bath with us.' But though she thanked them, she answered: 'Is there any bath which can wash away grief, or cure the hopeless sorrows of the world? There will be time enough to bathe, my sisters.'

As the girls turned away, an old woman entered the hammām, bearing a bowl upon her head, filled with fried earth-nuts and roast lupins. Some of the young women bought her goods for a penny, a half-penny, or two pence; and Dalāl, wishing to forget her trouble, called to her, saying: 'Give me a pennyworth of lupins, good aunt.' The old woman sat down by the bench and filled a horn measure with lupins; but, instead of giving her a penny, Dalāl handed her a necklace of pearls, saying: 'Take this for your children.'

Then, as the seller confounded herself in thanks and kissings of the hand, she said again: 'Will you give me your bowl and your ragged clothes in exchange for this gold basin, these linens, and all my jewelry and garments?' 'Why mock a poor old woman, my daughter?' asked the incredulous seller; but, when Dalāl had re-assured her, she hastily stripped off her rags. Dalāl dressed herself hastily in them, balanced the bowl of lupins upon her head, muffled herself in the old woman's filthy blue veil, blackened her hands with the mud of the vestibule pavement, and went out by the door near which the ghoul was sitting. Her whole body was one stupendous fright, but she schooled herself to cry: 'Lupins, roast lupins, pleasant distractions! Earth-nuts, delightful earth-nuts, piping hot!'

Though the ghoul had not recognised her, he smelt her smell after she had gone by, and said to himself: 'How can this old lupin-seller have my Dalāl's smell? As Allāh lives, I must look into this!' Then he cried aloud: 'Hi, lupin-seller! Earth-nuts, earth-nuts, come here!' But, as the woman did not turn her head, he said again to himself: 'It will be safer to make enquiry at the hammām.' He approached the guard, and asked: 'Why is the woman whom I gave into your charge so long?' 'She will come out later with the other women,' answered the guard. 'They do not leave till nightfall; for they have much to do, what with depilating themselves and tinting their fingers in henna, what with scenting themselves and tressing their hair.'

The ghoul was reassured and sat down again; but, when all the women had left and the guard came out to shut the door, he cried: 'What are you doing? Do you mean to shut my lady in?' 'There is no one left in the hammām,' she answered, 'except the old lupin-seller whom we always allow to sleep there, because she has no home.' The ghoul took the woman by the neck and shook her and made as if to strangle her, shouting in her face: 'O bawd, you are responsible for her! I gave her into your hands!' 'I am here to look after slippers,' she answered, 'I am no keeper of foul men's wives.' Then, as he in-creased the grip of his fingers about her neck, she cried: 'Help, help, good Mussulmāns!' The men of that village ran up from all sides; but the ogre took no heed of them and began to beat the slipper-guard. 'You shall give her back to me,' he bawled, 'even if she be in the seventh planet, O property of ancient whores!' So much for him.

Dalāl walked on across the country in the direction of her father's kingdom, until she came to a running stream, where she bathed her hands and face and feet. Then she made her way to a King's palace which stood near and sat down by the wall.

A negress slave, who came down for some purpose, saw her and returned to her mistress, saying: 'Dear mistress, were it not for the terror which I have of you, I would make bold to say that there is a woman below more beautiful even than yourself.' 'Bring her up here,' answered her mistress. So the negress went down, and said to Dalāl: 'My mistress bids you come and have speech with her.' 'Was my mother a black slave,' replied Dalāl, 'was my father a black slave, that I should walk with slaves?' The woman carried this answer to her mistress, who sent down a white slave with the same message. But when she had spoken, Dalāl answered: 'Was my mother a white slave, was my father a white slave, that I should walk with slaves?' When she heard of this, the Queen of that palace called her son to her and bade him go down to Dalāl.

The young prince, who was as handsome as the little star Canopus shining upon the sea, went down to the girl, and said to her: 'Dear lady, have the great goodness to visit the Queen, my mother, in her harīm.' And this time Dalāl answered: 'I will go up with you; for you are a King's son, even as I am a King's daughter.' So saying, she began to walk up the stairs before him.

At this point Shahrazād saw the approach of morning and discreetly fell silent.

But when the nine-hundred-and-forty-eighth night had come

SHE SAID:

When the prince saw Dalāl mounting the stairs in her beauty, a great love for her descended upon his heart. Also Dalāl opened her soul to the beauty of his regal youth. Also the Queen, the wife of the King of that palace, said to herself when she looked upon the girl: 'The slave was right. She is more beautiful than I.'

After a greeting and salutation, the prince said to his mother: 'I would marry this lady. The royalty of her line shines clearly forth from her.' 'That is your business, my son,' answered his mother. 'You are old enough to know what you are doing.'

The young prince called the kādī to write out a marriage contract, and the wedding was celebrated on that day. At night he went up into the bridal chamber.

But what, in the meanwhile, had happened to the ghoul?
You shall hear.

On the wedding day a man came to the palace, leading a fat white ram, and gave it to the King, saying: 'My lord, I am one of your farmers and have brought this as a gift for your son's marriage. We fattened him ourselves. But I must beg you to fasten him at the door of the harīm, for he was born and raised among women and, if you leave him below, he will bleat all night and trouble the sleep of your palace.' The King accepted this present and sent the farmer on his way with a robe of honour; then he handed over the ram to the āgah of the harīm, saying: 'Tie him at the door of the harīm, for he is only quiet and happy when he is among women.'

When the prince had entered the marriage chamber that night and accomplished that which there was to accomplish, he fell into a deep sleep at Dalāl's side. Then the white ram broke his cord and entered the room. He lifted Dalāl and carried her out into the court-yard, saying gently: 'Have you left me much of my honour, Dalāl?' 'Do not eat me,' she begged; but he replied: 'This time there is no help for it.' Then she prayed him to wait, before eating her, until she had satisfied a need in the privy; so the ghoul carried her to the courtyard privy and waited outside until she should have finished.

As soon as she was alone in the privy, Dalāl lifted her two hands on high, praying: 'O our Lady Zainab, O daughter of the blessed Prophet, come to my aid!' The saint heard her and sent down one of her following, a daughter of the Jinn, who came through the wall and asked: 'What is your desire, O Dalāl?' 'The ghoul is outside,' answered the princess, 'and he will eat me when I go forth.' Then said the Jinnīyah: 'If I save you from him, will you let me kiss you?' and, when Dalāl consented to this condition, she passed through the wall into the courtyard, threw herself upon the ghoul, and kicked him so violently in the testicles that he fell dead.

Then the Jinnīyah went back to the privy and led out Dalāl to see the body of the fat white ram. The two dragged him away from the courtyard and threw him into the ditch. So much, definitively, for him.

'Now I wish to ask a service of you,' said the Jinnīyah, as she kissed Dalāl upon the cheek. 'I am your humble servant, dear,' answered the princess. 'Come with me then,' urged the Jinnīyah, 'for one little hour, to the Emerald Sea. My son is ill, and the doctor has said that the only cure for him is a porringer of the water of the

Emerald Sea. But none save a human can fill a porringer at the Emerald Sea, my darling, and I ask your help in return for the trifling service which I have done you.' 'I will go willingly,' answered Dalāl, 'as long as I can return before my husband wakes.'

The Jinnīyah took up Dalāl upon her shoulders and carried her to the shores of the Emerald Sea, where she gave her a gold porringer; and Dalāl filled the porringer with that water of marvel, but, as she lifted the vessel, a little wave, which had been thus commanded, lapped over her hand so that it became as green as clover. Then the Jinnīyah took up Dalāl again and soon laid her upon her bride bed at the prince's side. So much for the servant of the Lady Zainab (upon whom be prayer and peace!).

Now there is a weigher of the Emerald Sea, who comes to measure and weigh it every morning, for he is responsible and wishes to know if any of the water has been stolen. Next day, when he had weighed and measured the sea, he found that there was a porringer missing. 'Who can have been the thief?' he cried. 'I will voyage the world until I catch him. If I can find a man, or more likely a woman, with a green hand, our Sultan will know the proper punishment.'

He provided himself with a tray of green glass rings and bracelets, and wandered over the world, crying under the windows of kings' palaces: 'Green glass bracelets, O princesses! O young ladies, emerald rings!'

After ten years of fruitless searching in all lands, he came to the palace where Dalāl dwelt in her content. As soon as he began to cry beneath the windows: 'Green glass bracelets, O princesses! O young ladies, emerald rings!', the princess came down to him and stretched forth her left hand, saying: 'Try some of your fairest bracelets.' But the weigher of the Emerald Sea recoiled, and cried: 'Lady, are you not ashamed to give me your left hand? I only try my bracelets on the right.' 'My right hand hurts,' answered Dalāl; but the weigher insisted, saying: 'I will only look and take the measure with my eye. I will not touch.' So the princess showed her right hand, and lo! it was as green as clover.

At once the weigher of the Emerald Sea lifted her in his arms and carried her, with the speed of light, into the presence of his King, saying: 'O Sultān of the Sea, she has stolen a porringer of your water. My lord knows the penalty.' The Sultān of the Emerald Sea prepared to look angrily upon Dalāl, but, as soon as his eyes beheld her, he was troubled by her beauty, and said: 'O young girl, I wish to marry you.' 'That is a pity,' she answered, 'for I am already law-fully married to a youth as fair as the little star Canopus shining upon the sea.' 'Have you a sister who at all resembles you?' asked the King, 'or a daughter, or even a son?' 'I have a daughter, ten years old,' answered Dalāl. 'To-day she has become ripe for mar-riage, and she is as beautiful as her father.' 'That is excellent,' said the Sultān of the Emerald Sea.

He took Dalāl's hand in his, and the weigher carried them both to the spot from which he had ravished the princess.

Dalāl led the King into the presence of her husband and, when the demand for their daughter's hand had been made in due form, the prince requested the stranger to name a dowry. Then said the lord of the miraculous water: 'I will give forty camels loaded with emeralds and hyacinths.'

Thus it came about that the Sultān of the Emerald Sea married the daughter of Dalāl and the starry prince. It is not recorded whether the four lived together in perfect harmony. But glory be to Allāh in any case!

Before Captain Jamāl al-Dīn had time to regain his place, Sultān Baibars cried: 'As Allāh lives, O Jamāl, that is the most beautiful story which I have ever heard!' 'It has become so, since it has pleased our master,' said Jamāl, as he took his seat. Then a seventh police-man, whose name was Fakhr al-Dīn, embraced the earth before the throne, saying: 'O our amīr and our King, I will tell you a personal anecdote, which has the single merit of being short.' And he told:

The Seventh Captain's Tale

ONE night an Arab thief broke into a farmer's house in my district, to steal a sack of corn; but the farm folk heard the noise he made and called me loudly, with cries of: 'Thief! Thief!' Yet the man managed to hide himself so cleverly that we could not find him, and I was already walking away from the door when I noticed a high heap of corn standing in the yard, with a copper measure on top of it. As I passed this heap, I heard an awe-inspiring fart proceed from the middle of it and saw the copper measure rise full five feet into the air. At once I searched among the corn and brought the thief to light, kneeling in the middle of it, bottom upwards. When I had bound him, I questioned him concerning the strange outburst which had betrayed his presence to me. 'It was intentional, my lord,' he answered. 'Intentional?' I cried. 'Whoever heard of a man farting to his own disadvantage?' 'It was for your advantage,' he retorted. 'Whoever heard of a fart being to anyone's advantage?' I cried again. 'I did it to make things easy for you,' declared the thief, 'and I trust that you will be fair-minded enough to make things easy for me.' What could I do but let him go?

Such is my story.

'By Allāh, you acted rightly!' cried Sultān Baibars, when he had heard this tale. Then, as Fakhr al-Dīn returned to his place, an eighth policeman, named Nizām al-Dīn, came forward, saying: 'O King of time, I will tell you a tale which has nothing in common with those which you have heard already.' 'Did you see the thing, or only hear of it?' asked Baibars. 'I heard of it, my Lord,' answered Nizām. And he said:

The Tale of the Eighth Captain

THERE was once a strolling clarinet-player, whose wife became pregnant by his works and, with Allāh's help, was delivered of a son. As the man had no money at all to pay the midwife or to buy food for the mother, he left the house, intending to beg two copper pieces from the charitably disposed on Allāh's way, that he might give one to the midwife on account and the other to the poultry merchant in earnest for a fowl.

As he walked through a field, he saw a hen sitting on a hillock; creeping up behind her, he lifted her and found a freshly laid egg on the grass beneath. Slipping the egg into his pocket and tucking the bird beneath his arm, he retraced his footsteps, saying to himself: 'There is a blessing upon the day! My wife can have the fowl, and I will sell the egg to pay the midwife something on account.'

As he passed through the jewellers' market on his way to the egg market, he met a Jew of his acquaintance, who asked him what he carried. 'A hen and an egg,' he answered, and at once the Jew wished to know if he would sell the egg. 'Yes,' said he. 'How much?' asked the Jew. 'Speak first,' said he. 'It is not worth more than ten gold dīnārs,' said the Jew. Thinking that the infidel mocked him, the poor man cried: 'You know that that is no price for an egg!' The Jew thought that he was demanding more, so he raised his offer to fifteen dīnārs. 'Allāh open another door!' cried the clarinet-player, and the Jew, with bitter hatred in his heart, exclaimed: 'Twenty dīnārs of new gold; take them or leave them!' The delighted clarinet-player saw that the offer was serious, so he handed over the egg, received the money, and began hastily to move away. But the Jew ran after him, and asked: 'Have you many eggs like that at home?' 'I can bring you one to-morrow, when the hen has laid again,' answered the man, 'and I will only charge you the same price, though to anyone else it would be thirty dīnārs.' Then said the Jew: 'Point out your house to me and I will come every morning to buy an egg for twenty dīnārs.' The clarinet-player pointed out his house, and then bought another and ordinary hen, which he cooked for the child's mother, at the same time paying the midwife handsomely for her trouble.

Next morning, he leaned over the bed, saying: 'O daughter of my uncle, take great care not to kill the black hen which lives in the kitchen, for she is the blessing of our house and lays eggs worth twenty dīnārs each. The Jew has promised to buy all that we can give him at that price.'

At this point Shahrazād saw the approach of morning and discreetly fell silent.

But when the nine-hundred-and-forty-ninth night had come

SHE SAID:

The Jew came every morning and bought the black hen's egg for twenty dīnārs, so that in a short time the clarinet-player's circumstances became most comfortable, and he was able to open a fair shop in the market.

When the son, who had been born on the day of the hen's discovery, was old enough to go to school, his father had a handsome seminary built at his own expense and called together the children of the poor, that they might learn to read and write with his own child. He hired an excellent master for them, one who knew the Koran by heart and could even recite it backwards.

Then he resolved to go on pilgrimage and, after cautioning his wife lest the Jew should try to cozen her of the hen, left with a caravan for Mecca.

Soon after his departure, the Jew said to the woman: 'I have a trunk full of gold to give you if you will let me have the hen in exchange.' 'How can I do such a thing?' she asked. 'My husband bade me only give you the eggs.' 'If he is angry I will take the responsibility,' pleaded the Jew. 'My shop is known in the market; I will not run away from him.' With that he opened the trunk and showed the glorious gold within. As soon as she saw it, the woman handed over the black hen, and the Jew gave her the trunk with its contents, saying: 'Now clean the bird and cook it. I will come back in a few hours and, if a single part of it be missing, I will slit up the belly of the eater rather than lose it.' After that he went his way.

At noon the lad returned from school and saw his mother take the hen from the pot, set it in a porcelain dish, and cover it with muslin. His schoolboy's appetite clamoured for a portion of the enticing bird; but, when he asked to be allowed to take a piece, his mother told him that the dish was not for them.

Yet, when she went away to satisfy a need, her son lifted the muslin and, with a single snap of his teeth, removed the hen's hot rump and swallowed it whole. One of the slaves saw him in the act, and cried: 'O my master, what misfortune, what dire calamity! If you do not flee the house, the Jew will slit your belly to recover the rump!' 'You are right,' replied the boy, 'it would be better to depart than to lose that pleasant rump.' So he mounted his mule and rode away.

When the Jew returned for his property and asked after the missing rump, the woman told him that her son had bitten it off, in her absence, and swallowed it. Then cried the Jew: 'Woe, woe upon you! It was for the rump that I paid you all that gold. Where is your son?' 'He has fled in terror,' she replied.

The Jew departed hastily and journeyed through towns and villages, until he came upon the boy sleeping in a field. He crept up softly to kill him, but the lad, who was sleeping with one eye open, jumped up and made as if to flee. 'Come here, my child,' said the Jew. 'Who asked you to eat that rump? I gave your mother a chest full of gold for the thing, and the bargain can only be completed by your death.' 'Be gone, O Jew!' answered the boy, without a sign of fear. 'Are you not ashamed to journey so far for a hen's rump? Are you not ashamed to wish to open my belly for so small a thing?' Then, as the Jew drew a knife from his belt, the courageous child seized him with one hand and, lifting him high, pashed him against the earth (curse him!) so that his bones were broken and he died.

The boy was soon to feel further effects of the hen's rump; for, in attempting to return to his mother's house, he lost his way and came to a King's palace, the door of which was decorated with forty severed heads save one. When he asked concerning these, the people said to him: 'The King has a daughter who is a very strong wrestler; she has consented to marry the man who can conquer her in this sport, but those whom she defeats are always beheaded.' Without hesitation the youth sought the presence of the King, saying: 'I wish to measure my strength against your daughter's strength.' 'My boy,' answered the King, 'if you take my advice you will depart. Many strong grown men have come here and lost to my daughter. I would not wish to have to cut you off before your prime.' 'If I am beaten,' answered the boy, 'I am quite willing to have my head severed and hung upon the gate.' 'Then write an undertaking to that effect and seal it with your seal,' said the King.

As soon as the undertaking had been signed and sealed, a carpet was spread in the inner court, and the boy and girl stood facing each other upon it, with arms about each other's waists and armpit locked in armpit. Their wrestling was a marvel to be seen; sometimes the boy lifted the princess and threw her to the ground, but she would ever slip from under him like a serpent and throw him in her turn. For two hours they strove together, and neither could press the adverse shoulder to the carpet. Therefore the King became angry, seeing that his daughter did not distinguish herself, and cried: 'Enough for to-day! To-morrow you shall wrestle again.'

Then he retired to his apartment and called his doctors to him, saying: 'To-night while that boy is asleep, you must give him narcotic banj and carefully examine his body. If you can find the amulet which makes him powerful against one who has thrown thirty-nine of the strongest men, I will reward you; but, if you fail to discover anything, I will cast you from my palace and my city.'

So, when night came and the boy slept, the physicians made him breathe narcotic banj and sounded his body as a man might sound a jar. They came at length upon the hen's rump, bedded among the entrails, and, recognising it, sent for their scissors and their instruments. They made an incision and withdrew the rump; then they sewed up the wound, sprinkled it with powerful vinegar, and left all as it had been.

In the morning the boy woke from his drugged sleep and found his force abated, for his remarkable strength had been due entirely to the hen's rump, which had the property of making the eater invincible. Knowing full well that he could not hold his own in his present state, he fled from the palace and the city, and kept on running till he came upon three men who were quarrelling violently among themselves. 'Why do you quarrel?' he asked, and they replied: 'For a thing.' 'What sort of thing?' he asked, and they replied: 'For this carpet. It is a magic carpet; if any beat it with this stick and bid it remove to such-and-such a place, were it even to the top of Kāf, it will remove.' 'Instead of wringing each other's necks for the carpet,' said the boy, 'let me be your arbiter.' 'We consent,' they answered, and he said again: 'Spread out the carpet on the ground that I may see its length and breadth.' When this had been done, he stood in the middle of the carpet and told the three claimants that he would cast a stone for them to race for and bring back; but, when he had done so and they were far off, running their hardest, he beat the carpet with the stick, crying: 'Take me straight to the interior of the palace which I left this morning.' In the twinkling of an eye he found himself in the courtyard where he had wrestled on the previous day.

'The champion! The champion!' he cried. 'Who will meet him?' and presently the young girl came down, in the presence of the whole court, and stood before him on the carpet. Without giving her time to engage him, he struck down with his stick, saying: 'Fly with us to the top of Kāf!' The carpet rose into the air and, leaving the sea of upturned stupid faces below, bore the youth and maiden to the top of Kāf.

'Who wins now?' cried the boy. 'She who had the hen's rump filched from my belly, or he who has filched the princess from her palace?'

At this point Shahrazād saw the approach of morning and discreetly fell silent.

But when the nine-hundred-and-fiftieth night had come

SHE SAID:

'I claim your protection,' said the girl meekly, 'I ask you to pardon me. If you will take me back to my father's palace, I will proclaim that you have thrown me, and marry you at once.' 'That is all very well,' replied the boy, 'but there is a proverb which says: *Beat the bolt while it is soft.* I wish to do you know what before I take you back.' With that he took the seemingly consenting girl and was fumbling for a soft bolt in order to beat it, when she kicked upwards violently, so that he rolled off the carpet. Before he had time to rise, she struck the magic fabric with the stick, and cried: 'Fly back to my father's palace.' Thus, in the twinkling of an eye, the boy was left alone.

The clarinet-player's son stayed lonely on the top of the mountain, so far from the world that even the ants might not have found him, until he began to feel hunger and thirst. Then he scrambled down, gnawing his hand for rage. In a day and a night he reached to the middle height of Kāf and, on the morning of the second day, came upon two date palms bowed with their abundance of ripe fruit. One of them bore red dates, and the other yellow.

The boy plucked a branch of each and, as he preferred yellow dates, swallowed one of them with great delight. But hardly had it passed his lips when he had an itching of his scalp and, carrying his hand to the place, felt a horn rapidly growing out of his head. This horn wound itself round one of the palms, and the unfortunate youth found himself a prisoner. 'If I am doomed,' he said to himself, 'I would rather die fed than fasting.' And he fell upon the red dates. But, no sooner had he eaten one of them, than the horn writhed away from about the palm and, leaving him free, grew small and disappeared.

He ate the red dates until his hunger was satisfied and then, after filling his pockets with fruit of each colour, went on walking so vigorously that, by the end of two months, he had come back to the palace of the wrestling princess.

He strode beneath the windows, crying: 'Dates, early dates, oh, dates! Girls' fingers, oh, dates! Riders' friends, oh, dates!'

When the King's daughter heard this call, she said to her maidens: 'Run quickly and buy me some dates. Be careful to pick out the crisp ones.' So the maidens went down and bought sixteen, paying a dīnār each because of their rarity at that season.

The princess saw that the dates were yellow, the kind that she loved best; so she ate the whole sixteen, one after the other, as quickly as she could carry them to her mouth. 'My heart, but they are excellent!' she said; but, even as she spoke, she had an itching in sixteen parts of her head and felt sixteen horns growing out of her scalp, from sixteen different spots symmetrically placed. Before she could speak again or move, the horns had branched off, four by four, and solidly pierced the walls of her room.

At the shrill cries of his daughter and her following, the King ran in great haste, and the maidens cried to him: 'Dear master, we saw these sixteen horns come out of our lady's head and instantly pierce the wall!'

The distracted father called together those skilful physicians who had stolen away the hen's rump from the lad's belly, and they tried to saw through the horns; but the things would not be sawn. Then they made use of other means; but nothing would free the princess.

So the King had no choice but to send a herald about the city, to cry: 'He who shall cure the princess of her sixteen horns may marry her, and shall be considered worthy to succeed the King!'

Now, what do you think happened?

The clarinet's son, who had eagerly expected this proclamation, entered the palace, saying: 'I will cure the horns.' When he was in the presence of the girl he loved, he broke one of the red dates and placed the fragments between her teeth. At once a horn detached itself from the wall and dwindled towards the princess's head, until it vanished utterly.

All the court, with the King at its head, joyfully cried out: 'A doctor of doctors!' and the boy replied: 'To-morrow I will cure the second horn.' He was kept in the palace with all honour and high entertainment, curing a horn each day, until the last had disappeared.

Finding his daughter free and undisfigured, the grateful King had his city illuminated with coloured fires, and married the princess to her preserver. Then came the night of penetration.

When the boy entered the chamber where his bride waited for him, he said: 'And who wins now? She who had the hen's rump filched from my belly and stole my magic carpet; or he who grew full sixteen horns upon your head and made them go again?' 'It is you, then?' she asked, and he replied: 'Yes, it is I, the son of the clarinet!' Then said the princess: 'By Allāh, you have beaten me!'

They lay down, and their strength was equal. They became King and Queen. They lived together in a perfect happiness.

Such is my story.

When Sultān Baibars had listened to this, he cried: 'As Allāh lives, I am not sure that this tale is not the fairest I have ever heard!' Then a ninth policeman, whose name was Jalāl al-Dīn, came forward, saying: 'O King of time, if Allāh wills, my tale shall please you greatly.' And he said:

The Ninth Captain's Tale

THERE was once a woman who could not conceive, for all her husband's assaulting. So one day she prayed to Allāh, saying: 'Give me a daughter, even if she be not proof against the smell of flax!'

In speaking thus of the smell of flax she meant that she would have a daughter, even if the girl were so delicate and sensitive that the anodyne smell of flax would take hold of her throat and kill her.

Soon the woman conceived and easily bore a daughter, as fair as the rising moon, as pale and delicate as moonlight.

When little Sittukhān, for such they called her, grew to be ten years old, the Sultān's son passed beneath her window and saw her and loved her, and went back ailing to the palace.

Doctor succeeded doctor fruitlessly beside his bed; but, at last, an old woman, who had been sent by the porter's wife, visited him and said, after close scrutiny: 'You are in love, or else you have a friend who loves you.' 'I am in love,' he answered. 'Tell me her name,' she begged, 'for I may be a bond between you.' 'She is the fair Sittukhān,' he replied; and she comforted him, saying: 'Refresh your eyes and tranquillise your heart, for I will bring you into her presence.'

Then she departed and sought out the girl, who was taking the air before her mother's door. After compliment and greeting, she said: 'Allāh protect so much beauty, my daughter! Girls like you, and with such lovely fingers, should learn to spin flax; for there is no more delightful sight than a spindle in spindle fingers.' Then she went her way.

At once the girl went to her mother, saying: 'Mother, take me to the mistress.' 'What mistress?' asked her mother. 'The flax mistress,' answered the girl. 'Do not say such a thing!' cried the woman. 'Flax is a danger to you; its smell is fatal to your breast, a touch of it will kill you.' But her daughter reassured her, saying: 'I shall not die,' and so wept and insisted that her mother sent her to the flax mistress.

The white girl stayed there for a day, learning to spin; and her fellow pupils marvelled at her beauty and the beauty of her fingers. But, when a morsel of flax entered behind one of her nails, she fell swooning to the floor.

They thought her dead and sent to her father and mother, saying:

'Allāh prolong your days! Come and take up your daughter, for she is dead.'

The man and his wife tore their garments for the loss of their only joy, and went, beaten by the wind of calamity, to bury her. But the old woman met them, and said: 'You are rich folk and it would be shame on you to lay so fair a girl in dust.' 'What shall we do then?' they asked, and she replied: 'Build her a pavilion in the midst of the waves of the river and couch her there upon a bed, that you may come to visit her.'

So they built a pavilion of marble, on columns rising out of the river, and planted a garden about it with green lawns, and set the girl upon an ivory bed, and came there many times to weep.

What happened next?

The old woman went to the King's son, who still lay sick of love, and said to him: 'Come with me to see the maiden. She waits you, couched in a pavilion above the waves of the river.'

The prince rose up and bade his father's wazīr come for a walk with him. The two went forth together and followed the old woman to the pavilion. Then the prince said: 'Wait for me outside the door, for I shall not be long.'

He entered the pavilion and began to weep by the ivory bed, recalling verses in the praise of so much beauty. He took the girl's hand to kiss it and, as he passed her slim white fingers through his own, noticed the morsel of flax lodged behind one of her nails. He wondered at this and delicately drew it forth.

At this point Shahrazād saw the approach of morning and discreetly fell silent.

But when the nine-hundred-and-fifty-first night had come

SHE SAID:

At once the girl came out of her swoon and sat up upon the ivory bed. She smiled at the prince, and whispered: 'Where am I?' 'You are with me,' he answered, as he pressed her all against him. He kissed her and lay with her, and they stayed together for forty days and forty nights. Then the prince took leave of his love, saying: 'My wazīr is waiting outside the door. I will take him back to the palace and then return.'

He found the wazīr and walked with him across the garden towards the gate, until he was met by white roses growing with jasmine. The sight of these moved him, and he said to his companion: 'The roses and the jasmine are white with the pallor of Sittukhān's cheeks! Wait here for three days longer, while I go to look upon the cheeks of Sittukhān.'

He entered the pavilion again and stayed three days with Sittu-khān, admiring the white roses and the jasmine of her cheeks.

Then he rejoined the wazīr and walked with him across the garden towards the gate, until the carob, with its long black fruit, rose up to meet him. He was moved by the sight of it, and said: 'The carobs are long and black like the brows of Sittukhān. O wazīr, wait here for three more days, while I go to view Sittukhān's brows.'

He entered the pavilion again and stayed three days with the girl, admiring her perfect brows, long and black like carobs hanging two by two.

Then he rejoined the wazīr and walked with him towards the gate, until a springing fountain with its solitary jet rose up to meet him. He was moved by this sight and said to the wazīr: 'The jet of the fountain is as Sittukhān's waist. Wait here for three days longer, while I go to gaze again upon the waist of Sittukhān.'

He went up into the pavilion and stayed three days with the girl, admiring her waist, for it was as the slim jet of the fountain.

Then he rejoined the wazir and walked with him across the garden towards the gate. But Sittukhān, when she saw her lover come again a third time, had said to herself: 'What brings him back?' So now she followed him down the stairs of the pavilion, and hid behind the door which gave on the garden to see what she might see. The prince happened to turn and catch sight of her face; he returned to-wards her, pale and distracted, and said sadly: 'Sittukhān, Sittukhān, I shall never see you more, never, never again.' Then he departed with the wazīr, and his mind was made up that he would not return.

Sittukhān wandered in the garden, weeping, lonely and re-gretting that she was not dead in very truth. As she walked by the water, she saw something sparkle in the grass and, on raising it, found it to be a talismanic ring. She rubbed the engraved carnelian of it, and the ring spoke, saying: 'Behold, here am I! What do you wish?' 'O ring of Sulaimān,' answered Sittukhān, 'I require a palace next to the palace of the prince who used to love me, and a beauty greater than my own.' 'Shut your eye and open it!' said the ring; and, when the girl had done so, she found herself in a magnificent palace, next to the palace of the prince. She looked in a mirror which was there and marvelled at her beauty.

Then she leaned at the window until her false love should pass by on his horse. When the prince saw her, he did not know her; but he loved her and hastened to his mother, saying: 'Have you not some very beautiful thing which you can take as a present to the lady who dwells in the new palace? And can you not beg her, at the same time, to marry me?' 'I have two pieces of royal brocade,' answered his mother, 'I will take them to her and urge your suit with them.'

Without losing an hour, the Queen visited Sittukhān, and said to her: 'My daughter, I pray you to accept this present, and to marry my son.' The girl called her negress and gave her the pieces of brocade, bidding her cut them up for floor cloths; so the Queen became angry and returned to her own dwelling. When the son learned that the woman of his love had destined the cloth of gold for menial service, he begged his mother to take some richer present, and the Queen paid a second visit, carrying a necklace of unflawed emeralds.

'Accept this gift, my daughter, and marry my son,' she said; and Sittukhān answered: 'O lady, your present is accepted.' Then she called her slave, saying: 'Have the pigeons eaten yet?' 'Not yet, mistress,' answered the slave. 'Take them these green trifles!' said Sittukhān.

When she heard this outrageous speech, the Queen cried: 'You have humbled us, my daughter. Now, at least, tell me plainly whether you wish to marry my son or no.' 'If you desire me to marry him,' answered Sittukhān, 'bid him feign death, wrap him in seven winding-sheets, carry him in sad procession through the city, and let your people bury him in the garden of my palace.' 'I will tell him your conditions,' said the Queen.

'What do you think!' cried the mother to her son, when she had returned to him. 'If you wish to marry the girl, you must pretend to be dead, you must be wrapped in seven winding-sheets, you must be led in sad procession through the city, and you must be buried in her garden!' 'Is that all, dear mother?' asked the prince in great delight. 'Then tear your clothes and weep, and cry: "My son is dead!"'

The Queen rent her garments and cried in a voice shrill with pain: 'Calamity and woe! My son is dead!' All the folk of the palace ran to that place and, seeing the prince stretched upon the floor with the Queen weeping above him, washed the body and wrapped it in seven winding-sheets. Then the old men and the readers of the Koran came together and formed a procession, which went throughout the city, carrying the youth covered with precious shawls. Finally they set down their burden in Sittukhān's garden and went their way.

As soon as the last had departed, the girl, who had once died of a morsel of flax, whose cheeks were jasmine and white roses, whose brows were carobs two by two, whose waist was the slim jet of the fountain, went down to the prince and unwrapped the seven winding-sheets from about him, one by one. Then 'Is it you?' she said. 'You are ready to go very far for women; you must be fond of them!' The prince bit his finger in confusion, but Sittukhān reassured him, saying: 'It does not matter this time!'

And they dwelt together in love delight.

'In the very name of Allāh,' cried the Sultān Baibars to Jalāl al-Dīn, 'I do not think that I have ever heard a better tale!' Then a tenth policeman, whose name was Hilāl al-Dīn, came forward to the foot of the throne, saying: 'I have a tale which is the elder sister of all these!' And he told:

The Tenth Captain's Tale

THERE was once a King who had a son called Muhammad. One day the boy said to his father: 'I wish to marry.' 'That is right,' answered the King, 'but you must wait until your mother has passed the maidens of the harīms in review.' 'I would rather choose for myself and see with my own eyes,' objected the prince. So, when the King gave him leave, he mounted his horse, which was as beautiful as if it had come from fairy stock, and rode away from that city.

At the end of two days' journey he came upon a man sitting in a field, who cut leeks while his young daughter bound them into bundles. After greeting, the prince sat down beside the two and asked the girl for water. She rose and fetched him a cup, and he drank. Then, because the maiden pleased him, he turned to her father, saying: 'O sheikh, will you give me the hand of your daughter in marriage?' 'We are your servants,' answered the old man. 'I am rejoiced, O sheikh!' said the delighted prince. 'Have the goodness to stay here while I go to my native city and make preparations for the wedding. I will soon return.'

Prince Muhammad returned to his father, saying: 'I am betrothed to the daughter of the Sultān of leeks.' 'So they have a Sultān, then?' asked the king, and his son replied: 'Yes, and I am going to marry his daughter.' Then cried his father: 'Glory be to Allāh, my son, that He has given a Sultān to the leeks! Since the daughter pleases you, we will send your mother to leek-land, to see father leek, mother leek, and the leek girl.' 'Very well,' answered Muhammad.

The Queen set forth and found the daughter of the Sultān of leeks charming in each respect and fitted by Allāh to be the consort of a King's son. Her heart went out to the girl and she embraced her, saying: 'I am the Queen, my dear, I am the mother of the prince who visited you a short time ago. I have come to marry you to him.' But the girl replied: 'If your son is a prince, I will not marry him.' 'Why?' asked the astonished Queen. 'Because,' answered the girl, 'I will never wed a man who does not work with his hands.'

The Queen returned in anger to the city, and said to her husband: 'The chit of leek-land will not marry our son.' 'Why?' asked the King. 'Because,' answered the Queen bitterly, 'she will only wed one who practises a trade.' 'She is quite right!' exclaimed the King. But the prince fell ill when he learnt of this refusal.

So the King ordered the sheikhs of all the corporations into his presence, and said to the first, who was the sheikh of the carpenters: 'You, how long would it take you to teach my son your trade?' 'Two years, at least,' answered the man. The King bade him step aside, and asked the sheikh of the blacksmiths: 'How long would it take you to teach my son your trade?' 'Exactly a year,' replied the man. So the King bade him step aside, and questioned all the other sheikhs in turn; but they all asked one year, two years, three years or four years, in which to teach their trades. The King was about to give way to despair when he saw a little man, obscured by all the rest, who was dancing up and down, and clicking his fingers. 'Why do you dance up and down, and click your fingers?' he demanded, and the little man replied: 'So that our lord the King might notice me. I am poor, and the sheikhs of the corporations did not tell me of this meeting. I am a weaver, and will teach my trade to your son in one hour.'

The King sent away all the sheikhs and provided the weaver with coloured silks and a loom, saying: 'Teach my son your art.' So the weaver turned to the prince, and said: 'Watch me! I do not say do this, or do that; I simply say, open your eyes and watch me! Watch the way my hands go in and out!'

In less time than it takes to tell, the weaver wove a handkerchief under the attentive eyes of the lovesick prince; then he said to his pupil: 'Come here now and weave a handkerchief yourself.' The youth sat down immediately at the loom and wove a most remarkable handkerchief, working in pictures of the palace and the gardens.

At this point Shahrazād saw the approach of morning and discreetly fell silent.

But when the nine-hundred-and-fifty-second night had come

SHE SAID:

The weaver took the two handkerchiefs to the King and asked him to decide which was the prince's work and which his own. Without a moment's hesitation, the King pointed to the one which bore the design of the palace and the gardens, saying: 'This is your work, and the other is also your work.' But the weaver cried: 'By the merits of your glorious ancestors, O King, I swear that the handsome handkerchief was woven by your son, and the other one, the ugly one, by me.'

The pleased King appointed the weaver to be sheikh of all the sheikhs of the corporations, and then said to his wife: 'Take our son's work and show it to the daughter of the Sultān of leeks; tell her that he is by trade a weaver.'

The prince's mother carried the handkerchief and the message to the leek girl, who marvelled and exclaimed: 'I am ready to marry him now!'

The King's wazīrs sent for the kādī and bade him write out a marriage contract. The wedding took place, and the prince went in to the leek girl, who bore him numerous sons, each marked upon the thigh with the semblance of a leek. Every one of these children learnt a trade, and, consequently, passed his life in prosperous content. But Allāh knows all!

Then said Sultān Baibars: 'This tale of the daughter of the Sultān of leeks has an excellent moral. But have the rest of you no tales?' So another policeman, the eleventh, whose name was Salāh al-Dīn, kissed the earth, and said:

The Eleventh Captain's Tale

A SON was born to a certain Sultān at the same time as a blood mare in the royal stables dropped a foal. So the Sultān said: 'The foal is written in the luck of my new-born son and shall belong to him.'

Now, while the boy grew up, his mother died, and the mare died at the same moment.

Days passed and the Sultān married another wife from among the palace slaves. And after that he put the boy to school, neither loving him nor setting a watch upon him. So, whenever the child returned from school, he would go into the stable and greet his horse; he would caress him, give him food and drink, and tell him of his grief and loneliness.

The slave who had become queen kept a lover, a Jewish doctor (Allāh curse the same!). And these two found themselves hindered in their unlawful meetings by the presence of the boy. Therefore they took counsel together and resolved to poison him.

That day, when the prince returned from school, he found his horse in tears. So, as he gentled him, he asked why he was weeping. 'For your death,' answered the horse. 'Your stepmother and that vile Jew have distilled a poison from a black man's skin, and mean to put it in your food. Beware, dear master!'

Thus it happened that the prince was on his guard when the Queen set food before him, and, before she could prevent the act, he threw the contents of his plate to the palace cat, who ate greedily and died upon her hour. Then the prince rose up and left the apartment, as if he had noticed nothing.

The woman and the Jew asked each other: 'Who can have told him?' and answered each other: 'None but his horse.' So the woman pretended to be ill, and the King summoned the foul Jew to examine her, because he was the court physician. 'There is but one cure for her,' said the Jew, 'the heart of a foal dropped by a blood mare, of such and such a colour.' 'There is but one animal in my kingdom which fulfils that condition,' answered the King, 'and it belongs to my motherless son.' So, when the boy came home from school, his father said to him: 'Your stepmother, the Queen, is very ill, and the heart of your horse is the only cure for her.' 'It is permitted,' replied the prince, 'but I have never ridden him and would like to do so once before he dies.' The King gave his permission, and the lad mounted his horse, in the presence of the whole court, and galloped across the polo-ground, and beyond, until he disappeared from the sight of men. Riders were sent after him, but could not come up with him.

At length the prince came to another kingdom and halted to rest by the garden of another King. Then his horse gave him a tuft of his hairs and a fire stone, saying: 'If you have need of me, burn one of these hairs. For the time being, it will be better if I leave you, so that my presence may not interfere with the progress of your Destiny.' When they had come to this agreement, horse and rider embraced and separated.

The prince sought out the chief gardener of those royal gardens, and said to him: 'I am a stranger here. Can you not take me into your service?' 'I can,' answered the man, 'for I have need of someone to drive the bullock of the water-wheel.' So the prince went to the water-wheel and drove the bullock.

Now the King's daughters were walking in the garden, and the youngest looked upon the boy who drove the bullock and loved him. Without showing her feelings, she said to her sisters: 'How long are we to stay without husbands? Does our father mean to let us sour? Our blood will turn upon us!' 'What you say is true,' answered her sisters, 'we are souring and our blood is turning upon us.' So the seven went to their mother, and said to her: 'Does our father wish us to sour, and our blood to turn upon us? Can he not find us husbands who will prevent such accidents?'

The Queen repeated this conversation to the King, who at once sent out a herald to summon all the young men of the city to pass beneath the palace windows, because the princesses wished to marry. All the young men passed beneath the palace windows, and, when one of them pleased a princess, she dropped her handkerchief upon him. Soon six of them had chosen husbands and were content.

When the King was told that his youngest daughter had not thrown her handkerchief, he asked: 'Is there no other youth left in the city?' and they answered: 'There is none except the beggar boy who drives the bullock of the water-wheel.' Then said the King: 'He also must pass, although I know full well that no daughter of mine would choose him.' The servants of the palace immediately fetched the prince and hustled him below the palace windows. But, behold! the youngest princess threw her handkerchief to him. And the King, her father, fell ill from shame and vexation.

The court physicians came together and ordered their royal

patient to drink bear's milk, fetched in the skin of a virgin bear.
'That should be an easy matter,' said the King. 'I have six sons-in-
law, heroic horsemen, quite unlike that seventh, that water-wheel
brat. Tell them to bring me the milk!'

The six sons-in-law mounted their handsome steeds to ride forth
in quest of the bear's milk, and the prince departed after them
mounted upon a lame mule, so that all the people mocked him. But,
when he had come to a place apart, he struck the fire stone and burnt
one of the hairs. Then his horse appeared, and, after the two had embraced, the boy asked him for his advice.

At the end of a certain time the six-sons-in-law returned, bringing
with them a bearskin bottle filled with bear's milk. But when the
Queen had sent her eunuchs with this bottle, that the physicians
might examine its contents, the wise men said: 'It is the milk of an
old bear, and the skin is the skin of an old bear. These things would
only harm the King.'

Soon the eunuchs brought up a second bottle to the Queen, saying: 'This was left at the door by a youth more beautiful than the
angel Hārūt.' 'Take it to the doctors,' said the Queen. When the
doctors had examined the second bottle and its contents, they cried:
'This is what we sought! The milk is the milk of a young bear, and
the skin is the skin of a virgin bear.' They gave the King to drink
and he was cured instantly. 'Who brought my cure?' he asked, and
they replied: 'A youth more beautiful than the angel Hārūt.' 'Give
him the ring of my succession,' cried the King, 'and beg him to sit
upon my throne. As soon as my youngest daughter is divorced from
the water-wheel brat, I will marry her to my preserver.'

When enough time had passed for the fulfilment of his orders, the
King went into the throne hall and fell at the feet of a youth who sat
in the seat of his royalty. Seeing his youngest daughter smiling beside the stranger, he said to her: 'Well done, my child! I see that you
have divorced yourself already from the water-wheel brat, and made
free choice of my delightful saviour.' 'Dear father,' she answered,
'the water-wheel brat, the youth who brought you virgin bear's
milk, and the prince who sits upon your throne, are one and the
same person.'

'Is that true?' asked the astonished King, and the prince replied:
'It is most true. But, if you do not wish me to enter your line, your
daughter is still a virgin and may be restored to you.' But the King
embraced him and took him to his heart; he celebrated the wedding

of the two with great magnificence (for previously it had been without ceremony).

And, in the matter of penetration, the youth carried himself so valiantly that his young bride was for ever prevented from souring and having her blood turn upon her.

After certain weeks the prince returned to his father's kingdom at the head of a mighty army. He found that the King was dead and that his stepmother reigned, with the stinking Jew for wazīr. Without a second thought, he had them seized and impaled above an ardent fire, so that they were consumed as it were upon spits. So much for them.

But glory be to Allāh, Who lives and can never be consumed!

When he had heard this story, Sultān Baibars cried: 'It is a pity that there are no more tales!' So a twelfth policeman, whose name was Nasr al-Dīn, came forward and said: 'So far, I have spoken nothing, O King of time. And, after me, there will be nothing spoken, for nothing will be left to say.' And he began:

The Twelfth Captain's Tale

IT is related—but is there knowledge save with Allah?—that there was once a King who had a barren Queen. One day a Moor sought audience with him, saying: 'If I give you a remedy by which your Queen shall conceive and bear, will you give me your first son?' 'Certainly,' answered the King. So the Moor handed him two sweetmeats, one green and the other red, with these words: 'Eat the green yourself, make your wife eat the red, and Allāh will do the rest.' Then he departed.

When the King had eaten the green sweetmeat and given his wife the red one, the woman conceived and bore a son, whom his father called Muhammad (a blessing be upon that name!). And the child grew up rich in all learning and with a most sweet voice.

Then the Queen bore a second son, whom his father called Alī; and the child grew up unhandy in everything. Finally, she bore a third son, Mahmūd, who grew up as an idiot.

At the end of ten years the Moor sought audience of the King again, saying: 'Give me my son.' So the King went to the Queen and told her of the Moor's demand. 'Never, never,' she cried. 'Let us rather give him Alī, the unhandy.'

The Moor left the palace with Alī and walked with him along the roads in the great heat, till noon. Then he asked: 'Are you not hungry or thirsty?' 'By Allāh, what a question!' exclaimed the boy. 'How can you expect me not to be both, after half a day without food and drink?' Then the Moor exclaimed: 'Hum!' and led Alī back to his father, saying: 'That is not my son. Let me see the three of them together and I will know my own.' So the King made the three boys stand in line, and the Moor picked out Muhammad, the eldest, rich in all learning and with a most sweet voice.

The Moor walked for half a day, and then asked: 'Are you hungry? Are you thirsty?' 'If you are hungry or thirsty,' answered Muhammad, 'then I am hungry and thirsty also.' The magician embraced him, saying: 'That is well, that is very well, O Learned! You are indeed my son.'

He led Muhammad into his own land in the heart of Morocco and, taking him to a garden, gave him food and drink. Then he put a grimoire into his hand, and said: 'Read this book!' The boy turned the pages but could not read a word; so the Moor flew into a rage, and cried: 'You are my son, and yet you cannot read this grimoire? By Gog and Magog, and by the fire of the turning stars, if you have not learnt it by heart in thirty days, I shall cut off your right arm!' Then he left Muhammad and walked out of the garden.

The boy pored over the grimoire for twenty-nine days, but, at the end of that time, he did not even know which way up to hold it. Suddenly he cast it from him, crying: 'If there be only one day left before my loss, I would rather spend it in the garden than wearying my eyes with this old thing!'

He began to walk under the heavy trees, deep in the garden, and saw a young girl hanging by her hair from one of them. He hastened to free her and she embraced him, saying: 'I am a princess who fell into the power of the Moor. He hung me up here because I learnt his grimoire by heart.' 'And I am a King's son,' answered Muhammad. 'The sorcerer gave me thirty days in which to learn the grimoire, but I cannot read it and my loss is certain to-morrow.' 'I will teach you,' said the girl with a smile, 'but, when the Moor comes back, you must say that you have not been able to read one word.' She sat down by his side and taught him the grimoire, kissing him much the while. Then she said: 'Hang me up as I was before,' and Muhammad did so.

At this point Shahrazād saw the approach of morning and discreetly fell silent.

But when the nine-hundred-and-fifty-third night had come

SHE SAID:

When the Moor returned at the end of the thirtieth day, he bade the boy recite the grimoire. 'How can I recite it,' asked Muhammad, 'when I cannot read a word of it?' Then the Moor cut off his right arm, and cried: 'I give you another thirty days! If, at the end of that time, you have not learnt the grimoire, you may say farewell to your head.' As soon as the sorcerer had departed for a second time, Muhammad went out to the girl, carrying his right arm in his left hand. When he had taken her down, she said: 'Here are three leaves of a plant which I have found by chance. The Moor has been seeking it for forty years, to complete his knowledge of the chapters of magic. Apply them to the two parts of your arm, my dear.' The boy did as he was told, and his arm was restored to its former state.

Then the girl read out of the grimoire and rubbed another of the magic leaves the while. Hardly had she spoken when two racing camels came up out of the earth and knelt down near them. At once the princess mounted one of these, and said: 'Let us each return to our parents. Afterwards you can come and ask for my hand in marriage. My father's palace is in such a place, in such a land.' She kissed him tenderly, and they departed, one riding to the right and the other to the left.

Muhammad came to his father's palace, shaking the earth with the formidable gallop of his camel. But there, instead of telling his story, he handed over his mount to the chief eunuch, saying: 'Sell it in the camel market, but be sure to keep the halter of its nose.'

When the eunuch offered the camel for sale, a hashīsh-seller came along and wished to buy it. After a great deal of chatting and chaffering, the animal changed hands at a very moderate price, for the eunuch, like all his kind, was no great hand at a bargain. He even sold the halter as a make-weight.

The hashīsh-seller led the camel to the space in front of his shop and showed it off to the hashīsh-eaters, his habitual customers. He set a bowl of water before it, while the takers of the drug laughed as if their hearts would break. But the camel placed its fore feet in the bowl and, when its new owner beat it and cried: 'Back, back, you pimp!' threw up its hind legs and, diving head first into the water, disappeared.

The hashīsh-seller beat his hands together, showing the halter which still remained to him, and crying: 'Help, help, good Mussulmāns! My camel is drowning in the bowl!'

Folk ran up from all sides, and said to him: 'Be quiet, O man, for you are mad! How could a camel drown in a bowl?' 'Be gone!' he answered. 'What are you doing here? I tell you that he dived in head first and disappeared. If you want further proof than this halter, ask the honourables who were with me.' But the sensible merchants departed, calling over their shoulders: 'You and your honourables are all mad together!'

While this scene was in the happening, the Moor bit his finger for rage at the disappearance of the prince and the princess. 'By Gog and Magog,' he exclaimed, 'and by the fire of the turning stars, I will catch them, even if they are on the seventh planet!' He hastened to Muhammad's city and entered the market just as the hashīsh-seller was bewailing his loss. Hearing talk of a halter and of a bowl which was both sea and tomb, he approached the man, saying: 'My poor fellow, if you have lost your camel, I am ready, for Allāh's sake, to reimburse you. Give me the halter which remains to you, and I will refund the price you paid for the animal, with a hundred dīnārs in addition.' The bargain was quickly concluded, and the Moor danced off with the halter, so light for joy that his toes scarcely touched the ground.

Now, beside other powers, this halter had the power of capture. The Moor had only to hold it out towards the palace, and Muhammad came at once to pass his nose into the loop of it; also at contact with the cord the boy was changed into a camel which knelt before the sorcerer.

The Moor mounted his new steed and urged it towards the dwelling of the princess. When the two came below the walls of the garden which surrounded the palace, the magician worked the cord to make the camel kneel; but this movement brought the halter within reach of Muhammad's teeth and he at once snapped it through, so that its power of capture was destroyed. Then, to escape his persecutor, the prince used the virtue of the cord to change into a large pomegranate and hang himself among the pomegranate flowers in the garden.

The Moor at once sought audience with the princess's father and, after humble greeting, said to him: 'O King of time, I come to beg you for a pomegranate; my wife is pregnant and ardently desires to eat one. You know how great a sin it is to thwart the yearning of a woman in her state!' 'But, my good man,' answered the astonished King, 'the season of pomegranates is not yet! All the trees of my garden are in flower only.' Then said the Moor: 'O King of time, if there is no pomegranate in your garden, I give you leave to cut off my head.'

The King called his chief gardener, and asked: 'Are there any pomegranates in my garden?' and, when the man answered: 'But master, this is no time for pomegranates!' he turned to the Moor, saying: 'Your head is forfeit!'

At this point Shahrazād saw the approach of morning and discreetly fell silent.

But when the nine-hundred-and-fifty-fourth night had come

SHE SAID:

But the Moor cried: 'O King, before you cut off my head, will you not tell the gardener to look among the pomegranate trees?' The King consented to do this, and the gardener, going down to his trees, found a large pomegranate, the like of which he had never seen before.

When the King received the fruit, he was so astonished that he did not know whether to keep it for himself or to cede it to the childing woman. He sought the advice of his wazīr, and the man asked him this question in return: 'If the pomegranate had not been found, would you have cut off this Moor's head?' 'Certainly,' said the King, and the wazīr replied: 'Then justice demands that he be given the pomegranate.'

The King held forth the fruit in his hand, but, as soon as the Moor touched it, it burst asunder, and all the grains were scattered on the floor. The sorcerer picked them up, one by one, until he came to the last grain, which had sought refuge in a little hole near the throne's foot, and which contained the vital essence of Muhammad. As the vile magician stretched out his neck towards this final grain, a dagger came up out of it and stabbed him to the heart, so that he spat out his unbelieving soul in a stream of blood.

Then Prince Muhammad appeared in his own delightful form and kissed the earth between the King's hands. At that moment the princess entered and said to her father: 'This was the youth who loosed me when I was hung by my hair from a tree.' 'Since that is so, you cannot do less than marry him,' answered the King.

The wedding was celebrated with all due pomp, and that night for the young lovers was blessed among all other nights.

They dwelt together in sweet content, and had many sons and daughters. This is the end.

But praise and glory to the Only, to the One, Who knows neither end nor beginning!

When Nasr al-Dīn, the twelfth captain of police, had made an end of his tale, Sultān Baibars so exulted in his pleasure that he named all the captains chamberlains of his palace, with monthly stipends of a thousand dīnārs from the royal treasure. He made them his cup-companions, and was never separated from them either in war or peace. The mercy of Allāh be upon them all!

Then Shahrazād smiled and fell silent; and King Shahryār cried: 'O Shahrazād, surely the nights are short when we get no more than this from your sweet mouth!' 'O King of time, if such be your wish,' answered Shahrazād, 'I will begin another tale at once, and you shall find that it leaves those which you have already heard far, far behind.' 'I am sure that it will be admirable!' replied King Shahryār. So Shahrazād said . . .

The Tale of the Sea Rose of the Girl of China

IT is related, O King of time, that there was once in a certain land of Sharkastān,—but Allāh on high knows all!—a King called Zain al-Mulūk, whose fame had gone out to the horizons of the world and who was the very brother of lions for valour and generosity. Though he was still young, he had two upstanding sons already, and a time came when, by the grace of Allāh, a third was born to him, a child picked out among ten thousand, whose beauty dispelled the shadows as a girl moon at her full dispels them. As the boy's years increased, his eyes, those cups of drunkenness, troubled the wise with the sweet fires of their regard, his lashes shone like curved dagger blades, the curls of his musk black hair confused the heart like nard, his cheeks mocked the cheeks of young girls; his smiles were arrows, he walked nobly and daintily; the sun had dexterously painted a freckle on the left commissure of his lips; his breast was smooth and white as a crystal tablet, and hid a lively heart.

Zain al-Mulūk delighted in his youngest son, and called together the court astrologers to cast his horoscope. They shook their sand and traced their figures in it; they murmured the major forms of divination, and then said to the King: 'His lot is fortunate, and his star assures him infinite happiness. But it is written in his Destiny that if you, his father, look upon him in his boyhood, your sight shall be destroyed.'

The world grew dark before the King's face; he had the child taken from his presence and ordered his wazīr to install him, with his mother, in a far away palace, so that he might never chance to see him in his goings to and fro.

These things were done, and years passed in which this flower of the royal garden, under the delicate guidance of his mother, blossomed in health and beauty. But no man may escape his Destiny, and a day came when young prince Nūrgihān mounted his horse and galloped after game in the forest. King Zain al-Mulūk had gone there also, hunting the deer, and, in spite of the many miles of trees, Fate willed that he should meet his son. He glanced at him, without recognition, and sight forsook his eyes. He became a prisoner in the kingdom of night.

Knowing, by this terrible proof, that the young rider must be his son, he wept and cried: 'The eyes of all fathers become brighter when they behold their sons; but mine are blind, are blind!'

He called the great doctors of that time to his palace, physicians more skilful than Ibn Sīnā, and consulted them concerning his blindness. When they had questioned him and considered together, they declared that the King was not to be cured by ordinary means. 'The one remedy is so difficult to come by,' they said, 'that we cannot advise our lord to dream of it. It is the sea rose of the girl of China.'

At this point Shahrazād saw the approach of morning and discreetly fell silent.

But when the nine-hundred-and-fifty-fifth night had come

SHE SAID:

And they explained to the King that there dwelt in the far interior of China a princess, daughter of King Fīrūz-Shāh, who had in her garden the only known tree of that magic sea rose which could cure the sight, even of those who had been born blind.

At once Zain al-Mulūk sent heralds through his kingdom to announce that the man who brought the King the sea rose of the girl of China should receive half of the empire as a recompense.

Then he sat down to await the issue, weeping like Jacob, wasting like Job, and drinking the blood of his heart's either lobe.

Among those who set forth to seek the sea rose in China were the king's two eldest sons, and young Prince Nūrgihān departed also. For he said to himself: 'I wish to prove the gold of my Destiny on the touchstone of danger, and also, as I was the unwitting cause of my father's blindness, it is only right that I should risk my life to cure him.'

Prince Nūrgihān, that son of the fourth sky, mounted his wind-swift courser at that hour when the moon, riding the black palfrey of the night, had pulled his bridle to the East.

He journeyed for days and months, across plains and deserts and through solitudes peopled only by wild grass and the presence of God, until he came to a limitless forest, darker than the wit of ignorance and so obscure that in it was neither night nor day, black nor white. But the prince's shining face lit up the shadows, and he advanced, with a heart of steel, among trees bearing living heads which grinned and laughed and fell as he passed by, and other trees whose fruits were earthen pots, which cracked and let out birds with golden eyes. Suddenly he found himself face to face with an old and mountainous Jinnī, seated on the trunk of an enormous carob. The youth saluted this figure, and dropped from the ruby casket of his mouth words which melted in the mind of the Ifrīt like sugar in milk. Pleased by the boy's beauty, the giant bade him rest beside him; so Nūrgihān got down from his horse and, taking a cake of flour and melted butter from his food sack, offered it to his new acquaintance as a token of friendship. The Jinnī made one mouthful of it and then jumped for joy, saying: 'This human food gives me more pleasure than an inheritance of that red sulphur which formed the stone of Sulaimān's ring! By Allāh, I am so delighted that, if each of my hairs turned to a hundred thousand tongues and each of those tongues were to sing your praise, the whole concert would fall short of the gratitude I feel. If you do not ask for some favour in return my heart will be as a porcelain plate dropped from a high terrace!'

Nūrgihān thanked the Jinnī for his engaging discourse, and answered: 'O chief and crown of all the Jinn, O careful guardian of the forest, since you permit me to express a wish, I ask you to take me without delay to the kingdom of Fīrūz-Shāh, for there I hope to pluck the sea rose of the girl of China.'

When he heard these words, the guardian of the forest heaved a cold sigh, beat his head with his hand, and lost consciousness. The prince heaped the most delicate cares upon him but they were unavailing until he thought to place a second sugar-and-butter cake in the giant's mouth. At once the large eyes opened, and the Ifrīt, with his mind troubled by the excellence of the cake and the difficulty of the wish which he had heard, said sorrowfully to Nūrgihān: 'O my master, the sea rose of the royal girl of China is guarded by certain aerial Jinn, whose business it is, day and night, to prevent the birds from flying above it, to ward off the drops of rain from its cup, to forbid the sun to burn its petals. Even if I transport you to the garden, I do not see how we are to elude the vigilance of those guards, for they greatly love the sea rose. I am perplexed in the extreme; but if you will give me another of those excellent cakes, which have done me so much good, perhaps the inspiration of it will bear some scheme. I have made a promise, I have sworn to bring you to the rose of your desire.'

Prince Nūrgihān gave the guardian of the forest another cake, which he dropped into the cavern of his throat, before wrapping his head in the hood of cogitation. Suddenly he lifted his eyes, and said: 'The cake has done its work! Seat yourself on my arm and we will fly together to China; for I have found the simplest of all ways to distract the attention of those Jinn: I will throw them one of these astonishing sugar-and-butter cakes.'

At these words, the boy, who had known great anxiety when the Jinnī of the forest swooned, grew calm again and blossomed like the young rose and freshened like the grass of the garden after rain. 'It is permitted,' he said to the Jinnī.

So the giant took the prince on his left arm and flew through the air towards China, shielding his burden from the near rays of the sun with his right hand, devouring distance in his flight. Soon he came to the capital city of China and set Nūrgihān down at the entrance of that marvellous garden where dwelt the sea rose. 'You can enter with a calm heart,' he said, 'for I go to distract the guards with that cake. You will find me waiting for you here, when you have finished your business.'

The prince entered the garden and found it a morsel of high Paradise, as lovely as a vermilion evening.

At this point Shahrazād saw the approach of morning and discreetly fell silent.

But when the nine-hundred-and-fifty-sixth night had come

SHE SAID:

In the middle of this garden was a lake filled to the brim with rose-water, and in these scented waves a fire red flower bloomed from a single stem. This was the admirable sea rose; none but the nightingale could find description for it.

Drunken with the beauty and smell of it, Prince Nūrgihān threw aside his clothes and, plunging into the scented water, pulled up the rose tree by its roots. Then he swam back with his delicate burden, dried and dressed in the shade of the trees, and hid his prize in his mantle, while the birds among the reeds gave the stream tidings of the rape.

But he would not leave the garden until he had visited a delightful pavilion, built of Yemen carnelians, which stood beside the water. Entering, he found himself in a high hall, containing an ivory bed studded with jewels and shaded by artfully-embroidered curtains. He opened these curtains with his hand and stood spellbound at the sight of a tender girl, who lay couched upon cushions with no vest or ornament save beauty. She slept deeply, little knowing that a human gaze had pierced the veil of her mystery. Her hair was in disorder, and her white hand with its five dimples was thrown up carelessly to touch her brow. The negro of night had fled into her musk-tinted hair; the sisters, the Pleiades, had veiled themselves in cloud before the bright chaplet of her teeth.

This was none other than Lily-Brow, the girl of China, and the sight of her nakedness cast Nūrgihān to the floor in a swoon. When, at length, he came to himself with a cold sigh, he whispered in the sleeping ear of the princess:

> They would sell silks to me,
> But I came by your bed
> And with my fingers tested the dark subtlety
> Of your hair instead.
> You are dressed in the narcissus and the rose
> And those
> Appear to me
> As cool as the palm-tree.

You sleep on purple tissue;
Surely to me
Your face is the fair issue
Of dawn from thence
And your light eyes the excellence
Of stars above the sea.

Then, as he wished to leave the sleeper some token of his entrance to that place, he changed rings with her. As he left the pavilion, he said over to himself:

I leave this garden with a blood-red tulip
Deep in my heart for wound and ornament.
Unhappy he, who from a greater garden
Were called with no flower in his tunic fold,
Nor time to gather one before he went.

He found the guardian of the forest waiting for him at the gate, and begged him to fly straight to the kingdom of Zain al-Mulūk in Sharkastān. 'To hear is to obey!' answered the Jinnī. 'But not until you have given me another cake.' So Nūrgihān gave him the last cake, and was instantly borne aloft and carried towards Sharkastān.

They came, without difficulty, to the palace of the blind King, and there the Jinnī said to his young friend: 'O capital of my life and joy, I will not leave you without one mark of my solicitude. Take this tuft of my beard hairs, and, when you have need of me, burn one of them.' So saying, he kissed the hands which had fed him, and went upon his way.

Nūrgihān sought audience of his father and, when he was introduced into the royal presence, drew the miraculous sea rose from under his mantle and handed it to the blind King. No sooner had the sufferer brought his eyes close to the blossom, whose odour and beauty drifted the soul of all who stood there, than his eyes became as bright as stars and beheld the colours of the world again.

In joyful thanks the King kissed his son upon the brow and pressed him to his heart in tenderness. He made proclamation throughout his kingdom that henceforth he but shared the empire with Nūrgihān, and gave order that royal rejoicings should be held for a whole year, to open the door of pleasure to all his subjects, rich and poor, and shut the door of heaviness against them.

Now that there was no danger of his father becoming blind

again, Nūrgihān was re-established in the King's favour, and had no thought but to plant the sea rose so that it should not die. To this end he burnt one of the Jinnī's beard hairs and, when the guardian of the forest appeared, begged him to see to the matter. So the giant hollowed out a fountain basin between two rocky peaks of the garden, in a single night. Its cement was of pure gold, and the foundations of it were jewels. The prince planted the sea rose in the midst of it, and she became again an enchantment to the nose and eyes.

At this point Shahrazād saw the approach of morning and discreetly fell silent.

But when the nine-hundred-and-fifty-seventh night had come

SHE SAID:

But, in spite of their father's cure, the two eldest sons, who had returned from China with drooping noses, pretended that the sea rose had no miraculous virtue, and that the King had only recovered his sight through sorcery and the intervention of the Stoned One.

Zain al-Mulūk was equally angry at their insinuation and their lack of discernment. He brought them together in the presence of their brother Nūrgihān, and talked to them severely, saying: 'How can you doubt the effects of the sea rose on my sight? Do you not believe that Allāh, Who brings forth woman out of man and man from woman, may as easily set healing in the heart of a rose? Listen, and I will tell you the apt adventure of an Indian princess.

'There was once, in the antiquity of time, a King of India who held in his harīm a hundred women, chosen from the myriad beauties of that land. But none of these conceived or bore a child; and this was a grief to the King, for he was old and bent. At length, however, Allāh permitted the youngest of his wives to become pregnant and bear a daughter of exceptional loveliness.

'Fearing that her lord would be vexed that her offspring was not a son, the mother put about the statement that she had borne a boy, and concerted with the astrologers to make the King believe that he must not look upon his heir until he was ten years old.

'When the girl approached that age, her mother taught her carefully how she might pass as a boy; and the quick child learned her lesson so well that she came and went in the royal apartments, dressed in a prince's garments, and a very prince in all her behaviour.

'The King rejoiced more and more each day at the beauty of his heir and, when five more years had passed, determined and made preparation to marry him to the daughter of a neighbouring Sultān.

'At the time appointed, he had his son dressed in a magnificent robe, and set out with him, in a gold palanquin upon an elephant's back, to the country of the bride. And in such embarrassing circumstance the counterfeit prince wept and laughed by turns.

'One night, when the royal procession had halted in a leafy forest, the princess left the palanquin and went apart among the trees to satisfy a need which is imperative even upon princesses. Suddenly she found herself face to face with a young and handsome Jinnī who sat on the ground below the branches, and was the guardian of that forest. Dazzled by her beauty, the creature gave her gentle greeting, and asked who she was and what might be her business in that place. Wooed to confidence by his engaging air, she told her story in all its details and gave expression to those fears which she had for the bridal night.

'The Jinnī was moved by her embarrassment and, after a moment's reflexion, generously offered to lend her his sex in its entirety and to take hers, on condition that she would hold the former in strict trust and return it when it had served her purpose. The princess gratefully accepted this proposition, and, by Allāh's grace, the exchange was effected without difficulty or complication. Light with delight and heavy with her new merchandise, the girl returned to her father and climbed up again into the palanquin; but, as she was not yet used to her novel ornaments, she sat down clumsily upon them and rose with a cry of pain. Yet she controlled herself so quickly that the accident was not noticed; and she took great care to run no such risk in future, to avoid both suffering and any harm she might do to a thing which she was engaged to return in working order to its owner.

'A few days after this, the train arrived at the bride's city, the marriage was celebrated with great pomp, and the groom made such good use of his borrowed instrument that the bride became pregnant on that night, and all concerned rejoiced.

'At the end of nine months the girl gave birth to a delightful boy, and, when she had risen from her bed, her husband said to her: "It is time that you came with me to my father's court to see my mother and my kingdom." This he said only as an excuse to set out; for his real intention was to return the Jinnī's sex, which, during these nine agreeable months, had developed and improved in beauty.

'The young wife consented to her lord's proposal, and the two set forth. When they reached the forest where the Jinnī dwelt, the prince left the caravan and betook himself to the spot where the exchange had been made. There he found the Jinnī, sitting in the same place, visibly fatigued and with a monstrous belly. After greeting, he said: "O chief and crown of the Jinn, thanks to your benevolence I have done my duty well; now I come to return your property, greater and improved in beauty, and to receive my own." He would have handed over the thing, but the Jinnī answered: "Your faith is a great faith and your honour is commendable, but I regret to have to tell you that I am no longer anxious to reverse the exchange which we made. Destiny has ruled that the matter should end with the first barter. After we parted something happened which forbids any resumption of our former states." "And what was that, great Jinnī?" asked the prince. "O one time maiden," answered the Ifrīt, "I waited here for you, sedulously guarding the thing which you had left in my care and sparing no pains to keep it in its original state of white virginity. But one day a fellow Ifrīt, the intendant of these regions, passed through the forest and came to see me. He knew by my changed smell that I was carrying a sex hitherto foreign, and fell violently in love with me. When he had excited a like sentiment in my heart, he joined himself to me in the usual manner and broke the precious seal of the packet which I had in care. I felt all that a woman would feel in like circumstances, and determined that a female's pleasure is more durable and more delicate than a male's. I am now pregnant by my future husband and could not possibly give back your sex without running the risk of great pain and tearing in my labour. Therefore I can only beg you to keep my loan and to give thanks to Allāh that no harm at all has come from our exchange." '

When he had told this story to his two eldest sons in the presence of their brother Nūrgihān, the King continued: 'Thus it is proved that nothing is impossible to the might of the Creator. He Who can change a girl into a boy, and a Jinnī into a pregnant woman, could, without difficulty, set a cure for blindness in the heart of a rose.' He dismissed his two other sons and kept Nūrgihān by him to receive all the love and prerogative of his reign. So much for Zain al-Mulūk and his sons.

Now we must return to Princess Lily-Brow, the girl of China, the bereft mistress of the sea rose.

When the Perfumer of the sky had set the sun's gold plate, filled

with the camphor of the dawn, within the eastern window, Princess
Lily-Brow opened the magic of her eyes and stepped from bed. She
plied her comb, tressed her hair, and walked, with the pleasant
balance of a swan, to the sheet of water which nourished her sea rose.
For her first thought each morning was of that flower. She walked
through the garden. Its air blew as from some aromatic shop, and the
fruits of its branches were flasks of dyed sugar hung in the wind.
The morning was fairer than all mornings and the alchemic sky had
the colour of glass and turquoise. Flowers sprang up where the rose
feet of the girl had trodden, and the dust which the fringes of her
robe sent flying was a balm for the eyes of the nightingale.

At this point Shahrazād saw the approach of morning and
discreetly fell silent.

But when the nine-hundred-and-fifty-eighth night had come

SHE SAID:

So she came to the rose-water lake and saw that her dear flower
had gone. She was ready to melt like gold in the crucible, to fade like
a flower in the hot wind; for, at the same moment that she perceived
the flame flower's place empty, she noticed that the ring she wore
was strange.

Remembering the nakedness of her sleep and realising that
treacherous eyes had violated the delightful mystery of her form, she
was tossed by the waves of confusion and wept in her pavilion all
that day. But, after this, reflection brought her reasonable thoughts,
and she said to herself: 'How false is the proverb which says: *There
is no track where no track has been left, for, were there track, it had been
left!* And a greater lie is the saying: *One must lose oneself to find a
lost thing.* For, as Allāh lives, though I am weak and young, I will
set out in quest of the thief of my sea rose and punish the man who
has slaked the desire of his eyes on the maidenhead of a sleeping
princess.'

She left her father's kingdom on the wings of impatience, followed
by a train of girl slaves dressed as warriors; and, by dint of questioning, came at last to Sharkastān and to the kingdom of Zain al-Mulūk,
father of Nūrgihān.

She found the capital gay for the year-long festival of rejoicing,
and heard the playing of music from each door. Still in her man's disguise, she asked the reason of this excitement, and people answered:

'The King was blind, but his excellent son Nūrgihān succeeded, after incredible adventures, in curing him with the sea rose of the girl of China. It is to celebrate the return of his sight that we are commanded to rejoice for a whole year at the royal expense and to play music at our doors from morning to night.'

Lily-Brow rejoiced to hear these certain tidings of her rose, and went down to bathe in the river after the fatigues of her journey. Then she dressed again as a youth and walked delightfully through the markets towards the palace. Those who saw her were effaced with admiration more quickly than the marks of her little feet upon the sand, and the coiled ringlets of her hair twisted about the hearts of the merchants.

Thus she came to the royal garden and saw the sea rose blossoming, as of old, in the scented water of its gold pond. After a rapturous recognition of it, she murmured: 'I will hide under the trees to catch a sight of the pert fellow who stole my rose and ring.'

Soon the prince came down to the rose's pond. His eyes, those cups of drunkenness, troubled the wise with the sweet fires of their regards, his lashes shone like curved dagger blades, the curls of his musk black hair confused the heart like nard, his cheeks mocked the cheeks of young girls, his smiles were arrows, he walked nobly and daintily; the sun had dexterously painted a freckle on the left commissure of his lips; his breast was smooth and white like a crystal tablet, and hid a lively heart. Lily-Brow fell into a kind of amazement when she saw him, and almost lost her wits; for the poet had done this boy no more than justice, when he wrote:

> If in a throng of base and true men mixed
> > He sped his shafts, that are in madness bathed,
> All noble hearts thereby would be transfixed
> > And all unworthy hearts would go unscathed.

When Lily-Brow came to herself, she rubbed her eyes and looked for the youth, but he was no longer there. 'Oh, oh,' she murmured to herself, 'the man who stole my rose has taken my heart also! He who broke the rare flask of my honour upon the stone of his eyes' seduction has sent an arrow to my heart as well. Alas, from whom shall I seek justice for these assaults? I have no mother to do me right in this strange land.'

Her heart was burning with passion as she went back to her maidens; she sat down among them and, taking paper and reed, wrote a letter to Nūrgihān. This she sent with the changeling ring by the hand of her favourite follower, who found the prince sitting and dreaming, it must have been, of Lily-Brow. He was thrown into a trouble of the heart when he recognised his ring, and this became more intense when he opened the paper, and read:

'After homage to the free Master of How and Why, who has given beauty to maidens and the dark eye of seduction to young men, lighting a lamp in the heart of both so that the moth of wisdom shall be destroyed.

'I die of my love for your eyes of languor; the flame devours me. How false is the proverb which says: *A heart will hear a heart*; for I am consumed, and you know nothing of it. What defence will you make if I accuse you of assassination?

'But write no further, O pen; for you have said too much.'

An answering fire took hold of Nūrgihān as he read these words. As restless as quicksilver, he took paper and answered thus:

'To her who queens it over all the silver-bodied fair, the curve of whose brows is as a sword in the hands of a drunken soldier!

'Star-fronted lady of light, jealousy of China, your letter has torn open the wound in my lonely heart. My lonely heart beats for you as many times as there are freckles on the full of the moon.

'A spark from your heart has fallen upon my wound, and the blaze of my desire has caught your harvest. Only a lover knows the joy of wasting away. I am like a half-killed fowl which rolls on the ground day and night, and will die if it be not lifted.

'O Lily-Brow, there is no veil upon your face, but you are your-self your veil! Come forth from behind it, for the heart is an admirable matter, and, though it be very small, Allāh has made His house there!

'O charm, I must not speak more clearly or confide more secrets to my pen, for he is of too masculine a shape to be allowed into the harīm of a lover's heart.'

Nūrgihān folded this letter, sealed it with his favourite seal, and, as he gave it to the messenger, begged her to say all the delicacies of passion to her mistress as a supplement to what he had written.

At this point Shahrazād saw the approach of morning and discreetly fell silent.

But when the nine-hundred-and-fifty-ninth night had come

SHE SAID:

The girl found her mistress waiting with eyes like the hearts of jonquils bathed in tears; so she greeted her with a smile, saying: 'O rose upon the tree of joy, may the reason for these tears staining the petals of your face recoil on me and leave you ever laughing! I bring good news!' And she gave Nūrgihān's letter, together with all the delicacies of passion as a supplement to what he had written.

As soon as Lily-Brow had read and had her joy confirmed by the slave's words, she rose and bade her girls prepare her.

The pretty women used all their art; they combed and scented her hair until the musk of Tartary had fumed off in mist for jealousy, and hearts danced to see her braids falling below her hips, tressed like palm trees on a day of festival. They put a belt of red lawn about her waist, and each of its threads was a hunting noose. They draped her in rose-tinted gauze which confessed her body, and put drawers upon her of royal amplitude and a more cloudy texture, sewn to enslave the world. They braided the long division of her hair with pearls until the stars of the milky way were cast into confusion. They put a diadem upon her brow, and then were thrown into a trance by the picture they had made. Yet her beauty was more than all their art.

Thus dressed, Lily-Brow went again with beating heart to the garden trees about the rose's pond. When Nūrgihān saw her below the branches, he swooned away, but the scent of her sighs brought his lids fluttering open again, and he lay upon the zenith of delight as he looked up at her. Lily-Brow found the prince so exact a counterfeit of the picture graven upon the leaves of her heart that she set aside the veil of reserve and gave him all her gifts: lips more to be desired than rose petals, silver arms, the moonlight of her smile, her cheeks' gold, the musk of her breathing, passing the musk of Tartary; the almonds of her eyes, her curls' black amber, the apple of her chin, the diamonds of her glances, and the thirty-six carven poses of her maiden body. Love bound his threads about their breasts and brows, and none may know what happened under the trees that night between so fair a two.

As neither love nor musk can be ignored for ever, parents on both sides learned of the affair and hastened to wed them.

They passed the remainder of their lives between loving and looking at the sea rose.

Glory be to Allāh Who sends both love and roses! And prayer and peace be upon our master lord Muhammad, the Prince of Messengers, and upon all his line!

When Shahrazād fell silent, little Dunyazād cried: 'O my sister, your words are sweet and delicate, fair and refreshing! How admirable is this tale of the sea rose and the girl of China! Please, please tell us another like it while there is yet time to-night.' 'I have a better, little one, should our King permit,' answered Shahrazād with a smile; and Shahryār cried: 'Have no doubt of my permission, Shahrazād! Henceforth, shall I ever be able to pass a night without your speech in my ears and your body before my eyes?' Shahrazād thanked him with another smile, and said: 'In that case I will tell you The Tale of the Honey Cake and the Cobbler's Calamitous Wife.'

And she said:

The Tale of the Honey Cake and the Cobbler's Calamitous Wife

IT is related, O auspicious King, that there was once, in the fortunate city of Cairo, a cobbler of liberal sympathies and excellent disposition, who earned his bread by patching old slippers. His name was Maarūf, and Allāh—may His name be exalted!—had afflicted him with a calamitous wife. She was called Fātimah, but her soul had been so steeped in tar and pitch that the neighbours nicknamed her Hot-Slop, knowing that she was an itching plaster upon the cobbler's heart and a black misfortune to any eye. This shrew used and abused the patience of her man, cursed him a thousand times a day, and never gave him any sleep at night. As time went on, therefore, Maarūf began to tremble at her evil deeds and fear her wickedness. He was a wise and sensitive man, jealous of his good name even in its poverty; so he would hand over all his money to the caprices of this dry wasp to avoid dispute. If, by ill fortune, he did not earn enough during his day's work, his ears were doomed that night to be filled with shrieking and his eyes with formidable domestic scenes. Sometimes the hours which should have been spent in sleep were darker for the poor man than the book of his Destiny, and he might well have murmured these words of the poet:

Hopeless at night I squirm
Beside the rough-legged worm
    I call my wife.
On that dark funeral day
When we were wedded, say
    Where was my knife?
Where the cold poison cup
For her to tipple up
    And sneeze out life?

You shall hear one of the many afflictions suffered by this Job of patience.

At this point Shahrazād saw the approach of morning and discreetly fell silent.

But when the nine-hundred-and-sixtieth night had come

SHE SAID:

His wife came into his presence one day—Allāh remove such days!—and said to him: 'O Maarūf, I wish you to bring me back a kunāfah cake to-night. Let it be dripping with bee honey.' 'O daughter of my uncle,' answered poor Maarūf, 'if Allāh of His generosity allows me to make enough money to-day, I will gladly bring you the kunāfah. At present I have not one copper piece, yet perhaps He will take compassion upon me.' But the shrew cried: 'What is all this talk of Allāh? Do you think I am going to wait upon a benediction? If you do not bring me an ounce of kunāfah, dripping with bee honey, your night shall be blacker than the Destiny which betrayed you into my hands! I am not going without, to please Allāh or anyone else!' 'He is merciful and generous!' sighed the cobbler with the sweat of affliction streaming down his brow.

When he had opened his shop in the cobblers' market, he lifted his hands on high, praying: 'O lord, grant that I earn enough to buy an ounce of kunāfah, and save myself from the hands of that vile woman!' But, in spite of this, no man brought him any work that day and he did not earn even enough to buy a crust of bread for supper. It was with trembling fingers that he locked his shop, and upon trembling feet that he set out towards his home.

But his way lay past the shop of a pastrycook whose shoes he had often mended, and the man, seeing him walk by in evident despair with his back bent under some heavy weight of grief, called to him, saying: 'Master Maarūf, why do you weep? What is your trouble? Come in here and rest while you tell me all about it.' Maarūf approached the delightful counter, and exclaimed after greeting: 'There is no power or might save in Allāh, the Merciful, the Compassionate! Destiny pursues me and will not even allow me supper.' Then, as the pastrycook insisted on further details, he told him of his wife's demand and how impossible it was of obedience.

When the man had heard all, he answered with a good-natured laugh: 'At least you might tell me how many ounces of kunāfah your good lady requires.' 'Perhaps five would be enough,' answered Maarūf. 'Then let it not trouble you,' cried the benevolent cook. 'I will let you have the five ounces and you can give me the price when Allāh returns to you with His favour.' He cut off a large slab of kunāfah and set it in a dish, where it swam among butter and honey. As he set the dish in Maarūf's hand, he said: 'This is worthy of a king's table. I have not made it with bee honey but with sugarcane honey, a change from the usual which improves it greatly.' The cobbler, who had known neither sort of sweetening in his life, would have kissed his saviour's hand, but the man prevented him, saying: 'The cake is written in the Destiny of your wife, O Maarūf. You yourself have nothing for supper and I insist on handing you this trifle of bread and cheese which Allāh intended for you.' He added to his other splendid present a fresh warm-smelling roll and a round of white cheese wrapped in fig leaves; and Maarūf, who had never been so rich in all his days, could find no words with which to thank such charity. As he left, he lifted his eyes to heaven to make it witness of his gratitude.

As soon as he entered his house, his wife cried in a harsh and menacing voice: 'Have you brought the kunāfah?' 'Allāh has been generous and it is here,' he replied, as he set the crisp and bearded sweet before her in its golden bath.

But the calamitous woman had no sooner set eyes on the dish than she uttered a cry of strident indignation and, beating her cheeks, exclaimed: 'Allāh curse the Stoned One! Did I not tell you it must be made with bee honey? You have brought me golden syrup to spite me! Did you imagine that I could not tell the difference? Do you wish to thwart me into my grave, you dog?' Poor Maarūf, who had certainly expected a very different reception, babbled excuses with a trembling tongue, and said: 'O daughter of excellent parents,

I did not buy this kunāfah; one of Allāh's compassionate pastry-cooks had pity on me and gave it to me with indefinite credit.' But, even so, the terrifying shrew thus broke in upon him: 'These are but words and help you not at all! Take your dirty treacle kunāfah!' With that she threw the confection at her husband's head, dish and all, and bade him rise up for a pimp and bring her another made with honey. At the same time she buffeted him so heartily on the jaw that she broke one of his front teeth and caused the blood to spurt over his beard and breast.

At this last aggression poor Maarūf ever so little lost his patience and gave an instinctive gesture with his hand which lightly brushed the woman's head. This natural reaction to his pain increased her rage; she seized his beard with both hands and hung from it with all her weight, crying: 'Help, O Mussulmāns, help! He is killing me!'

At this point Shahrazād saw the approach of morning and discreetly fell silent.

But when the nine-hundred-and-sixty-first night had come

SHE SAID:

The neighbours ran in answer to her cries and, coming between the two, had great difficulty in freeing the cobbler's tortured beard from the clutching fingers of his wife. Seeing the broken tooth, the bloody beard, and the wrenched hairs, and being well aware, from old experience, of the terrible life which Maarūf led with the woman, they lectured her with so much reason and eloquence that surely any but herself would have been shamed and converted. 'We all most gladly eat treacle kunāfah,' they said, 'and find it better than the other kind. What crime has your husband committed to deserve a broken tooth and a plucked beard?' Then they cursed her in chorus and went their way.

When they had gone, the raging termagant, who had sat silent in a corner during their harangue, muttered at Maarūf with suffocating hate: 'So you raise up the neighbours against me! You shall see, you shall see!'

As she sat glaring at him with tigress eyes, the cobbler tried to placate her by collecting the kunāfah from the broken bits of the dish and assembling it cleanly upon one of their own plates. Then he offered it to his wife, saying timidly: 'Eat a little of this one, sweetheart, and to-morrow, if Allāh wills, I shall bring you the other.' But she repulsed him with a kick, and answered: 'Begone with it, O dog of botchers! Do you think that I will touch the wages of your shameful trade with pastrycooks? To-morrow, by Allāh's grace, I shall destroy you utterly!'

After this, the wretched Maarūf, who found truce with his wife more difficult than any other job of patching, gave up the attempt and turned his thoughts to the hunger which had been gnawing him all day. He sat down before the plate and ate, first, all the delicious mouthfuls of the kunāfah, then the roll, and finally the cheese until not a fragment remained. This meal he made to the accompaniment of: 'May it choke you!' and: 'May it poison you!' delivered with flaming eyes. He did not answer any of these amenities, and the woman's disappointment culminated in a paroxysm of fury, during which she cast the furniture of the room at her husband's head. At last she threw herself upon the couch, where she continued to curse him in her sleep all through the night.

Maarūf rose early and dressed in haste; he opened his shop betimes, hoping that Allāh might send him money with which to satisfy his wife's extravagant demand. But he had not been seated long before two policemen arrested him by order of the kādī, bound his hands behind his back, and led him to the tribunal. When he had been hustled into the judge's presence, he beheld his wife standing with her arm bandaged, her head wrapped in a bloodstained rag, and a broken tooth held in her fingers. As soon as the kādī saw the terrified cobbler, he cried: 'Come here! Have you no fear of Allāh that you violently attack this poor young woman, and wound her arms and break her teeth?' Maarūf wished the ground might open and swallow him; his confusion, his desire for peace, his regard for his good name which would not let him call the neighbours as witnesses, led him to keep silence. The kādī, construing this silence as confession, bade his guards cast the afflicted man to the floor and give him a hundred stripes with the stick on the soles of his feet. While this sentence was cruelly carried out, Hot-Slop Fātimah watched with gloating eyes.

Maarūf dragged himself away from the tribunal to a ruined house on the banks of the Nile, where he waited for the swelling of his feet to die down. He would rather have tasted red death than seek his home again and, therefore, when he could walk, he hired himself to the captain of a river boat. He dropped down the Nile, and came in good time to Damietta, where he signed on as sail-mender aboard a certain felucca and confided his destiny to Allāh.

After a voyage of several weeks, the felucca was stricken by a terrible tempest and sent to the bottom of the sea. All were drowned save Maarūf, whom Allāh delivered by placing a fragment of the mainmast beneath his hand as he struggled in the water. Thanks to the unnatural strength which the love of dear life will give a man, the cobbler was able to climb astride this piece of wreckage. He beat the water with his feet as if they had been oars. The waves made him their plaything and cast him dizzily to left and right; for a day and a night he wrestled with the deep; but, on the second morning, the wind and the current set him ashore near a well-built seaside city.

He lay motionless on the sand and soon fell into a deep sleep; when he woke, he saw a richly-dressed stranger bending above him, flanked by two slaves with folded arms. This man was examining Maarūf's body with singular attention, and as soon as he saw the cobbler's eyes open, he cried aloud: 'Glory to Allāh! O wanderer, be welcome to our city!' Then, in a lower voice, he said: 'In Allah's name, tell me your land and city, for, by the remnants of your clothes, you would seem to be an Egyptian.' 'You are right, master,' answered Maarūf, 'I am an Egyptian, and Cairo is the city of my birth and dwelling.' 'Would it be indiscreet to ask in what part of Cairo you live?' asked the rich man in a trembling voice. 'In the Red Street, master,' replied the cobbler. 'What folk do you know in that street?' demanded the man. 'And what is your trade, my brother?' 'I am a cobbler; I patch old shoes,' said Maarūf. 'The folk I know are of the commoners, of my own kind, but honoured and respectable for all that. Here, if you wish them, are some of their names.' And he said over the names of several neighbours who lived in Red Street.

The rich man, whose face had more and more lighted at these answers, asked again: 'O brother, do you know sheikh Ahmad, the perfume-seller?' 'Allah increase you!' cried Maarūf. 'He is my neighbour, our walls are one.' 'Is he well?' asked the rich man. 'Thanks to Allāh, he is very well,' answered Maarūf. 'How many children has he now?' asked the man. 'Still three, may Allāh preserve them!' answered Maarūf. 'Still Mustafā, Muhammad, and Alī.' 'What do they do with themselves?' asked the man, and Maarūf answered: 'The eldest, Mustafā, is a schoolmaster in a monastery. He has fame as a scholar; he knows the Holy Book by heart and can recite it in seven different manners. Muhammad, the second, is a druggist and perfume-seller, like his father. The old man has just opened a shop for him near his own, to celebrate the birth of a grandson in Muhammad's house. As for little Alī—may Allāh shower blessings upon him!—he was the companion of my childhood; we amused ourselves together every day, and played a thousand tricks upon the people. But a time came when Alī did what he did with a little Coptic boy, a child of the Nazarenes, who ran to his parents and told them that he had been humbled and outraged in a disgraceful way. Poor Alī had to fly the city to escape the vengeance of those Christians. He has not been heard of for twenty years. Allāh shower blessings upon him, I say again!'

At these words the rich man threw his arms about Maarūf's neck and drew him to his breast, weeping and saying: 'Glory be to Allāh, to the Reuniter! O Maarūf, I am Alī, the son of Ahmad!'

At this point Shahrazād saw the approach of morning and discreetly fell silent.

But when the nine-hundred-and-sixty-second night had come

SHE SAID:

After the first mutual transports of joy, Alī begged Maarūf to explain his presence on that coast. When he learned that the cobbler had not eaten for a day and a night, he took him up behind him on his mule and carried him to his own splendid palace, where the servants magnificently entreated him. It was not until next morning that Alī was free to talk again with his old friend, but eventually the two sat together in comradeship and Maarūf told the torments of his life since his calamitous marriage. He explained how he had chosen to abandon his shop and native land rather than remain any longer a prey to that vixen, how he had been beaten on the feet, how he had been wrecked and well-nigh drowned.

Then, in his turn, Alī told his friend that they were in Ikhtiyān al-Khatan, that Allāh had favoured him in his dealings, and that he was now the richest merchant and the most respected noble in all the city.

When each had given rein to his memories, Alī, the rich merchant, said to his friend: 'Maarūf, my brother, the blessings which Allāh has showered upon me are not mine, I only hold them in trust for Him. Can I make better use than to give a great part of them to you?' He presented him with a bag of a thousand gold dīnārs, dressed him in sumptuous garments, and then said: 'To-morrow morning you shall mount my best mule and ride to the market, where you will find me sitting among the most substantial merchants of the city. When I see you I will rise and greet you, I will hold the reins of your mule, I will kiss your hands, and pay you every possible respect. This proceeding will gain you great consideration at the outset, and I will complete the effect by lending you a vast and well-stocked shop. You will speedily become acquainted with the best people, your affairs will prosper under Allāh, and you will rejoice in that calm which only wealth and far absence from a nagging wife can give.' Maarūf could find no words with which to thank his friend; he would have kissed the hem of his robe but Alī prevented him and embraced him. Afterwards they talked of this and that, reviewing their childish past, until it was time to sleep.

Next morning Maarūf dressed magnificently to appear as some rich foreign merchant, mounted a superb grey mule and rode to the market at the appointed time. Then the little drama played itself as arranged between himself and Alī, until all the merchants were overwhelmed with admiration and respect for the stranger. When they saw Alī kiss his hand and help him from his mule, when they saw the newcomer seat himself slowly and gravely on a prepared seat in front of Ali's shop, they came one after another to their old friend, saying in a low voice: 'Surely he is some great merchant!' Alī looked at them in pity as he answered: 'Some great merchant, did you say? He is one of the first merchants of the world. He has more shops and storehouses over the earth than the fires of the earth could well destroy! I am only a wretched pedlar when compared with him. His partners and agents and counting-houses are the honour of every city, from Egypt and Yemen to India and the far frontiers of China. By Allāh, you will see what kind of a man he is, when you get to know him well!'

Hearing this testimonial delivered in the accents of exact truth, the merchants flocked round Maarūf with salute, congratulation, and welcome. Each hurried to ask him to dinner, while he smiled complacently and begged to be excused on the ground that he had already accepted the hospitality of his friend Alī. The syndic of the merchants came to greet him in his place, contrary to the custom which demands that the first visit be paid by the newcomer, and exerted himself to give particulars of prices current and the principal industries of that land. Then, to show that he was ready to help this stranger to make a brisk trade in the goods which he had brought so far, the syndic said: 'Doubtless, my master, you have many bales of yellow cloth? There is a great demand for yellow cloth in this city.' 'Yellow cloth?' answered Maarūf without a moment's pause. 'I have, I believe, a vast quantity of it.' 'And gazelle blood red?' asked the syndic. 'As for gazelle blood red,' answered Maarūf with assurance, 'I do not think that my customers will have any complaint to make on that score. We are supposed to have the finest gazelle blood red in all the world.' To all such questions, he returned the same answer: 'Plenty! Plenty!' until the syndic timidly asked: 'Would you be so good as to show us a few samples?' Maarūf took this difficulty in his stride, and replied with a certain condescension: 'Certainly, as soon as my caravan arrives, certainly!' Then he explained to his questioner and the other merchants that he expected a caravan of a thousand camels in a few days. And the very thought of this held them spellbound.

But their marvel at him did not reach its limit until they witnessed the following prodigy. While they chatted together, opening wide eyes at the details of the caravan, a beggar approached them and held out his hand to each in turn. Some gave the man a copper piece, some half a copper piece, and the majority contented themselves with saying: 'May Allāh pay you!' But Maarūf drew out a great fistful of gold dīnārs and gave them as simply to the afflicted man as if they had been a copper. After this a silence fell upon that company, and all were thinking over and over again: 'How rich this man must be!'

In this way Maarūf's reputation increased from hour to hour, until it reached the ears of the King, who called his wazīr to him, saying: 'O wazīr, a caravan of extraordinary richness is expected at my city, to the address of a merchant stranger. Now I do not wish those wolves of the market to make their profit from this coming, for they are already far too rich. This time I am determined that we of the court shall benefit, my wife your mistress, my daughter the princess, and myself.' 'There seems no harm in that,' answered the wazīr, who was a wise and prudent man, 'but do you not think that it would be better, O King of time, to wait until the caravan comes, before taking the necessary steps?' The King grew angry at this, and cried: 'Are you mad? Does one buy the meat when the dogs have devoured it? Bring the rich merchant instantly into my presence and I will speak to him!'

When the wazīr, in spite of his nose, had brought Maarūf into the presence, the cobbler bowed low and kissed the earth before the throne, making a delicious compliment. The King marvelled at his choice language and distinguished manner, and asked him many questions concerning his business and great wealth. But Maarūf was content to answer with a smile: 'Our lord the King shall see and be satisfied when my caravan arrives.' Therefore the King believed in Maarūf and, to test him, showed him a wonderful great pearl worth at least a thousand dīnārs. 'Are there such pearls in your caravan?' he asked. Maarūf held the jewel in his fingers for a moment, examining it disdainfully, and then threw it to the earth and broke it with a strong blow of his heel. 'What are you doing, O man?' cried the stupefied Sultān. 'You have broken a pearl worth a thousand dīnārs.' 'Yes, it was worth quite that,' replied the cobbler with a laugh, 'but I have whole sacks of infinitely larger and more beautiful in my caravan.'

After this the King's greed knew no bounds, and he said to himself: 'I must catch this prodigious fellow for my daughter.'

At this point Shahrazād saw the approach of morning and discreetly fell silent.

But when the nine-hundred-and-sixty-third night had come

SHE SAID:

Therefore he turned to Maarūf, saying: 'O honoured and most distinguished amīr, will you accept my only daughter, your slave, as a gift to celebrate your coming to our land? If you are willing, I will marry you to her and you shall reign over the kingdom after my death.' Maarūf, who had adopted a pose of modest reserve, answered discreetly: 'The King's suggestion honours his slave. But do you not think, my lord, that it would be better to wait until my great caravan arrives before celebrating the marriage? The dowry of a princess, such as your daughter, would entail an expenditure which I am not in a position to undertake for the moment. You will understand that I must give my wife a bridal portion of at least two hundred thousand purses of a thousand dīnārs each. Beyond that, I shall have to distribute a thousand purses of a thousand dīnārs to the poor and needy on the night of penetration, a thousand further purses to those who come with gifts, and a thousand purses for the price of the feast. Then there will be necklets of a hundred large pearls for each of the women in the harīm, and compliments to you and my aunt the queen of uncounted jewels and sumptuous novelties. It is an expense which I can hardly compass before my caravan comes in.'

This prodigious enumeration won the King's heart even more than the delicacy of Maarūf's attitude. 'No, by Allāh,' he cried, 'I myself will pay all the expenses of the marriage! You can give me my daughter's dowry when your caravan comes in. I insist on the marriage taking place as soon as possible, and give you free leave to take all that you require of ready money from the royal treasury. Have no scruple, my son, for all that is mine is yours.'

He called his wazīr, and said to him: 'Tell the sheikh al-Islām that I wish to speak with him concerning the immediate marriage of my daughter and the amīr Maarūf.' The wazīr lowered a disconsolate head and said nothing; but, when the King began to grow impatient, he came closer, and whispered in his ear: 'O King of time, this fellow does not please me, his manner bodes no good to the court. I pray you, by your dear life, to wait at least until we have more certain proof of the existence of this caravan; for a princess like your daughter, O King, is worth more than the convenience of an unknown adventurer.'

The King saw the world darken before his face, and cried angrily: 'O execrable traitor, O you who loathe us, you only say these things because you wish to marry my daughter yourself. But that is far from your nose's destiny, I tell you. If you do not instantly cease from troubling my mind and swaying it against this polished, high-souled, and exceedingly wealthy gentleman, I shall become vexed and utterly destroy you.' He paused, and then cried on in rising excitement: 'Perhaps you wish my daughter to be left on my hands until she is old and unacceptable? How could I ever find a more perfect son-in-law than this generous, charming, and discreet young man? Not only is he almost certain to love the princess, but he will make us all rich, I tell you, make us all rich! Begone and fetch the sheikh al-Islām instantly!'

So the wazīr went out, his nose trailing well-nigh to his feet, and fetched the sheikh al-Islām, who wrote out a marriage contract for Maarūf and the princess.

The city was decked and lighted by the King's orders, festival and rejoicing sounded everywhere, and Maarūf, the cobbler, who had seen black death, red death and all calamity, sat on a throne in the courtyard of the palace. A crowd of ballad-singers, wrestlers,

players, drummers, clowns, buffoons and jolly mountebanks, surged
round to entertain the court, and Maarūf had the wazīr bring sack
after sack of gold to cast among the shouting, singing, dancing mob.
Nor did the wazīr have any rest that day, for no sooner had he come
to Maarūf's throne, bending under the weight of a thousand thousand dīnārs, than he was sent back for another load. These extravagant celebrations lasted for three days and far into the fourth
night, which was the night of penetration. The bride's procession
was of great magnificence, for the King had willed it so. Each
woman, as she passed, showered presents about the princess, and
her girls gathered them up and set them aside. But, when the girl
was taken to the bridal chamber, Maarūf went himself to a corner of
it, and muttered: 'Plague on plague on plague on plague! Come
what will, it is no fault of mine! This is Destiny, O slipper-patcher, O
wife-beaten, O Maarūf, O you ape!'

When the two were left alone and the princess lay at ease beneath
the silken curtains of the couch, Maarūf sat down upon the ground
and beat his hands together in despair. As he made no move to join
her, the girl thrust her delightful head out of the curtains, saying:
'Why so far off and sad, my handsome lord?'

At this point Shahrazād saw the approach of morning and
discreetly fell silent.

But when the nine-hundred-and-sixty-fourth night had come

SHE SAID:

Maarūf heaved a sigh and answered, as if with effort: 'There is
no power or might save in Allāh!' 'How so, my master?' asked the
girl in a trembling voice. 'Do you find me ill-made or ugly, or is it
some other grief which tortures you?' 'It is your father's fault,' said
Maarūf with another sigh. 'What harm has he done?' she demanded;
and he replied: 'Harm? Surely everyone has noticed my disgusting
meanness, my niggardly treatment of you and your ladies? The
King was very wrong when he did not let me wait the coming of my
caravan. At least I should have been able to give you a few necklaces
with five or six rows of mighty pearls, at least a few fair robes un-
dreamed of by princesses, at least a few jewelled toys not quite unworthy of you; at least I could have appeared before your guests as
something better than a cheese-parer. But your father would hurry
on the match and betray me into a false position. It was like burning

green grass.' At once the princess answered: 'Instead of bothering about such trifles, undress and come to me. Leave this thought of presents and the like, for I am indifferent to your caravan and all your wealth. That which I want is much more simple, my dear, and much more interesting. Strengthen your loins for the fight, my darling!'

'Here it is at last!' cried Maarūf, as he threw off his clothes and advanced at the tilt towards the princess; but, as he lay down beside the tender girl, he thought: 'Can this be Maarūf, the cobbler of Red Street?'

Then rose a hot struggle of legs and arms and thighs and hands. Maarūf set his fingers on the girl's knee, and she came forward to him, so that lip spoke to lip in that hour when we forget our mothers. He clasped her strongly, to let out all the honey and that the titbits might be face to face. When he slipped his hand under her left armpit, his essential thews grew taut and hers were stretched. When he put his left hand in the fold of her groin, all the strings of their bows groaned in concert. He aimed between her breasts, but it was between her thighs,—Allāh knows how!—that the shot told. He put on the legs of the princess as a belt, and took both forks of the road, crying: 'Charge, O father of kisses!' He baited the hook and lit the fuse. He threaded the needle, he cooked the eel, he let the valiant trumpet peel. His tongue said: 'Squeal!' his teeth said: 'Feel!' and his eyes said: 'Burn 'em up with zeal!' One hand bade kneel, one hand bade steal, and both of his lips cried: 'Give us veal!' The drilling steel said: 'Dance a reel beneath my quick descending wheel, O pearl in peal, O daughter leal, O jewel of the royal seal! Come, chirp and leap, my dainty!' And thus the citadel was ta'en, whose towers shall not be held again. The battle rolled upon the plain (that is to say, the counterpane) with banging but with little bane, with mighty wound but little pain, with piercing, but with no one slain, with lightning and with hurricane, with stain and strain of vein and brain; and yet the end of the campaign was neither's loss and either's gain. So 'Praise to Him,' be our refrain, 'Who makes the maiden ripe and fain and swells the muscles of the swain that, by the playing of these twain, the world may be fulfilled again!'

Then, after a night of such sucking and milking, Maarūf rose and went to the hammām, followed by the happy sighing of his bride. After he had bathed and dressed himself in a magnificent robe, he entered the dīwān and sat upon the right hand of the King, his father-in-law, to receive the felicitations of the amīrs and great folk. On his own authority he sent for the wazīr and ordered him to distribute robes of honour to all who were present, to make vast gifts of money to the amīrs and the wives of the amīrs, to the great folk and the wives of the great folk, to the guards and the wives of the guards, and to all the eunuchs great and small, and old and young. Also he had sacks of dīnārs brought to him and pressed handfuls of them on any who would take them. Thus all the people loved him and prayed for his long life.

He filled twenty days with incalculable generosity, and twenty nights with attendance upon his wife, so that she loved him also.

At the end of this time there was no news of Maarūf's caravan, and his insane prodigalities had gone so far that, one morning, the royal treasure was found by the wazīr to be quite empty. He went in perplexity of spirit and burning with concealed rage, to say to the King: 'May Allāh spare us all ill news! But I must tell you, since silence would be culpable, that the treasure has run dry and that the marvellous caravan of your son-in-law has not yet come to fill the empty sacks.' The King became a little disquieted, and answered: 'By Allāh, it is true that the caravan is a few days late, but it will surely come.' Then said the wazīr with an evil smile: 'Allāh prolong your days, my master, and shower His blessings upon you! But you must confess that we have fallen on evil times since the amīr Maarūf came among us. And I see no way out of our embarrassment, for there is no more money, and your daughter is already married to this unknown man. Allāh save us all from the Evil One, the Far One, the Stoned One!' 'Your words weary me,' answered the King, who was by this time very frightened indeed. 'Instead of showing off your powers of speech, you would be more useful if you suggested some way to remedy the situation and to prove, if such be the case, that my son-in-law is a liar and a fraud.' 'You are very right, O King,' agreed the wazīr. 'A man should not be condemned before he is found guilty. In my opinion none but your daughter can come to the truth of the matter. Call her here, I beg, and let me question her from behind the modesty of a curtain.' 'It is permitted,' cried the King, 'and, by the life of my head, if that Maarūf be proved to have deceived us, his death shall be dark indeed!'

As Maarūf was absent from the palace at the time, the King at once had a curtain stretched across the hall and caused his daughter, the princess, to sit behind it.

When the wazīr had thought out his plan of attack, the King called across the curtain to his daughter, bidding her speak with the wazīr. 'What do you wish, fellow?' she cried back; and the wazīr answered: 'Dear mistress, the treasure of the reign is empty, thanks to the prodigalities of the amīr Maarūf; also the caravan, of which he has spoken so much, has not yet given any sign. Therefore the King, your father, has empowered me to ask what your opinion is of this stranger, what effect he has produced upon your mind, and what suspicions you may have formed of him during the twenty nights which you have had together.'

'Allāh bless the amīr Maarūf! Allāh preserve my husband!' answered the princess. 'You ask me what I think of him? I answer, nothing but good. There is no sugarstick on earth to be compared with him for sweetness and pleasure. Since I have been his bride, I have become fat and beautiful, so that, when I pass them, people say: "Allāh preserve such beauty from the evil-eye!" My husband is a compost of all delights; he is my joy and I am his. Long may we dwell together!'

The King turned to the disconcerted wazīr, saying: 'You see? My son-in-law is entirely to be trusted. You deserve to be impaled for your suspicions.' But the wazīr questioned again through the curtain, saying: 'And what of the caravan, my mistress?' 'What can that matter to me?' she answered. 'Will my delight be less or more because of its coming?' 'Yet, if it does not come,' asked the wazīr, 'who will provide food for my lady now that the treasure chests are empty? Who will find money for the expenses of her husband?' 'Allāh is generous and will not forsake His own,' retorted the princess, and the King checked the wazīr, saying: 'Hold your tongue! My daughter is quite right.' Then he continued through the curtain: 'Yet there would be no harm, my dear, in trying to find out approximately on what day your husband expects his caravan. I would like to know, simply in order to regulate my payments and see if it will be necessary to levy new taxes to bridge the interval.' 'I hear and I obey,' replied the princess. 'I will ask Maarūf to-night and tell you what he says.'

So, at nightfall, when the two lay side by side, the princess put her hand below her husband's armpit, and took on that pleasant, tender, caressing, honey-sweet air which every woman has at her command when she would gain an end.

At this point Shahrazād saw the approach of morning and discreetly fell silent.

But when the nine-hundred-and-sixty-fifth night had come

SHE SAID:

'Light of my eyes,' she said, 'fruit of my liver, seed of my heart's berry, life of my soul, the fires of your love compass my breast and I am ready to give my life for you, to share your Destiny however dark. Hide nothing from me, I beg by your sweet life. Tell me, sweet, that I may guard the secret in my heart of hearts, why that great caravan, of which my father and his wazīr talk so much, has not yet come. If you are doubtful or embarrassed concerning it, confide in me and I will discover a way to help you.' Then she pressed him to her breasts and melted in his arms. 'My dear,' answered Maarūf, with a burst of laughter, 'why go by-ends to ask so simple a thing? I am quite ready to tell you the truth.'

He stayed silent for a moment, to swallow his spit, and then went on: 'Sweetheart, I am no merchant, no master of caravans; I own no wealth or other calamity. In my own country I am a jobbing cobbler, married to a pest of a woman called Fātimah Hot-Slop, a blister on my heart, a black calamity before my eyes. It happened one day . . .' And he told the princess of his life with the woman in Cairo and the whole adventure of the honey cake. He omitted no detail of his shipwreck, of his meeting with the merchant Alī; but nothing would be gained by repeating his story in this place.

When the princess had heard all, she laughed so heartily that she fell over on her backside, and Maarūf laughed also. 'Allāh is the Dealer of Destiny!' he cried. 'You were written in my fate, O mistress!' 'Indeed, Maarūf,' answered the girl, 'you are a perfect master of stratagem; you have no equal for wisdom, cunning and good luck. But what will my father say? And, above all, what will the wazīr say, if the truth comes to be known! They will surely kill you and I will as surely die of grief. For the moment, your only course is to leave the palace and retire to some far country, until I can find a way of arranging matters and explaining your most inexplicable conduct. . . . Take these fifty thousand dīnārs and, when you have ridden to some safe retreat, let me know its position that I may send a daily courier with news and for news. That will be best, my dear.' 'I lie under your protection, mistress,' replied the cobbler. 'I put my trust in you.' So the princess embraced him, and he did his ordinary with her until midnight.

Then she bade him rise, clothed him in the garments of a mamlūk, and gave him the best horse in her father's stables. We will leave him riding away from the city, and pursue the tale of the princess, the King, the wazīr and the mythical caravan.

Early on the following morning, the King sat in the hall, with the wazīr by his side, and summoned the princess into his presence. She took her place behind the curtain as before, and asked: 'What is it, O father?' 'Tell us what you have found out, my daughter,' answered the King, and the princess exclaimed: 'What have I found out? Allāh confound the Evil One, the Stoned One! May he curse all calumniators and especially blacken the black face of your wazīr, who would have blackened mine and my husband's!' 'How? Why?' asked the King, and his daughter continued: 'Why? How? By Allāh, is it possible that you confide at all in this sinister wazīr? Do you not see that his whole business and hobby in life is to discredit my husband?' She fell silent for a moment, as if stifled by indignation, and then said: 'If you must hear the secrets of my marriage, father, I will prove to you that there is no more upright and truthful man on earth than the amīr Maarūf, whom may Allāh bless! At nightfall yesterday, just as my dear husband had entered my apartment, the eunuch of my service begged speech on a most urgent matter and brought in a letter which had been given to him by ten foreign mamlūks in costly raiment, who desired an audience with their master Maarūf. My husband read the letter and then passed it to me. I found it to be from the commander of that very caravan which you so greedily expect. Now this commander was accompanied by five hundred young mamlūks to guard the riches of the caravan, and it appeared that these had been attacked by a band of cut-throat Badāwī, who would have disputed their right to pass. That was the first cause of delay. A few nights after they had beaten off this band, they were attacked by a second, greater and better armed. A bloody fight took place, in which the caravan lost fifty of the mamlūks, two hundred camels and four hundred bales of price.

'Yet, at this distressing news, my husband only smiled and tore up the letter; he did not even ask further particulars from those who waited below. "What are four hundred bales and two hundred camels?" he said to me. "All told it cannot be more than a loss of nine hundred thousand dīnārs. It is not worth speaking of; above all, it is not worth a moment's thought from you, my dearest. One aspect of the matter alone annoys me, that I shall have to leave you for a few days in order to go myself and hurry on the arrival of the caravan." He rose with a jolly laugh and petted me a little, because I wept. When the stone of my heart's fruit had departed from me, I leaned from the window and saw him talking in the courtyard with ten mamlūks, as handsome as white moons. Soon he mounted his horse and rode away at the head of them, to hasten the coming of his caravan.'

Here the princess blew her nose loudly, as one who has wept much, and continued in sudden spleen: 'So tell me what would have happened had I been indiscreet enough to question my husband in the way you wished? Or rather in the way your pitch-faced wazīr wished? He would have looked askance at me, he would have ceased to trust me, he would have loved me no more, he would have very rightly hated me! And all because that calamitous old beard has an offensive mind!' So saying, she rose and went her way with a noise of angry draperies. 'Son of a dog,' cried the King to his wazīr, 'do you see what you have done now? As Allāh lives, only my too clement heart preserves you from a merited death! Breathe but one further word of suspicion against my son-in-law, and see what you will get!' He gave him a terrible look from the corner of his eye, and left the dīwān. So much for the King, the wazīr, and the princess.

When Maarūf had ridden far through desert places away from Ikhtiyān al-Khatan, he began to be assailed by great fatigue, for he was not used to riding royal horses and his cobbling had not fitted him for princely exercise. Also he began bitterly to regret that he had told the truth to the princess. 'Now you must take to the road again,' he grumbled, 'instead of rejoicing in the arms of your butter-sweet bride, whose kisses had made you forget the calamitous Hot-Slop.'

He fell to dreaming of dead lovers, whose hearts had been burnt by separation, until he wept tears of self-pity and broke into despairing verses. He groaned and exhaled his anguish in suitable mournful songs, until he came at sunrise to the outskirts of a little village. By this time he was famishing; for, in his haste to leave Ikhtiyān al-Khatan, he had forgotten to provide himself with food. Therefore, seeing a peasant ploughing behind two oxen in a field, he approached him and said: 'Greeting, O sheikh!' 'Greeting and the mercy of Allāh and His blessings!' answered the peasant. 'Doubtless, my master, you are one of the Sultān's mamlūks?' When Maarūf had answered that he was, the peasant continued: 'Be very welcome,

O milk-white countenance! Be so good as to dismount and accept my hospitality.'

But the cobbler, who saw with the same glance that the man was generous and that his house was poor, excused himself, saying: 'My brother, I fear I am too hungry to be content with what you could spare.' 'Allāh's food is all found,' replied the man. 'If you will dismount and let me entertain you in His name, I will run instantly to the village, for it is near, and bring back provision for yourself and your noble horse.' 'Since the village is so close, my brother,' objected Maarūf, 'would it not be better for me to ride there, than for you to run there? I could easily buy food in the market.' But so great was the native generosity of the peasant that he could not persuade himself to let any stranger of Allāh pass his dwelling; he went upon another tack, and answered: 'But what is this market of which you speak, my master? There is no market in a miserable little village like ours, its houses all built of cowdung, or anything in the least like a market. We hardly buy and sell at all, for our poverty is self-supporting. I beg you, by Allāh and His blessed Prophet, to alight at my house and give me the pleasure of receiving you. I can go swiftly to the village and come back twice as swiftly.' Seeing that further refusal would grieve the good man, Maarūf dismounted and sat down at the entrance of the dung hut, while the peasant made off towards the village as fast as his legs would carry him.

As he waited for his food, Maarūf reflected: 'I am a cause of loss and embarrassment to this poor man, whose state is much as mine was when I cobbled in Red Street. Why should I not make up for his lost time by working a little in his place?'

So he rose, dressed all in the gilded garments of a royal mamlūk, and guided the plough along the line of the furrow. But the oxen had not taken many steps before the share came to a sudden standstill, striking with a curious sound against some obstacle. The beasts were thrown to their knees and, though Maarūf goaded them up and they strained strongly against the yoke, the plough remained immovable as the Day of Judgment.

Maarūf shifted the earth about the share and found that it had caught in a mighty copper ring, strongly sealed into a marble slab on a level with the tillage.

After he had tugged this way and that for a little, the slab moved to one side, and he saw below him a flight of marble stairs, leading down into a square vault as large as a hammām. Calling upon the name of Allāh, Maarūf went down into this place and found it composed of four separate and abutting halls. The first was filled from floor to ceiling with gold pieces, the second with pearls, emeralds, and coral, the third with hyacinths, rubies, turquoises, and diamonds; but the fourth, which was the greatest and best conditioned, held nothing save an ebony pedestal bearing a crystal box no larger than a lemon.

The cobbler rejoiced prodigiously at this discovery, but it was the little crystal box which first and most strongly tempted him. Forgetting the incalculable masses of treasure in the other halls, he lifted the transparent lid and found within the box a gold ring, bearing a carnelian bezel on which was engraved, in fine lines, certain talismanic writings which looked like the legs of ants. With an instinctive movement he passed the ring upon his finger and, as he fitted it, rubbed the stone.

At once a loud voice came from the bezel, saying: 'I am here! I am here! For pity's sake do not rub me any more! Speak and I will obey! What do you lack? Shall I destroy or shall I build, shall I kill kings and queens or shall I bring them, shall I take forth a mighty city from the earth or shall I annihilate an empire, shall I root up a continent or cover it with flowers, shall I raze a mountain or dry up all the seas? I am your slave, by leave of the Master of the Jinn, Creator of the day and night. What do you lack? . . . But I beg you not to rub me hard, my lord.' When Maarūf realised that this voice came from the bezel of the ring, he asked: 'O creature of God, who are you?' 'I am the Father of Fortune, the slave of the ring,' answered the carnelian voice. 'Blindly I execute the orders of my master, and my master is he who holds the ring. Nothing is impossible to me; for I am the supreme captain of seventy-two bands of Jinn, Afārīt, Shaitāns, Auns, and Marids. Each of these bands is composed of twelve million lusty irresistibles, stronger than elephants and subtler than quicksilver. But, though my power is thus enormous, I obey my master as a child obeys its mother. Of one thing only I must warn you; if you rub the bezel twice instead of once, I shall be consumed in the fire of the terrible names which are engraved upon this ring, and you will lose me for ever.'

At this point Shahrazād saw the approach of morning and discreetly fell silent.

But when the nine-hundred-and-sixty-seventh night had come

SHE SAID:

'O excellent and powerful Father of Fortune, I have stored your words in the heart of my memory,' answered the cobbler. 'Will you tell me who shut you into this carnelian and bent you to the power of the ring's master?' Then said the Jinnī from the depths of the bezel: 'The place where we now are, my master, is the ancient treasure of Shaddād ibn Ad, who built the city of Many-Columned Irām. While he lived I was his slave and dwelt in his ring, the ring you have upon your finger now.'

The one time cobbler of Red Street in Cairo had now become, thanks to the ring, direct heir to the line of Nimrod, and of Shaddād, the proud hero who lived to the age of seven eagles. As he wished to make immediate trial of the bezel's power, he said to the Jinnī of the carnelian: 'O slave of the ring, could you carry all the treasure from this cave and lay it in the light?' 'With the greatest ease,' answered the Father of Fortune. 'Then,' said Maarūf, 'I bid you bear all these marvels above ground, so that not the littlest is left for any who may come after me.' And the voice cried: 'Ho, little boys, little boys!'

Maarūf saw twelve lads of surpassing beauty appear before him, carrying mighty baskets upon their heads. They kissed the earth between his hands and then, in a series of lightning journeys, emptied the three halls of their treasure. Finally, they made new obeisance to the delighted cobbler and disappeared.

'This is perfection,' said Maarūf to the dweller in the carnelian. 'Now I require chests, mules with drivers, and camels with their camel-boys, to carry these things to Ikhtiyān al-Khatan.' The slave of the ring gave an immediate cry and there appeared mules with drivers, camels with their camel-boys, chests and baskets, and six hundred moon-fair mamlūks, gloriously clad. In the time that it takes to open and close an eye, the chests and baskets were loaded with treasure and placed upon the backs of the mules and camels, and the caravan stood in order, guarded by mounted mamlūks in a symmetrical square.

'And now, O Father of Fortune,' continued the cobbler, 'I require a thousand other beasts, loaded with silks and the precious fabrics of Syria, Egypt, Greece, Persia, India, and China.' Hardly had the wish been spoken before a thousand camels and mules appeared at the tail of the caravan, laden with the required merchandise and guarded by a further square of mamlūks. Then Maarūf was content, and said to the slave of the ring: 'Now I wish to eat. Pitch me a silk pavilion and serve me there with cool wines and chosen dishes.'

He had entered the consequent pavilion and was sitting down to his magic feast, when the benevolent peasant returned from the village. He carried on his head a wooden bowl of lentils cooked in oil, a black loaf and onions under his right arm, and, under his left, a peck sack of hay for the horse. When he saw the prodigious caravan drawn up before his house, and Maarūf sitting in a silk tent, served by quick slaves and still slaves, he was troubled in his mind, and thought: 'Surely the Sultān has come already, and that first mamlūk was sent to announce him! It is a dishonour to me that I never thought of killing my two fowls and cooking them in cow butter.' He determined to remedy this omission and was going towards the birds, when Maarūf saw him, and said to his slaves: 'Bring that man to me!'

At this point Shahrazād saw the approach of morning and discreetly fell silent.

But when the nine-hundred-and-sixty-eighth night had come

SHE SAID:

The slaves led the peasant to the pavilion with his bowl of lentils, his onions, his black bread, and his peck sack; and Maarūf rose in his honour and embraced him, saying: 'What is it you carry, O my brother in misery?' The poor man was astounded at such affection from so great a personage and, when he heard himself spoken of as a brother in misery, could not help thinking: 'If this man is poor, what am I?' Then he answered: 'My master, I was bringing the food of hospitality and a ration for your horse. You must excuse my ignorance; if I had known that you were the Sultān, I should not have hesitated to sacrifice my two fowls and roast them in cow butter. But poverty takes the wits from a man and leaves him blind.' And he hung his head in shamed confusion.

Maarūf remembered his old condition, which had been even lower than this peasant's, and wept so that the tears fell down abundantly through the hairs of his beard into the magic dishes. 'Be of good cheer, brother,' he said, 'I am not the Sultān, but only his son-in-law. Certain difficulties rose between us and I left the palace. But now he has sent these slaves and these presents after me in sign that we are reconciled. I am about to turn back to the city, and I would have you know, O generous, who would have fed me without knowing me, that you have not sown in barren and ungrateful soil.'

He made the peasant sit upon his right hand, and said: 'You see a profusion of meats, but I swear by Allāh that I will eat nothing save your lentils, your onions, and the good black bread!' He ordered the slaves to serve his friend with the sumptuous courses and, as he ate the lentils himself, with the onions and the good black bread, rejoiced to see the other's rapture at the unknown dainties.

When the two meals had been eaten, Maarūf gave thanks to Allāh and led the peasant from the tent towards the caravan. There he obliged him to choose for himself a pair of camels and a pair of mules from each group, as they stood according to their loads. 'These are your property, my brother,' he said, 'and I leave you the silk pavilion with all its contents.' Then, turning a deaf ear to the man's thanks and excuses, he took leave and, galloping his horse to the head of the caravan, sent a rapid courier ahead to announce his coming to the King.

Maarūf's messenger arrived at the palace just as the wazīr was saying to the King: 'Be no longer deceived, I pray, dear master. Give no belief to your daughter's report of her husband's setting forth. For I swear, by the life of your head, that it was not to hasten his caravan (for there is no caravan) that the amīr fled secretly by night, it was to save the skin of a liar and a cheat.' The King, already half persuaded, was opening his mouth to answer, when the courier entered the presence and prostrated himself before the throne, saying: 'O King of time, I come with good news! My master, the great and generous amīr, the celebrated hero Maarūf, rides behind me. But he stays with his caravan, which needs must go somewhat slowly because of its heavy splendour.' So saying the young mamlūk kissed the earth between the King's hands and departed as he had come.

The King rejoiced, but his joy hardly kept pace with his fury against the wazīr. 'Allāh blacken your face until it be as dark as your soul!' he cried. 'May he curse your traitorous beard until you confess your lies!' Without a word the wazīr threw himself at his master's feet, and the King left him to lie there, as he went forth to give orders for the lighting and decoration of the city, and for a procession to meet his son-in-law.

He visited his daughter's apartment and told her the good news. But, when the princess heard her father speak of the caravan which she thought she had invented piece by piece, she did not know what to say or how to answer. Was her husband mocking the Sultān once again? Or had he tested her love with an invented tale of poverty? In either event, she thought it best to show a face of happy confidence and to hasten her father forth to meet the caravan.

But the most astonished of them all was incontestably the excellent Alī, the companion of Maarūf's childhood. When he saw the whole city one bustle of preparation and learnt that it was being decked because the amīr Maarūf would soon come in at the head of a splendid caravan, he beat his hands together, and said to himself: 'What new cobbler's trick is this? By Allāh, I did not know that the botching of old slippers led to caravans! Yet all is possible to God, and I trust that He will at least preserve my old friend's honour from a public shaming!' Then he sat down to wait like all the rest.

At this point Shahrazād saw the approach of morning and discreetly fell silent.

But when the nine-hundred-and-sixty-ninth night had come

SHE SAID:

Soon the escort, which had gone out to meet the caravan, returned to the city, and Maarūf pranced at its head, triumphant, magnificent, a thousand times more splendid than a king, so that a pig, on beholding him, would have burst its gall bladder out of envy. As the caravan wound slowly in, with its vast complement of mamlūk outriders in their costly uniform, the people held their breath, and the merchant Alī murmured to himself: 'I have it, he has fixed up some new trick with his wife, some new jest against the King!' He pushed his way through the packed crowd and came near enough to whisper to his friend: 'What is all this, O sheikh of fortunate rascals, O cleverest of jugglers? And yet, by Allāh, you deserve the glory! Make the most of it, and may He increase your tricks for our delight!' His old companion answered with a laugh and arranged a meeting with Alī for the morrow.

Maarūf rode to the palace by the King's side and sat with him upon a throne set in the great audience hall. First he bade fill all the sacks of the treasury from the cases of gold and jewels, and then, with his own hands, began opening the boxes of wealth and bales of precious stuffs. Their contents he distributed in a frenzy of generosity to the great folk and their wives, to the members of the dīwān, to all the merchants whom he knew, and to the poor and lowly. In spite of the curses of the King, who hopped from one foot to another in an agony at this dispersal, he did not cease from giving, until the load of the caravan had been exhausted. As he threw double handfuls of gold or emeralds to left and right, the King would grimace and cry: 'Enough, my son, enough! There will be nothing left for us!' But Maarūf would always answer with a smile: 'My wealth is inexhaustible.'

Soon the wazīr came and told the King that the treasure chamber was full and could hold no more. 'Choose another hall and fill that,' answered the King; and Maarūf added, without looking up from his distribution: 'Fill a third hall, fill a fourth! If the King did not mind, I could fill the whole palace with these worthless things.' The wazīr departed to garnish more and more halls for the reception of the treasure, and the King stood in a daze between sleeping and waking.

As soon as he had proved the worth of his caravan, Maarūf hastened to his wife, who met him with tears of joy and kissed his hand, saying: 'Was it sheer jest, my husband, or was it to try my love, that you told me that tale of poverty and despair with the calamitous Fātimah Hot-Slop? Whichever it was, I thank Allāh that I behaved as I did!' Maarūf embraced her and gave her a magnificent robe, a necklace formed of ten strings of forty orphan pearls as large as pigeons' eggs, and anklets chiselled by the hands of sorcerers. The princess cried out for joy as she saw these things, but said: 'I must keep them for special occasions only.' 'Not so, my dear,' answered the smiling Maarūf, 'I will give you them fresh and fresh each day, until your chests and cupboards can hold no more.' And he did his business with her until the morning.

He had not yet come from under the curtains when he heard the voice of the King demanding admittance. He opened the door to him and saw him standing with terrified aspect and a yellow face. He helped him to a couch, and the princess sprinkled her father's face with rose-water until he was able to speak. At length he said distractedly: 'Alas, alas, my son, I bring bad news! Shall I tell or shall I not tell?' 'Tell, certainly,' answered Maarūf, and the King sadly continued: 'All your mamlūks, your camels, and your mules disappeared in the night, leaving less trace upon the roads than a bird when it quits a branch. You are lost for ever, and I am so upset that I do not know what I am saying.' But Maarūf laughed aloud. 'Calm your dear spirit and refresh your eyes!' he said. 'The disappearance of these things is nothing to me. It is as the loss of one drop of water from the ocean. To-day, to-morrow, the next day, and all the days of my life, might be filled with caravans and mamlūks, if I but wished it so. Calm your dear spirit, and let us dress in peace!'

The King was thrown into a greater amaze than ever by these words. He reported them to the wazīr, and said to him: 'What have you to say this time? Does not the power of my son-in-law pass all understanding?' 'Here is my chance of revenge,' thought the wazīr, who had not forgotten his many humiliations, and aloud he answered: 'O King of time, my poor advice can hardly be expected to throw light upon your darkness. But, since you ask me, I suggest that you make the amīr Maarūf drunk if you wish to know the source of his riches. When his reason goes to dancing, you may question him skilfully and he will tell the truth.' 'An excellent plan!' exclaimed the King.

So, when evening came, the King sat with Maarūf and the wazīr before dishes of wine cups. And when these were passed and passed, the cobbler's throat became a barrel and his state a woeful state. As soon as his tongue went like a windmill and he could not tell his right hand from his left, the Sultān said to him: 'My son, you have never told us the adventurous story of your life. I can well believe it to contain marvellous changes of fortune, which would rejoice us in the hearing.'

At this point Shahrazād saw the approach of morning and discreetly fell silent.

But when the nine-hundred-and-seventieth night had come

SHE SAID:

Maarūf, with his mind hind-part-before and up-side-down, let the wine carry him to an extravagant vaunting (for that is the way of drinkers) and he told his life's story, from his marriage to Hot-Slop to the finding of the magic ring in the peasant's field.

The King and his wazīr bit their hands as they looked at each other, and at length the wazīr said to Maarūf: 'My dear sir, may we not be honoured with one little sight of the ring?' Immediately the foolish cobbler took the heirloom of Shaddād from his finger and handed it to his enemy, saying: 'Look at the carnelian! My old friend, Father of Fortune, lives there!' With glittering eyes the wazīr slipped the ring on to his own finger and rubbed the bezel.

Then said the voice from the carnelian: 'Here am I! Ask and have! Shall I ruin a city, build an empire, or kill a King?' 'O slave of the ring,' answered the wazīr, 'I bid you take up this pimping King and cobbling bawd, and cast them down upon some waterless desert.' Instantly the King and the cobbler were lifted like wisps of straw and set down on a savage plain, a desert of thirst, where red death and desolation kept house together. So much for them.

The wazīr summoned the dīwān and explained that the good of the State demanded the exile of the King and his son-in-law, together with his own accession to the throne. 'Also,' said he, 'if one of you dares to be slow to recognise the new order, I shall send him to join them in the red wilderness of thirst and death!'

The nobles swore fealty in spite of themselves, and the wazīr, after appointing some and abasing others, sent this word to the princess: 'Prepare to receive me, for my desire is great.' The princess, who had already heard of the wazīr's revolt, sent back a eunuch to say for her: 'Soon I will receive you with great pleasure, but for the moment I have that monthly evil which is common to women and young girls. When I am clean of all taint, I will send for you.' But the wazīr made reply: 'I know nothing of monthly evils, or of yearly evils for that matter, and desire to visit you at once.' 'Come then and find me,' said the princess by her eunuch.

She dressed herself with great magnificence, scented herself sweetly, and received the wazīr with a smiling face. 'What an honour!' she said. 'What a delightful night we shall have together!' She used her eyes as snares for the traitor's heart and, when he pressed her to undress, began to do so with a thousand voluptuous delays. Suddenly she uttered a cry of terror and started back, veiling her face. 'What is the matter, my mistress,' demanded the wazīr. 'Why this cry, this veiling of the face?' 'Do you not see?' she answered, from below her coverings. 'As Allāh lives, I see nothing!' swore the wazīr, but she cried again: 'O shame! O great dishonour! Would you show me naked to that strange man?' 'Where, where?' shouted the wazīr, looking to left and right. 'There, in the carnelian of your ring,' said she. 'By Allāh, that is true. I had not thought of it,' confessed the wazīr. 'But, dear lady, that is no man, no human; that is an Ifrīt!' 'An Ifrīt, oh, my sorrow!' moaned the princess, burying her face in the cushions. 'I am terribly afraid of Afārīt! For my sake,

put him away!' So the wazīr, in his eagerness to come to conclusions
with her, took off the ring and hid it under the pillow of the bed.
Then he came nearer to her joyfully.

She let him approach, and then kicked him so violently in the
belly that he rolled head over heels on the floor. With a movement
as of light, she snatched up the ring and rubbed the bezel, saying to
the Ifrīt: 'Cast this pig into the lowest dungeon of the palace, and
then bring me back my father and my husband, safe and well!'

At this point Shahrazād saw the approach of morning and
discreetly fell silent.

But when the nine-hundred-and-seventy-first night had come

SHE SAID:

At once the wazīr was plucked up, like a bundle of old clothes,
and cast into the lowest dungeon of the palace. At the same time the
King and Maarūf appeared suddenly in the princess's room, the King
in the last stages of fright and Maarūf hardly recovered from his
drunkenness. She received them with expressions of delight and,
seeing that their swift journey from the desert had roused hunger
and thirst in them, set them down to eat and drink, while she told
them how she had outwitted the wazīr. 'We will impale him and
burn him at once!' cried the King. 'It is permitted,' murmured
Maarūf, and then to his wife he said: 'First, give me back my ring,
sweetheart.' 'I do not think so,' answered the princess. 'Since you
could not keep it when you had it, I will look after it in future.' 'That
is but just,' said Maarūf.

The impaling stake was set up in the polo-ground, opposite the
great door of the palace, and the wazīr was fitted to it in sight of the
whole people. While the instrument was at work, a large fire was
lighted below the stake, so that the traitor was both spitted and
grilled, like any pigeon. So much for him.

The King shared the government with Maarūf and appointed him
sole heir to the throne. The ring stayed on the princess's finger, and
Maarūf lived for some time in pleasurable ease.

But one night, when he had finished his usual with the princess
and retired to his own apartment to sleep, an old woman jumped out
of his bed and fell upon him with a menacing arm. He had hardly
time to recognise her by her terrible jaw, her long teeth and black
ugliness as Fātimah Hot-Slop, his calamitous wife, before she gave

him a couple of sounding blows in the face which broke two more of his teeth. 'Where have you been, O wretch?' she cried. 'How dared you leave me without farewell? Son of a dog, I have you now!' Maarūf turned tail and ran towards the bedchamber of the princess, his crown awry upon his head and his royal robes flying out behind him. 'Help, help!' he shouted. 'Help, O Ifrīt of the ring!' Then he darted like a madman into the girl's presence and fell swooning at her feet.

As the princess was sprinkling rose-water upon Maarūf's brow to bring him to himself, the terrifying shrew burst in upon them, brandishing a cudgel which she had brought all the way from Egypt. 'Where is that son of adultery?' she cried. 'Where is that pimp?' At first sight of Fātimah's pitchy cheeks, the princess rubbed the carnelian of the ring and gave a quick order to the Father of Fortune. Instantly the woman was frozen in her place, her arm thrown up, her face tortured with anger, as if she had been held by forty arms.

Maarūf came slowly to himself, but, when he saw Hot-Slop's threatening attitude, he swooned again. At once the wise princess knew that she had to do with her husband's former wife, and she gave a further order to the Ifrīt, whereby that vixen was lifted from her place and carried into the garden. There she was fastened, as if she had been a wild bear, to the trunk of a stout carob tree by an enormous chain. And thus she was left, either to mend her manners or to die. So much for her.

Maarūf and his wife lived together through many joyful years, until they were visited by the Separator of Friends, the Destroyer, the Tomb Builder, Death the Inevitable.

Glory be to Him Who sits throned in eternity above life and death!

And that night, as Shahrazād was not weary and saw that King Shahryār was still disposed to listen, she began this tale of the rich young man who looked out by Windows on the Garden of History. She said:

Windows on the Garden of History

IT is related that there was once a youth in the city of Alexandria, who inherited great possessions and riches from his father in well-watered fields and solid buildings. As he was born in benediction, with a right spirit and a knowledge of the Holy Book, which bids a generosity of alms to the people of Allāh, he hesitated for a long time as to the best use which he might make of his inheritance. At length, in his perplexity, he decided to consult a venerable sheikh who had been a friend of his father. He displayed his scruples and hesitations to the old man, who reflected for an hour after hearing them, and then said: 'O son of Abd al-Rahmān—whom may Allāh bless—to give gold and silver to the needy with full hands is an action which finds great favour in the sight of God. But such merit is possible to any rich man. It is not necessary to have great virtue in order to give away the surplus of one's goods. There is another generosity, the savour of which is more agreeable to the Master of All, and that is the generosity of the intellect. He who can scatter the benefits of his intelligence upon those who grope in darkness has the highest merit of all in the accounts of heaven. Only a cultivated mind is capable of such an alms, and a cultivated mind is only possible to one who has read and meditated deeply. Enrich your mind, O son of my old friend, and let your alms-giving lie in that direction. Such is my counsel under Allāh!'

The rich youth wished to ask for further explanation, but the sheikh would say no more. Therefore he was forced to retire, and inspiration led him to the market of the booksellers. He assembled all the merchants (some of them, indeed, had books belonging to the library which the Christians burnt when Amr ibn al-Âs entered Alexandria) and bade them carry to his house all the most precious volumes in their possession. He paid them what they asked, without bargaining or hesitation, but his eagerness was not satisfied. He sent messengers to Cairo, Damascus, Baghdād, Persia, Morocco and India, and even among the lands of the Christians, to purchase at any price the best-reputed books of all these peoples. When his messengers returned, loaded with bales of precious manuscripts, the young man had these well arranged in the presses of a magnificent dome which he had built for their reception. Above the principal entrance of the place, these simple words were painted in great letters of blue and gold: 'The Dome of Books.'

At this point Shahrazād saw the approach of morning and discreetly fell silent.

But when the nine-hundred-and-seventy-second night had come

SHE SAID:

The young man consecrated his days to methodical reading, and, as he had been born under benediction, with his feet pointed towards the way of happiness, he remembered all he read. Soon he was as learned as any sage of his time, and had a mind stored with far greater riches than he had inherited from his father. Then, in order to share this bounty with others, he gave a great feast in the Dome of Books and invited all his friends and acquaintances, his relations far and near, his slaves and his grooms, and the customary beggars upon his threshold. When they had eaten and drunken and thanked Allāh, the youth rose in the attentive circle of them, saying: 'O my guests, let wisdom preside for us to-night instead of music and singing! A wise man has said: "Bring forth your knowledge that the ear of him who hears may be nourished. He that obtains learning has obtained great riches. God gives wisdom to whom it pleases Him, and intellect is created at His word; but there are few of the sons of men who have been honoured with these things." Also Allāh Himself, speaking by the mouth of His Prophet (upon whom be prayer and peace!), has said: "O my Faithful, give alms of your best, for he shall not obtain perfection who has not divided that which pleases him most. But give not with ostentation, for the proud giver is like a stony hill covered with a little earth: the rain beats upon that hill and nothing but the naked rock remains. Such men have no profit from their works. But those who give alms for the strengthening of their own souls are like a garden planted upon a hill, which is watered by the abundant rains of heaven and whose fruit hangs double upon the bough. If no rain falls, there shall be dew. And they shall enter into the gardens of Paradise."

'That is why I have called you together this evening, dear guests. I do not wish to keep the fruits of learning to myself; I desire you to taste them with me, that we may walk together in the way of the spirit.'

And he added:

'Let us look out together by the windows of learning upon the garden of history, and watch the marvellous procession of old time pass by, that our souls may be enlightened by that passing and may journey on by that light towards perfection. Amen.'

Then all the guests carried their hands to their faces, and replied: 'Amen.'

The youth sat down amid silence, and thus addressed the circle of his company: 'My friends, I do not know how I can better begin than by giving you some particulars of the life of our fathers in the days of chivalry. They were the true Arabs of the sands; their mighty poets could neither read nor write, inspiration was a vehement gift with them, and, without inks or pens or critics, they built up this Arab speech of ours, which Allāh chose by preference when He would dictate His words to His Prophet (upon whom be prayer and peace and benediction!). Amen.'

When the guests had again replied Amen, 'Here is one tale of the thousand tales of chivalry,' he said:

The Poet Duraid, His Generosity, and His Love for Tumādir Al-Khansah

THE poet Duraid ibn Simmah, sheikh of the tribe of the Banū Jusham, lived in the age of chivalry and was equally famous as a warrior and a poet. He was the master of many tents and rich pastures.

One day he set forth on a raid against the rival tribe of the Banū Firās, whose sheikh was Rabīah, the bravest fighter in all the deserts. As he journeyed at the head of his chosen troop, he came out into a valley belonging to the enemy, and saw, far off at its opposing end, an unmounted man leading a camel ridden by a woman. After the first glance, Duraid turned to one of his horsemen, saying: 'Go forward and fall upon that man!'

The horseman galloped ahead and, when he had come within shouting distance, cried out: 'Leave that woman and run, if you would save your life!' He gave this challenge three times, but the man walked calmly on until the horse was near. Then he passed the camel's halter to the woman, and sang this song:

> Ride on in pride, heart ignorant of fear,
>   Ride on, hips rounded in our tranquil day.
> But first, as chance has brought a meeting here,
>   Enjoy the sword-play of a Firasid. . . .
>
> Now all is safety, lady, now you may
>   Ride on in pride.

With that he charged Duraid's warrior and stretched him lifeless in the dust with a single blow of his lance. He mounted the riderless horse, bowing to the woman as he did so, and led the camel forward again with no sign of haste or emotion.

At this point Shahrazād saw the approach of morning and discreetly fell silent.

But when the nine-hundred-and-seventy-third night had come
SHE SAID:

When Duraid saw that his rider did not return, he sent out a second warrior, who found his comrade lying in the path and galloped forward to do battle with the slayer. He cried out his challenge, but the man upon the captured horse seemed not to have heard. He rode towards him with levelled lance, but the man passed the camel's halter to the woman, and suddenly charged, crying:

> Although the iron teeth of chance
>   Drove you, O spew, to take this road
> And sicken with your countenance
>   My lady of the free abode,
>   The iron of Rabīah's lance
> Is fiercer than the teeth of chance!

The warrior fell, pierced through the liver, and died tearing at the sand with his nails. Then Rabīah went forward with unhurried pace.

Duraid presently became anxious and sent a third rider to look for the other two. The man soon found his comrades lying dead, and perceived a stranger jogging quietly at a little distance, leading a camel by the halter and carelessly trailing his lance. 'Yield your prize, O dog of the tribes!' he cried; but Rabīah, without turning, said to his companion: 'Dear friend, go forward to our nearest tents.' Then he wheeled sharply upon his foe, and chanted:

> Have you not seen, O eyeless head,
>   Your brothers welter in their clots,
>   And how the Vulture's breathing blots
> The scarlet from the cheeks of dread?
>
> Did you hope lessons from my wrath,
>   Or any teaching from my frowns
>   Save how a lance-head flourish drowns
> Dead kidneys in a crow-black bath?

He pierced Duraid's third warrior through and through the chest, and his lance broke off short with the violence of that assault; but Rabīah, this fighter of the valleys, knowing himself to be near his tribe, scorned to pick up the weapon of his dead foe. Instead he rode forward, armed only with the splintered shaft.

Astonished that none of his messengers returned, Duraid himself rode out to look for them, and soon found their lifeless bodies lying at intervals upon the sand. As he went pondering on their death, Rabīah himself came round the side of a little hill and recognised the poet of the Jushamids. Though the sheikh of the Banū Firās regretted that he had not armed himself from the corpse of his third adversary, yet he halted straight in the saddle, and faced Duraid with the broken wood of his lance firmly at tilt.

When he saw how ill-equipped Rabīah was for conflict, the grandeur of his soul urged Duraid to exclaim: 'O father of riders, one does not kill such men as you; but my troop is seeking vengeance, and soon it may come upon you, alone, unarmed, and very young. Therefore take this lance of mine, and I will ride back to call off my men from the pursuit.'

He galloped to his band, and said to them: 'That brave knew how to defend his woman! He killed three of us and disarmed me. He is too strong to be attacked.'

Then he bade the warriors follow him back to their own territory, and there was no raid.

Years passed and Rabīah died, as fearless soldiers die, in a bloody engagement with the tribe of Duraid. To avenge his death a troop of Firasids set out upon a fresh raid against the Banū Jusham. They fell upon the camp at night, made a great slaughter, and rode off with many captives and a booty of women and goods. Duraid himself, the sheikh of the Jushamids, walked as one of the prisoners.

When he came among his conquerors, Duraid was careful to hide his name and quality; but, as he lay under heavy guard, the women of the Firasids were struck by his nobility and walked past him provocatively, triumphing at his discomfiture. 'By the black death,' cried one of them, 'you have done a fair day's work, O children of the Firasids! Do you know this man?' The warriors ran up and examined their captive. 'He was one of those who scouted against our band,' they said; and the woman answered: 'Past question he scouted bravely! This is the man who gave a lance to Rabīah in the valley.' She threw her veil over the prisoner as a sign of protection, and cried: 'Children of Firās, I claim this captive for myself.' So the warriors pressed round the poet, and asked his name. 'I am Duraid ibn Simmah,' he answered, 'but who are you, O lady?' Then said the woman: 'I am Raytah, the daughter of al-ijlān. I rode upon that camel. Rabīah was my husband.'

She visited all the tents of her tribe, and said to the horsemen: 'Children of Firās, remember the generosity of the son of Simmah, for he gave Rabīah his long and costly lance. Now is the time to return clemency for clemency, lest the mouths of men swell with disgust when they tell the story of Duraid and the Firasids. You must break his bonds and buy his freedom from the hands of his captor, if you do not wish to raise a stepping-stone to long repentance and regret!'

The Firasids contributed money to pay Muhārik, the warrior who had taken Duraid; and, when he had been set at liberty, Raytah gave the poet the arms of her dead husband.

Duraid returned to his tribe and never more waged war on the Banū Firās. Years passed, and he became an old man, though his strength in song was unabated.

Now there dwelt in the tribe of the Banū Sulaim that Tumādir al-Khansah, daughter of Amr, who was renowned in all the deserts for her high poetic ecstasy. And one day, as Duraid rode near the tents of the Sulamī, he came upon this girl anointing one of her father's camels with pitch, labouring almost naked because of the heat, and trusting to the loneliness of that place. The poet was able to examine and marvel at her beauty from a hidden vantage, and as he gazed he improvised this song:

> Sing to the Sulamī,
>   Sing for this Tumādir,
>   Make for this light gazelle
> Verses of pride!
>
> Unveiled her young bloom,
>   Never the riding tribes,
>   Seeking a prodigy,
> Found such a camel groom.
>
> Brown girl of high race,
>   Smooth as an image's
>   Under the hair stream
> Brightens her gold face.

Like the black waves we see
    Tailing our stallions
    Is the wind-beaten tress.
Let to go carelessly

It floats in glancing chains;
    When it is kissed with combs
    Then you would call it grapes
Polished by little rains.

Her brows are symmetries
    Drawn with a heavy pen,
    Black crowns of queenship
Over the deep eyes.

Modelled with leaf shadows,
    Her cheeks are scarce flecked,
    As by rose purple dawn
Rising on white meadows.

Her lips' red pigment
    Lends the small teeth pallor,
    Straight jasmine petals
Moistened in honey scent.

And the neck's silver, see,
    Balance above breasts
    Like the proud breasts on
Girls smoothed in ivory.

Her arms are firm for us,
    Firm for me, white for me,
    And of her finger-tips
Red dates are envious.

Belly with white valleys
    Folded of song paper,
    Ranged round the navel's
Deep box of essences!

Where can her waist borrow
    Strength for its slenderness,
    When to such glory
Falls the slim back furrow?

Mountains of white sands
  Drag her to sit on them,
  And when she would sit
Swift she again stands.

Yet on two slender
  Columns of smoothness,
  Stems of papyrus
Sprinkled with tender

Brown hair, two pearl stalks,
  Two filed and fine
  Feet that are lance blades,
The pride of her walks.

Sing to the Sulamī,
  Sing for this Tumādir,
  Make for this light gazelle
Verses of pride!

Next day the noble Duraid took the chiefs of his tribe with him and visited Tumādir's father in formal glory, to ask for the hand of his daughter. Old Amr answered the poet readily, saying: 'O Duraid, a man as generous as yourself is not repulsed, so great a chief is never thwarted, so signal a stallion no man would turn from the manger of his desire. But I must tell you that Tumādir has thoughts and angles of her own.'

At this point Shahrazād saw the approach of morning and discreetly fell silent.

But when the nine-hundred-and-seventy-fourth night had come

SHE SAID:

'As such thoughts and angles are not common in women, I always let my daughter do as she pleases. I will tell her of your request and use all the persuasion of my tongue, but I cannot answer for her consent, for in that I leave her free.' When Duraid had thanked him, the old man visited al-Khansah, saying: 'O al-Khansah, a mighty warrior, a man of noble blood, a chief of the Banū Jusham, one venerated for his bravery and his great age, has come to my tents seeking you in marriage. He is none other than Duraid, Simmah's noble son, whose warlike odes and ravishing songs you have by heart. The alliance would do us honour, my child, but I shall make no attempt to influence your decision.' 'Dear father,' answered Tumādir, 'let me take a few days to consider the matter before I answer.'

So Amr returned to Duraid, saying: 'Al-Khansah wishes for a few days in which to consider your proposal, but I have a hope that she will accept your suit. Speak to me again when the time has gone by.' 'Willingly, O father of heroes,' answered Duraid, and he retired to the tent which had been placed at his disposal.

As soon as the poet had left her father's tent, the fair Sulamī called one of her girls to her, saying: 'Go out now, and watch Duraid. Follow him when he leaves the tents to satisfy his need; look carefully at the jet, determine its strength, and bring me news of its track upon the sand. Your report will tell us whether he be still a man or no.'

The girl obeyed with such diligence that she was back in a few minutes. 'Finished,' was her report.

When Duraid returned for his answer, Amr left him in the men's part of the tent and went to take her answer from Tumādir. 'I have considered,' she said, 'and am determined not to marry out of my tribe. I would not forsake a union with one of my cousins, youths as handsome as great lances, to take this ancient Jushamid, this Duraid, to my bed. To-morrow, or the day after, he will be gasping out his owl's soul. By the greatness of our warriors, I would rather become an old maid than marry a grey spindle-shanks!'

Though Duraid was in the other part of the tent, he heard this contemptuous reply and was wounded to the quick. His pride would suffer him to give no sign of his discontent, but, when he returned to his tribe, he answered Tumādir's cruelty with this satire:

> Duraid is old, too old, you say,
> (He never claimed he was born yesterday)
> While you desire—and, faith, you're right—
> A splayfoot clown to fork your dung at night.
> Take my advice and be afraid
> To choose as strong a husband as Duraid,
> For his great strength, when all is said,
> Is kept for nobler matters than his bed.
> He's one whom, in the throes of fate,
> Fear cannot chain nor haste precipitate.

The wretch to whom Duraid has lent
The shade of his protection or his tent,
Be he the greatest thief unscotched,
Walks in the tribe unquestioned and unwatched.
Even in the hungry months of dearth,
When the new-born go starving from their birth,
His camps are victualled to desire
And many cookpots chatter at his fire.
Again I counsel, be afraid
To take a man, and bear sons, like Duraid,
For you desire—it is your right—
A splayfoot clown to fork your dung at night,
And I am old, too old, you say . . .
At least this proves me not born yesterday.

When these lines became known among the tribes, all men advised Tumādir to accept the maker for her husband, but she never went back on her decision.

It was soon after this that Muāwiyah, Tumādir's brother, a notable warrior, perished in a battle against the hostile tribe of the Banū Murrah. He was slain by the hand of Hāshim, the opposing chief, father of that beautiful Asmā whom the youth had at one time outraged. It was for her brother that Tumādir made this funeral song, chanted slowly in the tonic of the ring-finger string:

Weep! Weep! Weep!
These tears are for my brother,
Henceforth that veil which lies between us,
That recent earth,
Shall not be lifted again.

You have gone down to the bitter water
Which all must taste,
And you went pure, saying:
'Life is a buzz of hornets about a lance point.'

But my heart remembers, O son of my father and mother,
I wither like Summer grass,
I shut myself in the tent of consternation.

He is dead, who was the buckler of our tribe
And the foundation of our house,
He has departed in calamity.

He is dead, who was the lighthouse of courageous men,
Who was for the brave
As fires lighted upon the mountains.

He is dead, who rode costly horses,
Shining in his garments.
The hero of the long shoulder belt is dead,
The young man of valiance and beauty breathes no more;
The right hand of generosity is withered,
And the beardless king of our tribe shall breathe no more.

He shall be cold beneath his rock.

Say to his mare Alwah
That she must weep
As she runs riderless for ever.

O son of Amr,
Glory has galloped with you knee to knee.
When you passed with your brothers to the flame of war
You were as demons riding upon vultures.

You threw your life against the sun,
You sought out unperturbed
Horrors as dark as the tar colour of the storm
And whirlwinds great with steel.

Though you were young like a gold-ringed lance,
Though you were strong and slight
Like a lance-shaft of Rudainah,
Death trailed the hems of her mantle deep in blood
After your feet.

When the red millstone ground the flowers of youth,
You shattered a thousand horses against the squadrons;
High on the groaning flanks of Alwah
You lifted the bright skirts of your silver mail.

You made the lances live,
You shook their beams,
You quenched their beams in red,
O tiger of the double panoply.

White women wandered with disordered veils
And you saved them in the morning.
Your captives were as troops of antelopes
Whose beauty troubles the first drops of rain.

Your sword was our wall against distress,
How many mothers would have borne no more
If your sword had perished!

How effortless were your rhymes of combat
Chanted in tumult, O my brother!
They pierced like lances,
They live among our hearts for ever.

Let the stars go out,
Let the sun withdraw his rays,
He was our star and sun.

Who now will gather in the strangers at dusk
When the sad North whistles with her winds?
You have laid down and left in the dust, O wanderers,
Him who nourished you with his flocks
And bared his sword for your salvation.
You set him low in the terrible house
Among a few stakes planted,
You threw down boughs of salāmah upon him.
He lies among the tombs of our fathers,
Where the days and the years shall pass over him
As they have passed over our fathers.

Your loss is a great distress to me,
Child of the Sulamī,
I shall be glad no more.

Tell me, are the meharas comforted
By the little images
When their new-born are taken away?

While you have tears, O daughters of the Sulamī,
Weep! Weep! Weep!

It was because of this song that the poet Nābigah al-Dhubyānī
and the other poets, assembled at the great fair of Ukāz for the
annual recitation of their works before all the tribes of Arabia, said

of this Tumādir when they were asked of her: 'In her verse she surpasses both men and angels!'

Tumādir lived on until after the preaching of Islām in Arabia. In the eighth year of the Hijrah of Muhammad (upon whom be prayer and peace!) she came with her son Abbās, who had then become paramount chief of the Sulamī, to make her submission to the Prophet and to become ennobled in the Faith. Muhammad treated her with honour and, though he had no appreciation of poetry, delighted to hear her say her verses. He even congratulated her on her inspiration and renown.

It was in repeating some of Tumādir's lines that the Prophet showed himself insensitive to the rhythm of prosody. He falsified the quantity of the line he was quoting, by transposing the last two words. The venerable Abū Bakr, who heard this violence done to metrics, would have corrected the mistake, but Muhammad (upon whom be prayer and peace!) answered him: 'What does it matter? It is all one.' Then said Abū Bakr: 'Indeed, O Prophet of Allāh, you have fulfilled the word which God revealed to you in His Holy Book: *We have not taught our Prophet the art of verses, for he has no need of this. The Koran is a teaching, and the reading of it is a simple reading!*'

But Allāh knows all!

Then the young man said to his guests: 'Here is another admirable tale from the chivalrous life of our fathers.'

And he began:

Ufairah the Suns, and Hudhailah the Moons, the Warrior Daughters of the Poet Find

IT has come down to us that the poet Find, chief of the Banū Zimmān, which were a branch of the tribe of the Bakrids, who were sprung from Rabīah, had two young daughters, Ufairah the Suns, the elder, and Hudhailah the Moons. When Find was a hundred years old, the whole tribe of the Banū Bakr went to war with the more numerous Banū Taghlab, and Find, in spite of his great age, was considered worthy, because of his renown, to ride at the head of the seventy horsemen which his tribe sent to the rally of the

Banū Bakr. His two daughters rode with him, and the messenger, who was sent forward to announce his coming, said to the Banū Bakr: 'We of the Banū Zimmān are sending a contingent of a thousand warriors and seventy horsemen.' By this he meant that Find was alone equal to an army of a thousand men.

When the fighting tribe of the Banū Bakr was complete, war was loosed like a hurricane, and a battle took place which is famous even to our time as the Yaum al-tahāluk, because the captive Banū Taghlab had their foretops shaven and were then liberated, that all might see the disgrace of their defeat. It was in this engagement that Find's two daughters, the petulant fighters, mistresses of the field, achieved their immortality.

At this point Shahrazād saw the approach of morning and discreetly fell silent.

But when the nine-hundred-and-seventy-fifth night had come

SHE SAID:

In the hottest hour of the battle, when the issue hung in balance, these two young girls leapt from their horses and began to strip off their garments and coats of mail. When they were quite naked, save for the green anklets and bracelets upon them, one ran forward in the midst of the right wing of the Bakrid army, one in the midst of the left wing, and stood there white and panting. In the thick of the fight each improvised a war song, and since then both of these songs have been sung to the rhythm ramal, on the tonic of the mean string of the tetrachord, alternating with a second rhythm beaten low upon the drum.

This was the war song of Ufairah the Suns:

> Red swords, children of Bakr! Red swords!
> Heat the battle red, O sons of Zimmān!
> The heights are drowned in horses,
> Heat the battle red!
>
> Put on red robes of honour
> And our arms shall be white for you,
> Lay on red swords this morning, sons of Bakr!
> Let your wounds be wide as the rent garment
> Of a mad mistress,

> And we will prepare our bodies for you
> On soft cushions.
> Let your swords be red!
>
> Red swords, red roses, sons of Bakr!
> Children of Zimmān, heat the battle red!

Hudhailah the Moons stayed by her father, who had cut the hamstrings of his camel in the van of the left wing, so that he might not at all retreat. This was the war song of her anger, to exalt those who ringed the standard of her tribe:

> Carve all, carve all, O children of Zimmān,
> Carve with your cutting swords!
> Shake down the red thunderbolts,
> O sons of Bakr!
>
> We are the daughters of the morning star
> Nard-haired,
> Pearls are about us . . .
> Shake down the red thunderbolts, O riders,
> And we are yours!
>
> Mow us a red carpet for our feet,
> O riders of Rabīah!
> Hudhailah of Moons is for the reddest sword!

This double chant of death heated a new ardour in the veins of the Banū Bakr, the slaughter waxed, and victory came to rest with them.

That is how our fathers fought in the days of chivalry. That was the fashion of their daughters. May the fires of Hell lie not too sore upon them!

Then the rich youth said to his stirred guests: 'Now listen to the love story of the Princess Fātimah with the poet Murakkish, who both lived also in that heroic age.'

And he began:

The Love Story of Princess Fātimah and the Poet Murakkish

IT is related that Numān, King of Hīrah in Irāk, had a daughter named Fātimah, who was as ardent as she was beautiful. Knowing the young princess's dangerous temperament, her father kept her shut up in a remote palace, as a precaution against calamity, and had the approaches guarded day and night by armed men, both to do his daughter honour and to preserve that quality in her. None but Fātimah's personal servant had the right of entry into this stronghold of virtue; and, that assurance might be doubly sure, the guards had orders to trail large woollen garments all about the sand at evening, so that the handmaid's little footprints might disappear and a surface be left for the detection of any larger ones.

The beautiful captive would often climb up to the top of her cloister, and sigh as she gazed upon the men walking far off. One day, while she was thus engaged, she saw her servant, whose name was Ibnat-Ijlan, talking to a youth of most attractive appearance. When she questioned the girl, she discovered that this was none other than the celebrated poet Murakkish, and that much joy of love had passed between the two. Ibnat, who was both charming and vivacious, boasted to her mistress of her lover's beauty and the great wealth of his falling hair, until Fātimah burned to see for herself, and to share the favours of this prodigy. Yet, because she was a princess of refined delicacy, she would do nothing in the matter until she was sure that the poet had some pretension to noble birth. This is an example of that breeding which guided each action of the Arab nobility in those days. Contrast it with the careless acceptance of the less scrupulous handmaid.

In order to prove the poet, Fātimah talked with Ibnat-Ijlan concerning her chance of introducing him into the palace, and ended by saying: 'When he is with you to-morrow, give him a toothpick of scented wood and a brazier with a little perfume burning in it. If he uses the toothpick without snipping it and fraying the end, or if he places the brazier under his garments and gets right over it, he will have proved himself a man of humble origin. As such he would be unworthy of a princess, even were he the greatest poet alive.'

Next morning, when the handmaid went to find her lover, she set a brazier in the middle of the chamber where they met and, after

462

throwing grains of perfume upon it, bade the poet come near and scent himself. But, instead of moving, he answered: 'Bring it here to me.' When Ibnat had done so, he scented his beard and hair only, making no movement to set the brazier below his clothes. Then he accepted the toothpick which his mistress gave him and, after cutting off a portion of it, frayed out the end into a small flexible brush, with which he rubbed his teeth and perfumed his gums.

When the act of kind had taken place between these two, the little one returned to her petulant mistress and reported the result of the double test. 'Bring this noble Arab to me instantly!' cried Fātimah.

But the guards were armed and watchful, and every morning the King's diviners came to scrutinise the footprints left upon the sand. 'O King of time,' they would say to Numān on their return, 'we could only read the passing of the little feet of the girl Ibnat-Ijlan.'

What did that astute handmaid do to achieve the introduction of Murakkish? On the night appointed she took the young man strongly upon her back, fastened a mantle about both of them in order to secure him, and carried him thus safely into the presence of the princess. The poet passed a white night of benediction, a night of sweetness and flame in the arms of that vehement king's daughter. Then he departed at dawn as he had come, on the back of the handmaid.

In the morning what happened? The King's diviners examined the sand about the palace, and then reported to King Numān: 'O King of time, we could only read the passing of the little feet of the girl Ibnat-Ijlan; but she must be putting on weight at the palace, for her footprints are becoming noticeably deeper.'

By this ruse the princess and the poet loved each other in all delight for many weeks, and the diviners continued to talk of the fattening effect of life in the palace. This joy might never have known a period, had not Murakkish pulled down his happiness with his own hands.

He had a friend, so dear that he could refuse him nothing, and, when this friend learned of the princess's love making, nothing would satisfy him but that he should go, trusting to the darkness, to take the poet's place. At length Murakkish was persuaded and gave his oath. So, that night, it was the friend who climbed upon the handmaid's back and was carried to the bed of Fātimah.

In the obscurity, that began which was fated to begin, but the expert princess, feeling softness where there should have been iron, coldness where there should have been great heat, and poverty where there should have been abundance, immediately detected the substitution. She leapt from the bed, disdainfully kicked the intruder, and had Ibnat-Ijlan carry him away upon her shoulders.

At this point Shahrazād saw the approach of morning and discreetly fell silent.

But when the nine-hundred-and-seventy-sixth night had come

SHE SAID:

After that, Fātimah would never allow the poet to come near her, or for one moment forgive his betrayal of their love. This was a song he wrote in his great grief.

> Farewell Fātimah, Numān's daughter
>> With a cadenced ostrich walk
>> And a waist of nabk stalk,
> Teeth wet with the mouth's dew water.
> Farewell fairness, a pool water,
>> Farewell Numān's daughter.
>
> Farewell cheeks of surface silver,
>> Golden wrists with copper bangles,
>> Lake hair lying in black angles
> Deep to drain my heart's bright river.
> Farewell glorying glittering river,
>> Farewell surface silver.
>
> Dreams are the pictures in the book of sleep,
>> And no more mine for ever.

The poet Murakkish was one of those lovers who died for love.

Then said the young man to his guests: 'Before we come to the time of Islām, listen to this tale of the King of the Kindis and his wife Hind."

And he began:

The Vengeance of King Hujr

IT is handed down in the annals of our fathers that King Hujr, chief of the Kindis and father of that Imru al-Kais who was the greatest poet of chivalry, had renown among the Arabs for his ferocity and signal boldness. He was so harsh with his family that his son, Prince Imru, had to flee the paternal tents, before he could give rein to his genius, for King Hujr considered that a public assumption of the poetic title was a derogation from nobility.

Once, when the King was far from his own territory on a warlike expedition against the dissenting Banū Asad, his ancient enemies the Kudaid, with Ziyād at their head, raided his home lands and made off with a large booty of dried dates, horses, camels, oxen, and young girls. And Hind, the jewel of the tribe, the King's favourite wife, was among the captives.

As soon as the news of this disaster reached Hujr, he hastened back with all his warriors and made for a spot where he might hope to come up with his foe. When he was within a short distance of the camp of the Kudaid, he sent two proven spies, Sālih and Sadūs, to collect information concerning the strength and movement of Ziyād's band.

The two spies succeeded in entering the hostile camp, and there collected many invaluable particulars of the enemy's number and disposition. After a few hours of close research, Sālih said to his companion: 'I think that we have gathered enough to outline Ziyād's plans to our master. I intend to return with my news.' But Sadūs answered: 'I will not return without more detailed information.' And he stayed on alone in the camp of the Kudaid.

At nightfall a detachment of Ziyād's men posted themselves on guard round their chief's tent, and Sadūs was in peril of discovery; therefore he took a bold course and brought his hand down heavily on the shoulder of one of the guards, asking in a tone of sharp command: 'Who are you?' 'Such and such, son of such and such,' answered the man. 'Good!' cried Sadūs, and he sat down right against the tent, sure now that none would care to disturb him.

At once he heard voices talking within, the voices of Ziyād and Hind as they kissed and played together. Among other matters Sadūs marked the following dialogue: the voice of Ziyād said: 'Tell me what your husband Hujr would do, if he knew that we were occupied so sweetly?' 'By death,' answered Hind, 'he would run upon your track like a wolf, he would never stay till he came to your red tents! He would rage and thirst for vengeance, he would scatter foam from his mouth, as a rutting camel which has eaten bitter herbs.' Ziyād was jealous at this answer and gave his captive a buffet in the face, saying: 'I understand! That bald ape pleases you, you love him, and wish to humiliate me!' But Hind vehemently denied this accusation. 'I swear by Lāt and Izzah,' she cried, 'that I have never loathed a man as I loathe my husband. But, at the same time, I must warn you that I have never known a man, sleeping or waking, more vigilant and circumspect.' 'How is that?' asked Ziyād, and Hind continued: 'Hujr sleeps with one eye open and with half of his mind awake. I will give you an example: one night, as he slept by my side and I watched over his sleep, a black snake came from below the mat and made straight as if to crawl over his face. Without waking Hujr turned his head away. Then the snake crawled towards the open palm of his hand. Hujr closed his hand. The snake went down towards his stretched foot, but Hujr bent his leg in his sleep and pulled his foot away. Disturbed by these movements, the snake made for a pitcher of milk which the King had always by his bed. It swallowed greedily and then vomited back the milk into the jar, while I rejoiced in my soul, saying: "When he wakes, he will drink the poisoned milk and then die. I shall be free from this wolf for ever." Soon Hujr woke in a great thirst and lifted the pitcher; but, before he drank, he sniffed at the milk, his hand trembled, the pitcher dropped, and he was saved. He is like this in all things; he thinks of everything, foresees everything, and never can be taken unawares.'

As the spy heard nothing after this save the noise of sighs and kisses, he rose softly and left the camp. By hastening his steps he reached his master before the dawn, and told him what he had seen and heard. 'When I left them,' he said, 'Ziyād had his head upon the knees of Hind; he was playing with her and she was answering.'

A grating sigh rumbled in the breast of Hujr at this news, and he ordered an immediate attack to be made upon the Kudaid camp.

At this point Shahrazād saw the approach of morning and discreetly fell silent.

But when the nine-hundred-and-seventy-seventh night had come

SHE SAID:

The full force of the Kindis fell upon the followers of Ziyād, who were worsted in that furious engagement and put to flight. Their tents were sacked and burnt. Many were slain and much was driven down the wind of anger.

Hujr found Ziyād in the mass, attempting to rally the retreat; with a bellow of rage he stooped from his horse and lifted his rival high in air. He held him thus suspended for a breath by the strength of his wrists, and then dashed him to the earth, so that his bones were broken. He cut off Ziyād's head and fastened it to the tail of his war-horse.

As soon as this part of his vengeance had been satisfied, he sought for Hind until he found her. He bound her between two horses and lashed them in opposite directions; as she was torn in sunder, he cried: 'Your tongue was sweet, the secrets of your heart were bitter!'

When he had told them of this wild revenge, the young man said to his guests: 'Since I am still dealing with the times before the bene-diction of Islam, I will tell you a tale to illustrate the thoughts of Arab women at that period. It is reported by our Lady Āishah, the cherished wife of the Prophet (upon whom be prayer and peace!). She was the fairest and most noble woman of primitive Islām; she was tender, courageous, passionate, and wise; her brilliant speech had male vigour combined with the wholesome eloquence of a young girl.'

Then the young man described in the very words of Āishah:

Men in the Judgment of their Wives

ONE day certain noble women of Yemen met at my house and agreed on oath to tell the whole truth concerning their hus-bands, without dissimulation whether for good or evil.

The first said: 'My husband, is it? An ugly and inaccessible man, as it were camel meat perched on a difficult mountain. And so dry with it all, that there is not a morsel of marrow to be found in him. A worn straw mat!'

The second said: 'Even to speak of mine is sickening to me. An intractable brute, he threatens divorce if I answer him one word; and, if I keep silence, he bustles me until I feel as if I were balanced on a naked lance point.'

Then said the third: 'Here is a description of my charming lord: if he eats he licks the bottoms of the plates, if he drinks he sucks out the last drop, if he stoops he squats like a parcel, if he kills for our food it is ever the dryest and leanest of the flock. Otherwise he is nothing; even his hand does not touch me to find out how I do.'

The fourth said: 'Be he far off from me! He is a heavy burden upon my eyes and upon my heart, both day and night. He is a store-house of defects, extravagances, idiocies. He will give you a slap over the side of the head as soon as look at you, or prick and tear your belly, or rush at you, or slap and tear and rush at the same time. A dangerous animal, Allāh destroy him!'

But the fifth said: 'My man is both good and pleasant, like the fairest of the nights of Tihāmah; he is as generous as the rain, he is honoured and feared by all our warriors. He is a lion going forth in his magnificence. His heart burns for all men; the column of his name is high and glorious. He hoards his hunger even at feast times; he watches in the night of danger. He has built his house near the public square so that it shall be the first resort of every traveller. Oh, he is great and handsome! His skin is a soft rabbit silk, it tickles me deliciously. The perfume of his breath is the scent of the zarnab; yet, in spite of all these things, I do as I like with him.'

The sixth lady of Yemen smiled sweetly, as she said: 'My husband is Mālik Abū Zār, that Abū Zār whom the tribes love. He found me the child of a poor house, he led me to his tent of colours, and en-riched my ears with rings of splendour; he put ornaments upon my breasts, and his love brought fatness to my wasted arms. He honoured me as his bride, he led me to a dwelling filled with the singing of lively songs and the shining of the lances of Samhar. Ever in my ears I hear the noises of horses, and of camels collected in great parks, the noise of milling and threshing, the noise of twenty flocks. With him I speak to my desire and he does not check me. When I lie down he does not leave me dry, and when I sleep he lets me sleep on. He has quickened my flanks with an excellent little son, so small that his bed seems a sliver of reed plucked from the mat, so behaved that the ration of a new-born kid suffices him, so delightful that, when he walks, balancing in his little coat of mail, he drags after him the hearts of all beholders. And the daughter which Abū Zār gave me! The delicacy, the jewel of our tribe! Her plumpness exquisitely fills her garment, she is bound in her small mantle like a tress of hair. Her belly is firm and straight, the line of her body is a pleasure under her coat, her thighs are rich and free, her little arms are rounded. She has a wide and open eye, a deep black eye with brows of gentle arch. Her nose is curved a little, the blade of a costly sabre. Fair and sincere is her mouth, beautiful and generous are her hands, her gaiety flashes in freedom. Her speech refreshes like a shadow at noonday, her breath is softer than silk, a soul-ensnaring musk. May Allāh keep them for my tenderness and joy, the daughter of Abū Zār, the son of Abū Zār, and Abū Zār!'

When the sixth had thus spoken, I thanked all my guests for the pleasure they had given me and then, taking up the discourse, said:

At this point Shahrazād saw the approach of morning and discreetly fell silent.

But when the nine-hundred-and-seventy-eighth night had come

SHE SAID:

'My sisters, may Allāh in the highest preserve the Prophet for our blessing! My mouth is not pure enough to sing his praise; I will content myself with repeating words of his concerning us, us women who are for the most part fuel for the fires of Hell. One day I begged him to give me counsel which should lead me into the path of righteousness, and he said to me:

' "O Āishah of my heart, let the women of the Mussulmāns keep watch upon themselves, to have patience in adversity and to be not unmindful in the day of their fortune, to give many children to their husbands, to surround their husbands with honour and attention, and never to be ungrateful for the gifts of Allāh. For God shall drive out from His mercy the ungrateful woman. Also that woman who looks with an insolent regard upon her husband, saying to him or concerning him: 'An ugly face! A hideous body!' God will twist out one of her eyes on the Day of Judgment, He will lengthen and deform her body, He will cause it to know an ignoble heaviness, to be a repulsive mass of flaccid flesh, dirtily lumped upon a rumpled, hanging base. Also the woman who opposes her husband in the marriage bed, or vexes him with bitter words, or profanes his mood, Allāh shall pull forth her tongue upon the last day into a foul and fleshy thong, sixty cubits in length, which shall wind its horrible, livid meat about her neck.

' "But the virtuous woman, who never troubles the peace of her husband, who never stays from the house at night without permission, who despises dear-bought garments and precious veils, who wears no costly circles about her arms and ankles, who does not angle for the glances of Believers, who is content with the natural beauty God has given her, whose words are soft, whose riches lie in works of charity, who eagerly foresees in all that concerns her husband, who has a tender love for her children, who keeps good counsel for her neighbour, and who is well disposed to each creature of Allāh—that woman, my dear Āishah, shall enter into Paradise with the prophets and the chosen of the Lord!"

'Then I was moved to cry: "O Prophet of Allāh, you are dearer to me than the blood of my father and mother!" '

'And now,' continued the young man, 'that we have reached the time of the benediction of Islām, let us consider certain aspects of the life of the Khalīfah Umar ibn al-Khattāb (whom may Allāh bless!). In an age which was stern and pure he was the purest and the sternest; he was the most upright of all Commanders of the Faithful.'

And he told:

Tales of Umar Ibn Al-Khattāb

IT is related that the Commander of the Faithful, Umar ibn al-Khattāb, the most upright Khalīfah and disinterested servant of Islām, was also called al-Farrūkh, or the Separator, because it was his custom to cut in two with his sword any man who refused to bow to sentence pronounced against him by the Prophet (upon whom be prayer and peace!).

His unworldly simplicity was such that, when he had made himself master of the treasures of the kings of Yemen, he distributed all this booty equally among the Mussulmāns, without making distinction of any. Among other things, each received a portion of striped cloth, and Umar had his portion made into a new garment. He was dressed in this garment when he went up into the pulpit at Madinah and harangued his hearers to a new raid against the Infidels. As he was speaking, a man of the congregation rose and interrupted him, saying: 'We will not obey you.' 'Why so?' asked Umar. 'Because,' answered the man, 'when you divided the striped cloth of Yemen, you said that each should have an equal share, but now we see you in a new garment which would have taken more than one man's share to make, for you are very tall. We will not obey you, because you have taken more than your share of the striped cloth.' Umar turned to his son Abdallāh, saying: 'Answer this man, for his complaint is just.' So Abdallāh rose, and cried: 'O Mussulmāns, when the Commander of the Faithful wished to have a garment sewn of his share of the cloth and it was found insufficient, I gave him a portion of mine, for I knew that otherwise he would have no suitable dress in which to preach before you to-day.' Then he sat down, and the interrupter exclaimed: 'Glory be to Allāh! Umar, we will obey you!'

On another occasion, when Umar had conquered Syria, Mesopotamia, Egypt, Persia, and all the lands of the Rūms, and had founded Basrah and Kūfah in Irāk, he returned to Madinah in a robe so tattered that it hung in twelve pieces, and sat all day upon the steps leading up to the mosque, listening to the complaints of the humblest and weighing out equal justice to amīr and camel-boy.

Now Harkal al-Kaisar, who ruled the Christians at Constantinople, had sent an ambassador with secret instructions to report the means, the strength, and the behaviour of the Arab prince. When this man arrived in Madinah, he asked: 'Where is your King?' and the people answered: 'We have no King, for we have a Prince! He is the Prince of Believers, Umar ibn al-Khattāb, the Khalīfah of Allāh!' 'Where is he?' asked the ambassador. 'Lead me to him.' 'He does justice, or he sleeps,' they answered, as they pointed out the road to the mosque.

So al-Kaisar's ambassador walked to the mosque and saw Umar sleeping in the noonday sun on the hot steps of the temple, with his head lying directly upon the stone. The sweat fell from the sleeper's brow and made a pool of moisture about his head.

Fear descended upon the heart of al-Kaisar's ambassador, and he could not help but cry: 'All the kings of the earth have bowed their heads before this beggar; he is the master of the world's great empire. When a people is governed by such a man, other nations must put on mourning.'

During the conquest of Persia, many objects of marvel were taken from the palace of King Yazdijard at Istakhr, and among them was a carpet, sixty cubits square, which pictured a garden whose every flower was made of precious stones and rose from a stalk of pure gold. Though Saad ibn Abū Wakkās, the Mussulmān general, had no practice in estimating the value of precious furnishings, he understood that here was a thing of price, and saved it from the looting of the palace as a present for Umar. But the upright Khalīfah (whom may Allāh be pleased to favour!) feared, if he accepted such a gift, to encourage that luxury which he had always dreaded for his people. (You will remember that, after the subjection of Yemen, he would touch nothing but a share of coarse striped cloth.) So, as soon as he received the carpet, he had it cut into as many pieces as there were chiefs in Madinah, and refused even one portion for himself. Though its value was depreciated by such treatment, the materials of the carpet were so costly that Alī (upon whom be prayer and peace!) was able to sell his small square to the Syrian merchants for twenty thousand dirhams.

In this invasion of Persia, the satrap Harmuzān was one of the last to surrender and only gave himself up at length on the understanding that the Khalīfah himself should decide his fate. Umar was at Madinah, and thither Harmuzān was conducted by two of the most courageous of our amīrs. These good men wished the Khalīfah to understand the importance and high rank of their prisoner, so they allowed him to resume his gold-embroidered mantle and tall, bright tiara, which were such as the satraps used to wear at the Persian court. When Harmuzān appeared before the steps of the mosque thus nobly clad, he refused to believe that the figure sitting in rags and alone upon an old mat in the courtyard could be the Commander of the Faithful; and the Khalīfah, for his part, when he raised his eyes at the rumour that some personage approached, and saw before him a prisoner dressed in those proud trappings which had so long overawed the noblest Arab tribes, cried in a great voice: 'Glory be to Allāh Who has raised up Islām to humble you, and such as you!' He had the Persian stripped of his gilded robe and muffled in a coarse blanketing of the desert; then he said: 'Now that you are clad according to your deserts, do you acknowledge the hand of that Lord to Whom alone is grandeur?' 'I easily recognise His hand in this,' answered Harmuzān. 'If God had remained neutral, I know that we would have vanquished you; our past triumphs and greater glory tell me so. This Lord must have fought on your side, since you conquered us.' Hearing this confession of Faith and finding it somewhat too ironical, Umar frowned so fiercely that the Persian was stricken by a sudden foreboding. Dreading that his conversation might have earned him death, he feigned a violent thirst and asked for water; when an earthen jar was handed to him, he fixed his eyes on the Khalīfah and seemed to hesitate. 'Of what are you afraid?' asked Umar.

At this point Shahrazād saw the approach of morning and discreetly fell silent.

But when the nine-hundred-and-seventy-ninth night had come

SHE SAID:

'I fear that someone will stab me while I am occupied in drinking,' answered the satrap; but Umar said: 'Allāh preserve me from such a suspicion! I at least grant you grace until this water has cooled your lips and quenched your thirst.' At once the subtle Persian threw the jar upon the steps and shattered it. Umar felt bound by his oath to harry the man no more, and, touched by such generosity, Harmuzān ennobled himself in Islām. Thenceforward he received from Umar a pension of two thousand dirhams.

At the time of the taking of Jerusalem, the city sacred to Jesus, son of Mary, the greatest prophet before the coming of Muhammad (upon whom be prayer and peace!), the city towards which the primitive Believers turned in prayer, the patriarch Sophronios consented to surrender if the Khalīfah in person would come to take possession of the holy place. Hearing of this condition, Umar set out from Madinah, and, though he was Allāh's Khalīfah upon earth, though he had bowed the heads of kings before the standard of Islām, he went alone. The camel upon which he rode bore two sacks, one of fodder for itself and another of dates. With a wooden platter slung before him and a waterskin behind, the Commander of the Faithful went forward day and night, stopping only for prayer or to deliver justice to some chance-met tribe, until he came to the gates of Jerusalem. He signed the treaty of capitulation, and the city was opened to him. As he passed the Christian church, he perceived that the time of prayer was at hand, and asked Sophronios in what place he might humble himself before Allāh. The Christian suggested the church, but Umar refused, saying: 'Though your faith is false, I will not pray in your church, for, when the Khalīfah prays upon any spot, the Mussulmāns take it at once into their possession.' After he had humbled himself towards the holy Kaabah, he said to the patriarch: 'Now show me some spot where I may build a mosque, that the Mussulmāns may assemble for prayer without troubling you in the exercise of your devotions.' Sophronios led him to the site of the temple of Sulaiman, in that place where Jacob, the son of Abraham, once laid his head. Seeing that the stone of Jacob served as a receptacle for all the filth of the city, Umar lifted some of the dung, as an example to the workmen, and bore it away in the folds of his garment. Thus it was that he cleared the place for that mosque which is the fairest upon earth and bears his name.

Umar used to walk through the markets and streets of Mecca and Madinah, leaning on a stick and dressed in rags. This he did in order to detect those merchants who cheated or overcharged; sometimes he would sternly lecture the delinquent and sometimes, if the case were bad, beat him severely with the stick.

One day, as he passed through the milk and curd market, he saw an old woman who had jars of milk for sale. When he had watched her doings for some time, he went up to her, saying: 'O woman, be very careful never again to cheat the Faithful as I have seen you cheating; be very careful never again to put water in your milk.' 'I hear and I obey, O Prince of Believers,' answered the woman, and Umar went upon his way. But the next morning, he approached the milk-seller again, saying: 'Daughter of evil, did I not warn you not to put water in your milk?' 'I swear I have not done so, O Commander of the Faithful,' cried the old woman; but a girl's voice came angrily from the interior of the shop, saying: 'Mother, how dare you lie to the Prince of Believers? How dare you add untruth to fraud, and disrespect to both? May Allāh pardon you!'

Umar's heart was moved by these words. Instead of reproaching the old woman further, he turned to his two sons, Abdallāh and Akim, saying: 'Which of you wishes to marry this virtuous maiden? It is certain that Allāh will grant the child, by the perfumed bestowal of His grace, a posterity as virtuous as herself.' 'I will marry her, my father,' answered Akim, who was Umar's younger son. Thus it was that a marriage took place between a milk-seller's daughter and a Khalīfah's son; and that marriage was blessed, for the daughter of it married Abd al-Azīz ibn Marwān and bore Umar ibn Abd al-Azīz. He ascended the throne of the Umayyads, being the eighth of that dynasty, and was one of the five great Khalīfahs of Islām. Glory be to Him Who raises to honour!

Umar used to say: 'I will never let the murder of a Mussulmān go unavenged.' One day, while he sat in judgment on the steps of the mosque, they brought him the murdered body of a beardless boy, tender and girlish, saying that they had found it in the road.

Umar investigated the crime with zeal, but could come upon no clue to the murderer. His unsuccess weighed on his justice-loving soul, and he would often be heard to pray: 'O our Lord Allāh, grant that I may run the man to earth.'

At the beginning of the next year, a living new-born child was brought to him who had been found abandoned on the place where the boy's body had been thrown down. 'Glory be to Allāh!' cried Umar. 'Now am I master of the victim's blood, and the murder shall not go unavenged.'

He handed over the child to a woman in whom he had confidence, saying: 'Look after this poor orphan at my expense. Never let him be taken away from you, and listen very carefully to all that any person may say concerning him. If you notice that some woman kisses the infant and clasps him to her breast, find out discreetly where she lives and inform me at once.' The nurse took the child, and laid the Khalīfah's instructions in the heart of her memory.

At this point Shahrazād saw the approach of morning and discreetly fell silent.

But when the nine-hundred-and-eightieth night had come

SHE SAID:

The child grew sturdily, and, when he was two years old, a slave came one day to the nurse, saying: 'My mistress begs you to allow me to take your little son to her. She is pregnant and, because your child is beautiful—Allāh preserve him from the evil-eye!—wishes to look upon him for a short time, that the life in her womb may be moulded to resemble him.' 'It is permitted, but I must accompany you,' answered the nurse.

They set forth together, and, as soon as the slave's mistress saw the boy, she ran to him weeping and took him in her arms, covering him with kisses and rocking over him.

The nurse hastened to the Khalīfah with this news, 'And the woman,' she said, 'is none other than that most virtuous Sālihah, daughter of the venerable Ansarī, the sheikh Sālih, who knew and followed our master the Prophet (upon whom be prayer and peace!).'

After reflection Umar concealed a sword under his mantle and sought out the house of the Ansārī, whom he found sitting in meditation before his door. 'What has your daughter done, O venerable sheikh?' he asked after greeting; and the sheikh replied: 'O Commander of the Faithful, may Allāh reward her for her works of charity! She is known far and wide for her exemplary conduct and her piety, for her deep sense of duty towards Allāh and her father, for her zeal in prayer and all religious observance, for the purity of her Faith.' 'That is well,' said Umar, 'but I wish to see her, in order that I may increase in her, even, the love of good.' 'Allāh pour His blessings upon you, O Prince of Believers!' answered Sālih. 'May He reward your benevolence towards my daughter! If you will stay here till my return, I will go and warn Sālihah to expect you.'

When he was introduced into the girl's presence, Umar ordered all who were there to depart and leave him quite alone with her. Then, uncovering his sword, he said: 'I wish to hear your theory concerning the death of the boy who was found in the road, for I know you have a theory. If you try to hide the truth from me, there is this sword between us, O Sālihah.' 'Commander of the Faithful,' answered the girl calmly, 'your investigations have led you to the right quarter. I swear, by the great name of Allāh and by the virtues of His blessed Prophet (upon whom be prayer and peace!) that I will tell you the whole truth.' Then she lowered her voice, and said:

'I had an old woman to live with me, and she went with me everywhere. I loved her as if I had been her daughter, and she was devoted to my service. We were together for a long time in mutual care, and I listened to her every word with veneration.

'One day she came to me, saying: "My child, I must go for a short time to my kinsfolk. But I have a daughter, and I fear that, in the house where now she stays, she may be exposed to some irrevocable disaster. I pray you to let me bring her here and leave her in your charge, until I return." When I had given permission, she went upon her visit.

'Next morning the daughter came to my house, and I found her both tall and beautiful. I grew fond of her, and let her sleep in the room where I myself slept.

'One afternoon I rested upon my bed and felt myself assaulted in my sleep. I was being ravished by some man who lay upon me with all his weight and held me helpless. When I could free myself, I was already soiled and dishonoured. In my agony of shame, I seized a knife and plunged it into the belly of my assailant, a beardless youth who had entered my household in disguise, feigning to be the old woman's daughter.

'When I had killed him I had the body thrown down in the place where it was found. Allāh permitted that I should become with child by that rape, but, when I bore a son, I abandoned him in the spot where his father's corpse had lain, for I would not raise a son who had been gotten upon me by force. That is the story of those two, O Prince of Believers. Allāh is my witness that I have told you the truth!'

'You have told me the truth, my daughter!' cried Umar. 'May Allāh shower down His blessings upon you!' In a great admiration for the virtue and courage of the girl, he recommended her to persevere in her pious works, and also prayed for her. As he passed out of the house, he said to her father: 'May Allāh bless your house, my friend, because of the virtue of your daughter! I have exhorted her as far as in me lies, and will trouble her no further.' 'May Allāh lead you in the way of all content, O Commander of the Faithful,' answered the unsuspecting Ansārī, 'may He bestow such blessings as your soul desires!'

After a short rest, the rich young man continued: 'I will now tell you quite a different tale, the tale of Blue Salāmah the Singer.'

And he said:

Blue Salāmah the Singer

MUHAMMAD of Kūfah, the poet, singer, and musician, tells the story thus:

Of all the girls and slaves to whom I gave music and singing lessons, Blue Salāmah was my most beautiful and vivacious pupil, my most fascinating, witty, and most promising. We called this brown child Blue because she bore on her upper lip a blue trace of dainty hair, as if the light hand of an illuminator had rubbed a morsel of musk upon it. At the time when I taught her she was quite young, a maiden on the eve of flower time, with little breasts just large enough to make a rising and falling in her garment. To look at her was a ravishment, a disturbance of the soul, the eyes were dazzled, and the brain reeled. Though all the renowned beauties of Kūfah were in her company, no man had eyes for any but Salāmah. 'See,

see, the Blue!' we would exclaim when she appeared. She was passionately and vainly loved by all who knew her; I loved her to distraction. Though she was my pupil, I was her devoted and obedient slave; if she had asked me for a human fry of brains and marrow, I would have rummaged all the gallows' heads and mossy bones of the world.

At this point Shahrazād saw the approach of morning and discreetly fell silent.

But when the nine-hundred-and-eighty-first night had come

SHE SAID:

When her master, Ibn Ghānim, went on pilgrimage and took her with him among his other slaves, I composed the words and music of this song:

> O Ghānim, you have left behind your caravan
> A lifeless lover but a living man,
> With bitter-apple and wormwood you have undone
> Such love as has not often seen the sun,
> And you allowed your camel-boy to break my heart
> When with a grin he drove two souls apart.

But my case was not as dark as that of another of Blue's lovers, Yazīd ibn Auf, the money-changer.

One day Ibn Ghānim took it into his head to say: 'O Blue, did any of all those who have fruitlessly loved you ever obtain a secret meeting or a kiss? Tell me the truth!' Fearing that her lord had become aware of some little licence which she had allowed herself before indiscreet witnesses, Salāmah answered truthfully: 'No one has ever had anything from me except Yazīdi bn Auf, the money-changer, who took a single kiss. I should never have given it to him, if he had not slipped two magnificent pearls into my mouth by way of exchange. I sold them afterwards for eighty thousand dirhams.'

'Was that so?' said Ibn Ghānim, and, without a word to show the jealous hatred which he felt, he settled down on the trail of Yazīd ibn Auf. He followed him until a suitable occasion offered, and then had him beaten to death.

These were the circumstances of that fatal kiss:

As I was going one day towards Ibn Ghānim's house to give Blue Salāmah a singing lesson, I met Yazīd ibn Auf in the street and asked him: 'Whither away, O Yazīd, in such brave garments?' 'We are bound for the same place,' he answered, and I said: 'Then let us go together.'

We were shown into the guest chamber, and Salāmah came to us there, dressed in an orange mantle and a rose red kaftān so that she seemed one stormy sun from head to foot. A slave girl followed, carrying a lute.

While Blue was singing in a new mode which I had taught her, while her voice rang rich and deep and moving in our ears, her master left us to give orders for the midday meal. Then Yazīd, whose heart was burning for the singer, went nearer to her, begging for a look. Though she did not break off her song, her answering glance so intoxicated the changer that he drew two unparalleled pearls from his belt and said, waiting until the song was over: 'O Blue, I have just paid sixty thousand dirhams for these pearls. If they take your fancy, they are yours.' 'What must I do to please you?' she asked, and he answered: 'Sing for me.'

So Salāmah carried her hand to her brow in acquiescence, and sang a trifle whose words and music she had made herself:

> The aching wound in my heart is red
>> Although Blue Salāmah made it.
> I showed my wound, and the doctors said
>> Nothing on earth could aid it;
> So I took my wound to love, instead,
> But he only looked wise and shook his head.
> 'I can do nothing for that,' he said,
>> 'I suppose Blue Salāmah made it?'

She sang this, looking at Yazīd, and then said: 'Now give me what you have to give.' 'Your will is mine,' he answered, 'but I have sworn an oath, a sacred oath, that I will only pass the pearls from my lips to yours.' The slave rose in indignation to admonish the audacious lover, but I caught her by the arm, saying: 'Let them be, my girl! Matters are in fine train and they are both bound for great profit with little loss.'

Salāmah laughed, and said: 'So be it! You may give them in any way you please.'

Yazīd placed the pearls between his lips and then approached Salāmah on hands and knees, as if he had been a dog; she fled from him to right and left, with her robes held up, and uttering little frightened cries. But, when she had nearly worn him out with this pretty game and had maddened him with the thousand coquetries of her retreat, she made a sign to her slave, who caught the changer by the shoulders and pinioned him in his place. Having proved herself the victor, Blue Salāmah went forward, in a little confusion, her brow diamonded with sweat, and kissed the pearls from the lover's lips to her own. Then she recovered countenance, and cried with a laugh: 'See, you are beaten all along the line, O Yazīd!' 'That does not trouble me,' answered Yazīd, 'I have caught a delight of perfume from your lips which will stay in my heart for ever.'

Allāh have Yazīd ibn Auf in His compassion! He died for love.

'And now you shall hear an example of Tufailism,' said the rich young man. 'The word was coined by our fathers, who lived in the age of Tufail the Glutton, to express the habit of going to feasts as an uninvited guest.'

And he told:

The Tale of the Parasite

IT is related that the Khalīfah al-Walīd, son of Yazīd, of the dynasty of Umar, greatly rejoiced to sit with Tufail of the Feasts, the lover of good dishes and fine flavours, the famous voluptuary who gave his name to the profession of parasite. Apart from his deep knowledge of foods, this Tufail had a learned wit, a cynical malice, and was ever ready with an apposite retort. His mother, by the way, had been taken in adultery. He expressed the whole art and shamelessness of sponging in these lines:

> He who's invited to a wedding feast
> Must look about as if he felt no least
>   Shade of uncertainty,
> Must enter jauntily and take the best
> Seat, catching no one's eye, that every guest
>   May think him quality;
> Must quell the porter if he will not quail,
> Must scorn the dishes as but poor regale
>   For such a man as he,
> Yet clutch the wine jars close to him, and sit
> Nearer the smoking roast than was the spit
>   Which turned it tenderly;

> Then, as his steel-tipped fingers rip and thrust
> And dig the chicken stuffing up, he must
> Cast well-bred glances of surprised disgust
>   At all the company.

Such was the code for perfect sponges, drawn up in the city of Kūfah by Tufail, the crown and father of them all. Here, from a thousand, is one example of his method.

At this point Shahrazād saw the approach of morning and discreetly fell silent.

But when the nine-hundred-and-eighty-second night had come

SHE SAID:

A notable citizen once invited a few intimate friends to dine off a marvellous confection of mixed fishes. When the well-known voice of Tufail was heard talking to the slave at the door, one of the guests cried: 'Allāh preserve us from the sponge! Let us at least save these fine big fishes from his fabulous appetite. Let us set them down in that dark corner, and only leave the little ones before us. When he has devoured the small fry and gone his way, we can finish our feast.'

The bigger fish had scarcely been hidden when Tufail entered, assured and smiling, and threw a casual greeting to the company. After calling upon the name of Allāh, he set his hand to the dish, but contented himself with one small worthless sprat. The guests were delighted, and said to him: 'Well, master Tufail, what do you think of these fish? They hardly seem to take your fancy.' 'I have not been on good terms with fish for a long time,' answered Tufail, 'my anger against fish is very terrible. My poor father was drowned at sea, and the savage brutes devoured him.' 'Then surely this is a good chance to avenge your father by devouring them,' said one of the guests. 'Perhaps you are right,' exclaimed Tufail, 'but wait a moment.' His parasitic eye had already searched out the fine and hidden fishes in the corner, so he lifted the smallest sprat from the dish and held it close to his ear, seeming to listen to its conversation. 'Do you know what this little bit of a sprat has been saying?' he asked at length, and the guests answered: 'As Allāh lives, how should we know?' Then said Tufail: 'This is what he said: "I was much too young to have eaten your good father, whom may Allāh have in mercy! If you want revenge, apply to the big fish in the corner, for they were the very ones who threw themselves upon the poor old man and gobbled him up!" '

The host and his guests realised that the trained nostrils of the parasite had winded their device; so, as well as they could for laughter, they set the fine big fish before him, saying: 'Eat in Allāh's name, and may they give you horrible indigestion!'

'And now,' said the young man, 'I will tell you the mournful tale of the fair Slave of Destiny.'

And he began:

The Tale of the Slave of Destiny

IT is related by the annalists that the third Abbāsid Khalīfah, al-Mahdī, Commander of the Faithful, left his throne to his eldest son, al-Hādi, whom he loved not and even hated; but insisted that, after al-Hādi's death, his own younger and favourite son, Hārūn al-Rashīd, should ascend the throne, and not an heir of al-Hādi's body.

When al-Hādi was proclaimed Prince of Believers, he looked upon his brother al-Rashīd with growing jealousy and suspicion, and did all in his power to cheat him out of his right of succession. But Hārūn's mother, the wise and holy Khayzarān, checkmated these designs, and with such consistency that the Khalīfah soon held her in equal detestation with her son, and only waited an opportunity for destroying both.

One day al-Hādi sat in his garden, beneath a costly dome carried on eight columns and having four doors, each giving upon one of the cardinal points of the sky. The fair Ghādir, his favourite slave, sat at his feet; he had only possessed her for forty days. The musician, Ishāk of Mosul, was present also, and it was to his accompaniment upon the lute that Ghādir sang and threw al-Hādi into transports of delight. Outside the night fell, the moon rose among the trees, and water ran lisping in broken shadows to the murmur of the sunset breeze.

Suddenly joy was stricken from the Khalīfah's face, and he frowned. He sat in a silence dark as the oakum of an inker, and then said harshly: 'Each has a fixed term, and none remains save the Eternal.' After another interval of ill-omened reflection, he cried aloud: 'Send Masrūr to me quickly!' This Masrūr, who was the in-strument of al-Hādi's anger and justice, had watched over the childhood of al-Rashīd, had borne him in his arms and on his shoulders. When he came into the presence, the Khalīfah said to him: 'Go to my brother, al-Rashīd, and bring back his head.'

At this point Shahrazād saw the approach of morning and discreetly fell silent.

But when the nine-hundred-and-eighty-third night had come

SHE SAID:

When he heard this sentence of death passed on his beloved, Masrūr stood stockstill, as if he had been struck by lightning. 'We come from Allāh,' he murmured, 'and to Him we return at last!' Yet in the end he went out, though staggering like a drunken man.

He ran straight to the Princess Khayzarān, al-Hādi's and al-Rashīd's mother, and, when she asked him why he had come so late and in such terror, answered: 'O my mistress, there is no power or might save in Allāh! Your son, our master the Khalīfah, has bidden me bring him the head of his brother al-Rashīd.'

These words so beat upon the heart of Khayzarān that she had to lower her head and collect herself, before she said: 'Run to al-Rashīd and bring him here at once.'

Masrūr hastened to Hārūn's apartment and, finding him already in bed, cried out: 'In Allāh's name rise up, my master, and come with me to your royal mother!'

Al-Rashīd rose and dressed in haste; when he had come to his mother's presence, Khayzarān embraced him without a word and thrust him unresisting into a little secret room. Then she sent to fetch all the amīrs and principal personages of the court, from where they were sleeping in their houses. When they were assembled in her apartment, she addressed them from behind the silk curtain of the harīm, in these simple words: 'I require you, in the name of Allāh, the Merciful, the Compassionate, and in the name of His Prophet, to say if you have ever heard tell that my son al-Rashīd had lot or part with the enemies of the throne or with the Zandakah heresy, or that he has ever made the least movement of insubordination and revolt against his lord, al-Hādi, your master and my son.' When they had all answered with one voice that they had never heard any of these things, Khayzarān said: 'Yet, even at this hour, my son al-Hādi has sent for the head of his brother al-Rashīd.' The amīrs and notables were dumb with fear, but the wazīr Rabīah rose and whispered to

Masrūr: 'Go at once to the Khalīfah and, when he asks you if you have done the deed, tell him that our Lady Khayzarān saw you about to fall upon al-Rashīd and, pushing you away, prevented you from striking off his head.'

So Masrūr returned to al-Hādi, and the Khalīfah cried: 'Have you obeyed my order?' 'O my master,' answered Masrūr, 'the Princess Khayzarān, my mistress, saw me as I was about to throw myself upon your brother and, pushing me back, prevented me from doing the deed.' When he heard this, al-Hādi rose, at the limit of his anger, and said to Ishāk and the slave: 'Stay here, for I shall soon return.'

The amīrs and notables rose at the sudden entry of the Khalīfah, but al-Hādi took no notice of them and turned to his mother, saying in a voice which trembled for rage: 'When I have given an order, how dare you gainsay it?' 'Allāh preserve me from gainsaying you in anything, O Commander of the Faithful,' answered Khayzarān, 'I only wished to know why you have condemned my second son to death. He is your blood brother, he is of the same vital and spiritual essence as yourself.' Then said al-Hādi: 'If you must know, I was decided in my course by a terrible dream which I had last night. I saw al-Rashīd sitting upon my throne, drinking and playing with my favourite slave Ghādir. As I love both my throne and my favourite, I will allow no dangerous rival near me, were he ten times my brother.' 'These are the false illusions of sleep, my lord,' urged Khayzarān. 'These are the visions born of heating meats. A dream is seldom true, my son.' She spoke on in this way, while the amīrs looked approval at her, until she had calmed al-Hādi and relieved his fears. Then she fetched al-Rashīd out of the little secret room and made him swear before his brother that he had never had the least thought of treachery, or lightest ambition for the throne.

When the last wisp of his anger had dissipated, al-Hādi returned to his pleasure dome and, sending Ishāk away, prepared to bathe himself with Ghādir in the waters of night and love. But suddenly he felt a sharp pain on the sole of one foot and, carrying his hand to the spot, began to scratch the itching of it. In a few moments a little tumour formed, which grew to the size of a nut; this burned and itched intolerably so that al-Hādi was forced to scratch again. At once the tumour increased to the size of a walnut, and burst of its own accord. Then al-Hādi fell back lifeless upon the floor.

The reason of al-Hādi's death was this: during the few minutes for which the Khalīfah had remained with her after the reconciliation, Khayzarān had made him drink of a tamarind sherbert which held the sentence of Destiny.

The first to learn of his death was the eunuch Masrūr; he ran at once to his mistress, saying: 'Allāh prolong your days, O mother of the Khalīfah! My master al-Hādi is dead.' 'That is well,' answered the Queen, 'but keep the news secret until you have fetched al-Rashīd to me again.'

So Masrūr went to al-Rashīd and roused him out of sleep, saying: 'The Queen calls you, my lord.' 'As Allāh lives,' cried Hārūn in a panic, 'my brother has told her something else against me; he has accused me of some new plot of which I am quite innocent.' But Masrūr interrupted, saying: 'O Hārūn, follow me quickly. Calm your dear spirit and refresh your eyes, for all goes very well and nought but joy awaits you.'

Hārūn rose and dressed; then Masrūr bowed before him, kissing the earth between his hands, as he cried: 'Greeting and salutation, O Commander of the Faithful, O Imām of the servants of God, O Khalīfah of Allāh upon earth, Defender of the Faith, and Weapon of the Law!' 'What do you mean, Masrūr?' demanded al-Rashīd, swaying between astonishment and uncertainty. 'A moment ago you called me by my simple name, and now you hail me as Commander of the Faithful. What is this sudden change?'

At this point Shahrazād saw the approach of morning and discreetly fell silent.

But when the nine-hundred-and-eighty-fourth night had come

SHE SAID:

'Master,' answered Masrūr, 'each life is put out into the world with a Destiny and a term. May the Giver prolong your days, for your brother is dead!' 'Allāh have him in pity,' said al-Rashīd. Freed for the first time from fear and care, he hastened to his mother, and she cried when she saw him: 'Delight and happiness! Delight and happiness for the Prince of Believers!' She put the royal mantle upon him and gave him the sceptre and the supreme seal. As she was thus decking him in his sovereignty, the chief eunuch of the harīm entered, saying to Hārūn: 'I bring good news, my master! a son has been born to you by Marājil, your slave!' Doubly rejoicing, the Khalīfah gave his son the name of Abdallāh al-Mamūn.

News of al-Hādi's death and the accession of al-Rashīd had gone about all Baghdād before the dawn. Hārūn received with royal dignity the allegiance of his amīrs and nobles and, in the same hour, raised al-Fadl and Jafar, two sons of Yahyā the Barmakid, to the post of wazīr. All the lands and dependencies of the empire and all peoples who confessed Islām swore obedience to the new Khalīfah, and the world's most powerful and glorious reign began.

Now I will tell you about Ghādir, the slave in whose arms al-Hādi died.

On the evening of his elevation to the throne al-Rashīd, who had heard of her beauty, wished to behold her while his eyes were still fresh to the delights of royalty. He went to her, and said: 'I wish you to come with me to the garden and the dome where my brother al-Hādi—Allāh pity him!—delighted to take his pleasure and his ease.' Ghādir, who was already wearing garments of deep mourning, lowered her head, and answered: 'The Commander of the Faithful is my lord and I am his slave.' She changed her robes of grief for ones more suitable, and then hurried to the pleasure dome. Al-Rashīd bade her sit by his side, and feasted his eyes upon her unrivalled beauty until his heart was dancing for joy. But, when the wines which he loved were handed about and Hārūn would have had her drink, Ghādir refused. 'Why do you refuse?' asked the Khalīfah, and she answered: 'Wine without music loses a little of its generosity. I would be glad if that excellent Ishāk were here to bear us musical company.' 'It is permitted,' said al-Rashīd graciously, and he sent Masrūr for the musician, who soon entered and stood before him. When Ishāk had kissed the earth between his hands, the Khalīfah bade him seat himself opposite the favourite.

The wine cup passed about, and they drank it out until the night was dark about them. Suddenly Ishāk cried under the inspiration of the wine: 'Eternal praise to Him who with His hand alters the course of life, bringing about succession and demission!' 'Of what are you thinking, O son of Ibrāhīm?' asked al-Rashīd, and the singer answered: 'Alas, my lord, yesterday, at this hour, your brother leaned from that window and watched the streams pass lisping to the night, beneath the womanish moon; and these glad things so terrified him that he would have made you drink a bitter cup.' Then said al-Rashīd: 'O Ishāk, the lives of all men are written in the Book of Destiny. How could my brother have killed me, since my time had not yet come?' Then he turned to the fair Ghādir, and asked her:

'What do you say, my girl?' For answer, Ghādir took up her lute and sang in a trembling voice:

> In life of time two rivers join,
>   One muddy and one clear;
> Two days in time of life there are,
>   The soft and the severe;
> You may trust time and life as far
> As you would trust the spinning of a coin,
>   Or very near.

And when she had made an end of this song, al-Hādi's favourite fell to the ground and lay there without movement. They shook her and succoured her, but she lived no longer; she had taken refuge in the breast of Allāh. 'She loved the dead, my lord,' said Ishāk. 'It is a poor love which lasts only till the grave is digged. Allāh grant His mercy to al-Hādi, and to his favourite, and to all of us!'

A tear dropped from al-Rashīd's eye; he ordered the body to be washed and set in the same tomb with al-Hādi. 'Yes,' he said, 'Allāh grant His mercy to al-Hādi, and his favourite, and to all of us!'

When he had finished this moving history, the young man said to his guests: 'Now hear another manifestation of Destiny in the tale of the Fatal Collar.'

And he said:

The Tale of the Fatal Collar

ONE day the Khalīfah Hārūn al-Rashīd, who had heard tell of the great talent of Hāshim ibn Sulaimān, the singer, sent for him and begged for a taste of his quality in composition. Hāshim sang a melody in three stanzas, with so much art and in so exquisite a voice that al-Rashīd cried: 'Blessed be your father's spirit, for you have excelled, O son of Sulaimān!' So saying, he lifted a magnificent collar, enriched with drop emeralds as large as musk pears, from about his neck and fastened it upon that of the singer.

But, instead of rejoicing at this gift, Hāshim allowed his eyes to fill with tears. A weight of sadness descended upon his heart, and his cheeks became yellow.

At this point Shahrazād saw the approach of morning and discreetly fell silent.

But when the nine-hundred-and-eighty-fifth night had come

SHE SAID:

Al-Rashīd, who had expected delight, supposed that this ornament was not to the other's taste, so he said: 'Why these sad tears,
O Hāshim, and why, if the collar does not please you, do you keep a
silence which is equally awkward for us both?' 'May Allāh increase
His favour upon the most generous of all Kings!' answered the
musician. 'My grief is not such as you suppose, dear master. If you
allow me, I will tell you the tale of this collar, and you will understand why the sight of it saddens me so much.' 'You have my leave
to speak,' replied al-Rashīd, 'for surely the story must be astonishing
if it explains how an heirloom of my race can cause so great a grief.'

So the singer collected his memories, and then said:

The matter of the collar dates back to my first youth, when I
dwelt in my native land of Sham. One evening, as I walked at dusk
on the borders of our lake, dressed as an Arab of that desert and
having my face muffled to the eyes, I met a man magnificently clad,
and accompanied, against all usage, by two most beautiful girls,
singers, to judge them by the lutes they carried. At first glance I
recognised the Khalīfah al-Walīd, second of that name, who had left
Damascus to hunt gazelles beside this Lake Tabarīah.

When he saw me, the Khalīfah turned to his two companions,
saying in a voice intended for them alone: 'Here is an Arab just in
from the desert, one of those foolish savages. As Allāh lives, I will
call him to keep us company, and we can jest a little at his expense.'
He signed to me with his hand and, when I had come near, made me
sit down beside him on the grass, facing the two singers.

Then, at her lord's command, one of the girls tuned her lute and
sang a song of mine, in a moving voice but with a few mistakes and
certain mutilations of the air. Although I had put on a mask of im-
passivity, in order not to draw down the Khalīfah's raillery before
its time, I could not help crying: 'That was by no means perfect,
girl.' The singer gave a mocking laugh, and said to the Khalīfah:
'O Commander of the Faithful, this camel-boy has dared to accuse
me of mistakes!' Al-Walīd looked at me, at once frowning and
smiling, and asked: 'Do they teach singing and the delicate art of
music in your tribe?' 'They do not, O Prince of Believers,' I answered with a respectful inclination, 'but, if you give me leave, I can
convict this admirable player of certain errors.' The Khalīfah gave

his permission, and I said to the girl: 'Tighten your second string a quarter and loose your fourth the same; then begin with the lower mode of the melody. You will find the passages which you muddled come straight of themselves, and the run and expression of the whole vastly improved.'

In a dumb surprise to hear a savage talk so, the young woman tuned her lute again, according to my direction, and sang the song a second time. When it came forth with all perfection of beauty, she threw herself at my feet, crying: 'You are Hāshim ibn Sulaimān, I swear it by the Lord of the Kaabah!' I was no less moved than she and could say no word; but, when the Khalīfah asked me if her guess were correct, I uncovered my face and answered: 'O Commander of the Faithful, I am indeed your slave Hāshim.'

Al-Walīd was delighted to make my acquaintance, and said: 'I give thanks to Allāh that He has set you upon my way, O son of Sulaimān. This girl admires you above all the musicians of your time, and will play and sing your compositions only. I would have you for my friend.'

When I had kissed his hand in sign of thanks, the singer turned towards al-Walīd, saying: 'O Prince of Believers, have I your permission to mark a happy meeting by giving a token to this master?' 'The wish is most suitable,' replied the Khalīfah. So the charming child took a magnificent collar from about her neck and fastened it on mine, saying: 'Excuse the poverty, and accept the homage!' This collar had been given to her by al-Walīd himself, and was the same which you have hung about my neck to-day.

And now for the reason of my tears:

At this point Shahrazād saw the approach of morning and discreetly fell silent.

But when the nine-hundred-and-eighty-sixth night had come

SHE SAID:

When we had sung together for a little, the breeze came cool from the water, and al-Walīd said: 'Let us row upon the lake.' Slaves, who had stood far off, ran down and brought round a boat to us. The Khalīfah boarded her first and I followed him; when the girl who had given me the collar put forth her foot to embark, she was troubled by the great veil in which she had muffled herself because of the rowers, and missed her footing. Before any of us could help her, she had disappeared below the water, and, in spite of all our searchings, her body was never found. Allāh have her in His mercy!

Al-Walīd wept abundantly in his bitter grief, and I wept also. After a long silence, he said to me: 'The loss would have been heavier, if we had not still that collar to serve as a memory of her short life. I will not take it back from you, but I beg that you will sell it to me.'

I handed the emerald toy to the Khalīfah, and, when we returned to the city, he paid me thirty thousand silver dirhams, and added precious gifts to them.

Now you know the reason of my tears, O Commander of the Faithful. Allāh in His wisdom dispossessed the dynasty of Umar and gave the throne to your glorious ancestors. That is how the collar came to be among your treasures and to return to me so strangely.

Al-Rashīd was moved by this tale, and said: 'Allāh have mercy on all who have deserved mercy!' By this general formula he avoided the naming of a name which belonged to a rival dynasty.

'And, since we are on the subject of music and singing,' said the rich young man, 'I will tell you one tale, out of a thousand, concerning the life of Ishāk ibn Ibrāhīm of Mosul, the greatest musician of any age.'

And he said:

Ishāk of Mosul and the Lost Melody

AMONG the many writings which have come down to us in the hand of Ishāk ibn Ibrāhīm of Mosul, we find the following:

I entered the presence one day and found Hārūn al-Rashīd sitting with his wazīr al-Fadl and a sheikh of al-Hijāz, whose handsome face was marked with grave nobility. After greeting, I leaned towards al-Fadl and asked the stranger's name, for his appearance pleased me and I had never seen him before. 'He is the grandson of Maabad of al-Hijāz, the poet and singer,' answered al-Fadl. 'The name should be familiar to you.' He must have seen by my face that I was delighted to meet the descendant of one whom I had so admired in youth, for he whispered to me presently: 'O Ishāk, if you make yourself agreeable to this old man, he will sing you all his grandfather's songs, for he has a fine memory as well as a charming voice.'

So, wishing to make trial of the man's method and to be reminded of the old songs which had charmed my adolescence, I made myself pleasant to the sheikh of al-Hijāz and, after friendly talk of this and that, was bold to say: 'Most noble sheikh, can you tell me how many songs your grandfather composed?' 'Just sixty,' answered the old man, and I asked again: 'Would it be trespassing too far upon your patience if I begged you to name your favourite?' 'Easily the finest of them all,' said he, 'is the forty-third song, which begins with the line: *Beauty of the neck of Mulaikah, my Mulaikah of the breasts . . .*'

Then, as if this simple saying over of the line inspired him, he took the lute from my hand and sang the whole song through to a very light accompaniment. His voice was astonishingly full and true, and he brought such deep emotion from the old music that I was rapt quite outside myself to hear him. As I could rely upon my memory, which retains the most complicated air when I have heard it once, I did not trouble to sing the song over after him, but contented myself with thanking the old man from the bottom of my heart. Soon we parted, he for Madinah and I, still drunken with the melody, to my own house.

At this point Shahrazād saw the approach of morning and discreetly fell silent.

But when the nine-hundred-and-eighty-seventh night had come

SHE SAID:

When I got home, I took down and burnished my lute, and tuned it to perfection. But, as Allāh lives, I could not play that air of al-Hijāz which had moved me so, I could not remember one note of it, I could not even call to mind the mode in which it had been written. I can usually retain a hundred couplets and their melody when I have listened once with a negligent ear, but this time it was as if an impenetrable woollen curtain had fallen between the music and my mind.

Night and day I racked my brains and spurred them to remember, but all to no purpose. At last, in despair, I left my lute and my singing lessons behind, and went journeying through Baghdād, through Mosul and Basrah, and finally through the whole of Irāk, questioning the oldest singers concerning Maabad's forty-third song. But none of them could help me to it.

Rather than be ridden eternally by this obsession, I made up my mind to cross the desert to far Madinah and beg the poet's grandson to sing me the song again. I was in Basrah at the time, and rode by the river as I came to this decision. Suddenly two young women in rich robes, seeming of high rank, seized the bridle of my ass and brought him to a standstill.

Having no thought except for the song, I answered their greeting with a gruff: 'Leave go!' and would have snatched away the bridle. But one of the beauties smiled below her discreet veil, saying: 'Where is your passion for Maabad's song, O Ishāk? What has come to: *O beauty of the neck of Mulaikah?* Have you given up your search?' Then, before I had time to answer, she said again: 'I was behind the lattice of the harīm, Ishāk. I was watching you when the old man of al-Hijāz sang his song to the Khalīfah and al-Fadl. I saw you twitch, I saw the cushions dancing; you wagged your head and balanced on your feet, O Ishāk! I thought that you were mad.'

'By the memory of my father, I am madder now than ever after that song!' I cried. 'I would give anything to hear it, even if it were sung off the key, even if it were cut. I would give ten years of my life for a single note! You have fanned the flame of my regret, O tenderness, you have breathed upon the coal of my despair. Why did you remind me of it, why did you bring the whole scene back to me? For pity's sake, let me go to Madinah!'

But the girl laughed, instead of loosing the bridle, and then asked: 'If I can sing you the song, will you still go to Madinah?' 'Do not torture me so, O daughter of excellent parents!' I entreated. 'I have told you that I am mad already.'

Then the woman suddenly started singing the song of my infatuation, and the voice and skill of her were a thousand times more wonderful than the sheikh's. Yet it was only at half voice she sang! As I listened, a great calm fell upon my troubled heart, I threw myself from the saddle at the girl's feet and kissed the hem of her robe, saying: 'I am your slave, bought by your generosity. Will you allow me to entertain you at my house? You can sing me the song of Mulaikah, and I will sing all day and all night to you. Yes, all day and all night!' But the girl answered: 'O Ishāk, we know your character, we know the greed with which you hoard your compositions. No pupil has ever learnt more than one song from your own lips, or been allowed to sing more than one song which you have made yourself. The rest of their stock is the work of others and taught by others, Allawaihi, Wahj al-Karah, Mukhārik, or the like. I fear you are too jealous to treat us suitably, O Ishāk. If your only desire is to learn the song, I will gladly sing it to you, until you have it pat.' 'And I will pour out my blood for you, O daughter of heaven!' I cried. 'But who are you? What is your name?'

At this point Shahrazād saw the approach of morning and discreetly fell silent.

But when the nine-hundred-and-eighty-eighth night had come

SHE SAID:

'I am a simple singer,' she answered, 'one of those who have overheard what the leaves say to the birds, and the breezes to the leaves. My name is Wahbah; I am she whom the poet praised in the song which bears my name.' And she sang:

> Joy stays all night by your white side to sigh:
>   'Now not an hour is wasted, Wahbah.'
> He knows the water of your mouth, which none but I
>   Have tasted, Wahbah.
>
> He knows it rarer than the silver rain
>   When thirst expects her visit, Wahbah.
> You brimmed its scarlet chalice once, and not again;
>   I miss it, Wahbah.
>
> Oh, be not like the fabled cock which lays
>   Once in a lifetime only, Wahbah;
> Come and perfume my dwelling, for the laggard days
>   Are lonely, Wahbah.
>
> And bring that softer dew than morning's is
>   Which weighs no tenderest fronds down, Wahbah,
> That dew more light than karkafah or kandaris
>   Or swan's-down, Wahbah.

The words of this song were by the poet Farrūh, and Wahbah herself had composed a delicate air to them. The words and their melody and the singing of them quite maddened me, and I begged so hard that at last the girl consented to come to my house with her sister. We passed the rest of that day and all the night in an ecstasy of music, and I found in Wahbah talent which I have not yet seen equalled. Love of her ate even to my soul, and a time came when she gave me her flesh as she had given me her voice. She was an ornament to my life for many happy years.

'And now,' said the rich young man, 'I will tell you an anecdote concerning court dancers.'

And he began:

The Two Dancers

THERE was in Damascus during the reign of Abd al-Malik ibn Marwān, a poet musician called Ibn Abī Atīk, who spent all the gains of his art and all the charity of the Damascene amīrs in a mad profusion of prodigalities. Thus, in spite of his considerable earnings, he lived in perpetual want and was hard put to it to find food for his large family. Gold in the hands of a poet and patience in the heart of a lover are like water in a sieve.

One of the poet's friends was Abdallāh the chamberlain, an intimate of the Khalīfah, and this good man, after interesting many of the city's notables on the rake's behalf, resolved at length to gain for him the favour of his royal master. One day, when the Khalīfah was in the best possible humour, Abdallāh broached the subject and painted in sombre colours the destitution of one who had a right to be considered the greatest poet at that time living in the land of Shām. 'You may send him to me,' said Abd al-Malik ibn Marwān.

The chamberlain ran with this good news to his friend, and the poet, with many expressions of thanks, prepared to present himself at the palace.

When he was introduced into the presence, he found the Khalīfah sitting between two superb dancing girls, who balanced as gracefully upon their feet as if they had been two branches of the ban, and moved with languid grace two palm-leaf fans to cool their master.

On one of the fans was painted in letters of blue and gold:

> Cool and light the air I fling to
> The rose-modest girls I kiss.
> Sometimes I relent and bring, too,
> Shield for other kisses—this.

And on the other fan was painted in letters of blue and gold:

> I desire pale hands and palaces,
>   All inelegance I despise;
> Girls, then? No, that's one of your fallacies—
>   With cool sleep I kiss his eyes.

When the poet had considered these two breathing miracles, he began to shiver with pleasure and felt himself snatched, as it were, into a comfortable blaze of light. He thought himself in Paradise, with two hūrīs who had been specially set aside, and looked back on all the women whom he had known as ugly fools.

After the first homage and greeting, the Khalīfah said: 'O Ibn Abī Atīk, I have heard from Abdallāh of the deep misery into which you and yours have fallen, and have called you into my presence to satisfy any desire you may express to me.' The poet was so dazzled by the dancers that he hardly understood what the Khalīfah was saying; indeed, had he done so clearly, his mind would not have dwelt for an instant upon the idea of money or food. His soul had but one inspiration, the beauty of the dancers, his body but one desire, to hold them and grow drunk beneath their eyes.

Therefore he answered: 'Allāh prolong your days, O Commander of the Faithful! Your slave has already been greatly blessed by the Giver; he is rich, he lacks for nothing, he is as an amīr! His eyes are content, his soul is content, his heart is content. Standing thus in the presence of the sun between two moons, he is the richest man in all your kingdom.'

Abd al-Malik was pleased by this answer. Also, as he saw the poet's eyes craving for that which his lips dared not express, he rose up from between the dancers, saying: 'O Ibn Abī Atīk, I received these girls from the King of Rūm to-day; they are yours, they are your fields. It is lawful to enter into your fields by any road you wish.' And he left them there together.

After the poet had taken his dancers home, Abdallāh returned to the palace, and the Khalīfah said to him. 'O Abdallāh, surely you a little exaggerated the wretched state of your friend the poet? He swore to me that he was utterly happy and lacked for nothing at all.' Abdallāh felt his face covered with confusion and stood silent, as al-Malik continued: 'Yes, yes, Abdallāh, the man was happier than anyone I have ever seen.' He repeated the poet's extravagant words of satisfaction, and Abdallāh replied, half smiling and half offended:

'I swear by the dear life of your head, O Commander of the Faithful, that the man has lied! He has lied very shamelessly! He is the most wretched, the most entirely destitute of your subjects; the sight of his wife and children would make you weep. There is no beggar upon the road who has such need of the crumbs of your charity.'

When Abdallāh was dismissed from the presence, he hastened to Ibn Abī Atīk's house.

At this point Shahrazād saw the approach of morning and discreetly fell silent.

But when the nine-hundred-and-eighty-ninth night had come

SHE SAID:

He found the poet sitting in an expansion of delight, with a dancer on each knee and a great tray of wine cups in front of him. 'You madman,' he cried roughly, as he entered, 'why did you give me the lie before the Khalīfah? You have darkened my face until it can be no blacker.' 'My friend,' answered the poet joyfully, 'who could whine about poverty or sing of misery in those very glorious surroundings? It would have been a poor compliment to these two ladies; and, moreover, I would not have been rewarded so richly. Joy is much better paid than sorrow, my friend.'

With that he held out an enormous cup, filled to the brim with a laughing and musk-scented wine. 'Drink beneath the black light of these eyes, my friend,' he said, 'the black light of my folly!' Then, with a double gesture, he continued: 'These are mine. How could I have asked for more without offending Allāh?'

As Abdallāh smiled in spite of himself and lifted the cup to his lips, the poet took up his lute and sang, after a sparkling prelude:

> Lively and light-foot as if sprayed
>   From dancing fountains,
>   Such is each slender-flanked gazelle;
> Her breasts are pear-shaped cups of jade
>   Against a sky of light.
>
> Should I not sing, then? If the bald
>   And ancient mountains
>   Had drunken of these girls as well,
> They would have jumped and sung and called
>   And danced in their delight.

And, from that time, the poet Ibn Abī Atīk lived as he had lived before, trusting his Destiny to the Master of all, and careless of the morrow. The two dancers remained his consolation in despair, and an abiding joy until his death.

'And I will also tell you the tale of The Pistachio Oil Cream,' said the young man.

The Pistachio Oil Cream, and the Legal Point

THE supreme Kādī of Baghdād during the reign of Hārūn al-Rashīd was Yakūb Abū Yūsuf. He possessed an acuter mind and a greater knowledge of the law than any other man in the city, and had been the pupil and dear companion of the Imām Abū Hanīfah. Indeed, it was he who clarified, assembled, and co-ordinated the admirable Hanafī doctrine, which is the basis of all orthodox procedure even in our own time.

He tells us the story of his youth and humble beginnings, and in it deals both with pistachio oil cream and an intricate legal difficulty. He says:

When my father died—Allāh have him in mercy and keep a chosen place for him!—I was still a little boy, but we were so poor that my mother soon apprenticed me to a dyer, and I was supporting our house at a much earlier age than is usual.

But Allāh had not worked any dye into my Destiny, and, instead of spending all my day at the vats, I would escape, as often as possible, to join the circle of listeners who met to receive religious teaching from the Imām Abū Hanīfah (Allah reward him!). My mother had her suspicions, and would sometimes follow my truantry and drag me from the presence of that venerable master. On these occasions she would beat and scold me, and force me back into the dyer's shop.

Yet I managed to attend the Imām's lessons regularly, and that holy man soon began to point me out as an example of zeal and thirst for knowledge. Indeed I spent so little time among the dyes that at length my mother came to the assembly and, in the scandalised silence of all his pupils, cursed Abū Hanīfah aloud, saying: 'It is you, O sheikh, who are corrupting this child and driving him into the way of penury. I can earn but little with my spindle, and, if this poor orphan does not hold by his trade, the two of us may soon expect to starve to death. It will be your responsibility at the Day of Judgment.' My master lost none of his calm at this tirade, but answered my mother pleasantly: 'Allāh shower down His blessings upon you, O woman of the poor! But it is not bread that this poor orphan is learning to eat here, it is pistachio oil cream.' These strange words persuaded my mother that the venerable Imām was not right in the head, and, as she retired, she threw this final insult over her shoulder: 'May Allāh shorten your days, old babbler! Your brains are softening upon you!' But I remembered the words of the Imām.

Allāh had planted the passion of study in my heart, and therefore it triumphed over every difficulty. I fervently frequented Abū Hanīfah, and the learning he gave me lifted me step by step until I became the supreme Kādī of Baghdād, and was the constant guest of the Khalīfah himself.

One day, as I sat at meat with Hārūn al-Rashīd, the slaves brought in a great porcelain dish where trembled a fair white cream, snowed with grated pistachios and giving forth a delightful smell. 'Taste some of this dish, O Yakūb,' said the Khalīfah. 'Even my most expert cooks cannot always succeed with it, but to-day I can see that it is excellent.' 'What is it called, O Commander of the Faithful?' I asked. 'What are its ingredients, that it should look and smell so very sweet?' Then said Hārūn: 'It is a baluza, prepared with cream, honey, fine white flour, and the oil of pistachios.'

At this point Shahrazād saw the approach of morning and discreetly fell silent.

But when the nine-hundred-and-ninetieth night had come

SHE SAID:

When I heard these words, I could not help smiling. 'Why do you smile, O Yakūb?' asked the Khalīfah; and I replied: 'For nothing but good, O Commander of the Faithful. A simple memory of childhood passed through my brain, and I smiled to see it pass.' 'Tell me of it quickly,' said al-Rashīd, 'for I am sure that it will be profitable to hear.'

So I told of my first steps under the guidance of Abū Hanīfah, of my mother's despair on seeing me forsake the vats, and of the Imām's prediction concerning pistachio oil cream.

Hārūm was delighted by my tale, and said: 'An application to learning will always bear fruit, and the advantage of that fruit will be both secular and religious. The venerable Abū Hanīfah was a wise prophet, he saw with the eyes of his soul what other men could not see with their eyes of flesh. May Allāh grant him mercy and the most scented of His pleasures in Paradise!'

So much for the pistachio oil cream. Now for the legal difficulty.

One evening, when I had retired early, being more weary than usual, I was woken from a deep sleep by a violent knocking upon my door. I wrapped my loins in a woollen izār and went down to find Harthamah, the confidential eunuch of the Khalīfah. Instead of taking time to answer my greeting, he threw me into great terror by crying: 'Come with me to our master at once, for he wishes to speak with you.' 'O my dear Harthamah,' I answered, 'have a little consideration for a sick old man. The night is far spent, and surely this matter can stay over till the morning. Perhaps by then the Prince of Believers will have forgotten, or have changed his mind.' But the eunuch answered: 'As Allāh lives, I dare not disobey.' 'Yet you can at least tell me why I am summoned,' I ventured. 'Masrūr came running to me,' replied Harthamah. 'He was quite out of breath and gave me the command without an explanation.'

This uncertainty perplexed me, and I said: 'O Harthamah, will you not at least allow me to wash quickly and perfume myself a little? If the business is serious, I shall then be suitably prepared to meet it; and if, as I hope, the affair is trivial, a trifle of washing and scenting will have done me no harm.'

The eunuch allowed me this favour, and I was washed, perfumed, and properly dressed when I rejoined him. We went swiftly to the palace and found Masrūr waiting for us at the door. 'Here is the kādī,' said Harthamah, and Masrūr bade me follow him. As we entered the palace, I made bold to say: 'O Masrūr, you know that I am a devoted servant to the Khalīfah, you know what is due to a man of my age and position, you know that I have always been your friend. Can you not tell me why our master requires me at this strange hour?' 'I myself do not know,' answered Masrūr. 'You can at least tell me who is with him,' I urged with my knees knocking together. 'Isā the chamberlain is alone with him,' he replied, 'and Isā's slave is in the neighbouring room.'

But I refused to understand yet, and cried: 'I put my trust in Allāh! There is no power or might save in Him!' As I came towards the Khalīfah's apartment, I stepped heavily so that I should be heard, and a voice cried: 'Who is there?' 'Your servant Yakūb, O Commander of the Faithful,' I answered, and Hārūn bade me enter.

I found the Khalīfah seated with his chamberlain Isā on his right hand. I prostrated myself and then gave greeting; to my great relief my greeting was returned, and al-Rashīd asked with a smile: 'We have troubled you, upset you, perhaps frightened you?' 'Only frightened, O Prince of Believers,' I replied. 'I and mine were quite bowled over by your message.' Then said the Khalīfah: 'Be seated, O father of the law.'

When I had taken my seat, with relief singing about my heart, the Khalīfah turned to me, saying: 'O Yakūb, do you know why we have called you thus in the dead of night?' 'I do not, O Commander of the Faithful,' I replied. 'I required you to bear witness to a solemn oath which I am about to take,' explained al-Rashīd, with a gesture towards his chamberlain. 'Isā here has a slave which he refuses either to give or sell to me; you, as the supreme kādī of Baghdād, must be present when I swear, by the most exalted name of Allāh, to kill this Isā if he will not let me have the slave in one of these two ways.'

Quite certain now that I was out of all danger, I gave Isā a stern glance and cried: 'Tell me what strange quality or virtue Allāh has given to this girl of yours, that you will not relinquish her to the Khalīfah. Do you not see that your refusal is degrading to you and much disparages your soul?' 'O our lord the kādī,' replied the unmoved chamberlain. 'There is something lamentable in a precipitation of judgment. Blame me, if you will, when you have heard my reason.' 'Can there be a valid reason for such conduct?' I demanded. 'There can be, and there is,' asserted Isā. 'An oath which is made with full consent and in all clarity of mind may not be set aside. I have sworn, by the triple divorce and on a promise to free all my slaves and to make over my riches to the poor, that I will never sell or give away this girl.'

At this point Shahrazād saw the approach of morning and discreetly fell silent.

But when the nine-hundred-and-ninety-first night had come

SHE SAID:

'O Yakūb, is there no way of resolving this difficulty?' asked the Khalīfah. 'There is,' I answered without a moment's hesitation, 'and a very easy way. Isā has only to give you half of the girl and sell you the other half, then he will be at one with his conscience.'

'But would that be legal, O father of jurisprudence? Would the law accept such a compromise?' asked Isā. But, when I had replied that the law most certainly would, he lifted his hand quickly, crying: 'Then I take you to witness, O kādī, that I give one half of my slave to the Khalīfah, and that I sell him the other half for that sum of a hundred thousand silver dirhams which the whole of her cost me.' 'I accept the gift,' al-Rashīd answered, 'but I pay a hundred thousand gold dīnārs for the second half. Bring me the girl!'

The money was counted out in sacks, and Isā fetched in the girl to his master, saying: 'Take her, O Prince of Believers, for she is yours. May Allāh abundantly bless you by her means!'

When the chamberlain had departed, al-Rashīd turned to me, and said anxiously: 'There remains a second difficulty. As this girl has been another man's slave, the law requires her to be set aside until it be proved that she is not pregnant by her former master. But, if I do not lie with her to-night, I am quite sure that my liver will burst and I shall die.'

I gave a moment to reflection, and then answered: 'There is nothing difficult about that, O Commander of the Faithful. The law is applicable to slaves, but not to free women. You can free her at once and then marry her.' The shadow cleared from al-Rashīd's face, and he cried: 'I free this slave.' Then the shadow returned, and he asked: 'But who can marry us at such an hour? It is now, and not to-morrow, that I wish to lie with her.' 'I can marry you myself,' I answered.

I called Masrūr and Husain as witnesses and, in their presence, performed the marriage ceremony, stipulating, as is customary, that the Khalīfah should give his bride an immediate dowry. The sum I assessed myself at twenty thousand dīnārs.

When this gold had been brought and handed over to the girl, I made as if to retire; but Hārūn called Masrūr to him, saying: 'As a recompense for the trouble which we have caused him, carry two hundred thousand dirhams to the house of the kādī, together with twenty robes of honour.' I bowed myself out with many thanks, leaving a delighted prince behind me, and returned home accompanied by slaves who bore the money and the robes.

Hardly had I crossed my threshold when an old woman entered to me, saying: 'O Abū Yūsuf, the happy child who has been freed and married to the Khalīfah by your advice, she who has gained the proud title of wife of the Commander of the Faithful, ranks herself now as your daughter and sends me with filial greeting. She begs you to accept half of the dowry which the Khalīfah has given her, and to excuse the poverty of her offering. She hopes to express her gratitude more fully in the future.' With that the old woman set down ten thousand golden dīnārs before me, and, after kissing my hand, departed upon her way.

I thanked Allāh for having, of His infinite mercy, changed my anxiety to joy, and in my heart I blessed the venerable memory of Abū Hanīfah, who had taught me all the subtleties of civil and religious law. May God be good to him!

'And now, my friends,' said the rich young man, 'listen to the tale of The Arab Girl at the Fountain.'

And he began:

The Arab Girl at the Fountain

THE accession to the throne of al-Mamūn, Hārūn al-Rashīd's son, proved a blessing to the empire, for he was incomparably the wisest and most brilliant of the Abbāsids. He made his lands fertile with peace and justice, he honoured and efficiently protected both scholars and poets, and started the intelligence of his time, as if it had been a ball, rolling in the polo-ground of knowledge. Yet, in spite of days filled with toil and study, he contrived to find hours for gaiety and feasting; and, at these times, it was the singers and musicians who won the chief part of his approbation and reward. He always chose his wives, the mothers of his children, from among the most beautiful and intellectual women of that age. Here is one example out of twenty of the way he selected a wife.

One day, as he was returning from a hunt with his escort, he came to a fountain, near which an Arab girl stood in the act of slinging a full waterskin to her shoulder. Allāh had given her a perfect figure of five spans, and a breast cast in the mould of perfection. For the rest she was a full moon on the night of full moon.

At this point Shahrazād saw the approach of morning and discreetly fell silent.

But when the nine-hundred-and-ninety-second night had come

SHE SAID:

When she saw this brilliant troop of riders, the girl walked away, but, in her haste, she did not take time to fasten the neck of the skin securely. Therefore she had hardly made a few steps before the water began to gush out noisily upon the ground. At once the girl turned in the direction of her dwelling, and cried: 'Father, father, come and arrange the neck of this skin! The neck has betrayed me! I am no longer mistress of the neck!'

These three cries for help showed such an excellent choice of words and were given in so delightful a voice that the Khalīfah reined in to listen. As there was no response to her calling, the girl set down the skin; and then it was that the Khalīfah spoke to her. 'What is your tribe, my child?' he asked, and she answered in a tone which delighted him: 'I belong to the Banū Kilab.' Though al-Mamūn was well aware that this tribe was one of the noblest of all, he wished to prove the mind of the girl and therefore played upon words, saying: 'Do you not mind belonging to the tribe of Dogsons?' 'Are you really so ignorant of the true meaning?' the girl demanded mockingly. 'If you are, I must tell you that the tribe of the Banū Kilab are the tribe of Faultless Generosity. They know how to entreat strangers with magnificence, they also know how to use the sword. But what is your own line and pedigree, O rider?' Instead of answering, the Khalīfah laughed and asked: 'Are you by chance as learned in genealogy as you are pre-eminent in beauty?' 'Answer my question and you shall see,' retorted the girl. So al-Mamūn, entering into the spirit of the game, and wishing to know whether the girl understood the ramifications of his royal lineage, condescended to reply: 'My line is the line of the Red Mudaris.' The maiden knew that this qualification of colour came from the red leather tent which Mudar, the father of those tribes which bear his name, had used in the desert; therefore she showed no surprise, and asked again: 'And to what tribe of the Mudaris do you belong?' 'To the most illustrious,' answered al-Mamūn, 'to the one which has the best breeding on the male and female sides, the one which all the other Mudaris revere.' 'Then your tribe is the tribe of the Kinānids,' exclaimed the girl. When al-Mamūn had admitted with some surprise that this was so, she smiled and asked again: 'To what branch of the Banū Kinānah do you belong?' 'To the purest,' he replied, 'to the most generous, to the most feared.' 'Then you must be one of the Kuraishids,' said the girl. 'You are right,' allowed al-Mamūn, marvelling more and more, 'I belong to the Banū Kuraish.' 'But the Kuraishids have many branches,' objected the girl. 'Which is your branch?' 'The one which received benediction,' he answered. 'Then, as Allāh lives,' cried the girl, 'you are descended from Hāshim the Kuraishid, who was the great-grandfather of the Prophet (on whom be prayer and peace!)'. 'I am in truth a Hashimid,' said al-Mamūn, and the girl asked: 'But what is your family among the Hashimids?' 'The noblest glory of them all,' he said, 'that which is venerated by each Believer in the world.' Immediately the maiden prostrated herself and kissed the earth between his hands, crying: 'Veneration and homage to the Commander of the Faithful, to Allāh's vicar upon earth, al-Mamūn, the glorious Abbāsid!'

The Khalīfah was profoundly and joyfully moved by this speech; in the hearing of all his escort he proclaimed: 'By the Lord of the Kaabah and the pure merit of my glorious ancestors, I will marry this admirable child! She is the noblest jewel which has been set in my Destiny.'

At this point Shahrazād saw the approach of morning and discreetly fell silent.

But when the nine-hundred-and-ninety-third night had come

SHE SAID:

He called the chief of the tribe, who was the girl's father, and obtained his consent to the marriage, paying him a hundred thousand golden dīnārs as a portion, and writing in his name all the taxes of al-Hijāz for five years.

The wedding was celebrated with a pomp which had never been equalled, even during the reign of al-Rashīd. On the night of penetration al-Mamūn gave the girl's mother a thousand pearls on a gold dish to pour over her daughter's head; and the bridal chamber was perfumed by an immense torch of ambergris, which weighed forty minas and had been bought with the whole taxes of Persia for one year.

The Khalīfah gave all his love and passion to this new bride, and she bore him a son, whom he called Abbās. The mother of Abbās was ever considered among the most learned and eloquent women whose names have honoured the history of Islām.

'I will tell you another and very different tale from the life of al-Mamūn,' said the youth, and he began:

The Perils of Insistence

WHEN the Khalīfah Muhammad al-Amīn, the son of Hārūn al-Rashīd and Zubaidah, had been slain after his defeat, by order of the general of al-Mamun's army, all the provinces which had held by al-Amīn hastened to submit themselves to al-Mamūn, who was the dead man's half-brother by a slave named Marājil. The new Khalīfah inaugurated his reign with a sweeping clemency towards his foes, and would often be heard to say: 'If my enemies knew my goodness of heart, they would place themselves in my hands and confess their deeds.'

Now the directing hand in all the oppressions which al-Mamūn had suffered, during the lifetime of his father al-Rashīd and of his brother al-Amīn, had been the hand of Zubaidah herself. When she heard of her son's lamentable end, her first thought was to take refuge from her stepson's vengeance upon the holy ground of Mecca; but, after many days of vacillation, she decided to leave her fate to the man who had disinherited her and to whom she had so long given the bitterest cup which it was within her power to mingle. So she wrote the following letter:

'O Commander of the Faithful, however great a fault may be, it looks a little thing to the vision of your mercy. Before your greatness of heart crime itself can appear but as an error.

'The sender of this supplication begs you to recall a memory as dear to you as it is to her, and to pardon the transgressor of to-day for the sake of him who was the darling of our common yesterdays.

'If you will take pity upon my weakness and destitution, if you will find mercy for one who has deserved no mercy, you will be acting as he would have acted who, were he alive to-day, would be the first to intercede for me. O son of your father, remember your father, and do not close your heart to the prayer of his unfortunate widow.'

When the Khalīfah al-Mamūn had read this letter, his heart was so moved with pity that he wept for the tragedy of his brother al-Amīn and for the straits to which Zubaidah had been reduced. He rose from his place at length and wrote this answer:

'*My mother, your words found my heart acrumble with regret. Allāh is my witness that I feel for my father's widow as I would feel towards my own mother.*

'*No man may call back the decisions of Destiny, but I will do my best to attenuate your grief. I have given order to restore your confiscated lands to you, your houses, your goods, and all which a contrary fate has taken from you. If you return among us, my mother, you will find your former state undimmed and the veneration of your subjects unabated.*

'*I wish you to know that you have lost one son only, and that another remains to you, who is to prove himself devoted as the dead.*

'*May peace and security abide with you!*'

At this point Shahrazād saw the approach of morning and discreetly fell silent.

But when the nine-hundred-and-ninety-fourth night had come

SHE SAID:

Also, when Zubaidah came weeping and failing to cast herself at his feet, al-Mamūn rose in her honour and kissed her hand and shed tears upon her breast. He gave back all those prerogatives due to the wife of al-Rashīd and a princess of the royal blood, and treated his stepmother, until the end of her life, as if he had been the child of her body. But, in spite of all this illusion of power, the Queen could never forget the former reality nor cease to mourn over the death of al-Amīn. Until her last hour she nursed a sort of resentment towards the Khalīfah and, though she hid this carefully, it could not but be apparent to al-Mamūn.

The Khalīfah suffered this smouldering enmity without complaint. Here is an example of Zubaidah's rancour and his clemency.

Al-Mamūn entered her apartment one day and saw that her lips moved as she looked towards him. Since he could not hear her words, he said: 'I am afraid, dear mother, that you are cursing me because the heretic Persians slew your son and left the throne vacant for my occupation. Yet there can be no fault with Allāh.' But Zubaidah denied this, saying: 'I swear by the holy memory of your father that no such thought was in my mind.' 'Then will you tell me,' urged the Khalīfah, 'what you muttered as you looked at me?'

Zubaidah lowered her head as one who will not speak. 'I beg to be excused from answering,' she said. But al-Mamūn was too curious to let the matter drop, and pressed so strongly that at last the Queen burst out: 'If you must know, I was cursing the folly of insistence. I was saying: "Allāh confound the importunity of man!" ' 'What put such a speech into your mind?' asked the Khalīfah, and Zubaidah answered:

'O Commander of the Faithful, one day I lost a game of chess which I was playing against your father, Hārūn al-Rashīd, and, as we had a wager on the result, he insisted that I should walk through the palace and the gardens quite naked at the dead of night. In spite of my supplications and entreaties, he refused to consider any other forfeit, and I was forced to obey. When I returned after this walk, I was mad with rage and half dead from weariness and cold.

'Next morning it was my turn to win and impose conditions.

'I took a long time to consider what was the most disagreeable action to which I could condemn my husband, and at last bade him pass the night in the arms of the ugliest and dirtiest of our kitchen slaves. A certain Marājil combined these two qualifications; so, at sunset, I led al-Rashīd to the stinking cellar where she had her being, and obliged him to lie down by her and to work all night. In the morning his state was lamentable and he smelt horribly.

'Now it was from that cohabitation in filth that you were born, O Commander of the Faithful.

'Thus blindly I brought into the world the death of my son al-Amīn and the cause of all our woe.

'This would not have happened, except for my insistence that your father should mount the slave and his insistence that I should walk naked at the dead of night.

'That is why I cursed the folly of insistence and the importunity of man.'

Al-Mamūn hastened from the Queen's presence to hide his confusion. As he went, he said to himself: 'As Allāh lives, the lesson is applicable to me also, for, had it not been for my insistence, I would not have been reminded of that disreputable episode.'

Then said the rich young man to his guests: 'I trust, my friends, that Allāh has used me as a pathway between true learning and your ears. I have given you a share of those riches which may be gathered without pain and enjoyed without danger. To-day I will say no more, but another time, if Allāh wills, I shall show you further of those marvels which are the most precious inheritance our fathers left us.'

Then he distributed a hundred gold pieces and a square of precious material to each of his hearers as a reward for their attention. 'One must encourage the seed,' he said to himself, 'and make the way easy when it leads to good.'

He regaled them all with an excellent supper and sent them upon their way in peace.

So much for them. But Allāh knows all!

When she had made an end of this admirable series of tales, Shahrazād fell silent, and King Shahryār cried: 'O Shahrazad, you have instructed me in many things, but I think that you have forgotten to speak of the wazīr Jafar. I have long desired to hear all that you know concerning him, for I find that he strangely resembles in his quality my own grand-wazīr, your excellent father. It is that likeness which urges me to hear the whole of his surely admirable story.' But Shahrazād hung her head, as she replied: 'Allāh keep us from calamity, O King of time, and have compassion upon Jafar the Barmakid and all his people! I beg you to excuse me from telling that story, for it is full of tears. Alas, who would not weep to hear of the end of Jafar, and of his father Yahya, and of his brother al-Fadl, and of all the Barmakids! So lamentable was their taking off that stone itself would become tender at the telling of it.' 'Yet tell me all the same, O Shahrazād,' said King Shahryār, 'and may Allāh keep us from all calamity!'

So Shahrazād said:

The End of Jafar and the Barmakids

HERE then, O auspicious King, is that sorry tale which mars the reign of the Khalīfah Hārūn al-Rashīd with a bloodstain which not even the four rivers shall wash away.

As is already known, O king of time, Jafar was one of the four sons of Yahya ibn Khālid ibn Barmak. His eldest brother, al-Fadl, was in some sort al-Rashīd's foster-brother, for, because of the great friendship which existed between the family of Yahya and that of the Abbāsids, and because of the tender affection which bound the two women themselves, al-Rashīd's mother, the Princess Khayzarān, and al-Fadl's mother, the noble Itabah, exchanged nurslings and each gave to her friend's son that milk which Allāh had destined for her own. That is why al-Rashīd always spoke of Yahya as: 'My father,' and al-Fadl as: 'My brother.'

At this point Shahrazād saw the approach of morning and discreetly fell silent.

But when the nine-hundred-and-ninety-fifth night had come

SHE SAID:

The most reliable chroniclers place the origin of the Barmakids in the city of Balkh in Khurāsān, where they occupied a position of great distinction. It was not until a little more than a hundred years after the Hijrah of our Prophet (upon whom be prayer and peace!) that the family moved to Damascus and took root there under the dynasty of Umar. In the reign of Hishām, the head of the house was converted from the Magian cult and became ennobled in Islām.

But it was not until the accession of the Abbāsids that the family was admitted into the counsels of the court, and began to brighten the earth with its glory. Khālid ibn Barmak was made grand-wazīr by Abū al-Abbās al-Saffah, the first of the Abbāsids; and, during the reign of al-Mahdī, the third in the line of Abbās, Yahya ibn Khālid was charged with the education of Hārūn al-Rashīd, the Khalīfah's favourite son, who was born only seven days after al-Fadl, Yahya's son.

When al-Rashīd was invested with the supreme power, after the unexpected death of his brother al-Hādi, he had no need to go back to the memories of his earliest youth, spent with the Barmakid children, before calling Yahya and his two sons to share in his aggrandizement; it was only necessary for him to recall his education by Yahya and the devotion which that good man had shown in braving the menaces of al-Hādi in order to assure his pupil's inheritance. On the very night of al-Hādi's death the tyrant had given order that Yahya and his children should be beheaded.

When Yahya went in the middle of the night with Masrūr to tell Hārūn that he was now master of the empire and Khalīfah of Allāh upon earth, al-Rashīd immediately named him grand-wazīr and raised his two sons, al-Fadl and Jafar, to be wazīrs under him. This action augured most happily for the new reign.

After that the Barmakids were an ornament for the brow of their century, and a crown upon its head. Destiny showered her most favourable gifts upon them, so that Yahya and his sons became bright stars, vast oceans of generosity, impetuous torrents of kindness, beneficent rains. The world lived at their breath, and under their hands the empire reached the pinnacle of its splendour. They were the refuge of the afflicted, the final resort of the comfortless. The poet Abū Nuwās said of them:

> Since earth has put you away, O sons of Barmak,
> The roads of morning twilight and evening twilight
> Are empty. My heart is empty, O sons of Barmak.

They were admirable wazīrs, wise administrators, they filled the public treasure. They were strong, eloquent, and of a good counsel; they surpassed in learning; their generosity equalled the generosity of Hātim Taiy. They were rivers of happiness, they were good winds bringing up the fruitful clouds; it was through them that the name and glory of Hārūn al-Rashīd clanged from the flats of Central Asia to the northern forests, from Morocco and Andalusia to the farthest bounds of China and Tartary.

And suddenly the sons of Barmak were cast from the greatest height which men have reached to the lowest depths of horror; they drank the most bitter cup which calamity can pour. Alas, for the unfaith of time, they had not only ruled a vast empire, they had been the dear friends, the inseparable companions of their King. Jafar was the life of al-Rashīd's eyes; his place was so great in the Khalīfah's mind and heart that, one day, Hārūn even had a double mantle made, so that they both could wear it and be, as it were, one man. Such were the terms on which they lived together until the final tragedy.

O pain of my soul, listen to the coming of that black cloud which veiled the sky of Islām and cast dismay upon every heart!

One day—be such days far from us!—al-Rashīd, returning from Mecca, went by water from Hīrah to the city of Anbār. He halted at the monastery of al-Umr, on the banks of the Euphrates, and night found him in feasts and pleasures, as so many other nights had found him.

But this time his dear companion Jafar was not with him; he had gone for a few days of hunting in the plains of the river. Gifts and messages from the Khalīfah followed him everywhere in his sport.

No hour passed without the arrival at his tent of some messenger, bearing a precious reminder of al-Rashīd's love.

Now that night—be such nights far from us!—Jafar sat in his tent with the doctor Jibrīl Bakhtiyāshū, al-Rashīd's personal physician, and with the Khalīfah's favourite poet, blind Abū Zakār. Hārūn had deprived himself of the company of both these men, in order that the one might watch over Jafar's health and the other entertain him with his improvisations.

It was the time of the evening meal, and Abū Zakār, the blind poet, was playing upon the mandoline and singing verses of fickle chance.

At this point Shahrazād saw the approach of morning and discreetly fell silent.

But when the nine-hundred-and-ninety-sixth night had come

SHE SAID:

Suddenly Masrūr, the Khalīfah's sword-bearer, the instrument of his anger, strode unceremoniously into the tent. When Jafar saw him thus enter, in defiance of all etiquette, without demanding an audience or even announcing his proposed visit, he turned yellow in the face, and said: 'You are welcome, Masrūr, your presence is ever a fresh delight. But I must confess, my brother, that I am astonished to see you come to me, for the first time in your life, without sending some servant to give news of your arrival.' 'The matter is too grave for ceremony,' replied Masrūr, without deigning the least salute to his old friend. 'Rise up now, Jafar, and testify to your Faith for the last time. The Commander of the Faithful demands your head from me.'

Jafar rose to his feet, and said: 'There is no God but Allāh, and Muhammad is the Prophet of Allāh! From His hands we come and, soon or late, to His hands we return again!' Then he faced his old friend of so many years and moments, and cried out: 'O Masrūr, it is impossible. Our master must have given you the order in a moment of drunkenness. I conjure you, by our walks together and our community of life by day and night, to return to the Khalīfah; for I believe that you will find he has forgotten what he said.' But Masrūr answered: 'It is my head or yours. I cannot return with my duty unfulfilled. Write your last wishes, for that is the only privilege I can accord you in memory of our ancient friendship.' Then said Jafar:

'We belong to Allāh! I have no last wishes to write. May Allāh prolong the span of the Commander of the Faithful by those days which are shorn from mine.'

He left the tent, knelt upon the leather of blood which Masrūr had already spread, and bandaged his eyes with his own hands. Then his head was struck off. Allāh have him in His mercy!

After this, Masrūr returned to the Khalīfah, and entered the royal presence bearing Jafar's head upon a shield. Al-Rashīd looked at the head of his old friend and, leaning forward suddenly, spat upon it.

But his resentment was stronger than death. He ordered the body to be crucified at one end of the bridge of Baghdād, and the head to be exposed at the other. This punishment was more degrading than any which had ever been inflicted upon even the worst of malefactors. At the end of six months he ordered that his wazīr's remains should be burnt on cattle dung and scattered among the privies.

O pitiful misery, that the scribe Imrānī should have been able to write on the same page of the register of treasury accounts: 'For a robe of state, given by the Commander of the Faithful to his wazīr Jafar, son of Yahya al-Barmakī, four hundred thousand dīnārs of gold,' and a little further down: 'Naphtha, reeds, and dung to burn the body of Jafar ibn Yahya, ten silver dirhams.'

Such was the end of Jafar. Yahya his father, the guide of al-Rashīd's infancy, and al-Fadl his brother, al-Rashīd's foster-brother, were arrested on the morning following the execution, and with them were taken all the rest of the Barmakids, to the number of about a thousand, who had any public charge or employment. They were thrown into foul dungeons, their great riches were confiscated, their wives and children were left without shelter, shunned by the regard of man. Some died of starvation, and others were strangled; but Yahya, his son al-Fadl and his brother Muhammad died under the torture. Allāh have them all in His mercy! Their fall was great!

And now, O King of Time, if you wish to hear me speak of the cause of this disgrace and lamentable death:

One day, some years after the end of the Barmakids, Alīyah, al-Rashīd's young sister, plucked up heart to say to him: 'My lord, I have not known you pass one tranquil day since the death of Jafar and the disappearance of his family. How did he come to merit such disgrace?' Al-Rashīd's face grew dark, and he pushed her away, saying: 'My child, my life, my sole remaining happiness, how would it advantage you to know the reason? If I thought that my shirt knew, I would tear my shirt in pieces.'

The historians and annalists are far from being agreed as to the cause of this catastrophe. Here are some of the differing versions which they give of the events which may be supposed to have led up to it.

According to some, al-Rashīd became offended at last by the extravagant liberalities of Jafar and the Barmakids, the tale of which became a weariness even in the ears of those who benefited, and which called forth rather envy and dislike than grateful friendship. There was never mention of any other house than theirs; one could not come to the royal favour save through them, directly or indirectly; members of their family filled all the highest positions at court and in the army, of the magistrature and about the provinces; the fairest properties near the city belonged to them; their palace was more encumbered by courtiers and petitioners than that of the Khalīfah himself. Al-Rashīd's doctor, that same Jibrīl Bakhtiyāshū who was with Jafar in his tent on the night of doom, has said concerning the splendour of the Barmakids:

'One day I entered al-Rashīd's apartments, in his palace called Kasr al-khuld at Baghdād. The Barmakids dwelt on the other bank of the Tigris, so that there was only the width of the river between the two dwellings. The Khalīfah, after remarking the number of horses which were being held near the steps of his favourites and the crowd pressing about their door, said in my hearing, but as if to himself: "May Allāh reward Yahya and his two sons! They bear all the burden of my reign, leaving me free to look about me and live at ease." But, on another occasion, I saw that he was beginning to regard the Barmakids in a different manner. As he looked out of the window upon the same affluence of men and horses, he said: "Yahya and his sons have taken the management of my reign away from me. They are the true power and I am only a figure." This I heard, and from that time made sure of the disgrace of the Barmakids.'

According to other historians, the growing jealousy of al-Rashīd was fanned by the many enemies which the pride of the Barmakids raised up against them, and by anonymous detractors, who allowed unsigned bitter verses and perfidious prose to come to the ears of the Khalīfah. These same annalists aver that it was a grave indiscretion on the part of Jafar which placed the final stone on the tower of his master's resentment. Once, when al-Rashīd had commanded him secretly to destroy a descendant of Alī and Fātimah, the daughter of the Prophet, a man named al-Saiyid Yahya ibn Abdallāh al-Husainī, Jafar had pity upon this Alid and allowed him to escape, although the Khalīfah had marked him as a danger to the dynasty of Abbās. This generous action was reported to al-Rashīd, with exaggeration and distortion; and it became that drop of gall which overflowed the angry cup. When he was questioned, Jafar frankly confessed what he had done, and said: 'I acted for the glory and good name of my master.' 'You acted well,' answered al-Rashīd, turning very pale, but he was heard to mutter to himself: 'Allāh do so to me and more also, if I do not destroy you, Jafar!'

Other historians would trace the fall of the Barmakids to their heretical opinions in the face of Islamic orthodoxy. It must not be forgotten that, when they lived in Balkh before their conversion to the Faith, they practised the Magian cult. During the expedition into Khurāsān, the birthplace of the Barmakids, al-Rashād noticed that Yahya and his sons exerted all their power to prevent the destruction of the temples and monuments of the Magi. His suspicion of their religious integrity grew greater afterwards, for he found that they always showed clemency to every kind of heretic, and especially to his personal enemies among the Jabarīyah and Zandakah. Those who hold this theory cite in proof of it the fact that serious religious troubles broke out in Baghdād immediately after the death of al-Rashīd, and almost proved the death-blow to orthodoxy.

But the most probable reason for the destruction of the Barmakids is adduced both by Ibn Khillikān, and by Ibn al-Athīr. They say:

'At the time when Jafar lay so near the heart of the Khalīfah that al-Rashīd had that double mantle made for the two of them, the Khalīfah could not abide to be separated from his favourite, and desired to look upon his face at all hours of the day and night. But al-Rashīd also loved, with a strange and deep tenderness, his own sister Abbāsah, perhaps the most beautiful and cultivated woman of her time. No other of her sex influenced al-Rashīd so greatly, and he was as incapable of living without her as if she had been a woman Jafar. These two loves made up his happiness; yet, for his joy's perfection, they had to be indulged at the same time. Thus it was necessary that the two favourites should be present together. But the law of our Faith forbids a man to look upon a woman, or for a woman to be looked upon by a man, unless he be her husband or near relation. To transgress this law is to lose honour, and therefore al-Rashīd, who was a strict observer of the law which it was his high privilege to administer, could not enjoy the simultaneous presence of Jafar and Abbāsah without the constraint of veils and the irksomeness of silence.

'That is why he one day said to Jafar: "My friend, I have no true pleasure save when I sit with you and my dear sister Abbāsah. I wish you to wed the girl; but I forbid you to come together save in my presence, and I insist that there shall be no consummation of the marriage, lest the noble sons of Abbās be cheated out of their inheritance." Jafar bowed before the desire of his master and had, perforce, to accept this marriage with all its unnatural conditions.

'The young husband and wife met only in the presence of the Khalīfah, and even then their glances hardly crossed. Al-Rashīd rejoiced at the new arrangement and seemed not to know that he was torturing his two best friends. How can love be controlled by a third person? How can such restraint between two young and handsome beings not break out into the flame of love?'

At this point Shahrazād saw the approach of morning and discreetly fell silent.

But when the nine-hundred-and-ninety-seventh night had come

SHE SAID:

'These two married lovers, who had every right to come together and yet could not, sighed more deeply every day, and felt that drunkenness which, when it is hidden, becomes a fever about the heart. Abbāsah, in her deprivation, became madly desirous of her husband. At length she told her love, coming upon Jafar in secret as often as she was able and soliciting him to grant her right; but the wazīr was too loyal and too prudent to give way to her. He was bound by his oath to al-Rashīd, and he also knew how hasty the Khalīfah could be in his anger.

'When Princess Abbāsah saw that her entreaties were in vain, she took the part of all women and sought out a devious way. She sent a message to the noble Itabah, the mother of Jafar, saying: "O our mother, I require you to introduce me into Jafar's household, as if I were one of those slaves which you procure for him every day." It was a fact that Itabah would send her dear son a fresh and chosen virgin slave each Thursday, and that the wazīr would not touch this child until he had eaten richly and partaken of generous wines.

'But Itabah vehemently refused to lend herself to the betrayal, and sent back word to the princess that danger for all the world might lurk in this affair. Then the young wife became insistent even to the point of using threats. "Reflect on the consequences of your refusal," she said. "My resolution is taken and I shall reach my end in spite of you and by any means. I would rather die than lose Jafar and my rights in him."

'So Itabah was forced to consent, for she realised that, if this trick had to be played, it would be better to play it under the most hopeful conditions. She promised the princess her help in that plot which was at once so innocent and so dangerous, and immediately told Jafar that she meant to send him a slave of unparalleled beauty. She painted the girl in such warm colours that her son kept on referring to this gift and showed every sign of impatience that the night should come. When she saw that she had worked upon him sufficiently, Itabah sent word to her daughter-in-law, saying: "Be ready for to-night."

'Abbāsah decked herself for her part, and then went to the house of Jafar's mother, who, at nightfall, introduced her into the apartment of her son. Jafar, whose senses were a little dulled by the fermentation of the wines, did not recognise his wife in the virgin slave who stood before him. It must be remembered that neither had looked often or directly on the other's face, for fear of the Khalīfah's resentment, and that modesty had ever caused Abbāsah to turn away from Jafar's furtive glances.

'The marriage became a marriage in fact, and, after a night of mutual transport, Abbāsah rose, saying: "How do you like King's daughters, my master? Are they different from slaves who are bought and sold?" "King's daughters?" asked the astonished Jafar. "Are you one yourself? Are you some captive of our victorious arms?" "O Jafar," she answered, "I am both a captive and a slave. I am Abbāsah, sister of al-Rashīd, daughter of al-Mahdī. I am of the blood of Abbās, uncle of the Prophet (upon whom be prayer and peace!)."

'These words cleared off the last clouds of Jafar's drunkenness, and he cried: "You have destroyed yourself, you have destroyed me, O daughter of my masters!"

'He hastened to Itabah, and said to her: "O mother, mother, you have sold me cheap!" For answer Yahya's trembling wife told her son how she had been forced to forward this stratagem, in order to save her household from a worse misfortune.

'In fulness of time Abbāsah bore a son whom she confided to Riyāsh, a man faithful in her service, and to the nursing of a woman called Barrah. Then, fearing lest a rumour of this birth should escape in spite of all her precautions, she sent her child to Mecca with his two guardians.

'Now Yahya, Jafar's father, was responsible for order in the palace and harīm of al-Rashīd. After a certain hour of night he would shut all the communicating doors and take away the keys, a severity of discipline which soon caused discontent among the women and especially in the Lady Zubaidah. When she complained to al-Rashīd and cursed the old man's misplaced zeal, he called Yahya to him, and asked: "My father, what grievance has Zubaidah against you?" "Does she complain that I am lax in my supervision of the harīm?" demanded Yahya. "Not so, my father," answered al-Rashīd with a smile. "In that case," cried the Barmakid, "take no notice of what she says, O Commander of the Faithful!" And, after that, he redoubled his severity in door locking.

'Zubaidah came to her lord a second time, crying out in bitter resentment against Yahya; so al-Rashīd tried to pacify her, saying: "O daughter of my uncle, my guide and father Yahya is only obeying orders and doing his duty, when he schools my harīm in this way." "If he is so deeply concerned with his duty," retorted Zubaidah with some feeling, "why does he not begin by schooling the imprudence of his son?" "What imprudence?" demanded al-Rashīd. Zubaidah at once told him the whole story of Abbāsah, though not as a matter of great importance. "Are there proofs of this?" asked the Khalīfah in a sombre voice. "What better proof could there be than the child himself?" demanded Zubaidah. "Where is he?" asked the Khalīfah, and she replied: "In the Holy City, the cradle of our race." "Does any beside you know of these things?" he asked, and she replied: "There is not a woman in the whole palace, not a slave who does not know."

'Al-Rashīd said no further word, but soon afterwards he departed on pilgrimage for Mecca and took Jafar with him.

'At once Abbāsah sent a letter to Riyāsh and the nurse, ordering them to leave the city and pass into Yemen with the child.

'As soon as the Khalīfah arrived at Mecca he bade certain of his trusted spies make enquiry concerning the infant, and these soon returned with the news that they had found proof of his existence, and that he was in perfect health. In a few days the child was seized in Yemen and sent secretly to Baghdād.

'It was on his return from that pilgrimage, when lying at the monastery of al-Umr near Anbār on the Euphrates, that al-Rashīd gave his fateful command to Masrūr.

'Abbāsah was buried alive with her son in a ditch dug in the floor of her own apartment.

'Allāh have them both in His compassion!'

It remains for me to say, O auspicious King, that other and quite worthy historians contend that Jafar and the Barmakids had done nothing to deserve their fate, and that it would not have come upon them if it had not been written in their Destiny.

But Allāh knows all!

The celebrated poet, Muhammad of Damascus, gives this final word concerning the Barmakids:

'One day I entered a hammām to take a bath, and the master detailed a handsome boy to serve me. As the cleansing proceeded, I began to chant to myself, led on by I know not what whim of the mind, certain verses which I had composed to celebrate the birth of a son to my benefactor, al-Fadl ibn Yahya al-Barmakī. Suddenly the boy who was washing me fell to the floor in a swoon. When he came to himself a few moments later, his face was wet with tears, and he fled, leaving me alone in the water.'

At this point Shahrazād saw the approach of morning and discreetly fell silent.

But when the nine-hundred-and-ninety-eighth night had come

SHE SAID:

'In some astonishment I left the water and sharply reproached the master of the hammām for allowing me to be attended by an epilept. But the man swore that he had never noticed a sign of that malady in the youth and, to prove his words, recalled the fugitive to my presence. "What has happened to make this lord so discontented with you?" he asked. The boy hung his head and then turned to me, saying: "O my master, do you know the author of those verses which you were chanting while I bathed you?" "I am the author," I replied, and he continued: "Then you are the poet Muhammad of

Damascus. You made those verses to celebrate the birth of a son to al-Fadl the Barmakid. I beg you to excuse me if the sudden hearing of those lines gripped me about the heart and caused me to fall. I am that son, of whose coming you sang so excellently." Then he fell into a second swoon.

'Moved to the soul to see the lad so reduced, and mindful that I owed to his father all my riches and the greater part of my fame, I lifted him and clasped him to my breast, saying: "O son of that great generosity, I am old and have no heir. Come with me to the kādī, and I will adopt you as my son. You shall inherit all my goods when I am dead."

'But the young Barmakid answered with further tears: "May Allāh pour His blessings upon you, O son of virtue! It would not sort with my dignity in His eyes to take back a single dirham which my father gave."

'In spite of all my prayers, the child would accept nothing. They were of true blood, those Barmakids! Allāh reward them according to their great deserts!'

As for the Khalīfah Hārūn al-Rashīd: after his cruel vengeance for some wrong known only to himself and Allāh, he returned to Baghdād, but passed it by. He found that he could not live any longer in that city which it had been his delight through so many years to embellish. He established himself at Rākah and never returned to the Place of Peace. This sudden abandonment of his capital by al-Rashīd inspired the poet Abbās ibn al-Ahnaf, who was of his train, to write the following lines:

> Scarce had we made the camels kneel
> Before we had to ride again,
> The friends who watched our coming
> Saw us turn the camels round.
>
> They cried us welcome, but it was
> 'Farewell,' that we replied again,
> 'Farewell, O city of Baghdād,
> O consecrated ground.'

Since the disappearance of his friends, al-Rashīd got no good of his sleep; his regrets burned him day and night, and he would have given his kingdom to bring back Jafar. If any courtiers had the misfortune to speak even a little slightingly of the Barmakids, the

Khalīfah would angrily cry out on them: 'Allāh damn your fathers! Either cease from blaming them, or try to fill the place which they left empty.'

Though he remained all-powerful until his death, al-Rashīd imagined that he was surrounded by traitors. He feared to be poisoned by his sons, who were indeed no cause for pride. At the beginning of a punitive expedition into Khurāsān, from which he was not destined to return alive, he sadly admitted his doubts to al-Tabarī, the annalist, who was one of the courtiers most in his confidence. When al-Tabarī tried to reassure him as to certain presages of death which he had received, he drew the chronicler into the shadow of a great tree, where they might be rid of prying glances, and opened his robe to show him a silk bandage wrapped about his belly. 'I have a deep and incurable disease,' he said. 'No one knows of it save you. And I have spies round me, sent by al-Amīn and al-Mamūn to filch away the little remainder of my life. They feel that I have lived too long. They have corrupted my most faithful servants. Masrūr is the spy of my favourite son al-Mamūn, my doctor Jibrīl Bakhtiyāshū is al-Amīn's spy. And there are many more. Would you have proof of their plots? I have ordered a riding horse to be sent to me, and instead of choosing one with a strong and easy action, you will see them bring to me a worn beast, having a broken pace to aggravate my suffering.'

This prophecy was fulfilled; al-Rashīd was given such a horse as he described, and he accepted it with a look of sad understanding to al-Tabarī.

A few weeks after this incident, Hārūn saw in his dreams a hand stretched out above his head, holding a little red earth. A voice cried: 'This shall be his sepulchre.' 'Where?' asked another voice, and the first replied: 'In Tūs.'

Some days later the course of his malady obliged al-Rashīd to halt at Tūs. At once he showed signs of grave disquiet, and sent Masrūr to bring him a little earth from the outskirts of the city. The eunuch returned in an hour, bearing a handful of red soil, and al-Rashīd cried: 'There is no God but Allāh, and Muhammad is the Prophet of Allāh! My vision is accomplished, my death is very near!'

He did not see Irāk again. The next day he was weaker, and said to those about him: 'The moment is at hand. I was envied by all the world, but now the world might pity me.'

He died at Tūs on the third day of Jumāda, second in the one

hundred-and-ninety-third year of the Hijrah. According to Abul-
fidā, he was forty-seven years, five months, and five days old at the
time of his death. Allāh pardon his mistakes and have him in pity!
He was an orthodox Khalīfah.

Then, as Shahrazād saw that her story had moved King Shahryār
to sorrow, she hastened to begin The Tender Tale of Prince Jasmine
and Princess Almond.

SHE SAID:

The Tender Tale of Prince Jasmine and Princess Almond

IT is related—but Allāh in the Highest knows all!—that there was
once, in a certain Mussulmān country, an old king whose heart
was as the ocean, who had the wisdom of Aflātūn, whose nature was
the nature of the Sages, whose glory surpassed the glory of Farīdūn,
whose star was the star of Alexander, whose fortune was the fortune
of the Persian Ānūshīrwān. This King had seven sons, seven fires of
the Pleiades. But the youngest was in everything the most excellent.
He was white and rose, and his name was Prince Jasmine.

The lily faded when he was by, for he stood like a cypress and his
cheeks were new tulips. The musk curls of his violet-tendrilled hair
borrowed their darkness from a thousand nights, his colouring was
blond amber, his lashes were curved arrows, his eyes were the long
eyes of the jonquils, two pistachios formed the seduction of his lips.
His brow shamed the moonlight, blotting the face of the full moon
with blue; his mouth, whose teeth were diamonds and whose tongue
was a rose, distilled a language sweeter than the sugarcane. Bold and
active and beautiful, he was made to be the god of lovers.

Prince Jasmine had been chosen from among his brothers to guard
the vast buffalo herds of his father, King Nujūm-Shāh. As he sat
one day in the lonely pasturage, watching his charges and playing
upon the flute, a venerable darwīsh approached him and, after greeting, begged him to draw off a little milk. 'O holy man,' answered the
prince, 'it grieves me bitterly that I cannot satisfy your need. I have
milked all my buffaloes this morning, and there is nothing left with
which to quench your thirst.' 'Nevertheless, call upon Allāh's name,'
said the darwīsh, 'and milk one of the animals a second time. I think

that benediction will follow.' At once the jonquil prince did as the
old man suggested. He invoked the name of Allāh and worked the
udder of the fairest cow. Benediction followed, and the pail filled
with foaming blue milk. Jasmine set the pail before his chance guest,
and the darwīsh drank until he was satisfied. Then he smiled and
turned to the prince, saying: 'Delicate child, you have not wasted
your milk; by giving it you have advanced your fortune. I came to
you as a messenger of love and now I see that you deserve love's
gift, which is the first gift and the last. A poet has said:

> Love was before the light began,
> When light is over, love shall be;
> O warm hand in the grave, O bridge of truth,
> O ivy's tooth
> Eating the green heart of the tree
> Of man!

'Yes, my son, I approach your heart as a messenger of love, and
yet no one sent me. If I have crossed plains and deserts it was but to
find a youth worthy to come near a girl, a fairy girl I chanced to see
one morning as I passed her garden. You must know, O lighter than
the breeze, that in the kingdom which marches with your father's, a
girl of royal blood has seen you in her dreams. Her face is the moon's
shame, she is one pearl lying in the casket of excellence, a spring of
fair weather, a niche of beauty. Her slight body has the colour of
silver, and stands like a box-tree; her waist is a hair's breadth, her
station is the station of the sun, she has the walk of a partridge. Her
hair is of hyacinth, her eyes are sabres of Isfahān; her cheeks resemble the verse of Beauty in the Book; the bows of her brows recall
the chapter of the Pen. Her mouth, carved from a ruby, is an astonishment; a dimpled apple is her chin, its beauty spot avails against
the evil-eye. Her very small ears wear lovers' hearts instead of jewels,
the ring of her nose is a slave ring about the moon. The soles of her
little feet are altogether charming. Her heart is a sealed flask of perfume, her soul is wise. Her approach is the tumult of the Resurrection! She is the daughter of King Akbar, and her name is Princess
Almond. Such names are blessed!'

At this point Shahrazād saw the approach of morning and
discreetly fell silent.

But when the nine-hundred-and-ninety-ninth night had come

SHE SAID:

After drawing a long breath the darwīsh said again: 'But I should tell you, O river of sympathy, that it is within a liver burnt by sorrow that the child lodges her love; a mountain lies upon her heart because of a dream. She was as desolate as the sumbul when I left her. . . . And now that my words have cast the seed of love into your heart, may Allāh preserve you and lead you towards your Destiny!'

The darwīsh rose and departed, leaving Prince Jasmine's heart transfixed and bleeding. As did Majnūn in his love for Lailah, he tore his robes from neck to waist, and sighed and cried, strangling in the curls of Princess Almond. He wandered away from his herd, drunk without wine, shaken and dazed by the whirlwind of his passion. The shield of wisdom is proof against many wounds, but not against the bow of love. The medicine of good counsel is unavailing to a soul stricken by that pure sentiment. So much for Prince Jasmine.

One night, as Princess Almond slept upon the terrace of her father's palace, she saw a dream sent by the Jinn of love, and in it a youth fairer than Zulaikah's lover, a counterpart, line for line and beauty for beauty, of Prince Jasmine. As this vision became ever more clear to the eyes of her maiden soul, her careless heart slipped from her fingers and became enmeshed in the twined curls of the boy. She woke with her pulse beating to the rose of dreams, and, as she cried into the darkness like a nightingale, tears came to bathe the hot silver of her cheeks. Her maidens ran to her, crying: 'In Allāh's name, what are these tears upon the face of Almond? What has passed in her heart as it slept? Alas, alas, the bird of her reason has flown away!'

Their lamentation lasted till morning, and at dawn the King and Queen were told of the princess's grief. They ran in their anxiety to her chamber, where she sat with disordered hair and robes, with no news of her body and no attention for her heart. She answered all their questions with silence and a modest shaking of the head, so that they sorrowed exceedingly.

They brought doctors and conjurers to her, but these made her worse, for they thought it necessary to bleed her. They bound her arm and pricked it with their lancet, but not one drop of blood came from that charming vein. They ceased from their operation and went their way, shaking their heads and saying that there was no hope.

Some days passed without any coming forward to understand this malady. Then her maidens led the fevered Almond to the garden, hoping that this might be a distraction for her. But, wherever her eyes glanced, they recognised her love: the roses told her of his body, the jasmine spoke of the perfume of his garments, the cypress called to mind his balance, and the narcissus looked upon her with his eyes. She seemed to see his lashes in thorns, and pressed them to her heart.

When the greenness of the garden had a little recovered her parched heart, and the stream of which they made her drink had cooled her mind, her girls sat in a circle about her and sang a light ghazal for her delight.

Then, seeing that she was more ready to take heed, her dearest servant moved near to her, saying: 'O our mistress, a few days ago a young flute player came to our fields from the land of the noble Hazārah; the melody of his voice would bring back reason, would check the flowing of water and the flight of swallows. He is white and rose, and his name is Jasmine. The lily fades when he is by, for he stands like a cypress and his cheeks are new tulips. The musk curls of his violet-tendrilled hair borrow their darkness from a thousand nights. His colouring is blond amber, his lashes are curved arrows, his eyes are the long eyes of the jonquils, two pistachios form the seduction of his lips. His brow shames the moonlight, blotting the face of the full moon with blue; his mouth, whose teeth are diamonds and whose tongue is a rose, distils a language sweeter than sugar-cane. Bold and active and beautiful, he is made to be the god of lovers. . . . This princely flute-player has come, lighter and more agile than the morning breeze, over difficult mountains to our land. He has crossed the running of great rivers, where the swan herself would have no confidence, where the waterfowl and wild drakes would turn giddy and undergo a thousand astonishments. Would he have faced these ardours had it not been for love?'

The girl fell silent, and Akbar's ailing daughter rose up, happy and dancing, upon her two feet. Her cheeks were lighted by a red fire within, her drunken soul looked from her eyes. No trace of her malady remained, the simple words of a girl speaking of love had scattered it like smoke.

She entered her own apartment, as light and swift as a gazelle. She wrote with the pen of joy upon the paper of meeting. She wrote to Prince Jasmine, who had stolen her reason, who had glowed before the eyes of her spirit. She wrote this white-winged letter:

'*After praise to Him Who, without ink or pen, has written the life of His creatures within the garden of beauty.*

'*Greeting to the rose who has made drunk the nightingale!*

'*When I heard tell of your beauty, my heart slipped from my hand.*

'*When I saw your face in dreams, I forgot my father and my mother, and became a stranger in my own house. What are father or mother, when a maiden is made stranger even to herself?*

'*In your presence the fair are swept down as by a torrent; the arrows of your eyes have cleft my heart in twain.*

'*Oh, show me the beauty of yourself in my waking, that my living eyes may see. You, who are learned in the science of love, must know that the heart's road leads to the heart.*

'*You are the water and clay of my being; the roses of my bed have turned to thorns; the seal of silence is upon my lips, and I have forgotten my careless walking.*'

At this point Shahrazād saw the approach of morning and discreetly fell silent.

But when the thousandth night had come

SHE SAID:

She folded the wings of this letter, slipping a grain of musk between them, and gave it to her favourite. The girl carried it over her heart and went, like a homing pigeon, to the wood where Jasmine played his flute. She found him seated below a cypress, singing this short ghazal:

> I see in my heart
> Clouds and lights dart,
> Part quicksilver, part
>   Blood on the sea.
> When the night has gone
> We shall be joined anon
> Like river and swan,
>   I and she.

He read the letter and well-nigh swooned for joy, knowing not if he slept or waked. His heart glowed like a furnace and waves troubled the surface of his soul; it was in a daze that he heard the plans and instructions of his mistress.

At the determined hour the angel of meeting led Jasmine along the path to Almond's garden. He scaled the walls into this fragment of Paradise, just as the sun was sinking in the western haze and the moon showed her face below the veils of the East. He walked, as lightly as a fawn, to a certain tree which the young confidant had described, and climbed up to hide himself in the branches.

Princess Almond came with night into the garden. She was dressed in blue and held a blue rose in her hand. She trembled like the leaves of a willow, as she lifted her head towards the tree; she could not determine whether she saw the full moon caught in the branches or whether Jasmine waited for her there. But soon, as a flower ripened by desire, a fruit heavy with its precious weight, the boy slipped from the branches, and covered the pale feet of the princess with his violet-tendrilled hair. She recognised her dream and found the truth of its image fairer. Jasmine saw that the darwīsh had not lied, and that this moon was the crown of moons. Their hearts were bound together tenderly, their happiness was as great as the happiness of Majnūn and Lailah, as pure as the friendship of old men.

After most sweet kisses and blossoming of the soul, they prayed to the Master of perfect love that the tyrant sky should never rain his bolts upon them, to ravish the seam of their enchantment. As a first resource against separation, they decided that Almond should immediately interview her father, the King, as he loved her and could refuse her nothing.

She left Jasmine beneath the trees and entered her father's presence as a suppliant, joining her hands, and saying: 'O high noon of the two worlds, your servant wishes to ask a favour.' The King was both astonished and delighted; he lifted her in his hands and pressed her to his bosom, as he answered: 'Surely, O Almond of my heart, it must be an urgent favour which brings you from your bed in the midst of night to beg for it. But whatever it may be, light of my eye, trust in your father and speak fearlessly.' The gentle Almond hesitated for a little, and then, raising her face to the King's, spoke thus with subtlety: 'My strength and health have returned to me after taking an evening walk in the meadow with my girls. I have interrupted you thus unseasonably to tell you that I noticed how ill our cattle and sheep were kept. It came into my mind that, if I should meet a worthy herd or shepherd, I would bring him to your notice. Hardly had I had this thought, when, by a happy chance, I came upon a most diligent and active man. He is young and well-disposed; he fears neither trouble nor fatigue, laziness and carelessness are removed by many parasangs from his heart. O father, I beg you to put him in charge of our flocks and herds.'

King Akbar listened to this discourse with astonished, bulging eyes. 'By my life,' he cried, 'I have never heard of a shepherd being engaged in the middle of the night. But your recovery has so delighted me that I swear to employ the herd of your choice, if I think him suitable when I have seen him.'

Princess Almond went on the wings of joy to find Jasmine under the trees. She took him by the hand and led him into her father's presence, saying: 'Here is the excellent shepherd of whom I spoke; his heart is proved, his crook is strong.' Now Allāh had graced King Akbar with intelligence, and he was puzzled to see that the youth whom his daughter brought to him was quite unlike the run of herd boys. As he was determining to keep silence concerning these important differences, rather than distress his child, the princess read his thought and, joining her hands together, said in a most moving voice: 'Father, the outside is not always an index to the inside. I assure you that this young man is used to herding lions.' So, to please her, King Akbar put the finger of consenting to his eye and, in the middle of the night, engaged Prince Jasmine to watch his flocks and herds.

At this point Shahrazād saw the approach of morning and discreetly fell silent.

And her sister, little Dunyazād, who had become in all things desirable, a girl each day and every night more ripe and charming, more silent, more understanding, and more attentive, half rose from her carpet, saying: 'O Shahrazād, how sweet and delectable are your words, how pleasant to our taste!' Shahrazād smiled and embraced her, as she answered: 'They are as nothing to those which I should use to-morrow night, if our master, this exquisitely mannered King, were not weary of my talking.' 'O Shahrazād,' cried King Shahryār, 'how can you hint at such a possibility? You have calmed my heart and taught my soul. There has been a blessing upon the land since you came to me. Rest assured that you may finish your delightful tale to-morrow; even to-night, if you are not too tired. I am eager to know what happened to Prince Jasmine and Princess Almond.' But Shahrazād said no more that night.

The King pressed her to his heart and slept by her side until the morning. When he rose and went to sit in judgment, he saw his wazīr come, bearing a winding-sheet destined for Shahrazād; for the old man every day expected that he would hear of her death, because of the oath which Shahryār had sworn. The King said nothing to allay his fear, but entered the dīwān and sat there, giving judgment, raising some and debasing others, commanding and concluding cases, until the fall of day.

But when the thousand-and-first night had come

AND KING SHAHRYĀR had done his usual with Shahrazād, little Dunyazād said to her sister: 'Please, please tell us the rest of the tender tale of Prince Jasmine and Princess Almond, if you are not too weary.' Shahrazād caressed the little one's hair, as she answered: 'With all my heart and as in duty bound to this magnanimous King.' And she continued:

AFTER THAT TIME Prince Jasmine lived the outer life of a shepherd, but his interior being was occupied with love. By day he pastured his sheep and cattle at three or four parasangs from the palace, but, when evening came, he called them together with his flute, and led them back to the stables of the King. At night he stayed in the garden with his mistress Almond, that rose of excellence. Such was the tenor of his life.

But who may hold even the most hidden happiness to be safe for ever from the jealousy of censure?

In her love for him, Almond would send her herd boy food and drink into the woods. One day her passion led her to an imprudence, and she bore the dish herself, delicacies fit for his sugar lips, fruit, nuts and pistachios, pleasantly arranged upon the silver spaces. As she gave these things, she said: 'May they be of easy digestion, eloquent little parrot, O comfit-eater!' With that she disappeared like camphor.

When this peeled almond had disappeared like camphor, Jasmine made ready to taste the delicacies; but he had hardly lifted the first of them to his mouth before he saw the princess's uncle coming towards him, a hostile and ill-intentioned old man, who spent his days in detestation of the world, preventing musicians from their instruments and singers from their singing.

This vile busybody suspiciously asked what the herd was doing with the King's dish; but Jasmine, who thought no evil and had a heart as generous as an Autumn rose, only supposed that his questioner wished to eat, and therefore gave him all the good things for himself.

The calamitous uncle carried the dish to King Akbar and, by its means, proved there to be some relation between Almond and Jasmine.

The King raged at this discovery, and called his daughter into his presence. 'Shame of your fathers,' he cried, 'you have brought disgrace upon our house! Until to-day our dwelling was free from the thorns and bitter herbs of shame. But you have caught my neck in the running noose of your deceit, and have veiled the lamp of my intelligence with your cajolery. What man may boast that he is safe from women? The Prophet (on whom be prayer and peace!) has said: "My Faithful, your wives and daughters are the chief of your foes. They lack both reason and probity. They were born of a twisted rib. It is your duty to reprimand them and, when they disobey, to beat them." What shall I do to you, now that you have played the wanton with a stranger, a herd boy, whom it would be beneath your dignity to marry? Shall I cut off your heads with a single blow of my sword? Shall I burn the two of you in the fires of death?' Then, as she wept, he added: 'Go from my presence now and bury yourself behind the curtain of the harīm. Do not come out until I give you leave.'

When he had thus punished his daughter, King Akbar gave orders for the destruction of her shepherd. There was a wood near that city, a lair of wild and terrifying beasts. Brave men shook and felt their hair stand upon end when the name of that wood was spoken before them. In its shade morning appeared as night, and night as the sinister dawn of Resurrection. Among the horrors of it were two pig-deer, which terrorised both bird and beast, and sometimes carried devastation into the city.

At their father's order, Almond's brothers sent Jasmine to perish in this terrifying place. Thinking no evil, he led the sheep and cattle of his charge into the wood, at that hour when the two-horned star shows upon the horizon and the Ethiopian of the night turns round his face to flee away. He left his flocks to feed at their will, and sat down upon a white skin, to draw the wine notes from his flute. Suddenly the two ravening pig-deer, who had been guided by his human smell, bounded into the clear space where he sat, bellowing like thunder clouds. The sweet-eyed prince drew them with the sounds of his flute and tamed them with the glory of his playing. When he rose silently and left the forest, the two fierce beasts accompanied him, going upon his right and left, and the flocks and herds came after. At last beneath the very windows of the King, Jasmine enticed the pig-deer into an iron cage.

When Jasmine offered his captives to the King, Akbar felt himself to be in a difficulty, and revoked the sentence of death which he had passed.

But the princes, who would not so easily forgo their resentment, plotted together to marry their sister to a detested cousin, the son of that calamitous uncle. 'We must bind the feet of this mad girl with the marriage rope,' they said, 'then perhaps she will forget her other and inordinate affection.' For this purpose they assembled musicians and singers, fife-players and drummers, and made ready the procession.

Watched by her tyrannical brothers, the desolate Almond, who had been clothed against her will in splendid robes and the gold ornaments of marriage, sat on an elegant couch of gold brocade, a flower upon a bed of flowers, silent as a lily, motionless as an idol. She seemed as one dead among the living, her heart beat like a captive bird; her soul was mantled in grey dusk, and her breast torn by the nail of grief; her urgent spirit gloomily foreshadowed the muddy crow who should soon lie with her. She sat throned upon a very Caucasus of grief.

But Jasmine, who had come with the other servants to the bridal of his mistress, gave her hope to drink from a single glance of his eyes. Surely the looks of lovers can say twenty things.

When night came and the princess had been led to the marriage chamber, Destiny turned a fortunate face to the lovers and stayed their hearts with the eight odours. Taking advantage of the little moment before her bridegroom should come to her, Almond glided from the chamber in her gold robes and fled to Jasmine. These two delightful children took hands and vanished, more lightly than the dew-wet breeze of morning.

Nothing has since been heard of them, or their abiding place. There are few upon this earth worthy of happiness, worthy to take the road which leads to happiness, worthy to draw near the house of happiness.

Therefore glory and everlasting praise be to the Master of happiness! Amen.

Conclusion

'Such, O auspicious King,' said Shahrazād, 'is the tender tale of Prince Jasmine and Princess Almond. I have told it as I heard it. But Allāh knows all!'

Then she fell silent, and King Shahryār cried: 'O Shahrazād, that was a noble and admirable story! O wise and subtle one, you have taught me many lessons, letting me see that every man is at the call of Fate; you have made me consider the words of kings and peoples passed away; you have told me some things which were strange, and many that were worthy of reflection. I have listened to you for a thousand nights and one night, and now my soul is changed and joyful, it beats with an appetite for life. I give thanks to Him Who has perfumed your mouth with so much eloquence and has set wisdom to be a seal upon your brow!'

Little Dunyazād rose quite up from her carpet, and ran to throw her arms about her sister, crying: 'O Shahrazād, how soft and delicate are your words, how moving and delightful! With what a savour they have filled our hearts! Oh, how beautiful are your words, my sister!'

Shahrazād leaned over the child and, as she embraced her, whispered some words which caused her to glide from the room, as camphor melts before the sun.

Shahrazād stayed alone with Shahryār, but, as he was preparing to take this marvellous bride between his joyful arms, the curtains opened and Dunyazād reappeared, followed by a nurse with twin children hanging at her breasts. A third child hurried after them on all fours.

Shahrazād embraced the three little ones and then ranged them before Shahryār; her eyes filled with tears, as she said: 'O King of time, behold these three whom Allāh has granted to us in three years.'

While Shahryār kissed the children and was moved with joy through all his body to touch them, Shahrazād said again: 'Your eldest son is more than two years old, and these twins will soon be one. Allāh protect them from the evil-eye! You remember, O King of time, that I was absent through sickness for twenty days between the six hundred and seventy-ninth night of my telling and the seven hundredth. It was during that absence that I gave birth to the twins. They pained and wearied me a great deal more than their elder brother in the previous year. With him I was so little disturbed

531

that I had no need to interrupt the tale of Sympathy the Learned, even for one night.'

She fell silent, and King Shahryār, looking from her to his sons and from his sons to her, could say no word.

Then little Dunyazād turned from kissing the infants a twentieth time, and said to Shahryār: 'Will you cut off my sister's head, O King? Will you destroy the mother of your sons, and leave three little kings to miss her love?'

'Be quiet and have no fear, young girl,' answered King Shahryār, between two fits of sobbing. It was not for a long time that he could master his emotion, and say: 'O Shahrazād, I swear by the Lord of Pity that you were already in my heart before the coming of these children. He had given you gifts with which to win me; I loved you in my soul because I had found you pure, holy, chaste, tender, straightforward, unassailable, ingenious, subtle, eloquent, discreet, smiling, and wise. May Allāh bless you, my dear, your father and mother, your root and race! O Shahrazād, this thousand and first night is whiter for us than the day!' When he had said these things, he rose and embraced the woman's head.

Shahrazād took her King's hand and carried it to her lips, her heart, and her brow, saying: 'O lord of time, I beg you to call your old wazīr, that he may rejoice at my salvation and partake in the benediction of this night.'

So the King sent for his wazīr, and the old man entered carrying Shahrazād's winding-sheet over his arm, for he was sure that her hour had come at last. Shahryār rose in his honour and kissed him between the eyes, saying: 'O father of Shahrazād, O begetter of benediction, Allāh has raised up your daughter to be the salvation of my people. Repentance has come to me through her!' Joy penetrated the old man's heart so suddenly that he fell into a swoon. When rose-water had brought him to himself, Shahrazād and Dunyazād kissed his hand, and he blessed them. The rest of that night passed for them all in a daze of happiness.

Shahryār sent for his brother Shahzamān, King of Samarkand al-Ajam, and went out to meet his coming with a glorious retinue. The city was gay with flags, and in the streets and markets the people burnt incense, sublimated camphor, aloes, Indian musk, nard and ambergris. They put fresh henna upon their fingers and saffron upon their faces. Drums, flutes, clarinets, fifes, cymbals and dulcimers filled every ear with a rejoicing sound.

While great feasts were being given at the royal expense, King Shahryār took his brother aside and spoke of the life which he had led with Shahrazād for the last three years. He recounted for Shahzamān's benefit some of the maxims, phrases, tales, proverbs, jests, anecdotes, characteristics, marvels, poems, and recitations which he had heard during that time. He praised the wazīr's daughter for her eloquence, wisdom, purity, piety, sweetness, honesty and discretion. 'She is my wife,' he said, 'the mother of my children.'

When King Shahzamān had a little recovered from his astonishment, he said: 'Since you have been so fortunate, I too will marry. I will marry Shahrazād's sister, the little one, I do not know her name. We shall be two brothers married to two sure and honest sisters; we will forget our old misfortune. That calamity touched me first, and then through me it reached to you. If I had not discovered mine, you would never have known of yours. Alas, my brother, I have been mournful and loveless during these years. Each night I have followed your example by taking a virgin to my bed, and every morning I have avenged our ills upon her life. Now I will follow you in a better deed, and marry your wazīr's second daughter.'

Shahryār went joyfully to Shahrazād and told her that his brother had, of his own accord, elected Dunyazād for his bride. 'We consent, O King of time,' she said, 'on condition that your brother stays henceforth with us. I could not bear to be separated from my little sister, even for one hour. I brought her up and educated her; she could not part from me. If Shahzamān will give this undertaking, Dunyazād shall be his slave. If not, we will keep her.'

When Shahzamān heard Shahrazād's answer, he said: 'As Allāh lives, my brother, I had intended no less than to remain with you always. I feel now that I can never abide to be parted from you again. As for the throne of Samarkand, Allāh will send to fill it.' 'I have longed for this,' answered King Shahryār. 'Join with me in thanks to Allāh, my brother, that He has brought our hearts together again after so many months!'

The kādī and witnesses were summoned, and a marriage contract was written out for King Shahzamān and Dunyazād. Rejoicing and illuminations with coloured fire followed upon the news of this; and all the city ate and drank at the King's expense for forty days and forty nights. The two brothers and two sisters entered the hammām and bathed there in rose-water, flower-water, scented willow-water,

533

and perfumed water of musk, while eagle wood and aloes were burned about them.

Shahrazād combed and tressed her little sister's hair, and sprinkled it with pearls. Then she dressed her in a robe of antique Persian stuff, stitched with red gold and enhanced by drunken animals and swooning birds embroidered in the very colours of life. She put a fairy collar about her neck, and Dunyazād became below her fingers fairer than Alexander's wife.

When the two Kings had left the hammām and seated themselves upon their thrones, the bridal company, the wives of the amīrs and notables, stood in two motionless lines to right and left. Time came, and the sisters entered between these living walls, each sustaining the other, and having the appearance of two moons in one night sky.

Then the noblest ladies there took Dunyazād by the hand and, after removing her robes, dressed her in a garment of blue satin, a sea tint to make reason fail upon her throne. A poet said of her:

> Her veil is torn from the bright blue
> Which all the stars are hasting to,
> Her lips control a hive of bees,
> And roses are about her knees,
> The white flakes of the jasmine twine
> Round her twin sweetness carnaline,
> Her waist is a slight reed which stands
> Swayed on a hill of moving sands.

Shahzamān came down to be the first to look upon her. When he had admired her in this dress, he sat upon his throne again, and this was a signal for the second change. So Shahrazād and the women clad their bride in a robe of apricot silk. As she passed before her husband's throne, she justified the words of the poet:

> You are more fair than a summer moon
> On a winter night, you are more fair.
> I said when I saw your falling hair:
> 'Night's black fain wing is hiding day.'
> 'A cloud, but lo! the moon is there,'
> You, rose child, found to say.

When Shahzamān had come down and admired her in this dress, Shahrazād put a tunic of grenade velvet upon her sister. A poet said:

Red and slight as a running deer,
   Small as a child with his father's bow,
   Yet you so shine that when you go
The sun will fly and night appear.

After this Dunyazād was habited in citron yellow silk with lines of pictures. A poet has said:

You are the fortunate moon which shone
   On the road I used to take
   Many a glad night for the sake
Of a once desirous one;
Yet if now a lover nears,
   Unrecking silver fire,
Your breasts' two crimson granite spears
   Are proof against desire.

Shahrazād led her slowly before the Kings and all the company of guests. Shahzamān looked upon his bride and then, by returning to his place, gave signal for the final change. Shahrazād kissed the child long upon the mouth, and then dressed her in a robe of green, sewn with red gold and pearls. With careful fingers she pulled out the lines of this, and then set a light diadem of emeralds on her sister's brow. It was upon her arm that this small branch of ban, this camphor girl, walked through the hall. A poet has been inspired to sing:

Green leaves as fairly shade the red pomegranate flowers
   As you your light chemise.
I ask its name which suits your golden check,
   You ponder and then speak:
   'It has no name, for it is my chemise.'
Yet I will call it murderer of ours,
   A murderous chemise . . . .

Shahrazād slipped her hand to her sister's waist, and they walked before the Kings and between the guests toward the inner chambers. Then the Queen undressed little Dunyazād and laid her upon the bed with such recommendations as were suitable. They kissed and wept in each other's arms for a little, as it was the first night for which they had been separated.

That was a white and joyful night for the two brothers and the two sisters, it was a fair continuation of the thousand and one which had gone before, a love tale better than them all, the dawn of a new era for the subjects of King Shahryār.

When the brothers had come from the hammām in the morning and joined their wives, the wazīr sought permission to enter. They rose in his honour and the two women kissed his hand; but, when he asked for the day's orders, the four said with one voice: 'O father, we wish that you should give commands in the future and not receive them. That is why we make you King of Samarkand al-Ajam.' 'I yield my throne to you,' said Shahzamān; and Shahryār cried: 'I will only give you leave to do so, my brother, if you will consent to share my royalty and reign with me day and day about.' 'I hear and I obey,' said Shahzamān.

The wazīr kissed his daughters in farewell, embraced the three little sons, and departed for Samarkand al-Ajam at the head of a magnificent escort. Allāh had written him security in his journey, and the inhabitants of his new kingdom hailed his coming with delight. He reigned over them in all justice and became a King among great Kings. So much for him.

After these things, King Shahryār called together the most renowned annalists and proficient scribes from all the quarters of Islām, and ordered them to write out the tales of Shahrazād from beginning to end, without the omission of a single detail. So they sat down and wrote thirty volumes in gold letters, and called this sequence of marvels and astonishments: THE BOOK OF THE THOUSAND NIGHTS AND ONE NIGHT. Many faithful copies were made, and King Shahryār sent them to the four corners of his empire, to be an instruction to the people and their children's children. But he shut the original manuscript in the gold cupboard of his reign and made his wazīr of treasure responsible for its safe keeping.

King Shahryār and Queen Shahrazād, King Shahzamān and Queen Dunyazād, and Shahrazād's three small sons, lived year after year in all delight, knowing days each more admirable than the last and nights whiter than days, until they were visited by the Separator of friends, the Destroyer, the Builder of tombs, the Inexorable, the Inevitable.

Such are the excellent tales called THE THOUSAND NIGHTS AND ONE NIGHT, together with all that is in them of wonder and instruction, prodigy and marvel, astonishment and beauty.

CONCLUSION

But Allah knows all! He alone can distinguish between the true and the false. He knows all!

Now everlasting glory and praise be unto Him
Who rests Intangible amid Eternity;
Who, changing all things, yet Himself changes not;
Who is the Master of the Seen and of the Unseen;
Who alone Lives!
And prayer and peace with benediction
be upon the King's Chosen,
our Lord Muhammad,
Prince of Messengers,
Jewel of the World,
our hope for an auspicious
E N D !